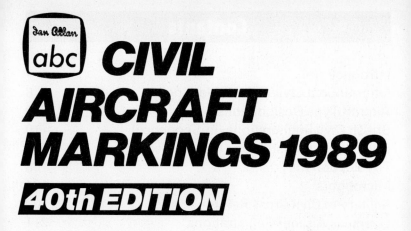

Ian Allan abc CIVIL AIRCRAFT MARKINGS 1989

40th EDITION

Alan J. Wright

LONDON

IAN ALLAN LTD

Contents

This fortieth edition published 1989

ISBN 0 7110 1833 2

Published by Ian Allan Ltd, Shepperton, Surrey;
and printed by Ian Allan Printing Ltd at their works
at Coombelands in Runnymede, England.

Cover photo: Austin J. Brown/Aviation Picture Library

Introduction

The 'G' prefixed four letter registration system was adopted in 1919 after a short-lived spell of about three months with serial numbers beginning at K-100. Until July 1928 the UK allocations were in the G-Exxx range, but as a result of further International agreements, this series was ended at G-EBZZ, the replacement being G-Axxx. From this point the registrations were issued in a reasonably orderly manner through to G-AZZZ, reached in July 1972. There were two exceptions. To avoid possible confusion with signal codes, the G-AQxx sequence was omitted, while G-AUxx was reserved for Australian use originally. In recent years however, an individual request for a mark in the latter range has been granted by the Authorities.

Although the next logical sequence was started at G-Bxxx, it was not long before the strictly applied rules relating to aircraft registration began to be relaxed. Permission was readily given for personalised marks to be issued incorporating virtually any four letter combination, while re-registration has also become a common feature, a practice almost unheard of in the past. In this book, where this has taken place at some time, the previous UK civil identity appears in parenthesis after the owner's/operator's name. An example of this is One-Eleven G-BBMG which originally carried G-AWEJ.

Some aircraft have also been allowed to wear military markings without displaying their civil identity. In this case the serial number actually carried is shown in parenthesis after the type's name. For example Gladiator G-AMRK flies as L8082 in RAF colours. As an aid to the identification of these machines, a military conversion list is provided.

Other factors caused a sudden acceleration in the number of registrations allocated by the Civil Aviation Authority in the early 1980s. The first surge came with the discovery that it was possible to register plastic bags and other items even less likely to fly, on payment of the standard fee. This erosion of the main register was checked in early 1982 by the issue of a special sequence for such devices commencing at G-FYAA. Powered hang-gliders provided the second glut of allocations as a result of the decision that these types should be officially registered. Although a few of the early examples penetrated the normal in-sequence register, the vast majority were given marks in other special ranges, this time G-MBxx, G-MGxx, G-MJxx, G-MMxx, G-MNxx, G-MTxx, G-MVxx, G-MWxx, G-MYxx and G-MZxx. At first it was common practice for microlights to ignore the requirement to carry their official identity. However the vast majority now display their registration somewhere on the structure, the size and position depending on the dimensions of the component to which it is applied.

Throughout the UK section of this book, there are many instances where the probable base of the aircraft has been included. This is positioned at the end of the owner/operator details preceded by an oblique stroke. It must of course be borne in mind that changes do take place and that no attempt has been made to record the residents at the many private strips. The base of airline equipment has been given as the company's headquarter's airport, although frequently aircraft are outstationed for long periods.

Non-airworthy preserved aircraft are shown with a star after the type.

Any new registrations issued by the CAA after this publication went to press will inevitably not be included until the next edition.

The three-letter codes used by airlines to prefix flight numbers are included for those carriers appearing in the book. Radio frequencies for the larger airfields/airports are also listed.

Acknowledgements

Once again thanks are extended to the Registration Department of the Civil Aviation Authority for their assistance and allowing access to their files. The comments and amendments flowing from Wal Gandy have as always proved of considerable value, while Ian Checkley, Duncan Cummings and Howard Curtis also contributed useful facts. The help given by numerous airlines or their information agencies has been much appreciated. The work of A. S. Wright and C. P. Wright during the update of this edition must not go unrecorded, since without it, deadlines would probably become impossible.   **AJW**

International Civil Aircraft Markings

A2-	Botswana	P-	Korea (North)
A3-	Tonga	P2-	Papua New Guinea
A5-	Bhutan	PH-	Netherlands
A6-	United Arab Emirates	PJ-	Netherlands Antilles
A7-	Qatar	PK-	Indonesia and West Irian
A9-	Bahrain	PP-, PT-	Brazil
A40-	Oman	PZ-	Surinam
AP-	Pakistan	RDPL-	Laos
B-	China/Taiwan	RP-	Philippine Republic
C-F, C-G	Canada	S2-	Bangladesh
C2-	Nauru	S7-	Seychelles
C3	Andora	S9-	São Tomé
C5-	Gambia	SE-	Sweden
C6-	Bahamas	SP-	Poland
C9-	Mozambique	ST-	Sudan
CC-	Chile	SU-	Egypt
CCCP-*	Soviet Union	SX-	Greece
CN-	Morocco	T2	Tuvalu
CP-	Bolivia	T3-	Kiribati
CR-	Portuguese Overseas Provinces	T7-	San Marino
CS-	Portugal	TC-	Turkey
CU-	Cuba	TF-	Iceland
CX-	Uruguay	TG-	Guatemala
D-	German Federal Republic (West)	TI-	Costa Rica
D2-	Angola	TJ-	United Republic of Cameroon
D4	Cape Verde Islands	TL-	Central African Republic
D6-	Comores Islands	TN-	Republic of Congo (Brazzaville)
DDR-	German Democratic Republic (East)	TR-	Gabon
DQ-	Fiji	TS-	Tunisia
EC-	Spain	TT-	Chad
EI-, EJ-	Republic of Ireland	TU-	Ivory Coast
EL-	Liberia	TY-	Benin
EP-	Iran	TZ-	Mali
ET-	Ethiopia	V2-	Antigua
F-	France, Colonies and Protectorates	V3-	Belize
G-	United Kingdom	V8-	Brunei
H4-	Solomon Islands	VH-	Australia
HA-	Hungarian People's Republic	VN-	Vietnam
HB-	Switzerland and Liechtenstein	VP-F	Falkland Islands
HC-	Ecuador	VP-LKA/	
HH-	Haiti	LLZ	St Kitts-Nevis
HI-	Dominican Republic	VP-LMA/	
HK-	Colombia	LUZ	Montserrat
HL-	Korea (South)	VP-LVA/	
HP-	Panama	LZZ	Virgin Islands
HR-	Honduras	VQ-T	Turks & Caicos Islands
HS-	Thailand	VR-B	Bermuda
HV-	The Vatican	VR-C	Cayman Islands
HZ-	Saudi Arabia	VR-G	Gibraltar (not used: present
I-	Italy		Gibraltar Airways aircraft
J2-	Djibouti		registered G-)
J3-	Grenada	VR-H	Hong Kong
J5-	Guinea Bissau	VT-	India
J6-	St Lucia	XA-, XB-,	
J7-	Dominica	XC-,	Mexico
J8-	St Vincent	XT-	Burkina Faso
JA-	Japan	XU-	Kampuchea
JY-	Jordan	XY-, XZ-	Burma
LN-	Norway	YA-	Afghanistan
LQ-, LV-	Argentine Republic	YI-	Iraq
LX-	Luxembourg	YJ-	Vanuatu
LZ-	Bulgaria	YK-	Syria
MI-	Marshall Islands	YN-	Nicaragua
N-	United States of America	YR-	Romania
OB-	Peru	YS-	El Salvador
OD-	Lebanon	YU-	Yugoslavia
OE-	Austria	YV-	Venezuela
OH-	Finland	Z-	Zimbabwe
OK-	Czechoslovakia	ZA-	Albania
OO-	Belgium	ZK-	New Zealand
OY-	Denmark		

* Cyrillic letters for SSSR.

8

ZP-	Paraguay	6O-	Somalia
ZS-	South Africa	6V-	Senegal
3A-	Monaco	6Y-	Jamaica
3B-	Mauritius	7O-	Democratic Yemen
3C-	Equatorial Guinea	7P-	Lesotho
3D-	Swaziland	7Q-	Malawi
3X-	Guinea	7T-	Algeria
4R-	Sri Lanka	8P-	Barbados
4U-	United Nations Organisation	8Q-	Maldives
4W-	Yemen Arab Republic	8R-	Guyana
4X-	Israel	9G-	Ghana
4YB	Jordanian-Iraqi Co-op Treaty	9H-	Malta
5A-	Libya	9J-	Zambia
5B-	Cyprus	9K-	Kuwait
5H-	Tanzania	9L-	Sierra Leone
5N-	Nigeria	9M-	Malaysia
5R-	Malagasy Republic (Madagascar)	9N-	Nepal
5T-	Mauritania	9Q-	Zaire
5U-	Niger	9U-	Burundi
5V-	Togo	9V-	Singapore
5W-	Western Somoa (Polynesia)	9XR-	Rwanda
5X-	Uganda	9Y-	Trinidad and Tobago
5Y-	Kenya		

Aircraft Type Designations

(eg PA-28 Piper Type 28)

A.	Beagle, Auster	GY	Gardan
AA-	American Aviation, Grumman American	H	Helio
		HM.	Henri Mignet
AB	Agusta-Bell	HP.	Handley Page
AS	Aerospatiale	HR.	Robin
A.S.	Airspeed	H.S.	Hawker Siddeley
A.W.	Armstrong Whitworth	IL	Ilyushin
B.	Blackburn, Bristol Boeing, Beagle	J.	Auster
		L.	Lockheed
BAC	British Aircraft Corporation	L.A.	Luton
BAe	British Aerospace	M.	Miles, Mooney
BAT	British Aerial Transport	MBB	Messerschmitt-Bölkow-Blohm
BN	Britten-Norman	MJ	Jurca
Bo	Bolkow	M.S.	Morane-Saulnier
Bu	Bucker	NA	North American
CAARP	Co-operative des Ateliers Aer de la Région Parisienne	P.	Hunting (formerly Percival), Piaggio
		PA-	Piper
CCF	Canadian Car & Foundry Co	PC.	Pilatus
C.H.	Chrislea	QAC	Quickie Aircraft Co
CHABA	Cambridge Hot-Air Ballooning Association	R.	Rockwell
		S.	Short, Sikorsky
CLA	Comper	SA., SE, SO.	Sud-Aviation, Aérospatiale, Scottish Aviation
CP.	Piel		
D.	Druine	SC	Short
DC-	Douglas Commercial	SCD	Side Cargo Door
D.H.	de Havilland	S.R.	Saunders-Roe, Stinson
D.H.C.	de Havilland Canada	ST	SOCATA
DR.	Jodel (Robin-built)	T.	Tipsy
EMB	Embraer	TB	SOCATA
EoN	Elliotts of Newbury	Tu	Tupolev
EP	Edgar Percival	UH.	United Helicopters (Hiller)
F.	Fairchild, Fokker	V.	Vickers-Armstrongs, BAC
G.	Grumman	V.S.	Vickers-Supermarine
GA	Gulfstream American	WAR	War Aircraft Replicas
G.A.L.	General Aircraft	W.S.	Westland
G.C.	Globe	Z.	Zlin

British Civil Aircraft Registrations

Notes	Reg.	Type (†False registration)	Owner or Operator
	G-EACN	BAT BK23 Bantam (K123) ★	Shuttleworth Trust/O. Warden
	G-EASQ	Bristol Babe (replica) (BAPC87)★	Bomber County Museum
	G-EAVX	Sopwith Pup (B1807)	K. A. M. Baker
	G-EBHX	D.H.53 Humming Bird	Shuttleworth Trust/O. Warden
	G-EBIA	S.E.5A (F904)	Shuttleworth Trust/O. Warden
	G-EBIB	S.E.5A (F939) ★	Science Museum
	G-EBIC	S.E.5A (F938) ★	RAF Museum
	G-EBIR	D.H.51	Shuttleworth Trust/O. Warden
	G-EBJE	Avro 504K (E449)★	RAF Museum
	G-EBJG	Parnall Pixie III ★	Midland Aircraft Preservation Soc
	G-EBJO	ANEC II ★	Shuttleworth Trust/O. Warden
	G-EBKY	Sopwith Pup (N5180)	Shuttleworth Trust/O. Warden
	G-EBLV	D.H.60 Cirrus Moth	British Aerospace/Hatfield
	G-EBMB	Hawker Cygnet I ★	RAF Museum
	G-EBNV	English Electric Wren	Shuttleworth Trust/O. Warden
	G-EBQP	D.H.53 Humming Bird ★	Russavia Collection/Duxford
	G-EBWD	D.H.60X Hermes Moth	Shuttleworth Trust/O. Warden
	G-EBYY	Cierva C.8L ★	Musée de l'Air, Paris
	G-EBZM	Avro 594 Avian IIIA ★	Greater Manchester Museum of Science & Technology
	G-AAAH	D.H.60G Gipsy Moth (replica) (BAPC 168) ★	Hilton Hotel/Gatwick
	G-AAAH	D.H.60G Gipsy Moth ★	Science Museum
	G-AACN	H.P.39 Gugnunc ★	Science Museum/Wroughton
	G-AADR	D.H.60GM Moth	H. F. Moffatt
	G-AAHY	D.H.60M Moth	M. E. Vaisey
	G-AAIN	Parnall Elf II	Shuttleworth Trust/O. Warden
	G-AAMX	D.H.60GM Moth	R. J. Parkhouse
	G-AAMY	D.H.60M Moth	R. Twisleton-Wykeham Fiennes
	G-AAMZ	D.H.60G Moth	C. C. & J. M. Lovell
	G-AANF	D.H.60GMW Moth	A. Lloyd
	G-AANG	Blériot XI	Shuttleworth Trust/O. Warden
	G-AANH	Deperdussin Monoplane	Shuttleworth Trust/O. Warden
	G-AANI	Blackburn Monoplane	Shuttleworth Trust/O. Warden
	G-AANJ	L.V.G.-C VI (7198/18)	Shuttleworth Trust/O. Warden
	G-AANL	D.H.60M Moth	D. & P. Ellis
	G-AANM	Bristol 96A F.2B (D7889)	Aero Vintage Ltd
	G-AANO	D.H.60GMW Moth	R. I. & J. O. Souch
	G-AANV	D.H.60G Moth	R. I. Souch
	G-AAOK	Curtiss Wright Travel Air 12Q	Shipping & Airlines Ltd/Biggin Hill
	G-AAOR	D.H.60G Moth (EM-01)	J. A. Pothecary/Shoreham
	G-AAPZ	Desoutter I (mod.) ★	Shuttleworth Trust/O. Warden
	G-AAUP	Klemm L.25-1A	J. I. Cooper
	G-AAVJ	D.H.60GMW Moth	R. W. Livett/Sywell
	G-AAWO	D.H.60G Gipsy Moth	N. J. W. Reid & L. A. Fenwick
	G-AAXK	Klemm L.25-1A	C. C. Russell-Vick
	G-AAYX	Southern Martlet	Shuttleworth Trust/O. Warden
	G-AAZP	D.H.80A Puss Moth	R. P. Williams
	G-ABAA	Avro 504K (H2311) ★	RAF Museum/Henlow
	G-ABAG	D.H.60G Moth	Shuttleworth Trust/O. Warden
	G-ABDW	D.H.80A Puss Moth (VH-UQB) ★	Museum of Flight/E. Fortune
	G-ABDX	D.H.60G Moth	M. D. Souch
	G-ABEE	Avro 594 Avian IVM (Sports) ★	Aeroplane Collection Ltd
	G-ABEV	D.H.60G Moth	Wessex Aviation & Transport Ltd
	G-ABLM	Cierva C.24 ★	Mosquito Aircraft Museum
	G-ABLS	D.H.80A Puss Moth	R. C. F. Bailey
	G-ABMR	Hart 2 (J9941)★	RAF Museum
	G-ABNT	Civilian C.A.C.1 Coupe	Shipping & Airlines Ltd/Biggin Hill
	G-ABNX	Redwing 2	J. Pothecary (stored)
	G-ABOI	Wheeler Slymph ★	Midland Air Museum
	G-ABOX	Sopwith Pup (N5195)	Museum of Army Flying/Middle Wallop
	G-ABSD	D.H.60G Moth	M. E. Vaisey
	G-ABTC	CLA.7 Swift	P. Channon (stored)
	G-ABUS	CLA.7 Swift	R. C. F. Bailey
	G-ABUU	CLA.7 Swift	H. B. Fox
	G-ABVE	Arrow Active 2	J. D. Penrose
	G-ABWP	Spartan Arrow	R. E. Blain/Barton

10

Reg.	Type	Owner or Operator	Notes
G-ABXL	Granger Archaeopteryx ★	Shuttleworth Trust/O. Warden	
G-ABZB	D.H.60G-III Moth Major	R. E. & B. A. Ogden	
G-ACBH	Blackburn B.2 ★	R. Coles	
G-ACCB	D.H.83 Fox Moth ★	E. A. Gautrey	
G-ACDA	D.H.82A Tiger Moth	R. J. Biddle	
G-ACDC	D.H.82A Tiger Moth	Tiger Club Ltd/Redhill	
G-ACDJ	D.H.82A Tiger Moth	F. J. Terry	
G-ACEJ	D.H.83 Fox Moth	J. I. Cooper	
G-ACFM	Avro 631 Cadet	R. Souch	
G-ACGT	Avro 594 Avian IIIA ★	Yorkshire Light Aircraft Ltd/Leeds	
G-ACIT	D.H.84 Dragon ★	Science Museum/Wroughton	
G-ACLL	D.H.85 Leopard Moth	D. C. M. & V. M. Stiles	
G-ACMA	D.H.85 Leopard Moth	S. J. Filhol/Sherburn	
G-ACMD	D.H.82A Tiger Moth	I. B. & J. M. Grace	
G-ACMN	D.H.85 Leopard Moth	H. D. Labouchere	
G-ACOJ	D.H.85 Leopard Moth	M. J. Abbott	
G-ACOL	D.H.85 Leopard Moth	M. J. Abbott	
G-ACSP	D.H.88 Comet	Saltair Ltd/Staverton	
G-ACSS	D.H.88 Comet	Shuttleworth Trust/Hatfield	
G-ACTF	CLA.7 Swift ★	Brooklands Museum of Aviation/ Weybridge	
G-ACUS	D.H.85 Leopard Moth	T. P. A. Norman/Panshanger	
G-ACUU	Cierva C.30A ★	G. S. Baker/Duxford	
G-ACUX	S.16 Scion (VH-UUP) ★	Ulster Folk & Transport Museum	
G-ACVA	Kay Gyroplane★	Glasgow Museum of Transport	
G-ACWM	Cierva C.30A ★	J. Eagles	
G-ACWP	Cierva C.30A (AP507) ★	Science Museum	
G-ACXE	B.K.L-25C Swallow	J. Wakefield	
G-ACYK	Spartan Cruiser III ★	Museum of Flight (front fuselage)/ E. Fortune/Henstridge	
G-ACZE	D.H.89A Dragon Rapide	Wessex Aviation & Transport Ltd (G-AJGS)/Henstridge	
G-ADAH	D.H.89A Dragon Rapide ★	Museum of Flight/E. Fortune	
G-ADCG	D.H.82A Tiger Moth	D. A. Lowe (stored)	
G-ADEV	Avro 504K (H5199)	Shuttleworth Trust (G-ACNB)/ O. Warden	
G-ADFO	Blackburn B-2 ★	R. Cole	
G-ADFV	Blackburn B-2 ★	Humberside Aircraft Preservation Soc	
G-ADGP	M.2L Hawk Speed Six	R. I. Souch	
G-ADGT	D.H.82A Tiger Moth	D. R. & Mrs M. Wood	
G-ADGV	D.H.82A Tiger Moth	K. J. Whitehead	
G-ADHA	D.H.83 Fox Moth	Wessex Aviation & Transport Ltd	
G-ADHD	D.H.60G-III Moth Major	M. E. Vaisey	
G-ADIA	D.H.82A Tiger Moth	Mithril Racing Ltd/Goodwood	
G-ADJJ	D.H.82A Tiger Moth	J. M. Preston	
G-ADKC	D.H.87B Hornet Moth	L. E. Day/Carlisle	
G-ADKK	D.H.87B Hornet Moth	C. P. B. Horsley & R. G. Anniss	
G-ADKL	D.H.87B Hornet Moth	L. J. Rice	
G-ADKM	D.H.87B Hornet Moth	L. V. Mayhead	
G-ADLY	D.H.87B Hornet Moth	M. V. Gauntlett/Goodwood	
G-ADMT	D.H.87B Hornet Moth	M. A. Livett	
G-ADMW	M.2H Hawk Major (DG590) ★	RAF Museum/Henlow	
G-ADND	D.H.87B Hornet Moth	Shuttleworth Trust/O. Warden	
G-ADNE	D.H.87B Hornet Moth	R. Twisleton-Wykeham Fiennes/ Biggin Hill	
G-ADNZ	D.H.82A Tiger Moth	R. W. & Mrs. S. Pullan	
G-ADOT	D.H.87B Hornet Moth ★	Mosquito Aircraft Museum	
G-ADPJ	B.A.C. Drone	P. G. Dunnington	
G-ADPR	P.3 Gull ★	Shuttleworth Trust Jean/O. Warden	
G-ADPS	B.A. Swallow 2	Wessex Aviation & Transport Ltd	
G-ADRA	Pietenpol Aircamper	A. J. Mason & R. J. Barrett	
G-ADRC	K. & S. Jungster J-1	J. J. Penney & L. R. Williams	
G-ADRG†	Mignet HM.14 replica (BAPC77) ★	Cotswold Aircraft Restoration Group	
G-ADRH	D.H.87B Hornet Moth	I. M. Callier	
G-ADRR	Aeronca C.3	D. S. Morgan	
G-ADRY†	Mignet HM.14 replica (BAPC29) ★	Brooklands Museum	
G-ADUR	D.H.87B Hornet Moth	Wessex Aviation & Transport Ltd	
G-ADWO	D.H.82A Tiger Moth	Wessex Aviation Soc	
G-ADXS	Mignet HM.14 ★	Rebel Air Museum/Earls Colne	
G-ADXT	D.H.82A Tiger Moth	J. & J. M. Pothecary/Shoreham	
G-ADYS	Aeronca C.3	B. Cooper	
G-AEBB	Mignet HM.14 ★	Shuttleworth Trust/O. Warden	

Notes	Reg.	Type	Owner or Operator
	G-AEBJ	Blackburn B-2	British Aerospace/Brough
	G-AEDB	B.A.C. Drone 2	M. C. Russell/Duxford
	G-AEDT	D.H.90 Dragonfly	Wessex Aviation & Transport Ltd
	G-AEDU	D.H.90 Dragonfly	T. Norman
	G-AEEG	M.3A Falcon	Vintage Aircraft Magazine Ltd/Denham
	G-AEEH	Mignet HM.14 ★	RAF Museum/St Athan
	G-AEFG	Mignet HM.14 (BAPC75) ★	N. Ponsford
	G-AEFT	Aeronca C.3	C. E. Humphreys & ptnrs/Henstridge
	G-AEGV	Mignet HM.14 ★	Midland Aircraft Preservation Soc
	G-AEHM	Mignet HM.14 ★	Science Museum/Wroughton
	G-AEJZ	Mignet HM.14 (BAPC120) ★	Bomber County Museum/Cleethorpes
	G-AEKR	Mignet HM.14 (BAPC121) ★	S. Yorks Aviation Soc
	G-AEKV	Kronfield Drone ★	Brooklands Museum of Aviation/Weybridge
	G-AELO	D.H.87B Hornet Moth	S. N. Bostock
	G-AEML	D.H.89 Dragon Rapide	M. V. Gauntlett/Goodwood
	G-AENP	Hawker Hind (K5414) (BAPC78)	Shuttleworth Trust/O. Warden
	G-AEOA	D.H.80A Puss Moth	P. & A. Wood/O. Warden
	G-AEOF†	Mignet HM.14 (BAPC22) ★	Aviodome/Schiphol, Holland
	G-AEOF	Rearwin 8500	Shipping & Airlines Ltd/Biggin Hill
	G-AEOH	Mignet HM.14 ★	Midland Air Museum
	G-AEPH	Bristol F.2B (D8096)	Shuttleworth Trust/O. Warden
	G-AERV	M.11A Whitney Straight ★	Ulster Folk & Transport Museum
	G-AESB	Aeronca C.3	C. E. & W. B. Cooper
	G-AESE	D.H.87B Hornet Moth	J. G. Green/Redhill
	G-AESZ	Chilton D.W.1	R. E. Nerou
	G-AETA	Caudron G.3 (3066) ★	RAF Museum
	G-AEUJ	M.11A Whitney Straight	R. E. Mitchell
	G-AEVS	Aeronca 100	A. J. E. Smith
	G-AEVZ	B. A. Swallow 2	C. D. J. Bland & T. S. Warren/Sandown
	G-AEXD	Aeronca 100	Mrs M. A. & R. W. Mills
	G-AEXF	P.6 Mew Gull	J. D. Penrose/Old Warden
	G-AEXT	Dart Kitten II	A. J. Hartfield
	G-AEXZ	Piper J-2 Cub	Mrs M. & J. R. Dowson/Leicester
	G-AEYY	Martin Monoplane ★	Martin Monoplane Syndicate/Hatfield
	G-AEZF	S.16 Scion 2 ★	Southend Historic Aircraft Soc
	G-AEZJ	P.10 Vega Gull	R. N. Goode & C. R. Wilson
	G-AEZX	Bucker Bu133C Jungmeister	A. J. E. Ditheridge
	G-AFAP†	C.A.S.A. C.352L ★	Aerospace Museum/Cosford
	G-AFAX	B. A. Eagle 2	J. G. Green
	G-AFBS	M.14A Hawk Trainer ★	G. D. Durbridge-Freeman (G-AKKU)/Duxford
	G-AFCL	B. A. Swallow 2	A. M. Dowson/O. Warden
	G-AFDO	Piper J-3F-60 Cub	R. Wald
	G-AFDX	Hanriot HD.1 (75) ★	RAF Museum
	G-AFEL	Monocoupe 90A	Fortune Holdings Ltd/Barton
	G-AFFD	Percival Q-6 ★	B. D. Greenwood
	G-AFFH	Piper J-2 Cub	M. J. Honeychurch
	G-AFFI	Mignet HM.14 replica (BAPC76) ★	Bomber County Museum/Cleethorpes
	G-AFGC	B. A. Swallow 2	H. Plain
	G-AFGD	B. A. Swallow 2	A. T. Williams & ptnrs/Shobdon
	G-AFGE	B. A. Swallow 2	G. R. French
	G-AFGH	Chilton D.W.1.	M. L. & G. L. Joseph
	G-AFGI	Chilton D.W.1. ★	J. E. McDonald
	G-AFGM	Piper J-4A Cub Coupé	A. J. P. Marshall/Carlisle
	G-AFHA	Mosscraft M.A.1. ★	C. V. Butler
	G-AFIN	Chrislea Airguard ★	Aeroplane Collection Ltd
	G-AFIU	Parker C.A.4 Parasol ★ (LA-3 Minor)	Aeroplane Collection Ltd/Warmingham
	G-AFJA	Watkinson Dingbat ★	K. Woolley
	G-AFJB	Foster-Wikner G.M.1. Wicko (DR613) ★	K. Woolley
	G-AFJR	Tipsy Trainer 1	M. E. Vaisey
	G-AFJV	Mosscraft MA.2	C. V. Butler
	G-AFLW	M.17 Monarch	N. I. Dalziel/Biggin Hill
	G-AFNG	D.H.94 Moth Minor	T. E. G. Buckett/White Waltham
	G-AFNI	D.H.94 Moth Minor	B. M. Welford
	G-AFOB	D.H.94 Moth Minor	Wessex Aviation & Transport Ltd
	G-AFOJ	D.H.94 Moth Minor	R. M. Long
	G-AFPN	D.H.94 Moth Minor	J. W. & A. R. Davy/Carlisle
	G-AFPR	D.H.94 Moth Minor	J. A. Livett
	G-AFRZ	M.17 Monarch	R. E. Mitchell (G-AIDE)
	G-AFSC	Tipsy Trainer 1	R. V. & M. H. Smith

Reg.	Type	Owner or Operator	Notes
G-AFSV	Chilton D.W.1A	R. Nerou	
G-AFSW	Chilton D.W.2 ★	R. I. Souch	
G-AFTA	Hawker Tomtit (K1786)	Shuttleworth Trust/O. Warden	
G-AFTN	Taylorcraft Plus C2 ★	Leicestershire County Council Museums	
G-AFUP	Luscombe 8A Silvaire	A. J. W. Sturgess	
G-AFVE	D.H.82 Tiger Moth	P. E. Swinstead/Blackbushe	
G-AFVN	Tipsy Trainer 1	W. Callow & ptnrs	
G-AFWH	Piper J-4A Cub Coupé	J. R. Edwards & D. D. Smith	
G-AFWI	D.H.82A Tiger Moth	N. E. Rankin & ptnrs	
G-AFWT	Tipsy Trainer 1	J. S. Barker/Redhill	
G-AFYD	Luscombe 8E Silvaire	J. D. Iliffe	
G-AFYO	Stinson H.W.75	R. N. Wright	
G-AFZA	Piper J-4A Cub Coupé	J. R. Joiner	
G-AFZE	Heath Parasol	K. C. D. St Cyrien	
G-AFZK	Luscombe 8A Silvaire	M. G. Byrnes	
G-AFZL	Porterfield CP.50	P. G. Lucas & ptnrs/White Waltham	
G-AFZN	Luscombe 8A Silvaire	R. V. Smith	
G-AGAT	Piper J-3F-50 Cub	Wessex Aviation & Transport Ltd	
G-AGBN	G.A.L.42 Cygnet 2 ★	Museum of Flight/E. Fortune	
G-AGEG	D.H.82A Tiger Moth	T. P. A. Norman	
G-AGFT	Avia FL.3	P. A. Smith	
G-AGHY	D.H.82A Tiger Moth	P. Groves	
G-AGIV	Piper J-3C-65 Cub	P. C. & F. M. Gill	
G-AGJG	D.H.89A Dragon Rapide	Russavia Ltd/Duxford	
G-AGLK	Auster 5D	W. C. E. Tazewell	
G-AGMI	Luscombe 8A	Bluegale Ltd	
G-AGNV	Avro 685 York 1 (MW100) ★	Aerospace Museum/Cosford	
G-AGOH	J/1 Autocrat	Leicestershire County Council Museums	
G-AGOS	R.S.4 Desford Trainer (VZ728)	Scottish Aircraft Collection/Perth	
G-AGOY	M.48 Messenger 3 (U-0247)	P. A. Brooks	
G-AGPG	Avro 19 Srs 2 ★	Brenzett Aviation Museum	
G-AGPK	D.H.82A Tiger Moth	P. D. Castle	
G-AGRU	V.498 Viking 1A ★	Aerospace Museum/Cosford	
G-AGSH	D.H.89A Dragon Rapide 6	Specialist Flying Training Ltd/Carlisle	
G-AGTM	D.H.89A Dragon Rapide 6 (NF875)	Russavia Ltd/Duxford	
G-AGTO	J/1 Autocrat	M. J. Barnett & D. J. T. Miller/Duxford	
G-AGTT	J/1 Autocrat	R. Farrer	
G-AGVG	J/1 Autocrat	RN Aviation (Leicester Airport) Ltd	
G-AGVN	J/1 Autocrat	S. Thursfield & K. E. Eld/Leicester	
G-AGVV	Piper J-3C-65 Cub	A. R. W. Taylor & D. Lofts/Sleap	
G-AGWE	Avro 19 Srs 2 ★	Phoenix Aviation Museum	
G-AGXN	J/1N Alpha	I. R. Walters/Cranwell	
G-AGXT	J/1N Alpha ★	Nene Valley Aircraft Museum	
G-AGXU	J/1N Alpha	R. J. Guess/Sibson	
G-AGXV	J/1 Autocrat	B. S. Dowsett	
G-AGYD	J/1N Alpha	P. Herring & ptnrs/Dishforth	
G-AGYH	J/1N Alpha	G. E. Twyman & P. J. Rae	
G-AGYK	J/1 Autocrat	D. A. Smith	
G-AGYL	J/1 Autocrat ★	Military Vehicle Conservation Group/Havant	
G-AGYT	J/1N Alpha	P. C. Davies & ptnrs/Lee-on-Solent	
G-AGYU	DH.82A Tiger Moth (DE208)	P. & A. Wood	
G-AGYY	Ryan ST.3KR	D. S. & I. M. Morgan	
G-AGZZ	D.H.82A Tiger Moth	G. P. L. Shea-Simonds/Netheravon	
G-AHAL	J/1N Alpha	Skegness Air Taxi Services Ltd/Ingoldmells	
G-AHAM	J/1 Autocrat	P. J. Stock/Goodwood	
G-AHAN	D.H.82A Tiger Moth	G. L. Owens	
G-AHAP	J/1 Autocrat (Rover) ★	V. H. Bellamy	
G-AHAU	J/1 Autocrat	J. F. Smith	
G-AHAV	J/1 Autocrat	C. J. Freeman/Headcorn	
G-AHBL	D.H.87B Hornet Moth	Dr Ursula H. Hamilton	
G-AHBM	D.H.87B Hornet Moth	P. A. & E. P. Gliddon	
G-AHCK	J/1N Alpha	P. A. Woodman/Shoreham	
G-AHCR	Gould-Taylorcraft Plus D Special	D. E. H. Balmford & D. R. Shepherd/Yeovil	
G-AHEC	Luscombe 8A Silvaire	C. C. Lovell	
G-AHED	D.H.89A Dragon Rapide (RL962) ★	RAF Museum (Cardington)	
G-AHGD	D.H.89A Dragon Rapide (Z7258)	M. R. L. Astor/Booker	

13

Notes	Reg.	Type	Owner or Operator
	G-AHGW	Taylorcraft Plus D (LB375)	C. V. Butler/Coventry
	G-AHGZ	Taylorcraft Plus D	S. J. Ball
	G-AHHH	J/1 Autocrat	H. A. Jones/Norwich
	G-AHHK	J/1 Autocrat	C. Johns
	G-AHHN	J/1 Autocrat	KK Aviation
	G-AHHP	J/1N Alpha	D. J. Hutcheson (G-SIME)
	G-AHHT	J/1N Alpha	R.A.E. Aero Club/Farnborough
	G-AHHU	J/1N Alpha ★	L. Groves & I. R. F. Hammond
	G-AHIP	Piper J-3C-65 Cub	R. E. Nerou/Coventry
	G-AHIZ	D.H.82A Tiger Moth	C.F.G. Flying Ltd/Cambridge
	G-AHKX	Avro 19 Srs 2	British Aerospace PLC/Woodford
	G-AHKY	Miles M.18 Series 2	Scottish Aircraft Collection/Perth
	G-AHLI	Auster 3	G. A. Leathers
	G-AHLK	Auster 3	E. T. Brackenbury/Leicester
	G-AHLT	D.H.82A Tiger Moth	R. C. F. Bailey
	G-AHMJ	Cierva C.30A (K4235) ★	Shuttleworth Trust/O. Warden
	G-AHMN	D.H.82A Tiger Moth (N6985)	Museum of Army Flying/Middle Wallop
	G-AHNH	Bucker Bu181 Bestmann	D. M. Fenton
	G-AHNR	Taylorcraft BC-12D	Bluegale Ltd
	G-AHOO	D.H.82A Tiger Moth	G. W. Bisshopp
	G-AHRI	D.H.104 Dove 1 ★	Lincolnshire Aviation Museum
	G-AHRO	Cessna 140	R. H. Screen/Kidlington
	G-AHSA	Avro 621 Tutor (K3215)	Shuttleworth Trust/O. Warden
	G-AHSD	Taylorcraft Plus D	A. Tucker
	G-AHSO	J/1N Alpha	Skegness Air Taxi Services Ltd/ Ingoldmells
	G-AHSP	J/1 Autocrat	D. S. Johnstone & ptnrs
	G-AHSS	J/1N Alpha	P. J. Wenman/Denham
	G-AHST	J/1N Alpha	C. H. Smith
	G-AHSW	J/1 Autocrat	K. W. Brown
	G-AHTE	P.44 Proctor V	J. G. H. Hassell
	G-AHTW	A.S.40 Oxford (V3388) ★	Skyfame Collection/Duxford
	G-AHUF	D.H.82A Tiger Moth	D. S. & I. M. Morgan
	G-AHUG	Taylorcraft Plus D	D. Nieman
	G-AHUI	M.38 Messenger 2A ★	Berkshire Aviation Group
	G-AHUJ	M.14A Hawk Trainer 3 (R1914)	Strathallan Aircraft Collection
	G-AHUN	Globe GC-1B Swift	B. R. Rossiter/White Waltham
	G-AHUV	D.H.82A Tiger Moth	W. G. Gordon
	G-AHVU	D.H.82A Tiger Moth (T6313)	Foley Farm Flying Group
	G-AHVV	D.H.82A Tiger Moth	R. Jones
	G-AHWJ	Taylorcraft Plus D (LB294)	Museum of Army Flying/Middle Wallop
	G-AHXE	Taylorcraft Plus D (LB312)	J. Pothecary/Shoreham
	G-AIBE	Fulmar II (N1854) ★	F.A.A. Museum/Yeovilton
	G-AIBM	J/1 Autocrat	J. K. Avis
	G-AIBR	J/1 Autocrat ★	A. Topen
	G-AIBW	J/1N Alpha	W. E. Bateson/Blackpool
	G-AIBX	J/1 Autocrat	Wasp Flying Group/Panshanger
	G-AIBY	J/1 Autocrat	D. Morris/Sherburn
	G-AICX	Luscombe 8A Silvaire	R. V. Smith/Henstridge
	G-AIDL	D.H.89A Dragon Rapide 6	Snowdon Mountain Aviation Ltd
	G-AIDS	D.H.82A Tiger Moth	K. D. Pogmore & T. Dann
	G-AIEK	M.38 Messenger 2A (RG333)	J. Buckingham
	G-AIFZ	J/1N Alpha	C. P. Humphries
	G-AIGD	J/1 Autocrat	A. G. Batchelor
	G-AIGF	J/1N Alpha	A. R. C. Mathie
	G-AIGM	J/1N Alpha	Wickenby Flying Club Ltd
	G-AIGT	J/1N Alpha	B. D. Waller
	G-AIGU	J/1N Alpha	N. K. Geddes
	G-AIIH	Piper J-3C-65 Cub	J. A. de Salis
	G-AIJI	J/1N Alpha ★	C. Baker
	G-AIJM	Auster J/4	N. Huxtable
	G-AIJR	Auster J/4	B. A. Harris/Halfpenny Green
	G-AIJS	Auster J/4 ★	stored
	G-AIJT	Auster J/4 srs 100	Aberdeen Auster Flying Group
	G-AIJZ	J/1 Autocrat	stored
	G-AIKE	Auster 5	C. J. Baker
	G-AILL	M.38 Messenger 2A	H. Best-Devereux
	G-AIPR	Auster J/4	MPM Flying Group/Booker
	G-AIPV	J/1 Autocrat	J. Linegar
	G-AIPW	J/1 Autocrat	B. Hillman
	G-AIRC	J/1 Autocrat	A. G. Martlew/Barton
	G-AIRI	D.H.82A Tiger Moth	E. R. Goodwin
	G-AIRK	D.H.82A Tiger Moth	R. C. Teverson & ptnrs

Reg.	Type	Owner or Operator	Notes
G-AISA	Tipsy B Srs 1	J. W. Thomson & R. P. Aston	
G-AISB	Tipsy B Srs 1	D. M. Fenton	
G-AISC	Tipsy B Srs 1	Wagtail Flying Group	
G-AISS	Piper J-3C-65 Cub	K. R. Nunn	
G-AIST	V.S.300 Spitfire IA (AR213)	The Hon A. M. M. Lindsay/Booker	
G-AISX	Piper J-3C-65 Cub	R. I. Souch	
G-AITB	A.S.10 Oxford (MP425) ★	RAF Museum/Cardington	
G-AIUA	M.14A Hawk Trainer 3	P. A. Brook	
G-AIUL	D.H.89A Dragon Rapide 6	I. Jones	
G-AIXA	Taylorcraft Plus D	A. A. & M. J. Copse	
G-AIXD	D.H.82A Tiger Moth	Sark International Airways/Guernsey	
G-AIXN	Benes-Mraz M.1c Sokol	J. F. Evetts & D. Patel	
G-AIYR	D.H.89A Dragon Rapide	C. D. Cyster	
G-AIYS	D.H.85 Leopard Moth	Wessex Aviation & Transport Ltd	
G-AIZE	F.24W Argus 2 ★	RAF Museum/Henlow	
G-AIZF	D.H.82A Tiger Moth ★	stored	
G-AIZG	V.S. Walrus 1 (L2301) ★	F.A.A. Museum/Yeovilton	
G-AIZU	J/1 Autocrat	C. J. & J. G. B. Morley	
G-AIZY	J/1 Autocrat	B. J. Richards	
G-AIZZ	J/1 Autocrat ★	S. E. Bond	
G-AJAB	J/1N Alpha	Air Farm Ltd	
G-AJAC	J/1N Alpha	R. C. Hibberd	
G-AJAD	Piper J-3C-65 Cub	R. A. C. Hoppenbrouwers	
G-AJAE	J/1N Alpha	M. G. Stops	
G-AJAJ	J/1N Alpha	R. B. Lawrence	
G-AJAM	J/2 Arrow	D. A. Porter	
G-AJAO	Piper J-3C-65 Cub	T. G. Dixon	
G-AJAS	J/1N Alpha	C. J. Baker	
G-AJCP	D.31 Turbulent	H. J. Shaw	
G-AJDW	J/1 Autocrat	D. R. Hunt	
G-AJDY	J/1 Autocraft ★	stored	
G-AJEB	J/1N Alpha ★	Aeroplane Collection Ltd/Warmingham	
G-AJEE	J/1 Autocrat	A. R. C. De Albanoz/Bournemouth	
G-AJEH	J/1N Alpha	A. Beswick & N. Robinson	
G-AJEI	J/1N Alpha	Skegness Air Taxi Services Ltd/ Ingoldmells	
G-AJEM	J/1 Autocrat	J. C. Greenslade	
G-AJES	Piper J-3C-65 Cub (330485)	P. Crawford	
G-AJGJ	Auster 5 (RT486)	S. C. Challis & J. Lawless	
G-AJHJ	Auster 5	stored	
G-AJHO	D.H.89A Dragon Rapide	M. V. Gauntlett/Goodwood	
G-AJHS	D.H.82A Tiger Moth	Machine Music Ltd/Blackbushe	
G-AJHU	D.H.82A Tiger Moth	F. P. Le Coyte	
G-AJID	J/1 Autocrat	D. J. Ronayne/France	
G-AJIH	J/1 Autocrat	T. Boyd & A. H. Diver	
G-AJIS	J/1N Alpha	A. Tucker	
G-AJIT	J/1 Kingsland Autocrat	Kingsland Aviation Ltd	
G-AJIU	J/1 Autocrat	W. Greenhalgh & Son Ltd/Doncaster	
G-AJIW	J/1N Alpha	N. A. Roberts	
G-AJJP	Jet Gyrodyne (XJ389) ★	Aerospace Museum/Cosford	
G-AJJS	Cessna 120	L. G. Sharkey	
G-AJJT	Cessna 120	P. M. Hallett & J. S. Robson	
G-AJOA	D.H.82A Tiger Moth (T5424)	F. P. Le Coyte	
G-AJOC	M.38 Messenger 2A ★	Ulster Folk & Transport Museum	
G-AJOE	M.38 Messenger 2A	J. Eagles & P. C. Kirby/Staverton	
G-AJON	Aeronca 7AC Champion	R. D. Morcom	
G-AJOV†	Sikorsky S-51 ★	Aerospace Museum/Cosford	
G-AJOZ	F.24W Argus 2 ★	Lincolnshire Aviation Museum	
G-AJPI	F.24R-41a Argus 3	J. F. Read/White Waltham	
G-AJPZ	J/1 Autocrat ★	Wessex Aviation Soc	
G-AJRB	J/1 Autocrat	S. C. Luck/Sywell	
G-AJRC	J/1 Autocrat	S. W. Watkins & ptnrs	
G-AJRE	J/1 Autocrat (Lycoming)	T. A. Hodges	
G-AJRH	J/1N Alpha	Leicestershire County Council Museums	
G-AJRS	M.14A Hawk Trainer 3 (P6382)	Shuttleworth Trust/O. Warden	
G-AJTW	D.H.82A Tiger Moth	J. A. Barker	
G-AJUD	J/1 Autocrat	C. L. Sawyer	
G-AJUE	J/1 Autocrat	P. H. B. Cole	
G-AJUL	J/1N Alpha	M. J. Crees	
G-AJVE	D.H.82A Tiger Moth	M. J. Abbot & I. J. Jones/Dunkeswell	
G-AJVT	Auster 5	I. N. M. Cameron	
G-AJXC	Auster 5	J. E. Graves	
G-AJXV	Auster 4 (NJ695)	P. C. J. Farries/Leicester	

Notes	Reg.	Type	Owner or Operator
	G-AJXY	Auster 4	G. B. Morris
	G-AJYB	J/1N Alpha	P. J. Shotbolt
	G-AKAA	Piper J-3C-65 Cub	M. S. C. Ball
	G-AKAT	M.14A Magister (T9738)	A. J. E. Smith
	G-AKAZ	Piper J-3C-65 Cub	S. J. Johnstone
	G-AKBM	M.38 Messenger 2A ★	Bristol Plane Preservation Unit
	G-AKBO	M.38 Messenger 2A	B. Du Cros
	G-AKDN	D.H.C. 1A Chipmunk 10	K. R. Nunn/Seething
	G-AKEL	M.65 Gemini 1A ★	Ulster Folk & Transport Museum
	G-AKER	M.65 Gemini 1A ★	Berkshire Aviation Group
	G-AKEZ	M.38 Messenger 2A (RG333) ★	P. G. Lee
	G-AKGD	M.65 Gemini 1A ★	Berkshire Aviation Group
	G-AKGE	M.65 Gemini 3C ★	Ulster Folk & Transport Museum
	G-AKHP	M.65 Gemini 1A	P. G. Lee
	G-AKHW	M.65 Gemini 1A	Vintage Aircraft Magazine Ltd/Denham
	G-AKHZ	M.65 Gemini 7 ★	Berkshire Aviation Group
	G-AKIB	Piper J-3C-90 Cub (480015)	M. C. Bennett
	G-AKIF	D.H.89A Dragon Rapide	Airborne Taxi Services Ltd/Booker
	G-AKIN	M.38 Messenger 2A	A. J. Spiller/Sywell
	G-AKIU	P.44 Proctor V ★	N. Weald Aircraft Restoration Flight
	G-AKJU	J/1N Alpha	R. C. Lewis
	G-AKKB	M.65 Gemini 1A	S.A.C. Bristol Ltd
	G-AKKH	M.65 Gemini 1A	M. C. Russell/Duxford
	G-AKKR	M.14A Magister (T9707) ★	Greater Manchester Museum of Science & Technology
	G-AKKY	M.14A Hawk Trainer 3 (L6906) (BAPC44) ★	Berkshire Aviation Group/Woodley
	G-AKLW	SA.6 Sealand 1 ★	Ulster Folk & Transport Museum
	G-AKOE	D.H.89A Dragon Rapide 4	J. E. Pierce
	G-AKOT	Auster 5 ★	C. Baker
	G-AKOW	Auster 5 (TJ569) ★	Museum of Army Flying/Middle Wallop
	G-AKPF	M.14A Hawk Trainer 3 (N3788) ★	L. N. D. Taylor
	G-AKPI	Auster 5 (NJ703)	B. H. Hargrave/Doncaster
	G-AKRA	Piper J-3C-65 Cub	W. R. Savin
	G-AKSZ	Auster 5	A. R. C. Mathie
	G-AKTH	Piper J-3C-65 Cub	A. L. Wickens
	G-AKTI	Luscombe 8A Silvaire	C. C. & J. M. Lovell
	G-AKTJ	Piper J-3C-65 Cub	N. M. Bloom
	G-AKTL	Luscombe 8A Silvaire	R. W. Sage
	G-AKTM	Luscombe 8F Silvaire	B. R. Rossiter
	G-AKTN	Luscombe 8A Silvaire	C. J. Pollard
	G-AKTO	Aeronca 7AC Champion	P. R. B. Truscott
	G-AKTP	PA-17 Vagabond	L. A. Maynard
	G-AKTS	Cessna 120	B. A. Bower
	G-AKTT	Luscombe 8A Silvaire	T. G. Dixon
	G-AKUE	D.H.82A Tiger Moth	S. J. Ellis
	G-AKUF	Luscombe 8A Silvaire	R. D. Jones
	G-AKUG	Luscombe 8A Silvaire	J. F. D. Robbie
	G-AKUH	Luscombe 8E Silvaire	C. C. Lovell
	G-AKUI	Luscombe 8E Silvaire	C. C. Lovell
	G-AKUJ	Luscombe 8E Silvaire	D. Delaney & C. L. Cooper
	G-AKUK	Luscombe 8A Silvaire	C. C. Lovell
	G-AKUM	Luscombe 8F Silvaire	R. J. Willies
	G-AKUW	C.H.3 Super Ace	C. V. Butler (stored)
	G-AKVF	C.H.3 Super Ace	P. V. B. Longthorp/Bodmin
	G-AKVP	Luscombe 8A Silvaire	D. G. Anderson
	G-AKVZ	M.38 Messenger 4B	Shipping & Airlines Ltd/Biggin Hill
	G-AKWS	Auster 5-160	J. E. Homewood
	G-AKWT	Auster 5 ★	Loughborough & Leicester Aircraft Preservation Soc
	G-AKXP	Auster 5	F. E. Telling
	G-AKXS	D.H.82A Tiger Moth	P. A. Colman
	G-AKZN	P.34A Proctor 3 (Z7197) ★	RAF Museum/St Athan
	G-ALAH	M.38 Messenger 4A (RH377) ★	RAF Museum/Henlow
	G-ALAX	D.H.89A Dragon Rapide ★	Durney Aeronautical Collection/Andover
	G-ALBJ	Auster 5	R. H. Elkington
	G-ALBK	Auster 5	S. J. Wright & Co (Farmers) Ltd
	G-ALBN	Bristol 173 (XF785) ★	RAF Museum/Henlow
	G-ALCK	P.34A Proctor 3 (LZ766) ★	Skyfame Collection/Duxford
	G-ALCS	M.65 Gemini 3C ★	Stored
	G-ALCU	D.H.104 Dove 2 ★	Midland Air Museum

16

Reg.	Type	Owner or Operator	Notes
G-ALDG	HP.81 Hermes 4 ★	Duxford Aviation Soc (*Fuselage only*)	
G-ALEH	PA-17 Vagabond	A. D. Pearce/Redhill	
G-ALFA	Auster 5	Alpha Flying Group	
G-ALFM	D.H.104 Devon C.2	N. J. Taaffe & A. D. Hemley	
G-ALFT	D.H.104 Dove 6 ★	Torbay Aircraft Museum	
G-ALFU	D.H.104 Dove 6 ★	Duxford Aviation Soc	
G-ALGA	PA-15 Vagabond	M. J. Markey/Biggin Hill	
G-ALGT	V.S.379 Spitfire 14 (RM689)	Rolls-Royce Ltd	
G-ALIJ	PA-17 Vagabond	RFC Flying Group/Popham	
G-ALIW	D.H.82A Tiger Moth	D. I. M. Geddes & F. Curry/Booker	
G-ALJF	P.34A Proctor 3	J. F. Moore/Biggin Hill	
G-ALJL	D.H.82A Tiger Moth	C. G. Clarke	
G-ALNA	D.H.82A Tiger Moth	A. W. Kennedy	
G-ALND	D.H.82A Tiger Moth (N9191)	Arrow Air Services (Engineering) Ltd/ Shipdham	
G-ALNV	Auster 5 ★	*stored*	
G-ALOD	Cessna 140	J. R. Stainer	
G-ALRH	EoN Type 8 Baby	P. D. Moran	
G-ALRI	D.H.82A Tiger Moth (T5672)	Wessex Aviation & Transport Ltd	
G-ALSP	Bristol 171 (WV783) Sycamore ★	RAF Museum/Henlow	
G-ALSS	Bristol 171 (WA576) Sycamore ★	E. Fortune	
G-ALST	Bristol 171 (WA577) Sycamore ★	N.E. Aircraft Museum/Usworth	
G-ALSW	Bristol 171 (WT933) Sycamore ★	Newark Air Museum	
G-ALSX	Bristol 171 (G-48-1) Sycamore ★	British Rotorcraft Museum/Duxford	
G-ALTO	Cessna 140	J. E. Cummings/Popham	
G-ALTW	D.H.82A Tiger Moth ★	A. Mangham	
G-ALUC	D.H.82A Tiger Moth	D. R. & M. Wood/Shipdham	
G-ALVP	D.H.82A Tiger Moth ★	V. & R. Wheele (*stored*)	
G-ALWB	D.H.C.1 Chipmunk 22A	M. L. & J. M. Soper/Perth	
G-ALWC	Dakota 4	Visionair (International Aviation) Ltd	
G-ALWF	V.701 Viscount ★	Viscount Preservation Trust/Duxford	
G-ALWS	D.H.82A Tiger Moth ★	Airwork Services Ltd	
G-ALWW	D.H.82A Tiger Moth	F. W. Fay & ptnrs	
G-ALXT	D.H.89A Dragon Rapide ★	Science Museum/Wroughton	
G-ALXZ	Auster 5-150	B. J. W. Thomas & R. A. E. Witheridge	
G-ALYB	Auster 5 (RT520)★	S. Yorks Aircraft Preservation Soc	
G-ALYG	Auster 5D	A. L. Young	
G-ALYW	D.H.106 Comet 1 ★	RAF Exhibition Flight (*fuselage converted to Nimrod*)	
G-ALZE	BN-1F ★	M. R. Short/Southampton Hall of Aviation	
G-ALZO	A.S.57 Ambassador★	Duxford Aviation Soc	
G-AMAW	Luton LA-4 Minor	R. H. Coates	
G-AMBB	D.H.82A Tiger Moth	J. Eagles	
G-AMCA	Dakota 3	Air Atlantique Ltd/Coventry	
G-AMCM	D.H.82A Tiger Moth	G. C. Masterton	
G-AMDA	Avro 652A Anson 1 (N4877)★	Skyfame Collection/Duxford	
G-AMEN	PA-18 Super Cub 95	A. Lovejoy & W. Cook	
G-AMHF	D.H.82A Tiger Moth	L. Mayhead	
G-AMHJ	Dakota 6	Atlantic Air Transport Ltd/Coventry	
G-AMIU	D.H.82A Tiger Moth	R. & Mrs J. L. Jones	
G-AMKU	J/1B Aiglet	Southdown Flying Group (*stored*)	
G-AMLZ	P.50 Prince 6E ★	J. F. Coggins/Coventry	
G-AMMS	J/5F Aiglet Trainer	V. Long	
G-AMOG	V.701 Viscount ★	Aerospace Museum/Cosford	
G-AMPG	PA-12 Super Cruiser	R. Simpson	
G-AMPI	SNCAN Stampe SV-4C	J. Hewett	
G-AMPO	Dakota 4	Atlantic Air Transport Ltd/Coventry	
G-AMPP	Dakota 3 (G-AMSU) ★	Dan-Air Preservation Group/Lasham	
G-AMPW	J/5B Autocar ★	R. Neal (*stored*)	
G-AMPY	Dakota 4	Air Atlantique Ltd/Coventry	
G-AMPZ	Dakota 4	Janes Aviation Ltd/Blackpool	
G-AMRA	Dakota 6	Air Atlantique Ltd/Coventry	
G-AMRF	J/5F Aiglet Trainer	A. I. Topps/E. Midlands	
G-AMRK	G.37 Gladiator (L8032)	Shuttleworth Trust/O. Warden	
G-AMSG	SIPA 903	S. W. Markham	
G-AMSV	Dakota 4	Air Atlantique Ltd/Coventry	
G-AMTA	J/5F Aiglet Trainer	H. J. Jauncey/Rochester	
G-AMTD	J/5F Aiglet Trainer	C. I. Fray	
G-AMTK	D.H.82A Tiger Moth ★	A. Topen (*stored*)	
G-AMTM	J/1 Autocrat	R. Stobo & D. Clewley	
G-AMUF	D.H.C.1 Chipmunk 21	Redhill Tailwheel Flying Club Ltd	
G-AMVD	Auster 5	R. F. Tolhurst	

Notes	Reg.	Type	Owner or Operator
	G-AMVP	Tipsy Junior	A. R. Wershat
	G-AMVS	D.H.82A Tiger Moth	P. A. Crawford
	G-AMXT	D.H.104 Sea Devon C.20	Scoteroy Ltd/Southampton
	G-AMYA	Zlin Z.381	D. M. Fenton
	G-AMYD	J/5L Aiglet Trainer	G. H. Maskell
	G-AMYJ	Dakota 6	Janes Aviation Ltd/Blackpool
	G-AMYL	PA-17 Vagabond	P. J. Penn-Sayers/Shoreham
	G-AMZI	J/5F Aiglet Trainer	J. F. Moore/Biggin Hill
	G-AMZT	J/5F Aiglet Trainer	D. Hyde & J. W. Saull/Cranfield
	G-AMZU	J/5F Aiglet Trainer	J. A. Longworth & ptnrs
	G-ANAF	Dakota 3	Atlantic Air Transport Ltd/Coventry
	G-ANAP	D.H.104 Dove 6 ★	Brunel Technical College/Lulsgate
	G-ANCF	B.175 Britannia 308 ★	—/Weybridge
	G-ANCS	D.H.82A Tiger Moth (R4907)	M. F. Newman
	G-ANCX	D.H.82A Tiger Moth	D. R. Wood/Biggin Hill
	G-ANDE	D.H.82A Tiger Moth	A. J. & P. B. Borsberry
	G-ANDM	D.H.82A Tiger Moth	J. G. Green
	G-ANDP	D.H.82A Tiger Moth	A. H. Diver
	G-ANDX	D.H.104 Devon C.2	L. Richards
	G-ANEC	D.H.82A Tiger Moth ★	(stored)
	G-ANEF	D.H.82A Tiger Moth (T5493)	RAF College Flying Club Co Ltd/ Cranwell
	G-ANEH	D.H.82A Tiger Moth ★	A. Topen/Cranfield
	G-ANEL	D.H.82A Tiger Moth (N9238)	Chauffair Ltd
	G-ANEM	D.H.82A Tiger Moth	P. J. Benest
	G-ANEW	D.H.82A Tiger Moth	A. L. Young
	G-ANEZ	D.H.82A Tiger Moth	C. D. J. Bland & T. S. Warren/Sandown
	G-ANFC	D.H.82A Tiger Moth (DE363) ★	Mosquito Aircraft Museum
	G-ANFH	Westland S-55 ★	British Rotorcraft Museum
	G-ANFI	D.H.82A Tiger Moth (DE623)	D. H. R. Jenkins
	G-ANFL	D.H.82A Tiger Moth	R. P. Whitby & ptnrs
	G-ANFM	D.H.82A Tiger Moth	S. A. Brook & ptnrs/Booker
	G-ANFP	D.H.82A Tiger Moth ★	Mosquito Aircraft Museum
	G-ANFU	Auster 5 ★	N.E. Aircraft Museum
	G-ANFV	D.H.82A Tiger Moth (DF155)	R. A. L. Falconer
	G-ANFW	D.H.82A Tiger Moth	G. M. Fraser/Denham
	G-ANHK	D.H.82A Tiger Moth	J. D. Iliffe
	G-ANHR	Auster 5	C. G. Winch
	G-ANHX	Auster 5D	D. J. Baker
	G-ANHZ	Auster 5	D. W. Pennell
	G-ANIE	Auster 5 (TW467)	S. A. Stibbard
	G-ANIJ	Auster 5D	H. A. Jones
	G-ANIS	Auster 5	J. Clarke-Cockburn
	G-ANJA	D.H.82A Tiger Moth (N9389)	J. J. Young
	G-ANJD	D.H.82A Tiger Moth	H. J. Jauncey/(stored)
	G-ANJK	D.H.82A Tiger Moth	A. D. Williams
	G-ANJV	W.S.55 Whirlwind 3 (VR-BET)★	British Rotorcraft Museum
	G-ANKK	D.H.82A Tiger Moth (T5854)	Halfpenny Green Tiger Group
	G-ANKT	D.H.82A Tiger Moth (T6818)	Shuttleworth Trust/O. Warden
	G-ANKZ	D.H.82A Tiger Moth (N6466)	Fortune Services Ltd/Barton
	G-ANLD	D.H.82A Tiger Moth	D. P. Parks
	G-ANLH	D.H.82A Tiger Moth	The Aeroplane Co (Hamble) Ltd
	G-ANLS	D.H.82A Tiger Moth	P. A. Gliddon
	G-ANLW	W.B.1. Widgeon (MD497) ★	Helicopter Hire Ltd (stored)
	G-ANLX	D.H.82A Tiger Moth	B. J. Borsberry & ptnrs
	G-ANMO	D.H.82A Tiger Moth	E. Lay
	G-ANMV	D.H.82A Tiger Moth (T7404)	J. W. Davy/Cardiff
	G-ANMY	D.H.82A Tiger Moth	D. J. Elliott
	G-ANNB	D.H.82A Tiger Moth	Cormack (Aircraft Services) Ltd/ Glasgow
	G-ANNK	D.H.82A Tiger Moth	P. J. Wilcox/Cranfield
	G-ANNN	D.H.82A Tiger Moth	T. Pate
	G-ANOA	Hiller UH-12A ★	Redhill Technical College
	G-ANOD	D.H.82A Tiger Moth	D. R. & M. Wood
	G-ANOH	D.H.82A Tiger Moth	D. H. Parkhouse & ptnrs/White Waltham
	G-ANOK	S.91 Safir ★	Strathallan Aircraft Collection
	G-ANOM	D.H.82A Tiger Moth	P. A. Colman
	G-ANON	D.H.82A Tiger Moth (T7909)	A. C. Mercer/Sherburn
	G-ANOO	D.H.82A Tiger Moth	T. J. Hartwell & ptnrs
	G-ANOR	D.H.82A Tiger Moth	G. A. Black & C. L. Keith-Lucas
	G-ANOV	D.H.104 Dove 6 ★	Museum of Flight/E. Fortune
	G-ANPK	D.H.82A Tiger Moth	The D. & P. Group
	G-ANPP	P.34A Proctor 3	C. P. A. & J. Jeffery

Reg.	Type	Owner or Operator	Notes
G-ANRF	D.H.82A Tiger Moth	C. D. Cyster	
G-ANRM	D.H.82A Tiger Moth	C. A. Currie & D. G. Relf/Goodwood	
G-ANRN	D.H.82A Tiger Moth	J. J. V. Elwes	
G-ANRP	Auster 5 (TW439)	C. T. K. Lane	
G-ANRX	D.H.82A Tiger Moth ★	Mosquito Aircraft Museum	
G-ANSM	D.H.82A Tiger Moth	J. L. Bond	
G-ANTE	D.H.82A Tiger Moth	T. I. Sutton & B. J. Champion/ Chester	
G-ANTK	Avro 685 York ★	Duxford Aviation Soc	
G-ANTS	D.H.82A Tiger Moth (N6532)	J. G. Green	
G-ANUO	D.H.114 Heron 2D	Avtech Ltd/Biggin Hill	
G-ANUW	D.H.104 Dove 6 ★	Civil Aviation Authority/Stansted	
G-ANWB	D.H.C.1 Chipmunk 21	G. Briggs/Blackpool	
G-ANWO	M.14A Hawk Trainer 3 ★	P. A. Brook	
G-ANWX	J/5L Aiglet Trainer	Applied Fastenings & Components	
G-ANXB	D.H.114 Heron 1B ★	Newark Air Museum	
G-ANXC	J/5R Alpine	C. J. Repek & ptnrs	
G-ANXR	P.31C Proctor 4 (RM221)	L. H. Oakins/Biggin Hill	
G-ANYP	P.31C Proctor 4 (NP184) ★	Torbay Aircraft Museum	
G-ANZJ	P.31C Proctor 4 (NP303) ★	A. Hillyard	
G-ANZT	Thruxton Jackaroo ★	J. D. Illiffe (stored)	
G-ANZU	D.H.82A Tiger Moth	P. A. Jackson/Sibson	
G-ANZZ	D.H.82A Tiger Moth	IBC Transport Containers Ltd	
G-AOAA	D.H.82A Tiger Moth	Tiger Club Ltd/Redhill	
G-AOAR	P.31C Proctor 4 (NP181) ★	Historic Aircraft Preservation Soc	
G-AOBG	Somers-Kendall SK.1 ★	stored	
G-AOBH	D.H.82A Tiger Moth (T7997)	C. H. A. Bott	
G-AOBO	D.H.82A Tiger Moth	P. A. Brook	
G-AOBU	P.84 Jet Provost ★	Shuttleworth Trust/Loughborough	
G-AOBV	J/5P Autocar	P. E. Champney	
G-AOBX	D.H.82A Tiger Moth	M. Gibbs/Redhill	
G-AOCP	Auster 5 ★	C. Baker (stored)	
G-AOCR	Auster 5D	J. M. Edis	
G-AOCU	Auster 5	S. J. Ball/Leicester	
G-AODA	Westland S-55 Srs 3	Bristow Helicopters Ltd	
G-AODT	D.H.82A Tiger Moth	A. H. Warminger	
G-AOEH	Aeronca 7AC Champion	M. Weeks & ptnrs/Eglinton	
G-AOEI	D.H.82A Tiger Moth	C.F.G. Flying Ltd/Cambridge	
G-AOEL	D.H.82A Tiger Moth (N9510) ★	Museum of Flight/E. Fortune	
G-AOES	D.H.82A Tiger Moth	A. Twemlow & G. A. Cordery/Redhill	
G-AOET	D.H.82A Tiger Moth	Glylynn Ltd	
G-AOEX	Thruxton Jackaroo	A. T. Christian	
G-AOFE	D.H.C.1 Chipmunk 22A	M. L. Sargeant	
G-AOFJ	Auster 5	Miss M. R. Innocent/Perth	
G-AOFM	J/5P Autocar	Micro Rent Aviation Ltd	
G-AOFS	J/5L Aiglet Trainer	J. K. Avis	
G-AOGA	M.75 Aries ★	Irish Aviation Museum (stored)	
G-AOGE	P.34A Proctor 3	N. I. Dalziel/Biggin Hill	
G-AOGI	D.H.82A Tiger Moth	W. J. Taylor	
G-AOGR	D.H.82A Tiger Moth (T6099)	M. I. Edwards	
G-AOGV	J/5R Alpine	ABH Aviation	
G-AOHL	V.802 Viscount ★	British Air Ferries (Cabin Trainer)/ Southend	
G-AOHM	V.802 Viscount	British Air Ferries Viscount Sir George Edwards/Southend	
G-AOHT	V.802 Viscount	British Air Ferries/Southend	
G-AOHZ	J/5P Autocar	M. R. Gibbons & G. W. Brown	
G-AOIL	D.H.82A Tiger Moth	J. O. Souch	
G-AOIM	D.H.82A Tiger Moth	C. R. Hardiman/Shobdon	
G-AOIR	Thruxton Jackaroo	L. H. Smith	
G-AOIS	D.H.82A Tiger Moth	V. B. & R. G. Wheele/Shoreham	
G-AOIY	J/5G Autocar	P. E. Scott	
G-AOJC	V.802 Viscount ★	Wales Aircraft Museum/Cardiff	
G-AOJH	D.H.83C Fox Moth	J. S. Lewery/Bournemouth	
G-AOJJ	D.H.82A Tiger Moth (DF128)	E. Lay	
G-AOJK	D.H.82A Tiger Moth	P. A. de Courcy Swoffer	
G-AOJT	D.H.106 Comet 1 ★	Mosquito Aircraft Museum	
G-AOKH	P.40 Prentice 1	J. F. Moore/Biggin Hill	
G-AOKL	P.40 Prentice 1 (VS610)	J. R. Batt/Southend	
G-AOKO	P.40 Prentice 1 ★	J. F. Coggins/Coventry	
G-AOKZ	P.40 Prentice 1 (VS623) ★	Midland Air Museum	
G-AOLK	P.40 Prentice 1	Hilton Aviation Ltd/Southend	
G-AOLU	P.40 Prentice 1 (VS356) ★	Scottish Aircraft Collection/Perth	

Notes	Reg.	Type	Owner or Operator
	G-AORB	Cessna 170B	G. Lawry
	G-AORW	D.H.C.1 Chipmunk 22A	V. P. Butler/Biggin Hill
	G-AOSK	D.H.C.1 Chipmunk 22	A. M. S. Cullen
	G-AOSO	D.H.C.1 Chipmunk 22	Earl of Suffolk & Berkshire
	G-AOSU	D.H.C.1 Chipmunk 22 (Lycoming)	RAFGSA/Bicester
	G-AOSY	D.H.C.1 Chipmunk 22 (WB585)	Fletcher Aviation Ltd/Blackbushe
	G-AOSZ	D.H.C.1 Chipmunk 22A	D. M. Barnett
	G-AOTD	D.H.C.1 Chipmunk 22 (WB588)	Shuttleworth Trust/O. Warden
	G-AOTF	D.H.C.1 Chipmunk 23 (Lycoming)	RAFGSA/Bicester
	G-AOTI	D.H.114 Heron 2D	Avtech Ltd/Biggin Hill
	G-AOTK	D.53 Turbi	The T. K. Flying Group/Hatfield
	G-AOTR	D.H.C.1 Chipmunk 22	P. W. B. & M. A. R. Spearing
	G-AOTY	D.H.C.1 Chipmunk 22A	West London Aero Services Ltd/ White Waltham
	G-AOUJ	Fairey Ultra-Light ★	British Rotorcraft Museum
	G-AOUO	D.H.C.1 Chipmunk 22 (Lycoming)	RAFGSA/Bicester
	G-AOUP	D.H.C.1 Chipmunk 22	Wessex Flying Group
	G-AOUR	D.H.82A Tiger Moth ★	Ulster Folk & Transport Museum
	G-AOVF	B.175 Britannia 312F ★	Aerospace Museum/Cosford
	G-AOVT	B.175 Britannia 312F ★	Duxford Aviation Soc
	G-AOVW	Auster 5	B. Marriott/Cranwell
	G-AOXG	D.H.82A Tiger Moth (XL717)	FAA Museum/Yeovilton
	G-AOXN	D.H.82A Tiger Moth	S. L. G. Darch
	G-AOYG	V.806 Viscount	British Air Ferries Viscount Sir Peter Masefield/Southend
	G-AOYL	V.806 Viscount	British Air Ferries Viscount Churchill/ Southend
	G-AOYN	V.806 Viscount	British Air Ferries Viscount Jersey/ Southend
	G-AOYP	V.806 Viscount	British Air Ferries
	G-AOYR	V.806 Viscount	British Air Ferries Viscount Gatwick/ Southend
	G-AOZB	D.H.82A Tiger Moth	Structure Flex Ltd/Redhill
	G-AOZH	D.H.82A Tiger Moth (K2572)	V. B. & R. G. Wheele/Shoreham
	G-AOZL	J/5Q Alpine	E. A. Taylor/Southend
	G-AOZP	D.H.C.1 Chipmunk 22	M. E. Darlington
	G-APAA	J/5R Alpine ★	L. A. Groves (stored)
	G-APAF	Auster 5	J. E. Allen (G-CMAL)
	G-APAH	Auster 5	Executive Flying Services Ltd
	G-APAL	D.H.82A Tiger Moth (N6847)	L. H. Smith & D. S. Chapman
	G-APAM	D.H.82A Tiger Moth	R. P. Williams
	G-APAO	D.H.82A Tiger Moth	C. K. Irvine
	G-APAP	D.H.82A Tiger Moth	R. A. Slade
	G-APAS	D.H.106 Comet 1XB ★	Aerospace Museum/Cosford
	G-APBE	Auster 5	G. W. Clark/O. Warden
	G-APBI	D.H.82A Tiger Moth (EM903)	R. Devaney & ptnrs/Audley End
	G-APBO	D.53 Turbi	T. W. Harris
	G-APBW	Auster 5	N. Huxtable
	G-APCB	J/5Q Alpine	M. J. Wilson/Redhill
	G-APCC	D.H.82A Tiger Moth	L. J. Rice/Henstridge
	G-APDB	D.H.106 Comet 4 ★	Duxford Aviation Soc
	G-APDT	D.H.106 Comet 4 ★	British Aerospace PLC/Hatfield
	G-APEG	V.953C Merchantman	Air Bridge Carriers Ltd/E. Midlands
	G-APEJ	V.953C Merchantman	Air Bridge Carriers Ltd/E. Midlands
	G-APEK	V.953C Merchantman	Air Bridge Carriers Ltd Dreadnought/ E. Midlands
	G-APEM	V.953C Merchantman	Elan International Ltd Agamemnon/ E. Midlands
	G-APEP	V.953C Merchantman	Air Bridge Carriers Ltd/E. Midlands
	G-APES	V.953C Merchantman	Air Bridge Carriers Ltd Swiftsure (withdrawn)/E. Midlands
	G-APET	V.953C Merchantman	Air Bridge Carriers Ltd Temeraire/ E. Midlands
	G-APEY	V.806 Viscount	British Air Ferries/Virgin Atlantic Dublin Lady
	G-APFA	D.54 Turbi	A. Eastelow & F. J. Keitch/Dunkeswell
	G-APFG	Boeing 707-436 ★	Instructional airframe/Stansted
	G-APFJ	Boeing 707-436 ★	Aerospace Museum/Cosford
	G-APFU	D.H.82A Tiger Moth	Mithril Racing Ltd/Goodwood
	G-APGL	D.H.82A Tiger Moth	C. R. Hardiman
	G-APHV	Avro 19 Srs 2 (VM360) ★	Museum of Flight/E. Fortune

Reg.	Type	Owner or Operator	Notes
G-APIE	Tipsy Belfair B	P. A. Smith	
G-APIH	D.H.82A Tiger Moth (R5086)	A. J. Ditheridge	
G-APIK	J/1N Alpha	T. D. Howe/Redhill	
G-APIM	V.806 Viscount	British Air Ferries *Viscount Stephen Piercey*/Southend	
G-APIT	P.40 Prentice 1 (VR192) ★	WWII Aircraft Preservation Soc/Lasham	
G-APIU	P.40 Prentice 1 ★	J. F. Coggins/Coventry	
G-APIY	P.40 Prentice 1 (VR249) ★	Newark Air Museum	
G-APIZ	D.31 Turbulent	M. J. Abbott	
G-APJB	P.40 Prentice 1 ★	City Airways/Coventry	
G-APJJ	Fairey Ultra-light ★	Midland Aircraft Preservation Soc	
G-APJO	D.H.82A Tiger Moth	D. R. & M. Wood	
G-APJZ	J/1N Alpha	P. G. Lipman	
G-APKH	D.H.85 Leopard Moth	P. Franklin (G-ACGS)	
G-APKM	J/1N Alpha	D. E. A. Huggins	
G-APKN	J/1N Alpha	Felthorpe Auster Group	
G-APKY	Hiller UH-12B	D. A. George (*stored*)	
G-APLG	J/5L Aiglet Trainer	G. R. W. Brown	
G-APLO	D.H.C.1 Chipmunk 22A (WD379)	Channel Islands Aero Holdings Ltd	
G-APMB	D.H.106 Comet 4B ★	Gatwick Handling Ltd (*ground trainer*)	
G-APMH	J/1U Workmaster	R. E. Neal & E. R. Stevens/Leicester	
G-APML	Dakota 6	Air Atlantique Ltd	
G-APMM	D.H.82A Tiger Moth (K2568)	R. K. J. Hadlow	
G-APMX	D.H.82A Tiger Moth	For rebuild	
G-APMY	PA-23 Apache 160 ★	Kelsterton College (*instructional airframe*)/Clwyd	
G-APNJ	Cessna 310 ★	Chelsea College/Shoreham	
G-APNS	Garland-Bianchi Linnet	Paul Penn-Sayers Model Services Ltd	
G-APNT	Currie Wot	J. W. Salter	
G-APNZ	D.31 Turbulent	Tiger Club Ltd/Redhill	
G-APOA	J/1N Alpha	J. S. M. Norman	
G-APOD	Tipsy Belfair	L. F. Potts	
G-APOI	Saro Skeeter Srs 8	F. F. Chamberlain	
G-APOL	D.36 Turbulent	T. A. S. Rayner/Perth	
G-APPL	P.40 Prentice 1	S. J. Saggers/Biggin Hill	
G-APPM	D.H.C.1 Chipmunk 22	J. D. Frankel	
G-APRF	Auster 5	R. Giles & ptnrs/Clacton	
G-APRJ	Avro 694 Lincoln B.2 ★	Charles Church Displays Ltd/Cranfield	
G-APRL	AW.650 Argosy 101 ★	Midland Air Museum	
G-APRR	Super Aero 45 (A1+BT)	R. H. Jowett	
G-APSA	Douglas DC-6A	Instone Air Line Ltd/Coventry	
G-APSR	J/1U Workmaster	D. & K. Aero Services Ltd/Shobdon	
G-APTH	Agusta-Bell 47J	R. Windley	
G-APTP	PA-22 Tri-Pacer 150	A. J. Corr	
G-APTR	J/1N Alpha	C. J. & D. J. Baker	
G-APTS	D.H.C.1 Chipmunk 22A	Wycombe Air Centre Ltd	
G-APTU	Auster 5	B. G. F. King	
G-APTW	W.B.1 Widgeon ★	Cornwall Aero Park/Helston	
G-APTY	Beech G.35 Bonanza	G. E. Brennand	
G-APTZ	D.31 Turbulent	B. E. Francis	
G-APUD	Bensen B.7M (modified) ★	Greater Manchester Museum of Science & Technology	
G-APUE	L-40 Meta Sokol	S. E. & M. J. Aherne	
G-APUK	J/1 Autocrat	P. L. Morley	
G-APUP	Sopwith Pup (N5182) (replica)★	RAF Museum/Hendon	
G-APUR	PA-22 Tri-Pacer 160	G. A. Allen & ptnrs	
G-APUW	J/5V-160 Autocar	Anglia Auster Syndicate	
G-APUY	D.31 Turbulent	C. Jones & ptnrs/Barton	
G-APUZ	PA-24 Comanche 250	S. D. Quigley/Prestwick	
G-APVF	Putzer Elster B	K. P. Rusling	
G-APVG	J/5L Aiglet Trainer	Cranfield Institute of Technology	
G-APVN	D.31 Turbulent	R. Sherwin/Shoreham	
G-APVS	Cessna 170B	N. Simpson	
G-APVU	L-40 Meta-Sokol	D. Kirk	
G-APVV	Mooney M-20A	Telcom Associates (*wreck*) Barton	
G-APVW	Beech A35 Bonanza	R. A. O'Neill	
G-APVY	PA-25 Pawnee 150	KK Aviation	
G-APVZ	D.31 Turbulent	H. R. Oldland	
G-APWJ	HPR-7 Herald 201 ★	Duxford Aviation Soc	
G-APWN	WS-55 Whirlwind 3 ★	Midland Air Museum	
G-APWR	PA-22 Tri-Pacer 160	Airads/Goodwood	
G-APWY	Piaggio P.166 ★	Science Museum/Wroughton	
G-APWZ	EP.9 Prospector ★	Museum of Army Flying/Middle Wallop	
G-APXJ	PA-24 Comanche 250	T. Wildsmith/Netherthorpe	

Notes	Reg.	Type	Owner or Operator
	G-APXR	PA-22 Tri-Pacer 160	A. Troughton
	G-APXT	PA-22 Tri-Pacer 150 (modified)	J. W. & I. Daniels
	G-APXU	PA-22 Tri-Pacer 125	C. G. Stone/Biggin Hill
	G-APXW	EP.9 Prospector ★	Museum of Army Flying/Middle Wallop
	G-APXX	D.H.A.3 Drover 2 (VH-FDT) ★	WWII Aircraft Preservation Soc/ Lasham
	G-APXY	Cessna 150	Merlin Flying Club Ltd/Hucknall
	G-APYB	T.66 Nipper 2	B. O. Smith
	G-APYD	D.H.106 Comet 4B ★	Science Museum/Wroughton
	G-APYG	D.H.C.1 Chipmunk 22	E. J. I. Musty & P. A. Colman
	G-APYI	PA-22 Tri-Pacer 135	G. K. Hare/Fenland
	G-APYN	PA-22 Tri-Pacer 160	W. D. Stephens
	G-APYT	Champion 7FC Tri-Traveller	D. M. Griffiths
	G-APYU	Champion 7FC Tri-Traveller	K. Collins (stored)
	G-APYW	PA-22 Tri-Pacer 150	Fiddian Ltd
	G-APZG	PA-24 Comanche 250	Jewelbarron Ltd/Goodwood
	G-APZJ	PA-18 Super Cub 150	Southern Sailplanes
	G-APZK	PA-18 Super Cub 95	W. T. Knapton
	G-APZL	PA-22 Tri-Pacer 160	M. R. Coward & R. T. Evans
	G-APZR	Cessna 150 ★	Engine test-bed/Biggin Hill
	G-APZS	Cessna 175A	G. A. Nash/Booker
	G-APZX	PA-22 Tri-Pacer 150	L. A. Thompson/Sywell
	G-ARAD	Luton LA-5A Major	W. T. Sproat
	G-ARAM	PA-18 Super Cub 150	I. M. & D. S. Morgan
	G-ARAN	PA-18 Super Cub 150	A. P. Docherty/Kidlington
	G-ARAO	PA-18 Super Cub 95 (607327)	R. T. Bennett & N. Tyler
	G-ARAS	Champion 7EC Traveller	I. D. Daniels
	G-ARAT	Cessna 180C	R. E. Styles & ptnrs
	G-ARAU	Cessna 150	S. Lynn/Sibson
	G-ARAW	Cessna 182C Skylane	P. Channon
	G-ARAX	PA-22 Tri-Pacer 150	P. Fabish
	G-ARAY	H.S.748 Srs 1	Dan-Air Services Ltd/Gatwick
	G-ARAZ	D.H.82A Tiger Moth (R4959)	M. V. Gauntlett/Goodwood
	G-ARBE	D.H.104 Dove 8	A. Freeman & T. Howe
	G-ARBG	T.66 Nipper 2	Felthorpe Tipsy Group
	G-ARBN	PA-23 Apache 160	H. Norden & H. J. Liggins
	G-ARBO	PA-24 Comanche 250	D. M. Harbottle
	G-ARBP	T.66 Nipper 2	F. W. Kirk
	G-ARBS	PA-22 Tri-Pacer 160 (modified to PA-20 Pacer 160)	T. R. G. Barney & M. A. Sherry/Redhill
	G-ARBV	PA-22 Tri-Pacer 150	Piper Flyers/Biggin Hill
	G-ARBZ	D.31 Turbulent	D. G. H. Hilliard/Bodmin
	G-ARCC	PA-22 Tri-Pacer 150	RFC Flying Group/Popham
	G-ARCF	PA-22 Tri-Pacer 150	A. L. Scadding (stored)
	G-ARCH	Cessna 310D ★	Instructional airframe/Perth
	G-ARCI	Cessna 310D	Sandtoft Air Services Ltd
	G-ARCS	Auster D6/180	E. A. Matty/Shobdon
	G-ARCT	PA-18 Super Cub 95	M. Kirk
	G-ARCV	Cessna 175A	Michael Gardner Ltd
	G-ARCW	PA-23 Apache 160	D. R. C. Reeves
	G-ARCX	AW Meteor 14 ★	Museum of Flight/E. Fortune
	G-ARDB	PA-24 Comanche 250	R. A. Sareen/Booker
	G-ARDD	CP.301C1 Emeraude	F. P. L. Clauson
	G-ARDE	D.H.104 Dove 6	R. J. H. Small/Cranfield
	G-ARDG	EP.9 Prospector ★	Museum of Army Flying/Middle Wallop
	G-ARDJ	Auster D.6/180	RN Aviation (Leicester Airport) Ltd
	G-ARDO	Jodel D.112	P. J. H. McCraig
	G-ARDP	PA-22 Tri-Pacer 150	G. M. Jones
	G-ARDS	PA-22 Caribbean 150	D. V. Asher/Leicester
	G-ARDT	PA-22 Tri-Pacer 160	A. A. Whiter
	G-ARDV	PA-22 Tri-Pacer 160	D. M. Butcher & R. J. Kelly
	G-ARDY	T.66 Nipper 2	M. T. Groves
	G-ARDZ	Jodel D.140A	M. J. Wright
	G-AREA	D.H.104 Dove 8	British Aerospace/Hatfield
	G-AREB	Cessna 175B Skylark	R. J. Postlethwaite & ptnrs/ Wellesbourne
	G-AREE	PA-23 Aztec 250	W. C. C. Meyer/Biggin Hill
	G-AREF	PA-23 Aztec 250 ★	Southall College of Technology
	G-AREH	D.H.82A Tiger Moth	T. Pate
	G-AREI	Auster 3 (MT438)	R. Alliker & ptnrs/Bodmin
	G-AREJ	Beech 95 Travel Air	D. Huggett/Stapleford
	G-AREL	PA-22 Caribbean 150	H. H. Cousins/Fenland
	G-AREO	PA-18 Super Cub 150	Lasham Gliding Soc Ltd
	G-ARET	PA-22 Tri-Pacer 160	D. T. Daniels

Reg.	Type	Owner or Operator	Notes
G-AREV	PA-22 Tri-Pacer 160	Spatrek Ltd/Barton	
G-AREX	Aeronca 15AC Sedan	R. J. Middleton-Turnbull & P. Lowndes	
G-AREZ	D.31 Turbulent	J. St. Clair-Quentin/Shobdon	
G-ARFB	PA-22 Caribbean 150	C. T. Woodward & ptnrs	
G-ARFD	PA-22 Tri-Pacer 160	D. C. Long	
G-ARFG	Cessna 175A Skylark	R. J. Fray/Sibson	
G-ARFH	PA-24 Comanche 250	L. M. Walton	
G-ARFI	Cessna 150A	J. H. Fisher	
G-ARFL	Cessna 175B Skylark	Garflair Group	
G-ARFN	Cessna 150A ★	Instructional airframe/Perth	
G-ARFO	Cessna 150A	Moray Flying Club Ltd	
G-ARFT	Jodel DR. 1050	R. Shaw	
G-ARFV	T.66 Nipper 2	C. G. Stone/Biggin Hill	
G-ARGB	Auster 6A ★	C. Baker (stored)	
G-ARGG	D.H.C.1 Chipmunk 22 (WD305)	B. Hook	
G-ARGO	PA-22 Colt 108	B. E. Goodman/Liverpool	
G-ARGV	PA-18 Super Cub 150	Deeside Gliding Club (Aberdeenshire) Ltd/Aboyne	
G-ARGZ	D.31 Turbulent	K. P. & T. J. Roberts	
G-ARHC	Forney F-1A Aircoupe	A. P. Gardner/Elstree	
G-ARHF	Forney F-1A Aircoupe	R. A. Nesbitt-Dufort	
G-ARHI	PA-24 Comanche 180	W. H. Entress/Swansea	
G-ARHL	PA-23 Aztec 250	J. J. Freeman & Co Ltd/Headcorn	
G-ARHM	Auster 6A	D. Hollowell & ptnrs/Finmere	
G-ARHN	PA-22 Caribbean 150	D. B. Furniss & A. Munro/Doncaster	
G-ARHP	PA-22 Tri-Pacer 160	W. Wardle	
G-ARHR	PA-22 Caribbean 150	J. A. Hargraves/Fairoaks	
G-ARHT	PA-22 Caribbean 150 ★	Moston Technical College	
G-ARHU	PA-22 Tri-Pacer 160	B. L. Newbold & ptnrs	
G-ARHW	D.H.104 Dove 8	Film Image Ltd/Elstree	
G-ARHZ	D.62 Condor	M. J. Groome & ptnrs	
G-ARID	Cessna 172B	L. A. Buckley & ptnrs/Leeds	
G-ARIE	PA-24 Comanche 250	W. Radwanski (stored)/Coventry	
G-ARIF	Ord-Hume O-H.7 Minor Coupe	N. H. Ponsford	
G-ARIH	Auster 6A (TW591)	India Hotel Ltd	
G-ARIK	PA-22 Caribbean 150	C. J. Berry	
G-ARIL	PA-22 Caribbean 150	G. N. Richardson Motors/Shobdon	
G-ARIN	PA-24 Comanche 250	S. J. Savage	
G-ARIV	Cessna 172B	C. Taylor & ptnrs	
G-ARIW	CP.301B Emeraude	P. J. Marsh	
G-ARJB	D.H.104 Dove 8 ★	J. C. Bamford (stored)	
G-ARJE	PA-22 Colt 108	C. I. Fray	
G-ARJF	PA-22 Colt 108	M. J. Collins	
G-ARJH	PA-22 Colt 108	J. D. A. Sherburn & C. A. Gentry/Headcorn	
G-ARJR	PA-23 Apache 160 ★	Instructional airframe/Kidlington	
G-ARJS	PA-23 Apache 160	Bencray Ltd/Blackpool	
G-ARJT	PA-23 Apache 160	Hiveland Ltd	
G-ARJU	PA-23 Apache 160	Chantaco Ltd/Biggin Hill	
G-ARJV	PA-23 Apache 160	Smart Estates Ltd/Bristol	
G-ARJZ	D.31 Turbulent	N. H. Jones	
G-ARKG	J/5G Autocar	M. M. James & C. M. G. Ellis	
G-ARKJ	Beech N35 Bonanza	T. Hasleden	
G-ARKK	PA-22 Colt 108	M. F. Newman	
G-ARKM	PA-22 Colt 108	L. E. Usher/Ipswich	
G-ARKN	PA-22 Colt 108	S. R. Winder	
G-ARKP	PA-22 Colt 108	C. J. & J. Freeman/Headcorn	
G-ARKR	PA-22 Colt 108	J. C. Rimmel	
G-ARKS	PA-22 Colt 108	J. Dickenson	
G-ARLG	Auster D.4/108	Auster D4 Group	
G-ARLK	PA-24 Comanche 250	M. Walker & C. Robinson	
G-ARLO	A.61 Terrier 1 ★	stored	
G-ARLP	A.61 Terrier 1	T. L. Gray & ptnrs	
G-ARLR	A.61 Terrier 2	W. H. Dyozinski	
G-ARLU	Cessna 172B Skyhawk ★	Instructional airframe/Irish AC	
G-ARLV	Cessna 172B Skyhawk	P. D. Lowdon	
G-ARLW	Cessna 172B Skyhawk	S. Lancashire Flyers Ltd/Barton	
G-ARLX	Jodel D.140B	Shipping & Airlines Ltd/Biggin Hill	
G-ARLY	J/5P Autocar	P. J. Elliott & G. Green/Leicester	
G-ARLZ	D.31A Turbulent	R. S. Hatwell & A. F. Hall	
G-ARMA	PA-23 Apache 160 ★	Instructional airframe/Kidlington	
G-ARMB	D.H.C.1 Chipmunk 22A (WB660)	P. A. Layzell/Goodwood	
G-ARMC	D.H.C.1 Chipmunk 22A	stored	

Notes	Reg.	Type	Owner or Operator
	G-ARMD	D.H.C.1 Chipmunk 22A ★	K. & L. Aero Services (stored)
	G-ARMG	D.H.C.1 Chipmunk 22A	Chipmunk Preservation Group Ltd/ Wellesbourne
	G-ARMI	PA-23 Apache 160 ★	Stapleford Flying Club Ltd
	G-ARML	Cessna 175B Skylark	R. C. Convine
	G-ARMN	Cessna 175B Skylark ★	Southall College of Technology
	G-ARMO	Cessna 172B Skyhawk	Sangria Designs Ltd & BRM Plastics Ltd/Booker
	G-ARMP	Cessna 172B	Ryders Express Services Ltd/ Birmingham
	G-ARMR	Cessna 172B Skyhawk	N. Grantham/Sibson
	G-ARMZ	D.31 Turbulent	J. E. M. B. Millns
	G-ARNA	Mooney M.20B	R. Travers/Blackpool
	G-ARNB	J/5G Autocar	M. T. Jeffrey
	G-ARND	PA-22 Colt 108	A. Cambridge
	G-ARNE	PA-22 Colt 108	T. D. L. Bowden/Shipdham
	G-ARNI	PA-22 Colt 108	M. M. Wallis
	G-ARNJ	PA-22 Colt 108	MKM Flying Group/Leavesden
	G-ARNK	PA-22 Colt 108	R. J. Fox
	G-ARNL	PA-22 Colt 108	J. A. & J. A. Dodsworth/White Waltham
	G-ARNO	A.61 Terrier 1	M. B. Hill
	G-ARNP	A.109 Airedale	S. W. & M. Isbister
	G-ARNY	Jodel D.117	D. J. Lockett
	G-ARNZ	D.31 Turbulent	C. J. McArdle
	G-AROA	Cessna 172B Skyhawk	D. E. Partridge
	G-AROE	Aero 145	Panther Aviation
	G-AROF	L.40 Meta-Sokol	B. G. Barber
	G-AROJ	A.109 Airedale ★	D. J. Shaw (stored)
	G-AROM	PA-22 Colt 108	J. R. Colthurst
	G-ARON	PA-22 Colt 108	R. W. Curtis
	G-AROO	Forney F-1A Aircoupe	W. J. McMeekan/Newtownards
	G-AROW	Jodel D.140B	Kent Gliding Club Ltd/Challock
	G-AROY	Stearman A.75N.1	W. A. Jordan
	G-ARPD	H.S.121 Trident 1C ★	CAA Fire School/Teesside
	G-ARPH	H.S.121 Trident 1C ★	Aerospace Museum, Cosford
	G-ARPK	H.S.121 Trident 1C ★	Manchester Airport Authority
	G-ARPL	H.S.121 Trident 1C ★	British Airports Authority/Edinburgh
	G-ARPN	H.S.121 Trident 1C ★	British Airports Authority/Aberdeen
	G-ARPO	H.S.121 Trident 1C ★	CAA Fire School/Teesside
	G-ARPP	H.S.121 Trident 1C ★	British Airports Authority/Glasgow
	G-ARPR	H.S.121 Trident 1C ★	CAA Fire School/Teesside
	G-ARPW	H.S.121 Trident 1C ★	CAA Fire School/Teesside
	G-ARPX	H.S.121 Trident 1C ★	Airwork Services Ltd/Perth
	G-ARPZ	H.S.121 Trident 1C ★	RFD Ltd/Dunsfold
	G-ARRE	Jodel DR.1050	A. Luty & M. P. Edwards/Barton
	G-ARRF	Cessna 150A	Electrical Engineering Services
	G-ARRL	J/1N Alpha	G. N. Smith & C. Webb
	G-ARRM	Beagle B.206-X ★	Shoreham Airport Museum
	G-ARRP	PA-28 Cherokee 160	M. J. Flynn/Cardiff
	G-ARRS	CP.301A Emeraude	E. H. Booker/Sibson
	G-ARRT	Wallis WA-116-1	K. H. Wallis
	G-ARRU	D.31 Turbulent	P. I. Kempsey/Biggin Hill
	G-ARRY	Jodel D.140B	A. J. E. Ditheridge
	G-ARRZ	D.31 Turbulent	G. L. Winterbourne/Redhill
	G-ARSB	Cessna 150A	B. T. White/Andrewsfield
	G-ARSG	Roe Triplane Type IV replica	Shuttleworth Trust/O. Warden
	G-ARSJ	CP.301-C2 Emeraude	J. R. Ware
	G-ARSL	A.61 Terrier 2	R. A. Hutchinson & P. T. M. Hardy
	G-ARSP	L.40 Meta-Sokol	R. E. Carpenter
	G-ARSU	PA-22 Colt 108	P. C. Riggs
	G-ARSW	PA-22 Colt 108	R. W. Rushton & ptnrs
	G-ARSX	PA-22 Tri-Pacer 160	M. J. Blanchard
	G-ARTD	PA-23 Apache 160	Dr. D. A. Jones
	G-ARTF	D.31 Turbulent	J. R. D. Bygraves
	G-ARTG	Hiller UH-12C ★	White Hart Inn/Stockbridge
	G-ARTH	PA-12 Super Cruiser	A. Horsfall/Sherburn
	G-ARTJ	Bensen B.8 ★	Museum of Flight/E. Fortune
	G-ARTL	D.H.82A Tiger Moth (T7281)	P. A. Jackson
	G-ARTT	M.S.880B Rallye Club	R. N. Scott
	G-ARTW	Cessna 150B ★	Instructional airframe/Perth
	G-ARTX	Cessna 150B ★	Instructional airframe/Perth
	G-ARTY	Cessna 150B ★	Instructional airframe/Perth
	G-ARTZ	McCandless M.4 Gyrocopter	W. E. Partridge (stored)
	G-ARUG	J/5G Autocar	J. Cantellow & D. Hulme/Biggin Hill

Reg.	Type	Owner or Operator	Notes
G-ARUH	Jodel DR.1050	PFA Group/Denham	
G-ARUI	A.61 Terrier	Crossford Hotels (Dunfermline) Ltd	
G-ARUL	Cosmic Wind	P. G. Kynsey	
G-ARUO	PA-24 Comanche 180	Uniform Oscar Group/Elstree	
G-ARUR	PA-28 Cherokee 160	The G-ARUR Group/Redhill	
G-ARUV	CP.301A Emeraude	J. Tanswell	
G-ARUY	J/1N Alpha	D. L. Webley	
G-ARUZ	Cessna 175C Skylark	G. Cormack & C. C. Wagner/Glasgow	
G-ARVF	V.1101 VC10 ★	Hermeskeil Museum (nr Trier)/ W. Germany	
G-ARVM	V.1101 VC10 ★	Aerospace Museum/Cosford	
G-ARVO	PA-18 Super Cub 95	Mona Aviation Ltd	
G-ARVS	PA-28 Cherokee 160	Skyscraper Ltd/Stapleford	
G-ARVT	PA-28 Cherokee 160	A. G. Smithson	
G-ARVU	PA-28 Cherokee 160	D. J. Hockings/Biggin Hill	
G-ARVV	PA-28 Cherokee 160	G. E. Hopkins	
G-ARVW	PA-28 Cherokee 160	Victor Whiskey Flying Group	
G-ARVZ	D.62B Condor	C. Watson & W. H. Cole/Redhill	
G-ARWB	D.H.C.1 Chipmunk 22 (WK611)	B. Salter	
G-ARWH	Cessna 172C Skyhawk ★	Pizza Express, Golders Green Rd	
G-ARWM	Cessna 175C	J. Taylor	
G-ARWO	Cessna 172C Skyhawk	A. Philip & ptnrs/Bodmin	
G-ARWR	Cessna 172C Skyhawk	The Devanha Flying Group Ltd	
G-ARWS	Cessna 175C Skylark	E. N. Skinner	
G-ARWW	Bensen B.8M	B. McIntyre	
G-ARXD	A.109 Airedale	D. Howden	
G-ARXG	PA-24 Comanche 250	I. M. Callier	
G-ARXH	Bell 47G	A. B. Searle	
G-ARXN	T.66 Nipper 2	Griffon Flying Group/Hucknall	
G-ARXP	Luton LA-4A Minor	W. C. Hymas	
G-ARXT	Jodel DR.1050	CJM Flying Group	
G-ARXU	Auster 6A	Bath & Wilts Gliding Club Ltd	
G-ARXW	M.S.885 Super Rallye	M. A. Jones	
G-ARXX	M.S.880B Rallye Club	M. S. Bird	
G-ARYB	H.S.125 Srs 1★	British Aerospace PLC/Hatfield	
G-ARYC	H.S.125 Srs 1 ★	The Mosquito Aircraft Museum	
G-ARYD	Auster AOP.6 (WJ358) ★	Museum of Army Flying/Middle Wallop	
G-ARYF	PA-23 Aztec 250B	I. J. T. Branson/Biggin Hill	
G-ARYH	PA-22 Tri-Pacer 160	Filtration (Water Treatment Engineers) Ltd	
G-ARYI	Cessna 172C	J. Rhodes	
G-ARYK	Cessna 172C	D. C. Barker/Sandown	
G-ARYR	PA-28 Cherokee 180	M. L. Allford/Kidlington	
G-ARYS	Cessna 172C Skyhawk	R. S. Morgan	
G-ARYV	PA-24 Comanche 250	Ilford Business Machines Ltd	
G-ARYZ	A.109 Airedale	J. D. Reid	
G-ARZB	Wallis WA-116 Srs 1	K. H. Wallis	
G-ARZE	Cessna 172C ★	*Parachute jump trainer*/Cockermouth	
G-ARZM	D.31 Turbulent	Tiger Club Ltd/Redhill	
G-ARZN	Beech N35 Bonanza	Eurolink Aviation Ltd	
G-ARZP	A.109 Airedale	G. B. O'Neill/(*stored*)/Booker	
G-ARZW	Currie Wot	J. H. Blake	
G-ARZX	Cessna 150B	M. D. Corbett	
G-ASAA	Luton LA-4A Minor	D. F. Lingard	
G-ASAI	A.109 Airedale ★	A. C. Watt	
G-ASAJ	A.61 Terrier 2 (WE569)	S. J. B. White & V. M. Howard	
G-ASAK	A.61 Terrier 2	Rochford Hundred Flying Group/ Southend	
G-ASAL	SAL Bulldog 120	British Aerospace/Prestwick	
G-ASAM	D.31 Turbulent	Tiger Club Ltd/Redhill	
G-ASAN	A.61 Terrier 2	D. R. Godfrey	
G-ASAT	M.S.880B Rallye Club	M. Cutovic	
G-ASAU	M.S.880B Rallye Club	W. J. Armstrong	
G-ASAV	M.S.880B Rallye Club	A. L. Averill & ptnrs	
G-ASAX	A.61 Terrier 2	G. Strathdee	
G-ASAZ	Hiller UH-12E4	P. A. Boitel-Gill	
G-ASBA	Currie Wot	M. A. Kaye	
G-ASBB	Beech 23 Musketeer	D. Silver/Southend	
G-ASBH	A.109 Airedale	D. T. Smollett	
G-ASBY	A.109 Airedale	M. J. Barnett & ptnrs	
G-ASCC	Beagle E.3 AOP Mk 11	Old Training Plane Co	
G-ASCM	Isaacs Fury II (K2050)	D. Calabritto	
G-ASCU	PA-18A Super Cub 150	Farm Aviation Services Ltd	

Notes	Reg.	Type	Owner or Operator
	G-ASCZ	CP.301A Emeraude	Hylton Flying Group/Newcastle
	G-ASDA	Beech 65-80 Queen Air	Parker & Heard Ltd/Biggin Hill
	G-ASDF	Edwards Gyrocopter ★	B. King
	G-ASDK	A.61 Terrier 2	M. L. Rose
	G-ASDL	A.61 Terrier 2	T. J. Rilley & C. E. Mason
	G-ASDO	Beech 95-A55 Baron ★	No 2498 Sqn ATC/Jersey
	G-ASDY	Wallis WA-116/F	K. H. Wallis
	G-ASEA	Luton LA-4A Minor	T. G. Thompson/Ipswich
	G-ASEB	Luton LA-4A Minor	S. R. P. Harper
	G-ASEG	A.61 Terrier (VF548)	J. A. Stott
	G-ASEO	PA-24 Comanche 250	Planetalk Ltd
	G-ASEP	PA-23 Apache 235	Arrowstate Ltd/Denham
	G-ASEU	D.62A Condor	W. Grant & D. McNicholl
	G-ASFA	Cessna 172D	The Dakota Flying Club/Cranfield
	G-ASFD	L-200A Morava	M. Emery/Bournemouth
	G-ASFK	J/5G Autocar	S. J. Harris
	G-ASFL	PA-28 Cherokee 180	E. W. Pinchbeck & D. F. Ranger/Popham
	G-ASFR	Bo.208A1 Junior	S. T. Dauncey
	G-ASFX	D.31 Turbulent	E. F. Clapham & W. B. S. Dobie
	G-ASGC	V.1151 Super VC10 ★	Duxford Aviation Soc
	G-ASHA	Cessna F.172D	R. Soar & ptnrs
	G-ASHB	Cessna 182F	RN & Royal Marines Sport Parachute Association/Dunkeswell
	G-ASHD	Brantly B-2A ★	British Rotorcraft Museum
	G-ASHH	PA-23 Aztec 250	Leicestershire Thread & Trimming Manufacturers Ltd
	G-ASHS	Stampe SV-4B	L. W. Gruber & ptnrs/Goodwood
	G-ASHT	D.31 Turbulent	C. W. N. Huke
	G-ASHU	PA-15 Vagabond	G. J. Romanes
	G-ASHV	PA-23 Aztec 250B	R. J. Ashley & G. O'Gorman
	G-ASHX	PA-28 Cherokee 180	Sunsaver Ltd
	G-ASIB	Cessna F.172D	A. T. Jay
	G-ASII	PA-28 Cherokee 180	Worldwide Wheels Ltd & ptnrs/Bristol
	G-ASIJ	PA-28 Cherokee 180	Precision Products Ltd & Stormweld Ltd
	G-ASIL	PA-28 Cherokee 180	N. M. Barker & ptnrs/Leicester
	G-ASIS	Jodel D.112	E. F. Hazell
	G-ASIT	Cessna 180	A. & P. A. Wood
	G-ASIY	PA-25 Pawnee 235	RAFGSA/Bicester
	G-ASJL	Beech H.35 Bonanza	P. M. Coulton
	G-ASJM	PA-30 Twin Comanche 160 ★	Via Nova Ltd (stored)
	G-ASJO	Beech B.23 Musketeer	G-Air Ltd/Goodwood
	G-ASJV	V.S.361 Spitfire IX (MH434)	Nalfire Aviation Ltd/Booker
	G-ASJY	GY-80 Horizon 160	B. Rogalewski
	G-ASJZ	Jodel D.117A	V. K. Hardy & R. B. Spink/Barton
	G-ASKC	D.H.98 Mosquito 35 (TA719)	Skyfame Collection/Duxford
	G-ASKH	D.H.98 Mosquito T.3 (RR299)	British Aerospace/Chester
	G-ASKK	HPR-7 Herald 211 ★	Norwich Aviation Museum
	G-ASKL	Jodel D.150A	J. M. Graty
	G-ASKP	D.H.82A Tiger Moth	Tiger Club Ltd/Redhill
	G-ASKS	Cessna 336 Skymaster	M. J. Godwin
	G-ASKT	PA-28 Cherokee 180	A. Mattacks & T. Hood
	G-ASKV	PA-25 Pawnee 235	Southdown Gliding Club Ltd
	G-ASLF	Bensen B.7	S. R. Hughes
	G-ASLH	Cessna 182F	Celahurst Ltd
	G-ASLK	PA-25 Pawnee 235	Bristol Gliding Club (Pty) Ltd/ Nympsfield
	G-ASLL	Cessna 336 ★	stored
	G-ASLR	Agusta-Bell 47J-2	D. Jack
	G-ASLV	PA-28 Cherokee 235	C.S.E. Aviation Ltd/Kidlington
	G-ASLX	CP.301A Emeraude	K. C. Green/Panshanger
	G-ASMA	PA-30 Twin Comanche 160	B. D. Glynn/Redhill
	G-ASMC	P.56 Provost T.1.	W. Walker (stored)
	G-ASME	Bensen B.8M	J. Jordan
	G-ASMF	Beech D.95A Travel Air	Hawk Aviation Ltd
	G-ASMJ	Cessna F.172E	J. E. Tribe & Z. W. Jakubowski/ Audley End
	G-ASML	Luton LA-4A Minor	R. L. E. Horrell
	G-ASMM	D.31 Tubulent	K. A. Browne
	G-ASMN	PA-23 Apache 160	W. London Aero Services Ltd/ White Waltham
	G-ASMO	PA-23 Apache 160 ★	Aviation Enterprises/Fairoaks
	G-ASMS	Cessna 150A	K. R. & T. W. Davies
	G-ASMT	Fairtravel Linnet 2	A. F. Cashin
	G-ASMU	Cessna 150D	Telepoint Ltd/Barton

Reg.	Type	Owner or Operator	Notes
G-ASMV	CP.1310-C3 Super Emeraude	P. F. D. Waltham/Leicester	
G-ASMW	Cessna 150D	Yorkshire Light Aircraft Ltd/Leeds	
G-ASMY	PA-23 Apache 160	Hanseviter Aviation/Ipswich	
G-ASMZ	A.61 Terrier 2 (VF516)	Museum of Army Flying/Middle Wallop	
G-ASNB	Auster 6A (VX118)	M. Pocock & ptnrs	
G-ASNC	Beagle D.5/180 Husky	Peterborough & Spalding Gliding Club/ Boston	
G-ASND	PA-23 Aztec 250	Commercial Air (Woking) Ltd/ Fairoaks	
G-ASNE	PA-28 Cherokee 180	J. L. Dexter	
G-ASNH	PA-23 Aztec 250B	The Earl of Suffolk & Berkshire & J. Hoerner	
G-ASNI	CP.1310-C3 Super Emeraude	D. Chapman	
G-ASNK	Cessna 205	Justgold Ltd	
G-ASNU	H.S.125 Srs. 1	Flintgrange Ltd	
G-ASNW	Cessna F.172E	J. A. Gibbs	
G-ASNY	Bensen B.8M	D. L. Wallis	
G-ASNZ	Bensen B.8M	W. H. Turner	
G-ASOC	Auster 6A	J. A. Rayment/Finmere	
G-ASOH	Beech B.55A Baron	J. S. Goodsir & J. Mason/Biggin Hill	
G-ASOI	A.61 Terrier 2	D. I. H. Johnstone	
G-ASOK	Cessna F.172E	Okay Flying Group/Denham	
G-ASON	PA-30 Twin Comanche 160	Follandbeech Ltd	
G-ASOO	PA-30 Twin Comanche 160	K. H. Acketts	
G-ASOX	Cessna 205A	Dorglen Ltd/Wellesbourne	
G-ASPF	Jodel D.120	W. S. Howell	
G-ASPI	Cessna F.172E	Icarus Flying Group/Rochester	
G-ASPK	PA-28 Cherokee 140	Westward Airways (Lands End) Ltd/ St Just	
G-ASPP	Bristol Boxkite replica	Shuttleworth Trust/O. Warden	
G-ASPS	Piper J-3C-90 Cub	A. J. Chalkley/Blackbushe	
G-ASPU	D.31 Turbulent	I. Maclennan	
G-ASPV	D.H.82A Tiger Moth	B. S. Charters/Shipdham	
G-ASPX	Bensen B-8S	R. Williams	
G-ASRB	D.62B Condor	T. J. McRae	
G-ASRC	D.62B Condor	P. S. Milner	
G-ASRF	Jenny Wren	G. W. Gowland (*stored*)	
G-ASRH	PA-30 Twin Comanche 160	Island Aviation & Travel Ltd	
G-ASRI	PA-23 Aztec 250B ★	Graham Collins Associates Ltd	
G-ASRK	A.109 Airedale ★	M. J. Barnett & R. Skingley	
G-ASRO	PA-30 Twin Comanche 160	A. G. Perkins/Halfpenny Green	
G-ASRR	Cessna 182G	G. J. Richardson/Bourn	
G-ASRT	Jodel D.150	H. M. Kendall	
G-ASRW	PA-28 Cherokee 180	K. R. Deering/Shoreham	
G-ASSC	D.H.82A Tiger Moth	—	
G-ASSB	PA-30 Twin Comanche 160	Mercia Aviation	
G-ASSE	PA-22 Colt 108	J. B. King/Goodwood	
G-ASSF	Cessna 182G Skylane	Burbage Farms Ltd/Leicester	
G-ASSP	PA-30 Twin Comanche 160	R. W. English	
G-ASSR	PA-30 Twin Comanche 160	Rangebury Ltd	
G-ASSS	Cessna 172E	D. H. N. Squires/Bristol	
G-ASST	Cessna 150D	F. R. H. Parker	
G-ASSU	CP.301A Emeraude	R. W. Millward (*stored*)/Redhill	
G-ASSW	PA-28 Cherokee 140	C. J. Plummer/Biggin Hill	
G-ASTA	D.31 Turbulent	L. P. Townsley	
G-ASTH	Mooney M.20C ★	E. Martin (*stored*)	
G-ASTI	Auster 6A	M. Pocock	
G-ASTL	Fairey Firefly 1 (Z2033) ★	Skyfame Collection/Duxford	
G-ASTP	Hiller UH-12C	L. Goddard	
G-ASTV	Cessna 150D (tailwheel) ★	*stored*	
G-ASUB	Mooney M.20E Super 21	A. Smith & J. Robinson	
G-ASUD	PA-28 Cherokee 180	S. E. Hobbs & Co Ltd	
G-ASUE	Cessna 150D	D. Huckle/Panshanger	
G-ASUG	Beech E18S ★	Museum of Flight/E. Fortune	
G-ASUI	A.61 Terrier 2	M. Durand	
G-ASUL	Cessna 182G Skylane	Parafreight Ltd/Halfpenny Green	
G-ASUP	Cessna F.172E	GASUP Air/Cardiff	
G-ASUR	Dornier Do 28A-1	Sheffair Ltd	
G-ASVG	CP.301B Emeraude	K. R. Jackson	
G-ASVM	Cessna F.172E	A. P. D. Hynes & ptnrs/Cambridge	
G-ASVN	Cessna U.206 Super Skywagon	British Skysports	
G-ASVO	HPR-7 Herald 214	British Air Ferries Ltd/Southend	
G-ASVP	PA-25 Pawnee 235	Aquila Gliding Club Ltd	
G-ASVZ	PA-28 Cherokee 140	E. Shipley	

Notes	Reg.	Type	Owner or Operator
	G-ASWB	A.109 Airedale	C. Gene & G. Taylor/Teesside
	G-ASWF	A.109 Airedale	C. Baker
	G-ASWH	Luton LA-5A Major	D. G. J. Chisholm/Coventry
	G-ASWJ	Beagle 206 Srs 1 (8449M) ★	RAF Halton
	G-ASWL	Cessna F.172F	C. Wilson
	G-ASWN	Bensen B.8M	D. R. Shepherd
	G-ASWP	Beech A.23 Musketeer	H. Mendelsohn & ptnrs/Edinburgh
	G-ASWW	PA-30 Twin Comanche 160	Bristol & Wessex Flying Club Ltd/ Bristol
	G-ASWX	PA-28 Cherokee 180	A. F. Dadds
	G-ASXC	SIPA 901	B. L. Proctor
	G-ASXD	Brantly B.2B	Brantly Enterprises
	G-ASXI	T.66 Nipper 2	M. R. Holden/Biggin Hill
	G-ASXJ	Luton LA-4A Minor	J. S. Allison/Halton
	G-ASXR	Cessna 210	S. G. Brady (stored)
	G-ASXS	Jodel DR.1050	R. A. Hunter
	G-ASXU	Jodel D.120A	R. W. & J. Thompsett
	G-ASXX	Avro 683 Lancaster 7 (NX611) ★	Lincolnshire Aviation Heritage Centre/ E. Kirkby
	G-ASXY	Jodel D.117A	P. A. Davies & ptnrs/Cardiff
	G-ASXZ	Cessna 182G Skylane	P. M. Robertson/Perth
	G-ASYD	BAC One-Eleven 670	British Aerospace
	G-ASYG	A.61 Terrier 2 ★	stored
	G-ASYJ	Beech D.95A Travel Air	Crosby Aviation (Jersey) Ltd
	G-ASYK	PA-30 Twin Comanche 160	E. W. Pinchback & D. F. Ranger
	G-ASYL	Cessna 150E	D. Mallinson
	G-ASYP	Cessna 150E	J. R. Payne
	G-ASYW	Bell 47G-2	Bristow Helicopters Ltd
	G-ASYZ	Victa Airtourer 100	N. C. Grayson
	G-ASZB	Cessna 150E	Exmoor Flying Syndicate/Exeter
	G-ASZD	Bo 208A2 Junior	A. J. Watson & ptnrs/O. Warden
	G-ASZE	A.61 Terrier 2	P. J. Moore
	G-ASZJ	S.C.7 Skyvan 3A-100	GEC Avionics Ltd/Luton
	G-ASZR	Fairtravel Linnet	H. C. D. & F. J. Garner
	G-ASZS	GY.80 Horizon 160	Horizon Flyers Ltd/Denham
	G-ASZU	Cessna 150E	T. H. Milburn
	G-ASZV	T.66 Nipper 2	R. L. Mitcham/Elstree
	G-ASZX	A.61 Terrier 1	C. A. Bailey
	G-ATAD	Mooney M.20C	M. R. Burr/Swansea
	G-ATAF	Cessna F.172F	F. R. Pearson/Shipdham
	G-ATAG	Jodel DR. 1050	K. M. O'Sullivan
	G-ATAI	D.H.104 Dove 8	L. A. Wootton/France
	G-ATAS	PA-28 Cherokee 180	D. R. Wood/Biggin Hill
	G-ATAT	Cessna 150E	The Derek Pointon Group (stored)
	G-ATAU	D.62B Condor	M. A. Peare/Redhill
	G-ATAV	D.62C Condor	The Condor Syndicate
	G-ATBF	F-86E Sabre 4 (XB733) ★	T. Bracewell (stored)
	G-ATBG	Nord 1002 (17)	L. M. Walton
	G-ATBH	Aero 145	P. D. Aberbach
	G-ATBI	Beech A.23 Musketeer	R. F. G. Dent/Staverton
	G-ATBJ	Sikorsky S-61N	British International Helicopters Ltd
	G-ATBL	D.H.60G Moth	J. J. V. Elwes
	G-ATBP	Fournier RF-3	Dishforth Flying Group
	G-ATBS	D.31 Turbulent	D. R. Keene & J. A. Lear
	G-ATBU	A.61 Terrier 2	P. R. Anderson
	G-ATBW	T.66 Nipper 2	Stapleford Nipper Group
	G-ATBX	PA-20 Pacer 135	G. D. & P. M. Thomson
	G-ATBZ	W.S-58 Wessex 60 ★	Sykes Aviation Ltd (stored)
	G-ATCC	A.109 Airedale	J. F. Moore & ptnrs/Biggin Hill
	G-ATCD	D.5/180 Husky	Oxford Flying & Gliding Group/Enstone
	G-ATCE	Cessna U.206	J. Fletcher & D. Hickling/Langar
	G-ATCI	Victa Airtourer 100	B. & C. Building Materials (Canvey Island) Ltd
	G-ATCJ	Luton LA-4A Minor	R. M. Sharphouse
	G-ATCL	Victa Airtourer 100	A. D. Goodall
	G-ATCN	Luton LA-4A Minor	J. C. Gates & C. Neilson
	G-ATCR	Cessna 310 ★	ITD Aviation Ltd/Denham
	G-ATCU	Cessna 337	University of Cambridge
	G-ATCX	Cessna 182H Skylane	K. J. Fisher/Bodmin
	G-ATDA	PA-28 Cherokee 160	D. E. Siviter (Motors) Ltd/Coventry
	G-ATDB	Nord 1101 Noralpha	J. B. Jackson/Prestwick
	G-ATDN	A.61 Terrier 2 (TW641)	S. J. Saggers/Biggin Hill
	G-ATDO	Bo 208C Junior	H. Swift

Reg.	Type	Owner or Operator	Notes
G-ATDS	HPR-7 Herald 209	Channel Express/Bournemouth	
G-ATEF	Cessna 150E	M. Smith & ptnrs/Blackbushe	
G-ATEG	Cessna 150E	A. W. Woodward/Biggin Hill	
G-ATEM	PA-28 Cherokee 180	G. Wyles & W. Adams	
G-ATEP	EAA Biplane ★	E. L. Martin (stored)/Guernsey	
G-ATES	PA-32 Cherokee Six 260 ★	Parachute jump trainer/Ipswich	
G-ATEV	Jodel DR. 1050	B. A. Mills & G. W. Payne	
G-ATEW	PA-30 Twin Comanche 160	Air Northumbria Group/Newcastle	
G-ATEX	Victa Airtourer 100	Medway Victa Group	
G-ATEZ	PA-28 Cherokee 140	J. A. Burton/E. Midlands	
G-ATFA	Bensen B.8	J. Butler (stored)	
G-ATFD	Jodel DR. 1050	A. D. Edge	
G-ATFF	PA-23 Aztec 250C	Neatspin Ltd	
G-ATFG	Brantly B.2B ★	Museum of Flight/E. Fortune	
G-ATFK	PA-30 Twin Comanche 160	L. J. Martin/Redhill	
G-ATFL	Cessna F.172F	R. L. Beverley/Bournemouth	
G-ATFM	Sikorsky S-61N	British International Helicopters Ltd/ Aberdeen	
G-ATFR	PA-25 Pawnee 150	W. A. Braim Ltd	
G-ATFU	D.H.85 Leopard Moth	A. H. Carrington & C. D. Duthy-James	
G-ATFV	Agusta-Bell 47J-2A	Alexander Warren & Co Ltd	
G-ATFW	Luton LA-4A Minor	C. Kirk	
G-ATFX	Cessna F.172G	R. J. Keyte/Shoreham	
G-ATFY	Cessna F.172G	H. Bennett & P. McCabe	
G-ATGE	Jodel DR.1050	S. T. & B. J. Dangar	
G-ATGG	M.S.885 Super Rallye	B&C Plant Hire Ltd/Southend	
G-ATGH	Brantly B.2B	D. Nieman	
G-ATGO	Cessna F.172G	Planetalk Ltd	
G-ATGP	Jodel DR.1050	N. J. Heaton	
G-ATGY	GY.80 Horizon	P. W. Gibberson/Birmingham	
G-ATGZ	Griffiths GH-4 Gyroplane	G. Griffiths	
G-ATHA	PA-23 Apache 235 ★	Brunel Technical College/Bristol	
G-ATHD	D.H.C.1 Chipmunk 22 (WP971)	Spartan Flying Group Ltd/Cranfield	
G-ATHF	Cessna 150F ★	Lincolnshire Aircraft Museum	
G-ATHG	Cessna 150F	G. T. Williams	
G-ATHI	PA-28 Cherokee 180 ★	Instructional airframe/Dublin	
G-ATHK	Aeronca 7AC Champion	A. Corran	
G-ATHL	Wallis WA-116/F	W. Vinten Ltd	
G-ATHM	Wallis WA-116 Srs 1	Wallis Autogyros Ltd	
G-ATHN	Nord 1101 Noralpha	E. L. Martin (stored)/Guernsey	
G-ATHR	PA-28 Cherokee 180	Britannia Airways Ltd/Luton	
G-ATHT	Victa Airtourer 115	H. C. G. Munroe	
G-ATHU	A.61 Terrier 1	J. A. L. Irwin	
G-ATHV	Cessna 150F	P. P. D. Howard-Johnston/Edinburgh	
G-ATHX	Jodel DR. 100A	T. S. & L. M. Wilkins	
G-ATHZ	Cessna 150F	E. & R. D. Forster	
G-ATIA	PA-24 Comanche 260	L. A. Brown	
G-ATIC	Jodel DR.1050 ★	stored	
G-ATID	Cessna 337	M. R. Tarrant/Bourn	
G-ATIE	Cessna 150F ★	Parachute jump trainer/Chetwynd	
G-ATIG	HPR-7 Herald 214	Westair International Ltd	
G-ATIN	Jodel D.117	D. R. Upton & J. G. Kay/Barton	
G-ATIR	Stampe SV-4C	D. T. Kaberry/Barton	
G-ATIS	PA-28 Cherokee 160	S. Boon	
G-ATIZ	Jodel D.117	R. Frith & ptnrs	
G-ATJA	Jodel D.1050	S. J. Kew/Booker	
G-ATJC	Victa Airtourer 100	D. G. Palmer & D. C. Giles/Glasgow	
G-ATJG	PA-28 Cherokee 140	Royal Aircraft Establishment Dept/ Thurleigh	
G-ATJL	PA-24 Comanche 260	M. J. Berry/Blackbushe	
G-ATJM	Fokker DR.1 replica (152/17)	R. Lamplough/Duxford	
G-ATJN	Jodel D.119	R. F. Bradshaw/Sibson	
G-ATJR	PA-E23 Aztec 250C	W. A. G. Willbond/Bourn	
G-ATJT	GY.80 Horizon 160	P. J. Stephenson	
G-ATJV	PA-32 Cherokee Six 260	SMK Engineers Ltd	
G-ATKF	Cessna 150F	P. J. Egan	
G-ATKH	Luton LA-4A Minor	H. E. Jenner	
G-ATKI	Piper J-3C-65 Cub	A. C. Netting	
G-ATKS	Cessna F.172G	Blois Aviation Ltd	
G-ATKT	Cessna F.172G	P. J. Megson	
G-ATKU	Cessna F.172G	W. J. & S. K. Boettcher/Doncaster	
G-ATKX	Jodel D.140C	M. P. F. Norman	
G-ATKZ	T.66 Nipper 2	M. W. Knights	
G-ATLA	Cessna 182J Skylane	Shefford Transport Engineers Ltd/ Luton	

Notes	Reg.	Type	Owner or Operator
	G-ATLB	Jodel DR.1050-M1	Tiger Club Ltd/Redhill
	G-ATLC	PA-23 Aztec 250C ★	Alderney Air Charter Ltd (stored)
	G-ATLG	Hiller UH-12B	Bristow Helicopters Ltd
	G-ATLM	Cessna F.172G	Yorkshire Flying Services Ltd/Leeds
	G-ATLP	Bensen B.8M	C. D. Julian
	G-ATLT	Cessna U-206A	Army Parachute Association/ Netheravon
	G-ATLV	Jodel D.120	M. D. Hackworth
	G-ATLW	PA-28 Cherokee 180	Lima Whisky Flying Group
	G-ATMC	Cessna F.150F	H. E. Peacock
	G-ATMG	M.S.893 Rallye Commodore 180	D. R. Wilkinson & T. Coldwell
	G-ATMH	D.5/180 Husky	Devon & Somerset Gliding Club Ltd
	G-ATMI	H.S.748 Srs 2A	Dan-Air Services Ltd/Gatwick
	G-ATMJ	H.S.748 Srs 2A	Dan-Air Services Ltd/Gatwick
	G-ATML	Cessna F.150F	N. Grantham/Conington
	G-ATMM	Cessna F.150F	LAR Aviation Ltd
	G-ATMT	PA-30 Twin Comanche 160	D. H. T. Bain/Newcastle
	G-ATMU	PA-23 Apache 160	Southend Flying Club
	G-ATMW	PA-28 Cherokee 140	Bencray Ltd/Blackpool
	G-ATMX	Cessna F.150F	H. M. Synge
	G-ATMY	Cessna 150F	C. F. Read/Doncaster
	G-ATNB	PA-28 Cherokee 180	R. F. Hill
	G-ATNE	Cessna F.150F	J. & S. Brew
	G-ATNI	Cessna F.150F	Telepoint Ltd/Barton
	G-ATNJ	Cessna F.150F ★	Instructional airframe/Perth
	G-ATNK	Cessna F.150F	Pegasus Aviation Ltd
	G-ATNL	Cessna F.150F	S. M. Kemp & ptnrs
	G-ATNV	PA-24 Comanche 260	B. S. Reynolds & P. R. Fortescue
	G-ATNX	Cessna F.150F	P. Jenkins
	G-ATOA	PA-23 Apache 160	S. J. Green
	G-ATOE	Cessna F.150F	S. Armstrong
	G-ATOF	Cessna F.150F ★	Instructional airframe/Perth
	G-ATOG	Cessna F-150F ★	Instructional airframe/Perth
	G-ATOH	D.62B Condor	E. D. Burke
	G-ATOI	PA-28 Cherokee 140	O. & E. Flying Ltd/Stapleford
	G-ATOJ	PA-28 Cherokee 140	Firefly Aviation Ltd/Glasgow
	G-ATOK	PA-28 Cherokee 140	J. R. Hewitt
	G-ATOL	PA-28 Cherokee 140	L. J. Nation & G. Alford
	G-ATOM	PA-28 Cherokee 140	R. P. Synge
	G-ATON	PA-28 Cherokee 140	R. G. Walters
	G-ATOO	PA-28 Cherokee 140	P. J. Stead/Cark
	G-ATOP	PA-28 Cherokee 140	P. R. Coombs/Blackbushe
	G-ATOR	PA-28 Cherokee 140	T. A. J. Morgan & ptnrs/Shobdon
	G-ATOT	PA-28 Cherokee 180	J. B. Waterfield & G. L. Birch
	G-ATOU	Mooney M.20E Super 21	P. R. & M. R. Parr
	G-ATOY	PA-24 Comanche 260 ★	Museum of Flight/E. Fortune
	G-ATOZ	Bensen B.8M	J. Jordan
	G-ATPD	H.S.125 Srs 1B	Euroguard Ltd
	G-ATPE	H.S.125 Srs 1B	Colt Executive Aviation Ltd/Staverton
	G-ATPJ	BAC One-Eleven 301	Dan-Air Services Ltd/Gatwick
	G-ATPK	BAC One-Eleven 301	Dan-Air Services Ltd/Gatwick
	G-ATPL	BAC One-Eleven 301	Dan-Air Services Ltd/Gatwick
	G-ATPM	Cessna F.150F	Dan-Air Flying Club/Lasham
	G-ATPN	PA-28 Cherokee 140	R. W. Harris & A. Jahanfar/Southend
	G-ATPT	Cessna 182J Skylane	Western Models Ltd/Redhill
	G-ATPV	JB.01 Minicab	J. Bryant & ptnrs
	G-ATRC	Beech B.95A Travel Air	Beechair Ltd
	G-ATRG	PA-18 Super Cub 150	Lasham Gliding Soc Ltd
	G-ATRI	Bo 208C Junior	W. H. Jones/Shoreham
	G-ATRK	Cessna F.150F	J. Rees & F. Doncaster
	G-ATRL	Cessna F.150F	Loganair Ltd/Glasgow
	G-ATRO	PA-28 Cherokee 140	390th Flying Group
	G-ATRR	PA-28 Cherokee 140	Manx Flyers Aero Club Ltd
	G-ATRU	PA-28 Cherokee 180	L. D. Lawrence/Luton
	G-ATRW	PA-32 Cherokee Six 260	Eastern Enterprises
	G-ATRX	PA-32 Cherokee Six 260	Comet Flying Group/Panshanger
	G-ATSI	Bo 208C Junior	D. L. Swallow
	G-ATSL	Cessna F.172G	D. Le Cheminant/Guernsey
	G-ATSM	Cessna 337A	Anglo-European Trustees Ltd
	G-ATSR	Beech M.35 Bonanza	Alstan Aviation Ltd
	G-ATSU	Jodel D.140B	B. M. O'Brien & P. J. Sellar (stored)
	G-ATSX	Bo 208C Junior	R. J. C. Campbell
	G-ATSY	Wassmer WA41 Super Baladou IV	Acorn Aviation Services Ltd

Reg.	Type	Owner or Operator	Notes
G-ATTB	Wallis WA-116-1 (XR944)	D. A. Wallis	
G-ATTD	Cessna 182J Skylane	K. M. Brennan & ptnrs	
G-ATTF	PA-28 Cherokee 140	S. J. & H. Y. George	
G-ATTG	PA-28 Cherokee 140	Arrow Air Services Engineering Ltd/ Shipdham	
G-ATTI	PA-28 Cherokee 140	D. Newman & C. Babb	
G-ATTK	PA-28 Cherokee 140	G-ATTK Flying Group/Southend	
G-ATTM	Jodel DR.250-160	R. W. Tomkinson	
G-ATTP	BAC One-Eleven 207	Dan-Air Services Ltd/Gatwick	
G-ATTR	Bo 208C Junior 3	S. Luck	
G-ATTU	PA-28 Cherokee 140	Lion Flying Group/Elstree	
G-ATTV	PA-28 Cherokee 140	D. R. Winder	
G-ATTX	PA-28 Cherokee 180	A. Gray & ptnrs	
G-ATTY	PA-32 Cherokee Six 260	M. J. Lee & K. Erbsmail/Kidlington	
G-ATUB	PA-28 Cherokee 140	R. H. Partington & M. J. Porter	
G-ATUC	PA-28 Cherokee 140	S. J. Green	
G-ATUD	PA-28 Cherokee 140	E. J. Clempson	
G-ATUF	Cessna F.150F	C. J. Lynn/Sibson	
G-ATUG	D.62B Condor	C. B. Marsh & D. J. R. Williams	
G-ATUH	Tipsy T.66 Nipper 1	A. R. Lemmon	
G-ATUI	Bo 208C Junior	A. W. Wakefield	
G-ATUL	PA-28 Cherokee 180	R. F. W. Warner	
G-ATVF	D.H.C.1 Chipmunk 22	RAFGSA/Bicester	
G-ATVH	BAC One-Eleven 207	Dan-Air Services Ltd/Gatwick	
G-ATVK	PA-28 Cherokee 140	JRB Aviation Ltd/Southend	
G-ATVL	PA-28 Cherokee 140	West London Aero Services Ltd/White Waltham	
G-ATVO	PA-28 Cherokee 140	Firefly Aviation Ltd/Glasgow	
G-ATVP	F.B.5 Gunbus (2345) ★	RAF Museum/Hendon	
G-ATVS	PA-28 Cherokee 180	Marshalls Woodflakes Ltd/Bristol	
G-ATVW	D.62B Condor	J. P. Coulter & J. Chidley/Panshanger	
G-ATVX	Bo 208C Junior	M. J. Porter	
G-ATWA	Jodel DR.1050	Jodel Syndicate/Lasham	
G-ATWB	Jodel D.117	Andrewsfield Flying Club Ltd	
G-ATWE	M.S.892A Rallye Commodore	D. I. Murray	
G-ATWJ	Cessna F.172F	C. J. & J. Freeman/Headcorn	
G-ATWP	Alon A-2 Aircoupe	H. Dodd & I. Wilson	
G-ATWR	PA-30 Twin Comanche 160B	Lubair (Transport Services) Ltd E. Midlands	
G-ATWZ	M.S.892A Rallye Commodore	A. D. Lovell-Spencer	
G-ATXA	PA-22 Tri-Pacer 150	R. C. Teverson	
G-ATXD	PA-30 Twin Comanche 160B	Alphameric Systems Ltd	
G-ATXF	GY-80 Horizon 150	A. I. Milne	
G-ATXJ	H.P.137 Jetstream 300 ★	British Aerospace (display mock-up)/ Prestwick	
G-ATXM	PA-28 Cherokee 180	J. Khan/Ipswich	
G-ATXN	Mitchell-Proctor Kittiwake	C. Dews	
G-ATXO	SIPA 903	M. Hillam/Sherburn	
G-ATXZ	Bo 208C Junior	J. Dyson & M. Hutchinson	
G-ATYM	Cessna F.150G	J. F. Perry & Co	
G-ATYN	Cessna F.150G	Skegness Air Taxi Services Ltd	
G-ATYS	PA-28 Cherokee 180	R. V. Waite	
G-ATZA	Bo 208C Junior	R. Wilder/Jersey	
G-ATZG	AFB2 gas balloon	Flt Lt S. Cameron Aeolis	
G-ATZK	PA-28 Cherokee 180	BI Aviation Services/Blackbushe	
G-ATZM	Piper J-3C-65 Cub	R. W. Davison	
G-ATZS	Wassmer WA41 Super Baladou IV	G. R. Outwin & D. P. Bennett	
G-ATZY	Cessna F.150G	P. P. D. Howard-Johnston/Edinburgh	
G-ATZZ	Cessna F.150G	Routair Aviation Services Ltd/Southend	
G-AUTO	Cessna 441 Conquest	Faresavers Ltd	
G-AVAA	Cessna F.150G	A. C. Garrett	
G-AVAJ	Hiller UH-12B	R. White & P. Lancaster	
G-AVAK	M.S.893A Rallye Commodore 180	W. K. Anderson (stored)/Perth	
G-AVAP	Cessna F.150G	Seawing Flying Club Ltd/Southend	
G-AVAR	Cessna F.150G	J. A. Rees & F. Doncaster	
G-AVAU	PA-30 Twin Comanche 160B	L. Batin/Fairoaks	
G-AVAW	D.62B Condor	Avato Flying Group	
G-AVAX	PA-28 Cherokee 180	J. J. Parkes	
G-AVBG	PA-28 Cherokee 180	Transknight Ltd/Booker	
G-AVBH	PA-28 Cherokee 180	C. Ellerbrook & T. Smith	

Notes	Reg.	Type	Owner or Operator
	G-AVBP	PA-28 Cherokee 140	Bristol & Wessex Aeroplane Club Ltd/Bristol
	G-AVBS	PA-28 Cherokee 180	S. L. Robinson/St Just
	G-AVBT	PA-28 Cherokee 180	P. O. Hire & D. J. Spicer/Denham
	G-AVBZ	Cessna F.172H	J. Seville
	G-AVCE	Cessna F.172H	Damon Products
	G-AVCM	PA-24 Comanche 260	F. Smith & Sons Ltd/Stapleford
	G-AVCS	A.61 Terrier 1	A. Topen/Cranfield
	G-AVCT	Cessna F.150G	DJH Aviation Ltd/Biggin Hill
	G-AVCU	Cessna F.150G	P. R. Moss/Alderney
	G-AVCV	Cessna 182J Skylane	University of Manchester Institute of Science & Technology/Woodford
	G-AVCX	PA-30 Twin Comanche 160B	F. J. Stevens/Leicester
	G-AVCY	PA-30 Twin Comanche 160B	M. Dukes/Biggin Hill
	G-AVDA	Cessna 182K Skylane	J. W. Grant
	G-AVDF	Beagle Pup 100 ★	Shoreham Airport Museum
	G-AVDG	Wallis WA-116 Srs 1	K. H. Wallis
	G-AVDR	Beech B80 Queen Air	Shoreham Flight Simulation/Bournemouth
	G-AVDS	Beech B80 Queen Air	Shoreham Flight Simulation/Bournemouth
	G-AVDT	Aeronca 7AC Champion	D. Cheney & J. G. Woods
	G-AVDV	PA-22 Tri-Pacer 150 (modified to Pacer)	S. C. Brooks/Slinfold
	G-AVDW	D.62B Condor	Essex Aviation/Andrewsfield
	G-AVDY	Luton LA-4A Minor	D. E. Evans & ptnrs
	G-AVEB	Morane MS 230 (1076)	The Hon A. M. M. Lindsay/Booker
	G-AVEC	Cessna F.172H	W. H. Ekin (Engineering) Co Ltd
	G-AVEF	Jodel D.150	Tiger Club Ltd/Redhill
	G-AVEH	SIAI-Marchetti S.205	P. D. Winborne
	G-AVEM	Cessna F.150G	D. E. Bedford
	G-AVEN	Cessna F.150G	N. J. Budd/Aberdeen
	G-AVEO	Cessna F.150G	Computaplane Ltd/Glasgow
	G-AVER	Cessna F.150G	Telepoint Ltd/Manchester
	G-AVET	Beech 95-C55A Baron	Tunstall Telecom Ltd
	G-AVEU	Wassmer WA.41 Baladou	Baladou Flying Group/Aberdeen
	G-AVEX	D.62B Condor	Cotswold Roller Hire Ltd/Long Marston
	G-AVEY	Currie Super Wot	A. Eastelow/Dunkeswell
	G-AVEZ	HPR-7 Herald 210 ★	*Rescue Trainer*/Norwich
	G-AVFB	H.S.121 Trident 2E ★	Duxford Aviation Soc
	G-AVFE	H.S.121 Trident 2E ★	Belfast Airport Authority
	G-AVFH	H.S.121 Trident 2E ★	Mosquito Aircraft Museum (Fuselage only)
	G-AVFK	H.S.121 Trident 2E ★	Metropolitan Police Training Centre/Hounslow
	G-AVFM	H.S.121 Trident 2E ★	Brunel Technical College/Bristol
	G-AVFP	PA-28 Cherokee 140	H. D. Vince Ltd/Woodvale
	G-AVFR	PA-28 Cherokee 140	J. J. Ballagh/Newtownards
	G-AVFS	PA-32 Cherokee Six 300	A. V. Brown/Cambridge
	G-AVFU	PA-32 Cherokee Six 300	Couesnon Ltd/Biggin Hill
	G-AVFX	PA-28 Cherokee 140	R. A. Harris
	G-AVFY	PA-28 Cherokee 140	D. R. Davidson/Bournemouth
	G-AVFZ	PA-28 Cherokee 140	R. S. Littlechild & V. B. G. Childs
	G-AVGA	PA-24 Comanche 260	W. B. Baillie/Tees-side
	G-AVGB	PA-28 Cherokee 140	City Flying Group/Swansea
	G-AVGC	PA-28 Cherokee 140	B. A. Bennett/Redhill
	G-AVGD	PA-28 Cherokee 140	S. & G. W. Jacobs
	G-AVGE	PA-28 Cherokee 140	H. H. T. Wolf
	G-AVGH	PA-28 Cherokee 140	Phoenix Aviation Services Ltd
	G-AVGI	PA-28 Cherokee 140	K. Hope & ptnrs/Barton
	G-AVGJ	Jodel DR.1050	S. T. Gilbert & G. W. Camp
	G-AVGK	PA-28 Cherokee 180	S. Crowden & J. Atkinson/Liverpool
	G-AVGP	BAC One-Eleven 408	British Airways (*withdrawn*)
	G-AVGV	Cessna F.150G	J. P. Lassey
	G-AVGY	Cessna 182K Skylane	Clifford F. Cross (Wisbech) Ltd/Fenland
	G-AVGZ	Jodel DR.1050	Gordonair Ltd/Enstone
	G-AVHF	Beech A.23 Musketeer	S. Elston
	G-AVHH	Cessna F.172H	M. J. Mann & J. Hickinbotom
	G-AVHJ	Wassmer WA.41 Baladou	D. G. Pickering & ptnrs
	G-AVHL	Jodel DR.105A	G. L. Winterbourne/Redhill
	G-AVHM	Cessna F.150G	M. Tosh/Panshanger
	G-AVHN	Cessna F.150F ★	Brunel Technical College/Bristol
	G-AVHT	Auster AOP.9 (WZ711)	M. Somerton-Rayner/Middle Wallop
	G-AVHY	Fournier RF.4D	R. Swinn & J. Conolly

Reg.	Type	Owner or Operator	Notes
G-AVIA	Cessna F.150G	Cheshire Air Training School (Merseyside) Ltd/Liverpool	
G-AVIB	Cessna F.150G	D. W. Horton/Humberside	
G-AVIC	Cessna F.172H	Pembrokeshire Air/Haverfordwest	
G-AVID	Cessna 182J	T. D. Boyle	
G-AVIE	Cessna F.172H	M. P. Parker	
G-AVII	AB-206A JetRanger	Bristow Helicopters Ltd	
G-AVIL	Alon A.2 Aircoupe	D. W. Vernon/Woodvale	
G-AVIN	M.S.880B Rallye Club	R. Wilcock	
G-AVIO	M.S.880B Rallye Club	A. R. Johnston/Popham	
G-AVIP	Brantly B.2B	Cosworth Engineering Ltd	
G-AVIS	Cessna F.172H	Jon Paul Photography Ltd/Rochester	
G-AVIT	Cessna F.150G	Shropshire Aero Club Ltd/Sleap	
G-AVIZ	Scheibe SF.25A Motorfalke	D. C. Pattison & D. A. Wilson	
G-AVJE	Cessna F.150G	P. R. Green & ptnrs/Booker	
G-AVJF	Cessna F.172H	J. A. & G. M. Rees	
G-AVJG	Cessna 337B	P. R. Moss/Bournemouth	
G-AVJH	D.62 Condor	Lleyn Flying Group/Mona	
G-AVJI	Cessna F.172H	D. V. D. Reed	
G-AVJJ	PA-30 Twin Comanche 160B	A. H. Manser Ltd/Staverton	
G-AVJK	Jodel DR.1050 M.1	G. Wylde	
G-AVJO	Fokker E.III Replica (422-15)	Personal Plane Services Ltd/Booker	
G-AVJV	Wallis WA-117 Srs 1	K. H. Wallis (G-ATCV)	
G-AVJW	Wallis WA-118 Srs 2	K. H. Wallis (G-ATPW)	
G-AVKB	MB.50 Pipistrelle	R. A. Fairclough	
G-AVKD	Fournier RF-4D	Lasham RF4 Group	
G-AVKE	Gadfly HDW.1 ★	British Rotorcraft Museum	
G-AVKG	Cessna F.172H	P. E. P. Sheppard	
G-AVKI	Slingsby T.66 Nipper 3	P. Archer	
G-AVKJ	Slingsby T.66 Nipper 3	N. M. Yeo	
G-AVKK	Slingsby T.66 Nipper 3	C. Watson	
G-AVKN	Cessna 401	Merlin Marine Investments Ltd	
G-AVKP	A.109 Airedale	D. R. Williams	
G-AVKR	Bo 208C Junior	C. W. Grant	
G-AVKY	Hiller UH-12E	Agricopters Ltd/Chilbolton	
G-AVKZ	PA-23 Aztec 250C	AEW Engineering Co Ltd/Norwich	
G-AVLB	PA-28 Cherokee 140	J. A. Overton Ltd/Andrewsfield	
G-AVLC	PA-28 Cherokee 140	F. C. V. Hopkins/Swansea	
G-AVLD	PA-28 Cherokee 140	WLS Flying Group/White Waltham	
G-AVLE	PA-28 Cherokee 140	Hambrair Ltd	
G-AVLF	PA-28 Cherokee 140	G. H. Hughesdon	
G-AVLG	PA-28 Cherokee 140	R. Friedlander & D. C. Raymond	
G-AVLH	PA-28 Cherokee 140	P. Preece/Goodwood	
G-AVLI	PA-28 Cherokee 140	J. V. White	
G-AVLJ	PA-28 Cherokee 140	E. Berks Boat Company Ltd	
G-AVLM	B.121 Pup 2	R. Towle	
G-AVLN	B.121 Pup 2	C. A. Thorpe	
G-AVLO	Bo 208C Junior	J. A. Webb & K. F. Barnard/Popham	
G-AVLR	PA-28 Cherokee 140	Peter Dolan & Co Ltd/Conington	
G-AVLT	PA-28 Cherokee 140	R. W. Harris & ptnrs/Southend	
G-AVLU	PA-28 Cherokee 140	London Transport (CRS) Sports Association Flying Club/Fairoaks	
G-AVLW	Fournier RF-4D	M. R. Shelton	
G-AVLY	Jodel D.120A	P. Cawkwell	
G-AVMA	GY-80 Horizon 180	B. R. & S. Hildick	
G-AVMB	D.62B Condor	J. C. Mansell	
G-AVMD	Cessna 150G	T. E. Aviation (W. Yorkshire) Ltd	
G-AVMF	Cessna F. 150G	J. F. Marsh & M. J. Oliver	
G-AVMH	BAC One-Eleven 510	British Airways *County of Cheshire*/Manchester	
G-AVMI	BAC One-Eleven 510	British Airways *County of Avon*/Manchester	
G-AVMJ	BAC One-Eleven 510	British Airways *Strathclyde Region*/Manchester	
G-AVMK	BAC One-Eleven 510	British Airways *County of Kent*/Manchester	
G-AVML	BAC One-Eleven 510	British Airways *County of Surrey*/Manchester	
G-AVMM	BAC One-Eleven 510	British Airways *County of Antrim*/Manchester	
G-AVMN	BAC One-Eleven 510	British Airways *County of Essex*/Manchester	
G-AVMO	BAC One-Eleven 510	British Airways *Lothian Region*/Manchester	

Notes	Reg.	Type	Owner or Operator
	G-AVMP	BAC One-Eleven 510	British Airways *Bailiwick of Jersey*/ Manchester
	G-AVMR	BAC One-Eleven 510	British Airways *County of Tyne & Wear*/ Manchester
	G-AVMS	BAC One-Eleven 510	British Airways *County of West Sussex*/ Manchester
	G-AVMT	BAC One-Eleven 510	British Airways *County of Berkshire*/ Manchester
	G-AVMU	BAC One-Eleven 510	British Airways *County of Dorset*/ Manchester
	G-AVMV	BAC One-Eleven 510	British Airways *County of Powys*/ Manchester
	G-AVMW	BAC One-Eleven 510	British Airways *Grampian Region*/ Manchester
	G-AVMX	BAC One-Eleven 510	British Airways *County of East Sussex*/ Manchester
	G-AVMY	BAC One-Eleven 510	British Airways *County of Derbyshire*/ Manchester
	G-AVMZ	BAC One-Eleven 510	British Airways *County of Lancashire*/ Manchester
	G-AVNC	Cessna F.150G	J. Turner
	G-AVNE	W.S.58 Wessex Mk 60 Srs 1 ★	British Rotorcraft Museum
	G-AVNN	PA-28 Cherokee 180	Barum Alloys Ltd
	G-AVNO	PA-28 Cherokee 180	Allister Flight Ltd/Stapleford
	G-AVNP	PA-28 Cherokee 180	R. W. Harris & ptnrs
	G-AVNR	PA-28 Cherokee 180	L. R. Davies/Biggin Hill
	G-AVNS	PA-28 Cherokee 180	A. Walton/Conington
	G-AVNU	PA-28 Cherokee 180	F. E. Gooding/Biggin Hill
	G-AVNW	PA-28 Cherokee 180	Len Smith's School & Sports Ltd
	G-AVNX	Fournier RF-4D	O. C. Harris & C. G. Masterman
	G-AVNY	Fournier RF-4D	M. P. Dentith/Biggin Hill
	G-AVNZ	Fournier RF-4D	Aviation Special Developments (ASD) Ltd/Biggin Hill
	G-AVOA	Jodel DR.1050	D. A. Willies/Cranwell
	G-AVOD	Beagle D5/180 Husky	D. Bonsall & ptnrs/Netherthorpe
	G-AVOH	D.62B Condor	J. E. Hobbs/Sandown
	G-AVOM	Jodel DR.221	M. A. Mountford/Headcorn
	G-AVON	Luton LA-5A Major	G. R. Mee
	G-AVOO	PA-18 Super Cub 150	London Gliding Club Ltd/ Dunstable
	G-AVOZ	PA-28 Cherokee 180	J. R. Winning/Booker
	G-AVPC	D.31 Turbulent	J. Sharp (*stored*)
	G-AVPD	D.9 Bebe	S. W. McKay (*stored*)
	G-AVPE	H.S.125 Srs 3B	British Aerospace/Filton
	G-AVPH	Cessna F.150G	W. Lancashire Aero Club/Woodvale
	G-AVPI	Cessna F.172H	R. W. Cope
	G-AVPJ	D.H.82A Tiger Moth	C. C. Silk
	G-AVPK	M.S.892A Rallye Commodore	B. A. Bridgewater/Halfpenny Green
	G-AVPM	Jodel D.117	J. Houghton/Breighton
	G-AVPN	HPR-7 Herald 213	Nordic Oil Services Ltd
	G-AVPO	Hindustan HAL-26 Pushpak	A. & R. Rimington
	G-AVPR	PA-30 Twin Comanche 160B	Cold Storage (Jersey) Ltd
	G-AVPS	PA-30 Twin Comanche 160B	John Bisco (Cheltenham) Ltd
	G-AVPT	PA-18 Super Cub 150	Tiger Club Ltd/Redhill
	G-AVPV	PA-28 Cherokee 180	Robert Hinton & Partners Ltd
	G-AVRF	H.S.125 Srs 3B	S. Gill
	G-AVRK	PA-28 Cherokee 180	S. R. Culley Developments Ltd & Macdillens Ltd
	G-AVRN	Boeing 737-204	Britannia Airways Ltd *Capt James Cook*/Luton
	G-AVRP	PA-28 Cherokee 140	T. Hiscox
	G-AVRS	GY-80 Horizon 180	Horizon Flyers Ltd/Denham
	G-AVRT	PA-28 Cherokee 140	F. Clarke/Stapleford
	G-AVRU	PA-28 Cherokee 180	H. B. Holden & ptnrs/Biggin Hill
	G-AVRW	GY-20 Minicab	R. B. Pybus
	G-AVRY	PA-28 Cherokee 180	Brigfast Ltd/Blackbushe
	G-AVRZ	PA-28 Cherokee 180	Mantavia Group Ltd
	G-AVSA	PA-28 Cherokee 180	E. Barrow & J. Walker/Barton
	G-AVSB	PA-28 Cherokee 180	White House Garage Ashford Ltd
	G-AVSC	PA-28 Cherokee 180	Maidenhead Audio Visual Ltd/ White Waltham
	G-AVSD	PA-28 Cherokee 180	Landmate Ltd
	G-AVSE	PA-28 Cherokee 180	Yorkshire Light Aircraft Ltd/Leeds

Reg.	Type	Owner or Operator	Notes
G-AVSF	PA-28 Cherokee 180	Monday Club	
G-AVSI	PA-28 Cherokee 140	CR Aviation Ltd	
G-AVSP	PA-28 Cherokee 180	Trig Engineering Ltd	
G-AVSR	Beagle D 5/180 Husky	A. L. Young	
G-AVTC	Slingsby T.66 Nipper 3	M. K. Field	
G-AVTJ	PA-32 Cherokee Six 260	A. W. Chapman/Southend	
G-AVTK	PA-32 Cherokee Six 260	Mannix Aviation Ltd/E. Midlands	
G-AVTP	Cessna F.172H	J. H. A. Clarke & ptnrs	
G-AVTT	Ercoupe 415D	Wright's Farm Eggs Ltd/Andrewsfield	
G-AVTV	M.S.893A Rallye Commodore	D. B. Meeks	
G-AVUA	Cessna F.172H	Recreational Flying Centre (Popham) Ltd	
G-AVUD	PA-30 Twin Comanche 160B	F. M. Aviation/Biggin Hill	
G-AVUG	Cessna F.150H	Skyways Flying Group/Netherthorpe	
G-AVUH	Cessna F.150H	S. P. Mann	
G-AVUL	Cessna F.172H	The Lion Flying Group Ltd/Elstree	
G-AVUS	PA-28 Cherokee 140	R. Groat/Glasgow	
G-AVUT	PA-28 Cherokee 140	Bencray Ltd/Blackpool	
G-AVUU	PA-28 Cherokee 140	R. W. Harris	
G-AVUZ	PA-32 Cherokee Six 300	Ceesix Ltd/Jersey	
G-AVVB	H.S. 125 Srs 3B	Jetlease Ltd	
G-AVVC	Cessna F.172H	Kestrel Air Ltd/Swansea	
G-AVVE	Cessna F.150H ★	R. Windley (stored)	
G-AVVF	D.H.104 Dove 8	Sparline Agencies Ltd/Cranfield	
G-AVVI	PA-30 Twin Comanche 160B	G. G. Long	
G-AVVJ	M.S.893A Rallye Commodore	Herefordshire Gliding Club Ltd/ Shobdon	
G-AVVL	Cessna F.150H	Osprey Air Services Ltd/Cranfield	
G-AVVO	Avro 652A Anson 19 (VL348) ★	Newark Air Museum	
G-AVVT	PA-23 Aztec 250C	Kayglynn Investment Holdings Ltd	
G-AVVV	PA-28 Cherokee 180	Courtrun Ltd/Redhill	
G-AVVX	Cessna F.150H	Hatfield Flying Club	
G-AVVY	Cessna F.150H	Telepoint Ltd/Manchester	
G-AVWA	PA-28 Cherokee 140	W. London Aero Services Ltd/ White Waltham	
G-AVWD	PA-28 Cherokee 140	M. P. Briggs	
G-AVWE	PA-28 Cherokee 140	W. C. C. Meyer (stored)/Biggin Hill	
G-AVWG	PA-28 Cherokee 140	Bencray Ltd/Blackpool	
G-AVWH	PA-28 Cherokee 140	P. Elliott/Biggin Hill	
G-AVWI	PA-28 Cherokee 140	L. M. Veitch	
G-AVWJ	PA-28 Cherokee 140	M. J. Steer/Biggin Hill	
G-AVWL	PA-28 Cherokee 140	Bristol & Wessex Aeroplane Club Ltd/ Bristol	
G-AVWM	PA-28 Cherokee 140	N. Jahanfar/Southend	
G-AVWN	PA-28R Cherokee Arrow 180	Vawn Air Ltd/Jersey	
G-AVWO	PA-28R Cherokee Arrow 180	P. D. Cahill/Biggin Hill	
G-AVWR	PA-28R Cherokee Arrow 180	D. A. Howe	
G-AVWT	PA-28R Cherokee Arrow 180	Flamex Ltd	
G-AVWU	PA-28R Cherokee Arrow 180	Horizon Flyers Ltd/Denham	
G-AVWV	PA-28R Cherokee Arrow 180	Mapair Ltd/Birmingham	
G-AVWY	Fournier RF-4D	ASD Formaero Ltd/Biggin Hill	
G-AVXA	PA-25 Pawnee 235	Agricultural Aerial Services Ltd	
G-AVXB	Lovegrove PL-1 gyrocopter	A. Stone	
G-AVXC	Slingsby T.66 Nipper 3	T. P. W. Hyde	
G-AVXD	Slingsby T.66 Nipper 3	D. A. Davidson	
G-AVXF	PA-28R Cherokee Arrow 180	J. G. Stewart & I. M. S. Ferriman/ Cranfield	
G-AVXI	H.S.748 Srs 2A	Civil Aviation Authority/Stansted	
G-AVXJ	H.S.748 Srs 2A	Civil Aviation Authority/Stansted	
G-AVXV	Bleriot XI (BAPC 104) ★	Imperial War Museum/Duxford	
G-AVXW	D.62B Condor	A. J. Cooper/Rochester	
G-AVXX	Cessna FR.172E	Hadrian Flying Group/Newcastle	
G-AVXY	Auster AOP.9 (XK417) ★	R. Windley (stored)	
G-AVXZ	PA-28 Cherokee 140 ★	ATC Hayle (instructional airframe)	
G-AVYB	H.S.121 Trident 1E-140 ★	SAS training airframe/Hereford	
G-AVYE	H.S.121 Trident 1E-140 ★	Science Museum/Wroughton	
G-AVYK	A.61 Terrier 3	A. R. Wright/Booker	
G-AVYL	PA-28 Cherokee 180	N. J. Allcoat	
G-AVYM	PA-28 Cherokee 180	Carlisle Aviation (1985) Ltd/Crosby	
G-AVYP	PA-28 Cherokee 140	T. D. Reid (Braids) Ltd/Newtownards	
G-AVYR	PA-28 Cherokee 140	D.R. Flying Club Ltd/Staverton	
G-AVYS	PA-28R Cherokee Arrow 180	E. W. Passmore	
G-AVYT	PA-28R Cherokee Arrow 180	H. Stephenson	
G-AVYV	Jodel D.120	Long Mountain Aero Group	

Notes	Reg.	Type	Owner or Operator
	G-AVYX	AB-206A JetRanger	D. A. C. Pipe
	G-AVZB	Aero Z-37 Cmelak ★	Science Museum/Wroughton
	G-AVZC	Hughes 269B	*LRC* Mail Order Ltd
	G-AVZI	Bo 208C Junior	C. F. Rogers
	G-AVZM	B.121 Pup 1	ARAZ Group/Elstree
	G-AVZN	B.121 Pup 1	W. E. Cro & Sons Ltd/Shoreham
	G-AVZP	B.121 Pup 1	T. A. White
	G-AVZR	PA-28 Cherokee 180	W. E. Lowe/Halfpenny Green
	G-AVZU	Cessna F.150H	E. J. R. McDowell
	G-AVZV	Cessna F.172H	B. Schreiber
	G-AVZW	EAA Model P Biplane	R. G. Maidment & G. R. Edmundson/ Goodwood
	G-AVZX	M.S.880B Rallye Club	J. T. Hicks
	G-AWAA	M.S.880B Rallye Club	P. A. Cairns/Dunkeswell
	G-AWAC	GY-80 Horizon 180	R. D. Harper
	G-AWAD	Beech D 55 Baron	Aero Lease Ltd/Bournemouth
	G-AWAH	Beech D 55 Baron	B. J. S. Grey
	G-AWAI	Beech D 55 Baron	Alibear Ltd/Booker
	G-AWAJ	Beech D 55 Baron	Standard Hose Ltd/Leeds
	G-AWAO	Beech D 55 Baron	D. W. Clark/Wellesbourne
	G-AWAT	D.62B Condor	Tarwood Ltd/Redhill
	G-AWAU	Vickers F.B.27A Vimy (replica) (F8614) ★	Bomber Command Museum/Hendon
	G-AWAW	Cessna F.150F	G. M. White
	G-AWAZ	PA-28R Cherokee Arrow 180	C. J. Chapman
	G-AWBA	PA-28R Cherokee Arrow 180	March Flying Group/Stapleford
	G-AWBB	PA-28R Cherokee Arrow 180	J. Calverley
	G-AWBC	PA-28R Cherokee Arrow 180	B. Sharbati
	G-AWBE	PA-28 Cherokee 140	B. E. Boyle
	G-AWBG	PA-28 Cherokee 140	D. J. Smith
	G-AWBH	PA-28 Cherokee 140	R. C. A. Mackworth
	G-AWBJ	Fournier RF-4D	A. Hill
	G-AWBL	BAC One-Eleven 416	British Airways (*withdrawn*)
	G-AWBM	D.31 Turbulent	K. J. Medcroft
	G-AWBN	PA-30 Twin Comanche 160B	Stourfield Investments Ltd/Jersey
	G-AWBP	Cessna 182L Skylane	Bournemouth Aviation
	G-AWBS	PA-28 Cherokee 140	W. London Aero Services Ltd/ White Waltham
	G-AWBT	PA-30 Twin Comanche 160B	Fridaythorpe Feeds Ltd
	G-AWBU	Morane-Saulnier N (replica) (M.S.50)	Personal Plane Services Ltd/Booker
	G-AWBV	Cessna 182L Skylane	Aerofilms Ltd/Elstree
	G-AWBW	Cessna F.172H ★	Brunel Technical College/Bristol
	G-AWBX	Cessna F.150H	A. R. Musgrove
	G-AWCM	Cessna F.150H	Telepoint Ltd/Manchester
	G-AWCN	Cessna FR.172E	LEC Refrigeration Ltd
	G-AWCP	Cessna F.150H (tailwheel)	C. E. Mason/Shobdon
	G-AWCW	Beech E.95 Travel Air	H. W. Astor/White Waltham
	G-AWCY	PA-32 Cherokee Six 260	J. Harvey
	G-AWDA	Slingsby T.66 Nipper 3	J. A. Cheesebrough
	G-AWDD	Slingsby T.66 Nipper 3	T. D. G. Roberts/Inverness
	G-AWDI	PA-23 Aztec 250C	Air Foyle Ltd/Luton
	G-AWDO	D.31 Turbulent	E. J. Lloyd
	G-AWDP	PA-28 Cherokee 180	B. H. & P. M. Illston/Shipdham
	G-AWDR	Cessna FR.172E	Levendene Ltd
	G-AWDU	Brantly B.2B	G. E. J. Redwood
	G-AWEF	Stampe SV-4B	Tiger Club Ltd/Redhill
	G-AWEI	D.62B Condor	M. A. Pearce/Redhill
	G-AWEL	Fournier RF-4D	A. B. Clymo/Halfpenny Green
	G-AWEM	Fournier RF-4D	B. J. Griffin/Wickenby
	G-AWEN	Jodel DR.1050	L. G. Earnshaw & ptnrs
	G-AWEO	Cessna F.150H	Banbury Plant Hire Ltd
	G-AWEP	JB-01 Minicab	K. Atkinson
	G-AWER	PA-23 Aztec 250C	Woodgate Air Services (IOM) Ltd
	G-AWET	PA-28 Cherokee 180	Broadland Flying Group Ltd/ Shipdham
	G-AWEV	PA-28 Cherokee 140	Smith Engineering/Shipdham
	G-AWEX	PA-28 Cherokee 140	R. Badham
	G-AWEZ	PA-28R Cherokee Arrow 180	BTG Plant Hire & Repairs Ltd/Stapleford
	G-AWFB	PA-28R Cherokee Arrow 180	Luke Aviation Ltd/Bristol
	G-AWFC	PA-28R Cherokee Arrow 180	K. A. Goodchild/Southend
	G-AWFD	PA-28R Cherokee Arrow 180	J. L. Yourell
	G-AWFF	Cessna F.150H	DJH Aviation Ltd/Biggin Hill

Reg.	Type	Owner or Operator	Notes
G-AWFJ	PA-28R Cherokee Arrow 180	W. F. van Schoten/Sherburn	
G-AWFK	PA-28R Cherokee Arrow 180	J. A. Rundle (Holdings) Ltd/Kidlington	
G-AWFN	D.62B Condor	R. M. Johnston & H. R. Oldland	
G-AWFO	D.62B Condor	T. A. Major	
G-AWFP	D.62B Condor	Blackbushe Flying Club	
G-AWFR	D.31 Turbulent	L. W. Usherwood	
G-AWFT	Jodel D.9 Bebe	W. H. Cole	
G-AWFW	Jodel D.117	F. H. Greenwell	
G-AWFZ	Beech A23 Musketeer	R. Sweet & B D. Corbett	
G-AWGD	Cessna F.172H	Brook Shaw Ltd	
G-AWGJ	Cessna F.172H	J. & C. J. Freeman/Headcorn	
G-AWGK	Cessna F.150H	G. R. Brown/Shoreham	
G-AWGM	Arkle Kittiwake 2	A. F. S. Caldecourt	
G-AWGN	Fournier RF-4D	R. H. Ashforth/Staverton	
G-AWGP	Cessna T.210H	S. Harcourt/Elstree	
G-AWGR	Cessna F.172H	P. Bushell/Liverpool	
G-AWGZ	Taylor JT.1 Monoplane	A. Hill	
G-AWHV	Rollason Beta B.2A	Tiger Club Ltd/Redhill	
G-AWHX	Rollason Beta B.2	J. J. Cooke/White Waltham	
G-AWIF	Brookland Mosquito 2	—/Husbands Bosworth	
G-AWII	V.S.349 Spitfire VC (AR501)	Shuttleworth Trust/Duxford	
G-AWIN	Campbell-Bensen B.8MC	M. J. Cuttel & J. Deane	
G-AWIP	Luton LA-4A Minor	J. Houghton	
G-AWIR	Midget Mustang	K. E. Sword/Leicester	
G-AWIT	PA-28 Cherokee 180	Ashley Gardner School of Flying Ltd	
G-AWIV	Airmark TSR.3	C. J. Jesson/Redhill	
G-AWIW	Stampe SV-4B	R. E. Mitchell	
G-AWIY	PA-23 Aztec 250C	B. Anderson/Belfast	
G-AWJC	Brighton gas balloon	P. D. Furlong *Slippery William*	
G-AWJE	Slingsby T.66 Nipper 3	N. McArthur & T. Mosedale	
G-AWJF	Slingsby T.66 Nipper 3	R. Wilcock/Shoreham	
G-AWJI	M.S.880B Rallye Club	D. V. Tyler/Southend	
G-AWJV	D.H.98 Mosquito TT Mk 35 (TA634) ★	Mosquito Aircraft Museum	
G-AWJX	Zlin Z.526 Akrobat	Aerobatics International Ltd	
G-AWJY	Zlin Z.526 Akrobat	Elco Manufacturing Co/Redhill	
G-AWKB	M.J.5 Sirocco F2/39	G. D. Claxton	
G-AWKD	PA-17 Vagabond	A. T. & M. R. Dowie/ White Waltham	
G-AWKM	B.121 Pup 1	D. M. G. Jenkins/Swansea	
G-AWKO	B.121 Pup 1	P. A. Brook/Redhill	
G-AWKP	Jodel DR.253	R. C. Chandless	
G-AWKT	M.S.880B Rallye Club	D. C. Strain	
G-AWKX	Beech A65 Queen Air	Subtec Aviation Ltd/Shoreham	
G-AWLA	Cessna F.150H	Royal Artillery Aero Club Ltd/ Middle Wallop	
G-AWLE	Cessna F.172H	H. Mendelssohn & H. I. Shott	
G-AWLF	Cessna F.172H	Osprey Air Services Ltd	
G-AWLG	SIPA 903	S. W. Markham	
G-AWLI	PA-22 Tri-Pacer 150	H. J. W. Ellison/Biggin Hill	
G-AWLL	AB-206B JetRanger 2	Land Air Ltd	
G-AWLM	Bensen B.8MS	C. J. E. Ashby	
G-AWLO	Boeing N2S-5 Kaydet	N. D. Pickard/Shoreham	
G-AWLP	Mooney M.20F	Petratek Ltd	
G-AWLR	Slingsby T.66 Nipper 3	J. D. Lawther	
G-AWLS	Slingsby T.66 Nipper 3	Stapleford Nipper Group	
G-AWLY	Cessna F.150H	Banbury Plant Hire Ltd	
G-AWLZ	Fournier RF-4D	E. V. Goodwin & C. R. Williamson	
G-AWMD	Jodel D.11	K. Dawson & E. Chandler/Stapleford	
G-AWMF	PA-18 Super Cub 150	Booker Gliding Club Ltd	
G-AWMI	Glos-Airtourer 115	Airtourer Group 86/Cardiff	
G-AWMK	AB-206B JetRanger	Bristow Helicopters Ltd	
G-AWMM	M.S.893A Rallye Commodore 180	P. Luscombe	
G-AWMN	Luton LA-4A Minor	R. E. R. Wilks	
G-AWMP	Cessna F.172H	W. Rennie-Roberts/Ipswich	
G-AWMR	D.31 Turbulent	D. G. Curran	
G-AWMT	Cessna F.150H	R. V. Grocott/Sleap	
G-AWMZ	Cessna F.172H ★	*Parachute jump trainer*/Cark	
G-AWNA	Boeing 747-136	British Airways *Colliford Lake*/Heathrow	
G-AWNB	Boeing 747-136	British Airways *Llangorse Lake*/ Heathrow	
G-AWNC	Boeing 747-136	British Airways *Lake Windermere*/ Heathrow	
G-AWND	Boeing 747-136	British Airways *Conniston Water*/ Heathrow	

Notes	Reg.	Type	Owner or Operator
	G-AWNE	Boeing 747-136	British Airways *Derwent Water*/Heathrow
	G-AWNF	Boeing 747-136	British Airways *Blagdon Lake*/Heathrow
	G-AWNG	Boeing 747-136	British Airways *Rutland Water*/Heathrow
	G-AWNH	Boeing 747-136	British Airways *Devoke Water*/Heathrow
	G-AWNJ	Boeing 747-136	British Airways *Bassenthwaite Lake*/Heathrow
	G-AWNL	Boeing 747-136	British Airways *Ennerdale Water*/Heathrow
	G-AWNM	Boeing 747-136	British Airways *Ullswater*/Heathrow
	G-AWNN	Boeing 747-136	British Airways *Lowes Water*/Heathrow
	G-AWNO	Boeing 747-136	British Airways *Grafton Water*/Heathrow
	G-AWNP	Boeing 747-136	British Airways *Haningfield Water*/Heathrow
	G-AWNT	BN-2A Islander	Aerofilms Ltd/Elstree
	G-AWOA	M.S.880B Rallye Club	E. & M. Craven/Barton
	G-AWOE	Aero Commander 680E	J. M. Houlder/Elstree
	G-AWOF	PA-15 Vagabond	S. B. Churchill
	G-AWOH	PA-17 Vagabond	The High Flats Flying Group
	G-AWOL	Bell 206B JetRanger 2	J. Palmer
	G-AWOT	Cessna F.150H	J. M. Montgomerie & J. Ferguson
	G-AWOU	Cessna 170B	P. Chaplin/Booker
	G-AWOX	W.S.58 Wessex Mk 60 ★	Sykes Aviation Ltd (*stored*)
	G-AWPH	P.56 Provost T.1	J. A. D. Bradshaw
	G-AWPJ	Cessna F.150H	W. J. Greenfield
	G-AWPN	Shield Xyla	T. Brown
	G-AWPS	PA-28 Cherokee 140	M. Shipley
	G-AWPU	Cessna F.150J	Light Planes (Lancashire) Ltd/Barton
	G-AWPW	PA-12 Super Cruiser	J. E. Davies/Sandown
	G-AWPX	Cessna 150E	W. R. Emberton/Southampton
	G-AWPY	Bensen B.8M	J. Jordan
	G-AWPZ	Andreasson BA-4B	J. M. Vening
	G-AWRK	Cessna F.150J	Southern Strut Flying Club/Shoreham
	G-AWRL	Cessna F.172H	T. Hayselden (Doncaster) Ltd
	G-AWRS	Avro 19 Srs. 2 ★	N. E. Aircraft Museum
	G-AWRY	P.56 Provost T.1 (XF836)	Slymar Aviation & Services Ltd/Popham
	G-AWRZ	Bell 47G-5	Hammond Aerial Spraying Ltd
	G-AWSA	Avro 652A Anson 19 (VL349) ★	Norfolk & Suffolk Aviation Museum
	G-AWSD	Cessna F.150J	British Skysports
	G-AWSL	PA-28 Cherokee 180D	Fascia Ltd/Southend
	G-AWSM	PA-28 Cherokee 235	Firecrest Aviation Ltd/Leavesden
	G-AWSN	D.62B Condor	J. Leader
	G-AWSP	D.62B Condor	R. Q. & A. S. Bond/Wellesbourne
	G-AWSS	D.62C Condor	G. Bruce/Inverness
	G-AWST	D.62B Condor	Humberside Aviation/Doncaster
	G-AWSV	Skeeter 12 (XM553)	Maj. M. Somerton-Rayner/Middle Wallop
	G-AWSY	Boeing 737-204	Britannia Airways Ltd *General James Wolfe*/Luton
	G-AWTA	Cessna E.310N	Heliscott Ltd
	G-AWTJ	Cessna F.150J	Metropolitan Police Flying Club/Biggin Hill
	G-AWTL	PA-28 Cherokee 180D	S. J. Lambden/Southend
	G-AWTS	Beech A.23 Musketeer	M. Corbett & ptnrs
	G-AWTV	Beech A.23 Musketeer	A. Johnston/Blackbushe
	G-AWTW	Beech B.55 Baron	Ingham Aviation Ltd/Bristol
	G-AWTX	Cessna F.150J	R. D. & E. Forster
	G-AWUB	GY-201 Minicab	H. P. Burrill
	G-AWUE	Jodel DR.1050	S. Bichan
	G-AWUG	Cessna F.150H	P. P. D. Howard-Johnston/Edinburgh
	G-AWUH	Cessna F.150H	Airtime (Hampshire) Ltd
	G-AWUJ	Cessna F.150H	W. Lawton/Doncaster
	G-AWUL	Cessna F.150H	E. I. Bett
	G-AWUN	Cessna F.150H	Northamptonshire School of Flying Ltd/Sywell
	G-AWUO	Cessna F.150H	K. A. Ellis/Sibson
	G-AWUP	Cessna F.150H	R. H. Timmis (*stored*)/Shannon
	G-AWUS	Cessna F.150J	Recreational Flying Centre (Popham) Ltd

Reg.	Type	Owner or Operator	Notes
G-AWUT	Cessna F.150J	J. Bluff/Netherthorpe	
G-AWUW	Cessna F.172H	B. Stewart/Panshanger	
G-AWUX	Cessna F.172H	V. Gray & ptnrs/Headcorn	
G-AWUZ	Cessna F.172H	March Microwave Ltd/Andrewsfield	
G-AWVA	Cessna F.172H	S. Tagg	
G-AWVB	Jodel D.117	C. M. & T. R. C. Griffin	
G-AWVC	B.121 Pup 1	J. H. Marshall	
G-AWVE	Jodel DR.1050M.1	E. A. Taylor/Southend	
G-AWVF	P.56 Provost T.1 (XF877)	J. Harper/Bourn	
G-AWVG	AESL Airtourer T.2	C. J. Schofield & G. M. Gearing	
G-AWVN	Aeronca 7AC Champion	Bowker Air Services Ltd/Rush Green	
G-AWVZ	Jodel D.112	D. C. Stokes	
G-AWWE	B.121 Pup 2	J. M. Randle/Coventry	
G-AWWF	B.121 Pup 1	N. M. Morris & Keef & Co Ltd/Denham	
G-AWWI	Jodel D.117	R. L. Sambell/Coventry	
G-AWWM	GY-201 Minicab	J. S. Brayshaw	
G-AWWN	Jodel DR.1051	T. W. M. Beck & ptnrs	
G-AWWO	Jodel DR.1050	Whiskey Oscar Group/Barton	
G-AWWP	Aerosport Woody Pusher III	M. S. Bird & R. D. Bird	
G-AWWT	D.31 Turbulent	M. A. Sherry & J. Tring/Redhill	
G-AWWU	Cessna FR.172F	Westward Airways (Lands End) Ltd	
G-AWWW	Cessna 401	Westair Flying Services Ltd/Blackpool	
G-AWWX	BAC One-Eleven 509	Dan-Air Services Ltd/Gatwick	
G-AWWZ	BAC One-Eleven 509	British Island Airways PLC *Island Empress*/Gatwick	
G-AWXA	Cessna 182M	P. Cannon	
G-AWXO	H.S.125 Srs. 400B	Twinjet Aircraft Sales Ltd/Luton	
G-AWXR	PA-28 Cherokee 180D	J. D. Williams	
G-AWXS	PA-28 Cherokee 180D	Rayhenro Flying Group/Shobdon	
G-AWXU	Cessna F.150J	B. B. Burtenshaw & ptnrs	
G-AWXV	Cessna F.172H	BAe Warton Flying Club	
G-AWXX	W.S.58 Wessex Mk. 60 Srs. 1	Sykes Group Co Ltd/Bournemouth	
G-AWXY	M.S.885 Super Rallye	A. J. Langdon & B. R. Pearson	
G-AWXZ	SNCAN SV-4C (D88)	Personal Plane Services Ltd/Booker	
G-AWYB	Cessna FR.172F	C. W. Larkin/Southend	
G-AWYE	H.S.125 Srs 1B	Flamebird Ltd/Jersey	
G-AWYF	G.159 Gulfstream 1	Ford Motor Co Ltd/Stansted	
G-AWYJ	B.121 Pup 2	H. C. Taylor	
G-AWYL	Jodel DR.253B	A. P. Broyden	
G-AWYO	B.121 Pup 1	B. R. C. Wild/Popham	
G-AWYR	BAC One-Eleven 501	British Airways *County of Suffolk*	
G-AWYS	BAC One-Eleven 501	British Airways *County of Norfolk*	
G-AWYT	BAC One-Eleven 501	British Airways *County of Gwynedd*	
G-AWYU	BAC One-Eleven 501	British Airways *County of Avon*	
G-AWYV	BAC One-Eleven 501	British Airways *County of Powys*	
G-AWYX	M.S.880B Rallye Club	J. M. L. Edwards/Exeter	
G-AWYY	T.57 Camel replica (B6401)	FAA Museum/Yeovilton	
G-AWZE	H.S.121 Trident 3B ★	*Instructional airframe*/Heathrow	
G-AWZI	H.S.121 Trident 3B ★	Surrey Fire Brigade (*instructional airframe*)/Reigate	
G-AWZJ	H.S.121 Trident 3B ★	British Airports Authority/Prestwick	
G-AWZK	H.S.121 Trident 3B ★	*Ground trainer*/Heathrow	
G-AWZM	H.S.121 Trident 3B ★	Science Museum/Wroughton	
G-AWZN	H.S.121 Trident 3B ★	Cranfield Institute of Technology	
G-AWZO	H.S.121 Trident 3B ★	British Aerospace/Hatfield	
G-AWZP	H.S.121 Trident 3B ★	Greater Manchester Museum of Science & Technology (*nose only*)	
G-AWZR	H.S.121 Trident 3B ★	CAA Fire School/Teesside	
G-AWZU	H.S.121 Trident 3B ★	British Airports Authority/Stansted	
G-AWZX	H.S.121 Trident 3B ★	BAA Fire Services/Gatwick	
G-AWZZ	H.S.121 Trident 3B ★	Airport Fire Services/Birmingham	
G-AXAB	PA-28 Cherokee 140	Bencray Ltd/Blackpool	
G-AXAK	M.S.880B Rallye Club	R. L. & C. Stewart	
G-AXAN	D.H.82A Tiger Moth	Comarket Aviation Ltd/Staverton	
G-AXAO	Omega 56 balloon	P. D. Furlong	
G-AXAS	Wallis WA-116T	K. H. Wallis (G-AVDH)	
G-AXAT	Jodel D.117A	A. W. Chapman	
G-AXAU	PA-30 Twin Comanche 160C	Bartcourt Ltd (*derelict*)/Bournemouth	
G-AXAV	PA-30 Twin Comanche 160C	P. S. King/Guernsey	
G-AXAW	Cessna 421A	P. J. McGoldrick/Stansted	
G-AXAX	PA-23 Aztec 250D	Horizon Holidays Ltd	
G-AXBB	BAC One-Eleven 409	British Island Airways PLC *Island Entente*/Gatwick	

Notes	Reg.	Type	Owner or Operator
	G-AXBF	Beagle D.5/180 Husky	C. H. Barnes
	G-AXBH	Cessna F.172H	Photoair Ltd/Sibson
	G-AXBJ	Cessna F.172H	K. M. Brennan & C. Mackay/Leicester
	G-AXBW	D.H.82A Tiger Moth (T5879)	R. Venning
	G-AXBZ	D.H.82A Tiger Moth	D. H. McWhir
	G-AXCA	PA-28R Cherokee Arrow 200	N. D. Douglas & D. T. Wright
	G-AXCG	Jodel D.117	Charlie Golf Group/Andrewsfield
	G-AXCI	Bensen B.8M ★	Loughborough & Leicester Aircraft Museum
	G-AXCL	M.S.880B Rallye Club	L. A. Christie
	G-AXCM	M.S.880B Rallye Club	Avcom Developments Ltd/Denham
	G-AXCN	M.S.880B Rallye Club	J. E. Compton
	G-AXCX	B.121 Pup 2	R. S. Blackman/Elstree
	G-AXCY	Jodel D.117	C. Smith
	G-AXDB	Piper J-3C-65 Cub	J. R. Wraight
	G-AXDC	PA-23 Aztec 250D	N. J. Lilley/Bodmin
	G-AXDE	Bensen B.8	T. J. Hartwell
	G-AXDH	BN-2A Islander	J. P. Lewington
	G-AXDI	Cessna F.172H	M. F. & J. R. Leusby/Conington
	G-AXDK	Jodel DR.315	P. J. Checketts & T. J. Thomas
	G-AXDM	H.S.125 Srs 400B	Ferranti Ltd/Edinburgh
	G-AXDN	BAC-Sud Concorde 01 ★	Duxford Aviation Soc
	G-AXDU	B.121 Pup 2	R. Wilson/Cambridge
	G-AXDV	B.121 Pup 1	C. N. G. Hobbs & J. J. Teagle
	G-AXDW	B.121 Pup 1	Cranfield Institute of Technology
	G-AXDY	Falconar F-II	J. Nunn
	G-AXDZ	Cassutt Racer Srs IIIM	A. Chadwick/Little Staughton
	G-AXEB	Cassutt Racer Srs IIIM	G. E. Horder/Redhill
	G-AXEC	Cessna 182M	H. S. Mulligan & E. R. Wilson
	G-AXED	PA-25 Pawnee 235	Wolds Gliding Club Ltd
	G-AXEH	B.121 Pup ★	Museum of Flight/E. Fortune
	G-AXEI	Ward Gnome ★	Lincolnshire Aviation Museum
	G-AXEO	Scheibe SF.25B Falke	Newcastle & Tees-side Gliding Club Ltd
	G-AXES	B.121 Pup 2	P. A. G. Field/Nairobi
	G-AXEV	B.121 Pup 2	J. T. Hicks/Biggin Hill
	G-AXFD	PA-25 Pawnee 235	J.E.F. Aviation Ltd
	G-AXFG	Cessna 337D	Skyborne Ltd
	G-AXFH	D.H.114 Heron 1B/C	Topflight Aviation Co Ltd
	G-AXFN	Jodel D.119	D. J. Williams & H. R. Leafe
	G-AXGC	M.S.880B Rallye Club	Ian Richard Transport Services Ltd
	G-AXGE	M.S.880B Rallye Club	R. P. Loxton
	G-AXGG	Cessna F.150J	A. R. Nicholls
	G-AXGP	Piper J-3C-65 Cub	W. K. Butler
	G-AXGR	Luton LA-4A Minor	A. D. R. Coackley
	G-AXGS	D.62B Condor	Tiger Club Ltd/Redhill
	G-AXGT	D.62B Condor	P. J. Simpson & ptnrs
	G-AXGV	D.62B Condor	R. J. Wrixon
	G-AXGZ	D.62B Condor	Lincoln Condor Group/Sturgate
	G-AXHA	Cessna 337A	G. Evans
	G-AXHC	SNCAN Stampe SV-4C	W. R. Pointer
	G-AXHE	BN-2A Islander	NW Parachute Centre/Cark
	G-AXHI	M.S.880B Rallye Club	J. M. Whittard
	G-AXHO	B.121 Pup 2	L. W. Grundy/Stapleford
	G-AXHP	Piper J-3C-65 Cub	R. Giles
	G-AXHR	Piper J-3C-65 Cub (329601)	I. S. Hodge
	G-AXHS	M.S.880B Rallye Club	D. Horne & ptnrs
	G-AXHT	M.S.880B Rallye Club	J. A. Levey
	G-AXHV	Jodel D.117A	D. M. Cashmore & K. R. Payne
	G-AXHX	M.S.892A Rallye Commodore	D. W. Weever
	G-AXIA	B.121 Pup 1	Cranfield Institute of Technology
	G-AXIE	B.121 Pup 2	I. J. Ross & D. I. McBride
	G-AXIF	B.121 Pup 2	T. G. Hiscock/Elstree
	G-AXIG	B.125 Bulldog 104	George House (Holdings) Ltd
	G-AXIO	PA-28 Cherokee 140A	W. London Aero Services Ltd/White Waltham
	G-AXIR	PA-28 Cherokee 140B	M. F. L. Purse/Weston Zoyland
	G-AXIT	M.S.893A Rallye Commodore 180	South Wales Gliding Club Ltd
	G-AXIW	Scheibe SF.25B Falke	Kent Motor Gliding & Soaring Centre
	G-AXIX	Glos-Airtourer 150	J. C. Wood
	G-AXIY	Bird Gyrocopter	E. N. Grace
	G-AXJB	Omega 84 balloon	Hot-Air Group *Jester*
	G-AXJH	B.121 Pup 2	J. S. Chillingworth
	G-AXJI	B.121 Pup 2	Cole Aviation Ltd/Southend

Reg.	Type	Owner or Operator	Notes
G-AXJJ	B.121 Pup 2	The Bumpf Group/Crosland Moor	
G-AXJK	BAC One-Eleven 501	British Airways *County of Hereford*	
G-AXJM	BAC One-Eleven 501	British Airways *County of Durham*	
G-AXJN	B.121 Pup 2	D. M. Jenkins/Shoreham	
G-AXJO	B.121 Pup 2	J. A. D. Bradshaw	
G-AXJR	Scheibe SF.25B Falke	D. R. Chatterton	
G-AXJV	PA-28 Cherokee 140B	Mona Aviation Ltd	
G-AXJX	PA-28 Cherokee 140B	I. R. Smith/Barton	
G-AXJY	Cessna U-206D	Hereford Parachute Club Ltd/Shobdon	
G-AXKD	PA-23 Aztec 250D	Levenmere Ltd/Norwich	
G-AXKH	Luton LA-4A Minor	M. E. Vaisey	
G-AXKI	Jodel D.9 Bebe	A. F. Cashin	
G-AXKJ	Jodel D.9 Bebe	J. R. Surbey	
G-AXKK	Westland Bell 47G-4A	Bristow Helicopters Ltd	
G-AXKR	Westland Bell 47G-4A	Robert & Hewett Agriculture Ltd	
G-AXKS	Westland Bell 47G-4A ★	Museum of Army Flying/Middle Wallop	
G-AXKU	Westland Bell 47G-4A	Bristow Helicopters Ltd	
G-AXKX	Westland Bell 47G-4A	Bristow Helicopters Ltd	
G-AXKY	Westland Bell 47G-4A	Bristow Helicopters Ltd	
G-AXLG	Cessna 310K	Smiths (Outdrives) Ltd	
G-AXLI	Slingsby T.66 Nipper 3	N. J. Arthur/Finmere	
G-AXLL	BAC One-Eleven 523FJ	British Airways *County of Yorkshire*	
G-AXLN	BAC One-Eleven 523FJ	British Island Airways PLC *Island Enterprise*/Gatwick	
G-AXLS	Jodel DR.105A	E. Gee/Southampton	
G-AXLZ	PA-18 Super Cub 95	J. C. Quantrell/Shipdham	
G-AXMA	PA-24 Comanche 180	Tegrel Products Ltd/Newcastle	
G-AXMB	Slingsby T.7 Motor Cadet 2	I. G. Smith/Langar	
G-AXMD	Omega O-56 balloon ★	British Balloon Museum	
G-AXME	SNCAN SV-4C	D. W. Hawthorne/Oporto	
G-AXMG	BAC One-Eleven 518	British Island Airways PLC *Island Emblem*/Gatwick	
G-AXMN	J/5B Autocar	A. Phillips	
G-AXMP	PA-28 Cherokee 180	P. Taylor & ptnrs	
G-AXMS	PA-30 Twin Comanche 160C	Ernest Green International Ltd	
G-AXMU	BAC One-Eleven 432	British Island Airways PLC/Gatwick	
G-AXMW	B.121 Pup 1	DJP Engineering (Knebworth) Ltd	
G-AXMX	B.121 Pup 2	Susan A. Jones/Cannes	
G-AXNA	Boeing 737-204C	Britannia Airways Ltd *Robert Clive of India*/Luton	
G-AXNB	Boeing 737-204C	Britannia Airways Ltd *Charles Darwin*/Luton	
G-AXNC	Boeing 737-204	Britannia Airways Ltd *Isambard Kingdom Brunel*/Luton	
G-AXNJ	Wassmer Jodel D.120	Clive Flying Group/Sleap	
G-AXNK	Cessna F.150J	Fowler Aviation Ltd/Leavesden	
G-AXNL	B.121 Pup 1	D. C. Barber/St Just	
G-AXNM	B.121 Pup 1	J. Green	
G-AXNN	B.121 Pup 2	Romney Marsh Flying Group/Lydd	
G-AXNP	B.121 Pup 2	J. W. & K. E. Ellis	
G-AXNR	B.121 Pup 2	S. T. Raby & ptnrs	
G-AXNS	B.121 Pup 2	Derwent Aero/Netherthorpe	
G-AXNW	SNCAN SV-4C (E6452)	C. S. Grace	
G-AXNX	Cessna 182M	P. Reid/Halfpenny Green	
G-AXNZ	Pitts S.1C Special	W. A. Jordan	
G-AXOG	PA-E23 Aztec 250D	R. W. Diggens/Denham	
G-AXOH	M.S.894 Rallye Minerva	Bristol Cars Ltd/White Waltham	
G-AXOI	Jodel D.9 Bebe	P. R. Underhill	
G-AXOJ	B.121 Pup 2	K. Fitzsimons & ptnrs	
G-AXOL	Currie Wot	A. Kennedy & ptnrs/Andrewsfield	
G-AXOR	PA-28 Cherokee 180D	Axor Aviation Ltd/Compton Abbas	
G-AXOS	M.S.894A Rallye Minerva	T. E. H. Simmons & S. L. Laker	
G-AXOT	M.S.893 Rallye Commodore 180	P. Evans & D. Riley	
G-AXOV	Beech B55A Baron	S. Brod/Elstree	
G-AXOX	BAC One-Eleven 432	British Island Airways PLC *Island Endeavour*/Gatwick	
G-AXPB	B.121 Pup 1	C. N. Carter	
G-AXPF	Cessna F.150K	Y. Newell/Booker	
G-AXPG	Mignet HM-293	W. H. Cole (*stored*)	
G-AXPM	B.121 Pup 1	M. J. Coton	
G-AXPN	B.121 Pup 2	Isohigh Ltd	
G-AXPZ	Campbell Cricket	W. R. Partridge	
G-AXRA	Campbell Cricket ★	L. E. Schnurr	

Notes	Reg.	Type	Owner or Operator
	G-AXRC	Campbell Cricket	K. W. Hayr (stored)
	G-AXRK	Practavia Sprite 115	E. G. Thale
	G-AXRL	PA-28 Cherokee 160	T. W. Clark/Headcorn
	G-AXRO	PA-30 Twin Comanche 160C	Bartlett Land Co (Aviation) Ltd
	G-AXRP	SNCAN SV-4C	C. C. Manning
	G-AXRR	Auster AOP.9 (XR241)	British Aerial Museum/Duxford
	G-AXRT	Cessna FA.150K (tailwheel)	W. R. Pickett/Southampton
	G-AXRU	Cessna FA.150K	Arrival Enterprises Ltd/Denham
	G-AXSC	B.121 Pup 1	T. R. Golding & C. Spencer
	G-AXSD	B.121 Pup 1	A. C. Townend
	G-AXSF	Nash Petrel	Nash Aircraft Ltd/Lasham
	G-AXSG	PA-28 Cherokee 180	Shropshire Aero Club Ltd/Sleap
	G-AXSM	Jodel DR.1051	C. Cousten/White Waltham
	G-AXSV	Jodel DR.340	Leonard F. Jollye Ltd/Panshanger
	G-AXSW	Cessna FA.150K	Furness Aviation Ltd/Walney Island
	G-AXSZ	PA-28 Cherokee 140B	R. B. Cheek
	G-AXTA	PA-28 Cherokee 140B	P. Barry & I. Cameron/Shoreham
	G-AXTC	PA-28 Cherokee 140B	B. Mellor & J. Hutchinson
	G-AXTD	PA-28 Cherokee 140B	G. R. Walker/Southend
	G-AXTH	PA-28 Cherokee 140B	W. London Aero Services Ltd/ White Waltham
	G-AXTI	PA-28 Cherokee 140B	London Transport (CRS) Sports Association Flying Club/Fairoaks
	G-AXTJ	PA-28 Cherokee 140B	A. P. Merrifield/Stapleford
	G-AXTL	PA-28 Cherokee 140B	P. Murphy & R. Flower/Blackbushe
	G-AXTO	PA-24 Comanche 260	J. L. Wright
	G-AXTP	PA-28 Cherokee 180	E. R. Moore/Elstree
	G-AXTX	Jodel D.112	J. J. Penney
	G-AXUA	B.121 Pup 1	F. R. Blennerhassett & C. Wedlake/ Tees-side
	G-AXUB	BN-2A Islander	Headcorn Parachute Club
	G-AXUC	PA-12 Super Cruiser	J. J. Bunton
	G-AXUE	Jodel DR.105A	L. Lewis
	G-AXUF	Cessna FA.150K	A. J. Redknap/Blackbushe
	G-AXUI	H.P.137 Jetstream 1	Cranfield Institute of Technology
	G-AXUJ	J/1 Autocrat	R. G. Earp & J. W. H. Lee/Sibson
	G-AXUK	Jodel DR.1050	Ambassadeur Flying/Bicester
	G-AXUM	H.P.137 Jetstream 1	Cranfield Institute of Technology
	G-AXUW	Cessna FA.150K	Coventry Air Training School
	G-AXVB	Cessna F.172H	C. Gabbitas/Staverton
	G-AXVC	Cessna FA.150K	V. F. Lynn/Sibson
	G-AXVK	Campbell Cricket	L. W. Harding
	G-AXVM	Campbell Cricket	D. M. Organ
	G-AXVN	McCandless M.4	W. R. Partridge
	G-AXVU	Omega 84 balloon	Brede Balloons Ltd Henry VIII
	G-AXVV	Piper J-3C-65 Cub	J. MacCarthy
	G-AXVW	Cessna F.150K	J. M. R. Layton & A. Grant/Elstree
	G-AXVX	Cessna F.172H	Judgenote Ltd
	G-AXWA	Auster AOP.9 (XN437)	M. L. & C. M. Edwards/Biggin Hill
	G-AXWB	Omega 65 balloon	A. Robinson & M. J. Moore Ezekiel
	G-AXWH	BN-2A Islander	Midland Parachute Centre Ltd
	G-AXWP	BN-2A Islander	Isles of Scilly Skybus Ltd/St Just
	G-AXWR	BN-2A Islander	Aurigny Air Services/Guernsey
	G-AXWT	Jodel D.11	R. C. Owen
	G-AXWV	Jodel DR.253	J. R. D. Bygraves/O. Warden
	G-AXWZ	PA-28R Cherokee Arrow 200	W. S. Stanley
	G-AXXC	CP.301B Emeraude	J. R. R. Gale & J. Tetley
	G-AXXG	BN-2A Islander	Van Diemen International Racing Services Ltd
	G-AXXJ	BN-2A Islander	Air Wight Ltd/Bembridge
	G-AXXV	D.H.82A Tiger Moth (DE992)	J. I. Hyslop
	G-AXXW	Jodel D.117	D. J. & M. Watson
	G-AXYD	BAC One-Eleven 509	Dan-Air Services Ltd/Gatwick
	G-AXYK	Taylor JT.1 Monoplane	T. W. M. Beck & M. J. Smith
	G-AXYM	BN-2A Islander	Halfpenny Green Skydiving Centre
	G-AXYY	WHE Airbuggy	R. A. A. Chiles
	G-AXYZ	WHE Airbuggy	W. B. Lumb
	G-AXZA	WHE Airbuggy	B. Gunn
	G-AXZB	WHE Airbuggy	D. R. C. Pugh
	G-AXZD	PA-28 Cherokee 180E	M. D. Callaghan & ptnrs
	G-AXZF	PA-28 Cherokee 180E	E. P. C. & W. R. Rabson/Southampton
	G-AXZK	BN-2A Islander	Atlantic Air Transport Ltd/Coventry
	G-AXZM	Slingsby Nipper T.66 Srs 3	G. R. Harlow
	G-AXZO	Cessna 180	Brinkley Light Aircraft Services

Reg.	Type	Owner or Operator	Notes
G-AXZP	PA-E23 Aztec 250D	Aviation East Ltd	
G-AXZT	Jodel D.117	H. W. Baines	
G-AXZU	Cessna 182N	Earthlogic Ltd	
G-AYAA	PA-28 Cherokee 180E	Briskloom Ltd/Manchester	
G-AYAB	PA-28 Cherokee 180E	J. A. & J. C. Cunningham	
G-AYAC	PA-28R Cherokee Arrow 200	Fersfield Flying Group	
G-AYAI	Fournier RF-5	Exeter RF Group	
G-AYAJ	Cameron O-84 balloon	E. T. Hall *Flaming Pearl*	
G-AYAL	Omega 56 balloon ★	British Balloon Museum	
G-AYAN	Slingsby Motor Cadet Mk III	I. Stevenson	
G-AYAP	PA-28 Cherokee 180E	Gala Air Holidays Ltd/Stapleford	
G-AYAR	PA-28 Cherokee 180E	V. Dowd	
G-AYAT	PA-28 Cherokee 180E	P. J. Messervy/Norwich	
G-AYAU	PA-28 Cherokee 180E	Tiarco Ltd	
G-AYAV	PA-28 Cherokee 180E	Bawtry Road Service Station Ltd/ Netherthorpe	
G-AYAW	PA-28 Cherokee 180E	Wizard Air Services Ltd/Coventry	
G-AYBD	Cessna F.150K	D. G. & W. B. Adams	
G-AYBG	Scheibe SF.25B Falke	D. J. Rickman	
G-AYBK	PA-28 Cherokee 180E	Firecrest Aviation Ltd/Leavesden	
G-AYBO	PA-23 Aztec 250D	Twinguard Aviation Ltd/Elstree	
G-AYBP	Jodel D.112	Fairwood Flying Group/Swansea	
G-AYBU	Western 84 balloon	D. R. Gibbons	
G-AYBV	Chasle YC-12 Tourbillon	B. A. Mills	
G-AYCC	Campbell Cricket	D. J. M. Charity	
G-AYCE	CP.301C Emeraude	R. A. Austin/Bodmin	
G-AYCF	Cessna FA.150K	E. J. Atkins/Popham	
G-AYCG	SNCAN SV-4C	N. Bignall/Booker	
G-AYCJ	Cessna TP.206D	H. O. Holm/Bournemouth	
G-AYCK	Stampe SV-4C	J. A. Sykes	
G-AYCM	Bell 206A JetRanger	F. Owen	
G-AYCN	Piper J-3C-65 Cub	W. R. & B. M. Young	
G-AYCO	CEA DR.360	L. M. Gould/Jersey	
G-AYCP	Jodel D.112	D. J. Nunn	
G-AYCT	Cessna F.172H	Fife Airport Management & Kontrox Ltd/Glenrothes	
G-AYDG	M.S.894A Rallye Minerva	R. P. Coplestone	
G-AYDI	D.H.82A Tiger Moth	R. B. Woods & ptnrs	
G-AYDR	SNCAN SV-4C	A. J. Mcluskie	
G-AYDV	Coates SA.II-1 Swalesong	J. R. Coates/Rush Green	
G-AYDW	A.61 Terrier 2	A. Topen/Cranfield	
G-AYDX	A.61 Terrier 2	G. W. & M. M. Bisshopp	
G-AYDY	Luton LA-4A Minor	T. Littlefair & N. Clark	
G-AYDZ	Jodel DR.200	F. M. Ward	
G-AYEB	Jodel D.112	M. A. Watts	
G-AYEC	CP.301A Emeraude	R. S. Needham	
G-AYED	PA-24 Comanche 260	C. A. Saville	
G-AYEE	PA-28 Cherokee 180E	D. J. Beale	
G-AYEF	PA-28 Cherokee 180E	L. Cheetham	
G-AYEG	Falconar F-9	A. G. Thelwall	
G-AYEH	Jodel DR.1050	D. L. Riley/Barton	
G-AYEI	PA-31 Turbo Navajo	Stewart McDonald & Co	
G-AYEJ	Jodel DR.1050	J. M. Newbold	
G-AYEK	Jodel DR.1050	I. Shaw & B. Hanson/Sherburn	
G-AYEN	Piper J-3C-65 Cub	P. Warde & C. F. Morris	
G-AYEU	Brookland Hornet	M. G. Reilly	
G-AYEV	Jodel DR.1050	L. G. Evans/Headcorn	
G-AYEW	Jodel DR.1051	Taildragger Group/Halfpenny Green	
G-AYEY	Cessna F.150K	B&M Motors/Goodwood	
G-AYFA	SA Twin Pioneer 3	Flight One Ltd/Shobdon	
G-AYFC	D.62B Condor	R. A. Smith/Redhill	
G-AYFD	D.62B Condor	Tiger Club Ltd/Redhill	
G-AYFE	D.62C Condor	J. Abbess/Andrewsfield	
G-AYFF	D.62B Condor	A. F. S. Caldecourt	
G-AYFG	D.62C Condor	J. Burton	
G-AYFJ	M.S.880B Rallye Club	E. P. Browne/Sibson	
G-AYFP	Jodel D.140	S. K. Minocha/Sherburn	
G-AYFT	PA-39 Twin Comanche 160 C/R	S. C. & V. L. Garry	
G-AYFV	Crosby BA-4B	A. Fines/Norwich	
G-AYFZ	PA-31 Turbo Navajo	P. M. Doran	
G-AYGA	Jodel D.117	R. L. E. Horrell	
G-AYGB	Cessna 310Q	*Instructional airframe*/Perth	
G-AYGC	Cessna F.150K	Alpha Aviation/Manchester	

Notes	Reg.	Type	Owner or Operator
	G-AYGD	Jodel DR.1051	B. A. James
	G-AYGE	SNCAN SV-4C	The Hon A. M. J. Rothschild/Booker
	G-AYGG	Jodel D.120	J. T. Taylor
	G-AYGK	BN-2A Islander	Pathcircle Ltd/Langar
	G-AYGN	Cessna 210K	J. W. O'Sullivan/Jersey
	G-AYGX	Cessna FR.172G	J. A. Edwards/Blackpool
	G-AYHA	AA-1 Yankee	D. L. Harrisberg & I. J. Widger/Elstree
	G-AYHI	Campbell Cricket	J. F. MacKay/Inverness
	G-AYHX	Jodel D.117A	L. J. E. Goldfinch
	G-AYHY	Fournier RF-4D	Tiger Club Ltd/Redhill
	G-AYIA	Hughes 369HS	G. D. E. Bilton/Sywell
	G-AYIB	Cessna 182N Skylane	J. N. K. Eaton
	G-AYIF	PA-28 Cherokee 140C	The Hare Flying Group/Elstree
	G-AYIG	PA-28 Cherokee 140C	Snowdon Mountain Aviation Ltd
	G-AYIH	PA-28 Cherokee 140C	B. Lince/Elstree
	G-AYII	PA-28R Cherokee Arrow 200	Devon Growers Ltd & A. L. Bacon/Exeter
	G-AYIJ	SNCAN SV-4B	K. B. Palmer/Headcorn
	G-AYIO	PA-28 Cherokee 140C	Frontline Aviation Ltd
	G-AYIT	D.H.82A Tiger Moth	R. L. H. Alexander & ptnrs/Newtownards
	G-AYJA	Jodel DR.1050	G. I. Doake
	G-AYJB	SNCAN SV-4C	F. J. M. & J. P. Esson/Middle Wallop
	G-AYJD	Alpavia-Fournier RF-3	C. Wren/Southend
	G-AYJE	BN-2A-26 Islander	Fife Parachute Centre/Glenroths
	G-AYJP	PA-28 Cherokee 140C	RAF Brize Norton Flying Club Ltd
	G-AYJR	PA-28 Cherokee 140C	RAF Brize Norton Flying Club Ltd
	G-AYJS	PA-28 Cherokee 140C	W. R. Griffiths & Sons (Office Furnishers) Ltd
	G-AYJT	PA-28 Cherokee 140C	Jennifer M. Lesslie/Leicester
	G-AYJU	Cessna TP-206A	Balmar Aviation/Thruxton
	G-AYJY	Isaacs Fury II	A. V. Francis
	G-AYKA	Beech 95-B55A Baron	Morris Cohen (Underwear) Ltd
	G-AYKD	Jodel DR.1050	B. P. Irish & A. W. Humphries
	G-AYKF	M.S.880B Rallye Club	R. N. Preston/Cranfield
	G-AYKJ	Jodel D.117A	G. R. W. Monksfield/Stapleford
	G-AYKK	Jodel D.117	D. M. Whitham
	G-AYKL	Cessna F.150L	M. A. Judge
	G-AYKS	Leopoldoff L-7	C. E. & W. B. Cooper
	G-AYKT	Jodel D.117	G. Wright/Leeds
	G-AYKV	PA-28 Cherokee 140C	A. Wright/Liverpool
	G-AYKW	PA-28 Cherokee 140C	A. G. Hopwood
	G-AYKX	PA-28 Cherokee 140C	M. J. Garland & ptnrs/Woodford
	G-AYKZ	SAI KZ-8	R. E. Mitchell/Coventry
	G-AYLA	Glos-Airtourer 115	R. E. Parker
	G-AYLB	PA-39 Twin Comanche 160 C/R	Mercia Aviation/Wellesbourne
	G-AYLE	M.S.880B Rallye Club	B. Butler & P. J. Clements
	G-AYLF	Jodel DR.1051	A. C. Frost & ptnrs/Cranfield
	G-AYLG	H.S.125 Srs 400B	British Aerospace PLC
	G-AYLL	Jodel DR.1050	B. R. Cornes
	G-AYLP	AA-1 Yankee	D. Nairn & E. Y. Hawkins
	G-AYLV	Jodel D.120	R. E. Wray/Stapleford
	G-AYLX	Hughes 269C	Feastlight Ltd/Sywell
	G-AYLY	PA-23 Aztec 250C	British Island Airways PLC/Shoreham
	G-AYME	Fournier RF-5	R. D. Goodger/Biggin Hill
	G-AYMG	HPR-7 Herald 213	Securicor Ltd/Birmingham
	G-AYMK	PA-28 Cherokee 140C	The Piper Flying Group
	G-AYML	PA-28 Cherokee 140C	Transair (UK) Ltd
	G-AYMO	PA-23 Aztec 250C	RFS Transport Ltd
	G-AYMP	Currie Wot Special	H. F. Moffatt
	G-AYMR	Lederlin 380L Ladybug	J. S. Brayshaw
	G-AYMT	Jodel DR.1050	Merlin Flying Club Ltd/Hucknall
	G-AYMU	Jodel D.112	M. R. Baker
	G-AYMV	Western 20 balloon	G. F. Turnbull & ptnrs *Tinkerbelle*
	G-AYMW	Bell 206A JetRanger 2	Dollar Air Services Ltd/Coventry
	G-AYMZ	PA-28 Cherokee 140C	T. H. & M. G. Weetman/Prestwick
	G-AYNA	Currie Wot	J. M. Lister
	G-AYNC	W.S. 58 Wessex Mk 60 Srs 1	Sykes Group Co Ltd
	G-AYND	Cessna 310Q	Source Premium & Promotional Consultants Ltd/Fairoaks
	G-AYNF	PA-28 Cherokee 140C	J. J. Power
	G-AYNJ	PA-28 Cherokee 140C	Lion Flying Group Ltd/Elstree
	G-AYNN	Cessna 185B Skywagon	Bencray Ltd/Blackpool
	G-AYNP	W.S.55 Whirlwind Srs 3	Bristow Helicopters Ltd

Reg.	Type	Owner or Operator	Notes
G-AYOD	Cessna 172	E. N. Simmons	
G-AYOM	Sikorsky S-61N Mk 2	British International Helicopters Ltd/ Aberdeen	
G-AYOP	BAC One-Eleven 530	British Airways *County of Humberside*	
G-AYOW	Cessna 182N Skylane	C. H. Royal	
G-AYOY	Sikorsky S-61N Mk 2	British International Helicopters Ltd/ Aberdeen	
G-AYOZ	Cessna FA.150L	Exeter Flying Club Ltd	
G-AYPB	Beech C-23 Musketeer	Martlets Flying Group/Goodwood	
G-AYPD	Beech 95-B55 Baron	Sir W. S. Dugdale/Birmingham	
G-AYPE	Bo 209 Monsun	Papa Echo Ltd/Biggin Hill	
G-AYPF	Cessna F.177RG	S. J. Westley	
G-AYPG	Cessna F.177RG	D. Davies	
G-AYPH	Cessna F.177RG	R. J. Everett/Ipswich	
G-AYPI	Cessna F.177RG	Cardinal Aviation Ltd/Guernsey	
G-AYPJ	PA-28 Cherokee 180	Mona Aviation Ltd	
G-AYPM	PA-18 Super Cub 95	D. H. Pattison	
G-AYPO	PA-18 Super Cub 95	R. T. Love	
G-AYPR	PA-18 Super Cub 95	J. W. Hollingsworth	
G-AYPS	PA-18 Super Cub 95	Tony Dyer Television	
G-AYPT	PA-18 Super Cub 95	P. Shires	
G-AYPU	PA-28R Cherokee Arrow 200	Alpine Ltd/Jersey	
G-AYPV	PA-28 Cherokee 140D	R. S. Mennie/Newcastle	
G-AYPZ	Campbell Cricket	A. Melody	
G-AYRF	Cessna F.150L	D. T. A. Rees	
G-AYRG	Cessna F.172K	W. I. Robinson	
G-AYRH	M.S.892A Rallye Commodore 150	J. D. Watt	
G-AYRI	PA-28R Cherokee Arrow 200	E. P. Van Mechelen & Delta Motor Co (Windsor) Sales Ltd/White Waltham	
G-AYRK	Cessna 150J	K. A. Learmonth/Southend	
G-AYRM	PA-28 Cherokee 140D	E. S. Dignam/Biggin Hill	
G-AYRN	Schleicher ASK-14	T. M. Austin/Lasham	
G-AYRO	Cessna FA.150L Aerobat	Thruxton Flight Centre	
G-AYRP	Cessna FA.150L Aerobat	Andrewsfield Flying Club Ltd	
G-AYRS	Jodel D.120A	J. H. Tetley & G. C. Smith/Sherburn	
G-AYRT	Cessna F.172K	E. W. & S. M. Pinchbeck	
G-AYRU	BN-2A-6 Islander	Joint Services Parachute Centre/ Netheravon	
G-AYSA	PA-23 Aztec 250C	J. M. Yendall & R. Greenhill	
G-AYSB	PA-30 Twin Comanche 160C	R. Fotheringham & Finrad Ltd/Biggin Hill	
G-AYSD	Slingsby T.61A Falke	R. G. G. English	
G-AYSH	Taylor JT.1 Monoplane	C. J. Lodge	
G-AYSK	Luton LA-4A Minor	P. F. Bennison & ptnrs/Barton	
G-AYSX	Cessna F.177RG	Nasaire Ltd/Liverpool	
G-AYSY	Cessna F.177RG	Bernard Vermilio & Co	
G-AYSZ	Cessna FA.150L	E. J. Miller/Dubai	
G-AYTA	M.S.880B Rallye Club	Kemps Corrosion Services Ltd	
G-AYTJ	Cessna 207 Super Skywagon	Foxair/Perth	
G-AYTN	Cameron O-65 balloon	P. G. Hall & R. F. Jessett *Prometheus*	
G-AYTR	CP.301A Emeraude	P. J. Hall	
G-AYTT	Phoenix PM-3 Duet	Gp Capt A. S. Knowles	
G-AYTV	MJ.2A Tempete	Tempete Group/Barton	
G-AYTY	Bensen B.8	J. H. Wood (*Stored*)	
G-AYUB	CEA DR.253B	D. J. Brook	
G-AYUH	PA-28 Cherokee 180F	M. S. Bayliss/Coventry	
G-AYUI	PA-28 Cherokee 180	Routair Aviation Services Ltd/Southend	
G-AYUJ	Evans VP-1 Volksplane	P. D. Shand & R. D. Davidson/Perth	
G-AYUL	PA-23 Aztec 250E	Northern Executive Aviation Ltd/ Manchester	
G-AYUM	Slingsby T.61A Falke	The Burn Gliding Club	
G-AYUN	Slingsby T.61A Falke	C. W. Vigar & R. J. Watts	
G-AYUP	Slingsby T.61A Falke	Cranwell Gliding Club	
G-AYUR	Slingsby T.61A Falke	W. A Urwin	
G-AYUS	Taylor JT.1 Monoplane	R. R. McKinnon & A. D. Lincoln/ Southampton	
G-AYUT	Jodel DR.1050	R. Norris	
G-AYUV	Cessna F.172H	Klingair Ltd/Conington	
G-AYUW	BAC One-Eleven 476FM	—/Luton	
G-AYUY	Cessna FA.150L Aerobat	G. C. B. Weir	
G-AYVA	Cameron O-84 balloon	A. Kirk *April Fool*	
G-AYVI	Cessna T.210H	R. H. Laing/Glasgow	
G-AYVO	Wallis WA120 Srs 1	K. H. Wallis	
G-AYVP	Woody Pusher	J. R. Wraight	

45

Notes	Reg.	Type	Owner or Operator
	G-AYVT	Brochet MB.84 ★	Dunelm Flying Group (stored)
	G-AYVU	Cameron O-56 balloon	Shell-Mex & B.P. Ltd Hot Potato
	G-AYVY	D.H.82A Tiger Moth (PG617)	R. C. Button/Tollerton
	G-AYWA	Avro 19 Srs 2 ★	Strathallan Aircraft Collection
	G-AYWB	BAC One-Eleven 531FS	British Island Airways PLC Island Envoy/Gatwick
	G-AYWD	Cessna 182N	Trans Para Aviation Ltd
	G-AYWE	PA-28 Cherokee 140	L. J. Fisher
	G-AYWH	Jodel D.117A	J. M. Knapp & ptnrs
	G-AYWM	Glos-Airtourer Super 150	The Star Flying Group/Staverton
	G-AYWT	Stampe SV-4B	B. K. Lecomber/Denham
	G-AYWW	PA-28R Cherokee Arrow 200D	Acorn Aviation Ltd/Coventry
	G-AYXO	Luton LA-5A Major	A. C. T. Broomcroft
	G-AYXP	Jodel D.117A	G. N. Davies
	G-AYXS	SIAI-Marchetti S205-18R	D. P. & P. A. Dawson
	G-AYXT	W.S. 55 Whirlwind Srs 2	J. E. Wilkie
	G-AYXU	Champion 7KCAB Citabria	H. Fould & ptnrs
	G-AYXV	Cessna FA.150L	Wreck/Popham
	G-AYXW	Evans VP-1	J. S. Penny/Doncaster
	G-AYYD	M.S.894A Rallye Minerva	P. D. Lloyd & ptnrs
	G-AYYF	Cessna F.150L	D. T. A. Rees
	G-AYYK	Slingsby T.61A Falke	Cornish Gliding & Flying Club Ltd/ Perranporth
	G-AYYL	Slingsby T.61A Falke	C. Wood
	G-AYYO	Jodel DR.1050/M1	Bustard Flying Club Ltd/Old Sarum
	G-AYYT	Jodel DR.1050/M1	Sicile Flying Group/Sandown
	G-AYYU	Beech C23 Musketeer	P. Peck
	G-AYYW	BN-2A Islander	Foster Yeoman Ltd/Biggin Hill
	G-AYYX	M.S.880B Rallye Club	S. N. T. Dempsey & ptnrs
	G-AYYY	M.S.880B Rallye Club	T. W. Heffer/Panshanger
	G-AYZE	PA-39 Twin Comanche 160 C/R	J. E. Balmer/Staverton
	G-AYZH	Taylor JT.2 Titch	K. J. Munro
	G-AYZI	Stampe SV-4C	W. H. Smout & C. W. A. Simmons
	G-AYZJ	W.S. 55 Whirlwind Srs 2 (XM685) ★	Newark Air Museum
	G-AYZK	Jodel DR.1050/M1	G. Kearney & D. G. Hesketh
	G-AYZN	PA-23 Aztec 250D	International Institute of Tropical Agriculture
	G-AYZS	D.62B Condor	P. E. J. Huntley & M. N. Thrush
	G-AYZT	D.62B Condor	J. Abbess
	G-AYZU	Slingsby T.61A Falke	The Falcon Gliding Group/Enstone
	G-AYZW	Slingsby T.61A Falke	J. A. Dandie & R. J. M. Clement
	G-AZAB	PA-30 Twin Comanche 160B	T. W. P. Sheffield/Humberside
	G-AZAD	Jodel DR.1051	I. C. Young & ptnrs/Bodmin
	G-AZAJ	PA-28R Cherokee Arrow 200B	J. McHugh
	G-AZAV	Cessna 337F	W. T. Johnson & Sons (Huddersfield) Ltd
	G-AZAW	GY-80 Horizon 160	G. A. P. N. Barlow
	G-AZAZ	Bensen B.8M ★	FAA Museum/Yeovilton
	G-AZBA	T.66 Nipper 3	I. McKenzie
	G-AZBB	MBB Bo 209 Monsun 160FV	G. N. Richardson/Staverton
	G-AZBC	PA-39 Twin Comanche 160 C/R	Tenison Air Ltd
	G-AZBE	Glos-Airtourer Super 150	S. E. Marples
	G-AZBI	Jodel D.150	T. A. Rawson & W. H. Milner
	G-AZBK	PA-23 Aztec 250E	Qualitair Engineering Ltd/Blackbushe
	G-AZBL	Jodel D.9 Bebe	West Midlands Flying Group
	G-AZBN	AT-16 Harvard 2B (FT391)	The Old Flying Machine Co Ltd/ Duxford
	G-AZBT	Western O-65 balloon	D. J. Harris Hermes
	G-AZBU	Auster AOP.9	K. H. Wallis
	G-AZBY	Westland Wessex 60 Srs 1 ★	Sykes Aviation Ltd (stored)
	G-AZBZ	Westland Wessex 60 Srs 1 ★	Sykes Aviation Ltd (stored)
	G-AZCB	Stampe SV-4B	M. J. Cowburn/Redhill
	G-AZCI	Cessna 320A Skyknight	Landsurcon (Air Survey) Ltd
	G-AZCK	B.121 Pup 2	Berkley Hamilton & Co
	G-AZCL	B.121 Pup 2	E. G. A. Prance
	G-AZCP	B.121 Pup 1	Pup Group 87/Elstree
	G-AZCT	B.121 Pup 1	P. & P. A. Smith/Sywell
	G-AZCU	B.121 Pup 1	G. N. Richardson
	G-AZCV	B.121 Pup 2	N. R. W. Long/Elstree
	G-AZCZ	B.121 Pup 2	P. R. Moorehead
	G-AZDA	B.121 Pup 1	G. H. G. Bishop/Shoreham

Reg.	Type	Owner or Operator	Notes
G-AZDD	MBB Bo 209 Monsun 150FF	Double Delta Flying Group/Biggin Hill	
G-AZDE	PA-28R Cherokee Arrow 200B	Electro-Motion UK (Export) Ltd/ E. Midlands	
G-AZDF	Cameron O-84 balloon	K. L. C. M. Busemeyer	
G-AZDG	B.121 Pup 2	D. J. Sage/Coventry	
G-AZDK	Beech B55 Baron	Forbury Foods Ltd	
G-AZDX	PA-28 Cherokee 180F	M. Cowan	
G-AZDY	D.H.82A Tiger Moth	J. B. Mills	
G-AZEE	M.S.880B Rallye Club	P. L. Clements	
G-AZEF	Jodel D.120	J. R. Legge	
G-AZEG	PA-28 Cherokee 140D	Ashley Gardner Flying Club Ltd	
G-AZER	Cameron O-42 balloon	M. P. Dokk-Olsen & P. L. Jaye Shy Tot	
G-AZEU	B.121 Pup 2	P. Tonkin & R. S. Kinman	
G-AZEV	B.121 Pup 2	G. P. Martin/Shoreham	
G-AZEW	B.121 Pup 2	J. T. Reynolds	
G-AZEY	B.121 Pup 2	G. Huxtable/Elstree	
G-AZFA	B.121 Pup 2	K. F. Plummer	
G-AZFC	PA-28 Cherokee 140D	A. H. Lavender/Biggin Hill	
G-AZFF	Jodel D.112	P. D. Smoothy/Cranfield	
G-AZFI	PA-28R Cherokee Arrow 200B	Sherburn Aero Club Ltd	
G-AZFM	PA-28R Cherokee Arrow 200B	Linco Poultry Machinery Ltd/Biggin Hill	
G-AZFO	PA-39 Twin Comanche 160 C/R	Handhorn Ltd/Blackpool	
G-AZFP	Cessna F.177RG	Allen Aviation Ltd/Goodwood	
G-AZFR	Cessna 401B	S. Shorrock/Blackpool	
G-AZFZ	Cessna 414	Redapple Ltd/Fairoaks	
G-AZGA	Jodel D.120	G. B. Morris	
G-AZGB	PA-23 Aztec 250D	Qualitair Engineering Ltd/Blackbushe	
G-AZGC	Stampe SV-4C (No 120)	The Hon A. M. M. Lindsay	
G-AZGE	Stampe SV-4A	M. R. L. Astor/Booker	
G-AZGF	B.121 Pup 2	K. Singh	
G-AZGI	M.S.880B Rallye Club	J. & S. Cattle/Newcastle	
G-AZGJ	M.S.880B Rallye Club	P. Rose	
G-AZGL	M.S.894A Rallye Minerva	The Cambridge Aero Club Ltd	
G-AZGY	CP.301B Emeraude	Rodingair Flying Group/Stapleford	
G-AZGZ	D.H.82A Tiger Moth	F. R. Manning	
G-AZHB	Robin HR.100-200	C. & P. P. Scarlett/Sywell	
G-AZHC	Jodel D.112	J. A. Summer & A. Burton/Netherthorpe	
G-AZHD	Slingsby T.61A Falke	J. Sentance	
G-AZHH	SA 102.5 Cavalier	D. W. Buckle	
G-AZHI	Glos-Airtourer Super 150	H. J. Douglas/Biggin Hill	
G-AZHJ	S.A. Twin Pioneer Srs 3	Flight One Ltd/Staverton	
G-AZHR	Piccard Ax6 balloon	G. Fisher	
G-AZHT	Glos-Airtourer T.3	D. G. Palmer & D. C. Giles/Glasgow	
G-AZHU	Luton LA-4A Minor	W. Cawrey/Netherthorpe	
G-AZIB	ST-10 Diplomate	Wilmslow Audio Ltd/Wickenby	
G-AZID	Cessna FA.150L	Exeter Flying Club Ltd	
G-AZII	Jodel D.117A	J. S. Brayshaw	
G-AZIJ	Jodel DR.360	Rob Airway Ltd/Guernsey	
G-AZIK	PA-34-200 Seneca II	C.S.E. Aviation Ltd/Kidlington	
G-AZIL	Slingsby T.61A Falke	D. W. Savage	
G-AZIO	Stampe SV-4C (Lycoming) ★	/Booker	
G-AZIP	Cameron O-65 balloon	Dante Balloon Group Dante	
G-AZJC	Fournier RF-5	J. J. Butler/Biggin Hill	
G-AZJE	Ord-Hume JB-01 Minicab	J. B. Evans/Sandown	
G-AZJI	Western O-65 balloon	W. Davison Peek-a-Boo	
G-AZJN	Robin DR.300/140	Wright Farm Eggs Ltd	
G-AZJV	Cessna F.172L	J. A. & A. J. Boyd/Cardiff	
G-AZJW	Cessna F.150L	S. S. Delwarte/Shoreham	
G-AZJY	Cessna FRA.150L	G. Firbank	
G-AZJZ	PA-23 Aztec 250E	Encee Services Ltd/Cardiff	
G-AZKC	M.S.880B Rallye Club	L. J. Martin/Redhill	
G-AZKD	M.S.880B Rallye Club	P. Feeney/Kidlington	
G-AZKE	M.S.880B Rallye Club	B.'S. Rowden & W. L. Rogers	
G-AZKK	Cameron O-56 balloon	Gemini Balloon Group Gemini	
G-AZKN	Robin HR.100/200	South Coast Aviation Ltd/Goodwood	
G-AZKO	Cessna F.337F	Crispair Aviation Services Ltd	
G-AZKP	Jodel D.117	J. Lowe	
G-AZKR	PA-24 Comanche 180	K. W. Brigden	
G-AZKS	AA-1A Trainer	D. K. Jackson	
G-AZKV	Cessna FRA.150L	Penguin Flight/Bodmin	
G-AZKW	Cessna F.172L	Banbury Plant Hire Ltd/ Hinton-in-the-Hedges	
G-AZKZ	Cessna F.172L	R. Hill Farms Ltd/Swanton Morley	

Notes	Reg.	Type	Owner or Operator
	G-AZLE	Boeing N2S-5 Kaydet	Parker Airways Ltd/Denham
	G-AZLF	Jodel D.120	B. J. Edwards
	G-AZLH	Cessna F.150L	Skegness Air Taxi Service Ltd/Boston
	G-AZLL	Cessna FRA.150L	Air Service Training Ltd/Perth
	G-AZLM	Cessna F.172L	J. F. Davis
	G-AZLN	PA-28 Cherokee 180F	Liteflite Ltd/Kidlington
	G-AZLV	Cessna 172K	B. L. F. Karthaus
	G-AZLY	Cessna F.150L	Cleveland Flying School Ltd/Tees-side
	G-AZLZ	Cessna F.150L	Exeter Flying Club Ltd
	G-AZMB	Bell 47G-3B	Autair Ltd
	G-AZMC	Slingsby T.61A Falke	Essex Gliding Club Ltd
	G-AZMD	Slingsby T.61C Falke	R. A. Rice
	G-AZMF	BAC One-Eleven 530	British Airways County of Northumberland
	G-AZMH	Morane-Saulnier M.S.500 (ZA+WN)	Wessex Aviation & Transport Ltd
	G-AZMJ	AA-5 Traveler	R. T. Love/Bodmin
	G-AZMK	PA-23 Aztec 250E	Subtec Aviation Ltd
	G-AZMN	Glos-Airtourer T.5	W. Crozier & I. Young/Glasgow
	G-AZMV	D.62C Condor	Norfolk Gliding Club Ltd/Tibenham
	G-AZMX	PA-28 Cherokee 140 ★	Kelsterton College (instructional airframe)/Deeside
	G-AZMZ	M.S.893A Rallye Commodore 150	P. J. Wilcox/Cranfield
	G-AZNA	V.813 Viscount	Baltic British Air Ferries Ltd/Southend
	G-AZNF	Stampe SV-4C	H. J. Smith/Shoreham
	G-AZNK	Stampe SV-4A	R. H. Reeves/Barton
	G-AZNL	PA-28R Cherokee Arrow 200D	P. L. Buckley Ltd
	G-AZNO	Cessna 182P	M&D Aviation/Bournemouth
	G-AZNT	Cameron O-84 balloon	N. Tasker
	G-AZOA	MBB Bo 209 Monsun 150FF	R. J. O. Walker & R. P. Wilson
	G-AZOB	MBB Bo 209 Monsun 150FF	G. N. Richardson/Staverton
	G-AZOD	PA-23 Aztec 250D	Falcon Flying Services/Biggin Hill
	G-AZOE	Glos-Airtourer 115	R. J. Zukowski
	G-AZOF	Glos-Airtourer Super 150	J. Harper
	G-AZOG	PA-28R Cherokee Arrow 200D	J. G. Collins/Cambridge
	G-AZOH	Beech 65-B90 Queen Air	Clyde Surveys Ltd/White Waltham
	G-AZOL	PA-34-200 Seneca II	MTV Design Ltd/Bournemouth
	G-AZON	PA-34-200 Seneca II	Willowvale Electronics Ltd/Elstree
	G-AZOO	Western O-65 balloon	Southern Balloon Group Carousel
	G-AZOR	MBB Bo 105D	Bond Helicopters Ltd/Bourn
	G-AZOS	Jurca MJ.5-F1 Sirocco	B. W. Davies
	G-AZOT	PA-34-200 Seneca II	L. G. Payne/Elstree
	G-AZOU	Jodel DR.1051	Horsham Flying Group/Slinfold
	G-AZOZ	Cessna FRA.150L	Routair Aviation Services Ltd/Southend
	G-AZPA	PA-25 Pawnee 235	Black Mountain Gliding Co Ltd
	G-AZPC	Slingsby T.61C Falke	B. C. Dixon
	G-AZPF	Fournier RF-5	R. Pye/Blackpool
	G-AZPH	Craft-Pitts S-1S Special	N. M. Bloom
	G-AZPV	Luton LA-4A Minor	J. Scott/(Stored)
	G-AZPX	Western O-31 balloon	E. R. McCosh
	G-AZPZ	BAC One-Eleven 515	British Airways Dumfries of Galloway Region
	G-AZRA	MBB Bo 209 Monsun 150FF	Alpha Flying Ltd/Denham
	G-AZRD	Cessna 401B	Morbaine Ltd
	G-AZRG	PA-23 Aztec 250D	Woodgate Aviation (IOM) Ltd/Ronaldsway
	G-AZRH	PA-28 Cherokee 140D	Newcastle-upon-Tyne Aero Club Ltd
	G-AZRI	Payne balloon	G. F. Payne Shoestring
	G-AZRK	Fournier RF-5	Thurleigh Flying Group
	G-AZRL	PA-18 Super Cub 95	B. J. Stead
	G-AZRM	Fournier RF-5	A. R. Dearden & R. Speer/Shoreham
	G-AZRN	Cameron O-84 balloon	C. A. Butter & J. J. T. Cooke
	G-AZRP	Glos-Airtourer 115	A. W. Webster
	G-AZRR	Cessna 310Q	Routarrow Ltd/Norwich
	G-AZRS	PA-22 Tri-Pacer 150	E. A. Harrhy/Shoreham
	G-AZRU	AB-206B JetRanger 2	Dollar Air Services Ltd/Coventry
	G-AZRV	PA-28R Cherokee Arrow 200B	Designed for Sound Ltd
	G-AZRW	Cessna T.337C	R. C. Frazle/Southend
	G-AZRX	GY-80 Horizon 160	P. S. Cottrell
	G-AZRZ	Cessna U.206F	Cyprus Combined Services Parachute Club/Akrotiri
	G-AZSA	Stampe SV-4B	J. K. Faulkner/Biggin Hill
	G-AZSC	AT-16 Harvard IIB	Machine Music Ltd/Fairoaks

Reg.	Type	Owner or Operator	Notes
G-AZSD	Slingsby T.29B Motor Tutor	R. G. Boynton	
G-AZSF	PA-28R Cherokee Arrow 200D	W. T. Northorpe & R. J. Mills/Coventry	
G-AZSG	PA-28 Cherokee 180E	Cherokee Flying Group/Netherthorpe	
G-AZSH	PA-28R Cherokee Arrow 180	C. R. Hayward	
G-AZSK	Taylor JT.1 Monoplane	R. R. Lockwood	
G-AZSN	PA-28R Cherokee Arrow 200	Jetstream Air Couriers Ltd/Bristol	
G-AZSU	H.S.748 Srs 2A	Dan-Air Services Ltd/Gatwick	
G-AZSW	B.121 Pup 1	Northamptonshire School of Flying Ltd/Sywell	
G-AZSZ	PA-23 Aztec 250D	Ravenair/Manchester	
G-AZTA	MBB Bo 209 Monsun 150FF	R. S. Perks/Elstree	
G-AZTD	PA-32 Cherokee Six 300	Presshouse Publications Ltd/Enstone	
G-AZTF	Cessna F.177RG	J. Bolson & Son Ltd/Bournemouth	
G-AZTI	MBB Bo 105D	Bond Helicopters Ltd/Bourn	
G-AZTK	Cessna F.172F	M. J. Steele/Clacton	
G-AZTO	PA-34-200 Seneca II	Bulldog Aviation Ltd	
G-AZTR	SNCAN SV-4C	P. G. Palumbo/Booker	
G-AZTS	Cessna F.172L	J. F. Morgan/Humberside	
G-AZTV	Stolp SA.500 Starlet	A. C. Byrne	
G-AZTW	Cessna F.177RG	R. M. Clarke/Leicester	
G-AZUK	BAC One-Eleven 476FM	—/Luton	
G-AZUM	Cessna F.172L	D. J. Morris	
G-AZUO	Cessna F.177RG	Newbury Sand and Gravel Co Ltd	
G-AZUP	Cameron O-65 balloon	R. S. Bailey & ptnrs	
G-AZUT	M.S.893A Rallye Commodore 180	Rallye Flying Group	
G-AZUV	Cameron O-65 balloon ★	British Balloon Museum	
G-AZUX	Western O-56 balloon	M. W. H. Henton	
G-AZUY	Cessna E.310L	Stagecoach (Holdings) Ltd	
G-AZUZ	Cessna FRA.150L	D. J. Parker/Netherthorpe	
G-AZVA	MBB Bo 209 Monsun 150FF	K. H. Wallis	
G-AZVB	MBB Bo 209 Monsun 150FF	P. C. Logsdon/Dunkeswell	
G-AZVE	AA-5 Traveler	R. N. Morant	
G-AZVF	M.S.894A Rallye Minerva	R. C. Holmes	
G-AZVG	AA-5 Traveler	R. W. Somerville & A. F. Reid	
G-AZVH	M.S.894A Rallye Minerva	Bristol Cars Ltd/White Waltham	
G-AZVI	M.S.892A Rallye Commodore	W. A. McCartney & T. A. Pugh	
G-AZVJ	PA-34-200 Seneca II	Business Air Travel Ltd/Lydd	
G-AZVL	Jodel D.119	Forest Flying Group/Stapleford	
G-AZVM	Hughes 369HS	Diagnostic Reagents Ltd	
G-AZVP	Cessna F.177RG	R. G. Saunders/Biggin Hill	
G-AZVT	Cameron O-84 balloon	Sky Soarer Ltd *Jules Verne*	
G-AZWB	PA-28 Cherokee 140	Avon Flying Group/Bristol	
G-AZWD	PA-28 Cherokee 140	Airways Aero Associations Ltd/Booker	
G-AZWE	PA-28 Cherokee 140	Airways Aero Associations Ltd/Booker	
G-AZWF	SAN Jodel DR.1050	J. S. Hill	
G-AZWS	PA-28R Cherokee Arrow 180	J. E. Shepherd	
G-AZWT	Westland Lysander III (V9441)	Strathallan Aircraft Collection	
G-AZWW	PA-23 Aztec 250E	Phoenix Aviation (Bedford) Ltd/Cranfield	
G-AZWY	PA-24 Comanche 260	Keymer Son & Co Ltd/Biggin Hill	
G-AZXA	Beechcraft 95-C55 Baron	F.R. Aviation Ltd/Bournemouth	
G-AZXB	Cameron O-65 balloon	London Balloon Club Ltd *London Pride II*	
G-AZXC	Cessna F.150L	Sheffield Aero Club Ltd/Netherthorpe	
G-AZXD	Cessna F.172L	Birdlake Ltd/Wellesbourne	
G-AZXG	PA-23 Aztec 250D	K. J. Le Fevre/Norwich	
G-AZXR	BN-2A-9 Islander	Stanton Aircraft Management Ltd	
G-AZYA	GY-80 Horizon 160	T. Poole & ptnrs/Sywell	
G-AZYD	M.S.893A Rallye Commodore	Deeside Gliding Club/Aboyne	
G-AZYF	PA-28 Cherokee 180	J. C. Glynn/E. Midlands	
G-AZYM	Cessna E.310Q	Kingswinford Engineering Co Ltd	
G-AZYS	CP.301C-1 Emeraude	I. P. Burnett & J. Cook/White Waltham	
G-AZYU	PA-23 Aztec 250E	L. J. Martin/Biggin Hill	
G-AZYV	Burns O-77 balloon	B. F. G. Ribbans *Contrary Mary*	
G-AZYY	Slingsby T.61A Falke	J. A. Towers	
G-AZYZ	WA.51A Pacific	A. E. O'Broin	
G-AZZG	Cessna 188 Agwagon	N. C. Kensington	
G-AZZH	Practavia Pilot Sprite 115	K. G. Stewart	
G-AZZK	Cessna 414	D. O. McIntyre	
G-AZZO	PA-28 Cherokee 140	R. J. Hind/Elstree	
G-AZZP	Cessna F.172H	D. Bishop/Exeter	
G-AZZR	Cessna F.150L	J. B. Small/Swansea	
G-AZZS	PA-34-200 Seneca II	Robin Cook Aviation/Shoreham	

Notes	Reg.	Type	Owner or Operator
	G-AZZT	PA-28 Cherokee 180 ★	*Ground instruction airframe*/Cranfield
	G-AZZV	Cessna F.172L	Century Composites Ltd
	G-AZZW	Fournier RF-5	Aviation Special Developments
	G-AZZX	Cessna FRA.150L	J. E. Uprichard & ptnrs/Newtownards
	G-AZZZ	D.H.82A Tiger Moth	S. W. McKay
	G-BAAD	Evans Super VP-1	R. W. Husband/Netherthorpe
	G-BAAF	Manning-Flanders MF1 replica	Aviation Film Services Ltd/Booker
	G-BAAH	Coates SA.III Swalesong	J. R. Coates
	G-BAAI	M.S.893A Rallye Commodore	R. D. Taylor/Thruxton
	G-BAAK	Cessna 207	Balmar Aviation/Thruxton
	G-BAAL	Cessna 172A	Anglo Normandy Aeroengineering Ltd/ Guernsey
	G-BAAP	PA-28R Cherokee Arrow 200	Shirley A. Shelley/Biggin Hill
	G-BAAT	Cessna 182P Skylane	A. H. Hunt/St Just
	G-BAAU	Enstrom F-28C-UK	M. Upton
	G-BAAW	Jodel D.119	S. W. Ward/Ipswich
	G-BAAX	Cameron O-84 balloon	The New Holker Estate Co Ltd *Holker Hall*
	G-BAAY	Valtion Viima II (VI-3)	P. H. McConnell/White Waltham
	G-BAAZ	PA-28R Cherokee Arrow 200D	A. W. Rix/Guernsey
	G-BABB	Cessna F.150L	Seawing Flying Club Ltd/Southend
	G-BABC	Cessna F.150L	Suffolk Aero Club Ltd/Ipswich
	G-BABD	Cessna FRA.150L	Phoenix Aviation (Bedford) Ltd/ Cranfield
	G-BABE	Taylor JT.2 Titch	P. D. G. Grist/Sibson
	G-BABG	PA-28 Cherokee 180	M. F. R. Slater/Booker
	G-BABH	Cessna F.150L	Skyviews & General Ltd/Leeds
	G-BABK	PA-34-200 Seneca II	D. F. J. & N. R. Flashman/Biggin Hill
	G-BABY	Taylor JT.2 Titch	R. E. Finlay
	G-BACB	PA-34-200 Seneca II	London Flight Centre (Stansted) Ltd
	G-BACC	Cessna FRA.150L	Osprey Air Services Ltd/Cranfield
	G-BACE	Fournier RF-5	R. W. K. Stead/Perranporth
	G-BACH	Enstrom F.28A	Rotor Enterprises Ltd/Coventry
	G-BACJ	Jodel D.120	Wearside Flying Association/Newcastle
	G-BACL	Jodel D.150	M. L. Sargeant/Biggin Hill
	G-BACN	Cessna FRA.150L	Air Service Training Ltd/Perth
	G-BACO	Cessna FRA.150L	W. R. Burgess & ptnrs/Sibson
	G-BACP	Cessna FRA.150L	B. A. Mills
	G-BADC	Luton Beta B.2A	H. M. Mackenzie
	G-BADH	Slingsby T.61A Falke	E. M. Andrew & ptnrs/Old Sarum
	G-BADI	PA-23 Aztec 250D	W. London Aero Services Ltd/ White Waltham
	G-BADJ	PA-E23 Aztec 250E	CKS Air Ltd/Southend
	G-BADK	BN-2A-8 Islander	CB Helicopters
	G-BADL	PA-34-200 Seneca II	Cartographical Services (Southampton) Ltd/Birmingham
	G-BADO	PA-32 Cherokee Six 300	B. J. Haylor & ptnrs/Southampton
	G-BADP	Boeing 737-204	Britannia Airways Ltd *Sir Arthur Whitten Brown*/Luton
	G-BADR	Boeing 737-204	Britannia Airways Ltd *Capt Robert Falconer Scott*/Luton
	G-BADT	Cessna 402B	British Aircraft Corp Ltd/Warton
	G-BADU	Cameron O-56 balloon	J. Philp *Dream Machine*
	G-BADV	Brochet MB-50	P. A. Cairns/Dunkeswell
	G-BADW	Pitts S-2A Special	R. E. Mitchell/Coventry
	G-BADZ	Pitts S-2A Special	A. L. Brown & ptnrs/Wellesbourne
	G-BAEB	Robin DR.400/160	W. D. Nightingale/Bodmin
	G-BAEC	Robin HR.100/210	Autographics Ltd/Booker
	G-BAED	PA-23 Aztec 250C	Trial Rapid Ltd/Norwich
	G-BAEE	Jodel DR.1050/M1	J. B. Randle
	G-BAEF	Boeing 727-46	Dan-Air Services Ltd/Gatwick
	G-BAEM	Robin DR.400/125	Store Equipment (London) Ltd/Booker
	G-BAEN	Robin DR.400/180	B. T. & L. M. Spreckley/Shoreham
	G-BAEP	Cessna FRA.150L	J. Calverley
	G-BAER	Cosmic Wind	R. S. Voice/Redhill
	G-BAET	Piper J-3C-65 Cub	C. M. G. Ellis
	G-BAEU	Cessna F.150L	Skyviews & General Ltd
	G-BAEV	Cessna FRA.150L	B. F. Axford/Bournemouth
	G-BAEW	Cessna F.172M	Northamptonshire School of Flying Ltd/ Sywell
	G-BAEY	Cessna F.172M	R. Fursman/Southampton
	G-BAEZ	Cessna FRA.150L	J. C. Glynn/E. Midlands
	G-BAFA	AA-5 Traveler	C. F. Mackley/Stapleford

Reg.	Type	Owner or Operator	Notes
G-BAFD	MBB Bo 105D	Gleneagle Helicopter Services (Scotland) Ltd	
G-BAFG	D.H.82A Tiger Moth	J. E. Shaw & ptnrs	
G-BAFH	Evans VP-1	C. M. Gibson	
G-BAFI	Cessna F.177RG	Grandsystem Ltd/Bristol	
G-BAFL	Cessna 182P	Ingham Aviation Ltd/Bristol	
G-BAFM	AT-16 Harvard IIB (FS728)	Parker Airways Ltd/Denham	
G-BAFP	Robin DR.400/160	N. R. Haines	
G-BAFS	PA-18 Super Cub 150	M. D. Morris/Sandown	
G-BAFT	PA-18 Super Cub 150	Cambridge University Gliding Trust Ltd/ Duxford	
G-BAFU	PA-28 Cherokee 140	Goshawk Aviation Ltd/Southend	
G-BAFV	PA-18 Super Cub 95	P. Elliott	
G-BAFW	PA-28 Cherokee 140	H. T. Boal & ptnrs/Cambridge	
G-BAFX	Robin DR.400/140	Nicholas Advertising Ltd	
G-BAGB	SIAI-Marchetti SF.260	British Midland Airways Ltd/ E. Midlands	
G-BAGC	Robin DR.400/140	Hempalm Ltd/Headcorn	
G-BAGF	Jodel D.92 Bebe	G. R. French	
G-BAGG	PA-32 Cherokee Six 300E	Hornair Ltd	
G-BAGI	Cameron O-31 balloon	D. C. & S. J. Boxall	
G-BAGL	SA.341G Gazelle Srs 1	Autokraft Ltd	
G-BAGN	Cessna F.177RG	R. W. J. Andrews	
G-BAGO	Cessna 421B	Donington Aviation Ltd/E. Midlands	
G-BAGR	Robin DR.400/140	F. C. Aris & J. D. Last/Mona	
G-BAGS	Robin DR.400/180 2+2	Headcorn Flying School Ltd	
G-BAGT	Helio H.295 Courier	B. J. C. Woodall Ltd	
G-BAGU	Luton LA-5A Major	J. Gawley	
G-BAGV	Cessna U.206F	Scottish Parachute Club/Strathallan	
G-BAGX	PA-28 Cherokee 140	T. R. Lister & A. Bradshaw	
G-BAGY	Cameron O-84 balloon	P. G. Dunnington *Beatrice*	
G-BAHD	Cessna 182P Skylane	S. Brunt (Silverdale Staffs) Ltd/Sleap	
G-BAHE	PA-28 Cherokee 140	A. H. Evans & A. O. Jones/Sleap	
G-BAHF	PA-28 Cherokee 140	S. J. Green/Halfpenny Green	
G-BAHG	PA-24 Comanche 260	Friendly Aviation (Jersey) Ltd	
G-BAHH	Wallis WA-121	K. H. Wallis	
G-BAHI	Cessna F.150H	M. D. Barrow/Exeter	
G-BAHJ	PA-24 Comanche 250	K. Cooper	
G-BAHL	Robin DR.400/160	Norvett Electronics Ltd	
G-BAHN	Beech 58 Baron	Cammac Coal Ltd/E. Midlands	
G-BAHO	Beech C.23 Sundowner	G-ATJG Private Aircraft Syndicate Ltd	
G-BAHP	Volmer VJ.22 Sportsman	W. St G. V. Stoney	
G-BAHS	PA-28R Cherokee Arrow 200-II	A. A. Wild & ptnrs	
G-BAHU	Enstrom F-28A	Allen Timpany Racing	
G-BAHX	Cessna 182P	A. Dunkerley & ptnrs/Blackpool	
G-BAHZ	PA-28R Cherokee Arrow 200-II	Rutland Properties Ltd/Leicester	
G-BAIA	PA-32 Cherokee Six 300E	Langham International (Aircraft) Ltd/ Southend	
G-BAIB	Enstrom F-28A	Blades Helicopters Ltd	
G-BAIH	PA-28R Cherokee Arrow 200-II	D. L. Claydon	
G-BAII	Cessna FRA.150L	Air Service Training Ltd/Perth	
G-BAIK	Cessna F.150L	Wickenby Aviation Ltd	
G-BAIL	Cessna FR.172J	D. R. Elphick/O. Warden	
G-BAIM	Cessna 310Q	Air Service Training Ltd/Perth	
G-BAIN	Cessna FRA.150L	Air Service Training Ltd/Perth	
G-BAIP	Cessna F.150L	W. D. Cliffe & J. F. Platt/Wellesbourne	
G-BAIR	Thunder Ax7-77 balloon	P. A. & Mrs M. Hutchins	
G-BAIS	Cessna F.177RG	I. H. Bewley	
G-BAIU	Hiller UH-12E (Soloy)	Heliwork Finance Ltd/Thruxton	
G-BAIW	Cessna F.172M	Humber Aviation Ltd	
G-BAIX	Cessna F.172M	R. A. Nichols/Elstree	
G-BAIY	Cameron O-65 balloon	Budget Rent A Car (UK) Ltd *Lady Budget*	
G-BAIZ	Slingsby T.61A Falke	W. L. C. O'Neill & ptnrs	
G-BAJA	Cessna F.177RG	Don Ward Productions Ltd/Biggin Hill	
G-BAJB	Cessna F.177RG	K. D. Horton/Staverton	
G-BAJC	Evans VP-1	J. R. Clements/Rochester	
G-BAJE	Cessna 177 Cardinal	J. E. Cull	
G-BAJN	AA-5 Traveler	Janacrew Ltd/Sherburn	
G-BAJO	AA-5 Traveler	A. Townson/Blackpool	
G-BAJR	PA-28 Cherokee 180	G-Air Ltd/Lydd	
G-BAJT	PA-28R Cherokee Arrow 200-II	P. H. Tavener	
G-BAJW	Boeing 727-46	Dan-Air Services Ltd/Gatwick	

Notes	Reg.	Type	Owner or Operator
	G-BAJY	Robin DR.400/180	F. Birch & K. J. Pike/Sturgate
	G-BAJZ	Robin DR.400/125	Rochester Aviation Ltd
	G-BAKD	PA-34-200 Seneca II	Andrews Professional Colour Laboratories/Elstree
	G-BAKF	Bell 206B JetRanger 2	M. J. K. Belmont/Coventry
	G-BAKG	Hughes 269C	W. K. MacGillivray
	G-BAKH	PA-28 Cherokee 140	Woodgate Air Services (IoM) Ltd/Ronaldsway
	G-BAKJ	PA-30 Twin Comanche 160B	M. F. Fisher & W. R. Lawes/Biggin Hill
	G-BAKK	Cessna F.172H ★	Parachute jump trainer/Coventry
	G-BAKL	F.27 Friendship Mk 200	Air UK Ltd/Norwich
	G-BAKM	Robin DR.400/140	MKS Syndicate
	G-BAKN	SNCAN SV-4C	M. Holloway
	G-BAKO	Cameron O-84 balloon	D. C. Dokk-Olsen Pied Piper
	G-BAKP	PA-23 Aztec 250E	J. J. Woodhouse
	G-BAKR	Jodel D.117	A. B. Bailey/White Waltham
	G-BAKS	AB-206B JetRanger 2	Dollar Air Services Ltd/Coventry
	G-BAKT	AB-206B JetRanger 2	Gleneagle Helicopter Services (Scotland) Ltd
	G-BAKV	PA-18 Super Cub 150	Pounds Marine Shipping Ltd/Goodwood
	G-BAKW	B.121 Pup 2	The KW Group/Shoreham
	G-BAKY	Slingsby T.61C Falke	G. A. Schulz & A. Jones/Leicester
	G-BALA	Stampe SV-4C	Full Bore Productions Ltd
	G-BALC	Bell 206B JetRanger 2	Dollar Air Services Ltd/Coventry
	G-BALF	Robin DR.400/140	F. A. Spear/Panshanger
	G-BALG	Robin DR.400/180	R. Jones
	G-BALH	Robin DR.400/140B	J. D. Copsey
	G-BALI	Robin DR.400 2+2	R. A. Gridley
	G-BALJ	Robin DR.400/180	D. A. Bett & D. de Lacey-Rowe
	G-BALK	SNCAN SV-4C	L. J. Rice
	G-BALM	Cessna 340	Manro Transport Ltd/Manchester
	G-BALN	Cessna T.310Q	O'Brien Properties Ltd/Shoreham
	G-BALS	T.66 Nipper 3	L. W. Shaw
	G-BALT	Enstrom F-28A	Codnor Pet-Aquatics
	G-BALW	PA-28R Cherokee Arrow 200-II	Cresthale Group Ltd
	G-BALX	D.H.82A Tiger Moth (N6848)	Toadair
	G-BALY	Practavia Pilot Sprite 150	A. L. Young
	G-BALZ	Bell 212	B.E.A.S. Ltd/Redhill
	G-BAMB	Slingsby T.61C Falke	Universities of Glasgow & Strathclyde Gliding Club/Strathaven
	G-BAMC	Cessna F.150L	D. F. Smith
	G-BAME	Volmer VJ-22 Sportsman	A. McLeod
	G-BAMF	MBB Bo 105D	Bond Helicopters Ltd/Bourn
	G-BAMG	Avions Lobet Ganagobie	J. A. Brompton
	G-BAMJ	Cessna 182P	Graham Cook Aviation Ltd/Shoreham
	G-BAML	Bell 206B JetRanger 2	Peter Scott Agriculture Ltd
	G-BAMM	PA-28 Cherokee 235	Holmfield Wakefield Ltd/Sherburn
	G-BAMR	PA-16 Clipper	H. Royce
	G-BAMS	Robin DR.400/160	G-BAMS Ltd/Headcorn
	G-BAMU	Robin DR.400/160	The Alternative Flying Group/Sywell
	G-BAMV	Robin DR.400/180	W. J. Gooding/Rochester
	G-BAMY	PA-28R Cherokee Arrow 200-II	G. R. Gilbert & ptnrs/Birmingham
	G-BANA	Robin DR.221	G. T. Pryor
	G-BANB	Robin DR.400/180	Time Electronics Ltd/Biggin Hill
	G-BANC	GY-201 Minicab	J. T. S. Lewis & J. E. Williams
	G-BAND	Cameron O-84 balloon	Mid-Bucks Farmers Balloon Group Clover
	G-BANE	Cessna FRA.150L	Osprey Air Services Ltd/Cranfield
	G-BANF	Luton LA-4A Minor	W. McNally
	G-BANG	Cameron O-84 balloon	R. F. Harrower
	G-BANK	PA-34-200 Seneca II	Cleveland Flying School Ltd/Teesside
	G-BANL	BN-2A-8 Islander	Loganair Ltd/Glasgow
	G-BANS	PA-34-200 Seneca II	G. Knowles/Halfpenny Green
	G-BANT	Cameron O-65 balloon	M. A. Dworski & R. M. Bishop
	G-BANU	Wassmer Jodel D.120	C. E. McKinney
	G-BANV	Phoenix Currie Wot	K. Knight
	G-BANW	CP.1330 Super Emeraude	D. M. Upfield
	G-BANX	Cessna F.172M	D. Sharp
	G-BAOB	Cessna F.172M	A. S. Bamrah/Biggin Hill
	G-BAOG	M.S.880B Rallye Club	T. Copland
	G-BAOH	M.S.880B Rallye Club	S. P. Bryant & ptnrs/Shobdon
	G-BAOJ	M.S.880B Rallye Club	B. J. Clark & D. J. Stevenson
	G-BAOM	M.S.880B Rallye Club	D. H. Tonkin

Reg.	Type	Owner or Operator	Notes
G-BAOP	Cessna FRA.150L	S. A. Cooper & T. Bamber/Shoreham	
G-BAOS	Cessna F.172M	F. W. Ellis & ptnrs	
G-BAOU	AA-5 Traveler	W. H. Ingram/St Just	
G-BAOV	AA-5A Cheetah	G. C. Rogers & J. P. Martin	
G-BAOW	Cameron O-65 balloon	P. I. White Winslow Boy	
G-BAOY	Cameron S-31 balloon	Shell-Mex BP Ltd New Potato	
G-BAPA	Fournier RF-5B Sperber	S. T. Evans & ptnrs	
G-BAPB	D.H.C.1 Chipmunk 22	R. C. P. Brookhouse/Redhill	
G-BAPC	Luton LA-4A Minor	Midland Aircraft Preservation Soc	
G-BAPF	V.814 Viscount	Baltic British Air Ferries Ltd/Southend	
G-BAPG	V.814 Viscount	Baltic British Air Ferries Ltd/Southend	
G-BAPI	Cessna FRA.150L	Industrial Supplies (Peterborough) Ltd	
G-BAPJ	Cessna FRA.150L	M. D. Page/Manston	
G-BAPK	Cessna F.150L	Andrewsfield Flying Club Ltd	
G-BAPL	PA-23 Turbo Aztec 250E	Medici Spa Marine & Exploration Ltd	
G-BAPM	Fuji FA.200-160	R. P. Munday/Biggin Hill	
G-BAPP	Evans VP-1	K. McNaughton	
G-BAPR	Jodel D.11	R. G. Marshall	
G-BAPS	Campbell Cougar ★	British Rotorcraft Museum	
G-BAPT	Fuji FA.200-180	J. F. Thurlow & J. H. Pickering/Ipswich	
G-BAPV	Robin DR.400/160	J. D. & M. Millne	
G-BAPW	PA-28R Cherokee Arrow 180	D. R. C. Reeves	
G-BAPX	Robin DR.400/160	M. A. Musselwhite	
G-BAPY	Robin HR.100/210	M. P. Hasted	
G-BARB	PA-34-200 Seneca II	H. McC. Clarke	
G-BARC	Cessna FR.172J	G. N. Hopcraft	
G-BARD	Cessna 337C	Jadealto Ltd	
G-BARF	Jodel D.112 Club	A. F. Scott	
G-BARG	Cessna E.310Q	Sally Marine Ltd	
G-BARH	Beech C.23 Sundowner	T. R. Sage	
G-BARJ	Bell 212	Autair International Ltd/Panshanger	
G-BARN	Taylor JT.2 Titch	R. G. W. Newton	
G-BARP	Bell 206B JetRanger 2	S.W. Electricity Board/Bristol	
G-BARS	D.H.C.1 Chipmunk 22	T. I. Sutton/Chester	
G-BARV	Cessna 310Q	Old England Watches Ltd/Elstree	
G-BARZ	Scheibe SF.28A Tandem Falke	J. A. Fox & ptnrs/Dishforth	
G-BASB	Enstrom F-28A	Blades Helicopters Ltd/Goodwood	
G-BASD	B.121 Pup 2	C. C. Brown/Leicester	
G-BASE	Bell 206B JetRanger 2	Air Hanson Ltd/Brooklands	
G-BASG	AA-5 Traveler	ASG Aviation/Glenrothes	
G-BASH	AA-5 Traveler	M. J. Metham/Blackbushe	
G-BASI	PA-28 Cherokee 140	S. J. Green	
G-BASJ	PA-28 Cherokee 180	Guildhaven Ltd/Staverton	
G-BASL	PA-28 Cherokee 140	Air Navigation & Trading Ltd/Blackpool	
G-BASM	PA-34-200 Seneca II	Poplar Aviation/Ipswich	
G-BASN	Beech C.23 Sundowner	M. F. Fisher	
G-BASO	Lake LA-4 Amphibian	E. P. Beck/Glasgow	
G-BASP	B.121 Pup 1	Northamptonshire School of Flying Ltd/Sywell	
G-BASU	PA-31-350 Navajo Chieftain	Streamline Aviation/E. Midlands	
G-BASX	PA-34-200 Seneca II	A. Smith	
G-BATC	MBB Bo 105D	Bond Helicopters Ltd/Swansea	
G-BATJ	Jodel D.119	E. G. Waite/Shobdon	
G-BATM	PA-32 Cherokee Six 300	Patgrove Ltd/Bolney	
G-BATN	PA-23 Aztec 250E	Marshall of Cambridge Ltd	
G-BATS	Taylor JT.1 Monoplane	J. Jennings	
G-BATT	Hughes 269C	Fairglobe Ltd	
G-BATU	Enstrom F-28A-UK	Rotor Enterprises Ltd/Coventry	
G-BATV	PA-28 Cherokee 180D	J. N. Rudsdale	
G-BATW	PA-28 Cherokee 140	N. Paxton & T. Jarman	
G-BATX	PA-23 Aztec 250E	Tayside Aviation Ltd/Dundee	
G-BAUA	PA-23 Aztec 250D	David Parr & Associates Ltd/Shobdon	
G-BAUC	PA-25 Pawnee 235	Southdown Gliding Club Ltd	
G-BAUD	Robin DR.400/160	R. E. Delvis/Shoreham	
G-BAUE	Cessna 310Q	A. J. Dyer/Elstree	
G-BAUH	Jodel D.112	G. A. & D. Shepherd	
G-BAUI	PA-23 Aztec 250D	SFT Aviation Ltd/Bournemouth	
G-BAUJ	PA-23 Aztec 250E	A. J. Costick	
G-BAUK	Hughes 269C	Curtis Engineering (Frome) Ltd	
G-BAUR	F.27 Friendship Mk 200	Air UK Ltd/Norwich	
G-BAUV	Cessna F.150L	Skyviews & General Ltd	
G-BAUW	PA-23 Aztec 250E	R. E. Myson	
G-BAUY	Cessna FRA.150L	The PMM Group/Glenrothes	
G-BAUZ	Nord NC.854S	W. A. Ashley & D. Horne	

53

Notes	Reg.	Type	Owner or Operator
	G-BAVB	Cessna F.172M	T. J. Nokes & T. V. Phillips
	G-BAVC	Cessna F.150L	Butler Associates (Aviation) Ltd
	G-BAVE	Beech A.100 King Air	Northern Executive Aviation Ltd/ Manchester
	G-BAVF	Beech 58 Baron	Eagle Tugs Ltd
	G-BAVH	D.H.C.1 Chipmunk 22	Portsmouth Naval Gliding Club/ Lee-on-Solent
	G-BAVL	PA-23 Aztec 250E	J. J. Woodhouse
	G-BAVO	Boeing Stearman N2S (26)	A. A. Hodgson
	G-BAVR	AA-5 Traveler	Rabhart Ltd/Carlisle
	G-BAVS	AA-5 Traveler	V. J. Peake/Headcorn
	G-BAVU	Cameron A-105 balloon	J. D. Michaelis
	G-BAVX	HPR-7 Herald 214	British Air Ferries Ltd/Southend
	G-BAVZ	PA-23 Aztec 250E	Merseyside Air Charter Ltd/Liverpool
	G-BAWB	PA-23 Aztec 250C	P. D. Bruce/Biggin Hill
	G-BAWG	PA-28R Cherokee Arrow 200-II	Solent Air Ltd
	G-BAWI	Enstrom F-28A-UK	Southern Air Ltd/Shoreham
	G-BAWK	PA-28 Cherokee 140	Newcastle-upon-Tyne Aero Club Ltd
	G-BAWN	PA-30C Twin Comanche 160C	Status Mail Order Services Ltd/ Manchester
	G-BAWR	Robin HR.100/210	Yarmouth Marine Service/Sandown
	G-BAWU	PA-30 Twin Comanche 160B	CCH Aviation Ltd
	G-BAWW	Thunder Ax7-77 balloon	M. L. C. Hutchins *Taurus*/Holland
	G-BAWX	PA-28 Cherokee 180	I. D. Slack & ptnrs/Leeds
	G-BAXD	BN-2A Mk III Trislander	Aurigny Air Services/Guernsey
	G-BAXE	Hughes 269A	Reethorpe Engineering Ltd
	G-BAXF	Cameron O-77 balloon	R. D. Sargeant & M. F. Lasson
	G-BAXH	Cessna 310Q	D. A. Williamson
	G-BAXJ	PA-32 Cherokee Six 300	UK Parachute Services/Ipswich
	G-BAXK	Thunder Ax7-77 balloon	Newbury Balloon Group *Jack O'Newbury*
	G-BAXL	H.S.125 Srs 3B	Dennis Vanguard International (Switchgear) Ltd/Coventry
	G-BAXP	PA-23 Aztec 250E	Subtec Aviation Ltd/Shoreham
	G-BAXS	Bell 47G-5	Helicopter Supplies & Engineering Ltd/ Bournemouth
	G-BAXT	PA-28R Cherokee Arrow 200-II	Williams & Griffin Ltd
	G-BAXU	Cessna F.150L	W. Lancs Aero Club Ltd/Woodvale
	G-BAXY	Cessna F.172M	Merrett Aviation Ltd
	G-BAXZ	PA-28 Cherokee 140	H. Martin & D. Norris/Halton
	G-BAYC	Cameron O-65 balloon	D. Whitlock & R. T. F. Mitchell
	G-BAYL	Nord 1203/III Norecrin	D. M. Fincham
	G-BAYO	Cessna 150L	Cheshire Air Training School Ltd/ Liverpool
	G-BAYP	Cessna 150L	Three Counties Aero Club Ltd/ Blackbushe
	G-BAYR	Robin HR.100/210	Gilbey Warren Co Ltd/Stapleford
	G-BAYT	H.S.125 Srs 600B	Genavco Ltd (G-BNDX)
	G-BAYV	SNCAN 1101 Noralpha (1480)★	Booker Aircraft Museum
	G-BAYZ	Bellanca 7GCBC Citabria	Cambridge University Gliding Trust Ltd/ Duxford
	G-BAZB	H.S.125 Srs 400B	Short Bros PLC/Sydenham
	G-BAZC	Robin DR.400/160	Southern Sailplanes
	G-BAZG	Boeing 737-204	Britannia Airways Ltd *Florence Nightingale*/Luton
	G-BAZH	Boeing 737-204	Britannia Airways Ltd *Sir Frederick Handley Page*/Luton
	G-BAZJ	HPR-7 Herald 209 ★	Guernsey Airport Fire Services
	G-BAZM	Jodel D.11	Bingley Flying Group/Leeds
	G-BAZS	Cessna F.150L	Sherburn Aero Club Ltd
	G-BAZT	Cessna F.172M	M. Fraser/Exeter
	G-BAZU	PA-28R Cherokee Arrow 200	S. C. Simmons/White Waltham
	G-BBAE	L.1011-385 TriStar	Caledonian Airways *Loch Earne*/ Gatwick
	G-BBAF	L.1011-385 TriStar	British Airways *Babbacombe Bay*/ Heathrow
	G-BBAG	L.1011-385 TriStar	British Airways *Bridgwater Bay*/ Heathrow
	G-BBAH	L.1011-385 TriStar	British Airways *Lyme Bay*/Heathrow
	G-BBAI	L.1011-385 TriStar	Caledonian Airways *Loch Inver*/Gatwick
	G-BBAJ	L.1011-385 TriStar	Caledonian Airways *Loch Rannoch*/ Gatwick
	G-BBAK	M.S.894A Rallye Minerva	W. G. Henderson/Dundee

Reg.	Type	Owner or Operator	Notes
G-BBAW	Robin HR.100/210	Scoba Ltd/Goodwood	
G-BBAX	Robin DR.400/140	S. R. Young	
G-BBAY	Robin DR.400/140	G. A. Pentelow & D. B. Roadnight	
G-BBAZ	Hiller UH-12E	Copley Farms Ltd	
G-BBBC	Cessna F.150L	T. Hayselden (Doncaster) Ltd	
G-BBBI	AA-5 Traveler	C. B. Dew	
G-BBBK	PA-28 Cherokee 140	Bencray Ltd/Blackpool	
G-BBBM	Bell 206B JetRanger 2	D. M. Leasing Co	
G-BBBN	PA-28 Cherokee 180	Medallion Meat Products Ltd/Luton	
G-BBBO	SIPA 903	J. S. Hemmings	
G-BBBW	FRED Series 2	D. L. Webster/Sherburn	
G-BBBX	Cessna E310L	Atlantic Air Transport Ltd/Coventry	
G-BBBY	PA-28 Cherokee 140	R. A. E. Tremlett/Guernsey	
G-BBCA	Bell 206B JetRanger 2	Hecray Ltd/Southend	
G-BBCB	Western O-65 balloon	M. Westwood Cee Bee	
G-BBCC	PA-23 Aztec 250D	Dorglen Ltd/Coventry	
G-BBCD	Beech 95-B55 Baron	L. M. Tulloch	
G-BBCF	Cessna FRA.150L	Yorkshire Light Aircraft Ltd	
G-BBCH	Robin DR.400/2+2	Headcorn Flying School Ltd	
G-BBCI	Cessna 150H	N. R. Windley	
G-BBCJ	Cessna 150J	Jones Aviation Services Ltd	
G-BBCK	Cameron O-77 balloon	R. J. Leathart The Mary Gloster	
G-BBCN	Robin HR.100/210	K. T. G. Atkins/Teesside	
G-BBCP	Thunder Ax6-56 balloon	J. M. Robinson Jack Frost	
G-BBCS	Robin DR.400/140	J. A. Thomas	
G-BBCW	PA-23 Aztec 250E	JDT Holdings Ltd/Sturgate	
G-BBCY	Luton LA-4A Minor	J. M. Jones	
G-BBCZ	AA-5 Traveler	Stronghill Flying Group/Bournemouth	
G-BBDB	PA-28 Cherokee 180	T. D. Strange/Newtownards	
G-BBDC	PA-28 Cherokee 140	G. Webster	
G-BBDD	PA-28 Cherokee 140	Midland Air Training School	
G-BBDE	PA-28R Cherokee Arrow 200-II	R. L. Coleman	
G-BBDG	Concorde 100 ★	British Aerospace PLC/Filton	
G-BBDH	Cessna F.172M	Eurohale Ltd/Biggin Hill	
G-BBDI	PA-18 Super Cub 150	Scottish Gliding Union Ltd	
G-BBDJ	Thunder Ax6-56 balloon	S. W. D. & H. B. Ashby Jack Tar	
G-BBDK	V.808C Viscount Freightmaster	British Air Ferries Viscount Linley/ Southend	
G-BBDL	AA-5 Traveler	A. M. Truslove & R. V. Bowles	
G-BBDM	AA-5 Traveler	J. Pettit/Stapleford	
G-BBDN	Taylor JT.1 Monoplane	T. Barnes	
G-BBDO	PA-23 Turbo Aztec E	R. Long/Bristol	
G-BBDP	Robin DR.400/160	Jarrett & Plumb Aviation (Rochester) Ltd	
G-BBDS	PA-31 Turbo Navajo	Broad Oak Air Services/Rochester	
G-BBDT	Cessna 150H	J. M. McCloy/Sherburn	
G-BBDU	PA-31 Turbo Navajo	G-Air Ltd/Goodwood	
G-BBDV	SIPA S.903	W. McAndrew	
G-BBEA	Luton LA-4A Minor	C. R. Greenaway	
G-BBEB	PA-28R Cherokee Arrow 200-II	R. D. Rippingale/Thruxton	
G-BBEC	PA-28 Cherokee 180	J. H. Kimber	
G-BBED	M.S.894A Rallye Minerva 220	Sky-Ad Ltd/Birmingham	
G-BBEF	PA-28 Cherokee 140	Air Navigation & Trading Co Ltd/ Blackpool	
G-BBEI	PA-31 Turbo Navajo	BKS Surveys Ltd/Exeter	
G-BBEL	PA-28R Cherokee Arrow 180	G. R. Cole & A. Grimshaw/Ronaldsway	
G-BBEN	Bellanca 7GCBC Citabria	W. K. Peters	
G-BBEO	Cessna FRA.150L	R. H. Ford	
G-BBEV	PA-28 Cherokee 140	Telepoint Ltd/Manchester	
G-BBEW	PA-23 Aztec 250E	Air Furness/Walney Island	
G-BBEX	Cessna 185A Skywagon	Westward Airways (Lands End) Ltd	
G-BBEY	PA-23 Aztec 250	Glasgow Air Leasing	
G-BBFC	AA-1B Trainer	R. C. Gillingham & G. Mobey/Lydd	
G-BBFD	PA-28R Cherokee Arrow 200-II	D. J. Ball	
G-BBFL	GY-201 Minicab	D. B. Busfield	
G-BBFS	Van Den Bemden gas balloon	A. J. F. Smith Le Tomate	
G-BBFV	PA-32 Cherokee Six 260	Southend Securities Ltd	
G-BBFW	PA-E23 Aztec 250B	T. Bartlett/Stapleford	
G-BBFZ	PA-28R Cherokee Arrow 200-II	Larkfield Garage (Chepstow) Ltd	
G-BBGB	PA-E23 Aztec 250E	Subtec Aviation Ltd	
G-BBGC	M.S.893E Rallye Commodore 180	A. Somerville	
G-BBGE	PA-23 Aztec 250D	Dollar Air Services Ltd/Coventry	
G-BBGH	AA-5 Traveler	Falcon Flying Services/Biggin Hill	

Notes	Reg.	Type	Owner or Operator
	G-BBGI	Fuji FA.200-160	J. J. Young/Seething
	G-BBGJ	Cessna 180	S. K. Stewart
	G-BBGL	Baby Great Lakes	F. Ball
	G-BBGR	Cameron O-65 balloon	M. L. & L. P. Willoughby
	G-BBGX	Cessna 182P Skylane	WOC Hire Ltd
	G-BBGZ	CHABA 42 balloon	G. Laslett & ptnrs
	G-BBHB	PA-31 Turbo Navajo	Photomap (Jersey) Ltd
	G-BBHC	Enstrom F-28A	Blades Helicopters Ltd/Goodwood
	G-BBHD	Enstrom F-28A	Farm Supply Co (Thirsk) Ltd
	G-BBHF	PA-23 Aztec 250E	Bevan Lynch Aviation Ltd/Birmingham
	G-BBHG	Cessna E310Q	Delta Aviation Ltd/Elstree
	G-BBHI	Cessna 177RG	ATS Air Charter Ltd/Blackbushe
	G-BBHJ	Piper J-3C-65 Cub	R. V. Miller & R. H. Heath
	G-BBHK	AT-16 Harvard IIB (FH153)	Bob Warner Aviation/Exeter
	G-BBHL	Sikorsky S-61N Mk II	Bristow Helicopters Ltd Glamis
	G-BBHM	Sikorsky S-61N Mk II	Bristow Helicopters Ltd Braemar
	G-BBHW	SA.341G Gazelle 1	McAlpine Aviation Ltd/Hayes
	G-BBHX	M.S.893E Rallye Commodore	H. H. Elder/Exeter
	G-BBHY	PA-28 Cherokee 180	Air Operations Ltd/Guernsey
	G-BBIA	PA-28R Cherokee Arrow 200-II	A. G. (Commodities) Ltd/Stapleford
	G-BBIC	Cessna 310Q	Angus Motor Co/Dundee
	G-BBID	PA-28 Cherokee 140	R. K. Tamlinson/Elstree
	G-BBIF	PA-23 Aztec 250E	Northern Executive Aviation Ltd/ Manchester
	G-BBIH	Enstrom F-28A-UK	Nunkeeling Ltd
	G-BBII	Fiat G-46-3B	The Hon A. M. M. Lindsay/Booker
	G-BBIL	PA-28 Cherokee 140	D. Arlette/Stapleford
	G-BBIN	Enstrom F-28A	Southern Air Ltd/Shoreham
	G-BBIO	Robin HR.100/210	R. A. King/Headcorn
	G-BBIT	Hughes 269B	Contract Development & Projects (Leeds) Ltd
	G-BBIV	Hughes 269C	W. R. Finance Ltd
	G-BBIX	PA-28 Cherokee 140	R. J. Hill/Biggin Hill
	G-BBJB	Thunder Ax7-77 balloon	St Crispin Balloon Group Dick Darby
	G-BBJI	Isaacs Spitfire	A. N. R. Houghton & ptnrs
	G-BBJU	Robin DR.400/140	J. C. Lister
	G-BBJV	Cessna F.177RG	Pilot Magazine/Biggin Hill
	G-BBJW	Cessna FRA.150L	Coventry School of Flying Ltd
	G-BBJX	Cessna F.150L	Yorkshire Flying Services Ltd/Leeds
	G-BBJY	Cessna F.172M	J. Lucketti/Barton
	G-BBJZ	Cessna F.172M	Burks, Green & ptnrs
	G-BBKA	Cessna F.150L	Sherburn Aero Club Ltd
	G-BBKB	Cessna F.150L	Shoreham Flight Simulation/ Bournemouth
	G-BBKC	Cessna F.172M	W. F. Hall
	G-BBKE	Cessna F.150L	Wickenby Aviation Ltd
	G-BBKF	Cessna FRA.150L	Compton Abbas Airfield Ltd
	G-BBKG	Cessna FR.172J	Cabledraw Ltd/Lydd
	G-BBKI	Cessna F.172M	C. W. & S.A. Burman
	G-BBKL	CP.301A Emeraude	R. Wells & H. V. Hunter
	G-BBKR	Scheibe SF.24A Motorspatz	P. I. Morgans
	G-BBKU	Cessna FRA.150L	LAR Aviation Ltd/Shoreham
	G-BBKV	Cessna FRA.150L	Skegness Air Taxi Service Ltd
	G-BBKX	PA-28 Cherokee 180	P. E. Eglington
	G-BBKY	Cessna F.150L	Telepoint Ltd/Manchester
	G-BBKZ	Cessna 172M	Exeter Flying Club Ltd
	G-BBLA	PA-28 Cherokee 140	Woodgate Aviation Co Ltd/Woodvale
	G-BBLE	Hiller UH-12E	Agricopters Ltd/Chilbolton
	G-BBLH	Piper J-3C-65 Cub	Shipping & Airlines Ltd/Biggin Hill
	G-BBLL	Cameron O-84 balloon	University of East Anglia Hot-Air Ballooning Club Boadicea
	G-BBLM	SOCATA Rallye 100S	R. J. Lewis & P. Walker
	G-BBLP	PA-23 Aztec 250D	Donnington Aviation Ltd/E. Midlands
	G-BBLS	AA-5 Traveler	Turnhouse Flying Club/Edinburgh
	G-BBLU	PA-34-200 Seneca II	F. Tranter/Manchester
	G-BBMB	Robin DR.400/180	G. A. Mason
	G-BBME	BAC One-Eleven 401	British Airways (G-AZMI) (withdrawn)
	G-BBMF	BAC One-Eleven 401	British Airways (G-ATVU) (withdrawn)
	G-BBMG	BAC One-Eleven 408	British Airways (G-AWEJ) (withdrawn)
	G-BBMH	E.A.A. Sports Biplane Model P.1.	K. Dawson
	G-BBMJ	PA-23 Aztec 250E	Tindon Ltd/Little Snoring
	G-BBMK	PA-31 Turbo Navajo	Steer Aviation Ltd/Biggin Hill
	G-BBMN	D.H.C.1 Chipmunk 22	R. Steiner/Panshanger
	G-BBMO	D.H.C.1 Chipmunk 22	A. J. Hurst/Holland

Reg.	Type	Owner or Operator	Notes
G-BBMR	D.H.C.1 Chipmunk T.10 ★ (WB763)	Southall Technical College	
G-BBMT	D.H.C.1 Chipmunk 22	A. T. Letts & ptnrs/Dunstable	
G-BBMV	D.H.C.1 Chipmunk 22 (WG348)	P. J. Morgan (Aviation) Ltd	
G-BBMW	D.H.C.1 Chipmunk 22	M. S. Evans	
G-BBMX	D.H.C.1 Chipmunk 22	A. L. Brown & P. S. Murchison	
G-BBMZ	D.H.C.1 Chipmunk 22	Wycombe Gliding School Syndicate/ Booker	
G-BBNA	D.H.C.1 Chipmunk 22 (Lycoming)	Coventry Gliding Club Ltd/Husbands Bosworth	
G-BBNC	D.H.C.1 Chipmunk T.10 ★ (WP790)	Mosquito Aircraft Museum	
G-BBND	D.H.C.1 Chipmunk 22	A. J. Organ/Bourn	
G-BBNG	Bell 206B JetRanger 2	Helicopter Crop Spraying Ltd	
G-BBNH	PA-34-200 Seneca II	Lawrence Goodwin Machine Tools Ltd Wellesbourne	
G-BBNI	PA-34-200 Seneca II	Colnenay Ltd/Guernsey	
G-BBNJ	Cessna F.150L	Sherburn Aero Club	
G-BBNN	PA-23 Aztec 250D	J. W. B. Wimble	
G-BBNO	PA-23 Aztec 250E	Hedley & Ellis Ltd/Conington	
G-BBNR	Cessna 340	Morris Cohen (Underwear) Ltd	
G-BBNT	PA-31-350 Navajo Chieftain	Northern Executive Aviation Ltd/ Manchester	
G-BBNV	Fuji FA.200-160	G. C. Thomas/Kidlington	
G-BBNX	Cessna FRA.150L	General Airline Ltd	
G-BBNY	Cessna FRA.150L	Air Tows Ltd/Lasham	
G-BBNZ	Cessna F.172M	Anchor Plastics (UK) Ltd	
G-BBOA	Cessna F.172M	J. W. J. Adkins/Southend	
G-BBOB	Cessna 421B	R. F. Gregory/Cardiff	
G-BBOC	Cameron O-77 balloon	J. A. B. Gray	
G-BBOD	Thunder O-5 balloon	B. R. & M. Boyle	
G-BBOE	Robin HR.200/100	Aberdeen Flying Group	
G-BBOH	Pitts S-1S Special	P. Meeson	
G-BBOI	Bede BD-5B	Heather V. B. Wheeler	
G-BBOJ	PA-23 Aztec 250E ★	Instructional airframe/Cranfield	
G-BBOK	PA-23 Aztec 250E	Merion Property Developments Ltd	
G-BBOL	PA-18 Super Cub 150	Lakes Gliding Club Ltd	
G-BBOO	Thunder Ax6-56 balloon	K. Meehan Tigerjack	
G-BBOR	Bell 206B JetRanger 2	Land Air Ltd	
G-BBOX	Thunder Ax7-77 balloon	R. C. Weyda Rocinante	
G-BBOY	Thunder Ax6-56A balloon	N. C. Faithfull Eric of Titchfield	
G-BBPJ	Cessna F.172M	B. W. Aviation Ltd/Cardiff	
G-BBPK	Evans VP-1	P. D. Kelsey	
G-BBPM	Enstrom F-28A	Wardell Holdings Ltd	
G-BBPN	Enstrom F-28A	D. S. Chandler/Shoreham	
G-BBPO	Enstrom F-28A	J. Morton & E. Ryan	
G-BBPP	PA-28 Cherokee 180	Hartmann Ltd	
G-BBPS	Jodel D.117	A. Appleby/Redhill	
G-BBPU	Boeing 747-136	British Airways Virginia Water/ Heathrow	
G-BBPW	Robin HR.100/210	The Character Premium Co Ltd	
G-BBPX	PA-34-200 Seneca II	Richel Investments Ltd/Guernsey	
G-BBPY	PA-28 Cherokee 180	George Hill (Oldham) Ltd	
G-BBRA	PA-23 Aztec 250D	W. London Aviation Services/ White Waltham	
G-BBRB	D.H.82A Tiger Moth (DF198)	R. Barham/Biggin Hill	
G-BBRC	Fuji FA.200-180	W. & L. Installations & Co Ltd/Fairoaks	
G-BBRH	Bell 47G-5A	Helicopter Supplies & Engineering Ltd	
G-BBRI	Bell 47G-5A	Camlet Helicopters Ltd/Fairoaks	
G-BBRN	Procter Kittiwake	Vari-Prop (GB) Ltd/Exeter	
G-BBRV	D.H.C.1 Chipmunk 22	HSA (Chester) Sports & Social Club	
G-BBRW	PA-28 Cherokee 140	P. R. Wernham/Elstree	
G-BBRX	SIAI-Marchetti S.205-18F	B. D. North/Goodwood	
G-BBRZ	AA-5 Traveler	C. P. Osbourne	
G-BBSA	AA-5 Traveler	K. Lynn	
G-BBSB	Beech C23 Sundowner	Sundowner Group/Manchester	
G-BBSC	Beech B24R Sierra	Beechcombers Flying Group	
G-BBSE	D.H.C.1 Chipmunk 22	Felthorpe Flying Group Ltd	
G-BBSM	PA-32 Cherokee Six 300	R. Robson/Biggin Hill	
G-BBSS	D.H.C.1A Chipmunk 22	Coventry Gliding Club Ltd/ Husbands Bosworth	
G-BBSU	Cessna 421B	Hamdanair Ltd	
G-BBSV	Cessna 421B	World Carrier (London) Ltd	
G-BBSW	Pietenpol Air Camper	J. K. S. Wills	

Notes	Reg.	Type	Owner or Operator
	G-BBTB	Cessna FRA.150L	Compton Abbas Airfield Ltd
	G-BBTG	Cessna F.172M	D. H. Laws
	G-BBTH	Cessna F.172M	S. Gilmore/Newtownards
	G-BBTJ	PA-23 Aztec 250E	GCA Survey Group Ltd/Shoreham
	G-BBTK	Cessna FRA.150L	Air Service Training Ltd/Perth
	G-BBTL	PA-23 Aztec 250C	Air Navigation & Trading Co Ltd/ Blackpool
	G-BBTS	Beech V35B Bonanza	Charles Lock Motors Ltd/Stapleford
	G-BBTU	ST-10 Diplomate	P. Campion/Stapleford
	G-BBTW	PA-31P Pressurised Navajo	M. G. Tyrell & Co Ltd/Leavesden
	G-BBTX	Beech C23 Sundowner	R. D. Rooke
	G-BBTY	Beech C23 Sundowner	Torlid Ltd/Biggin Hill
	G-BBTZ	Cessna F.150L	Woodgate Air Services Ltd
	G-BBUD	Sikorsky S-61N Mk II	British International Helicopters Ltd/ Aberdeen
	G-BBUE	AA-5 Traveler	S. J. Southwell-Gray/Blackpool
	G-BBUF	AA-5 Traveler	W. J. Brogan
	G-BBUG	PA-16 Clipper	A. G. Palmer/Coventry
	G-BBUJ	Cessna 421B	Expressflight Ltd/Southend
	G-BBUL	Mitchell-Procter Kittiwake 1	R. Bull
	G-BBUT	Western O-65 balloon	Wg. Cdr. G. F. Turnbull & Mrs K. Turnbull *Christabelle II*
	G-BBUU	Piper J-3C-65 Cub	Cooper Bros/Little Snoring
	G-BBVA	Sikorsky S-61N Mk II	Bristow Helicopters Ltd *Vega*
	G-BBVE	Cessna 340	R. M. Cox Ltd/Biggin Hill
	G-BBVF	SA Twin Pioneer III ★	Museum of Flight/E. Fortune
	G-BBVG	PA-E23 Aztec 250D	R. F. Wanbon & P. G. Warmerdan/ Panshanger
	G-BBVH	V.807 Viscount	GB Airways Ltd/Gibraltar
	G-BBVI	Enstrom F-28A ★	*Ground trainer*/Kidlington
	G-BBVJ	Beech B24R Sierra	J. G. Kelwick/Gamston
	G-BBVM	Beech A.100 King Air	Northern Executive Aviation Ltd/ Manchester
	G-BBVO	Isaacs Fury II	R. A. Bowes/Dunkeswell
	G-BBVP	Westland-Bell 47G-3B1	CKS Air Ltd/Southend
	G-BBWM	PA-E23 Aztec 250E	Guernsey Air Search Ltd
	G-BBWN	D.H.C.1 Chipmunk 22	D. C. Budd
	G-BBXB	Cessna FRA.150L	M. L. Swain/Bourn
	G-BBXG	PA-34-200 Seneca II	London Flight Centre (Stansted) Ltd
	G-BBXH	Cessna FR.172F	H. H. Metal Finishing (Wales) Ltd
	G-BBXK	PA-34-200 Seneca II	Aerobatic Displays Ltd
	G-BBXL	Cessna E310Q	Chatsworth Studios Ltd/Newcastle
	G-BBXO	Enstrom F-28A	Southern Air Ltd/Shoreham
	G-BBXS	Piper J-3C-65 Cub	M. J. Butler (G-ALMA)/Langham
	G-BBXT	Cessna F.172M	I. B. Wilkens/Netherthorpe
	G-BBXU	Beech B24R Sierra	B. M. Russell/Coventry
	G-BBXV	PA-28-151 Warrior	London Flight Centre (Stansted) Ltd
	G-BBXW	PA-28-151 Warrior	Shropshire Aero Club Ltd
	G-BBXX	PA-31-350 Navajo Chieftain	Natural Environment Research Council
	G-BBXY	Bellanca 7GCBC Citabria	J. Turner/Shoreham
	G-BBXZ	Evans VP-1	J. D. Kingston
	G-BBYB	PA-18 Super Cub 95	J. Taylor
	G-BBYE	Cessna 195	R. J. Willies
	G-BBYH	Cessna 182P	Sanderson (Forklifts) Ltd
	G-BBYK	PA-23 Aztec 250E	Kraken Air/Cardiff
	G-BBYL	Cameron O-77 balloon	Buckingham Balloon Club *Jammy*
	G-BBYM	H.P.137 Jetstream 200	British Aerospace PLC (G-AYWR)/ Woodford
	G-BBYO	BN-2A Mk III Trislander	Aurigny Air Services (G-BBWR)/ Guernsey
	G-BBYP	PA-28 Cherokee 140	A. J. Bamrah/Biggin Hill
	G-BBYS	Cessna 182P Skylane	Traffic Management Services
	G-BBYU	Cameron O-56 balloon	C. J. T. Davey *Chieftain*
	G-BBYW	PA-28 Cherokee 140	C.S.E. Aviation Ltd/Kidlington
	G-BBZF	PA-28 Cherokee 140	J. A. Havers & ptnrs/Elstree
	G-BBZH	PA-28R Cherokee Arrow 200-II	Mightycraft Ltd
	G-BBZI	PA-31-310 Turbo Navajo	—/Cardiff
	G-BBZJ	PA-34-200 Seneca II	Three Counties Aero Club Ltd/ Blackbushe
	G-BBZK	Westland-Bell 47G-3B1	Autair Helicopters Ltd/Cranfield
	G-BBZN	Fuji FA.200-180	J. Westwood & P. D. Wedd
	G-BBZO	Fuji FA.200-160	D. G. Lewendon/Bournemouth
	G-BBZS	Enstrom F-28A	Southern Air Ltd/Shoreham
	G-BBZV	PA-28R Cherokee Arrow 200-II	Unicol Engineering/Kidlington

Reg.	Type	Owner or Operator	Notes
G-BCAC	M.S.894A Rallye Minerva 220	R. S. Rogers/Cardiff	
G-BCAH	D.H.C.1 Chipmunk 22 (WG316)	E. Conroy/Shoreham	
G-BCAN	Thunder Ax7-77 balloon	Wessex Hot-Air Team	
G-BCAP	Cameron O-56 balloon	S. R. Seager	
G-BCAR	Thunder Ax7-77 balloon	T. J. Woodbridge/Australia	
G-BCAT	PA-31-310 Turbo Navajo	Hubbardair Ltd	
G-BCAZ	PA-12 Super Cruiser	A. D. Williams	
G-BCBD	Bede BD-5B	Brockmore-Bede Aircraft (UK) Ltd/ Shobdon	
G-BCBG	PA-23 Aztec 250E	M. J. L. Batt/Booker	
G-BCBH	Fairchild 24R-46A Argus III	Bluegale Ltd/Biggin Hill	
G-BCBJ	PA-25 Pawnee 235	Deeside Gliding Club (Aberdeenshire) Ltd	
G-BCBK	Cessna 421B	Robinson Publications Ltd	
G-BCBL	Fairchild 24R-46A Argus III (HB751)	J. Turner/Shoreham	
G-BCBM	PA-23 Aztec 250C	S. Lightbrown & M. Kavanagh	
G-BCBR	AJEP/Wittman W.8 Tailwind	D. A. Hood	
G-BCBW	Cessna 182P	E. Reed	
G-BCBX	Cessna F.150L	J. Kelly/Newtownards	
G-BCBY	Cessna F.150L	Scottish Airways Flyers (Prestwick) Ltd	
G-BCBZ	Cessna 337C	Westward Airways (Land End) Ltd/ St Just	
G-BCCB	Robin HR.200/100	A. M. Bailey & D. E. Ashton	
G-BCCC	Cessna F.150L	J. C. Glynn	
G-BCCD	Cessna F.172M	Lota Ltd	
G-BCCE	PA-23 Aztec 250E	Hymore Hodson Antiques	
G-BCCF	PA-28 Cherokee 180	J. T. Friskney Ltd/Skegness	
G-BCCG	Thunder Ax7-65 balloon	N. H. Ponsford	
G-BCCK	AA-5 Traveler	Prospect Air Ltd/Barton	
G-BCCP	Robin HR. 200/100	Northampton School of Flying Ltd/ Sywell	
G-BCCR	CP.301A Emeraude	A. B. Fisher/Dishforth	
G-BCCU	BN-2A Mk III-1 Trislander	Kondair/Stansted	
G-BCCX	D.H.C.1 Chipmunk 22 (Lycoming)	RAFGSA/Dishforth	
G-BCCY	Robin HR.200/100	Bristol Strut Flying Group	
G-BCDA	Boeing 727-46	Dan-Air Services Ltd/Gatwick	
G-BCDB	PA-34-200 Seneca II	A. & G. Aviation Ltd/Bournemouth	
G-BCDC	PA-18 Super Cub 95	Cotswold Aero Club Ltd/Staverton	
G-BCDJ	PA-28 Cherokee 140	J. A. Renelt/Southend	
G-BCDK	Partenavia P.68B	Nottingham Offshore Marine	
G-BCDL	Cameron O-42 balloon	D. P. & Mrs B. O. Turner *Chums*	
G-BCDN	F.27 Friendship Mk 200	Air UK/Norwich	
G-BCDO	F.27 Friendship Mk 200	Air UK *Lord Butler*/Norwich	
G-BCDR	Thunder Ax7-77 balloon	W. G. Johnston & ptnrs *Obelix*	
G-BCDY	Cessna FRA.150L	Air Service Training Ltd/Perth	
G-BCEA	Sikorsky S-61N Mk II	British International Helicopters Ltd/ Aberdeen	
G-BCEB	Sikorsky S-61N Mk II	British International Helicopters Ltd/ Penzance	
G-BCEC	Cessna F.172M	United Propedent Ltd/Manchester	
G-BCEE	AA-5 Traveler	Echo Echo Ltd/Bournemouth	
G-BCEF	AA-5 Traveler	Echo Fox Ltd/Jersey	
G-BCEN	BN-2A Islander	Atlantic Air Transport Ltd/Coventry	
G-BCEO	AA-5 Traveler	Regishire Ltd/Southampton	
G-BCEP	AA-5 Traveler	Nottingham Industrial Cleaners Ltd/ Tollerton	
G-BCER	GY-201 Minicab	D. Beaumont/Sherburn	
G-BCEU	Cameron O-42 balloon	Entertainment Services Ltd *Harlequin*	
G-BCEX	PA-23 Aztec 250E	Weekes Bros (Welling) Ltd/Biggin Hill	
G-BCEY	D.H.C.1 Chipmunk 22	D. O. Wallis	
G-BCEZ	Cameron O-84 balloon	Anglia Aeronauts Ascension Association *Stars and Bars*	
G-BCFB	Cameron O-77 balloon	J. J. Harris & P. Pryce-Jones *Teutonic Turkey*	
G-BCFC	Cameron O-65 balloon	B. H. Mead *Candy Twist*	
G-BCFD	West balloon ★	British Balloon Museum *Hellfire*	
G-BCFF	Fuji FA-200-160	G. W. Brown & M. R. Gibbons	
G-BCFN	Cameron O-65 balloon	W. G. Johnson & H. M. Savage	
G-BCFO	PA-18 Super Cub 150	Bristol & Gloucestershire Gliding Club (Pty) Ltd/Nympsfield	
G-BCFR	Cessna FRA.150L	J. J. Baumhardt/Southend	
G-BCFW	Saab 91D Safir	D. R. Williams	

Notes	Reg.	Type	Owner or Operator
	G-BCFY	Luton LA-4A Minor	R. J. Wrixon
	G-BCGB	Bensen B.8	A. Melody
	G-BCGC	D.H.C.1 Chipmunk 22 (WP903)	Culdrose Gliding Club
	G-BCGG	Jodel DR.250 Srs 160	C. G. Gray (G-ATZL)
	G-BCGH	Nord NC.854S	T. J. N. H. Palmer & G. W. Oliver
	G-BCGI	PA-28 Cherokee 140	A. Dodd/Redhill
	G-BCGJ	PA-28 Cherokee 140	I. T. D. Hall & B. R. Sedgeman Tees-side
	G-BCGK	PA-28 Cherokee 140	CSE Aviation Ltd/Kidlington
	G-BCGL	Jodel D.112	J. Harris
	G-BCGM	Jodel D.120	D. N. K. Symon
	G-BCGN	PA-28 Cherokee 140	Oxford Flyers Ltd/Kidlington
	G-BCGS	PA-28R Cherokee Arrow 200	MAP Thompson (Roofing) Ltd
	G-BCGT	PA-28 Cherokee 140	T. D. Bugg
	G-BCGW	Jodel D.11	G. H. & M. D. Chittenden
	G-BCGX	Bede BD-5A/B	R. Hodgson
	G-BCHK	Cessna F.172H	N. Yorks Aviation Ltd/Grindale
	G-BCHL	D.H.C.1 Chipmunk 22A (WP788)	Shropshire Soaring Ltd
	G-BCHM	SA.341G Gazelle	Bristol Helicopters Ltd/Yeovil
	G-BCHP	CP.1310C-3 Super Emeraude	R. F. Sothcott (G-JOSI)
	G-BCHT	Schleicher ASK.16	K. M. Barton & ptnrs/Dunstable
	G-BCHU	Dawes VP-2	G. Dawes
	G-BCHV	D.H.C.1 Chipmunk 22	N. F. Charles/Sywell
	G-BCHX	SF.23A Sperling	R. L. McClean
	G-BCID	PA-34-200 Seneca II	Comanche Air Services Ltd/Lydd
	G-BCIE	PA-28-151 Warrior	J. A. & J. V. Bridger/Exeter
	G-BCIF	PA-28 Cherokee 140	Fryer-Robins Aviation Ltd/E. Midlands
	G-BCIH	D.H.C.1 Chipmunk 22 (WD363)	J. M. Hosey & R. A. Schofield/Stansted
	G-BCIJ	AA-5 Traveler	W. J. McCollum
	G-BCIK	AA-5 Traveler	S. F. Lister/Tollerton
	G-BCIN	Thunder Ax7-77 balloon	P. G & R. A. Vale
	G-BCIO	PA-39 Twin Comanche 160 C/R	Rabhart Ltd
	G-BCIR	PA-28-151 Warrior	St Angelo Flight Centre
	G-BCIT	CIT/A1 Srs 1	Cranfield Institute of Technology
	G-BCIW	D.H.C.1 Chipmunk 22 (WZ868)	R. K. J. Hadlow & ptnrs/Duxford
	G-BCJF	Beagle B.206 Srs 1	A. A. Mattacks/Biggin Hill
	G-BCJH	Mooney M.20F	S. R. Cannell/Panshanger
	G-BCJM	PA-28 Cherokee 140	Paragraph Typesetting Ltd
	G-BCJN	PA-28 Cherokee 140	A. J. Steed/Goodwood
	G-BCJO	PA-28R Cherokee Arrow 200	P. C. Trott
	G-BCJP	PA-28 Cherokee 140	G. C. Smith/Bourn
	G-BCJS	PA-23 Aztec 250C	Woodgate Air Services (IoM) Ltd/ Ronaldsway
	G-BCKF	SA.102.5 Cavalier	K. Fairness
	G-BCKN	D.H.C.1A Chipmunk 22	RAFGSA/Bicester
	G-BCKO	PA-23 Aztec 250E	Planning & Mapping Ltd
	G-BCKP	Luton LA-5A Major	J. Horovitz & ptnrs
	G-BCKS	Fuji FA.200-180	J. T. Hicks/Goodwood
	G-BCKT	Fuji FA.200-180	Littlewick Green Service Station Ltd/ Booker
	G-BCKU	Cessna FRA.150L	Air Service Training Ltd/Perth
	G-BCKV	Cessna FRA.150L	Air Service Training Ltd/Perth
	G-BCLC	Sikorsky S-61N	Bristow Helicopters Ltd
	G-BCLD	Sikorsky S-61N	Bristow Helicopters Ltd
	G-BCLI	AA-5 Traveler	R. A. Williams/Panshanger
	G-BCLJ	AA-5 Traveler	M. E. Woodroffe/Shoreham
	G-BCLL	PA-28 Cherokee 180	Stu Davidson & Son Plant Hire Ltd
	G-BCLS	Cessna 170B	C. W. Proffitt-White/Shotteswell
	G-BCLU	Jodel D.117	N. A. Wallace
	G-BCLV	Bede BD-5A	R. A. Gardiner
	G-BCLW	AA-1B Trainer	E. J. McMillan
	G-BCMD	PA-18 Super Cub 95	R. G. Brooks/Dunkeswell
	G-BCMJ	SA.102.5 Cavalier (tailwheel)	R. G. Sykes/Shoreham
	G-BCMT	Isaacs Fury II	M. H. Turner
	G-BCNC	GY.201 Minicab	J. R. Wraight
	G-BCNP	Cameron O-77 balloon	M. L. J. Ritchie
	G-BCNR	Thunder Ax7-77A balloon	S. J. Miliken & ptnrs
	G-BCNT	Partenavia P.68B	Welsh Airways Ltd
	G-BCNX	Piper J-3C-65 Cub	K. J. Lord/Ipswich
	G-BCNZ	Fuji FA.200-160	J. Bruton & A. Lincoln/Manchester
	G-BCOB	Piper J-3C-65 Cub	R. W. & Mrs J. W. Marjoram
	G-BCOE	H.S.748 Srs 2B	British Airways *Glen Livet*/Glasgow
	G-BCOF	H.S.748 Srs 2B	British Airways *Glen Fiddich*/Glasgow
	G-BCOG	Jodel D.112	B. A. Bower & ptnrs

Reg.	Type	Owner or Operator	Notes
G-BCOH	Avro 683 Lancaster 10 (KB976)	Charles Church (Spitfires) Ltd	
G-BCOI	D.H.C.1 Chipmunk 22	D. S. McGregor & A. T. Letham	
G-BCOJ	Cameron O-56 balloon	T. J. Knott & M. J. Webber	
G-BCOL	Cessna F.172M	Calros Ltd	
G-BCOM	Piper J-3C-65 Cub	M. D. Blows	
G-BCOO	D.H.C.1 Chipmunk 22	T. G. Fielding & M. S. Morton/Blackpool	
G-BCOP	PA-28R Cherokee Arrow 200-II	E. A. Saunders/Halfpenny Green	
G-BCOR	SOCATA Rallye 100ST	H. J. Pincombe/Dunkeswell	
G-BCOU	D.H.C.1 Chipmunk 22 (WK522)	P. J. Loweth	
G-BCOX	Bede BD-5A	H. J. Cox	
G-BCOY	D.H.C.1 Chipmunk 22	Coventry Gliding Club Ltd/ Husbands Bosworth	
G-BCPB	Howes radio-controlled model free balloon	R. B. & Mrs C. Howes *Posbee 1*	
G-BCPD	GY-201 Minicab	A. H. K. Denniss/Halfpenny Green	
G-BCPE	Cessna F.150M	Routair Aviation Services Ltd/Southend	
G-BCPF	PA-23 Aztec 250D	M. A. Bonsall/E. Midlands	
G-BCPG	PA-28R Cherokee Arrow 200-II	Roses Flying Group/Liverpool	
G-BCPH	Piper J-3C-65 Cub (329934)	I. R. March	
G-BCPJ	Piper J-3C-65 Cub	P. Turton	
G-BCPK	Cessna F.172M	Skegness Air Taxi Services Ltd	
G-BCPN	AA-5 Traveler	B.W. Agricultural Equipments Ltd	
G-BCPO	Partenavia P.68B	Mondiale Aviation Ltd	
G-BCPU	D.H.C.1 Chipmunk T.10	P. Waller/Booker	
G-BCPX	Szep HFC.125	A. Szep/Netherthorpe	
G-BCRA	Cessna F.150M ★	Three Counties Aero Club/Blackbushe	
G-BCRB	Cessna F.172M	Specialised Laboratory Equipment Ltd	
G-BCRE	Cameron O-77 balloon	A. R. Langton	
G-BCRH	Alaparma Baldo B.75	A. L. Scadding/(*stored*)	
G-BCRI	Cameron O-65 balloon	V. J. Thorne *Joseph*	
G-BCRJ	Taylor JT.1 Monoplane	K. J. Jarrett	
G-BCRK	SA.102.5 Cavalier	T. Barlow/Blackpool	
G-BCRL	PA-28-151 Warrior	F. N. Garland/Biggin Hill	
G-BCRN	Cessna FRA.150L	Air Service Training Ltd/Perth	
G-BCRP	PA-E23 Aztec 250E	ReFair/Sibson	
G-BCRR	AA-5B Tiger	ReFair/Sibson	
G-BCRT	Cessna F.150M	Suffolk Aero Club Ltd/Ipswich	
G-BCRX	D.H.C.1 Chipmunk 22	J. R. Chapman & ptnrs	
G-BCSA	D.H.C.1 Chipmunk 22	RAFGSA/Dishforth	
G-BCSB	D.H.C.1 Chipmunk 22	RAFGSA/Bicester	
G-BCSL	D.H.C.1 Chipmunk 22	Jalawain Ltd/Barton	
G-BCSM	Bellanca 8GCBC Scout	Buckminster Gliding Club	
G-BCST	M.S.893A Rallye Commodore 180	P. J. Wilcox/Cranfield	
G-BCSX	Thunder Ax7-77 balloon	A. T. Wood *Whoopski*	
G-BCSY	Taylor JT.2 Titch	T. Hartwell & D. Wilkinson	
G-BCSZ	PA-28R Cherokee Arrow 200-II	J. Pownall/Tollerton	
G-BCTA	PA-28-151 Warrior	T. G. Aviation Ltd/Manston	
G-BCTF	PA-28-151 Warrior	Eastern Air Executive Ltd/Sturgate	
G-BCTI	Schleicher ASK.16	R. J. Steward	
G-BCTJ	Cessna 310Q	S. E. Clark/Biggin Hill	
G-BCTK	Cessna FR.172J	D. F. Ball	
G-BCTR	Taylor JT.2 Titch	D. H. Greenwood	
G-BCTT	Evans VP-1	B. J. Boughton	
G-BCTU	Cessna FRA.150M	J. H. Fisher & N. D. Hall	
G-BCTV	Cessna F.150M	C. E. Derbyshire & T. L. Morris/ Andrewsfield	
G-BCTW	Cessna F.150M	Woodgate Air Services Ltd/Aldergrove	
G-BCUB	Piper J-3C-65 Cub	A. L. Brown & G. Attwell/Bourn	
G-BCUF	Cessna F.172M	G. H. Kirke Ltd	
G-BCUH	Cessna F.150M	Heathgrange Ltd/Elstree	
G-BCUI	Cessna F.172M	Hillhouse Estates Ltd	
G-BCUJ	Cessna F.150M	T. Hayselden (Doncaster) Ltd	
G-BCUL	SOCATA Rallye 100ST	C. A. Ussher	
G-BCUW	Cessna F.177RG	Pageday Ltd/Cranfield	
G-BCUY	Cessna FRA.150M	S. R. Cameron	
G-BCVA	Cameron O-65 balloon	J. C. Bass & ptnrs *Crepe Suzette*	
G-BCVB	PA-17 Vagabond	A. T. Nowak/Popham	
G-BCVC	SOCATA Rallye 100ST	Brettshire Ltd/Southend	
G-BCVE	Evans VP-2	D. Masterson & D. B. Winstanley	
G-BCVF	Practavia Pilot Sprite	C. S. Carleton-Smith & H. C. U. Vonwiller	
G-BCVG	Cessna FRA.150L	Air Service Training Ltd/Perth	
G-BCVH	Cessna FRA.150L	Yorkshire Light Aircraft Ltd/Leeds	

Notes	Reg.	Type	Owner or Operator
	G-BCVI	Cessna FR.172J	R. M. Savage
	G-BCVJ	Cessna F.172M	D. S. Newland & J. Rothwell/Blackpool
	G-BCVW	GY-80 Horizon 180	P. M. A. Parrett/Dunkeswell
	G-BCVY	PA-34-200T Seneca II	C.S.E. Aviation Ltd/Kidlington
	G-BCWA	BAC One-Eleven 518	Dan-Air Services Ltd (G-AXMK)/ Gatwick
	G-BCWB	Cessna 182P	British Car Auctions (Aviation) Ltd/ Blackbushe
	G-BCWF	S.A. Twin Pioneer 1	Flight One Ltd (G-APRS)/Shobdon
	G-BCWH	Practavia Pilot Sprite	R. Tasker/Blackpool
	G-BCWI	Bensen B.8M	C. J. Blundell
	G-BCWK	Alpavia Fournier RF-3	D. I. Nickolls & ptnrs
	G-BCWL	Westland Lysander III (V9281)	Wessex Aviation & Transport Ltd
	G-BCWM	AB-206B JetRanger 2	Dollar Air Services Ltd/Coventry
	G-BCWR	BN-2A-21 Islander	Pilatus BN Ltd/Bembridge
	G-BCXB	SOCATA Rallye 100ST	A. Smails
	G-BCXE	Robin DR.400/2+2	Headcorn Flying School Ltd
	G-BCXF	H.S.125 Srs 600B	Beecham International Aviation Ltd/ Heathrow
	G-BCXH	PA-28 Cherokee 140F	C. P. Marshall
	G-BCXJ	Piper J-3C-65 Cub (413048)	W. F. Stockdale/Compton Abbas
	G-BCXN	D.H.C.1 Chipmunk 22	J. D. Featherby/Norwich
	G-BCXO	MBB Bo 105D	Bond Helicopters Ltd/Bourn
	G-BCXR	BAC One-Eleven 517	Dan-Air Services Ltd (G-BCCV)/Gatwick
	G-BCYH	DAW Privateer Mk. 2	D. B. Limbert
	G-BCYI	Schleicher ASK-16	J. Fox & J. Harding/Lasham
	G-BCYJ	D.H.C.1 Chipmunk 22 (WG307)	R. A. L. Falconer
	G-BCYK	Avro CF.100 Mk 4 Canuck (18393) ★	Imperial War Museum/Duxford
	G-BCYM	D.H.C.1 Chipmunk 22	C. R. R. Eagleton/Headcorn
	G-BCYR	Cessna F.172M	Donne Enterprises
	G-BCZH	D.H.C.1 Chipmunk 22 (WK622)	A. C. Byrne & D. Featherby/Norwich
	G-BCZI	Thunder Ax7-77 balloon	R. G. Griffin & ptnrs
	G-BCZM	Cessna F.172M	Cornwall Flying Club Ltd/Bodmin
	G-BCZN	Cessna F.150M	Mona Aviation Ltd
	G-BCZO	Cameron O-77 balloon	W. O. T. Holmes Leo
	G-BDAB	SA.102.5 Cavalier	A. H. Brown
	G-BDAC	Cameron O-77 balloon	D. Fowler & J. Goody Chocolate Ripple
	G-BDAD	Taylor JT.1 Monoplane	W. H. Greenwood/Shoreham
	G-BDAE	BAC One-Eleven 518	Dan-Air Services Ltd (G-AXMI)/Gatwick
	G-BDAG	Taylor JT.1 Monoplane	R. S. Basinger
	G-BDAH	Evans VP-1	A. M. Carter
	G-BDAI	Cessna FRA.150M	Scotia Safari Ltd/Prestwick
	G-BDAK	R. Commander 112A	D. P. Williams
	G-BDAL	R. 500S Shrike Commander	Quantel Ltd
	G-BDAM	AT-16 Harvard IIB (FE992)	N. A. Lees & E. C. English
	G-BDAP	AJEP Tailwind	J. Whiting
	G-BDAR	Evans VP-1	S. C. Foggin & M. T. Dugmore
	G-BDAS	BAC One-Eleven 518	Dan-Air Services Ltd (G-AXMH)/ Gatwick
	G-BDAT	BAC One-Eleven 518	Dan-Air Services Ltd (G-AYOR)/ Gatwick
	G-BDAV	PA-23 Aztec 250C	Air Ipswich
	G-BDAX	PA-23 Aztec 250C	Astra Management Ltd
	G-BDAY	Thunder Ax5-42A balloon	T. M. Donnelly Meconium
	G-BDBD	Wittman W.8 Tailwind	E. D. Bond
	G-BDBF	FRED Srs 2	R. G. Boyton
	G-BDBH	Bellanca 7GCBC Citabria	Inkpen Gliding Club Ltd/Thruxton
	G-BDBI	Cameron O-77 balloon	C. A. Butter & J. J. Cook
	G-BDBJ	Cessna 182P	H. C. Wilson
	G-BDBL	D.H.C.1 Chipmunk 22	B. E. Simpson
	G-BDBP	D.H.C.1 Chipmunk 22	Sherwood Flying Club Ltd/Tollerton
	G-BDBS	Short SD3-30	Short Bros PLC/Sydenham
	G-BDBU	Cessna F.150M	Routair Aviation Services Ltd/Southend
	G-BDBX	Evans VP-1	Montgomeryshire Ultra-Light Flying Club
	G-BDBZ	WS.55 Whirlwind Srs 2 ★	Ground instruction airframe/Kidlington
	G-BDCA	SOCATA Rallye 150ST	B. W. J. Pring & ptnrs/Dunkeswell
	G-BDCB	D.H.C.1 Chipmunk 22	R. F. Tolhurst
	G-BDCC	D.H.C.1 Chipmunk 22	Coventry Gliding Club Ltd/ Husbands Bosworth
	G-BDCD	Piper J-3C-85 Cub (480133)	Suzanne C. Brooks/Slinfold
	G-BDCE	Cessna F.172H	Lord Valentine William Cecil

Reg.	Type	Owner or Operator	Notes
G-BDCI	CP.301A Emeraude	D. L. Sentance	
G-BDCK	AA-5 Traveler	Low & Duff (Developments) Ltd	
G-BDCM	Cessna F.172RG	P. R. Gunnel	
G-BDCO	B.121 Pup 1	Dr R. D. H. & Mrs K. N. Maxwell/Leeds	
G-BDCS	Cessna 421B	Mainland Car Delivery Services Ltd	
G-BDCT	PA-25 Pawnee 235C	Apple Aviation Ltd/Sibson	
G-BDCU	Cameron O-77 balloon	H. P. Carlton	
G-BDDD	D.H.C.1 Chipmunk 22	RAE Aero Club Ltd/Farnborough	
G-BDDF	Jodel D.120	Sywell Skyriders Flying Group	
G-BDDG	Jodel D.112	A. J. Daley & J. A. Sumner/Burnaston	
G-BDDJ	Luton LA-4A Minor	D. D. Johnson	
G-BDDS	PA-25 Pawnee 235	Vale of Neath Gliding Club	
G-BDDX	Whittaker MW.2B Excalibur ★	Cornwall Aero Park/Helston	
G-BDDZ	CP.301A Emeraude	V. W. Smith & E. C. Mort	
G-BDEA	Boeing 707-338C	Anglo Cargo Airlines Ltd/Gatwick	
G-BDEC	SOCATA Rallye 100ST	Cambridge Chemical Co Ltd	
G-BDEF	PA-34-200T Seneca II	European Paper Sales Ltd/Biggin Hill	
G-BDEH	Jodel D.120A	D. W. Parkinson & ptnrs/Barton	
G-BDEI	Jodel D.9 Bebe	A. S. Walton	
G-BDEN	SIAI-Marchetti SF.260	Quantel Ltd/Biggin Hill	
G-BDEU	D.H.C.1 Chipmunk 22 (WP808)	A. Taylor	
G-BDEV	Taylor JT.1 Monoplane	D. A. Bass	
G-BDEW	Cessna FRA.150M	Compton Abbas Airfield Ltd	
G-BDEX	Cessna FRA.150M	Compton Abbas Airfield Ltd	
G-BDEY	Piper J-3C-65 Cub	Ducksworth Flying Club	
G-BDEZ	Piper J-3C-65 Cub	D. V. Wallis	
G-BDFB	Currie Wot	D. F. Faulkner-Bryant/Shoreham	
G-BDFC	R. Commander 112A	R. Fletcher	
G-BDFG	Cameron O-65 balloon	N. A. Robertson *Golly II*	
G-BDFH	Auster AOP.9 (XR240)	R. O. Holden/Booker	
G-BDFI	Cessna F.150M	Coventry Civil Aviation Ltd	
G-BDFJ	Cessna F.150M	T. J. Lynn/Sibson	
G-BDFM	Caudron C.270 Luciole	G. V. Gower	
G-BDFR	Fuji FA.200-160	C.S.E. Aviation Ltd/Kidlington	
G-BDFS	Fuji FA.200-160	R. W. Struth & A. H. Biggs	
G-BDFU	Dragonfly MPA Mk 1 ★	Museum of Flight/E. Fortune	
G-BDFW	R. Commander 112A	DTR Audio Visual Ltd/Blackbushe	
G-BDFX	Auster 5	C. W. Udale/Leicester	
G-BDFY	AA-5 Traveler	Edinburgh Flying Club Ltd	
G-BDFZ	Cessna F.150M	Skyviews & General Ltd	
G-BDGA	Bushby-Long Midget Mustang	J. R. Owen	
G-BDGB	GY-20 Minicab	D. G. Burden	
G-BDGH	Thunder Ax7-77 balloon	The London Balloon Club Ltd *London Pride III*	
G-BDGK	Beechcraft D.17S	P. M. J. Wolf/Biggin Hill	
G-BDGM	PA-28-151 Warrior	A. J. Breakspear & ptnrs	
G-BDGN	AA-5B Tiger	C. Zantow	
G-BDGO	Thunder Ax7-77 balloon	International Distillers & Vintners Ltd *J. & B. Rare*	
G-BDGP	Cameron V-65 balloon	Warwick Balloons Ltd	
G-BDGY	PA-28 Cherokee 140	R. E. Woolridge/Staverton	
G-BDHB	Isaacs Fury II	D. H. Berry	
G-BDHJ	Pazmany PL.1	C. T. Millner	
G-BDHK	Piper J-3C-65 Cub (329417)	A. Liddiard	
G-BDHL	PA-23 Aztec 250E	Cheshire Flying Services Ltd/Manchester	
G-BDHM	SA.102.5 Cavalier	D. H. Mitchell	
G-BDIC	D.H.C.1 Chipmunk 22	Woodvale Aviation Co Ltd	
G-BDIE	R. Commander 112A	T. D. Saveker/Birmingham	
G-BDIG	Cessna 182P	D. P. Cranston & Bob Crowe Aircraft Sales Ltd/Cranfield	
G-BDIH	Jodel D.117	J. Chisholm/Booker	
G-BDIJ	Sikorsky S-61N	Bristow Helicopters Ltd	
G-BDIM	D.H.C.1 Chipmunk 22	Protechnic Computers Ltd/Cambridge	
G-BDIW	D.H.106 Comet 4C ★	Air Classik/Dusseldorf	
G-BDIX	D.H.106 Comet 4C ★	Museum of Flight/E. Fortune	
G-BDIY	Luton LA-4A Minor	M. A. Musselwhite	
G-BDJB	Taylor JT.1 Monoplane	J. F. Barber	
G-BDJC	AJEP W.8 Tailwind	M. Risdale & S. J. Pugh	
G-BDJD	Jodel D.112	C. Davidson	
G-BDJF	Bensen B.8MV	R. P. White	
G-BDJN	Robin HR.200/100	Northampton School of Flying Co Ltd/Sywell	
G-BDJP	Piper J-3C-90 Cub	J. M. Pothecary (*stored*)/Shoreham	

Notes	Reg.	Type	Owner or Operator
	G-BDJR	Nord NC.858	R. F. M. Marson & ptnrs
	G-BDKB	SOCATA Rallye 150ST	N. C. Anderson
	G-BDKC	Cessna A185F	Bridge of Tilt Co Ltd
	G-BDKD	Enstrom F-28A	Normans Ltd
	G-BDKH	CP.301A Emeraude	P. G. & F. M. Morris
	G-BDKJ	SA.102.5 Cavalier	H. B. Yardley
	G-BDKK	Bede BD-5B	A. W. Odell (stored)/Headcorn
	G-BDKM	SIPA 903	S. W. Markham
	G-BDKU	Taylor JT.1 Monoplane	A. C. Dove
	G-BDKV	PA-28R Cherokee Arrow 200-II	H. Wilson/Bristol
	G-BDKW	R. Commander 112A	Denny Bros Printing Ltd
	G-BDLO	AA-5A Cheetah	S. & J. Dolan/Denham
	G-BDLR	AA-5B Tiger	McAlpine Aviation Ltd/Luton
	G-BDLS	AA-1B Trainer	P. W. Vaughan & J. M. Fraser/ Andrewsfield
	G-BDLT	R. Commander 112A	Wintergrain Ltd/Exeter
	G-BDLY	SA.102.5 Cavalier	J. A. Espin/Popham
	G-BDMB	Robin HR.100/210	R. J. Hitchman & Son
	G-BDMM	Jodel D.11	P. N. Marshall
	G-BDMS	Piper J-3C-65 Cub	A. T. H. Martin & K. G. Harris
	G-BDMW	Jodel DR.100	J. T. Nixon/Blackpool
	G-BDNC	Taylor JT.1 Monoplane	G. A. Stanley
	G-BDNF	Bensen B.8M	W. F. O'Brien
	G-BDNG	Taylor JT.1 Monoplane	D. J. Phillips/Lasham
	G-BDNO	Taylor JT.1 Monoplane	W. R. Partridge
	G-BDNP	BN-2A Islander ★	Ground parachute trainer/Headcorn
	G-BDNR	Cessna FRA.150M	Cheshire Air Training School Ltd/ Liverpool
	G-BDNT	Jodel D.92	D. J. Park
	G-BDNU	Cessna F.172M	Vectaphone Manufacturing Ltd/ Sandown
	G-BDNW	AA-1B Trainer	Partlease Ltd
	G-BDNX	AA-1B Trainer	R. M. North
	G-BDNY	AA-1B Trainer	M. R. Langford/Doncaster
	G-BDNZ	Cameron O-77 balloon	I. L. McHale
	G-BDOC	Sikorsky S-61N Mk II	Bristow Helicopters Ltd
	G-BDOD	Cessna F.150M	Latharp Ltd/Booker
	G-BDOE	Cessna FR.172J	Rocket Partnership
	G-BDOF	Cameron O-56 balloon	New Holker Estates Co Fred Cavendish
	G-BDOG	SA Bullfinch Srs 2100	I. Drake/Netherthorpe
	G-BDOH	Hiller UH-12E (Soloy)	D. A. H. Jack
	G-BDOI	Hiller UH-12E	T. J. Clark
	G-BDOL	Piper J-3C-65 Cub	U. E. Allman & M. C. Jordan/Shoreham
	G-BDON	Thunder Ax7-77A balloon	J. R. Henderson & ptnrs
	G-BDOR	Thunder Ax6-56A balloon	M. S. Drinkwater & G. Fitzpatrick
	G-BDOS	BN-2A Mk III-2 Trislander	Kondair/Stansted
	G-BDOW	Cessna FRA.150M	J. E. & A. P. Heywood
	G-BDOY	Hughes 369HS	B. Wronski
	G-BDPA	PA-28-151 Warrior	Noon (Aircraft Leasing) Ltd/ Shoreham
	G-BDPB	Falconar F-II-3	N. M. Hitchman
	G-BDPC	Bede BD-5A	P. R. Cremer
	G-BDPF	Cessna F.172M	Semloh Aviation Services/Andrewsfield
	G-BDPK	Cameron O-56 balloon	K. J. & G. R. Ibbotson
	G-BDPL	Falconar F-II	W. C. Brown
	G-BDPV	Boeing 747-136	British Airways Blea Water/Heathrow
	G-BDRB	AA-5B Tiger	G-BDRB Group/Leeds
	G-BDRC	V.724 Viscount ★	Fire School/Manston
	G-BDRD	Cessna FRA.150M	Air Service Training Ltd/Perth
	G-BDRE	AA-1B Trainer	P. J. Webb/Elstree
	G-BDRF	Taylor JT.1 Monoplane	N. T. Walter
	G-BDRG	Taylor JT.2 Titch	D. R. Gray
	G-BDRJ	D.H.C.1 Chipmunk 22 (WP857)	J. C. Schooling
	G-BDRK	Cameron O-65 balloon	D. L. Smith Smirk
	G-BDRL	Stitts SA-3 Playboy	D. L. MacLean
	G-BDSB	PA-28-181 Archer II	Testair Ltd/Blackbushe
	G-BDSD	Evans VP-1	J. E. Worthington
	G-BDSE	Cameron O-77 balloon	British Airways Concorde
	G-BDSF	Cameron O-56 balloon	A. R. Greensides & B. H. Osbourne
	G-BDSH	PA-28 Cherokee 140	BCF Roofing Ltd
	G-BDSK	Cameron O-65 balloon	Southern Balloon Group Carousel II
	G-BDSL	Cessna F.150M	Cleveland Flying School Ltd/Tees-side
	G-BDSM	Slingsby Cadet III	D. W. Savage
	G-BDSN	Wassmer WA.52 Europa	Sierra November Group (G-BADN)

Reg.	Type	Owner or Operator	Notes
G-BDSO	Cameron O-31 balloon	Budget Rent-a-Car *Baby Budget*	
G-BDSP	Cessna U.206F Stationair	J. E. Leakey/Biggin Hill	
G-BDTB	Evans VP-1	A. Toomer	
G-BDTL	Evans VP-1	A. K. Lang	
G-BDTN	BN-2A Mk III-2 Trislander	Aurigny Air Services Ltd/Guernsey	
G-BDTU	Omega III gas balloon	Mrs K. E. Turnbull *Omega II*	
G-BDTV	Mooney M.20F	J. P. McDermott & ptnrs/Biggin Hill	
G-BDTW	Cassutt Racer	B. E. Smith & C. S. Thompson/Redhill	
G-BDTX	Cessna F.150M	A. A. & R. N. Croxford/Southend	
G-BDUI	Cameron V-56 balloon	D. C. Johnson	
G-BDUJ	PA-31-310 Turbo Navajo	Frantham Property Ltd	
G-BDUL	Evans VP-1	D. Beevers & ptnrs	
G-BDUM	Cessna F.150M	SFG Ltd/Shipdham	
G-BDUN	PA-34-200T Seneca II	Air Medical Ltd	
G-BDUO	Cessna F.150M	Sandown Aero Club	
G-BDUX	Slingsby T.31B motor glider	J. C. Anderson (*stored*)/Southend	
G-BDUY	Robin DR.400/140B	Wing Task Ltd/Seething	
G-BDUZ	Cameron V-56 balloon	Balloon Stable Ltd *Hot Lips*	
G-BDVA	PA-17 Vagabond	I. M. Callier	
G-BDVB	PA-15 (PA-17) Vagabond	B. P. Gardner	
G-BDVC	PA-17 Vagabond	A. R. Caveen	
G-BDVG	Thunder Ax6-56A balloon	R. F. Pollard *Argonaut*	
G-BDVS	F.27 Friendship Mk 200	Air UK Ltd/Norwich	
G-BDVU	Mooney M.20F	Uplands Video Ltd/Stapleford	
G-BDWA	SOCATA Rallye 150ST	H. Cowan/Newtownards	
G-BDWE	Flaglor Scooter	D. W. Evernden	
G-BDWG	BN-2A Islander	Wilsons Transport Ltd	
G-BDWH	SOCATA Rallye 150ST	M. A. Jones	
G-BDWJ	SE-5A replica (F8010)	S. M. Smith/Booker	
G-BDWK	Beech 95-B58 Baron	Cammac Coal Ltd	
G-BDWL	PA-25 Pawnee 235	J. E. F. Aviation	
G-BDWM	Mustang ⅔ scale replica	D. C. Bonsall	
G-BDWO	Howes Ax6 balloon	R. B. & Mrs C. Howes *Griffin*	
G-BDWP	PA-32R Cherokee Lance 300	Trendgreen Ltd/Conington	
G-BDWV	BN-2A Mk III-2 Trislander	Aurigny Air Services Ltd/Guernsey	
G-BDWX	Jodel D.120A	J. P. Lassey	
G-BDWY	PA-28 Cherokee 140	Cleveland Flying School/Teeside	
G-BDXA	Boeing 747-236B	British Airways *City of Peterborough*/Heathrow	
G-BDXB	Boeing 747-236B	British Airways *City of Liverpool*/Heathrow	
G-BDXC	Boeing 747-236B	British Airways *City of Manchester*/Heathrow	
G-BDXD	Boeing 747-236B	British Airways *City of Plymouth*/Heathrow	
G-BDXE	Boeing 747-236B	British Airways *City of Glasgow*/Heathrow	
G-BDXF	Boeing 747-236B	British Airways *City of York*/Heathrow	
G-BDXG	Boeing 747-236B	British Airways *City of Oxford*/Heathrow	
G-BDXH	Boeing 747-236B	British Airways *City of Elgin*/Heathrow	
G-BDXI	Boeing 747-236B	British Airways *City of Cambridge*/Heathrow	
G-BDXJ	Boeing 747-236B	British Airways *City of Birmingham*/Heathrow	
G-BDXK	Boeing 747-236B	British Airways *City of Canterbury*/Heathrow	
G-BDXL	Boeing 747-236B	British Airways *City of Winchester*/Heathrow	
G-BDXM	Boeing 747-236B	British Airways *City of Derby*/Heathrow	
G-BDXN	Boeing 747-236B	British Airways *City of Stoke on Trent*/Heathrow	
G-BDXO	Boeing 747-236B	British Airways *City of Bath*/Heathrow	
G-BDXP	Boeing 747-236B (SCD)	British Airways *City of Salisbury*/Heathrow	
G-BDXW	PA-28R Cherokee Arrow 200-II	Directflight Ltd	
G-BDXX	Nord NC.858S	S. F. Elvins	
G-BDXY	Auster AOP.9 (XR269)	B. A. Webster	
G-BDYC	AA-1B Trainer	N. F. Whisler	
G-BDYD	R. Commander 114	SRS Aviation	
G-BDYF	Cessna 421C	Nullifire Ltd/Coventry	
G-BDYG	P.56 Provost T.1 (WV493)	Museum of Flight/E. Fortune	
G-BDYH	Cameron V-56 balloon	B. J. Godding	

Notes	Reg.	Type	Owner or Operator
	G-BDYM	Skysales S-31 balloon	Miss A. I. Smith & M. J. Moore *Cheeky Devil*
	G-BDYZ	MBB Bo 105D	Bond Helicopters Ltd/Bourn
	G-BDZA	Scheibe SF.25E Super Falke	Norfolk Gliding Club Ltd/Tibenham
	G-BDZB	Cameron S-31 balloon	Kenning Motor Group Ltd *Kenning*
	G-BDZC	Cessna F.150M	Air Tows Ltd/Blackbushe
	G-BDZD	Cessna F.172M	M. T. Hodges/Blackbushe
	G-BDZF	G.164 Ag-Cat B	Miller Aerial Spraying Ltd/Wickenby
	G-BDZS	Scheibe SF.25E Super Falke	A. D. Gubbay/Panshanger
	G-BDZU	Cessna 421C	Page & Moy Ltd & ptnrs/Leicester
	G-BDZX	PA-28-151 Warrior	E. Shipley
	G-BDZY	Phoenix LA-4A Minor	P. J. Dalby
	G-BEAA	Taylor JT.1 Monoplane	R. C. Hobbs/Bembridge
	G-BEAB	Jodel DR.1051	C. Fitton
	G-BEAD	WG.13 Lynx ★	*Instructional airframe*/Middle Wallop
	G-BEAG	PA-34-200T Seneca II	C.S.E. Aviation Ltd/Kidlington
	G-BEAH	J/2 Arrow	W. J. & Mrs M. D. Horler
	G-BEAK	L-1011-385 TriStar	British Airways *Carmarthen Bay*
	G-BEAL	L-1011-385 TriStar	Caledonian Airways *Loch May*/Gatwick
	G-BEAM	L-1011-385 TriStar	British Airways *Swansea Bay*
	G-BEAU	Pazmany PL.4A	B. H. R. Smith
	G-BEBC	WS.55 Whirlwind 3 (XP355) ★	Norwich Aviation Museum
	G-BEBE	AA-5A Cheetah	Biblio Graphic Ltd/Booker
	G-BEBF	Auster AOP.9	M. D. N. & Mrs A. C. Fisher
	G-BEBG	WSK-PZL SDZ-45A Ogar	The Ogar Syndicate
	G-BEBI	Cessna F.172M	Calder Equipment Ltd/Hatfield
	G-BEBL	Douglas DC-10-30	British Airways *Forest of Dean*/Gatwick
	G-BEBM	Douglas DC-10-30	British Airways *Sherwood Forest*/Gatwick
	G-BEBN	Cessna 177B	M. A. Berriman
	G-BEBO	Turner TSW-2 Wot	The Turner Special Flying Group
	G-BEBR	GY-201 Minicab	A. S. Jones & D. R. Upton
	G-BEBS	Andreasson BA-4B	J. H. Boulton
	G-BEBT	Andreasson BA-4B	A. Horsfall
	G-BEBU	R. Commander 112A	M. Rowland & J. K. Woodford
	G-BEBZ	PA-28-151 Warrior	Goodwood Terrena Ltd/Goodwood
	G-BECA	SOCATA Rallye 100ST	J. M. Gale/Exeter
	G-BECB	SOCATA Rallye 100ST	A. J. Trible
	G-BECC	SOCATA Rallye 150ST	Lapwing Flying Group Ltd/Denham
	G-BECD	SOCATA Rallye 150ST	A. J. Liddle
	G-BECF	Scheibe SF.25A Falke	D. A. Wilson & ptnrs
	G-BECG	Boeing 737-204ADV	Britannia Airways Ltd *Amy Johnson*/Luton
	G-BECH	Boeing 737-204ADV	Britannia Airways Ltd *Viscount Montgomery of Alamein*/Luton
	G-BECJ	Partenavia P.68B	Hereford Parachute Club Ltd/Shobdon
	G-BECK	Cameron V-56 balloon	D. W. Allum
	G-BECN	Piper J-3C-65 Cub (480480)	Harvest Air Ltd/Ipswich
	G-BECO	Beech A.36 Bonanza	Thorney Machinery Co Ltd
	G-BECT	C.A.S.A.1.131 Jungmann	Rendermere Ltd/Shoreham
	G-BECW	C.A.S.A.1.131 Jungmann	N. C. Jensen/Redhill
	G-BECZ	CAARP CAP.10B	Aerobatic Associates Ltd
	G-BEDA	C.A.S.A.1.131 Jungmann	M. G. Kates & D. J. Berry
	G-BEDB	Nord 1203 Norecrin	B. F. G. Lister
	G-BEDD	Jodel D.117A	A. T. Croy/Kirkwall
	G-BEDE	Bede BD-5A	Biggin Hill BD5 Syndicate
	G-BEDF	Boeing B-17G-105-VE (485784)	B-17 Preservation Ltd/Duxford
	G-BEDG	R. Commander 112A	L. E. Blackburn
	G-BEDJ	Piper J-3C-65 Cub (44-80594)	D. J. Elliott
	G-BEDL	Cessna T.337D	Wilford Aviation Ltd
	G-BEDV	V.668 Varsity T.1 (WJ945) ★	D. S. Selway/Duxford
	G-BEDZ	BN-2A Islander	Loganair Ltd/Glasgow
	G-BEEE	Thunder Ax6-56A balloon	I. R. M. Jacobs *Avia*
	G-BEEG	BN-2A Islander	D. W. Higgins
	G-BEEH	Cameron V-56 balloon	B. & N. V. Moreton
	G-BEEI	Cameron N-77 balloon	Hedgehoppers Balloon Group
	G-BEEJ	Cameron O-77 balloon	DAL (Builders Merchants) Ltd *Dal's Pal*
	G-BEEL	Enstrom 280C-UK-2 Shark	K. E. Wills
	G-BEEO	Short SD3-30	Fairflight Ltd/Biggin Hill
	G-BEEP	Thunder Ax5-42 balloon	Mrs B. C. Faithful/Holland

Reg.	Type	Owner or Operator	Notes
G-BEER	Isaacs Fury II	J. C. Lister	
G-BEEU	PA-28 Cherokee 140E	Berkshire Aviation Services Ltd	
G-BEEV	PA-28 Cherokee 140E	V. M. Lambeth/Dunkeswell	
G-BEEW	Taylor JT.1 Monoplane	K. Wigglesworth/Breighton	
G-BEFA	PA-28-151 Warrior	Firmbeam Ltd/Booker	
G-BEFC	AA-5B Tiger	Portway Aviation/Shobdon	
G-BEFF	PA-28 Cherokee 140	Sherwood Flying Club Ltd/Tollerton	
G-BEFP	BN-2A Mk III-2 Trislander	Kondair/Stansted	
G-BEFR	Fokker DR.1 Replica (425/17)	R. A. Bowes & P. A. Crawford	
G-BEFT	Cessna 421C	Specialist Flying Training Ltd/Carlisle	
G-BEFV	Evans VP-2	Yeadon Aeroplane Group	
G-BEFY	Hiller UH-12E	Wells (PF) Ltd	
G-BEGA	Westland-Bell 47G-3B1	Durlime Ltd/Glasgow	
G-BEGG	Scheibe SF.25E Super Falke	R. Culley & ptnrs	
G-BEGV	PA-23 Aztec 250F	Lanacre Ltd/Coventry	
G-BEHG	AB-206B JetRanger 2	Compass Helicopters/Bristol	
G-BEHH	PA-32R Cherokee Lance 300	SMK Engineering Ltd/Leeds	
G-BEHJ	Evans VP-1	K. Heath	
G-BEHK	Agusta-Bell 47G-3B1 (Soloy)	Dollar Air Services Ltd/Coventry	
G-BEHM	Taylor JT.1 Monoplane	H. McGovern	
G-BEHN	Westland-Bell 47G-3B1 (Soloy)	Dollar Air Services Ltd/Coventry	
G-BEHS	PA-25 Pawnee 260C	Sussex AG/Shoreham	
G-BEHU	PA-34-200T Seneca II	Appleby Glade Ltd	
G-BEHV	Cessna F.172N	P. P. D. Howard-Johnston/Edinburgh	
G-BEHW	Cessna F.150M	Westair Flying Services Ltd/Blackpool	
G-BEHX	Evans VP-2	G. S Adams	
G-BEIA	Cessna FRA.150M	Air Service Training Ltd/Perth	
G-BEIB	Cessna F.172N	R. L. Orsborn & Son Ltd/Sywell	
G-BEIC	Sikorsky S-61N	British International Helicopters Ltd/ Aberdeen	
G-BEIE	Evans VP-2	F. G. Morris	
G-BEIF	Cameron O-65 balloon	C. Vening	
G-BEIG	Cessna F.150M	C. W. & S. A. Burman	
G-BEIH	PA-25 Pawnee 235D	MPW Aviation Ltd	
G-BEII	PA-25 Pawnee 235D	Burn Gliding Club Ltd	
G-BEIL	SOCATA Rallye 150T	The Rallye Flying Group	
G-BEIP	PA-28-181 Archer II	M. Ferguson Ltd/Newtownards	
G-BEIS	Evans VP-1	G. G. Bigwood	
G-BEIZ	Cessna 500 Citation	Solid State Logic Ltd	
G-BEJA	Thunder Ax6-56A balloon	P. A. Hutchins *Jackson*	
G-BEJB	Thunder Ax6-56A balloon	International Distillers & Vinters Ltd	
G-BEJD	H.S.748 Srs 1	Dan-Air Services Ltd/Gatwick	
G-BEJE	H.S.748 Srs 1	Dan-Air Services Ltd/Gatwick	
G-BEJK	Cameron S-31 balloon	Rango Balloon & Kite Co	
G-BEJL	Sikorsky S-61N	British International Helicopters Ltd/ Aberdeen	
G-BEJM	BAC One-Eleven 423	Ford Motor Co Ltd/Stansted	
G-BEJP	D.H.C.6 Twin Otter 310	Loganair Ltd/Glasgow	
G-BEJV	PA-34-200T Seneca II	C.S.E. Aviation Ltd/Kidlington	
G-BEJW	BAC One-Eleven 423	Ford Motor Co Ltd/Stansted	
G-BEKA	BAC One-Eleven 520	Dan-Air Services Ltd/Gatwick	
G-BEKC	H.S.748 Srs 1	Dan-Air Services Ltd/Gatwick	
G-BEKE	H.S.748 Srs 1	Dan-Air Services Ltd/Gatwick	
G-BEKG	H.S.748 Srs 1	Air Atlantique/Euroair (G-VAJK)	
G-BEKL	Bede BD-4E	H. B. Carter	
G-BEKM	Evans VP-1	G. J. McDill/Glenrothes	
G-BEKN	Cessna FRA.150M	RFC (Bourn) Ltd	
G-BEKO	Cessna F.182Q	Tyler International	
G-BEKR	Rand KR-2	A. N. Purchase	
G-BELF	BN-2A Islander	Atlantic Air Transport Ltd/Coventry	
G-BELP	PA-28-151 Warrior	Coventry Civil Aviation Ltd	
G-BELR	PA-28 Cherokee 140	H. M. Clarke	
G-BELT	Cessna F.150J	Yorkshire Light Aircraft Ltd (G-AWUV)/ Leeds	
G-BELX	Cameron V-56 balloon	R. J. O. Evans	
G-BEMB	Cessna F.172M	P. B. Hollands Associates Ltd	
G-BEMD	Beech 95-B55 Baron	Vaux (Aviation) Ltd/Newcastle	
G-BEMM	Slingsby T.31B Motor Cadet	M. N. Martin	
G-BEMR	BN-2A-26 Islander	W. Midlands Police/Birmingham	
G-BEMU	Thunder Ax5-42 balloon	P. W. Limpus & ptnrs	
G-BEMW	PA-28-181 Archer II	Charta Furniture Ltd/Goodwood	
G-BEMY	Cessna FRA.150M	L. G. Sawyer/Blackbushe	
G-BEND	Cameron V-56 balloon	Dante Balloon Group *Le Billet*	
G-BENJ	R. Commander 112B	F. T. Arnold	

Notes	Reg.	Type	Owner or Operator
	G-BENK	Cessna F.172M	Graham Churchill Plant Ltd
	G-BENN	Cameron V-56 balloon	S. H. Budd
	G-BENO	Enstrom 280C-UK Shark	Red Baron Property Ltd/Shoreham
	G-BENT	Cameron N-77 balloon	N. Tasker
	G-BEOD	Cessna 180	M. E. Mortlock
	G-BEOE	Cessna FRA.150M	J. R. Nicholls/Sibson
	G-BEOH	PA-28R-201T Turbo Arrow III	Larksfell Ltd
	G-BEOI	PA-18 Super Cub 150	Southdown Gliding Club Ltd
	G-BEOK	Cessna F.150M	Seawing Flying Club Ltd/Southend
	G-BEOO	Sikorsky S-61N Mk. II	British International Helicopters Ltd
	G-BEOT	PA-25 Pawnee 235D	Moonraker Aviation Ltd/Thruxton
	G-BEOX	L-414 Hudson IV (A16-199) ★	RAF Museum/Hendon
	G-BEOY	Cessna FRA.150L	SM Reprographics Ltd/Elstree
	G-BEOZ	A.W.650 Argosy 101 ★	Aeropark/E. Midlands
	G-BEPB	Pereira Osprey II	J. J. & A. J. C. Zwetsloot
	G-BEPC	SNCAN SV-4-C	B. L. Procter/Dunkeswell
	G-BEPD	SA.102.5 Cavalier	P. & Mrs E. A. Donaldson
	G-BEPE	SC.5 Belfast	HeavyLift Cargo Airlines Ltd (G-ASKE) *(withdrawn)*/Southend
	G-BEPF	SNCAN SV-4A	L. J. Rice
	G-BEPH	BN-2A Mk III-2 Trislander	Aurigny Air Services Ltd/Guernsey
	G-BEPI	BN-2A Mk III-2 Trislander	Aurigny Air Services Ltd/Guernsey
	G-BEPO	Cameron N-77 balloon	G. Camplin & V. Aitken
	G-BEPS	SC.5 Belfast	HeavyLift Cargo Airlines Ltd/Stansted
	G-BEPV	Fokker S.11-1 Instructor	Strathallan Aircraft Collection
	G-BEPY	R. Commander 112B	W. Ewington & Co Ltd
	G-BEPZ	Cameron D-96 hot-air airship	D. W. Liddiard
	G-BERA	SOCATA Rallye 150ST	Surrey & Kent Flying Club (1982) Ltd/ Biggin Hill
	G-BERC	SOCATA Rallye 150ST	Severn Valley Aero Group
	G-BERD	Thunder Ax6-56A balloon	M. J. Betts
	G-BERF	Bell 212	Bristow Helicopters Ltd
	G-BERI	R. Commander 114	K. B. Harper/Blackbushe
	G-BERN	Saffrey S-330 balloon	B. Martin *Beeze*
	G-BERT	Cameron V-56 balloon	Southern Balloon Group *Bert*
	G-BERW	R. Commander 114	C. D. Allison
	G-BERY	AA-1B Trainer	R. H. J. Levi
	G-BESO	BN-2A Islander	Cranfield Aeronautical Services Ltd
	G-BESS	Hughes 369D	Flourishbest Ltd/Booker
	G-BETD	Robin HR.200/100	R. A. Parsons/Bourn
	G-BETE	Rollason B.2A Beta	T. M. Jones/Tatenhill
	G-BETF	Cameron 'Champion' balloon	Balloon Stable Ltd *Champion*
	G-BETG	Cessna 180K Skywagon	T. P. A. Norman/Panshanger
	G-BETI	Pitts S-1D Special	P. Metcalfe/Tees-side
	G-BETL	PA-25 Pawnee 235D	Crop Aviation (UK) Ltd/Wyberton
	G-BETM	PA-25 Pawnee 235D	Crop Aviation (UK) Ltd/Wyberton
	G-BETO	M.S.885 Super Rallye	R. Andrews
	G-BETP	Cameron O-65 balloon	J. R. Rix & Sons Ltd
	G-BETT	PA-34-200 Seneca II	Andrews Professional Colour Laboratories Ltd/Headcorn
	G-BETV	HS.125 Srs 600B	Rolls-Royce PLC/Filton
	G-BETW	Rand KR-2	T. A. Wiffen
	G-BEUA	PA-18 Super Cub 150	London Gliding Club (Pty) Ltd/ Dunstable
	G-BEUD	Robin HR.100/285R	E. A. & L. M. C. Payton/Cranfield
	G-BEUI	Piper J-3C-65 Cub	M. J. Whatley
	G-BEUK	Fuji FA.200-160	Dolphin Property (Management) Ltd
	G-BEUL	Beech 95-58 Baron	Basic Metal Co Ltd/Leavesden
	G-BEUM	Taylor JT.1 Monoplane	M. T. Taylor
	G-BEUN	Cassutt Racer IIIm	R. S. Voice/Redhill
	G-BEUP	Robin DR.400/180	A. V. Pound & Co Ltd
	G-BEUR	Cessna F.172M	B. V. Ruckstuhl
	G-BEUS	SNCAN SV-4C	G-BEUS Flying Group/Sibson
	G-BEUU	PA-18 Super Cub 95	F. Sharples/Sandown
	G-BEUV	Thunder Ax6-56A balloon	Silhouette Balloon Group
	G-BEUX	Cessna F.172N	Light Planes (Lancashire) Ltd/Barton
	G-BEUY	Cameron N-31 balloon	Southern Balloon Group
	G-BEVA	SOCATA Rallye 150ST	The Rallye Group
	G-BEVB	SOCATA Rallye 150ST	R. B. Tope & C. M. Blanchard
	G-BEVC	SOCATA Rallye 150ST	B. W. Walpole
	G-BEVG	PA-34-200T-2 Seneca	M. Smart
	G-BEVI	Thunder Ax7-77A balloon	The Painted Clouds Balloon Co Ltd
	G-BEVO	Sportavia-Pützer RF-5	T. Barlow
	G-BEVP	Evans VP-2	B. W. Webb

Reg.	Type	Owner or Operator	Notes
G-BEVS	Taylor JT.1 Monoplane	D. Hunter	
G-BEVT	BN-2A Mk III-2 Trislander	Aurigny Air Services Ltd/Guernsey	
G-BEVW	SOCATA Rallye 150ST	P. C. Goodwin	
G-BEWJ	Westland-Bell 47G-3B1	E. J. Mackelden	
G-BEWL	Sikorsky S-61N Mk II	British International Helicopters Ltd/ Aberdeen	
G-BEWM	Sikorsky S-61N Mk II	British International Helicopters Ltd	
G-BEWN	D.H.82A Tiger Moth	H. D. Labouchere	
G-BEWO	Zlin Z.326 Trener Master	Nimrod Group Ltd/Staverton	
G-BEWR	Cessna F.172N	Cheshire Air Training School Ltd/ Liverpool	
G-BEWX	PA-28R-201 Arrow III	A. Vickers	
G-BEXK	PA-25 Pawnee 235D	Howard Avis (Aviation) Ltd	
G-BEXN	AA-1C Lynx	Scotia Safari Ltd/Prestwick	
G-BEXO	PA-23 Apache 160	B. Burton/Bournemouth	
G-BEXR	Mudry/CAARP CAP-10B	R. P. Lewis/Booker	
G-BEXS	Cessna F.150M	Firecrest Aviation Ltd	
G-BEXW	PA-28-181 Archer II	P. F. Larkins	
G-BEXX	Cameron V-56 balloon	K. A. Schlussler	
G-BEXY	PA-28 Cherokee 140	Hillvine Ltd/Staverton	
G-BEXZ	Cameron N-56 balloon	D. C. Eager & G. C. Clark	
G-BEYA	Enstrom 280C Shark	Freshmay Ltd	
G-BEYB	Fairey Flycatcher (replica) (S1287)	John S. Fairey/Yeovilton	
G-BEYD	HPR-7 Herald 401	*Stored*/Southend	
G-BEYF	HPR-7 Herald 401	Channel Express Ltd/Bournemouth	
G-BEYK	HPR-7 Herald 401	British Air Ferries Ltd/Southend	
G-BEYL	PA-28 Cherokee 180	B. G. & G. Airlines Ltd/Jersey	
G-BEYN	Evans VP-2	C. D. Denham	
G-BEYO	PA-28 Cherokee 140	Solid State Logic Ltd/Kidlington	
G-BEYP	Fuji FA.200-180AO	A. C. Pritchard/Booker	
G-BEYV	Cessna T.210M	Valley Motors/Bournemouth	
G-BEYW	Taylor JT.1 Monoplane	R. A. Abrahams/Barton	
G-BEYY	PA-31 Turbo Navajo	Essex Leasing/Stansted	
G-BEYZ	Jodel DR.1051/M1	M. J. McCarthy & S. Aarons/ Biggin Hill	
G-BEZA	Zlin Z.226T Trener	L. Bezak	
G-BEZC	AA-5 Traveler	M. G. E. Hutton	
G-BEZE	Rutan Vari-Eze	J. Berry	
G-BEZF	AA-5 Traveler	KAL Aviation/Denham	
G-BEZG	AA-5 Traveler	B. A. & P. G. Osburn/Biggin Hill	
G-BEZH	AA-5 Traveler	H. & L. Sims Ltd	
G-BEZI	AA-5 Traveler	BEZI Flying Group/Cranfield	
G-BEZJ	MBB Bo 105D	Bond Helicopters Ltd/Bourn	
G-BEZK	Cessna F.172H	Zulu Kilo Flying Group	
G-BEZL	PA-31-310 Turbo Navajo C	Shopfitters (Lancashire) Ltd	
G-BEZO	Cessna F.172M	Staverton Flying Services Ltd	
G-BEZP	PA-32 Cherokee Six 300D	Falcon Styles Ltd/Booker	
G-BEZR	Cessna F.172M	Kirmington Aviation Ltd	
G-BEZS	Cessna FR.172J	R. E. Beeton & M. R. Cavinder	
G-BEZV	Cessna F.172M	Aberdeen Dairies Distribution Ltd	
G-BEZY	Rutan Vari-Eze	R. J. Jones	
G-BEZZ	Jodel D.112	G-BEZZ Jodel Group	
G-BFAA	GY-80 Horizon 160	Mary Poppins Ltd	
G-BFAB	Cameron N-56 balloon	Phonogram Ltd *Phonogram* Southend	
G-BFAC	Cessna F.177RG	J. J. Baumhardt/Southend	
G-BFAF	Aeronca 7BCM (7797)	D. C. W. Harper/Finmere	
G-BFAH	Phoenix Currie Wot	J. F. Dowe	
G-BFAI	R. Commander 114	D. S. Innes/Guernsey	
G-BFAK	M.S.892A Rallye Commodore 150	M. C. Aireton/Alderney	
G-BFAM	PA-31P Pressurised Navajo	Video Unlimited Motion Pictures	
G-BFAN	H.S.125 Srs 600F	British Aerospace (G-AZHS)/Hatfield	
G-BFAO	PA-20 Pacer 135	J. Day & ptnrs/Goodwood	
G-BFAP	SIAI-Marchetti S.205-20R	A. O. Broin	
G-BFAR	Cessna 500-1 Citation	Club Air (Europe) Ltd	
G-BFAS	Evans VP-1	A. I. Sutherland	
G-BFAW	D.H.C.1 Chipmunk 22	R. V. Bowles	
G-BFAX	D.H.C.1 Chipmunk 22 (WG422)	B. Earl/Biggin Hill	
G-BFBA	Jodel DR.100A	A. Brown & R. Wood	
G-BFBB	PA-23 Aztec 250E	Dollar Air Services Ltd/Coventry	

Notes	Reg.	Type	Owner or Operator
	G-BFBC	Taylor JT.1 Monoplane	D. Oxenham
	G-BFBD	Partenavia P.68B	Calmsafe Ltd
	G-BFBE	Robin HR.200/100	Charles Major Ltd/Blackpool
	G-BFBF	PA-28 Cherokee 140	F. R. Montgomery/Newtownards
	G-BFBM	Saffery S.330 balloon	B. Martin *Beeze II*
	G-BFBR	PA-28-161 Warrior II	Lowery Holdings Ltd/Fairoaks
	G-BFBU	Partenavia P.68B	W. Holmes & Son Ltd
	G-BFBV	Brügger M.B.2 Colibri	J. C. Lister
	G-BFBW	PA-25 Pawnee 235D	Scanrho Aviation
	G-BFBX	PA-25 Pawnee 235D	Oglesby Aviation Ltd/Bardney
	G-BFBY	Piper J-3C-65 Cub	L. W. Usherwood
	G-BFCT	Cessna TU.206F	Cecil Aviation Ltd/Cambridge
	G-BFCX	BN-2A Islander	Loganair Ltd/Glasgow
	G-BFCZ	Sopwith Camel (B7270) ★	FAA Museum/Yeovilton
	G-BFDA	PA-31-350 Navajo Chieftain	Streamline Aviation/E. Midlands
	G-BFDC	D.H.C.1 Chipmunk 22	N. F. O'Neill/Newtownards
	G-BFDE	Sopwith Tabloid (replica) (168) ★	Bomber Command Museum/Hendon
	G-BFDF	SOCATA Rallye 235E	J. H. Atkinson/Skegness
	G-BFDG	PA-28R-201T Turbo-Arrow III	Lantry Manor Hotels Ltd
	G-BFDI	PA-28-181 Archer II	Truman Aviation Ltd/Tollerton
	G-BFDL	Piper J-3C-65 Cub (454537)	K. A. Davies & N. C. Burman
	G-BFDM	Jodel D.120	Worcestershire Gliding Ltd
	G-BFDN	PA-31-350 Navajo Chieftain	Subtec Aviation Ltd
	G-BFDO	PA-28R-201T Turbo Arrow III	Grangewood Press Ltd
	G-BFDZ	Taylor JT.1 Monoplane	H. R. Leefe
	G-BFEB	Jodel D.150	D. Aldersea & ptnrs/Sherburn
	G-BFEC	PA-23 Aztec 250F	Techspan Aviation Ltd/Cambridge
	G-BFEE	Beech 95-E55 Baron	Interair (Aviation) Ltd/Bournemouth
	G-BFEF	Agusta-Bell 47G-3B1	Dollar Air Services Ltd/Coventry
	G-BFEH	Jodel D.117A	C. V. & S. J. Philpott
	G-BFEI	Westland-Bell 47G-3B1	Trent Air Services Ltd/Cranfield
	G-BFEK	Cessna F.152	Staverton Flying Services Ltd
	G-BFER	Bell 212	Bristow Helicopters Ltd
	G-BFEV	PA-25 Pawnee 235	Bowker Aircraft Services Ltd/ Rush Green
	G-BFEW	PA-25 Pawnee 235	Scanrho Aviation
	G-BFEX	PA-25 Pawnee 235	CKS Air Ltd/Southend
	G-BFEY	PA-25 Pawnee 235	Howard Avis Aviation Ltd
	G-BFFB	Evans VP-2	D. Bradley
	G-BFFC	Cessna F.152-II	Yorkshire Flying Services Ltd/Leeds
	G-BFFE	Cessna F.152-II	Doncaster Aero Club
	G-BFFG	Beech 95-B55 Baron	Beaucette Holdings Ltd
	G-BFFJ	Sikorsky S-61N Mk II	British International Helicopters Ltd/ Aberdeen
	G-BFFK	Sikorsky S-61N Mk II	British International Helicopters Ltd/ Aberdeen
	G-BFFP	PA-18 Super Cub 150	Booker Gliding Club Ltd
	G-BFFT	Cameron V-56 balloon	R. I. M. Kerr & D. C. Boxall
	G-BFFW	Cessna F.152	Midland Aircraft Leasing Ltd
	G-BFFY	Cessna F.150M	DJH Aviation Ltd/Biggin Hill
	G-BFFZ	Cessna FR.172 Hawk XP	Goodwood Terrena Ltd
	G-BFGD	Cessna F.172N-II	George Cross Services Ltd
	G-BFGF	Cessna F.177RG	Victree (V.M.) Ltd/Birmingham
	G-BFGG	Cessna FRA.150M	Air Service Training Ltd/Perth
	G-BFGH	Cessna F.337G	T. Perkins/Leeds
	G-BFGK	Jodel D.117	B. F. J. Hope
	G-BFGL	Cessna FA.152	Yorkshire Flying Services Ltd/Leeds
	G-BFGO	Fuji FA.200-160	Gt Consall Copper Mine Co Ltd
	G-BFGP	D.H.C.6 Twin Otter 310	National Airways/Southend
	G-BFGS	M.S.893E Rallye 180GT	K. M. & H. Bowen
	G-BFGW	Cessna F.150H	J. F. Morgan
	G-BFGX	Cessna FRA.150M	Air Service Training Ltd/Perth
	G-BFGZ	Cessna FRA.150M	Air Service Training Ltd/Perth
	G-BFHF	C.A.S.A. C.352L (N7+AA)	Junkers Ju.52/3m Flight Ltd
	G-BFHG	C.A.S.A. C.352L	Aces High Ltd/North Weald
	G-BFHH	D.H.82A Tiger Moth	P. Harrison & M. J. Gambrell/Redhill
	G-BFHI	Piper J-3C-65 Cub	J. M. Robinson
	G-BFHK	Cessna F.177RG-II	Facet Group Holdings Ltd/Southend
	G-BFHM	Steen Skybolt	R. F. Fisher & ptnrs
	G-BFHN	Scheibe SF.25E Super Falke	Booker Gliding Club Ltd
	G-BFHP	Champion 7GCAA Citabria	Rushett Flying Group/Redhill
	G-BFHR	Jodel DR.220/2+2	R. F. Huggett/Sibson
	G-BFHS	AA-5B Tiger	P. H. Johnson

Reg.	Type	Owner or Operator	Notes
G-BFHT	Cessna F.152-II	Riger Ltd/Luton	
G-BFHU	Cessna F.152-II	Deltair Ltd	
G-BFHV	Cessna F.152-II	Angelsword Ltd/Halfpenny Green	
G-BFHX	Evans VP-1	P. Johnson	
G-BFIB	PA-31 Turbo Navajo	Mann Aviation Ltd/Fairoaks	
G-BFID	Taylor JT.2 Titch Mk III	B. O. Smith	
G-BFIE	Cessna FRA.150M	RFC (Bourn) Ltd	
G-BFIF	Cessna FR.172K XPII	Michael Gardner Ltd	
G-BFIG	Cessna FR.172K XPII	Tenair Ltd	
G-BFIJ	AA-5A Cheetah	J. H. Wise/Redhill	
G-BFIN	AA-5A Cheetah	I. W. Lewis & ptnrs	
G-BFIP	Wallbro Monoplane 1909 replica	K. H. Wallis/Swanton Morley	
G-BFIR	Avro 652A Anson 21 (WD413)	G. M. K. Fraser/Bournemouth	
G-BFIT	Thunder Ax6-56Z balloon	J. A. G. Tyson	
G-BFIU	Cessna FR.172K XP	R. J. Weight	
G-BFIV	Cessna F.177RG	Kingfishair Ltd/Blackbushe	
G-BFIX	Thunder Ax7-77A balloon	E. Sowden Ltd	
G-BFJA	AA-5B Tiger	Sentry Courier Ltd/Blackbushe	
G-BFJH	SA.102-5 Cavalier	B. F. J. Hope	
G-BFJI	Robin HR.100/250	M. A. Egerton	
G-BFJJ	Evans VP-1	P. R. Pykett & B. J. Dyke/Thruxton	
G-BFJK	PA-23 Aztec 250F	R. Marsden	
G-BFJM	Cessna F.152	Tayside Aviation Ltd/Dundee	
G-BFJN	Westland-Bell 47G-3B1	Howden Helicopters	
G-BFJP	G.164B Ag-Cat	E. S. Axford/Nairobi	
G-BFJR	Cessna F.337G	C. J. Harling/Cranfield	
G-BFJV	Cessna F.172H	Southport & Merseyside Aero Club Ltd	
G-BFJW	AB-206B JetRanger	Autobase Rotary Ltd	
G-BFJZ	Robin DR.400/140B	Forge House Restaurant Ltd/Biggin Hill	
G-BFKA	Cessna F.172N	D. J. A. Seagram	
G-BFKB	Cessna F.172N	D. J. Allen	
G-BFKC	Rand KR.2	L. H. S. Stephens & I. S. Hewitt	
G-BFKD	R. Commander 114B	C. W. Ford/Guernsey	
G-BFKF	Cessna FA.152	Klingair Ltd/Conington	
G-BFKG	Cessna F.152	W. R. C. Foyle/Luton	
G-BFKH	Cessna F.152	T. G. Aviation Ltd/Manston	
G-BFKL	Cameron N-56 balloon	Merrythought Toys Ltd *Merrythought*	
G-BFKV	PA-25 Pawnee 235D	Moonraker Aviation Co Ltd/Thruxton	
G-BFKY	PA-34-200 Seneca II	S.L.H. Construction Ltd/Biggin Hill	
G-BFLH	PA-34-200T Seneca II	C.S.E. Aviation Ltd/Kidlington	
G-BFLI	PA-28R-201T Turbo Arrow III	Peter Walker (Heritage) Ltd	
G-BFLK	Cessna F.152	Falcon Flying Services/Biggin Hill	
G-BFLL	H.S.748 Srs 2A	Dan-Air Services Ltd/Gatwick	
G-BFLM	Cessna 150M	Cornwall Flying Club Ltd/Bodmin	
G-BFLN	Cessna 150M	Sherburn Aero Club Ltd	
G-BFLO	Cessna F.172M	W. A. Cook & ptnrs/Sherburn	
G-BFLP	Amethyst Ax6 balloon	K. J. Hendry *Amethyst*	
G-BFLU	Cessna F.152	Inverness Flying Services Ltd	
G-BFLV	Cessna F.172N	Cheshire Air Training School (Merseyside) Ltd)/Liverpool	
G-BFLX	AA-5A Cheetah	Abraxas Aviation Ltd/Denham	
G-BFLZ	Beech 95-A55 Baron	K. K. Demel Ltd/Kidlington	
G-BFMC	BAC One-Eleven 414	Ford Motor Co Ltd/Stansted	
G-BFME	Cameron V-56 balloon	Warwick Balloons Ltd	
G-BFMF	Cassutt Racer Mk IIIM	P. H. Lewis	
G-BFMG	PA-28-161 Warrior II	Bailey Aviation Ltd	
G-BFMH	Cessna 177B	Span Aviation	
G-BFMK	Cessna FA.152	RAF Halton Aeroplane Club Ltd	
G-BFMM	PA-28-181 Archer II	Bristol & Wessex Aeroplane Club Ltd/Bristol	
G-BFMR	PA-20 Pacer 125	B. C. & J. I. Cooper	
G-BFMX	Cessna F.172N	Colton Aviation Aero Spraying Ltd	
G-BFMY	Sikorsky S-61N	Bristow Helicopters Ltd	
G-BFMZ	Payne Ax6 balloon	G. F. Payne	
G-BFNC	AS.350B Ecureuil	Dollar Air Services Ltd/Coventry	
G-BFNG	Jodel D.112	M. Lomax/Booker	
G-BFNH	Cameron V-77 balloon	R. T. Revel	
G-BFNI	PA-28-161 Warrior II	C.S.E. Aviation Ltd/Kidlington	
G-BFNJ	PA-28-161 Warrior II	C.S.E. Aviation Ltd/Kidlington	
G-BFNK	PA-28-161 Warrior II	C.S.E. Aviation Ltd/Kidlington	
G-BFNM	Globe GC.1 Swift	Nottingham Flying Group/Tatenhill	
G-BFNU	BN-2B Islander	Isle of Scilly Sky Bus Ltd/St Just	
G-BFOD	Cessna F.182Q	Kington Productions Ltd	

Notes	Reg.	Type	Owner or Operator
	G-BFOE	Cessna F.152	B. W. Wells & Burbage Farms Ltd
	G-BFOF	Cessna F.152	Staverton Flying School Ltd
	G-BFOG	Cessna 150M	D. E. Tisdale
	G-BFOJ	AA-1 Yankee	A. J. Morton/Bournemouth
	G-BFOL	Beech 200 Super King Air	Bristow Helicopters Ltd
	G-BFOM	PA-31-325 Turbo Navajo C	Paramount Airways Ltd/Cardiff
	G-BFOP	Jodel D.120	R. J. Wesley & G. D. Western/Ipswich
	G-BFOS	Thunder Ax6-56A balloon	N. T. Petty
	G-BFOU	Taylor JT.1 Monoplane	G. Bee
	G-BFOV	Cessna F.172N	Gooda Walker Ltd/Shoreham
	G-BFOX	D.H.83 Fox Moth Replica	R. K. J. Hadlow
	G-BFOZ	Thunder Ax6-56 balloon	R. L. Harbord
	G-BFPA	Scheibe SF.25B Super Falke	Yorkshire Gliding Club (Pty) Ltd
	G-BFPB	AA-5B Tiger	Guernsey Aero Club
	G-BFPF	Sikorsky S-61N	Bristow Helicopters Ltd
	G-BFPH	Cessna F.172K	J. M. Reid
	G-BFPJ	Procter Petrel	S. G. Craggs
	G-BFPL	Fokker D.VII Replica (4253/18)	The Old Flying Machine Co Ltd/Duxford
	G-BFPM	Cessna F.172M	N. R. Havercroft
	G-BFPO	R. Commander 112B	J. G. Hale Ltd
	G-BFPP	Bell 47J-2	D. Fordham
	G-BFPS	PA-25 Pawnee 235D	Cranfield Aeronautical Services Ltd
	G-BFPX	Taylor JT.1 Monoplane	E. A. Taylor
	G-BFPZ	Cessna F.177RG	S. R. Cherry-Downes
	G-BFRA	R. Commander 114	Sabre Engines Ltd/Bournemouth
	G-BFRD	Bowers Flybaby 1A	F. R. Donaldson
	G-BFRF	Taylor JT.1 Monoplane	E. R. Bailey
	G-BFRI	Sikorsky S-61N	Bristow Helicopters Ltd
	G-BFRL	Cessna F.152	J. J. Baumhardt/Southend
	G-BFRM	Cessna 550 Citation II	Marshall of Cambridge (Engineering) Ltd
	G-BFRO	Cessna F.150M	Skyviews & General Ltd/Carlisle
	G-BFRR	Cessna FRA.150M	Interair Aviation Ltd/Bournemouth
	G-BFRS	Cessna F.172N	Poplar Toys Ltd
	G-BFRT	Cessna FR.172K XP II	B. J. Sharpe/Booker
	G-BFRV	Cessna FA.152	Rogers Aviation Ltd/Cranfield
	G-BFRX	PA-25 Pawnee 260	Yorkshire Gliding Club (Pty) Ltd
	G-BFRY	PA-25 Pawnee 260	C. J. Pearce
	G-BFSA	Cessna F.182Q	Clark Masts Ltd/Sandown
	G-BFSB	Cessna F.152	Seal Executive Aircraft Ltd/E. Midlands
	G-BFSC	PA-25 Pawnee 235D	Farm Aviation Services Ltd/Enstone
	G-BFSD	PA-25 Pawnee 235D	A. W. Evans
	G-BFSK	PA-23 Apache 160 ★	Oxford Air Training School/Kidlington
	G-BFSL	Cessna U.206F Stationair	J. M. Block/Nairobi
	G-BFSR	Cessna F.150J	Lamwood Aviation
	G-BFSS	Cessna FR.172G	Minerva Services
	G-BFSY	PA-28-181 Archer II	Downland Aviation/Goodwood
	G-BFTC	PA-28R-201T Turbo Arrow III	D. Hughes/Leeds
	G-BFTF	AA-5B Tiger	F. C. Burrow Ltd/Leeds
	G-BFTG	AA-5B Tiger	Freightflow International Ltd
	G-BFTH	Cessna F.172N	T. P. O. Nimenko/Ipswich
	G-BFTT	Cessna 421C	P&B Metal Components Ltd/Manston
	G-BFTX	Cessna F.172N	E. Kent Flying Group
	G-BFTY	Cameron V-77 balloon	Regal Motors (Bilston) Ltd *Regal Motors*
	G-BFTZ	MS.880B Rallye Club	R. & B. Legge Ltd
	G-BFUB	PA-32RT-300 Turbo Lance II	Jolida Holdings Ltd
	G-BFUD	Scheibe SF.25E Super Falke	S. H. Hart
	G-BFUG	Cameron N-77 balloon	Headland Services Ltd
	G-BFUZ	Cameron V-77 balloon	Skysales Ltd
	G-BFVA	Boeing 737-204ADV	Britannia Airways Ltd *Sir John Alcock*/Luton
	G-BFVB	Boeing 737-204ADV	Britannia Airways Ltd *Sir Thomas Sopwith*/Luton
	G-BFVF	PA-38-112 Tomahawk	Ipswich School of Flying
	G-BFVG	PA-28-181 Archer II	P. A. Cornah & S. Reed/Blackpool
	G-BFVH	D.H.2 Replica (5964)	Russavia Collection/Duxford
	G-BFVI	H.S.125 Srs 700B	Bristow Helicopters Ltd
	G-BFVM	Westland-Bell 47G-3B1	Pilotmoor Ltd
	G-BFVO	Partenavia P.68B	Travelair UK Ltd
	G-BFVP	PA-23 Aztec 250F	Ardsair Ltd/Newtownards
	G-BFVS	AA-5B Tiger	S. W. Biroth & T. Chapman/Denham
	G-BFVU	Cessna 150L	Thruxton Flight Centre Ltd
	G-BFVV	SA.365 Dauphin 2	Bond Helicopters Ltd/Bourn
	G-BFVW	SA.365 Dauphin 2	Bond Helicopters Ltd/Bourn

Reg.	Type	Owner or Operator	Notes
G-BFWB	PA-28-161 Warrior II	C.S.E. Aviation Ltd/Kidlington	
G-BFWD	Currie Wot	F. E. Nuthall	
G-BFWE	PA-23 Aztec 250D	Air Navigation & Trading Co Ltd/ Blackpool	
G-BFWF	Cessna 421B	Alcon Oil Ltd/Sibson	
G-BFWK	PA-28-161 Warrior II	Woodgate Air Services (IoM) Ltd	
G-BFWL	Cessna F.150L	J. Dolan/Eglinton	
G-BFWW	Robin HR.100/210	Willingair Ltd	
G-BFXC	Mooney M.20C	R. I. Craddock/Biggin Hill	
G-BFXD	PA-28-161 Warrior II	C.S.E. Aviation Ltd/Kidlington	
G-BFXE	PA-28-161 Warrior II	C.S.E. Aviation Ltd/Kidlington	
G-BFXF	Andreasson BA.4B	A. Brown/Sherburn	
G-BFXG	D.31 Turbulent	S. Griffin	
G-BFXH	Cessna F.152	Angelsword Ltd/Halfpenny Green	
G-BFXI	Cessna F.172M	Thanet Electronics/Manston	
G-BFXK	PA-28 Cherokee 140	G. S. & Mrs M. T. Pritchard/Southend	
G-BFXL	Albatross D.5A (D5397/17)	FAA Museum/Yeovilton	
G-BFXM	Jurca MJ.5 Sirocco	R. Bradbury & A. R. Greenfield	
G-BFXO	Taylor JT.1 Monoplane	A. S. Nixon	
G-BFXR	Jodel D.112	R. E. Walker & M. Riddin/Netherthorpe	
G-BFXS	R. Commander 114	Keats Printing Ltd	
G-BFXW	AA-5B Tiger	Crosswind Aviation Ltd/Leeds	
G-BFXX	AA-5B Tiger	George Cross Services Ltd	
G-BFYA	MBB Bo 105D	Veritair Ltd	
G-BFYB	PA-28-161 Warrior II	C.S.E. Aviation Ltd/Kidlington	
G-BFYC	PA-32RT-300 Lance II	Mastercraft Boat Co Ltd	
G-BFYE	Robin HR.100/285	J. Hackett/Jersey	
G-BFYI	Westland-Bell 47G-3B1	M&D Transport (Weston) Ltd	
G-BFYJ	Hughes 369HE	Wilford Aviation Ltd/Fairoaks	
G-BFYL	Evans VP-2	A. G. Wilford	
G-BFYM	PA-28-161 Warrior II	C.S.E. Aviation Ltd/Kidlington	
G-BFYN	Cessna FA.152	Phoenix Flying Services Ltd/Glasgow	
G-BFYO	Spad XIII replica (S3398) ★	FAA Museum/Yeovilton	
G-BFYP	Bensen B.7	A. J. Philpotts	
G-BFYU	SC.5 Belfast	HeavyLift Cargo Airlines Ltd/Stansted	
G-BFZB	Piper J-3C-85 Cub	Zebedee Flying Group/Shoreham	
G-BFZD	Cessna FR.182RG	R. B. Lewis & Co/Sleap	
G-BFZG	PA-28-161 Warrior II	C.S.E. Aviation Ltd/Kidlington	
G-BFZH	PA-28R Cherokee Arrow 200	R. E. & U. C. Mankelow	
G-BFZL	V.836 Viscount	Baltic British Air Ferries Ltd/Southend	
G-BFZM	R. Commander 112TC	Rolls-Royce Ltd/Filton	
G-BFZN	Cessna FA.152	Falcon Flying Services/Biggin Hill	
G-BFZO	AA-5A Cheetah	Heald Air Ltd/Manchester	
G-BFZT	Cessna FA.152	One Zero One Three Ltd/Guernsey	
G-BFZU	Cessna FA.152	George Cross Services Ltd	
G-BFZV	Cessna F.172M	R. Thomas	
G-BGAA	Cessna 152 II	Farr (Metal Fabrications) Ltd	
G-BGAB	Cessna F.152 II	TG Aviation Ltd/Manston	
G-BGAD	Cessna F.152 II	J. S. Develin & Z. Islam	
G-BGAE	Cessna F.152 II	Klingair Ltd/Conington	
G-BGAF	Cessna FA.152	Suffolk Aero Club Ltd/Ipswich	
G-BGAG	Cessna F.172N	F. E. P. Holmes	
G-BGAH	FRED Srs 2	G. A. Harris	
G-BGAJ	Cessna F.182Q II	Ground Airport Services Ltd/Guernsey	
G-BGAK	Cessna F.182Q II	Safari World Services Ltd	
G-BGAU	Rearwin 9000L	Shipping & Airlines Ltd/Biggin Hill	
G-BGAX	PA-28 Cherokee 140	Hillvine Ltd	
G-BGAY	Cameron O-77 balloon	Dante Balloon Group *Antonia*	
G-BGAZ	Cameron V-77 balloon	Cameron Balloons Ltd *Silicon Chip*	
G-BGBA	Robin R.2100A	D. Faulkner/Redhill	
G-BGBB	L.1011-385 TriStar 200	British Airways *Bridlington Bay*/ Heathrow	
G-BGBC	L.1011-385 TriStar 200	British Airways *St Andrews Bay*/ Heathrow	
G-BGBE	Jodel DR.1050	J. A. Wootton & ptnrs	
G-BGBF	D.31A Turbulent	N. A. D. Gribble	
G-BGBG	PA-28-181 Archer II	Harlow Printing Ltd/Newcastle	
G-BGBI	Cessna F.150L	Anglian Flight Training Ltd/Norwich	
G-BGBK	PA-38-112 Tomahawk	P. K. Pemberton	
G-BGBN	PA-38-112 Tomahawk	Leavesden Flight Centre Ltd	
G-BGBP	Cessna F.152	Stapleford Flying Club Ltd	
G-BGBR	Cessna F.172N	George Cross Services Ltd	
G-BGBU	Auster AOP.9 (XN435)	P. Neilson	

Notes	Reg.	Type	Owner or Operator
	G-BGBW	PA-38-112 Tomahawk	Truman Aviation Ltd/Tollerton
	G-BGBX	PA-38-112 Tomahawk	Ipswich School of Flying
	G-BGBY	PA-38-112 Tomahawk	Ravenair Ltd/Manchester
	G-BGBZ	R. Commander 114	R. S. Fenwick/Biggin Hill
	G-BGCG	Douglas C-47A	Datran Holdings
	G-BGCL	AA-5A Cheetah	Blackbushe School of Flying Ltd
	G-BGCM	AA-5A Cheetah	Pacific Associates Ltd/Blackbushe
	G-BGCO	PA-44-180 Seminole	J. R. Henderson
	G-BGCX	Taylor JT.1 Monoplane	G. M. R. Walters
	G-BGCY	Taylor JT.1 Monoplane	F. R. Donaldson
	G-BGDA	Boeing 737-236	British Airways *River Tamar*/Heathrow
	G-BGDB	Boeing 737-236	British Airways *River Tweed*/Heathrow
	G-BGDC	Boeing 737-236	British Airways *River Humber*/Heathrow
	G-BGDD	Boeing 737-236	British Airways *River Tees*/Heathrow
	G-BGDE	Boeing 737-236	British Airways *River Avon*/Heathrow
	G-BGDF	Boeing 737-236	British Airways *River Thames*/Heathrow
	G-BGDG	Boeing 737-236	British Airways *River Medway*/Heathrow
	G-BGDH	Boeing 737-236	British Airways *River Clyde*/Heathrow
	G-BGDI	Boeing 737-236	British Airways *River Ouse*/Heathrow
	G-BGDJ	Boeing 737-236	British Airways *River Trent*/Heathrow
	G-BGDK	Boeing 737-236	British Airways *River Mersey*/Heathrow
	G-BGDL	Boeing 737-236	British Airways *River Don*/Heathrow
	G-BGDN	Boeing 737-236	British Airways *River Tyne*/Heathrow
	G-BGDO	Boeing 737-236	British Airways *River Usk*/Heathrow
	G-BGDP	Boeing 737-236	British Airways *River Taff*/Heathrow
	G-BGDR	Boeing 737-236	British Airways *River Bann*/Heathrow
	G-BGDS	Boeing 737-236	British Airways *River Severn*/Heathrow
	G-BGDT	Boeing 737-236	British Airways *River Forth*/Heathrow
	G-BGDU	Boeing 737-236	British Airways *River Dee*/Heathrow
	G-BGEA	Cessna F.150M	Agricultural & General Aviation Ltd
	G-BGED	Cessna U.206F	Elecwind (Clay Cross) Ltd/E. Midlands
	G-BGEE	Evans VP-1	R. A. M. Purkis/Cranwell North
	G-BGEF	Jodel D.112	G. G. Johnson & S. J. Davies
	G-BGEH	Monnet Sonerai II	A. Dodd
	G-BGEI	Baby Great Lakes	I. H. Seach-Allen
	G-BGEK	PA-38-112 Tomahawk	Cheshire Flying Services Ltd/ Manchester
	G-BGEL	PA-38-112 Tomahawk	Ravenair Ltd/Manchester
	G-BGEM	Partenavia P.68B	AEW Engineering Co Ltd/Norwich
	G-BGEN	D.H.C.6 Twin Otter 310	Loganair Ltd/Glasgow
	G-BGEP	Cameron D-38 balloon	Cameron Balloons Ltd
	G-BGES	Currie Wot	K. E. Ballington
	G-BGET	PA-38-112 Tomahawk	Goodwood Terrena Ltd
	G-BGEW	Nord NC.854S	A. Doughty
	G-BGEX	Brookland Mosquito 2	R. T. Gough
	G-BGFC	Evans VP-2	A. Sharma
	G-BGFF	FRED Srs 2	G. R. G. Smith
	G-BGFG	AA-5A Cheetah	Fletcher Aviation Ltd/Biggin Hill
	G-BGFH	Cessna F.182Q	Mindon Engineering (Nottingham) Ltd/ Tollerton
	G-BGFI	AA-5A Cheetah	Maston Property Holdings Ltd
	G-BGFJ	Jodel D.9 Bebe	C. M. Fitton
	G-BGFK	Evans VP-1	I. N. M. Cameron
	G-BGFT	PA-34-200T Seneca II	C.S.E. Aviation Ltd/Kidlington
	G-BGFX	Cessna F.152	A. W. Fay/Cranfield
	G-BGGA	Bellanca 7GCBC Citabria	I. N. Jennison
	G-BGGB	Bellanca 7GCBC Citabria	N. A. & M. D. Cowburn
	G-BGGC	Bellanca 7GCBC Citabria	R. P. Ashfield & B. A. Jesty
	G-BGGD	Bellanca 8GCBC Scout	Bristol & Gloucestershire Gliding Club/Nympsfield
	G-BGGE	PA-38-112 Tomahawk	C.S.E. (Aircraft Services) Ltd/Kidlington
	G-BGGF	PA-38-112 Tomahawk	C.S.E. (Aircraft Services) Ltd/Kidlington
	G-BGGG	PA-38-112 Tomahawk	C.S.E. (Aircraft Services) Ltd/Kidlington
	G-BGGI	PA-38-112 Tomahawk	C.S.E. (Aircraft Services) Ltd/Kidlington
	G-BGGJ	PA-38-112 Tomahawk	C.S.E. (Aircraft Services) Ltd/Kidlington
	G-BGGL	PA-38-112 Tomahawk	Grunwick Ltd/Elstree
	G-BGGM	PA-38-112 Tomahawk	Grunwick Ltd/Elstree
	G-BGGN	PA-38-112 Tomahawk	C.S.E. Aviation Ltd/Kidlington
	G-BGGO	Cessna F.152	E. Midlands Flying School Ltd
	G-BGGP	Cessna F.152	E. Midlands Flying School Ltd
	G-BGGT	Zenith CH.200	P. R. M. Nind
	G-BGGU	Wallis WA-116R-R	K. H. Wallis

Reg.	Type	Owner or Operator	Notes
G-BGGV	Wallis WA-120 Srs 2	K. H. Wallis	
G-BGGW	Wallis WA-112	K. H. Wallis	
G-BGGY	AB-206B Jet Ranger ★	*Instructional airframe*/Cranfield	
G-BGHE	Convair L-13A	J. Davis/USA	
G-BGHF	Westland WG.30 ★	*Instructional airframe*/Yeovil	
G-BGHI	Cessna F.152	Taxon Ltd/Shoreham	
G-BGHK	Cessna F.152	Wilson Leasing/Biggin Hill	
G-BGHM	Robin R.1180T	H. Price	
G-BGHP	Beech 76 Duchess	J. J. Baumhardt Ltd	
G-BGHS	Cameron N-31 balloon	Balloon Stable Ltd	
G-BGHT	Falconar F-12	C. R. Coates	
G-BGHU	T-6G Texan (115042)	C. E. Bellhouse	
G-BGHV	Cameron V-77 balloon	E. Davies	
G-BGHW	Thunder Ax8-90 balloon	Edinburgh University Balloon Group *James Tytler*	
G-BGHY	Taylor JT.1 Monoplane	J. Prowse	
G-BGHZ	FRED Srs 2	A. Smith	
G-BGIB	Cessna 152 II	Mona Aviation Ltd	
G-BGIC	Cessna 172N	T. R. Sinclair	
G-BGID	Westland-Bell 47G-3B1	A. E. & B. G. Brown	
G-BGIG	PA-38-112 Tomahawk	Scotia Safari Ltd/Prestwick	
G-BGIH	Rand KR-2	G. & D. G. Park	
G-BGII	PA-32-300 Cherokee Six	Rosefair Electronics Ltd/Elstree	
G-BGIK	Taylor JT.1 Monoplane	M. C. Durand	
G-BGIO	Bensen B.8M	C. G. Johns	
G-BGIP	Colt 56A balloon	Capitol Balloon Club	
G-BGIU	Cessna F.172H	Metro Equipment (Chesham) Ltd/ Panshanger	
G-BGIV	Bell 47G-5	Autair Helicopters Ltd	
G-BGIX	H.295 Super Courier	Nordic Oil Services Ltd/Edinburgh	
G-BGIY	Cessna F.172N	W. Semple Son & Co Ltd/Glasgow	
G-BGIZ	Cessna F.152	Creaton Aviation Services Ltd	
G-BGJA	Cessna FA.152	Redhill Flying Club	
G-BGJB	PA-44-180 Seminole	George Cross Services Ltd	
G-BGJE	Boeing 737-236	British Airways *Sandpiper*/Gatwick	
G-BGJF	Boeing 737-236	Caledonian Airways *Loch Fyne*/Gatwick	
G-BGJG	Boeing 737-236	Caledonian Airways *Loch Avon*/Gatwick	
G-BGJH	Boeing 737-236	Caledonian Airways *Loch Loyal*/Gatwick	
G-BGJI	Boeing 737-236	Caledonian Airways *Loch Shiel*/Gatwick	
G-BGJJ	Boeing 737-236	British Airways *River Swale*/Gatwick	
G-BGJK	Boeing 737-236	British Airways *River Cherwell*/Gatwick	
G-BGJM	Boeing 737-236	British Airways *River Ribble*/Gatwick	
G-BGJU	Cameron V-65 Balloon	D. T. Watkins *Spoils*	
G-BGJV	H.S.748 Srs 2B	British Airways *Glen Avon*/Glasgow	
G-BGJW	GA-7 Cougar	Lambill Ltd	
G-BGKA	P.56 Provost T.1 (XF690)	D. W. Mickleburgh	
G-BGKD	SOCATA Rallye 110ST	M. A. Jones	
G-BGKE	BAC One-Eleven 539	British Airways *County of Gwynedd*/ Birmingham	
G-BGKF	BAC One-Eleven 539	British Airways *County of Warwickshire*/ Birmingham	
G-BGKG	BAC One-Eleven 539	British Airways *County of Staffordshire*/ Birmingham	
G-BGKJ	MBB Bo 105C	Bond Helicopters Ltd/Bourn	
G-BGKM	SA.365C-3 Dauphin	Bond Helicopters Ltd/Bourn	
G-BGKO	GY-20 Minicab	R. B. Webber	
G-BGKS	PA-28-161 Warrior II	Woodgate Air Services (IoM) Ltd	
G-BGKT	Auster AOP.9 (XN441)	K. H. Wallis	
G-BGKU	PA-28R-201 Arrow III	Caplane Ltd	
G-BGKV	PA-28R-201 Arrow III	G. E. Salter	
G-BGKW	Evans VP-1	I. W. Black	
G-BGKY	PA-38-112 Tomahawk	MSF Aviation	
G-BGKZ	J/5F Aiglet Trainer	R. C. H. Hibberd	
G-BGLA	PA-38-112 Tomahawk	Scotia Safari Ltd/Prestwick	
G-BGLB	Bede BD-5B	W. Sawney	
G-BGLD	Beech 76 Duchess	Devindale Ltd	
G-BGLE	Saffrey S.330 balloon	C. J. Dodd & ptnrs	
G-BGLF	Evans VP-1	B. P. Fraser-Newstead	
G-BGLG	Cessna 152	Skyviews & General Ltd	
G-BGLH	Cessna 152	Deltair Ltd/Chester	
G-BGLI	Cessna 152	Luton Flying Club (*stored*)	
G-BGLK	Monnet Sonerai II	G. L. Kemp & J. Beck	
G-BGLL	Bell 212	Bristow Helicopters Ltd/Aberdeen	
G-BGLN	Cessna FA.152	Bournemouth Flying Club	

Notes	Reg.	Type	Owner or Operator
	G-BGLO	Cessna F.172N	A. H. Slaughter/Southend
	G-BGLR	Cessna F.152	Horizon Flying Club Ltd/Ipswich
	G-BGLS	Super Baby Great Lakes	J. F. Dowe
	G-BGLW	PA-34-200 Seneca	P. C. Roberts
	G-BGLX	Cameron N-56 balloon	Sara A. G. Williams
	G-BGLZ	Stits SA-3A Playboy	J. R. Wynn
	G-BGMA	D.31 Turbulent	G. C. Masterton
	G-BGMB	Taylor JT.2 Titch	E. M. Bourne
	G-BGMD	D.H.C.6 Twin Otter 310	Hubbardair Ltd
	G-BGME	SIPA S.903	M. Emery (G-BCML)/Redhill
	G-BGMJ	GY-201 Minicab	P. Cawkwell
	G-BGMN	H.S.748 Srs 2A	Euroair/British Airways Glen Finnan/ Glasgow
	G-BGMO	H.S.748 Srs 2A	Euroair/British Airways Glen Goyne/ Glasgow
	G-BGMP	Cessna F.172G	S. G. Hoole
	G-BGMR	GY-201 Minicab	J. R. Large & ptnrs
	G-BGMS	Taylor JT.2 Titch	M. A. J. Spice
	G-BGMT	MS.894E Rallye 235GT	M. E. Taylor
	G-BGMU	Westland-Bell 47G-3B1	Carskiey Ltd
	G-BGMV	Scheibe SF.25B Falke	Wolds Gliding Club Ltd/Pocklington
	G-BGMW	Edgley EA-7 Optica	Edgley Aircraft Ltd/Old Sarum
	G-BGMX	Enstrom 280C-UK-2 Shark	P. V. Doman
	G-BGNB	Short SD3-30 Variant 100	Fairflight Ltd/National Airways/ Southend
	G-BGND	Cessna F.172N	Stansted Fluid Power Products Ltd
	G-BGNM	SA.365C-1 Dauphin 2	Bond Helicopters Ltd/Bourn
	G-BGNR	Cessna F.172N	Bevan Lynch Aviation Ltd/Birmingham
	G-BGNT	Cessna F.152	Klingair Ltd/Conington
	G-BGNV	GA-7 Cougar	R. W. Fairless/Southampton
	G-BGNW	Boeing 737-219ADV	Britannia Airways Ltd George Stephenson/Luton
	G-BGNZ	Cessna FRA.150L	P. P. D. Howard-Johnston/Edinburgh
	G-BGOA	Cessna FR.182RG	CDS Trading Co Ltd/Biggin Hill
	G-BGOC	Cessna F.152	Elliot Forbes (Kirkwall) Ltd
	G-BGOD	Colt 77A balloon	C. Allen & M. D. Steuer
	G-BGOE	Beech 76 Duchess	Niglon Ltd/Birmingham
	G-BGOF	Cessna F.152	Falcon Flying Services/Biggin Hill
	G-BGOG	PA-28-161 Warrior II	M. J. Cowham
	G-BGOH	Cessna F.182Q	Zonex Ltd/Blackpool
	G-BGOI	Cameron O-56 balloon	Balloon Stable Ltd Skymaster
	G-BGOL	PA-28R-201T Turbo Arrow III	Lonslow Dairy Ltd & ptnrs/Birmingham
	G-BGOM	PA-31-310 Turbo Navajo	Oxford Aero Charter Ltd/Kidlington
	G-BGON	GA-7 Cougar	C. Henry
	G-BGOO	Colt 56 SS balloon	British Gas Corporation
	G-BGOP	Dassault Falcon 20F	Nissan (UK) Ltd/Heathrow
	G-BGOR	AT-6D Harvard III	M. L. Sargeant
	G-BGOX	PA-31-350 Navajo Chieftain	Woodgate Aviation (IoM) Ltd
	G-BGOY	PA-31-350 Navajo Chieftain	Interflight (Air Charters) Ltd/Gatwick
	G-BGPA	Cessna 182Q	R. A. Robinson
	G-BGPB	AT-16 Harvard IV (385)	A. G. Walker & R. Lamplough/Sandown
	G-BGPD	Piper J-3C-65 Cub	P. D. Whiteman
	G-BGPF	Thunder Ax6-56Z balloon	Thunder Balloons Ltd Pepsi
	G-BGPH	AA-5B Tiger	A. J. Dales
	G-BGPI	Plumb BGP-1	B. G. Plumb
	G-BGPJ	PA-28-161 Warrior II	E. Green
	G-BGPK	AA-5B Tiger	Ann Green Manufacturing Co Ltd/ Elstree
	G-BGPL	PA-28-161 Warrior II	T. G. Aviation Ltd/Manston
	G-BGPM	Evans VP-2	M. G. Reilly
	G-BGPN	PA-18 Super Cub 150	Roy Moore Ltd/Blackpool
	G-BGPT	Parker Teenie Two	K. Atkinson
	G-BGPU	PA-28 Cherokee 140	Air Navigation & Trading Co Ltd/ Blackpool
	G-BGPZ	M.S.890A Rallye Commodore	J. A. Espin/Popham
	G-BGRA	Taylor JT.2 Titch	J. R. C. Thompson
	G-BGRC	PA-28 Cherokee 140	Arrow Air Centre Ltd/Shipdham
	G-BGRE	Beech A200 Super King Air	Martin-Baker (Engineering) Ltd/ Chalgrove
	G-BGRG	Beech 76 Duchess	Arrows Ltd/Manchester
	G-BGRH	Robin DR.400/2+2	T.M.A. Associates Ltd/Headcorn
	G-BGRI	Jodel DR.1051	B. Gunn & K. L. Burnett
	G-BGRK	PA-38-112 Tomahawk	Goodwood Terrena Ltd
	G-BGRL	PA-38-112 Tomahawk	Goodwood Terrena Ltd

Reg.	Type	Owner or Operator	Notes
G-BGRM	PA-38-112 Tomahawk	Goodwood Terrena Ltd	
G-BGRN	PA-38-112 Tomahawk	Goodwood Terrena Ltd	
G-BGRO	Cessna F.172M	Northfield Garage Ltd/Prestwick	
G-BGRR	PA-38-112 Tomahawk	MSF Aviation Ltd/Manchester	
G-BGRS	Thunder Ax7-77Z balloon	W. & J. Evans	
G-BGRT	Steen Skybolt	D. Callabritto	
G-BGRX	PA-38-112 Tomahawk	Leavesden Flight Centre Ltd	
G-BGSA	M.S.892E Rallye 150GT	Colin Draycott Group Ltd/Leicester	
G-BGSE	Pitts S-2A Special	P. H. Meeson	
G-BGSG	PA-44-180 Seminole	D. J. McSorley	
G-BGSH	PA-38-112 Tomahawk	Scotia Safari Ltd/Prestwick	
G-BGSI	PA-38-112 Tomahawk	Cheshire Flying Services Ltd/ Manchester	
G-BGSJ	Piper J-3C-65 Cub	W. J. Higgins/Dunkeswell	
G-BGSM	M.S.892E Rallye 150GT	G. T. Leedham & D. H. Rider	
G-BGSN	Enstrom F-28C-UK-2	Aircraft Sales International Ltd/Denham	
G-BGSO	PA-31-310 Turbo Navajo	B. Butler	
G-BGST	Thunder Ax7-65 balloon	L. H. T. Large & ptnrs *Eclipse*	
G-BGSV	Cessna F.172N	Wickenby Flying Club Ltd	
G-BGSW	Beech F33 Debonair	C. T. Wells/Stapleford	
G-BGSX	Cessna F.152	Midland Aircraft Leasing Ltd/ Birmingham	
G-BGSY	GA-7 Cougar	Van Allen Ltd/Guernsey	
G-BGTB	SOCATA TB.10 Tobago ★	D. Page/Reading	
G-BGTC	Auster AOP.9 (XP282)	Adrianair Ltd	
G-BGTF	PA-44-180 Seminole	New Guarantee Trust Ltd/Jersey	
G-BGTG	PA-23 Aztec 250F	R. J. Howard/Leeds	
G-BGTI	Piper J-3C-65 Cub	A. P. Broad	
G-BGTJ	PA-28 Cherokee 180	Serendipity Aviation/Staverton	
G-BGTK	Cessna FR.182RG	Kestrel Air Services Ltd/Denham	
G-BGTL	GY-20 Minicab	A. K. Lang	
G-BGTP	Robin HR.100/210	E. C. & C. E. E. Walker	
G-BGTR	PA-28 Cherokee 140	Liverpool Aero Club Ltd	
G-BGTS	PA-28 Cherokee 140	Liverpool Aero Club Ltd	
G-BGTT	Cessna 310R	Aviation Beauport Ltd/Jersey	
G-BGTU	BAC One-Eleven 409	Turbo Union Ltd/Filton	
G-BGTX	Jodel D.117	Madley Flying Group/Shobdon	
G-BGUA	PA-38-112 Tomahawk	Truman Aviation Ltd/Tollerton	
G-BGUB	PA-32-300 Cherokee Six	A. D. Liveras/Elstree	
G-BGUY	Cameron V-56 balloon	G. V. Beckwith	
G-BGVA	Cessna 414A	Royalair Services Ltd/Tollerton	
G-BGVB	Robin DR.315	Cedric P. Jones Ltd/Blackbushe	
G-BGVE	CP.1310-C3 Super Emeraude	E. J. A. Woolnough	
G-BGVF	Colt 77A balloon	Hot Air Balloon Co Ltd	
G-BGVH	Beech 76 Duchess	Velco Marketing	
G-BGVI	Cessna F.152	Farr (Metal Fabrications) Ltd	
G-BGVK	PA-28-161 Warrior II	F. G. Kaye & Son Ltd	
G-BGVL	PA-38-112 Tomahawk	Scotia Safari Ltd/Prestwick	
G-BGVN	PA-28RT-201 Arrow IV	Essex Aviation Ltd/Stapleford	
G-BGVP	Thunder Ax6-56Z balloon	A. Bolger	
G-BGVR	Thunder Ax6-56Z balloon	A. N. G. Howie	
G-BGVS	Cessna F.172M	P. D. A. Aviation Ltd/Tollerton	
G-BGVT	Cessna R.182RG	Barnes Plastics Group Ltd/Staverton	
G-BGVU	PA-28 Cherokee 180	Cheshire Flying Services Ltd/ Manchester	
G-BGVV	AA-5A Cheetah	A. H. McVicar	
G-BGVW	AA-5A Cheetah	D. Phillips/Biggin Hill	
G-BGVY	AA-5B Tiger	Porter Bell Ltd/Goodwood	
G-BGVZ	PA-28-181 Archer II	Midland Aircraft Leasing Ltd/ Birmingham	
G-BGWA	GA-7 Cougar	Lough Erne Aviation Ltd	
G-BGWC	Robin DR.400/180	E. F. Braddon & D. C. Shepherd/ Rochester	
G-BGWF	PA-18 Super Cub 150	E. D. Burke	
G-BGWH	PA-18 Super Cub 150	Clacton Aero Club (1988) Ltd	
G-BGWI	Cameron V-65 balloon	Army Balloon Club/W. Germany	
G-BGWJ	Sikorsky S-61N	British Executive Air Services Ltd	
G-BGWK	Sikorsky S-61N	Bristow Helicopters Ltd	
G-BGWM	PA-28-181 Archer II	Thames Valley Flying Club Ltd	
G-BGWN	PA-38-112 Tomahawk	Frontline Aviation Ltd/Teesside	
G-BGWO	Jodel D.112	A. J. Court	

NOTE: The G-BGUx sequence will not be issued unless specifically requested

Notes	Reg.	Type	Owner or Operator
	G-BGWP	MBB Bo 105C	Medical Aviation Services Ltd/Exeter
	G-BGWS	Enstrom 280C Shark	G. Firbank & N. M. Grimshaw
	G-BGWT	W.S.58 Wessex 60 Srs 1	Turbine Support Ltd
	G-BGWU	PA-38-112 Tomahawk	MSF Aviation Ltd/Manchester
	G-BGWV	Aeronca 7AC Champion	RFC Flying Group/Popham
	G-BGWW	PA-23 Turbo Aztec 250E	Ski Air Ltd/Biggin Hill
	G-BGWY	Thunder Ax6-56Z balloon	J. G. O'Connel
	G-BGWZ	Eclipse Super Eagle ★	FAA Museum/Yeovilton
	G-BGXA	Piper J-3C-65 Cub (329471)	E. F. Fryer & K. Nicholls
	G-BGXB	PA-38-112 Tomahawk	Signtest Ltd/Cardiff
	G-BGXC	SOCATA TB.10 Tobago	A. J. Halliday/Shoreham
	G-BGXD	SOCATA TB.10 Tobago	Selles Dispensing Chemists Ltd
	G-BGXJ	Partenavia P.68B	Cecil Aviation Ltd/Cambridge
	G-BGXK	Cessna 310R	Air Service Training Ltd/Perth
	G-BGXL	Bensen B.8MV	B. P. Triefus
	G-BGXN	PA-38-112 Tomahawk	Panshanger School of Flying Ltd
	G-BGXO	PA-38-112 Tomahawk	A. Dodd & M. D. B. Spencer/Booker
	G-BGXP	Westland-Bell 47G-3B1	B. A. Hogan & ptnrs
	G-BGXR	Robin HR.200/100	J. P. Kistner
	G-BGXS	PA-28-236 Dakota	Debian Car Hire Ltd/Jersey
	G-BGXT	SOCATA TB.10 Tobago	County Aviation Ltd/Halfpenny Green
	G-BGXU	WMB-1 balloon	C. J. Dodd & ptnrs
	G-BGXX	Jodel DR.1051M1	C. Evans
	G-BGXZ	Cessna FA.152	Falcon Flying Services Ltd/Biggin Hill
	G-BGYG	PA-28-161 Warrior II	C.S.E. Aviation Ltd/Kidlington
	G-BGYH	PA-28-161 Warrior II	C.S.E. Aviation Ltd/Kidlington
	G-BGYJ	Boeing 737-204	Britannia Airways Ltd *Sir Barnes Wallis*/Luton
	G-BGYK	Boeing 737-204	Britannia Airways Ltd *R. J. Mitchell*/Luton
	G-BGYL	Boeing 737-204	Britannia Airways Ltd *Jean Batten*/Luton
	G-BGYN	PA-18 Super Cub 150	A. G. Walker
	G-BGYR	H.S.125 Srs 600B	British Aerospace/Warton
	G-BGYT	EMB-110P1 Bandeirante	Business Air Travel
	G-BGYV	EMB-110P1 Bandeirante	Business Air Travel
	G-BGZC	C.A.S.A. 1.131 Jungmann	J. E. Douglas
	G-BGZF	PA-38-112 Tomahawk	Cambrian Flying Club/Swansea
	G-BGZJ	PA-38-112 Tomahawk	W. R. C. Foyle
	G-BGZK	Westland-Bell 47G-3B1	Cavco Floors Ltd
	G-BGZL	Eiri PIK-20E	D. I. Liddell-Grainger
	G-BGZN	WMB.2 Windtracker balloon	S. R. Woolfries
	G-BGZO	M.S.880B Rallye Club	K. J. Underwood
	G-BGZP	D.H.C.6 Twin Otter 310	Hubbardair Ltd
	G-BGZR	Meagher Model balloon Mk.1	S. C. Meagher
	G-BGZS	Keirs Heated Air Tube	M. N. J. Kirby
	G-BGZW	PA-38-112 Tomahawk	Ravenair Ltd/Manchester
	G-BGZY	Jodel D.120	J. V. George
	G-BGZZ	Thunder Ax6-56 balloon	J. M. Robinson
	G-BHAA	Cessna 152	Herefordshire Aero Club Ltd/Shobdon
	G-BHAB	Cessna 152	Herefordshire Aero Club Ltd/Shobdon
	G-BHAC	Cessna A.152	Herefordshire Aero Club Ltd/Shobdon
	G-BHAD	Cessna A.152	Shropshire Aero Club Ltd/Sleap
	G-BHAF	PA-38-112 Tomahawk	Ravenair/Manchester
	G-BHAG	Scheibe SF.25E Super Falke	British Gliding Association/Lasham
	G-BHAI	Cessna F.152	P. P. D. Howard-Johnston/Edinburgh
	G-BHAJ	Robin DR.400/160	Rowantask Ltd
	G-BHAL	Rango Saffery S.200 SS	A. M. Lindsay *Anneky Panky*
	G-BHAM	Thunder Ax6-56 balloon	D. Sampson
	G-BHAR	Westland-Bell 47G-3B1	E. A. L. Sturmer
	G-BHAT	Thunder Ax7-77 balloon	C. P. Witter Ltd *Witter*
	G-BHAV	Cessna F.152	Iceni Leasing
	G-BHAW	Cessna F.172N	W. Lancs Aero Club Ltd/Woodvale
	G-BHAX	Enstrom F-28C-UK-2	Southern Air Ltd/Shoreham
	G-BHAY	PA-28RT-201 Arrow IV	Alpha Yankee Group/Newcastle
	G-BHBA	Campbell Cricket	S. M. Irwin
	G-BHBB	Colt 77A balloon	S. D. Bellew/USA
	G-BHBE	Westland-Bell 47G-3B1 (Soloy)	Dollar Air Services Ltd/Coventry
	G-BHBF	Sikorsky S-76A	Bristow Helicopters Ltd
	G-BHBG	PA-32R-300 Lance	D. A. Stewart/Birmingham

Reg.	Type	Owner or Operator	Notes
G-BHBI	Mooney M.20J	B. K. Arthur/Exeter	
G-BHBL	L.1011-385 TriStar 200	British Airways *Largs Bay*/Heathrow	
G-BHBM	L.1011-385 TriStar 200	British Airways *Poole Bay*/Heathrow	
G-BHBN	L.1011-385 TriStar 200	British Airways *Bideford Bay*/Heathrow	
G-BHBO	L.1011-385 TriStar 200	British Airways *St Magnus Bay*/ Heathrow	
G-BHBP	L.1011-385 TriStar 200	British Airways *Whitesand Bay*/ Heathrow	
G-BHBR	L.1011-385 TriStar 200	British Airways *Bude Bay*/Heathrow	
G-BHBS	PA-28RT-201T Turbo Arrow IV	MX Euromark Ltd	
G-BHBT	Marquart MA.5 Charger	R. G. & C. J. Maidment/Shoreham	
G-BHBZ	Partenavia P.68B	Alpine Press Ltd/Leavesden	
G-BHCC	Cessna 172M	T. Howard	
G-BHCE	Jodel D.112	D. M. Parsons	
G-BHCF	WMB.2 Windtracker balloon	C. J. Dodd & ptnrs	
G-BHCM	Cessna F.172H	The English Connection Ltd/ Panshanger	
G-BHCP	Cessna F.152	Sherburn Aero Club Ltd	
G-BHCT	PA-23 Aztec 250F	Metronote Aviation Ltd/Biggin Hill	
G-BHCW	PA-22 Tri-Pacer 150	B. Brooks	
G-BHCX	Cessna F.152	A. S. Bamrah/Biggin Hill	
G-BHCZ	PA-38-112 Tomahawk	R. F. N. Hamilton	
G-BHDD	V.668 Varsity T.1 (WL626)	Historic Flight/E. Midlands	
G-BHDE	SOCATA TB.10 Tobago	D. J. M. Wilson/Denham	
G-BHDH	Douglas DC-10-30	British Airways *Ben More Forest* /Gatwick	
G-BHDI	Douglas DC-10-30	British Airways *Forest of Ae*/Gatwick	
G-BHDJ	Douglas DC-10-30	British Airways *Glen Cap Forest*/Gatwick	
G-BHDK	Boeing B-29A-BN (461748) ★	Imperial War Museum/Duxford	
G-BHDM	Cessna F.152 II	Tayside Aviation Ltd/Dundee	
G-BHDO	Cessna F.182Q II	Armada Aviation Ltd	
G-BHDP	Cessna F.182Q II	Rimmer Aviation Ltd/Elstree	
G-BHDR	Cessna F.152 II	Tayside Aviation Ltd/Dundee	
G-BHDS	Cessna F.152 II	Tayside Aviation Ltd/Dundee	
G-BHDT	SOCATA TB.10 Tobago	W. R. C. Foyle/Luton	
G-BHDU	Cessna F.152 II	Falcon Flying Services/Biggin Hill	
G-BHDV	Cameron V-77 balloon	E. D. Price	
G-BHDW	Cessna F.152	Air South Flying Group/Shoreham	
G-BHDX	Cessna F.172N	J. R. Surbey/Cambridge	
G-BHDZ	Cessna F.172N	J. Bines	
G-BHEC	Cessna F.152	W. R. C. Foyle	
G-BHED	Cessna FA.152	TG Aviation Ltd/Manston	
G-BHEG	Jodel D.150	P. R. Underhill	
G-BHEH	Cessna 310G	Vidlow Ltd	
G-BHEK	CP.1315C-3 Super Emeraude	D. B. Winstanley/Barton	
G-BHEL	Jodel D.117	K. J. Cockrill/Ipswich	
G-BHEM	Bensen B.8M	A. Lumley	
G-BHEN	Cessna FA.152	T. N. Moores/Leicester	
G-BHEO	Cessna FR.182RG	Cosworth Engineering Ltd/Coventry	
G-BHEP	Cessna 172 RG Cutlass	E. A. L. Sturmer/Booker	
G-BHET	SOCATA TB.10 Tobago	Claude Hooper Ltd	
G-BHEU	Thunder Ax7-65 balloon	M. H. R. Govett	
G-BHEV	PA-28R Cherokee Arrow 200	E. & G. H. Kelk	
G-BHEX	Colt 56A balloon	A. S. Dear & ptnrs *Super Wasp*	
G-BHEY	Pterodactyl O.R.	High School of Hang Gliding Ltd	
G-BHEZ	Jodel D.150	D. R. Elpick/O. Warden	
G-BHFA	Pterodactyl O.R.	High School of Hang Gliding Ltd	
G-BHFB	Pterodactyl O.R.	High School of Hang Gliding Ltd	
G-BHFC	Cessna F.152	T. G. Aviation Ltd/Manston	
G-BHFE	PA-44-180 Seminole	Grunwick Ltd/Elstree	
G-BHFF	Jodel D.112	P. J. Swain	
G-BHFG	SNCAN SV-4C (45)	The Hon A. M. M. Lindsay/Booker	
G-BHFH	PA-34-200T Seneca II	Hendefern Ltd/Goodwood	
G-BHFI	Cessna F.152	The BAe (Warton) Flying Group/ Blackpool	
G-BHFJ	PA-28RT-201T Turbo Arrow IV	T. L. P. Delaney	
G-BHFK	PA-28-151 Warrior	Ilkeston Car Sales Ltd	
G-BHFL	PA-28 Cherokee 180	Grayswood Aviation Services Ltd/ Coventry	
G-BHFM	Murphy S.200 balloon	M. Murphy	
G-BHFR	Eiri PIK-20E-1	G. Mackie	
G-BHFS	Robin DR.400/180	Flair (Soft Drinks) Ltd/Shoreham	
G-BHFT	H.S.125 Srs 400B	British Aerospace PLC	
G-BHGA	PA-31-310 Turbo Navajo	Heltor Ltd	

Notes	Reg.	Type	Owner or Operator
	G-BHGC	PA-18 Super Cub 150	D. E. Schofield
	G-BHGF	Cameron V-56 balloon	I. T. & H. Seddon *Biggles*
	G-BHGG	Cessna F.172N	Bryan Aviation Ltd
	G-BHGJ	Jodel D.120	Q. M. B. Oswell
	G-BHGK	Sikorsky S-76A	Bond Helicopters Ltd/Bourn
	G-BHGM	Beech 76 Duchess	Bolton Stirland International Ltd
	G-BHGN	Evans VP-1	C. J. D. Edwards
	G-BHGO	PA-32 Cherokee Six 260	AM Aviation Ltd
	G-BHGP	SOCATA TB.10 Tobago	P. A. Bennett/Edinburgh
	G-BHGX	Colt 56B balloon	M. N. Dixon
	G-BHGY	PA-28R Cherokee Arrow 200	Inca Marketing Ltd/Southend
	G-BHHB	Cameron V-77 balloon	N. L. Betts
	G-BHHE	Jodel DR.1051/M1	P. Bridges
	G-BHHG	Cessna F.152	Northamptonshire School of Flying Ltd/ Sywell
	G-BHHH	Thunder Ax7-65 balloon	C. A. Hendley (Essex) Ltd
	G-BHHI	Cessna F.152	Andrewsfield Flying Club Ltd
	G-BHHK	Cameron N-77 balloon	S. Bridge & ptnrs
	G-BHHN	Cameron V-77 balloon	Itchen Valley Balloon Group
	G-BHHU	Short SD3-30	Fairflight Ltd/Biggin Hill
	G-BHHX	Jodel D.112	C. F. Walter
	G-BHHZ	Rotorway Scorpion 133	L. W. & O. Usherwood
	G-BHIA	Cessna F.152	W. H. Wilkins/Stapleford
	G-BHIB	Cessna F.182Q	Ingamells (Machinery Services) Ltd & Spittalgate Motors Ltd
	G-BHIC	Cessna F.182Q	General Building Services Ltd/Leeds
	G-BHID	SOCATA TB.10 Tobago	W. B. Pinckney
	G-BHIH	Cessna F.172N	Watkiss Group Aviation Ltd/ Biggin Hill
	G-BHII	Cameron V-77 balloon	Starcrete Ltd
	G-BHIJ	Eiri PIK-20E-1	R. W. Hall & ptnrs/Swanton Morley
	G-BHIK	Adam RA-14 Loisirs	L. Lewis
	G-BHIN	Cessna F.152	P. Skinner/Netherthorpe
	G-BHIR	PA-28R Cherokee Arrow 200	Cheshire Flying Services Ltd/ Manchester
	G-BHIS	Thunder Ax7-65 balloon	Hedgehoppers Balloon Group
	G-BHIT	SOCATA TB.9 Tampico	Air Touring Services Ltd/Biggin Hill
	G-BHIY	Cessna F.150K	W. H. Cole
	G-BHJA	Cessna A.152	Cellobay Ltd
	G-BHJB	Cessna A.152	E. E. Fenning & Son
	G-BHJF	SOCATA TB.10 Tobago	D. G. Dedman/Leavesden
	G-BHJI	Mooney M.20J	T. R. Bamber & B. Refson/Elstree
	G-BHJK	Maule M5-235C Lunar Rocket	G. A. & B. J. Finch
	G-BHJN	Fournier RF-4D	S. C. Cattlin
	G-BHJO	PA-28-161 Warrior II	Nairn Flying Services Ltd/Inverness
	G-BHJS	Partenavia P.68B	Tewin Aviation/Panshanger
	G-BHJU	Robin DR.400/2+2	Harlow Transport Services Ltd/ Headcorn
	G-BHJW	Cessna F.152	Leicestershire Aero Club Ltd
	G-BHJY	EMB-110P1 Bandeirante	National Airways/Southend
	G-BHJZ	EMB-110P2 Bandeirante	Jersey European Airways/Exeter
	G-BHKA	Evans VP-1	M. L. Perry
	G-BHKE	Bensen B.8MV	V. C. Whitehead
	G-BHKH	Cameron O-65 balloon	D. G. Body
	G-BHKJ	Cessna 421C	United Nations/Pakistan
	G-BHKR	Colt 14A balloon ★	British Balloon Museum
	G-BHKT	Jodel D.112	R. Featherstone & ptnrs/Old Sarum
	G-BHKV	AA-5A Cheetah	Metronote Business Machines Ltd/ Biggin Hill
	G-BHKX	Beech 76 Duchess	A.B. Plant (Aviation) Ltd/Bristol
	G-BHKY	Cessna 310R II	Air Service Training Ltd/Perth
	G-BHLE	Robin DR.400/180	L. H. Mayall
	G-BHLF	H.S.125 Srs 700B	The Marconi Co Ltd/Luton
	G-BHLH	Robin DR.400/180	Trinecare Ltd/Southend
	G-BHLJ	Saffery-Rigg S.200 balloon	I. A. Rigg
	G-BHLK	GA-7 Cougar	Autair Ltd
	G-BHLP	Cessna 441	Rogers Aviation Ltd/Cranfield
	G-BHLT	D.H.82A Tiger Moth	P. J. & A. J. Borsberry
	G-BHLU	Fournier RF-3	M. C. Roper
	G-BHLW	Cessna 120	S. M. Hannan & M. J. Cross
	G-BHLX	AA-5B Tiger	Tiger Aviation (Jersey) Ltd
	G-BHLY	Sikorsky S-76A	Bristow Helicopters Ltd
	G-BHMA	SIPA 903	H. J. Taggart
	G-BHMC	M.S.880B Rallye Club	The G-BHMC Group

Reg.	Type	Owner or Operator	Notes
G-BHMD	Rand KR-2	W. D. Francis	
G-BHME	WMB.2 Windtracker balloon	I. R. Bell & ptnrs	
G-BHMG	Cessna FA.152	Tiger Air Ltd	
G-BHMH	Cessna FA.152	Flairhire Ltd/Redhill	
G-BHMI	Cessna F.172N	W. Lancashire Aero Club Ltd (G-WADE)/ Blackpool	
G-BHMJ	Avenger T.200-2112 balloon	R. Light *Lord Anthony 1*	
G-BHMK	Avenger T.200-2112 balloon	P. Kinder *Lord Anthony 2*	
G-BHML	Avenger T.200-2112 balloon	L. Caulfield *Lord Anthony 3*	
G-BHMM	Avenger T.200-2112 balloon	M. Murphy *Lord Anthony 4*	
G-BHMO	PA-20M Cerpa Special (Pacer)	A. B. Holloway	
G-BHMR	Stinson 108-3	D. Holliday	
G-BHMT	Evans VP-1	P. E. J. Sturgeon	
G-BHMU	Colt 21A balloon	J. R. Parkington & Co Ltd	
G-BHMW	F.27 Friendship Mk 200	Air UK/Norwich	
G-BHMX	F.27 Friendship Mk 200	Air UK/Norwich	
G-BHMY	F.27 Friendship Mk 200	Air UK/Norwich	
G-BHMZ	F.27 Friendship Mk 200	Air UK *R. J. Mitchell*/Norwich	
G-BHNA	Cessna F.152	Sheffield Aero Club Ltd/Netherthorpe	
G-BHNC	Cameron O-65 balloon	D. & C. Bareford	
G-BHND	Cameron N-65 balloon	Hunter & Sons (Wells) Ltd	
G-BHNE	Boeing 727-2J4	Dan-Air Services Ltd/Gatwick	
G-BHNF	Boeing 727-2J4	Dan-Air Services Ltd/Gatwick	
G-BHNI	Cessna 404 Titan	Interflight (Air Charters) Ltd/Gatwick	
G-BHNK	Jodel D.120A	F. G. Miskelly	
G-BHNL	Jodel D.112	P. E. Barker	
G-BHNM	PA-44-180 Seminole	Cearte Tiles Ltd/Coventry	
G-BHNN	PA-32R-301 Saratoga SP	H. Young Transport Ltd/ Southampton	
G-BHNO	PA-28-181 Archer II	Davison Plant Hire Co/Compton Abbas	
G-BHNP	Eiri PIK-20E-1	M. Astley/Husbands Bosworth	
G-BHNR	Cameron N-77 balloon	Bath University Hot-Air Balloon Club	
G-BHNT	Cessna F.172N	I. J. Boyd & D. J. McCooke	
G-BHNU	Cessna F.172N	B. Swindell (Haulage) Ltd/Barton	
G-BHNV	Westland-Bell 47G-3B1	Leyline Helicopters Ltd	
G-BHNX	Jodel D.117	R. V. Rendall	
G-BHNY	Cessna 425	Eclipsol Oil Ltd/Birmingham	
G-BHOA	Robin DR.400/160	Ferguson Aviation Ltd	
G-BHOF	Sikorsky S-61N	Bristow Helicopters Ltd	
G-BHOG	Sikorsky S-61N	Bristow Helicopters Ltd	
G-BHOH	Sikorsky S-61N	Bristow Helicopters Ltd	
G-BHOL	Jodel DR.1050	B. D. Deubelbeiss	
G-BHOM	PA-18 Super Cub 95	C. H. A. Bott	
G-BHOO	Thunder Ax7-65 balloon	D. Livesey & J. M. Purves *Scraps*	
G-BHOP	Thunder Ax3 balloon	B. R. & M. Boyle	
G-BHOR	PA-28-161 Warrior II.	Severn Valley Aviation Group	
G-BHOT	Cameron V-65 balloon	Dante Balloon Group	
G-BHOU	Cameron V-65 balloon	F. W. Barnes	
G-BHOW	Beech 95-58P Baron	Anglo-African Machinery Ltd/ Coventry	
G-BHOZ	SOCATA TB.9 Tampico	M. Brown	
G-BHPJ	Eagle Microlite	G. Breen/Enstone	
G-BHPK	Piper J-3C-65 Cub (236800)	H. W. Sage/Sywell	
G-BHPL	C.A.S.A. 1.131E Jungmann	M. G. Jeffries	
G-BHPM	PA-18 Super Cub 95	P. I. Morgans	
G-BHPN	Colt 14 balloon	Colt Balloons Ltd	
G-BHPO	Colt 14A balloon	C. J. Boxall	
G-BHPS	Jodel D.120A	C. J. Francis/Swansea	
G-BHPT	Piper J-3C-65 Cub	Airmiles Ltd	
G-BHPX	Cessna 152	Air South Flying Group/Shoreham	
G-BHPY	Cessna 152	Christopher Lunn & Co	
G-BHPZ	Cessna 172N	O'Brian Properties Ltd/Redhill	
G-BHRA	R. Commander 114A	J. M. F. Lyon-Williams/Old Sarum	
G-BHRB	Cessna F.152	Light Planes (Lancashire) Ltd/ Barton	
G-BHRC	PA-28-161 Warrior II	Sherwood Flying Club Ltd/Tollerton	
G-BHRD	D.H.C.1 Chipmunk 22 (WP977)	A. J. Dunstan & ptnrs/Kidlington	
G-BHRF	Airborne Industries AB400 gas balloon	Balloon Stable Ltd	
G-BHRH	Cessna FA.150K	Merlin Flying Club Ltd/Hucknall	
G-BHRI	Saffery S.200 balloon	N. J. & H. L. Dunnington	
G-BHRM	Cessna F.152	Angelsword Ltd/Wellesbourne	
G-BHRN	Cessna F.152	P. P. D. Howard-Johnston/Edinburgh	

Notes	Reg.	Type	Owner or Operator
	G-BHRO	R. Commander 112A	John Raymond Transport Ltd/Cardiff
	G-BHRP	PA-44-180 Seminole	C. Henry
	G-BHRR	CP.301A Emeraude	T. W. Offen
	G-BHRS	ICA IS-28M2	British Aerospace PLC/Woodford
	G-BHRV	Mooney M.20J	Tecnovil Equipamentos Industriales
	G-BHRW	Jodel DR.221	Melton Concrete Floors Ltd
	G-BHRY	Colt 56A balloon	A. S. Davidson
	G-BHSA	Cessna 152	Skyviews & General Ltd/Sherburn
	G-BHSB	Cessna 172N	Campbell Distribution Ltd/Booker
	G-BHSD	Scheibe SF.25E Super Falke	Lasham Gliding Soc Ltd
	G-BHSE	R. Commander 114	604 Sqdn Flying Group Ltd
	G-BHSF	AA-5A Cheetah	D.S. Plant Hire Ltd (G-BHAS)
	G-BHSL	C.A.S.A. 1.131 Jungmann	Cotswold Flying Group/Badminton
	G-BHSM	AB-206B JetRanger 2	Dollar Air Services Ltd/Coventry
	G-BHSN	Cameron N-56 balloon	Ballooning Endeavours Ltd
	G-BHSP	Thunder Ax7-77Z balloon	Chicago Instruments Ltd
	G-BHSS	Pitts S-1C Special	Booker Pitts Syndicate
	G-BHST	Hughes 369D	J. J. Woodhouse
	G-BHSU	H.S.125 Srs 700B	Shell Aircraft Ltd/Heathrow
	G-BHSV	H.S.125 Srs 700B	Shell Aircraft Ltd/Heathrow
	G-BHSW	H.S.125 Srs 700B	Shell Aircraft Ltd/Heathrow
	G-BHSY	Jodel DR.1050	S. R. Orwin & T. R. Allebone
	G-BHTA	PA-28-236 Dakota	Stenloss Ltd/Sywell
	G-BHTC	Jodel DR.1050/M1	D. Masterson & ptnrs
	G-BHTD	Cessna T.188C AgHusky	ADS (Aerial) Ltd/Southend
	G-BHTG	Thunder Ax6-56 balloon	F. R. & Mrs S. H. MacDonald
	G-BHTH	T-6G Texan (2807)	A. Reynard/Kidlington
	G-BHTI	SA.102.5 Cavalier	R. Cochrane
	G-BHTM	Cameron 80 Can SS balloon	BP Oil Ltd
	G-BHTR	Bell 206B JetRanger 3	Huktra (UK) Ltd
	G-BHTT	Cessna 500 Citation	Paramount Executive Ltd/Birmingham
	G-BHTV	Cessna 310R	Aviation Beauport Ltd/Jersey
	G-BHUB	Douglas C-47 (315509) ★	Imperial War Museum/Duxford
	G-BHUE	Jodel DR.1050	M. J. Harris
	G-BHUG	Cessna 172N	McArgent Aviation Ltd
	G-BHUI	Cessna 152	J. MacDonald
	G-BHUJ	Cessna 172N	Three Counties Aero Club Ltd/ Blackbushe
	G-BHUM	D.H.82A Tiger Moth	S. G. Towers
	G-BHUN	PZL-104 Wilga 35	W. Radwanski/Lasham
	G-BHUO	Evans VP-2	R. A. Povall
	G-BHUP	Cessna F.152	Light Planes (Lancashire) Ltd/ Barton
	G-BHUR	Thunder Ax3 balloon	B. F. G. Ribbons
	G-BHUU	PA-25 Pawnee 235	Scanrho Aviation
	G-BHUV	PA-25 Pawnee 235	Farmwork Services (Eastern) Ltd
	G-BHVB	PA-28-161 Warrior II	R.J.S. Aviation/Halfpenny Green
	G-BHVC	Cessna 172RG Cutlass	Ian Willis Publicity Ltd/Panshanger
	G-BHVE	Saffery S.330 balloon	P. M. Randles
	G-BHVF	Jodel D.150A	C. A. Parker & ptnrs/Sywell
	G-BHVM	Cessna 152	Merrett Aviation Ltd
	G-BHVN	Cessna 152	Three Counties Aero Club Ltd/ Blackbushe
	G-BHVP	Cessna 182Q	Air Tows/Lasham
	G-BHVR	Cessna 172N	Air Tows/Blackbushe
	G-BHVT	Boeing 727-212	Dan-Air Services Ltd/Gatwick
	G-BHVV	Piper J-3C-65 Cub	A. E. Molton
	G-BHVZ	Cessna 180	R. Moore/Blackpool
	G-BHWA	Cessna F.152	Wickenby Aviation Ltd
	G-BHWB	Cessna F.152	Wickenby Aviation Ltd
	G-BHWE	Boeing 737-204ADV	Britannia Airways Ltd/ Sir Sidney Camm/Luton
	G-BHWF	Boeing 737-204ADV	Britannia Airways Ltd/ Lord Brabazon of Tara/Luton
	G-BHWG	Mahatma S.200SR balloon	H. W. Gandy Spectrum
	G-BHWH	Weedhopper JC-24A	G. A. Clephane
	G-BHWK	M.S.880B Rallye Club	H. R. Oldland
	G-BHWN	WMB.3 Windtracker 200 balloon	C. J. Dodd & G. J. Luckett
	G-BHWS	Cessna F.152	Stapleford Flying Club
	G-BHWW	Cessna U.206G	Aerotime Ltd/Glenrothes
	G-BHWY	PA-28R Cherokee Arrow 200-II	Rack Delta Ltd/Blackbushe
	G-BHWZ	PA-28-181 Archer II	Symtec Computer Service Ltd
	G-BHXD	Jodel D.120	D. R. Gilbert & ptnrs/Prestwick

Reg.	Type	Owner or Operator	Notes
G-BHXJ	Nord 1203/2 Norecrin	R. E. Coates/Booker	
G-BHXK	PA-28 Cherokee 140	GXK Flying Group	
G-BHXL	Evans VP-2	T. W. Woolley	
G-BHXN	Van's RV.3	P. R. Hing	
G-BHXO	Colt 14A balloon	Colt Balloons Ltd/Sweden	
G-BHXS	Jodel D.120	S. Billington	
G-BHXT	Thunder Ax6-56Z balloon	Ocean Traffic Services Ltd	
G-BHXU	AB-206B JetRanger 3	Castle Air Charters Ltd	
G-BHXV	AB-206B JetRanger 3	G. Greenall (G-OWJM)	
G-BHXY	Piper J-3C-65 Cub (44-79609)	D. J. J. Harwood	
G-BHYA	Cessna R.182RG II	MLP Aviation Ltd/Elstree	
G-BHYB	Sikorsky S-76A	British International Helicopters Ltd/Beccles	
G-BHYC	Cessna 172RG Cutlass	T. G. Henshall	
G-BHYD	Cessna R.172K XP II	Sylmar Aviation Services Ltd	
G-BHYE	PA-34-200T Seneca II	C.S.E. Aviation Ltd/Kidlington	
G-BHYF	PA-34-200T Seneca II	C.S.E. Aviation Ltd/Kidlington	
G-BHYG	PA-34-200T Seneca II	C.S.E. Aviation Ltd/Kidlington	
G-BHYI	Stampe SV-4A	P. A. Irwin & W. C. Medcalfe	
G-BHYN	Evans VP-2	A. B. Cameron	
G-BHYO	Cameron N-77 balloon	C. Sisson	
G-BHYP	Cessna F.172M	H. Hargreaves	
G-BHYR	Cessna F.172M	Alumvale Ltd/Stapleford	
G-BHYV	Evans VP-1	L. Chiappi	
G-BHYW	AB-206B JetRanger	Gleneagles Helicopter Services (Scotland) Ltd	
G-BHYX	Cessna 152 II	Stanton Aircraft Management Ltd	
G-BHZA	Piper J-3C-65 Cub	R. G. Warwick	
G-BHZE	PA-28-181 Archer II	G. R. K. Saigal/Leicester	
G-BHZF	Evans VP-2	R. G. Boyes/Dunkeswell	
G-BHZH	Cessna F.152	Havelet Leasing Ltd	
G-BHZK	AA-5B Tiger	Achandunie Farming Co/Elstree	
G-BHZM	Jodel DR.1050	G. H. Wylde/Manchester	
G-BHZO	AA-5A Cheetah	Scotia Safari Ltd/Prestwick	
G-BHZU	Piper J-3C-65 Cub	J. K. Tomkinson	
G-BHZV	Jodel D.120A	J. G. Munro/Perth	
G-BHZX	Thunder Ax7-65A balloon	S. C. Kinsey & G. E. Harns	
G-BHZY	Monnet Sonerai II	C. A. Keech	
G-BIAA	SOCATA TB.9 Tampico	B. D. Greenwood	
G-BIAB	SOCATA TB.9 Tampico	H. W. A. Thirlway	
G-BIAC	SOCATA Rallye 235E	Anpal Finance Ltd & Aerial Facilities Ltd/Biggin Hill	
G-BIAH	Jodel D.112	D. Mitchell	
G-BIAI	WMB.2 Windtracker balloon	I. Chadwick	
G-BIAK	SOCATA TB.10 Tobago	Trent Combustion Components Ltd/Tollerton	
G-BIAL	Rango NA.8 balloon	A. M. Lindsay	
G-BIAO	Evans VP-2	P. J. Hall	
G-BIAP	PA-16 Clipper	I. M. Callier & P. J. Bish/White Waltham	
G-BIAR	Rigg Skyliner II balloon	I. A. Rigg	
G-BIAU	Sopwith Pup Replica (N6452)	FAA Museum/Yeovilton	
G-BIAV	Sikorsky S-76A	British International Helicopters Ltd	
G-BIAW	Sikorsky S-76A	British International Helicopters Ltd	
G-BIAX	Taylor JT.2 Titch	G. F. Rowley	
G-BIAY	AA-5 Traveler	M. D. Dupay & ptnrs	
G-BIBA	SOCATA TB.9 Tampico	R. E. Pettit	
G-BIBB	Mooney M.20C	Gloucestershire Flying Club/Staverton	
G-BIBC	Cessna 310R	Air Service Training Ltd/Perth	
G-BIBD	Rotec Rally 2B	A. Clarke	
G-BIBG	Sikorsky S-76A	Bristow Helicopters Ltd	
G-BIBJ	Enstrom 280C-UK-2 Shark	Tindon Ltd/Little Snoring	
G-BIBK	Taylor JT.2 Titch	T. C. Horner	
G-BIBN	Cessna FA.150K	P. H. Lewis	
G-BIBO	Cameron V-65 balloon	Southern Balloon Group	
G-BIBP	AA-5A Cheetah	Scotia Safari Ltd/Prestwick	
G-BIBS	Cameron P-20 balloon	Cameron Balloons Ltd	
G-BIBT	AA-5B Tiger	Fergusons (Blyth) Ltd/Newcastle	
G-BIBU	Morris Ax7-77 balloon	K. Morris	
G-BIBV	WMB.3 Windtracker balloon	P. B. Street	
G-BIBW	Cessna F.172N	Deltair Ltd/Chester	
G-BIBX	WMB.2 Windtracker balloon	I. A. Rigg	

Notes	Reg.	Type	Owner or Operator
	G-BIBY	Beech F33A Bonanza	M. J. H. Raymont
	G-BIBZ	Thunder Ax3 balloon	F. W. Barnes
	G-BICB	Rotec Rally 2B	J. D. Lye & A. P. Jones
	G-BICC	Vulture Tx3 balloon	C. P. Clitheroe
	G-BICD	Auster 5	J. A. S. Baldry & ptnrs
	G-BICE	AT-6C Harvard IIA (CE)	C. M. L. Edwards/Ipswich
	G-BICG	Cessna F.152	Denham School of Flying Ltd
	G-BICI	Cameron R-833 balloon	Ballooning Endeavours Ltd
	G-BICJ	Monnet Sonerai II	D. J. Willison
	G-BICM	Colt 56A balloon	T. A. R. & S. Turner
	G-BICN	F.8L Falco	R. J. Barber
	G-BICP	Robin DR.360	Bravo India Flying Group/Woodvale
	G-BICR	Jodel D.120A	S. W. C. Hall & ptnrs/Redhill
	G-BICS	Robin R.2100A	AJE Gearing Co Ltd/Popham
	G-BICT	Evans VP-1	A. S. Coombe & D. L. Tribe
	G-BICU	Cameron V-56 balloon	I. S. Clarke
	G-BICW	PA-28-161 Warrior II	Fastraven Ltd/Cranfield
	G-BICX	Maule M5-235C Lunar Rocket	Stanton Aircraft Management Ltd/Biggin Hill
	G-BICY	PA-23 Apache 160	A. M. Lynn/Sibson
	G-BIDD	Evans VP-1	J. E. Wedgbury
	G-BIDE	CP.301A Emeraude	D. Elliott
	G-BIDF	Cessna F.172P	J. J. Baumhardt/Southend
	G-BIDG	Jodel D.150A	D. R. Gray/Barton
	G-BIDH	Cessna 152	Midland Aircraft Leasing Ltd/Birmingham
	G-BIDI	PA-28R-201 Arrow III	LBE Contract Tooling Ltd
	G-BIDJ	PA-18A Super Cub 150	Marchington Gliding Club
	G-BIDK	PA-18 Super Cub 150	Scottish Gliding Union Ltd
	G-BIDM	Cessna F.172H	D. A. Mortimore/Humberside
	G-BIDO	CP.301A Emeraude	A. R. Plumb
	G-BIDP	PA-28-181 Archer II	H. S. Elkins/Bristol
	G-BIDT	Cameron A-375 balloon	Ballooning Endeavours Ltd
	G-BIDU	Cameron V-77 balloon	E. Eleazor
	G-BIDV	Colt 14A balloon	International Distillers & Vintners (House Trade) Ltd
	G-BIDW	Sopwith 1½ Strutter replica (A8226) ★	RAF Museum/Hendon
	G-BIDX	Jodel D.112	H. N. Nuttall & R. P. Walley
	G-BIDY	WMB.2 Windtracker balloon	D. M. Campion
	G-BIDZ	Colt 21A balloon	Hot Air Balloon Co Ltd/S. Africa
	G-BIEC	AB-206A JetRanger 2	Autair Helicopters Ltd
	G-BIEF	Cameron V-77 balloon	D. S. Bush
	G-BIEH	Sikorsky S-76A	Bond Helicopters Ltd/Bourn
	G-BIEJ	Sikorsky S-76A	Bristow Helicopters Ltd
	G-BIEK	WMB.4 Windtracker balloon	P. B. Street
	G-BIEM	D.H.C.6 Twin Otter 310	Loganair Ltd/Glasgow
	G-BIEN	Jodel D.120A	Echo November Flight/Bristol
	G-BIEO	Jodel D.112	W. S. V. Stoney
	G-BIEP	PA-28-181 Archer II	Bickerton Aerodromes Ltd
	G-BIER	Rutan LongEz	V. Mossor
	G-BIES	Maule M5-235C Lunar Rocket	William Proctor Farms
	G-BIET	Cameron O-77 balloon	G. M. Westley
	G-BIEW	Cessna U.206G	G. D. Atkinson/Guernsey
	G-BIEX	Andreasson BA-4B	H. P. Burrill/Sherburn
	G-BIEY	PA-28-151 Warrior	J. A. Pothecary/Shoreham
	G-BIFA	Cessna 310R-II	E. A. Pitcher
	G-BIFB	PA-28 Cherokee 150	C. J. Reed/Elstree
	G-BIFC	Colt 14A balloon	Colt Balloons Ltd
	G-BIFD	R. Commander 114	K. E. Armstrong
	G-BIFN	Bensen B.8M	B. Gunn
	G-BIFO	Evans VP-1	A. N. Wells/Bristol
	G-BIFP	Colt 56C balloon	J. Philp
	G-BIFT	Cessna F.150L	Phoenix Aviation (Bedford) Ltd/Cranfield
	G-BIFV	Jodel D.150	J. H. Kirkham/Barton
	G-BIFY	Cessna F.150L	Phoenix Aviation (Bedford) Ltd/Cranfield
	G-BIFZ	Partenavia P.68C	ALY Aviation Ltd/Henstridge
	G-BIGD	Cameron V-77 balloon	D. L. Clark Frog
	G-BIGF	Thunder Ax7-77 balloon	M. D. Stever & C. A. Allen
	G-BIGH	Piper J-3C-65 Cub	W. McNally
	G-BIGJ	Cessna F.172M	Clacton Aero Club (1988) Ltd

Reg.	Type	Owner or Operator	Notes
G-BIGK	Taylorcraft BC-12D	H. L. M. & G. R. Williams	
G-BIGL	Cameron O-65 balloon	P. L. Mossman	
G-BIGM	Avenger T.200-2112 balloon	M. Murphy	
G-BIGN	Attic Srs 1 balloon	G. Nettleship	
G-BIGP	Bensen B.8M	R. H. S. Cooper	
G-BIGR	Avenger T.200-2112 balloon	R. Light	
G-BIGU	Bensen B.8M	J. R. Martin	
G-BIGX	Bensen B.8M	J. R. Martin	
G-BIGY	Cameron V-65 balloon	Dante Balloon Group	
G-BIGZ	Scheibe SF.25B Falke	K. Ballington	
G-BIHD	Robin DR.400/160	Alexander Howden Group Sports & Social Club/Biggin Hill	
G-BIHE	Cessna FA.152	Inverness Flying Services Ltd	
G-BIHF	SE-5A Replica (F943)	K. J. Garrett *Lady Di*/Booker	
G-BIHG	PA-28 Cherokee 140	T. M. Plewman	
G-BIHI	Cessna 172M	J. H. Ashby-Rogers	
G-BIHN	Skyship 500 airship	Airship Industries Ltd/Cardington	
G-BIHO	D.H.C.6 Twin Otter 310	Brymon Aviation Ltd/Plymouth	
G-BIHP	Van Den Bemden gas balloon	J. J. Harris	
G-BIHT	PA-17 Vagabond	R. S. T. Sears/Wellesbourne	
G-BIHU	Saffery S.200 balloon	B. L. King	
G-BIHX	Bensen B.8M	C. C. Irvine	
G-BIHY	Isaacs Fury	P. C. Butler	
G-BIIA	Fournier RF-3	T. M. W. Webster	
G-BIIB	Cessna F.172M	Civil Service Flying Club (Biggin Hill) Ltd	
G-BIID	PA-18 Super Cub 95	875 (Westhill) Squadron ATC/Aberdeen	
G-BIIE	Cessna F.172P	Shoreham Flight Simulation Ltd/ Bournemouth	
G-BIIF	Fournier RF-4D	J. A. Bridges & J. A. Taylor (G-BVET)/ Biggin Hill	
G-BIIG	Thunder Ax-6-56Z balloon	P. Rose	
G-BIIJ	Cessna F.152	Leicestershire Aero Club Ltd	
G-BIIK	M.S.883 Rallye 115	P. Rose	
G-BIIL	Thunder Ax6-56 balloon	G. W. Reader	
G-BIIT	PA-28-161 Warrior II	Tayside Aviation Ltd/Dundee	
G-BIIV	PA-28-181 Archer II	Stratton Motor Co Ltd	
G-BIIX	Rango NA.12 balloon	Rango Kite Co	
G-BIIZ	Great Lakes 2T-1A Sport Trainer	The Hon A. M. M. Lindsay/Booker	
G-BIJB	PA-18 Super Cub 150	Essex Gliding Club/North Weald	
G-BIJC	AB-206B JetRanger	Anglia Helicopters Ltd/Southend	
G-BIJD	Bo 208C Junior	A. L. Burton/Netherthorpe	
G-BIJE	Piper J-3C-65 Cub	K. G. & J. Wakefield	
G-BIJS	Luton LA-4A Minor	I. J. Smith	
G-BIJT	AA-5A Cheetah	Mid-Sussex Timber Co Ltd	
G-BIJU	CP.301A Emeraude	D. Brooker & ptnrs (G-BHTX)/ Southend	
G-BIJV	Cessna F.152 II	Falcon Flying Services/Biggin Hill	
G-BIJW	Cessna F.152 II	G. K. Mitchell Ltd	
G-BIJX	Cessna F.152 II	Civil Service Flying Club Ltd/ Biggin Hill	
G-BIKA	Boeing 757-236	British Airways *Dover Castle*/ Heathrow	
G-BIKB	Boeing 757-236	British Airways *Windsor Castle*/ Heathrow	
G-BIKC	Boeing 757-236	British Airways *Edinburgh Castle*/ Heathrow	
G-BIKD	Boeing 757-236	British Airways *Caernarvon Castle*/ Heathrow	
G-BIKE	PA-28R Cherokee Arrow 200	R. V. Webb Ltd/Elstree	
G-BIKF	Boeing 757-236	British Airways *Carrikfergus Castle*/ Heathrow	
G-BIKG	Boeing 757-236	British Airways *Stirling Castle*/ Heathrow	
G-BIKH	Boeing 757-236	British Airways *Richmond Castle*/ Heathrow	
G-BIKI	Boeing 757-236	British Airways *Tintagel Castle*/ Heathrow	
G-BIKJ	Boeing 757-236	British Airways *Conway Castle*/ Heathrow	
G-BIKK	Boeing 757-236	British Airways *Eilean Donan Castle*/ Heathrow	

Notes	Reg.	Type	Owner or Operator
	G-BIKL	Boeing 757-236	British Airways *Nottingham Castle*/Heathrow
	G-BIKM	Boeing 757-236	British Airways *Glamis Castle*/Heathrow
	G-BIKN	Boeing 757-236	British Airways *Bodiam Castle*/Heathrow
	G-BIKO	Boeing 757-236	British Airways *Harlech Castle*/Heathrow
	G-BIKP	Boeing 757-236	British Airways *Enniskillen Castle*/Heathrow
	G-BIKR	Boeing 757-236	British Airways *Bamburgh Castle*/Heathrow
	G-BIKS	Boeing 757-236	British Airways *Corfe Castle*/Heathrow
	G-BIKT	Boeing 757-236	British Airways*Carisbrooke Castle*/Heathrow
	G-BIKU	Boeing 757-236	British Airways *Inverrary Castle*/Heathrow
	G-BIKV	Boeing 757-236	British Airways *Raglan Castle*/Heathrow
	G-BIKW	Boeing 757-236	British Airways *Colchester Castle*/Heathrow
	G-BIKX	Boeing 757-236	British Airways *Warwick Castle*/Heathrow
	G-BIKY	Boeing 757-236	British Airways *Leeds Castle*/Heathrow
	G-BIKZ	Boeing 757-236	British Airways *Kenilworth Castle*/Heathrow
	G-BILA	Daletol DM.165L Viking	R. Lamplough (*stored*)
	G-BILB	WMB.2 Windtracker balloon	B. L. King
	G-BILE	Scruggs BL.2B balloon	P. D. Ridout
	G-BILF	Practavia Sprite 125	G. Harfield
	G-BILG	Scruggs BL.2B balloon	P. D. Ridout
	G-BILI	Piper J-3C-65 Cub (454467)	D. M. Boddy & G. R. Mills
	G-BILJ	Cessna FA.152	Shoreham Flight Simulation Ltd/Bournemouth
	G-BILK	Cessna FA.152	A. Blair/Biggin Hill
	G-BILL	PA-25 Pawnee 235	Bowker Air Services Ltd/Rush Green
	G-BILP	Cessna 152 II	Skyviews & General Ltd
	G-BILR	Cessna 152	Skyviews & General Ltd
	G-BILS	Cessna 152	Skyviews & General Ltd
	G-BILU	Cessna 172RG	Melrose Pigs Ltd
	G-BILX	Colt 31A balloon	Hot Air Balloon Co Ltd
	G-BILZ	Taylor JT.1 Monoplane	A. Petherbridge
	G-BIMK	Tiger T.200 Srs 1 balloon	M. K. Baron
	G-BIMM	PA-18 Super Cub 150	D. S. & I. M. Morgan
	G-BIMN	Steen Skybolt	C. R. Williamson
	G-BIMO	Stampe SV-4C	G. A. Breen
	G-BIMT	Cessna FA.152	Staverton Flying Services Ltd
	G-BIMU	Sikorsky S-61N	Bristow Helicopters Ltd
	G-BIMX	Rutan Vari-Eze	A. S. Knowles
	G-BIMZ	Beech 76 Duchess	Barrein Engineers Ltd/Lulsgate
	G-BINA	Saffery S.9 balloon	A. P. Bashford
	G-BINB	WMB.2A Windtracker balloon	S. R. Woolfries
	G-BINF	Saffery S.200 balloon	T. Lewis
	G-BING	Cessna F.172P	J. E. M. Patrick
	G-BINH	D.H.82A Tiger Moth	Arrow Air Services (Engineering) Ltd (*stored*)/Felthorpe
	G-BINI	Scruggs BL.2C balloon	S. R. Woolfries
	G-BINL	Scruggs BL.2B balloon	P. D. Ridout
	G-BINM	Scruggs BL.2B balloon	P. D. Ridout
	G-BINO	Evans VP-1	J. I. Visser
	G-BINR	Unicorn UE.1A balloon	Unicorn Group
	G-BINS	Unicorn UE.2A balloon	Unicorn Group
	G-BINT	Unicorn UE.1A balloon	Unicorn Group
	G-BINU	Saffery S.200 balloon	T. Lewis
	G-BINX	Scruggs BL.2B balloon	P. D. Ridout
	G-BINY	Oriental balloon	J. L. Morton
	G-BINZ	Rango NA.8 balloon	T. J. Sweeting & M. O. Davies
	G-BIOA	Hughes 369D	Weetabix Ltd/Sywell
	G-BIOB	Cessna F.172P	Aerofilms Ltd/Elstree
	G-BIOC	Cessna F.150L	Seawing Flying Club/Southend
	G-BIOI	Jodel DR.1051M	H. F. Hambling

Reg.	Type	Owner or Operator	Notes
G-BIOJ	R. Commander 112TCA	T. D. Stronge/Newtownards	
G-BIOK	Cessna F.152	Tayside Aviation Ltd/Dundee	
G-BIOM	Cessna F.152	Falcon Flying Services/Biggin Hill	
G-BION	Cameron V-77 balloon	Elliott's Pharmacy Ltd	
G-BIOO	Unicorn UE.2B balloon	Unicorn Group	
G-BIOP	Scruggs BL.2D balloon	J. P. S. Donnellan	
G-BIOR	M.S.880B Rallye Club	Aircraft Dept. Royal Aircraft Establishment/Farnborough	
G-BIOU	Jodel D.117A	M. S. Printing & Graphics Machinery Ltd/Booker	
G-BIOW	Slingsby T.67A	Slingsby Aviation Ltd/Kirkbymoorside	
G-BIOX	Potter Crompton PRO.1 balloon	G. M. Potter	
G-BIPA	AA-5B Tiger	J. Campbell/Barrow	
G-BIPB	Weedhopper JC-24B	E. H. Moroney	
G-BIPH	Scruggs BL.2B balloon	C. M. Dewsnap	
G-BIPI	Everett Blackbird Mk 1	G. C. Webber & N. V. de Candole	
G-BIPJ	PA-36-375 Brave	G. B. Pearce/Shoreham	
G-BIPK	Saffery S.200 balloon	P. J. Kelsey	
G-BIPM	Flamboyant Ax7-65 balloon	Pepsi Cola International Ltd/S. Africa	
G-BIPN	Fournier RF-3	S. N. Lawrence	
G-BIPO	Mudry/CAARP CAP.20LS-200	BIPO Aviation Ltd/Booker	
G-BIPS	SOCATA Rallye 100ST	McAully Flying Group/Little Snoring	
G-BIPT	Jodel D.112	C. R. Davies	
G-BIPU	AA-5B Tiger	M. A. Judge	
G-BIPV	AA-5B Tiger	Copyacre Ltd	
G-BIPW	Avenger T.200-2112 balloon	B. L. King	
G-BIPY	Bensen B.8	W. J. Pope	
G-BIPZ	McCandless Mk 4-4	B. McIntyre	
G-BIRA	SOCATA TB.9 Tampico	Goldangel Ltd/Swansea	
G-BIRB	M.S.880B Rallye 100T	E. Smith	
G-BIRD	Pitts S-1C Special	CB Helicopters Ltd	
G-BIRE	Colt 56 Bottle balloon	Hot Air Balloon Co Ltd	
G-BIRH	PA-18 Super Cub 135 (R-163)	I. R. F. Hammond/Lee-on-Solent	
G-BIRI	C.A.S.A. 1.131E Jungmann	M. G. & J. R. Jeffries	
G-BIRK	Avenger T.200-2112 balloon	D. Harland	
G-BIRL	Avenger T.200-2112 balloon	R. Light	
G-BIRM	Avenger T.200-2112 balloon	P. Higgins	
G-BIRN	Short SD3-30	Thurston Aviation Ltd/Stansted	
G-BIRO	Cessna 172P	M. C. Grant	
G-BIRP	Arena Mk 17 Skyship balloon	A. S. Viel	
G-BIRS	Cessna 182P	D. J. Tollafield (G-BBBS)	
G-BIRT	Robin R.1180TD	W. D'A. Hall/Booker	
G-BIRV	Bensen B.8MV	R. Hart	
G-BIRW	M.S.505 Criquet (F+IS)	Museum of Flight/E. Fortune	
G-BIRY	Cameron V-77 balloon	J. J. Winter	
G-BIRZ	Zenair CH.250	B. A. Arnall & M. Hanley/Biggin Hill	
G-BISB	Cessna F.152 II	Sheffield Aero Club Ltd/Netherthorpe	
G-BISC	Robinson R-22	Skyline Helicopters Ltd/Booker	
G-BISF	Robinson R-22	Computer Ltd	
G-BISG	FRED Srs 3	R. A. Coombe	
G-BISH	Cameron O-42 balloon	Zebedee Balloon Service	
G-BISI	Robinson R-22	Sloane Helicopters Ltd/Luton	
G-BISJ	Cessna 340A	Castle Aviation/Leeds	
G-BISK	R. Commander 112B ★	P. A. Warner	
G-BISL	Scruggs BL.2B balloon	P. D. Ridout	
G-BISM	Scruggs BL.2B balloon	P. D. Ridout	
G-BISN	Boeing Vertol 234LR Chinook	British International Helicopters Ltd/ (withdrawn) Aberdeen	
G-BISP	Boeing Vertol 234LR Chinook	British International Helicopters Ltd/ (withdrawn) Aberdeen	
G-BISR	Boeing Vertol 234LR Chinook	British International Helicopters Ltd/ (withdrawn) Aberdeen	
G-BISS	Scruggs BL.2C balloon	P. D. Ridout	
G-BIST	Scruggs BL.2C balloon	P. D. Ridout	
G-BISV	Cameron O-65 balloon	Hylyne Rabbits Ltd	
G-BISW	Cameron O-65 balloon	J. R. Christopher & S. M. Antony	
G-BISX	Colt 56A balloon	Long John International Ltd	
G-BISZ	Sikorsky S-76A	Bristow Helicopters Ltd	
G-BITA	PA-18 Super Cub 150	J. & S. A. S. McCullough	
G-BITE	SOCATA TB.10 Tobago	M. A. Smith & R. J. Bristow/Fairoaks	
G-BITF	Cessna F.152	Bristol & Wessex Aeroplane Club/Bristol	

Notes	Reg.	Type	Owner or Operator
	G-BITG	Cessna F.152	Bristol & Wessex Aeroplane Club/ Bristol
	G-BITH	Cessna F.152	Bristol & Wessex Aeroplane Club/ Bristol
	G-BITK	FRED Srs 2	R. B. Armitage
	G-BITL	Horncastle LL-901 balloon	M. J. Worsdell
	G-BITM	Cessna F.172P	D. G. Crabtree/Barton
	G-BITO	Jodel D.112D	A. Dunbar/Barton
	G-BITR	Sikorsky S-76A	Bristow Helicopters Ltd
	G-BITS	Drayton B-56 balloon	M. J. Betts
	G-BITV	Short SD3-30	Air Europe Express/Gatwick
	G-BITW	Short SD3-30	Short Bros PLC (G-EASI)/Sydenham
	G-BITX	Short SD3-30	Fairflight Ltd/Biggin Hill
	G-BITY	FD.31T balloon	A. J. Bell
	G-BIUL	Cameron 60 SS balloon	D. C. Patrick-Brown
	G-BIUM	Cessna F.152	Sheffield Aero Club Ltd/ Netherthorpe
	G-BIUN	Cessna F.152	Sheffield Aero Club Ltd/ Netherthorpe
	G-BIUP	SNCAN NC.854S	C. M. Mogg
	G-BIUV	H.S.748 Srs 2A	Dan-Air Services Ltd (G-AYYH)/ Gatwick
	G-BIUW	PA-28-161 Warrior II	D. R. Staley
	G-BIUX	PA-28-161 Warrior II	C.S.E. Aviation Ltd/Kidlington
	G-BIUY	PA-28-181 Archer II	Maidenhead Electrical Services Ltd/ White Waltham
	G-BIVA	Robin R.2112	Cotswold Aero Club Ltd/Staverton
	G-BIVB	Jodel D.112	R. J. Lewis/Bodmin
	G-BIVC	Jodel D.112	M. J. Barmby/Cardiff
	G-BIVF	CP.301C-3 Emeraude	J. Cosker
	G-BIVK	Bensen B.8	J. G. Toy
	G-BIVL	Bensen B.8	R. Gardiner
	G-BIVT	Saffery S.80 balloon	L. F. Guyot
	G-BIVU	AA-5A Cheetah	Fastglow Ltd/Biggin Hill
	G-BIVV	AA-5A Cheetah	W. Dass
	G-BIVY	Cessna 172N	Goodwood Aircraft Management Services Ltd
	G-BIVZ	D.31A Turbulent	J. Gillespie
	G-BIWB	Scruggs RS.5000 balloon	P. D. Ridout
	G-BIWC	Scruggs RS.5000 balloon	P. D. Ridout
	G-BIWD	Scruggs RS.5000 balloon	D. Eaves
	G-BIWF	Warren balloon	P. D. Ridout
	G-BIWG	Zelenski Mk 2 balloon	P. D. Ridout
	G-BIWJ	Unicorn UE.1A balloon	B. L. King
	G-BIWK	Cameron V-65 balloon	I. R. Williams & R. G. Bickerdike
	G-BIWL	PA-32-301 Saratoga	D. Hammant/Southampton
	G-BIWN	Jodel D.112	C. R. Coates
	G-BIWP	Mooney M.20J	Earl of Caledon
	G-BIWR	Mooney M.20F	C. W. Yarnton & J. D. Heykoop/ Redhill
	G-BIWS	Cessna 182R	P. S. Bubbear
	G-BIWU	Cameron V-65 balloon	J. T. Whicker & J. W. Unwin
	G-BIWW	AA-5 Traveler	B&K Aviation/Cranfield
	G-BIWX	AT-16 Harvard IV (FT239)	A. E. Hutton/White Waltham
	G-BIWY	Westland WG.30	British International Helicopters Ltd/ (stored)
	G-BIXA	SOCATA TB.9 Tampico	WPS Aviation/Staverton
	G-BIXB	SOCATA TB.9 Tampico	Kitchen Bros/Little Snoring
	G-BIXH	Cessna F.152	Cambridge Aero Club Ltd
	G-BIXI	Cessna 172RG Cutlass	J. F. P. Lewis/Sandown
	G-BIXJ	Saffery S.40 balloon	T. M. Pates
	G-BIXK	Rand KR.2	R. G. Cousins
	G-BIXL	P-51D Mustang (472216)	R. Lamplough/North Weald
	G-BIXN	Boeing A.75N1 Stearman	I. L. Craig-Wood & ptnrs
	G-BIXR	Cameron A-140 balloon	Skysales Ltd
	G-BIXS	Avenger T.200-2112 balloon	M. Stuart
	G-BIXT	Cessna 182R	M. L. J. Warwick
	G-BIXV	Bell 212	Bristow Helicopters Ltd
	G-BIXW	Colt 56B balloon	J. R. Birkenhead
	G-BIXX	Pearson Srs 2 balloon	D. Pearson
	G-BIXZ	Grob G-109	V. J. R. Day
	G-BIYH	Short SD3-30	Fairflight Ltd
	G-BIYI	Cameron V-65 balloon	Sarnia Balloon Group
	G-BIYJ	PA-18 Super Cub 95	S. Russell

Reg.	Type	Owner or Operator	Notes
G-BIYK	Isaacs Fury	R. S. Martin/Dunkeswell	
G-BIYM	PA-32R-301 Saratoga SP	R. H. van Dijk	
G-BIYO	PA-31-310 Turbo Navajo	Northern Executive Aviation Ltd/Manchester	
G-BIYP	PA-20 Pacer 135	R. A. Lloyd-Hubbard & R. J. Whitcombe	
G-BIYR	PA-18 Super Cub 135	Delta Foxtrot Flying Group/Dunkeswell	
G-BIYT	Colt 17A balloon	A. F. Selby	
G-BIYU	Fokker S.11.1 Instructor (E-15)	H. R. Smallwood & A. J. Lee/Denham	
G-BIYW	Jodel D.112	W. J. Tanswell	
G-BIYX	PA-28 Cherokee 140	Telepoint Ltd/Manchester	
G-BIYY	PA-18 Super Cub 95	A. E. & W. J. Taylor/Ingoldmells	
G-BIZB	AB-206 JetRanger 3	Martin Butler Associates Ltd/Fairoaks	
G-BIZF	Cessna F.172P	R. S. Bentley	
G-BIZG	Cessna F.152	M. A. Judge	
G-BIZI	Robin DR.400/120	Headcorn Flying School Ltd	
G-BIZJ	Nord 3202	—/Liverpool	
G-BIZK	Nord 3202	A. A. Hodgson	
G-BIZL	Nord 3202	—/Liverpool	
G-BIZM	Nord 3202	Magnificent Obsessions Ltd	
G-BIZN	Slingsby T.67A	Condor Club/Redhill	
G-BIZO	PA-28R Cherokee Arrow 200	Aviation Metals Ltd/Cranfield	
G-BIZR	SOCATA TB.9 Tampico	Air Touring Services Ltd/Biggin Hill	
G-BIZT	Bensen B.8M	J. Ferguson	
G-BIZU	Thunder Ax6-56Z balloon	S. L. Leigh	
G-BIZV	PA-18 Super Cub 95 (18-2001)	J. K. Davies	
G-BIZW	Champion 7GCBC Citabria	G. Read & Son	
G-BIZY	Jodel D.112	C. R. A. Wood	
G-BJAD	FRED Srs 2	C. Allison	
G-BJAE	Lavadoux Starck AS.80	D. J. & S. A. E. Phillips/Coventry	
G-BJAF	Piper J-3C-65 Cub	P. J. Cottle	
G-BJAG	PA-28-181 Archer II	K. F. Hudson & ptnrs	
G-BJAJ	AA-5B Tiger	Sco-Fro Foods Ltd/Glasgow	
G-BJAK	Mooney M.20C	J. Harty & R. G. Soloman/Stapleford	
G-BJAL	C.A.S.A. 1.131E Jungmann	R. H. Reeves/Barton	
G-BJAN	SA.102-5 Cavalier	J. Powlesland	
G-BJAO	Bensen B.8M	G. L. Stockdale	
G-BJAP	D.H.82A Tiger Moth	J. Pothecary	
G-BJAR	Unicorn UE.3A balloon	Unicorn Group	
G-BJAS	Rango NA.9 balloon	A. Lindsay	
G-BJAU	PZL-104 Wilga 35	Anglo Polish Sailplanes Ltd	
G-BJAV	GY-80 Horizon 160	R. Pickett/Leicester	
G-BJAW	Cameron V-65 balloon	G. W. McCarthy	
G-BJAX	Pilatus P2-05 (14)	C. J. Diggins & ptnrs/Redhill	
G-BJAY	Piper J-3C-65 Cub	K. L. Clarke/Ingoldmells	
G-BJBI	Cessna 414A	Borfin Ltd/Manchester	
G-BJBK	PA-18 Super Cub 95	M. S. Bird/Old Sarum	
G-BJBM	Monnet Sonerai II	J. Pickerell & B. L. Sims/Southend	
G-BJBO	Jodel DR.250/160	C. C. Gordon	
G-BJBP	Beech A200 Super King Air	All Charter Ltd (G-HLUB)/Bournemouth	
G-BJBR	Robinson R-22	Stenoak Fencing & Construction Co Ltd	
G-BJBS	Robinson R-22	Cosworth Engineering Ltd/Sywell	
G-BJBV	PA-28-161 Warrior II	C.S.E. Aviation Ltd/Kidlington	
G-BJBW	PA-28-161 Warrior II	C.S.E. Aviation Ltd/Kidlington	
G-BJBX	PA-28-161 Warrior II	C.S.E. Aviation Ltd/Kidlington	
G-BJBY	PA-28-161 Warrior II	C.S.E. Aviation Ltd/Kidlington	
G-BJBZ	Rotorway 133 Executive	Rotorway (UK) Ltd	
G-BJCA	PA-28-161 Warrior II	D. M. Smith	
G-BJCD	Bede BD-5BH	Brockmoor-Bede Aircraft (UK) Ltd	
G-BJCF	CP.1310-C3 Super Emeraude	K. M. Hodson & C. G. H. Gurney	
G-BJCI	PA-18 Super Cub 150	The Borders (Milfield) Aero-Tour Club Ltd	
G-BJCJ	PA-28-181 Archer II	Coolstead Ltd/Panshanger	
G-BJCM	FRED Srs 2	J. C. Miller	
G-BJCP	Unicorn UE.2B balloon	Unicorn Group	
G-BJCR	Partenavia P.68C	Nullifire Ltd/Coventry	
G-BJCT	Boeing 737-204ADV	Britannia Airways Ltd *The Hon C. S. Rolls*/Luton	

Notes	Reg.	Type	Owner or Operator
	G-BJCU	Boeing 737-204ADV	Britannia Airways Ltd *Sir Henry Royce*/Luton
	G-BJCV	Boeing 737-204ADV	Britannia Airways Ltd *Viscount Trenchard*/Luton
	G-BJCW	PA-32R-301 Saratoga SP	Viscount Chelsea/Kidlington
	G-BJDE	Cessna F.172M	S. Lynn
	G-BJDF	M.S.880B Rallye 100T	W. R. Savin & ptnrs
	G-BJDI	Cessna FR.182RG	Spoils Kitchen Reject Shops Ltd
	G-BJDJ	H.S.125 Srs 700B	Consolidated Contractors International Ltd/Heathrow
	G-BJDK	European E.14 balloon	Aeroprint Tours
	G-BJDM	SA.102-5 Cavalier	J. D. McCracken
	G-BJDO	AA-5A Cheetah	Border Transport/Southampton
	G-BJDT	SOCATA TB.9 Tampico	Tampico Group/Old Sarum
	G-BJDW	Cessna F.172M	Suffolk Aero Club Ltd/Ipswich
	G-BJEI	PA-18 Super Cub 95	H. J. Cox
	G-BJEL	Nord NC.854	N. F. & S. G. Hunter
	G-BJEN	Scruggs RS.5000 balloon	N. J. Richardson
	G-BJEO	PA-34-220T Seneca III	D. W. Clark Land Drainage Ltd (G-TOMF)
	G-BJES	Scruggs RS.5000 balloon	J. E. Christopher
	G-BJEU	Scruggs BL.2D-2 balloon	G. G. Kneller
	G-BJEV	Aeronca 11AC Chief	R. F. Willcox
	G-BJEX	Bo 208C Junior	G. D. H. Crawford/Thruxton
	G-BJEY	BHMED Srs 1 balloon	D. R. Meades & J. S. Edwards
	G-BJFB	Mk 1A balloon	Aeroprint Tours
	G-BJFC	European E.8 balloon	P. D. Ridout
	G-BJFE	PA-18 Super Cub 95	B. C. Stevens
	G-BJFI	Bell 47G-2A1	Helicopter Supplies & Engineering Ltd/Bournemouth
	G-BJFK	Short SD3-30	National Commuter Airways/Southend
	G-BJFL	Sikorsky S-76A	Bristow Helicopters Ltd
	G-BJFM	Jodel D.120	M. L. Smith & ptnrs/Popham
	G-BJGC	Mk IV balloon	Windsor Balloon Group
	G-BJGD	Mk IV balloon	Windsor Balloon Group
	G-BJGE	Thunder Ax3 balloon	K. A. Williams
	G-BJGF	Mk 1 balloon	D. & D. Eaves
	G-BJGG	Mk 2 balloon	D. & D. Eaves
	G-BJGK	Cameron V-77 balloon	A. Simpson & R. Bailey
	G-BJGL	Cremer balloon	G. Lowther
	G-BJGM	Unicorn UE.1A balloon	D. Eaves & P. D. Ridout
	G-BJGT	Mooney M.20K	C. & K. Software Ltd
	G-BJGW	M.H.1521M Broussard (92)	G. A. Warner/Duxford
	G-BJGX	Sikorsky S-76A	Bristow Helicopters Ltd
	G-BJGY	Cessna F.172P	Lucca Wines Ltd
	G-BJHA	Cremer balloon	G. Cape
	G-BJHB	Mooney M.20J	Zitair Flying Club Ltd/Redhill
	G-BJHC	Swan 1 balloon	C. A. Swan
	G-BJHD	Mk 3B balloon	S. Meagher
	G-BJHK	EAA Acro Sport	S. M. Riseborough
	G-BJHL	Osprey 1C balloon	E. Bartlett
	G-BJHN	Osprey 1B balloon	J. E. Christopher
	G-BJHO	Osprey 1C balloon	G. G. Kneller
	G-BJHP	Osprey 1C balloon	N. J. Richardson
	G-BJHS	S.25 Sunderland V	Sunderland Ltd/Chatham
	G-BJHT	Thunder Ax7-65 balloon	A. H. & L. Symonds
	G-BJHU	Osprey 1C balloon	G. G. Kneller
	G-BJHV	Voisin Replica	M. P. Sayer/O. Warden
	G-BJHW	Osprey 1C balloon	N. J. Richardson
	G-BJIA	Allport balloon	D. J. Allport
	G-BJIB	D.31 Turbulent	N. H. Lemon
	G-BJIC	Dodo 1A balloon	P. D. Ridout
	G-BJID	Osprey 1B balloon	P. D. Ridout
	G-BJIF	Bensen B.8M	H. Redwin
	G-BJIG	Slingsby T.67A	B. R. Chapman/Redhill
	G-BJIR	Cessna 550 Citation II	Supreme Securities Ltd
	G-BJIV	PA-18 Super Cub 150	Yorkshire Gliding Club (Pty) Ltd
	G-BJIY	Cessna T337D	S. G. Hoole/Cranfield
	G-BJJE	Dodo Mk 3 balloon	D. Eaves
	G-BJJN	Cessna F.172M	Ospreystar Ltd (*stored*)/Stapleford
	G-BJJO	Bell 212	British Executive Air Services Ltd
	G-BJJP	Bell 212	British Executive Air Services Ltd
	G-BJJW	Mk B balloon	S. Meagher
	G-BJJX	Mk B balloon	S. Meagher

Reg.	Type	Owner or Operator	Notes
G-BJJY	Mk B balloon	S. Meagher	
G-BJKA	SA.365C Dauphin 2	Bond Helicopters Ltd/Bourn	
G-BJKB	SA.365C Dauphin 2	Bond Helicopters Ltd/Bourn	
G-BJKF	SOCATA TB.9 Tampico	H. Bollman Ltd	
G-BJKW	Wills Aera II	J. K. S. Wills	
G-BJKX	Cessna F.152	Eglinton Flying Club	
G-BJKY	Cessna F.152	Westair Flying Services Ltd/Blackpool	
G-BJLC	Monnet Sonerai IIL	P. J. Robins & R. King/Sywell	
G-BJLE	Osprey 1B balloon	I. Chadwick	
G-BJLF	Unicorn UE.1C balloon	I. Chadwick	
G-BJLG	Unicorn UE.1B balloon	I. Chadwick	
G-BJLH	PA-18 Super Cub 95 (K-33)	D. S. Kirkham	
G-BJLJ	Cameron D-50 balloon	Cameron Balloons Ltd	
G-BJLK	Short SD3-30	Gill Air/Newcastle	
G-BJLO	PA-31-310 Turbo Navajo	Linco (Poultry Machinery) Ltd/ Biggin Hill	
G-BJLU	Featherlight Mk 3 balloon	T. J. Sweeting & N. P. Kemp	
G-BJLV	Sphinx balloon	L. F. Guyot	
G-BJLX	Cremer balloon	P. W. May	
G-BJLY	Cremer balloon	P. Cannon	
G-BJMA	Colt 21A balloon	Colt Balloons Ltd	
G-BJMG	European E.26C balloon	D. Eaves & A. P. Chown	
G-BJMI	European E.84 balloon	D. Eaves	
G-BJMJ	Bensen B.8M	J. I. Hewlett	
G-BJML	Cessna 120	D. F. Lawlor/Inverness	
G-BJMO	Taylor JT.1 Monoplane	R. C. Mark	
G-BJMR	Cessna 310R	J. McL. Robinson/Leeds	
G-BJMU	European E.157 balloon	A. C. Mitchell	
G-BJMV	BAC One-Eleven 531FS	Dan-Air Services Ltd/Gatwick	
G-BJMW	Thunder Ax8-105 balloon	G. M. Westley	
G-BJMX	Jarre JR.3 balloon	P. D. Ridout	
G-BJMZ	European EA.8A balloon	P. D. Ridout	
G-BJNA	Arena Mk 117P balloon	P. D. Ridout	
G-BJNB	WAR F4U Corsair	A. V. Francis	
G-BJND	Osprey Mk 1E balloon	A. Billington & D. Whitmore	
G-BJNF	Cessna F.152	Exeter Flying Club Ltd	
G-BJNG	Slingsby T.67A	Slingsby Aviation Ltd/Kirkbymoorside	
G-BJNL	Evans VP-2	K. Morris	
G-BJNN	PA-38-112 Tomahawk	Scotia Safari Ltd/Prestwick	
G-BJNP	Rango NA.32 balloon	N. H. Ponsford	
G-BJNX	Cameron O-65 balloon	B. J. Petteford	
G-BJNY	Aeronca 11CC Super Chief	P. I. & D. M. Morgans	
G-BJNZ	PA-23 Aztec 250F	Leavesden Flight Centre Ltd (G-FANZ)	
G-BJOA	PA-28-181 Archer II	Channel Islands Aero Holdings (Jersey) Ltd	
G-BJOB	Jodel D.140C	T. W. M. Beck & M. J. Smith	
G-BJOD	Hollman HA-2M Sportster	W. O'Riordan	
G-BJOE	Jodel D.120A	R. A. Yates	
G-BJOI	Isaacs Special	J. O. Isaacs	
G-BJOP	BN-2B Islander	Loganair Ltd/Glasgow	
G-BJOT	Jodel D.117	R. L. A. Davies	
G-BJOV	Cessna F.150K	R. J. Lock	
G-BJOZ	Scheibe SF.25B Falke	P. W. Hextall	
G-BJPB	Osprey Mk 4A balloon	C. B. Rundle	
G-BJPI	Bede BD-5G	M. D. McQueen	
G-BJPJ	Osprey Mk 3A	K. R. Bundy	
G-BJPL	Osprey Mk 4A balloon	M. Vincent	
G-BJPM	Bursell PW.1 balloon	I. M. Holdsworth	
G-BJPV	Haigh balloon	M. J. Haigh	
G-BJPW	Osprey Mk 1C balloon	P. J. Cooper & M. Draper	
G-BJRA	Osprey Mk 4B balloon	E. Osborn	
G-BJRB	European E.254 balloon	D. Eaves	
G-BJRC	European E.84R balloon	D. Eaves	
G-BJRD	European E.84R balloon	D. Eaves	
G-BJRF	Saffery S.80 balloon	C. F. Chipping	
G-BJRG	Osprey Mk 4B balloon	A. de Gruchy	
G-BJRH	Rango NA.36 balloon	N. H. Ponsford	
G-BJRI	Osprey Mk 4D balloon	G. G. Kneller	
G-BJRJ	Osprey Mk 4D balloon	G. G. Kneller	
G-BJRK	Osprey Mk 1E balloon	G. G. Kneller	
G-BJRL	Osprey Mk 4B balloon	G. G. Kneller	
G-BJRP	Cremer balloon	M. Williams	
G-BJRS	Cremer balloon	P. Wallbank	

Notes	Reg.	Type	Owner or Operator
	G-BJRT	BAC One-Eleven 528	British Airways *County of South Glamorgan*
	G-BJRU	BAC One-Eleven 528	British Airways *County of West Glamorgan*
	G-BJRV	Cremer balloon	M. D. Williams
	G-BJRW	Cessna U.206G	A. I. Walgate & Son Ltd
	G-BJRY	PA-28-151 Warrior	Eastern Counties Aero Club Ltd/ Southend
	G-BJRZ	Partenavia P.68C	Gledhill Water Storage Ltd & M. F. J. Watson/Blackpool
	G-BJSA	BN-2A Islander	Harvest Air Ltd/Southend
	G-BJSC	Osprey Mk 4D balloon	N. J. Richardson
	G-BJSD	Osprey Mk 4D balloon	N. J. Richardson
	G-BJSE	Osprey Mk 1E balloon	J. E. Christopher
	G-BJSF	Osprey Mk 4B balloon	N. J. Richardson
	G-BJSG	V.S.361 Spitfire LF.IXE (ML417)	B. J. S. Grey/Duxford
	G-BJSI	Osprey Mk 1E balloon	N. J. Richardson
	G-BJSK	Osprey Mk 4B balloon	J. E. Christopher
	G-BJSL	Flamboyant Ax7-65 balloon	Pepsi Cola International Ltd
	G-BJSP	Guido 1A Srs 61 balloon	G. A. Newsome
	G-BJSR	Osprey Mk 4B balloon	C. F. Chipping
	G-BJSS	Allport balloon	D. J. Allport
	G-BJST	CCF Harvard 4	V. Norman & M. Lawrence
	G-BJSU	Bensen B.8M	J. D. Newlyn
	G-BJSV	PA-28-161 Warrior II	A. F. Aviation Ltd/Stansted
	G-BJSW	Thunder Ax7-65 balloon	Sandcliffe Garage Ltd
	G-BJSX	Unicorn UE-1C balloon	N. J. Richardson
	G-BJSY	Beech C90 King Air	Dualstake Ltd/Manston
	G-BJSZ	Piper J-3C-65 Cub	H. Gilbert
	G-BJTA	Osprey Mk 4B balloon	C. F. Chipping
	G-BJTB	Cessna A.150M	Leisure Lease Aviation/Andrewsfield
	G-BJTG	Osprey Mk 4B balloon	M. Millen
	G-BJTH	Kestrel AC Mk 1 balloon	R. P. Waller
	G-BJTK	Taylor JT.1 Monoplane	E. N. Simmons (G-BEUM)
	G-BJTN	Osprey Mk 4B balloon	M. Vincent
	G-BJTO	Piper J-3C-65 Cub	K. R. Nunn
	G-BJTP	PA-18 Super Cub 95 (115302)	J. T. Parkins
	G-BJTV	M.S.880B Rallye Club	E. C. Hender
	G-BJTW	European E.107 balloon	C. J. Brealey
	G-BJTY	Osprey Mk 4B balloon	A. E. de Gruchy
	G-BJUB	BVS Special 01 balloon	P. G. Wild
	G-BJUC	Robinson R-22	A. C. Byrne
	G-BJUD	Robin DR.400/180R	Lasham Gliding Soc Ltd
	G-BJUE	Osprey Mk 4B balloon	M. Vincent
	G-BJUG	SOCATA TB.9 Tampico	R. Howton & B. P. Waites/Biggin Hill
	G-BJUI	Osprey Mk 4B balloon	B. A. de Gruchy
	G-BJUK	Short SD3-30	Gill Aviation Ltd (G-OCAS)/Newcastle
	G-BJUR	PA-38-112 Tomahawk	Truman Aviation Ltd/Tollerton
	G-BJUS	PA-38-112 Tomahawk	Panshanger School of Flying
	G-BJUU	Osprey Mk 4B balloon	M. Vincent
	G-BJUV	Cameron V-20 balloon	Cameron Balloons Ltd
	G-BJUW	Osprey Mk 4B balloon	C. F. Chipping
	G-BJUX	Bursell balloon	I. M. Holdsworth
	G-BJUY	Colt Ax-77 balloon	Colt Balloons Ltd
	G-BJUZ	BAT Mk II balloon	A. R. Thompson
	G-BJVA	BAT Mk I balloon	B. L. Thompson
	G-BJVC	Evans VP-2	R. G. Fenn/Leicester
	G-BJVF	Thunder Ax3 balloon	A. G. R. Calder & F. J. Spite
	G-BJVH	Cessna F.182Q	A. R. G. Brooker Engineering Ltd/ Wellesbourne
	G-BJVJ	Cessna F.152	Cambridge Aero Club Ltd
	G-BJVK	Grob G-109	B. Kimberley/Enstone
	G-BJVM	Cessna 172M	Angelsword Ltd/Wellesbourne
	G-BJVO	Cameron D-50 airship	Cameron Balloons Ltd
	G-BJVS	CP.1315C-3 Super Emeraude	M. W. Wooldridge & A. E. Futter/ Norwich
	G-BJVT	Cessna F.152	Cambridge Aero Club Ltd
	G-BJVU	Thunder Ax6-56 balloon	G. V. Beckwith
	G-BJVV	Robin R.1180	Medway Flying Group Ltd/Rochester
	G-BJVX	Sikorsky S-76A	Bristow Helicopters Ltd
	G-BJVZ	Sikorsky S-76A	Bristow Helicopters Ltd

Reg.	Type	Owner or Operator	Notes
G-BJWC	Saro Skeeter AOP.12 ★	J. E. Wilkie	
G-BJWD	Zenith CH.300	D. Winton	
G-BJWH	Cessna F.152	Butler Associates (Aviation) Ltd	
G-BJWI	Cessna F.172P	Shoreham Flight Simulation Ltd/ Bournemouth	
G-BJWJ	Cameron V-65 balloon	R. G. Turnbull & S. G. Forse	
G-BJWL	BN-2A-8 Islander	Region Airways Ltd (G-BBMC)/ Southend	
G-BJWM	BN-2A-26 Islander	Harvest Air Ltd (G-BCAE)/Southend	
G-BJWN	BN-2A-8 Islander	Harvest Air Ltd (G-BALO)/Southend	
G-BJWO	BN-2A-8 Islander	Harvest Air Ltd (G-BAXC)/Southend	
G-BJWP	BN-2A-26 Islander	Harvest Air Ltd (G-BCEJ)/Southend	
G-BJWR	D.H.82A Tiger Moth	D. R. Whitby & ptnrs	
G-BJWT	Wittman W.10 Tailwind	J. F. Bakewell & R. A. Shelley	
G-BJWV	Colt 17A balloon	Lighter-Than-Air Ltd	
G-BJWW	Cessna F.172N	Shireburn Carpets Ltd	
G-BJWX	PA-18 Super Cub 95	D. E. Lamb	
G-BJWY	S-55 Whirlwind HAR.21 (WV198)	J. E. Wilkie	
G-BJWZ	PA-18 Super Cub 95	G. V. Harfield/Thruxton	
G-BJXA	Slingsby T.67A	Slingsby Aviation Ltd/Kirkbymoorside	
G-BJXB	Slingsby T.67A	Light Planes (Lancs) Ltd/Barton	
G-BJXD	Colt 17A balloon	Hot Air Balloon Co Ltd	
G-BJXJ	Boeing 737-219	Britannia Airways Ltd/Luton	
G-BJXK	Fournier RF-5	P. Storey & ptnrs	
G-BJXN	Boeing 747-230B	British Airways City of Worcester	
G-BJXO	Cessna 441	Hatfield Executive Aviation Ltd	
G-BJXP	Colt 56B balloon	Birmingham Broadcasting Ltd	
G-BJXR	Auster AOP.9 (XR267)	Cotswold Aircraft Restoration Group	
G-BJXU	Thunder Ax7-77 balloon	Perdix Ltd	
G-BJXX	PA-23 Aztec 250E	Aztec Euro Ltd	
G-BJXZ	Cessna 172N	T. M. Jones	
G-BJYC	Cessna 425	Carters Aviation Ltd/E. Midlands	
G-BJYD	Cessna F.152 II	Cleveland Flying School Ltd/ Tees-side	
G-BJYF	Colt 56A balloon	Hot Air Balloon Co Ltd	
G-BJYG	PA-28-161 Warrior II	C. M. Pollett	
G-BJYK	Jodel D.120A	T. Fox & D. A. Thorpe	
G-BJYL	BAC One-Eleven 515FB	Dan-Air Services Ltd (G-AZPE)/Gatwick	
G-BJYM	BAC One-Eleven 531FS	Dan-Air Services Ltd/Gatwick	
G-BJYN	PA-38-112 Tomahawk	Panshanger School of Flying Ltd (G-BJTE)	
G-BJZA	Cameron N-65 balloon	A. D. Pinner	
G-BJZB	Evans VP-2	J. A. Macleod	
G-BJZC	Thunder Ax7-65Z balloon	Greenpeace (UK) Ltd/S. Africa	
G-BJZD	Douglas DC-10-10	Novair Ltd (G-GFAL)/Gatwick	
G-BJZE	Douglas DC-10-10	Novair Ltd (G-GSKY)/Gatwick	
G-BJZF	D.H.82A Tiger Moth	C. A. Parker/Sywell	
G-BJZK	Cessna T.303	Landlink Ltd	
G-BJZL	Cameron V-65 balloon	S. L. G. Williams	
G-BJZN	Slingsby T.67A	Light Planes (Lancs) Ltd/Barton	
G-BJZR	Colt 42A balloon	C. F. Sisson	
G-BJZT	Cessna FA.152	Butler Associates (Aviation) Ltd	
G-BJZX	Grob G.109	Oxfordshire Sport Flying Ltd/Enstone	
G-BJZY	Bensen B.8MV	D. E. & M. A. Cooke	
G-BKAC	Cessna F.150L	Seawing Flying Club Ltd/Southend	
G-BKAE	Jodel D.120	M. P. Wakem	
G-BKAF	FRED Srs 2	L. G. Millen	
G-BKAG	Boeing 727-217	Dan-Air Services Ltd/Gatwick	
G-BKAK	Beech C90 King Air	National Airways Ltd/Southend	
G-BKAM	Slingsby T.67M Firefly	A. J. Daley & R. K. Warren	
G-BKAN	Cessna 340A	Manchester Air Charter Ltd	
G-BKAO	Jodel D.112	E. Carter & G. Higgins	
G-BKAR	PA-38-112 Tomahawk	C.S.E. Aviation Ltd/Kidlington	
G-BKAS	PA-38-112 Tomahawk	C.S.E. Aviation Ltd/Kidlington	
G-BKAT	Pitts S-1C Special	I. M. G. Senior & J. G. Harper	
G-BKAY	R. Commander 114	Costello Gears Ltd/Biggin Hill	
G-BKAZ	Cessna 152	Skyviews & General Ltd	
G-BKBB	Hawker Fury replica (K1930)	The Hon A. M. M. Lindsay	
G-BKBD	Thunder Ax3 balloon	D. L. Clark Tow-Rite	

Notes	Reg.	Type	Owner or Operator
	G-BKBE	AA-5A Cheetah	G. W. Plowman & Sons Ltd/Elstree
	G-BKBF	M.S.894A Rallye Minerva 220	Callow Aviation/Shobdon
	G-BKBK	Stampe SV-4A	B. M. O'Brien/Redhill
	G-BKBN	SOCATA TB.10 Tobago	Cross Bros Ltd/Andrewsfield
	G-BKBO	Colt 17A balloon	J. Armstrong & ptnrs
	G-BKBP	Bellanca 7GCBC Scout	L. B. Jefferies
	G-BKBR	Cameron Chateau 84 SS balloon	Forbes Europe Ltd/France
	G-BKBS	Bensen B.8MV	Construction & Site Administration Ltd
	G-BKBV	SOCATA TB.10 Tobago	R. M. Messenger
	G-BKBW	SOCATA TB.10 Tobago	P. Murphy/Blackbushe
	G-BKCB	PA-28R Cherokee Arrow 200	Bristol & Wessex Aeroplane Club Ltd
	G-BKCC	PA-28 Cherokee 180	K. C. Boreland & Creative Logistics Enterprises/Staverton
	G-BKCE	Cessna F.172PII	M. Askanoglu
	G-BKCF	Rutan Long Ez	I. C. Fallows
	G-BKCH	Thompson Cassutt	S. C. Thompson/Redhill
	G-BKCI	Brugger MB.2 Colibri	E. R. Newall
	G-BKCJ	Oldfield Baby Great Lakes	S. V. Roberts/Sleap
	G-BKCL	PA-30 Twin Comanche 160C	J. & J. Cannings (G-AXSP)
	G-BKCN	Currie Wot	S. E. Tomlinson
	G-BKCR	SOCATA TB.9 Tampico	Surrey & Kent Flying Club (1982) Ltd/ Biggin Hill
	G-BKCT	Cameron V-77 balloon	Quality Products General Engineering (Wickwat) Ltd
	G-BKCU	Sequoia F.8L Falco	J. J. Anziani & D. F. Simpson
	G-BKCV	EAA Acro Sport II	M. J. Clark
	G-BKCW	Jodel D.120A	A. Greene & G. Kerr/Dundee
	G-BKCX	Mudry CAARP CAP.10	Mahon & Associates/Booker
	G-BKCY	PA-38-112 Tomahawk II	Wellesbourne Aviation Ltd
	G-BKCZ	Jodel D.120A	P. Penn-Sayers Model Services Ltd/ Shoreham
	G-BKDA	AB-206B JetRanger	J. E. Backhouse
	G-BKDC	Monnet Sonerai II	J. Boobyer/Blackbushe
	G-BKDD	Bell 206B JetRanger	Dollar Air Services Ltd/Coventry
	G-BKDE	Kendrick I Motorglider	J. K. Rushton
	G-BKDF	Kendrick II Motorglider	J. K. Rushton
	G-BKDH	Robin DR.400/120	W. R. C. Foyle/Thruxton
	G-BKDI	Robin DR.400/120	Cotswold Aero Club Ltd/Staverton
	G-BKDJ	Robin DR.400/120	W. R. C. Foyle/Thruxton
	G-BKDK	Thunder Ax7-77Z balloon	A. J. Byrne
	G-BKDP	FRED Srs 3	M. Whittaker
	G-BKDR	Pitts S.1S Special	T. R. G. Barnby & ptnrs/Redhill
	G-BKDT	S.E.5A replica (F943)	J. H. Tetley & W. A. Sneesby/Sherburn
	G-BKDX	Jodel DR.1050	F. A. L. Castleden & ptnrs
	G-BKEK	PA-32 Cherokee Six 300	Cruspane Ltd/Stapleford
	G-BKEM	SOCATA TB.9 Tampico	M. Tidman
	G-BKEN	SOCATA TB.10 Tobago	C. J. Madeley
	G-BKEP	Cessna F.172M	George Cross Services Ltd
	G-BKER	S.E.5A replica (F5447)	N. K. Geddes
	G-BKES	Cameron SS bottle balloon	Lighter-Than-Air Ltd
	G-BKET	PA-18 Super Cub 95	J. A. Wills/Inverness
	G-BKEU	Taylor JT.1 Monoplane	R. J. Whybrow & J. M. Springham
	G-BKEV	Cessna F.172M	One Zero One Three Ltd
	G-BKEW	Bell 206B JetRanger 3	N. R. Foster
	G-BKEX	Rich Prototype glider	D. B. Rich
	G-BKEY	FRED Srs 3	G. S. Taylor
	G-BKEZ	PA-18 Super Cub 95	A. N. G. Gardiner
	G-BKFA	Monnet Sonerai IIL	R. F. Bridge
	G-BKFC	Cessna F.152II	D. W. Walton/Husbands Bosworth
	G-BKFG	Thunder Ax3 balloon	P. Ray
	G-BKFI	Evans VP-1	F. A. R. de Lavergne
	G-BKFK	Isaacs Fury II	G. C. Jones
	G-BKFM	QAC Quickie	A. J. Briggs
	G-BKFN	Bell 214ST	Bristow Helicopters Ltd
	G-BKFP	Bell 214ST	Bristow Helicopters Ltd
	G-BKFR	CP.301C Emeraude	A. J. Stevens/Barton
	G-BKFV	Rand KR-2	F. H. French/Swansea
	G-BKFW	P.56 Provost T.1	Slymar Aviation & Services Ltd
	G-BKFX	Colt 17A balloon	Colt Balloons Ltd
	G-BKFY	Beech C90 King Air	Corgi Investments Ltd
	G-BKFZ	PA-28R Cherokee Arrow 200	Shacklewell Flying Group/Leicester
	G-BKGA	M.S.892E Rallye 150GT	Harwoods of Essex Ltd

Reg.	Type	Owner or Operator	Notes
G-BKGB	Jodel D.120	R. W. Greenwood	
G-BKGC	Maule M.6-235	Stol-Air Ltd/Sibson	
G-BKGD	Westland WG.30 Srs 100	British International Helicopters Ltd (G-BKBJ)/Beccles	
G-BKGL	Beech 18 (164)	G. A. Warner/Duxford	
G-BKGR	Cameron O-65 balloon	S. R. Bridge	
G-BKGT	SOCATA Rallye 110ST	Long Marston Flying Group	
G-BKGW	Cessna F.152-II	Leicestershire Aero Club Ltd	
G-BKGX	Isaacs Fury	I. L. McMahon	
G-BKGZ	Bensen B.8	C. F. Simpson	
G-BKHA	W.S.55 Whirlwind HAR.10 (XJ763)	L. Goddard	
G-BKHC	W.S.55 Whirlwind HAR.10 (XP328)	Flight C Helicopters Ltd	
G-BKHD	Oldfield Baby Great Lakes	P. J. Tanulak	
G-BKHE	Boeing 737-204	Britannia Airways Ltd Sir Francis Chichester/Luton	
G-BKHF	Boeing 737-204	Britannia Airways Ltd Sir Alliot Verdon Roe/Luton	
G-BKHG	Piper J-3C-65 Cub (479766)	K. G. Wakefield	
G-BKHH	Thunder Ax10-160Z balloon	R. Carr/France	
G-BKHI	BAe Jetstream 3102-02	British Aerospace PLC/Prestwick	
G-BKHL	Thunder Ax9-140 balloon	R. Carr/France	
G-BKHP	P.56 Provost T.1 (WW397)	M. J. Crymble/Lyneham	
G-BKHR	Luton LA-4 Minor	R. J. Parkhouse	
G-BKHT	BAe 146-100	Dan-Air Services Ltd/Gatwick	
G-BKHV	Taylor JT.2 Titch	P. D. Holt	
G-BKHW	Stoddard-Hamilton Glasair SH.2RG	N. Clayton	
G-BKHX	Bensen B.8M	D. H. Greenwood	
G-BKHY	Taylor JT.1 Monoplane	J. Hall	
G-BKHZ	Cessna F.172P	Warwickshire Flying Training Centre Ltd	
G-BKIA	SOCATA TB.10 Tobago	Redhill Flying School	
G-BKIB	SOCATA TB.9 Tampico	A. J. Baggerley & F. D. J. Simmons/ Goodwood	
G-BKIC	Cameron V-77 balloon	C. A. Butler	
G-BKIF	Fournier RF-6B	G. G. Milton	
G-BKII	Cessna F.172M	M. S. Knight/Goodwood	
G-BKIJ	Cessna F.172M	V. Speck	
G-BKIK	Cameron DG-10 airship	Airspace Outdoor Advertising Ltd	
G-BKIM	Unicorn UE.5A balloon	I. Chadwick & K. H. Turner	
G-BKIN	Alon A.2A Aircoupe	P. A. Williams/Blackbushe	
G-BKIR	Jodel D.117	R. Shaw & D. M. Hardaker/ Crosland Moor	
G-BKIS	SOCATA TB.10 Tobago	Ospreystar Ltd	
G-BKIT	SOCATA TB.9 Tampico	D. G. Bligh/Ipswich	
G-BKIU	Colt 17A balloon	Robert Pooley Ltd	
G-BKIV	Colt 21A balloon	Colt Balloons Ltd	
G-BKIX	Cameron V-31 balloon	M. N. J. Kirby	
G-BKIY	Thunder Ax3 balloon	A. Hornak	
G-BKIZ	Cameron V-31 balloon	A. P. Greathead	
G-BKJB	PA-18 Super Cub 135	Cormack (Aircraft Services) Ltd/ Glasgow	
G-BKJD	Bell 214ST	Bristow Helicopters Ltd	
G-BKJE	Cessna 172N	The G-BKJE Group/Burnaston	
G-BKJF	M.S.880B Rallye 100T	The Nova Flying Group	
G-BKJR	Hughes 269C	March Helicopters Ltd/Sywell	
G-BKJS	Jodel D.120A	S. Walmsley	
G-BKJT	Cameron O-65 balloon	K. A. Ward	
G-BKJW	PA-23 Aztec 250E	Alan Williams Entertainments Ltd	
G-BKKI	Westland WG.30 Srs 100	Westland Helicopters Ltd/Yeovil	
G-BKKM	Aeronca 7AC Champion	M. McChesney	
G-BKKN	Cessna 182R	R A. Marven/Elstree	
G-BKKO	Cessna 182R	B. & G. Jebson Ltd/Crosland Moor	
G-BKKP	Cessna 182R	ISF Aviation Ltd/Leicester	
G-BKKR	Rand KR-2	D. R. Trouse	
G-BKKS	Mercury Dart Srs 1	B. A. Mills	
G-BKKZ	Pitts S-1D Special	G. C. Masterton	
G-BKLB	R. S2R Thrush Commander	Ag-Air	
G-BKLC	Cameron V-56 balloon	M. A. & J. R. H. Ashworth	
G-BKLJ	Westland Scout AH.1 ★	J. E. Wilkie	

Notes	Reg.	Type	Owner or Operator
	G-BKLM	Thunder Ax9-140 balloon	Aerial Promotions Balloon Club
	G-BKLO	Cessna F.172M	George Cross Services Ltd
	G-BKLP	Cessna F.172N	George Cross Services Ltd
	G-BKLT	SA.341G Gazelle	No Mans Land Ltd
	G-BKLU	SA.341G Gazelle	Stratton Motor Co (Norfolk) Ltd
	G-BKLZ	Vinten-Wallis WA-116MC	W. Vinten Ltd
	G-BKMA	Mooney M.20J Srs 201	Clement Garage Ltd/Stapleford
	G-BKMB	Mooney M.20J Srs 201	W. A. Cook & ptnrs
	G-BKMD	SC.7 Skyvan Srs 3	Aviation Investments (G-BAHK)
	G-BKME	SC.7 Skyvan Srs 3	Flightspares PLC (G-AYJN)/Southend
	G-BKMG	Handley Page O/400 replica	M. G. King
	G-BKMH	Flamboyant Ax7-65 balloon	Pepsi-Cola International Ltd/S. Africa
	G-BKMI	V.S.359 Spitfire HF VIII (MV154)	Aerial Museum (North Weald) Ltd
	G-BKMM	Cessna 180K	G. Cormack/Glasgow
	G-BKMN	BAe 146-100	Dan-Air Services Ltd (G-ODAN)/ Gatwick
	G-BKMR	Thunder Ax3 balloon	B. F. G. Ribbons
	G-BKMS	Boeing 737-2Q8	Paramount Airways Ltd
	G-BKMT	PA-32R-301 Saratoga SP	Hillary Investments Ltd
	G-BKMX	Short SD3-60	Manx Airlines Ltd/Ronaldsway
	G-BKNA	Cessna 421	Young Investments Ltd
	G-BKNB	Cameron V-42 balloon	S. A. Burnett
	G-BKND	Colt 56A balloon	Flying Colours Balloon Group
	G-BKNH	Boeing 737-210	Dan-Air Services Ltd/Gatwick
	G-BKNI	GY-80 Horizon 160D	A. Hartigan & ptnrs/Fenland
	G-BKNJ	Grob G.109	Oxfordshire Sport Flying Ltd/Enstone
	G-BKNL	Cameron D-96 airship	Drawarm Ltd
	G-BKNN	Cameron Minar E Pakistan balloon	Forbes Europe Ltd/France
	G-BKNO	Monnet Sonerai IIL	S. Tattersfield & K. Bailey/Netherthorpe
	G-BKNX	SA.102.5 Cavalier	G. D. Horn
	G-BKNY	Bensen B.8M-P-VW	D. A. C. MacCormack
	G-BKNZ	CP.301A Emeraude	R. Evernden/Barton
	G-BKOA	M.S.893E Rallye 180GT	Cheshire Flying Services Ltd/ Manchester
	G-BKOB	Z.326 Trener Master	W. G. V. Hall
	G-BKOR	Barnes 77 balloon	Robert Pooley Ltd
	G-BKOS	P.56 Provost T.51 (178)	Sylmar Aviation & Services Ltd/Upavon
	G-BKOT	Wassmer WA.81 Piranha	B. D. Deubelbeiss
	G-BKOU	P.84 Jet Provost T.3 (XN637)	A. Topen/Cranfield
	G-BKOV	Jodel DR.220A	E. H. Ellis & G. C. Winter
	G-BKOW	Cameron 77A balloon	Hot Air Ballon Co Ltd
	G-BKPA	Hoffman H-36 Dimona	Airmark Aviation Ltd/Booker
	G-BKPB	Aerosport Scamp	R. Scroby
	G-BKPC	Cessna A.185F	Black Knights Parachute Centre
	G-BKPD	Viking Dragonfly	P. E. J. Sturgeon
	G-BKPE	Jodel DR.250/160	J. S. & J. D. Lewer
	G-BKPG	Luscombe Rattler Strike	Luscombe Aircraft Ltd/Lympne
	G-BKPH	Luscombe Valiant	Luscombe Aircraft Ltd/Lympne
	G-BKPK	John McHugh Gyrocopter	J. C. McHugh
	G-BKPM	Schempp-Hirth HS.5 Nimbus 2	J. L. Rolls
	G-BKPN	Cameron N-77 balloon	P. S. H. Frewer
	G-BKPS	AA-5B Tiger	Eyewitness Ltd/Southampton
	G-BKPT	M.H.1521M Broussard	J. Taylor
	G-BKPV	Stevex 250.1	A. F. Stevens
	G-BKPW	Boeing 767-204	Britannia Airways Ltd *The Earl Mountbatten of Burma*/Luton
	G-BKPX	Jodel D.120A	C. G. Richardson
	G-BKPY	Saab 91B/2 Safir (56321)★	Newark Air Museum Ltd
	G-BKPZ	Pitts S-1T Special	A. J. Whitehead
	G-BKRA	T-6G Texan (51-15227)	M. D. Faiers
	G-BKRB	Cessna 172N	Saunders Caravans Ltd
	G-BKRD	Cessna 320E	ITD Aviation Ltd
	G-BKRF	PA-18 Super Cub 95	K. M. Bishop
	G-BKRG	Beechcraft C-45G	Aces High Ltd/North Weald
	G-BKRH	Brugger MB.2 Colibri	M. R. Benwell
	G-BKRI	Cameron V-77 balloon	J. R. Lowe & R. J. Fuller
	G-BKRJ	Colt 105A balloon	Owners Abroad Group PLC
	G-BKRK	SNCAN Stampe SV-4C	J. M. Alexander & ptnrs/Aberdeen
	G-BKRL	Designability Leopard	Chichester-Miles Consultants Ltd
	G-BKRM	Boeing 757-236	Air Europe Ltd/Air Europa (*leased as EC-EGI*)

Reg.	Type	Owner or Operator	Notes
G-BKRN	Beechcraft D.18S ★	Scottish Aircraft Collection/Perth	
G-BKRR	Cameron N-56 balloon	S. L. G. Williams	
G-BKRS	Cameron V-56 balloon	D. N. & L. J. Close	
G-BKRT	PA-34-220T Seneca III	Paucristar Ltd	
G-BKRU	Ensign Crossley Racer	M. Crossley	
G-BKRV	Hovey Beta Bird	A. V. Francis	
G-BKRW	Cameron O-160 balloon	Bondbaste Ltd	
G-BKRX	Cameron O-160 balloon	Bondbaste Ltd	
G-BKRZ	Dragon 77 balloon	Anglia Balloon School Ltd	
G-BKSB	Cessna T.310Q	P. S. King	
G-BKSC	Saro Skeeter AOP.12 (XN351)	R. A. L. Falconer	
G-BKSD	Colt 56A balloon	M. J. & G. C. Casson	
G-BKSE	QAC Quickie Q-2	M. D. Burns	
G-BKSG	Hoffman H-36 Dimona	F. C. Y. Cheung/H. Kong	
G-BKSH	Colt 21A balloon	T. A. Gilmour	
G-BKSJ	Cameron N-108 balloon	Cameron Balloons Ltd	
G-BKSO	Cessna 421C	Aviation Beauport Ltd/Jersey	
G-BKSP	Schleicher ASK.14	J. H. Bryson & E. A. H. Boyle	
G-BKSR	Cessna 550 Citation II	Osiwell Ltd/Biggin Hill	
G-BKSS	Jodel D.150	D. H. Wilson-Spratt/Ronaldsway	
G-BKST	Rutan Vari-Eze	R. Towle	
G-BKSX	SNCAN Stampe SV-4C	C. A. Bailey & J. A. Carr	
G-BKSZ	Cessna P.210N	Clark Masts Ltd/Sandown	
G-BKTA	PA-18 Super Cub 95	A. W. Chapman/Southend	
G-BKTH	CCF Hawker Sea Hurricane IB (Z7015)	Shuttleworth Trust/Duxford	
G-BKTM	PZL SZD-45A Ogar	J. A. Evans	
G-BKTO	Beech 58P Baron	Gold Key Trust Ltd	
G-BKTR	Cameron V-77 balloon	G. F. & D. D. Bouten	
G-BKTS	Cameron O-65 balloon	C. H. Pearce & Sons (Contractors) Ltd	
G-BKTT	Cessna F.152	Stapleford Flying Club	
G-BKTU	Colt 56A balloon	E. Ten Houten	
G-BKTV	Cessna F.152	London Flight Centre Ltd/Stansted	
G-BKTW	Cessna 404 Titan II	Hawk Aviation Ltd (G-WTVE)/ E. Midlands	
G-BKTY	SOCATA TB.10 Tobago	F. J. Lingham/Biggin Hill	
G-BKTZ	Slingsby T.67M Firefly	Trent Air Services Ltd (G-SFTV)/ Cranfield	
G-BKUE	SOCATA TB.9 Tampico	W. J. Moore/Kirkbride	
G-BKUI	D.31 Turbulent	R. F. Smith	
G-BKUJ	Thunder Ax6-56 balloon	R. J. Bent	
G-BKUR	CP.301A Emeraude	P. Gilmour/Perth	
G-BKUS	Bensen B.8M	I. J. Lawson	
G-BKUT	M.S.880B Rallye Club	J. J. Hustwitt/Bodmin	
G-BKUU	Thunder Ax7-77-1 balloon	City of London Balloon Group	
G-BKUY	BAe Jetstream 3102	British Aerospace PLC/Prestwick	
G-BKUZ	Zenair CH.250	K. Morris	
G-BKVA	SOCATA Rallye 180T	T. Miller	
G-BKVB	SOCATA Rallye 110ST	Martin Ltd/Biggin Hill	
G-BKVC	SOCATA TB.9 Tampico	Martin Ltd/Biggin Hill	
G-BKVE	Rutan Vari-Eze	H. R. Rowley (G-EZLT)	
G-BKVF	FRED Srs 3	N. E. Johnson	
G-BKVG	Scheibe SF.25E Super Falke	G-BKVG Ltd	
G-BKVJ	Colt 21A balloon	Colt Balloons Ltd	
G-BKVK	Auster AOP.9 (WZ662)	J. D. Butcher	
G-BKVL	Robin DR.400/160	The Cotswold Aero Club Ltd/Staverton	
G-BKVM	PA-18 Super Cub 150	D. G. Caffrey	
G-BKVN	PA-23 Aztec 250F	B. A. Eastwell/Shoreham	
G-BKVO	Pietenpol Aircamper	M. J. Honeychurch	
G-BKVP	Pitts S-1D Special	P. J. Leggo	
G-BKVR	PA-28 Cherokee 140	Page Aviation Ltd/Andrewsfield	
G-BKVS	Bensen B.8M	V. Scott	
G-BKVT	PA-23 Aztec 250E	Crane Investments Ltd (G-HARV)	
G-BKVV	Beech 95-B55 Baron	L. Mc. G. Tulloch	
G-BKVW	Airtour 56 balloon	L. D. & H. Vaughan	
G-BKVX	Airtour 56 balloon	E. G. Woolnough	
G-BKVY	Airtour 31 balloon	Airtour Balloon Co Ltd	
G-BKVZ	Boeing 767-204	Britannia Airways Ltd *Sir Winston Churchill*/Luton	
G-BKWA	Cessna 404 Titan	Hawk Aviation Ltd (G-BELV)/ E. Midlands	
G-BKWB	EMB-110P2 Bandeirante	Alexandra Aviation Ltd (G-CHEV)/ Gatwick	

Notes	Reg.	Type	Owner or Operator
	G-BKWD	Taylor JT.2 Titch	E. Shouler
	G-BKWE	Colt 17A balloon	Hot-Air Balloon Co Ltd
	G-BKWG	PZL-104 Wilga 35A	Anglo-Polish Sailplanes Ltd
	G-BKWI	Pitts S-2A	R. A. Seeley/Denham
	G-BKWR	Cameron V-65 balloon	April & Gilbert Games Photographers
	G-BKWW	Cameron O-77 balloon	A. M. Marten
	G-BKWY	Cessna F.152	Cambridge Aero Club
	G-BKXA	Robin R.2100	G. J. Anderson & ptnrs
	G-BKXC	Cameron V-77 balloon	P. Sarretti
	G-BKXD	SA.365N Dauphin 2	Bond Helicopters Ltd/Bourn
	G-BKXE	SA.365N Dauphin 2	Bond Helicopters Ltd/Bourn
	G-BKXF	PA-28R Cherokee Arrow 200	P. L. Brunton
	G-BKXG	Cessna T.303	Sutton Windows Ltd
	G-BKXI	Cessna T.303	Simonstone Securities Ltd
	G-BKXL	Cameron Bottle 70 balloon	Cameron Balloons Ltd
	G-BKXM	Colt 17A balloon	R. G. Turnbull
	G-BKXN	ICA IS-28M2A	British Aerospace PLC/Filton
	G-BKXO	Rutan LongEz	P. J. Wareham
	G-BKXP	Auster AOP.6	R. Skingley
	G-BKXR	D.31A Turbulent	M. B. Hill
	G-BKXS	Colt 56A balloon	Hot-Air Balloon Co Ltd
	G-BKXT	Cameron D-50 airship	Cameron Balloons Ltd
	G-BKXX	Cameron V-65 balloon	A. J. Legg & C. H. Harbord
	G-BKYA	Boeing 737-236	British Airways *River Derwent*/Heathrow
	G-BKYB	Boeing 737-236	British Airways *River Stour*/Heathrow
	G-BKYC	Boeing 737-236	British Airways *River Wye*/Heathrow
	G-BKYD	Boeing 737-236	British Airways *River Conway*/Heathrow
	G-BKYE	Boeing 737-236	British Airways *River Lagan*/Heathrow
	G-BKYF	Boeing 737-236	British Airways *River Spey*/Heathrow
	G-BKYG	Boeing 737-236	British Airways *River Exe*/Heathrow
	G-BKYH	Boeing 737-236	British Airways *River Dart*/Heathrow
	G-BKYI	Boeing 737-236	British Airways *River Waveney*/Heathrow
	G-BKYJ	Boeing 737-236	British Airways *River Neath*/Heathrow
	G-BKYK	Boeing 737-236	British Airways *River Foyle*/Heathrow
	G-BKYL	Boeing 737-236	British Airways *River Isis*/Heathrow
	G-BKYM	Boeing 737-236	British Airways *River Cam*/Heathrow
	G-BKYN	Boeing 737-236	British Airways *River Ayr*/Heathrow
	G-BKYO	Boeing 737-236	British Airways *River Kennet*/Heathrow
	G-BKYP	Boeing 737-236	British Airways *River Ystwyth*/Heathrow
	G-BKYR	—	British Airways/Heathrow
	G-BKYS	—	British Airways/Heathrow
	G-BKYT	—	British Airways/Heathrow
	G-BKYU	—	British Airways/Heathrow
	G-BKYV	—	British Airways/Heathrow
	G-BKYW	—	British Airways/Heathrow
	G-BKYX	—	British Airways/Heathrow
	G-BKYY	—	British Airways/Heathrow
	G-BKYZ	—	British Airways/Heathrow
	G-BKZA	Cameron N-77 balloon	University of Bath Students Union
	G-BKZB	Cameron V-77 balloon	A. J. Montgomery
	G-BKZC	Cessna A.152	Montaguis Ltd/Kuwait
	G-BKZD	Cessna A.152	Montaguis Ltd/Kuwait
	G-BKZE	AS.332L Super Puma	British International Helicopters/Aberdeen
	G-BKZF	Cameron V-56 balloon	G. M. Hobster
	G-BKZG	AS.332L Super Puma	British International Helicopters/Aberdeen
	G-BKZH	AS.332L Super Puma	British International Helicopters/Aberdeen
	G-BKZI	Bell 206B JetRanger 2	Heliwork Services Ltd/Thruxton
	G-BKZJ	Bensen B.8MV	S. H. Kirkby
	G-BKZL	Colt AS-42 airship	Colt Balloons Ltd
	G-BKZM	Isaacs Fury II (K2060)	J. Evans
	G-BKZT	FRED Srs 2	A. E. Morris
	G-BKZV	Bede BD-4A	A. L. Bergamasco/Headcorn
	G-BKZW	Beech C90 King Air	National Airways/Southend
	G-BKZY	Cameron N-77 balloon	W. Counties Automobile Co Ltd
	G-BLAA	Fournier RF-5	A. D. Wren/Southend

Reg.	Type	Owner or Operator	Notes
G-BLAC	Cessna FA.152	Lancashire Aero Club/Barton	
G-BLAD	Thunder Ax7-77-1 balloon	V. P. Gardiner & I. K. Turner	
G-BLAF	Stolp V-Star SA.900	J. E. Malloy	
G-BLAG	Pitts S-1D Special	C. M. Evans	
G-BLAH	Thunder Ax7-77-1 balloon	T. Donnelly	
G-BLAI	Monnet Sonerai IIL	T. Simpson	
G-BLAJ	Pazmany PL.4A	J. D. LePine	
G-BLAM	Jodel DR.360	B. F. Baldock	
G-BLAS	V.S.361 Spitfire F.IX (MJ730)	Aero Vintage Ltd	
G-BLAT	Jodel D.150	R. Bennett/Ipswich	
G-BLAW	PA-28-181 Archer II	David Martin Couriers Ltd/Booker	
G-BLAX	Cessna FA.152	Shoreham Flight Simulation Ltd/ Bournemouth	
G-BLAY	Robin HR.100/200B	B. A. Mills	
G-BLCA	Bell 206B JetRanger 3	R.M.H. Stainless Ltd	
G-BLCC	Thunder Ax7-77Z balloon	P. Hassell Ltd	
G-BLCF	EAA Acro Sport 2	M. J. Watkins & ptnrs	
G-BLCG	SOCATA TB.10 Tobago	J. A. & D. I. Hope (G-BHES)/Shoreham	
G-BLCH	Colt 56D balloon	Balloon Flights Club Ltd	
G-BLCI	EAA Acro Sport	P. A. Falter/Biggin Hill	
G-BLCK	V.S.361 Spitfire F.IX (TE566)	Historic Aircraft Collection Ltd	
G-BLCM	SOCATA TB.9 Tampico	Repclif Aviation Ltd/Liverpool	
G-BLCT	Jodel DR.220 2+2	H. W. Jemmett	
G-BLCU	Scheibe SF.25B Falke	B. Lumb & ptnrs/Rufforth	
G-BLCV	Hoffman H-36 Dimona	A. D. Gubbay	
G-BLCW	Evans VP-1	K. D. Pearce	
G-BLCY	Thunder Ax7-65Z balloon	Thunder Balloons Ltd	
G-BLCZ	Cessna 441	Northair Aviation Ltd/Leeds	
G-BLDB	Taylor JT.1 Monoplane	C. J. Bush	
G-BLDC	K&S Jungster 1	A. W. Brown	
G-BLDD	WAG-Aero CUBy AcroTrainer	C. A. Laycock	
G-BLDE	Boeing 737-2E7	Dan-Air Services Ltd/Gatwick	
G-BLDG	PA-25 Pawnee 260C	Ouse Gliding Club Ltd/Rufforth	
G-BLDH	BAC One-Eleven 475EZ	McAlpine Aviation Ltd/Luton	
G-BLDJ	PA-28-161 Warrior II	SFT Aviation Ltd/Bournemouth	
G-BLDK	Robinson R-22	R. H. Cleare & Co Ltd	
G-BLDL	Cameron Truck 56 balloon	Cameron Balloons Ltd	
G-BLDM	Hiller UH-12E	G. & S. G. Neal (Helicopters) Ltd	
G-BLDN	Rand KR-2	R. Y. Kendal	
G-BLDP	Slingsby T.67M Firefly	Cavendish Aviation Ltd/Netherthorpe	
G-BLDT	BN-2B Islander	Pilatus BN Ltd/Bembridge	
G-BLDY	Bell 212	Bristow Helicopters Ltd	
G-BLEB	Colt 69A balloon	I. R. M. Jacobs	
G-BLEC	BN-2B-27 Islander	LEC Refrigeration PLC (G-BJBG)	
G-BLEI	BN-2B-26 Islander	Pilatus BN Ltd/Bembridge	
G-BLEJ	PA-28-161 Warrior II	Eglinton Flying Club Ltd	
G-BLEL	Ax7-77-245 balloon	T. S. Price	
G-BLEP	Cameron V-65 balloon	D. Chapman	
G-BLES	Stolp SA.750 Acroduster Too	R. W. L. & L. Breckell	
G-BLET	Thunder Ax7-77-1 balloon	Servatruc Ltd	
G-BLEV	AS.355F Twin Squirrel	Haydon-Baillie Naval & Aircraft Museum/Southampton	
G-BLEW	Cessna F.182Q	Interair Aviation Ltd/Bournemouth	
G-BLEY	SA.365N Dauphin 2	Bond Helicopters Ltd/Bourn	
G-BLEZ	SA.365N Dauphin 2	Bond Helicopters Ltd/Bourn	
G-BLFE	Cameron Sphinx SS balloon	Forbes Europe Inc	
G-BLFF	Cessna F.172M	Air Advertising UK Ltd	
G-BLFJ	F.27 Friendship Mk 100	Air UK Ltd (G-OMAN/G-SPUD)/Norwich	
G-BLFT	P.56 Provost T.1 (WV686)	B. W. H. Parkhouse	
G-BLFV	Cessna 182R	Goddard Kay Rogers & Associates Ltd/ Booker	
G-BLFW	AA-5 Traveler	M. Swanborough/Brough	
G-BLFY	Cameron V-77 balloon	A. N. F. Pertwee	
G-BLFZ	PA-31-310 Turbo Navajo C	Huktra UK Ltd	
G-BLGB	Short SD3-60	Loganair Ltd/Glasgow	
G-BLGH	Robin DR.300/180R	Booker Gliding Club Ltd	
G-BLGI	McCullogh J.2	R. J. Everett	
G-BLGM	Cessna 425	John Hanson Services Ltd	
G-BLGN	Skyhawk Gyroplane	S. M. Hawkins	
G-BLGO	Bensen B.8M	F. Vernon	
G-BLGP	WAG-Aero Super CUBy	International School of Choveifat	

The G-BLBA-BZ batch has been reserved for British Airways.

Notes	Reg.	Type	Owner or Operator
	G-BLGR	Bell 47G-4A	Land Air Ltd
	G-BLGS	SOCATA Rallye 180T	Lasham Gliding Society Ltd
	G-BLGT	PA-18 Super Cub 95	T. A. Reed/Dunkeswell
	G-BLGV	Bell 206B JetRanger	Land Air Ltd
	G-BLGW	F.27 Friendship Mk 200	Air UK Ltd/Norwich
	G-BLGX	Thunder Ax7-65 balloon	Harper & Co (Glasgow) Ltd
	G-BLHA	Thunder Ax10-160 balloon	Thunder Balloons Ltd
	G-BLHB	Thunder Ax10-160 balloon	Thunder Balloons Ltd
	G-BLHD	BAC One-Eleven 492GM	McAlpine Aviation Ltd/Luton
	G-BLHE	Pitts S-1E Special	W. R. Penaluna
	G-BLHF	Nott/Cameron ULD.2 balloon	J. R. P. Nott
	G-BLHH	Jodel DR.315	G. G. Milton
	G-BLHI	Colt 17A balloon	Thunder & Colt Ltd
	G-BLHJ	Cessna F.172P	P. P. D. Howard-Johnston/Edinburgh
	G-BLHK	Colt 105A balloon	Hale Hot-Air Balloon Club
	G-BLHM	PA-18 Super Cub 95	I. R. March
	G-BLHN	Robin HR.100/285	H. M. Bouquiere/Biggin Hill
	G-BLHO	AA-5A Cheetah	Andreason Racing & Tuning Ltd
	G-BLHR	GA-7 Cougar	Fotex Aviation Ltd
	G-BLHS	Bellanca 7ECA Citabria	J. W. Platten & E. J. Timmins
	G-BLHW	Varga 2150A Kachina	Willoughby Farms Ltd
	G-BLHZ	Varga 2150A Kachina	MLP Aviation Ltd/Elstree
	G-BLID	D.H.112 Venom FB.50	P. F. A. Hoar/Cranfield
	G-BLIE	D.H.112 Venom FB.50	R. J. Everett
	G-BLIG	Cameron V-65 balloon	W. Davison
	G-BLIH	PA-18 Super Cub 135	I. R. F. Hammond
	G-BLIK	Wallis WA-116/F/S	K. H. Wallis
	G-BLIO	Cameron R-42 gas balloon	Cameron Balloons Ltd
	G-BLIP	Cameron N-77 balloon	L. A. Beardall & G. R. Hunt
	G-BLIT	Thorp T-18 CW	A. J. Waller
	G-BLIV	Cameron O-105 balloon	A. M. Thompson
	G-BLIW	P.56 Provost T.51 (177)	Pulsegrove Ltd (*stored*)/Shoreham
	G-BLIX	Saro Skeeter Mk 12 (XL809)	A. P. Nowicki
	G-BLIY	M.S.892A Rallye Commodore	L. Everex & Sons Ltd
	G-BLIZ	PA-46-310P Malibu	C. Evans & Sons Ltd
	G-BLJD	Glaser-Dirks DG.400	P. A. Hearne & ptnrs
	G-BLJE	AB-206B JetRanger	Nexgen Ltd
	G-BLJF	Cameron O-65 balloon	D. Fowler
	G-BLJG	Cameron N-105 balloon	J. W. Cato
	G-BLJH	Cameron N-77 balloon	A. J. Clarke & J. M. Hallam
	G-BLJI	Colt 105A balloon	Colt Balloons Ltd
	G-BLJJ	Cessna 305 Bird Dog	P. Dawe
	G-BLJK	Evans VP-2	R. R. Pierce
	G-BLJM	Beech 95-B55 Baron	Elstree Aircraft Hire Ltd
	G-BLJN	Nott-Cameron ULD-1 balloon	J. R. P. Nott
	G-BLJO	Cessna F.152	M. J. Endacott
	G-BLJP	Cessna F.150L	F. & S. E. Horridge/Lasham
	G-BLJX	Bensen B.8M	R. Snow
	G-BLJY	Sequoia F.8L Falco	K. Morris
	G-BLKA	D.H.112 Venom FB.54 (WR410)	A. Topen/Cranfield
	G-BLKB	Boeing 737-3T5	Orion/Britannia Airways/Luton
	G-BLKC	Boeing 737-3T5	Orion/Britannia Airways/Luton
	G-BLKD	Boeing 737-3T5	Orion/Britannia Airways/Luton
	G-BLKE	Boeing 737-3T5	Orion/Britannia Airways/Luton
	G-BLKF	Thunder Ax10-160 balloon	Thunder Balloons Ltd
	G-BLKG	Thunder Ax10-160 balloon	Thunder Balloons Ltd
	G-BLKH	Thunder Ax10-160 balloon	Thunder Balloons Ltd
	G-BLKI	Thunder Ax10-160 balloon	Thunder Balloons Ltd
	G-BLKJ	Thunder Ax7-65 balloon	D. T. Watkins
	G-BLKK	Evans VP-1	R. W. Burrows
	G-BLKL	D.31 Turbulent	D. L. Ripley
	G-BLKM	Jodel DR.1051	T. C. Humphreys
	G-BLKP	BAe Jetstream 3102	British Aerospace Ltd/Prestwick
	G-BLKU	Colt 56 SS balloon	Hot-Air Balloon Co Ltd
	G-BLKV	Boeing 767-204	Britannia Airways Ltd/Luton
	G-BLKW	Boeing 767-204	Britannia Airways Ltd *Sir Frank Whittle*/Luton
	G-BLKY	Beech 95-58	Kebbell Holdings Ltd/Leavesden
	G-BLKZ	Pilatus P2-05	Autokraft Ltd
	G-BLLA	Bensen B.8M	K. T. Donaghey
	G-BLLB	Bensen B.8M	D. H. Moss
	G-BLLD	Cameron O-77 balloon	D. C. Strange
	G-BLLE	Cameron 60 Burger King SS balloon	Burger King UK Ltd

Reg.	Type	Owner or Operator	Notes
G-BLLH	Jodel DR.220A 2+2	D. R. Scott-Longhurst & V. D. Stotter	
G-BLLM	PA-23 Aztec 250E	C. & M. Thomas (G-BBNM)/Cardiff	
G-BLLN	PA-18 Super Cub 95	W. H. Henry & A. T. Jeans	
G-BLLO	PA-18 Super Cub 95	D. G. & M. G. Marketts/Shobdon	
G-BLLP	Slingsby T.67B	Biggin Hill School of Flying	
G-BLLR	Slingsby T.67B	Trent Air Services Ltd/Cranfield	
G-BLLS	Slingsby T.67B	Trent Air Services Ltd/Cranfield	
G-BLLT	AA-5B Tiger	Alpha Welding & Engineering Ltd	
G-BLLU	Cessna 421C	G. E. Walker	
G-BLLV	Slingsby T.67B	M. J. Clayton	
G-BLLW	Colt 56B balloon	J. C. Stupples	
G-BLLY	Cessna 340A	Thunder & Colt Ltd	
G-BLLZ	Rutan LongEz	G. E. Relf & ptnrs	
G-BLMA	Zlin 326 Trener Master	G. P. Northcott/Shoreham	
G-BLMC	Avro 698 Vulcan B.2A (XM575) ★	Aeropark/E. Midlands	
G-BLME	Robinson R-22	Skyline Helicopters Ltd	
G-BLMG	Grob G.109B	K. & A. Barton	
G-BLMI	PA-18 Super Cub 95	B. J. Borsberry	
G-BLMN	Rutan LongEz	D. J. Bowie	
G-BLMO	Cameron 60 Demistica Bottle SS balloon	Cameron Balloons Ltd	
G-BLMP	PA-17 Vagabond	M. Austin/Popham	
G-BLMR	PA-18 Super Cub 150	Skyfever Aviation Enterprises/ Biggin Hill	
G-BLMT	PA-18 Super Cub 135	I. S. Runnalls	
G-BLMV	Jodel DR.1051	S. Windsor	
G-BLMW	T.66 Nipper 3	S. L. Millar	
G-BLMX	Cessna FR.172H	A. J. Fuller & ptnrs/Felthorpe	
G-BLMZ	Colt 105A balloon	M. J. Hutchins	
G-BLNA	Beech B90 King Air	National Airways (G-BHGT/G-AWWK)/ Southend	
G-BLNB	V.802 Viscount	British Air Ferries (G-AOHV)/Southend	
G-BLNJ	BN-2B Islander	Loganair Ltd/Glasgow	
G-BLNN	PA-38-112 Tomahawk	Nalson Aviation Ltd (G-CGFC)/ Biggin Hill	
G-BLNO	FRED Srs 3	L. W. Smith	
G-BLNW	BN-2B Islander	Loganair Ltd/Glasgow	
G-BLNZ	BN-2B Islander	Pilatus BN Ltd/Bembridge	
G-BLOA	V.806 Viscount Freightmaster II	British Air Ferries Ltd (G-AOYJ) Viscount Jock Bryce OBE/Southend	
G-BLOB	Colt 31A balloon	Jacques W. Soukup Ltd	
G-BLOC	Rand KR-2	F. Woodhouse	
G-BLOE	PA-31-350 Navajo Chieftain	PW Cleaning Services Ltd (G-NITE)	
G-BLOG	Cameron O-77 balloon	Britannia Balloon Group	
G-BLOJ	Thunder Ax7-77 Srs 1 balloon	J. W. Cato	
G-BLOK	Colt 77A balloon	D. L. Clark Spritsa	
G-BLOL	SNCAN Stampe SV-4A	Skysport Engineering	
G-BLOO	Sopwith Dove Replica	Skysport Engineering	
G-BLOR	PA-30 Twin Comanche 160	S. B. McIntyre & K. W. Felton	
G-BLOS	Cessna 185A (also flown with floats)	E. Brun	
G-BLOT	Colt Ax6-56B balloon	Thunder & Colt Ltd	
G-BLOU	Rand KR-2	D. Cole	
G-BLOV	Colt Ax5-42 Srs 1 balloon	Thunder & Colt Ltd	
G-BLPA	Piper J-3C-65 Cub	G. A. Card	
G-BLPB	Turner TSW Hot Two Wot	J. R. Woolford & K. M. Thomas	
G-BLPE	PA-18 Super Cub 95	A. Haig-Thomas	
G-BLPF	Cessna FR.172G	N. Abram	
G-BLPG	J/1N Alpha	P. G. & A. Valentine (G-AZIH)	
G-BLPH	Cessna FRA.150L	Aerobat Group of Shoreham	
G-BLPI	Slingsby T.67B	W. F. Hall	
G-BLPK	Cameron V-65 balloon	A. J. & C. P. Nicholls	
G-BLPM	AS.332L Super Puma	Bristow Helicopters Ltd	
G-BLPN	M.S.894E Rallye 220GT	Midair Services Ltd	
G-BLPP	Cameron V-77 balloon	L. P. Purfield	
G-BLRB	D.H.104 Devon C.2 (VP962)	V. S. E. Norman/Kemble	
G-BLRC	PA-18 Super Cub 135	Grays (Pakefield) Ltd	
G-BLRD	MBB Bo.209 Monsun 150FV	M. D. Ward	
G-BLRF	Slingsby T.67C	Bristow Helicopters Ltd/Redhill	
G-BLRG	Slingsby T.67B	Denham School of Flying	
G-BLRH	Rutan Long Ez	G. L. Thompson	
G-BLRJ	Jodel DR.1051	M. P. Hallam	
G-BLRL	CP.301C-1 Emeraude	R. A. Abrahams/Barton	

Notes	Reg.	Type	Owner or Operator
	G-BLRM	Glaser-Dirks DG.400	R. L. McLean & J. N. Ellis
	G-BLRP	FMA IA.58-A Pucara	Grampian Helicopters International Ltd
	G-BLRS	—	
	G-BLRT	Short SD3-60	Guernsey Airlines Ltd
	G-BLRW	Cameron 77 Elephant balloon	Forbes Europe Inc
	G-BLRX	SOCATA TB.9 Tampico	Wiselock Ltd/Elstree
	G-BLRY	AS.332L Super Puma	Bristow Helicopters Ltd
	G-BLRZ	SOCATA TB.9 Tampico	Aldred Associates Ltd
	G-BLSC	Consolidated PBY-5A Catalina (JV928)	J. P. W. Wilson/Duxford
	G-BLSD	D.H.112 Venom FB.54	Aces High Ltd/North Weald
	G-BLSF	AA-5A Cheetah	J. P. E. Walsh (G-BGCK)
	G-BLSH	Cameron V-77 balloon	C. N. Luffingham
	G-BLSI	Colt AS-56 airship	Hot-Air Balloon Co Ltd
	G-BLSJ	Thunder Ax8-90 balloon	Thunder Balloons Ltd
	G-BLSK	Colt 77A balloon	G. M. Hutton
	G-BLSM	H.S.125 Srs 700B	Dravidian Air Services Ltd/Heathrow
	G-BLSN	Colt AS-56 airship	Colt Balloons Ltd
	G-BLSO	Colt AS-42 airship	K. L. C. M. Busemeyer
	G-BLSR	Everett autogyro	R. J. Everett
	G-BLST	Cessna 421C	Cecil Aviation Ltd/Cambridge
	G-BLSU	Cameron A-210 balloon	Skysales Ltd
	G-BLSX	Cameron O-105 balloon	B. J. Petteford
	G-BLSY	Bell 222A	Glen International PLC
	G-BLTA	Thunder Ax7-77A	M. J. Forster & K. A. Schlussler
	G-BLTC	D.31 Turbulent	G. P. Smith & A. W. Burton
	G-BLTF	Robinson R-22A	Forest Dale Hotels Ltd
	G-BLTG	WAR Sea Fury (WJ237)	P. J. Collins
	G-BLTK	R. Commander 112TC	B. Rogalewski/Denham
	G-BLTM	Robin HR.200/100	P. D. Wheatland/Barton
	G-BLTN	Thunder Ax7-65 balloon	J. A. Liddle
	G-BLTO	Short SD3-60	Guernsey Airlines Ltd
	G-BLTP	H.S.125 Srs 700B	Dravidian Air Services Ltd/Heathrow
	G-BLTR	Scheibe SF.25B Falke	V. Mallon/W. Germany
	G-BLTS	Rutan LongEz	R. W. Cutler
	G-BLTT	Slingsby T.67B	Denham School of Flying
	G-BLTU	Slingsby T.67B	The Neiderhein Powered Flying Club
	G-BLTV	Slingsby T.67B	Slingsby Aviation PLC/Kirkbymoorside
	G-BLTW	Slingsby T.67B	Slingsby Aviation PLC/Kirkbymoorside
	G-BLTZ	SOCATA TB.10 Tobago	Martin Ltd/Biggin Hill
	G-BLUA	Robinson R-22	J. R. Budgen
	G-BLUE	Colting Ax7-77A balloon	M. R. & C. Cumpston
	G-BLUF	Thunder Ax10-180 balloon	Thunder & Colt Ltd
	G-BLUG	Thunder Ax10-180 balloon	Thunder & Colt Ltd
	G-BLUH	Thunder Ax10-180 balloon	Thunder & Colt Ltd
	G-BLUI	Thunder Ax7-65 balloon	A. Stace
	G-BLUJ	Cameron V-56 balloon	J. N. W. West
	G-BLUK	Bond Sky Dancer	J. Owen
	G-BLUL	Jodel DR.1051/M1	J. Owen
	G-BLUM	SA.365N Dauphin 2	Bond Helicopters Ltd
	G-BLUN	SA.365N Dauphin 2	Bond Helicopters Ltd
	G-BLUO	SA.365N Dauphin 2	Bond Helicopters Ltd
	G-BLUP	SA.365N Dauphin 2	Bond Helicopters Ltd
	G-BLUV	Grob G.109B	Go-Grob Ltd
	G-BLUX	Slingsby T.67M	Slingsby Aviation Ltd/Kirkbymoorside
	G-BLUY	Colt 69A balloon	The Balloon Goes Up Ltd
	G-BLUZ	D.H.82B Queen Bee (LF858)	B. Bayes
	G-BLVA	Airtour AH-56 balloon	Airtour Balloon Co Ltd
	G-BLVB	Airtour AH-56 balloon	Airtour Balloon Co Ltd
	G-BLVC	Airtour AH-31 balloon	Airtour Balloon Co Ltd
	G-BLVE	Boeing 747-2B4B	British Airways City of Lincoln/Gatwick
	G-BLVF	Boeing 747-2B4B	British Airways City of Lancaster/Gatwick
	G-BLVG	EMB-110P1 Bandeirante	Alexandra Aviation Ltd (G-RLAY)
	G-BLVH	Boeing 757-236	Air Europe Ltd Jackie/Gatwick
	G-BLVI	Slingsby T.67M	Slingsby Aviation Ltd/Kirkbymoorside
	G-BLVK	CAARP CAP-10B	BAC Aviation Ltd/Southend
	G-BLVL	PA-28-161 Warrior II	C.S.E. Aviation Ltd/Kidlington
	G-BLVN	Cameron N-77 balloon	B. Hodge
	G-BLVR	—	
	G-BLVS	Cessna 150M	W. Lancashire Aero Club Ltd/Woodvale
	G-BLVT	Cessna FR.172J	T. R. Scorer & J. J. Booth/Cambridge
	G-BLVU	Pitts S-2A	A. J. E. Ditheridge

Reg.	Type	Owner or Operator	Notes
G-BLVV	Bell 206B JetRanger	Bristow Helicopters Ltd	
G-BLVW	Cessna F.172H	G. S. Evans	
G-BLVY	Colt 21A balloon	Colt Balloons Ltd	
G-BLWB	Thunder Ax6-56 balloon	G. G. Bacon	
G-BLWD	PA-34-200T Seneca	C.S.E. Aviation Ltd/Kidlington	
G-BLWE	Colt 90A balloon	Thunder & Colt Ltd	
G-BLWF	Robin HR.100/210	A. H. Kelle	
G-BLWG	Varga 2150A Kachina	MLP Aviation Ltd/Elstree	
G-BLWH	Fournier RF-6B-100	Gloster Aero Club Ltd/Staverton	
G-BLWL	Colt 31A balloon	Hot Air Balloon Co Ltd	
G-BLWM	Bristol M.1C replica (C4912) ★	RAF Museum store	
G-BLWO	Cameron N-77 balloon	A. B. Williams	
G-BLWP	PA-38-112 Tomahawk	A. Dodd/Booker	
G-BLWR	Currie Wot	H. Moffat	
G-BLWT	Evans VP-1	C. J. Bellworthy	
G-BLWV	Cessna F.152	Redhill Flying Club	
G-BLWW	Taylor Mini Imp Model C	M. K. Field	
G-BLWX	Cameron N-56 balloon	Skipton Building Soc	
G-BLWY	Robin 2161D	A. Walton	
G-BLWZ	M.S.883 Rallye 115	J. H. Betton	
G-BLXA	SOCATA TB.20 Trinidad	Street Construction (Wigan) Ltd	
G-BLXB	Colt 240A balloon	Colt Balloons Ltd	
G-BLXF	Cameron V-77 balloon	D. I. Gray-Fisk	
G-BLXG	Colt 21A balloon	Balloon & Airship Co Ltd	
G-BLXH	Fournier RF-3	D. T. Kaberry/Blackpool	
G-BLXI	CP.1310-C3 Super Emeraude	R. A. M. Purkis	
G-BLXK	Agusta-Bell 205	Autair Helicopters Ltd	
G-BLXL	Colt AS-105 airship	Thunder & Colt Ltd	
G-BLXM	—	—	
G-BLXO	Jodel D.150	P. R. Powell	
G-BLXP	PA-28R Cherokee Arrow 200	London Flight Centre (Stansted) Ltd	
G-BLXR	AS.332L Super Puma	Bristow Helicopters Ltd	
G-BLXS	AS.332L Super Puma	Bristow Helicopters Ltd	
G-BLXT	RAF SE-5A (B4863)	The Hon A. M. M. Lindsay/Booker	
G-BLXX	PA-23 Aztec 250F	ABR Aviation Ltd (G-PIED)	
G-BLXY	Cameron V-65 balloon	Gone With The Wind Ltd	
G-BLYB	Beech B200 Super King Air	Alfred McAlpine Aviation Ltd	
G-BLYC	PA-38-112 Tomahawk	D. R. Gliddon	
G-BLYD	SOCATA TB.20 Trinidad	R. J. Crocker	
G-BLYE	SOCATA TB.10 Tobago	Presspart Manufacturing Ltd	
G-BLYJ	Cameron V-77 balloon	E. E. Clark & J. A. Lomas	
G-BLYK	PA-34-220T Seneca III	P. G. Somers	
G-BLYM	B.121 Pup 2	D. J. Sage	
G-BLYP	Robin 3000/120	Lydd Air Training Centre Ltd	
G-BLYR	Airtour AH-77B balloon	Airtour Balloon Co Ltd	
G-BLYT	Airtour AH-77 balloon	Airtour Balloon Co Ltd	
G-BLYU	Airtour AH-31 balloon	Airtour Balloon Co Ltd	
G-BLYV	Airtour AH-56 balloon	Airtour Balloon Co Ltd	
G-BLYY	PA-28-181 Archer II	Fairway Graphics Ltd	
G-BLZA	Scheibe SF.25B Falke	P. Downes & D. Gardner	
G-BLZB	Cameron N-65 balloon	D. Bareford	
G-BLZD	Robin R.1180T	Dunsmere Developments Ltd	
G-BLZE	Cessna F.152	Flairhire Ltd (G-CSSC)/Redhill	
G-BLZF	Thunder Ax7-77 balloon	H. M. Savage	
G-BLZH	Cessna F.152	Butler Associates (Aviation) Ltd	
G-BLZJ	AS.332L Super Puma	British International Helicopters Ltd	
G-BLZM	Rutan Long Ez	B. C. Barton	
G-BLZN	Bell 206B JetRanger	Helicopter Services	
G-BLZP	Cessna F.152	W. H. & J. Rogers Group Ltd/Cranfield	
G-BLZR	Cameron A-140 balloon	Clipper Worldwide Trading Ltd	
G-BLZS	Cameron O-77 balloon	M. M. Cobbold	
G-BLZT	Short SD3-60	Air UK Ltd/Norwich	
G-BLZZ	CAARP CAP.21	D. M. Britten	
G-BMAA	Douglas DC-9-15	British Midland Airways Ltd *The Shah Diamond*/(G-BFIH)/E. Midlands	
G-BMAB	Douglas DC-9-15	British Midland Airways Ltd *The Great Mogul Diamond*/E. Midlands	
G-BMAC	Douglas DC-9-15	British Midland Airways Ltd *The Eugenie Diamond*/E. Midlands	
G-BMAD	Cameron V-77 balloon	F. J. J. Fielder	
G-BMAF	Cessna 180F	P. Scales (G-BDVR)	
G-BMAG	Douglas DC-9-15	British Midland Airways Ltd *The Nassau Diamond*/E. Midlands	

Notes	Reg.	Type	Owner or Operator
	G-BMAH	Douglas DC-9-14	British Midland Airways Ltd *The Florentine Diamond*/E. Midlands
	G-BMAI	Douglas DC-9-14	British Midland Airways Ltd *The Star of Este Diamond*/E. Midlands
	G-BMAK	Douglas DC-9-30	British Midland Airways Ltd *The Stewart Diamond*/E. Midlands
	G-BMAL	Sikorsky S-76A	Bond Helicopters Ltd/Bourn
	G-BMAM	Douglas DC-9-30	British Midland Airways Ltd *The Cullinan Diamond*/E. Midlands
	G-BMAO	Taylor JT.1 Monoplane	V. A. Wordsworth
	G-BMAR	Short SD3-60	Loganair Ltd (G-BLCR)/Glasgow
	G-BMAT	V.813 Viscount	Baltic British Air Ferries Ltd (G-AZLT)/Southend
	G-BMAV	AS.350B Ecureuil	Southern Trust Co Ltd/Jersey
	G-BMAX	FRED Srs 2	D. A. Arkley
	G-BMAY	PA-18 Super Cub 135	G. V. Harfield/Popham
	G-BMBB	Cessna F.150L	Telepoint Ltd
	G-BMBC	PA-31-350 Navajo Chieftain	Casair Aviation Ltd/Teesside
	G-BMBE	PA-46-310P Malibu	Artix Ltd
	G-BMBF	Nord 3202B	F. & H. Aircraft Ltd/Breighton
	G-BMBI	PA-31-350 Navajo Chieftain	Streamline Aviation Ltd/E. Midlands
	G-BMBJ	Schempp-Hirth Janus CM	Oxfordshire Sportflying Ltd/Enstone
	G-BMBP	Colt Whisky Bottle balloon	Thunder & Colt Ltd
	G-BMBR	Issoire D77-M Motor Iris	G. R. Horner
	G-BMBS	Colt 105A balloon	A. P. Hardiman & H. G. Davies
	G-BMBT	Thunder Ax8-90 balloon	Capital Balloon Club Ltd
	G-BMBW	Bensen B.80	M. Vahdat
	G-BMBY	Beech A36 Bonanza	Morse Computers Ltd
	G-BMBZ	Scheibe SF.25E Falke	Cairngorm Gliding Club
	G-BMCB	Partenavia P.68B	Air Kilroe Ltd/Manchester
	G-BMCC	Thunder Ax7-77 balloon	H. N. Harben Ltd
	G-BMCD	Cameron V-65 balloon	M. C. Drye
	G-BMCE	Bensen B.8M	J. Lee
	G-BMCG	Grob G.109B	Soaring (Oxford) Ltd/Enstone
	G-BMCH	AB-206B JetRanger	Autair Ltd
	G-BMCI	Cessna F.172H	P. P. D. Howard-Johnston
	G-BMCJ	PA-31-350 Navajo Chieftain	Chelsea Land (Finance) Ltd
	G-BMCK	Cameron O-77 balloon	D. L. Smith
	G-BMCM	Grob G.109B	Sonardyne Ltd/Blackbushe
	G-BMCN	Cessna F.152	Lincoln Aero Club Ltd/Sturgate
	G-BMCO	Colomban MC.15 Cri-Cri	G. P. Clarke/Enstone
	G-BMCS	PA-22 Tri-Pacer 135	W. A. P. Darbishire
	G-BMCT	Cameron D-50 airship	Cameron Balloons Ltd
	G-BMCV	Cessna F.152	Leicester Aero Club Ltd
	G-BMCW	AS.332L Super Puma	Bristow Helicopters Ltd
	G-BMCX	AS.332L Super Puma	Bristow Helicopters Ltd
	G-BMCZ	Colt 69A balloon	Thunder & Colt Ltd
	G-BMDB	SE-5A replica (F235)	D. Biggs
	G-BMDC	PA-32-301 Saratoga	Maclaren Aviation/Newcastle
	G-BMDD	Slingsby T.29	D. I. H. Johnstone & L. Ward
	G-BMDE	Pientenpol Aircamper	D. Silsbury
	G-BMDF	Boeing 737-2E7	Dan-Air Services Ltd/Gatwick
	G-BMDG	Cameron O-105 balloon	Buddy Bombard Balloons Ltd
	G-BMDH	Cameron O-105 balloon	Buddy Bombard Balloons Ltd
	G-BMDI	Thunder Ax8-105Z balloon	Buddy Bombard Balloons Ltd
	G-BMDJ	Price Ax7-77S balloon	T. S. Price
	G-BMDK	PA-34-220T Seneca III	Skyline Helicopters Ltd/Booker
	G-BMDM	Cessna 340A	Dominion Credit & Finance Ltd/Biggin Hill
	G-BMDO	ARV Super 2	H. L. Wensley
	G-BMDP	Partenavia P.64B Oscar 200	D. Foey
	G-BMDS	Jodel D.120	D. Stansfield & H. Greenwood
	G-BMDU	Bell 214ST	Bristow Helicopters Ltd
	G-BMDV	Bell 47G-5	Autair Ltd
	G-BMDW	Dangerous Sports Club/Colt Hoppalong 1 balloon	D. A. C. Kirke
	G-BMDY	GA-7 Cougar	Eastern Air Taxis/Elstree
	G-BMEA	PA-18 Super Cub 95	C. L. Towell
	G-BMEB	Rotorway Scorpion 145	I. M. Bartlett
	G-BMEE	Cameron O-105 balloon	A. G. R. Calder
	G-BMEF	Beech C90 King Air	National Airways/Southend
	G-BMEG	SOCATA TB.10 Tobago	G. H. N. & R. V. Chamberlain
	G-BMEH	Jodel Super Special Mascaret	E. J. Horsfall/Blackpool
	G-BMEJ	PA-28R Cherokee Arrow 200	London Flight Centre (Stansted) Ltd

Reg.	Type	Owner or Operator	Notes
G-BMEM	Fournier RF-4D	A. M. Witt	
G-BMET	Taylor JT.1 Monoplane	M. K. A. Blyth	
G-BMEU	Isaacs Fury II	A. W. Austin	
G-BMEV	PA-32RT-300T Turbo Lance II	Northwest Motorcaravans Ltd/ Blackpool	
G-BMEX	Cessna A.150K	R. Kirkham & N. Brain/Netherthorpe	
G-BMEZ	Cameron D-50 airship	Cameron Balloons Ltd	
G-BMFB	Douglas AD-4W Skyraider	Coys of Kensington (Petrol Sales) Ltd	
G-BMFC	Douglas AD-4W Skyraider	Coys of Kensington (Petrol Sales) Ltd	
G-BMFD	PA-23 Aztec 250F	Bomford & Evershed Ltd (G-BGYY)/ Coventry	
G-BMFG	Dornier Do.27A-4	Onderstar Aviation Ltd/Booker	
G-BMFH	Dornier Do.27A-4	Onderstar Aviation Ltd/Booker	
G-BMFI	PZL SZD-45A Ogar	Marrix Ltd/Redhill	
G-BMFJ	Thunder Ax7-77 balloon	Thunder & Colt Ltd	
G-BMFK	PA-28-236 Dakota	R. G. Gabriel	
G-BMFL	Rand KR-2	E. W. B. Comber & M. F. Leusby	
G-BMFN	QAC Quickie 200	W. Blair-Hickman	
G-BMFP	PA-28-161 Warrior II	T. J. Froggatt & ptnrs/Blackbushe	
G-BMFT	H.S.748 Srs 2A	Euroair/British Airways	
G-BMFU	Cameron N-90 balloon	J. J. Rudoni	
G-BMFW	Hughes 369E	Ford Helicopters Ltd	
G-BMFY	Grob G.109B	P. J. Shearer	
G-BMFZ	Cessna F.152	Cornwall Flying Club Ltd	
G-BMGB	PA-28R Cherokee Arrow 200	Malmesbury Specialist Cars	
G-BMGC	Fairey Swordfish Mk II (W5856)	Strathallan Aircraft Collection	
G-BMGD	Colt 17A balloon	Airbureau Ltd	
G-BMGG	Cessna 152	A. S. Bamrah/Biggin Hill	
G-BMGH	PA-31-325 Turbo Navajo C/R	Chaseside Holdings Ltd/Exeter	
G-BMGJ	—	—	
G-BMGK	—	—	
G-BMGL	—	—	
G-BMGM	—	—	
G-BMGN	—	—	
G-BMGO	—	—	
G-BMGP	Hughes 269C	A. H. Canvin	
G-BMGR	Grob G.109B	BMGR Group/Lasham	
G-BMGS	Boeing 747-283B	British Airways City of Swansea/ Heathrow	
G-BMGT	Cessna 310R	Air Service Training Ltd/Perth	
G-BMGV	Robinson R-22	Foreman Hart Ltd	
G-BMGY	Lake LA-4-200 Buccaneer	M. A. Ashmole (G-BWKS/G-BDDI)	
G-BMHA	Rutan Long Ez	S. F. Elvins	
G-BMHI	Cessna F.152	Skyviews & General Ltd/Leeds	
G-BMHJ	Thunder Ax7-65 balloon	D. Cole	
G-BMHK	Cameron V-77 balloon	B. J. Workman	
G-BMHL	Wittman W.8 Tailwind	T. G. Hoult	
G-BMHN	Robinson R-22A	Ainderfield Ltd	
G-BMHR	Grob G.109B	HRN Aviation Ltd	
G-BMHS	Cessna F.172M	C. H. Ludar-Smith	
G-BMHT	PA-28RT-201T Turbo Arrow IV	Relay Services Ltd	
G-BMHU	Viking Dragonfly	H. A. Bancroft-Wilson	
G-BMHX	Short SD3-60	Loganair Ltd/Manx Airlines	
G-BMHY	Short SD3-60	Short Bros PLC/Sydenham	
G-BMHZ	PA-28RT-201T Turbo Arrow IV	Bioeve Ltd	
G-BMIA	Thunder Ax8-90 balloon	A. G. R. Calder	
G-BMIB	Bell 206B JetRanger	Lee Aviation Ltd/Booker	
G-BMID	Jodel D.120	A. W. Cooke	
G-BMIF	AS.350B Ecureuil	Colt Car Co Ltd/Staverton	
G-BMIG	Cessna 172N	J. R. Nicholls/Conington	
G-BMIK	Dornier Do.27-A4	Wessex Aviation & Transport Ltd	
G-BMIL	—		
G-BMIM	Rutan Long Ez	R. M. Smith	
G-BMIO	Stoddard-Hamilton Glasair RG	A. H. Carrington	
G-BMIP	Jodel D.112	M. T. Kinch	
G-BMIR	Westland Wasp HAS.1 (XT788)	R. Windley	
G-BMIS	Monnet Sonerai II	B. A. Bower/Thruxton	
G-BMIU	Enstrom F-28A	Rotor Enterprises Ltd	
G-BMIV	PA-28R-201T Turbo Arrow III	Trindon Ltd/Little Snoring	
G-BMIW	PA-28-181 Archer II	Stone Air/Shoreham	
G-BMIY	Oldfield Baby Great Lakes	J. B. Scott (G-NOME)	
G-BMJA	PA-32R-301 Saratoga SP	Continental Cars (Stansted) Ltd	
G-BMJB	Cessna 152	RJS Aviation Ltd	
G-BMJC	Cessna 152	Cambridge Aero Club Ltd	

Notes	Reg.	Type	Owner or Operator
	G-BMJD	Cessna 152	Fife Airport Management Ltd/ Glenrothes
	G-BMJG	PA-28R Cherokee Arrow 200	D. J. D. Ritchie & ptnrs/Elstree
	G-BMJL	R. Commander 114	H. Snelson
	G-BMJM	Evans VP-1	J. A. Mawby
	G-BMJN	Cameron O-65 balloon	E. J. A. Machole
	G-BMJO	PA-34-220T Seneca III	Richard Arnold & Co Ltd
	G-BMJP	Colt AS-56 airship	Thunder & Colt Ltd
	G-BMJR	Cessna T.337H	John Roberts Services Ltd (G-NOVA)
	G-BMJS	Thunder Ax7-77 balloon	Anglia Balloon School Ltd
	G-BMJT	Beech 76 Duchess	Mike Osborne Insurance Services Ltd
	G-BMJV	Hughes 369D	Bristol Estates Ltd
	G-BMJW	AT-6D Harvard III (EZ259)	J. Woods
	G-BMJX	Wallis WA-116X	K. H. Wallis
	G-BMJY	Yakolev C18M	R. Lamplough/North Weald
	G-BMJZ	Cameron N-90 balloon	Windsor Pharmaceuticals Ltd
	G-BMKB	PA-18 Super Cub 135	C. Marsh
	G-BMKC	Piper J-3C-65 Cub (329854)	R. J. H. Springall
	G-BMKD	Beech C90A King Air	A. E. Bristow
	G-BMKE	PA-28RT-201 Arrow IV	P. A. Lancaster/Booker
	G-BMKF	Jodel DR.221	B. M. R. Clavel & J. M. A. Lassauze
	G-BMKG	PA-38-112 Tomahawk	R. J. Hickson
	G-BMKH	Colt 105A balloon	Thunder & Colt Ltd
	G-BMKI	Colt 21A balloon	Thunder & Colt Ltd
	G-BMKJ	Cameron V-77 balloon	R. C. Thursby
	G-BMKK	PA-28R Cherokee Arrow 200	Arrow Aviation
	G-BMKM	AB-206B JetRanger 3	Fizzle Ltd
	G-BMKN	Colt 31A balloon	Thunder & Colt Ltd
	G-BMKO	PA-28-181 Archer II	Anglosky Ltd
	G-BMKP	Cameron V-77 balloon	Jacques W. Soukup Enterprises Ltd
	G-BMKR	PA-28-161 Warrior II	Field Flying Group (G-BGKR)/ Goodwood
	G-BMKS	Aerosport Scamp	R. R. Walters/Ipswich
	G-BMKV	Thunder Ax7-77 balloon	A. Hornak & M. J. Nadel
	G-BMKW	Cameron V-77 balloon	A. C. Garnett
	G-BMKX	Cameron 77 Elephant balloon	Cameron Balloons Ltd
	G-BMKY	Cameron O-65 balloon	First Reflex Ltd
	G-BMLA	Bell UH-1H ★	Grampian Helicopters International Ltd
	G-BMLB	Jodel D.120A	W. O. Brown
	G-BMLC	Short SD3-60	Loganair Ltd/Glasgow
	G-BMLH	Mooney M.20C	G. D. Bowd
	G-BMLJ	Cameron N-77 balloon	J. Money-Kyrle
	G-BMLK	Grob G.109B	A. Batters
	G-BMLL	Grob G.109B	A. H. R. Stansfield
	G-BMLP	Boeing 727-264	Dan-Air Services Ltd/Gatwick
	G-BMLS	PA-28R-201 Arrow III	South Coast Aviation Ltd/Goodwood
	G-BMLT	Pietenpol Aircamper	R. A. & F. A. Hawke/Redhill
	G-BMLU	Colt 90A balloon	Danish Catering Services Ltd
	G-BMLV	Robinson R-22A	Skyline Helicopters Ltd/Booker
	G-BMLW	Cameron V-65 balloon	M. L. & L. P. Willoughby
	G-BMLX	Cessna F.150L	K. Gallo
	G-BMLY	Grob G.109B	P. H. Yarrow & D. G. Margetts
	G-BMLZ	Cessna 421C	Chaseside Holdings Ltd (G-OTAD/ G-BEVL)
	G-BMMC	Cessna T310Q	W. H. G. Nunn/Elstree
	G-BMMD	Rand KR-2	K. R. Wheatley
	G-BMMF	FRED Srs 2	J. M. Jones
	G-BMMI	Pazmany PL.4	M. L. Martin
	G-BMMJ	Siren PIK-30	J. D. S. Thorne
	G-BMMK	Cessna 182P	M. S. Knight/Goodwood
	G-BMML	PA-38-112 Tomahawk	Atlantic Aviation Ltd
	G-BMMM	Cessna 152	A. S. Bamrah/Biggin Hill
	G-BMMN	Thunder Ax8-105 balloon	R. C. Weyda
	G-BMMP	Grob G.109B	B. F. Fraser-Smith & B. F. Pearson
	G-BMMR	Dornier Do.228-200	Suckling Airways Ltd/Ipswich
	G-BMMU	Thunder Ax8-105 balloon	H. C. Wright
	G-BMMV	ICA-Brasov IS-28M2A	T. Cust
	G-BMMW	Thunder Ax7-77 balloon	P. A. Georges
	G-BMMX	ICA-Brasov IS-28M2A	M. Lee & ptnrs
	G-BMMY	Thunder Ax7-77 balloon	Double Glazing Components Ltd
	G-BMMZ	Boeing 737-2D6	Britannia Airways Ltd/Luton
	G-BMNB	Airbus A.300B4-103	Dan-Air Services Ltd/Gatwick
	G-BMNC	Airbus A.300B4-103	Dan-Air Services Ltd/Gatwick
	G-BMNE	—	—

Reg.	Type	Owner or Operator	Notes
G-BMNF	Beech B200 Super King Air	Bernard Matthews PLC/Norwich	
G-BMNL	PA-28R Cherokee Arrow 200	Airways Aero Associations Ltd/Booker	
G-BMNP	PA-38-112 Tomahawk	Seal Executive Aircraft Ltd	
G-BMNT	PA-34-220T Seneca III	R. J. Alford	
G-BMNU	Cameron V-77 balloon	B. K. & G. S. Palmer	
G-BMNV	SNCAN Stampe SV-4D	Wessex Aviation & Transport Ltd	
G-BMNW	PA-31-350 Navajo Chieftain	Fletcher Rentals Ltd/Coventry	
G-BMNX	Colt 56A balloon	M. Davies	
G-BMNY	Everett gyroplane	J. D. Colvin	
G-BMNZ	Cessna U206F	Macpara Ltd/Shobdon	
G-BMOE	PA-28R Cherokee Arrow 200	Modern Air/Panshanger	
G-BMOF	Cessna U206G	Integrated Hydraulics Ltd	
G-BMOG	Thunder Ax7-77A balloon	Anglia Balloon School Ltd	
G-BMOH	Cameron N-77 balloon	Legal & General PLC	
G-BMOI	Partenavia P.68B	Simmette Ltd	
G-BMOJ	Cameron V-56 balloon	S. R. Bridge	
G-BMOK	ARV Super 2	Nik Coates Ltd	
G-BMOL	PA-23 Aztec 250D	LDL Enterprises (G-BBSR)/Elstree	
G-BMOM	ICA-Brasov IS-28M2A	R. E. Todd	
G-BMON	Boeing 737-2K9	Monarch Airlines Ltd/Luton	
G-BMOO	FRED Srs 2	N. Purllant	
G-BMOP	PA-28R-201T Turbo Arrow III	Coleridge Self Service/Cardiff	
G-BMOR	Boeing 737-253	Air UK Leisure Ltd/Stansted	
G-BMOT	Bensen B.8M	R. S. W. Jones	
G-BMOV	Cameron O-105 balloon	I. M. Hughes	
G-BMOW	G.159 Gulfstream 1	Birmingham Executive Airways PLC	
G-BMOX	Hovey Beta Bird	A. D. Tatton	
G-BMOY	Cameron A-250 balloon	Gone With The Wind Ltd	
G-BMOZ	Cameron O-160 balloon	R. M. Bishop	
G-BMPA	G.159 Gulfstream 1	Peregrine Air Services Ltd/Aberdeen	
G-BMPC	PA-28-181 Archer II	Charles Setton Trading Co Ltd	
G-BMPD	Cameron V-65 balloon	Cameron Balloons Ltd	
G-BMPF	OA.7 Optica	Brooklands Aircraft Co Ltd/Old Sarum	
G-BMPI	OA.7 Optica	Optica Industries Ltd/Old Sarum	
G-BMPL	OA.7 Optica	Hampshire Police Authority (Air Support Unit)/Lee-on-Solent	
G-BMPM	OA.7 Optica	Optica Industries Ltd/Old Sarum	
G-BMPN	OA.7 Optica	Optica Industries Ltd/Old Sarum	
G-BMPO	Cessna 182Q	R. Evans	
G-BMPP	Cameron N-77 balloon	Sarnia Balloon Group	
G-BMPR	PA-28R-201 Arrow III	AH Flight Services Ltd	
G-BMPS	Strojnik S-2A	T. J. Gardiner	
G-BMPU	Robinson R-22	Sloane Helicopters Ltd/Luton	
G-BMPV	PA-31-325 Navajo C/R	Theocsbury Aviation Ltd/Staverton	
G-BMPY	D.H.82A Tiger Moth	S. M. F. Eisenstein	
G-BMRA	Boeing 757-236	British Airways Beaumaris Castle/Heathrow	
G-BMRB	Boeing 757-236	British Airways Colchester Castle/Heathrow	
G-BMRC	Boeing 757-236	British Airways Rochester Castle	
G-BMRD	Boeing 757-236	British Airways Bothwell Castle	
G-BMRE	Boeing 757-236	British Airways Killyleagh Castle	
G-BMRF	Boeing 757-236	British Airways Hever Castle	
G-BMRG	Boeing 757-236	British Airways Caerphilly Castle	
G-BMRH	Boeing 757-236	Caledonian Airways Loch Aline	
G-BMRI	Boeing 757-236	Caledonian Airways Loch Tummel	
G-BMRJ	Boeing 757-236	Caledonian Airways Loch Ryan	
G-BMRK	—	British Airways	
G-BMRL	—	British Airways	
G-BMSA	Stinson HW.75 Voyager	P. F. Bennison (G-BCUM)/Barton	
G-BMSB	V.S.509 Spitfire IX (MJ627)	M. S. Bayliss (G-ASOZ)	
G-BMSC	Evans VP-2	F. R. Donaldson	
G-BMSD	PA-28-181 Archer II	Courtridge Ltd	
G-BMSE	Valentin Taifun 17E	K. P. O'Sullivan & G. T. Birks/Booker	
G-BMSF	PA-38-112 Tomahawk	N. Bradley/Leeds	
G-BMSG	Saab 32A Lansen	Aces High Ltd/Cranfield	
G-BMSI	Cameron N-105 balloon	Direction Air Conditioning Ltd	
G-BMSK	Hoffman H-36 Dimona	J. P. Kovacs	
G-BMSL	FRED Srs 3	A. C. Coombe	
G-BMSO	—	R. Windley	
G-BMSP	Hughes 369HS	Peregrine Air Services Ltd/Aberdeen	
G-BMSR	G.159 Gulfstream 1		
G-BMSS	—	Hot Air Balloon Co Ltd	
G-BMST	Cameron N-31 balloon		

Notes	Reg.	Type	Owner or Operator
	G-BMSU	Cessna 152	M. T. Tidswell
	G-BMSV	PA-31-350 Navajo Chieftain	Regency Aviation Services Ltd
	G-BMSW	Cessna T.210M	Foxgrove Construction Ltd
	G-BMSX	PA-30 Twin Comanche 160	M. Sparks/Bristol
	G-BMSY	Cameron A-140 balloon	Duskytone Ltd
	G-BMSZ	Cessna 152	RJS Aviation Ltd/Halfpenny Green
	G-BMTA	Cessna 152	Basic Vale Ltd/Netherthorpe
	G-BMTB	Cessna 152	J. A. Pothecary/Shoreham
	G-BMTE	Boeing 737-3S3	Air Europe Ltd/Gatwick
	G-BMTF	Boeing 737-3S3	Air Europe Ltd/Gatwick
	G-BMTG	Boeing 737-3S3	Air Europe Ltd/Gatwick
	G-BMTH	Boeing 737-3S3	Air Europe Ltd/Gatwick
	G-BMTJ	Cessna 152	Creaton Aviation Services Ltd
	G-BMTK	Cessna 152	Cloudshire Ltd/Wellesbourne
	G-BMTL	Cessna 152	Agricultural & General Aviation/ Bournemouth
	G-BMTN	Cameron O-77 balloon	Industrial Services (MH) Ltd
	G-BMTO	PA-38-112 Tomahawk	K. J. Baron
	G-BMTP	PA-38-112 Tomahawk	London Flight Centre (Stansted) Ltd
	G-BMTR	PA-28-161 Warrior II	London Flight Centre (Stansted) Ltd
	G-BMTS	Cessna 172N	DJH Aviation Ltd/Biggin Hill
	G-BMTU	Pitts S-1E Special	O. R. Howe
	G-BMTW	PA-31-350 Navajo Chieftain	Air Northwest Ltd
	G-BMTX	Cameron V-77 balloon	J. A. Langley
	G-BMTY	Colt 77A balloon	L. D. Ormerod
	G-BMUD	Cessna 182P	Ingham Aviation Ltd
	G-BMUF	Cessna R182RG	Wilsons Feeds Ltd
	G-BMUG	Rutan LongEz	P. Richardson & J. Shanley
	G-BMUH	Bensen B.8M-R	J. M. Montgomerie
	G-BMUI	Brugger MB.2 Colibri	Carlton Flying Group/Netherthorpe
	G-BMUJ	Colt Drachenfisch balloon	Hot Air Balloon Co Ltd
	G-BMUK	Colt UFO balloon	Hot Air Balloon Co Ltd
	G-BMUL	Colt Kindermond balloon	Hot Air Balloon Co Ltd
	G-BMUN	Cameron Harley 78 balloon	Forbes Europe Inc/France
	G-BMUO	Cessna A.152	Redhill Flying Club
	G-BMUP	PA-31-350 Navajo Chieftain	National Airways/Southend
	G-BMUR	Cameron gas airship	Cameron Balloons Ltd
	G-BMUT	PA-34-200T Seneca 2	BI Aviation Services
	G-BMUU	Thunder Ax7-77 balloon	Thunder & Colt Ltd
	G-BMUZ	PA-28-161 Warrior II	Newcastle-upon-Tyne Aero Club Ltd
	G-BMVA	Schiebe SF.25B Falke	R. Brown
	G-BMVB	Cessna 152	Light Planes (Lancashire) Ltd/Barton
	G-BMVC	Beech 95-B55A Baron	T. N. Ellefson/Newcastle
	G-BMVE	PA-28RT-201 Arrow IV	F. E. Gooding/Biggin Hill
	G-BMVG	QAC Quickie Q.1	P. M. Wright
	G-BMVI	Cameron O-105 balloon	Taunton Hot Air Balloons Co Ltd
	G-BMVJ	Cessna 172N	Cloudshire Ltd/Wellesbourne
	G-BMVK	PA-38-112 Tomahawk	Airways Aero Associations Ltd/Booker
	G-BMVL	PA-38-112 Tomahawk	Airways Aero Associations Ltd/Booker
	G-BMVM	PA-38-112 Tomahawk	Airways Aero Associations Ltd/Booker
	G-BMVO	Cameron O-77 balloon	Warners Motors (Leasing) Ltd
	G-BMVS	Cameron 77 SS balloon	Shellrise Ltd
	G-BMVT	Thunder Ax7-77A balloon	M. L. & L. P. Willoughby
	G-BMVU	Monnet Moni	S. R. Jee
	G-BMVV	Rutan Vari-Viggen	G. B. Roberts
	G-BMVW	Cameron O-65 balloon	S. P. Richards
	G-BMVX	M.S.733 Alcyon Srs 1	J. D. Read
	G-BMVY	Beech B200 Super King Air	Colin Draycott Group Ltd
	G-BMWA	Hughes 269C	March Helicopters Ltd/Sywell
	G-BMWB	Cessna 421C	Capital Trading Aviation Ltd/Cardiff
	G-BMWD	Douglas DC-9-32	British Midland Airways Ltd/E. Midlands
	G-BMWE	ARV Super 2	Interair (Aviation) Ltd/Bournemouth
	G-BMWF	ARV Super 2	ARV Aviation Ltd/Sandown
	G-BMWG	ARV Super 2	Airspeed Aviation Ltd/Burnaston
	G-BMWJ	ARV Super 2	ARV Aviation Ltd/Sandown
	G-BMWN	Cameron 80 SS Temple balloon	Forbes Europe Inc
	G-BMWP	PA-34-200T Seneca II	G-Air Ltd/Lydd
	G-BMWR	R. Commander 112A	M. Edwards & B. Fields
	G-BMWU	Cameron N-42 balloon	The Hot Air Balloon Co Ltd
	G-BMWV	Putzer Elster B	E. A. J. Hibberd
	G-BMXA	Cessna 152	Chamberlain Leasing
	G-BMXB	Cessna 152	Andrewsfield Flying Club Ltd
	G-BMXC	Cessna 152	Vectair Aviation Ltd
	G-BMXD	F.27 Friendship Mk 500	Air UK Ltd Victor Hugo/Norwich

Reg.	Type	Owner or Operator	Notes
G-BMXE	—	—	
G-BMXF	Valentin Taifun 17E	Zone Contracts Ltd	
G-BMXH	Robinson R-22HP	Bailey Employment Services Ltd	
G-BMXJ	Cessna F.150L	J. W. G. Ellis	
G-BMXL	PA-38-112 Tomahawk	Airways Aero Associations Ltd/Booker	
G-BMXM	Colt 180A balloon	Thunder & Colt Ltd	
G-BMXN	Lake LA.4-200 Buccaneer	Cold Storage (Jersey) Ltd	
G-BMXO	Beech C90 King Air	National Airways/Southend	
G-BMXW	D.H.C.6 Twin Otter 310	Loganair Ltd/Glasgow	
G-BMXX	Cessna 152	Midland Aircraft Leasing Ltd	
G-BMXY	Scheibe SF.25B Falke	Marrix Ltd	
G-BMYA	Colt 56A balloon	Thunder & Colt Ltd	
G-BMYC	SOCATA TB.10 Tobago	Drake Organic Chemicals Ltd/ Southampton	
G-BMYD	Beech A36 Bonanza	F. B. Gibbons & Sons Ltd	
G-BMYE	BAe 146-200	British Aerospace PLC (G-WAUS/ G-WISC)/Hatfield	
G-BMYF	Bensen B.8M	S. J. Roberts	
G-BMYG	Cessna F.152	Rolim Ltd/Aberdeen	
G-BMYH	Rotorway 133 Executive	J. Netherwood	
G-BMYI	AA-5 Traveler	W. C. & S. C. Westran	
G-BMYJ	Cameron V-65 balloon	S. M. Antony & R. J. Christopher	
G-BMYK	BAe ATP	British Midland Airways Ltd/E. Midlands	
G-BMYL	BAe ATP	British Midland Airways Ltd/E. Midlands	
G-BMYM	BAe ATP	British Midland Airways Ltd/E. Midlands	
G-BMYN	Colt 77A balloon	J. D. Shapland & ptnrs	
G-BMYO	Cameron V-65 balloon	N. V. Moreton	
G-BMYP	Fairey Gannet AEW.3 (XL502)	N. G. R. Moffatt & R. King	
G-BMYR	Robinson R-22	B. Warrington	
G-BMYS	Thunder Ax7-77Z balloon	J. E. Weidema	
G-BMYU	Jodel D.120	G. Davies	
G-BMYV	Bensen B.8M	R. G. Cotman	
G-BMYW	Hughes 269C	William Tomkins Ltd	
G-BMYY	—	—	
G-BMZA	Air Command 503 Commander	R. W. Husband	
G-BMZB	Cameron N-77 balloon	D. C. Eager	
G-BMZC	Cessna 421C	Larwood Holdings Ltd	
G-BMZD	Beech C90 King Air	Colt Transport Ltd	
G-BMZE	SOCATA TB.9 Tampico	Air Touring Services Ltd/Biggin Hill	
G-BMZF	Mikoyan Gurevich MiG-15 ★	FAA Museum/Yeovilton	
G-BMZG	QAC Quickie Q.2	K. W. Brooker	
G-BMZH	Cameron A-140 balloon	The Balloon Stable Ltd	
G-BMZJ	Colt 400A balloon	Thunder & Colt Ltd	
G-BMZK	Airbus A.300B4-203	Orion/Britannia Airways/Gatwick	
G-BMZL	Airbus A.300B4-203	Orion/Britannia Airways/Gatwick	
G-BMZM	Rand KR-2	K. McNaughton	
G-BMZN	Everett gyroplane	R. J. Brown	
G-BMZO	—	—	
G-BMZP	Everett gyroplane	B. C. Norris	
G-BMZR	—	—	
G-BMZS	Everett gyroplane	C. W. Cload	
G-BMZT	—	—	
G-BMZV	Cessna 172P	Mid Shires Aviation Ltd	
G-BMZW	Bensen B.8	P. D. Widdicombe	
G-BMZX	Wolf W-II Boredom Fighter	J. J. Penney	
G-BMZZ	Stephens Akro Z	P. G. Kynsey & J. Harper	
G-BNAA	V.806 Viscount	British Air Ferries (G-AOYH)/Southend	
G-BNAB	GA-7 Cougar	Brod Gallery (G-BGYP)/Elstree	
G-BNAC	Jurca MJ-100 Spitfire	S. E. Richards	
G-BNAD	Rand KR-2	M. J. Field	
G-BNAG	Colt 105A balloon	R. W. Batcholer	
G-BNAI	Wolf W-II Boredom Fighter	P. J. D. Gronow	
G-BNAJ	Cessna 152	G. Duncan	
G-BNAL	F.27 Friendship Mk 600	Air UK Ltd/Norwich	
G-BNAM	Colt 8A balloon	Thunder & Colt Ltd	
G-BNAN	Cameron V-65 balloon	A. M. Lindsay	
G-BNAO	Colt AS-105 airship	Thunder & Colt Ltd	
G-BNAP	Colt 240A balloon	Thunder & Colt Ltd	
G-BNAR	Taylor JT.1 Monoplane	C. J. Smith	
G-BNAU	Cameron V-65 balloon	J. Buckle	
G-BNAV	Rutan Cozy	G. E. Broome	
G-BNAW	Cameron V-65 balloon	A. Walker	
G-BNAY	Grob G.109B	Microperm Ltd	

Notes	Reg.	Type	Owner or Operator
	G-BNAZ	SOCATA TB.20 Trinidad	Mainouter Ltd/Biggin Hill
	G-BNBD	Short SD3-60	Air Europe Express/Gatwick
	G-BNBI	AS.355F-1 Twin Squirrel	McAlpine Helicopters Ltd/Hayes
	G-BNBJ	AS.355F-1 Twin Squirrel	Coln Helicopters Ltd
	G-BNBL	Thunder Ax7-77 balloon	J. R. Henderson
	G-BNBM	Colt 90A balloon	Thunder & Colt Ltd
	G-BNBN	Replica P-38 Lightning	R. C. Cummings
	G-BNBP	Colt Snowflake balloon	Thunder & Colt Ltd
	G-BNBR	Cameron N-90 balloon	Morning Star Motors Ltd
	G-BNBT	Robinson R-22B	E. Wooton
	G-BNBU	Bensen B.8MV	D. T. Murchie
	G-BNBV	Thunder Ax7-77 balloon	J. M. Robinson
	G-BNBW	Thunder Ax7-77 balloon	Reeds Rains Prudential
	G-BNBY	Beech 95-B55A Baron	D. Starling (G-AXXR)
	G-BNBZ	LET L-200D Morava	M. Emery
	G-BNCA	Lightning F.2A ★	P. Hoar
	G-BNCB	Cameron V-77 balloon	Phoenix Tyre & Battery Co Ltd
	G-BNCC	Thunder Ax7-77 balloon	D. C. Chipping
	G-BNCE	G.159 Gulfstream 1	Peregrine Air Services Ltd/Aberdeen
	G-BNCG	QAC Quickie Q.2	T. F. Francis
	G-BNCH	Cameron V-77 balloon	Royal Engineers Balloon Club
	G-BNCJ	Cameron N-77 balloon	I. S. Bridge
	G-BNCK	Cameron V-77 balloon	G. W. G. C. Sudlow
	G-BNCL	WG.13 Lynx HAS.2 (XX469)	J. E. Wilkie/Blackpool
	G-BNCM	Cameron N-77 balloon	S. & A. Stone Ltd
	G-BNCN	Glaser-Dirks DG.400	M. C. Costin
	G-BNCO	PA-38-112 Tomahawk	Cambrian Flying Club/Swansea
	G-BNCR	PA-28-161 Warrior II	Airpart Supply Ltd
	G-BNCS	Cessna 180	Michael Gardner Ltd
	G-BNCU	Thunder Ax7-77 balloon	G. C. Scott
	G-BNCV	Bensen B.8	L. W. Cload
	G-BNCW	Boeing 767-204	Britannia Airways Ltd/Luton
	G-BNCX	Hunter T.7	Lovaux Ltd
	G-BNCY	F.27 Friendship Mk 500	Air UK Ltd/Norwich
	G-BNCZ	Rutan LongEz	R. M. Bainbridge/Sherburn
	G-BNDD	PA-31-310 Turbo Navajo B	W. F. Turnbull
	G-BNDG	Wallis WA-201/R Srs1	K. H. Wallis
	G-BNDH	Colt 21A balloon	Hot-Air Balloon Co Ltd
	G-BNDM	Short SD3-60 Srs 300	Capital Airlines Ltd/Leeds
	G-BNDN	Cameron V-77 balloon	J. A. Smith
	G-BNDO	Cessna 152 II	Sparrows Flying Services Ltd
	G-BNDP	Brugger MB.2 Colibri	M. Black
	G-BNDR	SOCATA TB.10 Tobago	Air Touring Services Ltd/Biggin Hill
	G-BNDS	PA-31-350 Navajo Chieftain	Havilland Air Ltd
	G-BNDT	Brugger MB.2 Colibri	G. Pearson & E. Wilks
	G-BNDV	Cameron V-77 balloon	R. Jones
	G-BNDW	D.H.82A Tiger Moth	N. D. Welch
	G-BNDY	Cessna 425-1	Standard Aviation Ltd/Newcastle
	G-BNED	PA-22 Tri-Pacer 135	P. Storey
	G-BNEE	PA-28R-201 Arrow III	Britannic Management (Aviation) Ltd
	G-BNEF	PA-31-310 Turbo Navajo B	G-Air Ltd/Lydd
	G-BNEH	H.S. 125 Srs 800B	Genavco Air Ltd/Heathrow
	G-BNEI	PA-34-200T Seneca II	A. Bucknole
	G-BNEJ	PA-38-112 Tomahawk	G. K. Swindell
	G-BNEK	PA-38-112 Tomahawk	Seal Executive Aircraft Ltd/E. Midlands
	G-BNEL	PA-28-161 Warrior II	J. A. Pothecary/Shoreham
	G-BNEM	Robinson R-22	G. N. Taylor
	G-BNEN	PA-34-200T Seneca II	Willall Ltd
	G-BNEO	Cameron V-77 balloon	Graham Tatum & Sons Ltd
	G-BNEP	PA-34-220T Seneca III	D. W. Clark Land Drainage Ltd
	G-BNER	PA-34-200T Seneca II	Compass Peripherial Systems Ltd
	G-BNES	Cameron V-77 balloon	G. Wells
	G-BNET	Cameron O-84 balloon	J. Bennett & Son (Insurance Brokers) Ltd
	G-BNEU	Colt 105A balloon	I. Lilja
	G-BNEV	Viking Dragonfly	N. W. Eyre
	G-BNEW	Cessna 421C	World Carriers (London) Ltd
	G-BNEX	Cameron O-120 balloon	The Balloon Club Ltd
	G-BNEZ	Cessna 421C	P. Mitchell
	G-BNFF	—	—
	G-BNFG	Cameron O-77 balloon	Capital Balloon Club Ltd
	G-BNFI	Cessna 150J	M. Jackson
	G-BNFK	Cameron 89 Egg SS balloon	Forbes Europe Inc
	G-BNFL	WHE Airbuggy	Roger Savage (Photography) (G-AXXN)

Reg.	Type	Owner or Operator	Notes
G-BNFM	Colt 21A balloon	M. E. Dworski	
G-BNFN	Cameron N-105 balloon	Western Counties Automobile Co Ltd	
G-BNFO	Cameron V-77 balloon	D. C. Patrick-Brown	
G-BNFP	Cameron O-84 balloon	A. J. & E. J. Clarke	
G-BNFR	Cessna 152 II	London Flight Centre (Stansted) Ltd	
G-BNFS	Cessna 152 II	London Flight Centre (Stansted) Ltd	
G-BNFV	Robin DR.400/120	Flight Training International Ltd/ Biggin Hill	
G-BNFW	H.S.125 Srs 700B	British Aerospace PLC	
G-BNFX	Colt 21A balloon	Thunder & Colt Ltd	
G-BNFY	Cameron N-77 balloon	Holker Estates Ltd	
G-BNGC	Robinson R-22	Rassler Aero Services/Booker	
G-BNGD	Cessna 152	AV Aviation Ltd	
G-BNGE	Auster AOP.6 (TW536)	R. W. W. Eastman	
G-BNGG	—	—	
G-BNGH	Boeing 707-321C	Tradewinds Airways Ltd (G-BFZF)/ Stansted	
G-BNGJ	Cameron V-77 balloon	Latham Timber Centres (Holdings) Ltd	
G-BNGL	Boeing 737-3Y0	Inter European Airways Ltd/Cardiff	
G-BNGM	Boeing 737-3Y0	Inter European Airways Ltd/Cardiff	
G-BNGN	Cameron V-77 balloon	E. N. Preece	
G-BNGO	Thunder Ax7-77 balloon	J. S. Finlan	
G-BNGP	Colt 77A balloon	Headland Services Ltd	
G-BNGR	PA-38-112 Tomahawk	Frontline Aviation Ltd/Teesside	
G-BNGS	PA-38-112 Tomahawk	Frontline Aviation Ltd/Teesside	
G-BNGT	PA-28-181 Archer II	Aviation Development & Management Ltd	
G-BNGV	ARV Super 2	Golf Victor Ltd/Guernsey	
G-BNGW	ARV Super 2	Southern Aero Club (Shoreham) Ltd	
G-BNGX	ARV Super 2	Southern Aero Club (Shoreham) Ltd	
G-BNGY	ARV Super 2	Southern Aero Club (Shoreham) Ltd (G-BMWL)	
G-BNHB	ARV Super 2	Engine Developments Ltd	
G-BNHC	ARV Super 2	ARV Aviation Ltd/Sandown	
G-BNHD	ARV Super 2	ARV Aviation Ltd/Sandown	
G-BNHE	ARV Super 2	ARV Aviation Ltd/Sandown	
G-BNHF	Cameron N-31 balloon	P. G. Dunnington	
G-BNHG	PA-38-112 Tomahawk	Cheltenham & Gloucester School of Flying Ltd	
G-BNHH	Thunder Ax7-77 balloon	Gee-Tee Signs Ltd	
G-BNHI	Cameron V-77 balloon	Cameron Balloons Ltd	
G-BNHJ	Cessna 152	Ladel Ltd	
G-BNHK	Cessna 152	Antler Enterprises Ltd	
G-BNHL	Colt 90 Beer Glass SS balloon	Thunder & Colt Ltd	
G-BNHM	Thunder Ax8-105 balloon	Thunder & Colt Ltd	
G-BNHN	Colt Aerial Bottle SS balloon	The Balloon Stable Ltd	
G-BNHO	Thunder Ax7-77 balloon	M. J. Forster	
G-BNHP	Saffrey S.330 balloon	N. H. Ponsford *Alpha II*	
G-BNHR	Cameron V-77 balloon	R. L. Rummery	
G-BNHS	Thunder Ax7-77 balloon	Airship Shop Ltd	
G-BNHT	Fournier RF-3	D. Harker	
G-BNHU	Thunder Ax10-180 balloon	Thunder & Colt Ltd	
G-BNHV	Thunder Ax10-180 balloon	Thunder & Colt Ltd	
G-BNHW	Thunder Ax10-180 balloon	Thunder & Colt Ltd	
G-BNHX	Thunder Ax10-180 balloon	Thunder & Colt Ltd	
G-BNHY	AMF Chevvron 232	J. Hatswell	
G-BNIB	Cameron A-105 balloon	A. G. E. Faulkner	
G-BNID	Cessna 152	Midland Aircraft Leasing Ltd	
G-BNIE	Cameron O-160 balloon	The Balloon Club Ltd	
G-BNIF	Cameron O-56 balloon	D. V. Fowler	
G-BNIH	RomBac One-Eleven 561RC	Ryanair Europe PLC/Luton	
G-BNII	Cameron N-90 balloon	DW (Direct Wholesale) PLC	
G-BNIJ	SOCATA TB.10 Tobago	Air Touring Services Ltd/Biggin Hill	
G-BNIK	Robin HR.200/120	W. C. Smeaton/Popham	
G-BNIL	—		
G-BNIM	PA-38-112 Tomahawk	P. Q. Owen	
G-BNIN	Cameron V-77 balloon	Cloud Nine Balloon Group	
G-BNIO	Luscombe 8A Silvaire	P. T. Szluha	
G-BNIP	Luscombe 8A Silvaire	P. J. Penn-Sayers/Shoreham	
G-BNIR	Bell 206B JetRanger	Dollar Air Services Ltd/Coventry	
G-BNIS	Bell 206B JetRanger	Tyringham Charter & Group Services	
G-BNIT	Bell 206B JetRanger	Dollar Air Services Ltd/Coventry	
G-BNIU	Cameron O-77 balloon	A. J. Matthews & D. S. Dunlop	
G-BNIV	Cessna 152	Cloudshire Ltd/Wellesbourne	

G-BNIW — G-BNLP

Notes	Reg.	Type	Owner or Operator
	G-BNIW	Boeing Stearman PT-17	AJD Engineering Ltd/Ipswich
	G-BNIX	EMB-110P1 Bandeirante	National Airways/Southend
	G-BNJA	Wag-Aero Wag-a-Bond	G. K. Hare
	G-BNJB	Cessna 152	Farringdon Creative Services Ltd
	G-BNJC	Cessna 152	Mercury Flying Club Ltd/Shoreham
	G-BNJD	Cessna 152	R. S. Lambert
	G-BNJE	Cessna A.152	Seawing Flying Club Ltd/Southend
	G-BNJF	PA-32RT-300 Turbo Lance II	Michael Car Centre Ltd/Ronaldsway
	G-BNJG	—	—
	G-BNJH	Cessna 152	Basic Vale Ltd
	G-BNJJ	Cessna 152	Merrett Aviation Ltd
	G-BNJK	Macavia BAe 748 Turbine Tanker	Macavia International Ltd
	G-BNJL	Bensen B.8	M. W. Joynes
	G-BNJM	PA-28-161 Warrior II	Frontline Aviation Ltd/Teesside
	G-BNJN	—	—
	G-BNJO	QAC Quickie Q.2	J. D. Crymble
	G-BNJP	PA-28-161 Warrior II	J. L. Vaughan
	G-BNJR	PA-28RT-201T Turbo Arrow IV	C. Evans & Sons Ltd
	G-BNJT	PA-28-161 Warrior II	Airways Aero Associations Ltd/Booker
	G-BNJU	Cameron 80 Bust SS balloon	Forbes Europe Inc
	G-BNJV	Cessna 152	London Flight Centre (Headcorn) Ltd
	G-BNJW	Rutan Cozy	J. Whiting
	G-BNJX	Cameron N-90 balloon	Mars UK Ltd
	G-BNJY	PA-38-112 Tomahawk	Merrett Aviation Ltd
	G-BNJZ	Cassutt IIIM	R. J. Lake
	G-BNKA	—	—
	G-BNKC	Cessna 152	Royal Air Services Ltd
	G-BNKD	Cessna 172N	Royal Air Services Ltd
	G-BNKE	Cessna 172N	Mosconstruction Ltd/Tollerton
	G-BNKF	Colt AS-56 airship	Thunder & Colt Ltd
	G-BNKG	Alexander Todd Steen Skybolt	Cavendish Aviation Ltd (G-RATS/G-RHFI)
	G-BNKH	PA-38-112 Tomahawk	Goodwood Terrena Ltd
	G-BNKI	Cessna 152	RAF Halton Aeroplane Club Ltd
	G-BNKL	Beech 58P Baron	E. L. Klinge/Fairoaks
	G-BNKN	G.159 Gulfstream 1	Birmingham Executive Airways PLC
	G-BNKO	G.159 Gulfstream 1	Birmingham Executive Airways PLC
	G-BNKP	Cessna 152	Clacton Aero Club (1988) Ltd
	G-BNKR	Cessna 152	S. J. Page
	G-BNKS	Cessna 152	Shropshire Aero Club Ltd/Shobdon
	G-BNKT	Cameron O-77 balloon	British Airtours Ltd
	G-BNKV	Cessna 152	I. C. Adams & Vectair Aviation Ltd
	G-BNKW	PA-38-112 Tomahawk	P. G. Greenslade
	G-BNKX	Robinson R-22	Katzeye Sport & Film Vehicle Hire Ltd
	G-BNKZ	Hughes 369HS	Reeds Motor Co/Sywell
	G-BNLA	Boeing 747-436	British Airways City of London/Heathrow
	G-BNLB	Boeing 747-436	British Airways City of Edinburgh/Heathrow
	G-BNLC	Boeing 747-436	British Airways City of Cardiff/Heathrow
	G-BNLD	Boeing 747-436	British Airways City of Belfast/Heathrow
	G-BNLE	Boeing 747-436	British Airways City of Newcastle/Heathrow
	G-BNLF	Boeing 747-436	British Airways City of Leeds/Heathrow
	G-BNLG	Boeing 747-436	British Airways City of Southampton/Heathrow
	G-BNLH	Boeing 747-436	British Airways City of Westminster/Heathrow
	G-BNLI	Boeing 747-436	British Airways City of Sheffield/Heathrow
	G-BNLJ	Boeing 747-436	British Airways City of Nottingham/Heathrow
	G-BNLK	Boeing 747-436	British Airways City of Bristol/Heathrow
	G-BNLL	Boeing 747-436	British Airways City of Leicester/Heathrow
	G-BNLM	Boeing 747-436	British Airways City of Durham/Heathrow
	G-BNLN	Boeing 747-436	British Airways City of Portsmouth/Heathrow
	G-BNLO	Boeing 747-436	British Airways City of Dundee/Heathrow
	G-BNLP	Boeing 747-436	British Airways City of Aberdeen/Heathrow

Reg.	Type	Owner or Operator	Notes
G-BNLR	Boeing 747-436	British Airways *City of Hull*/Heathrow	
G-BNLS	Boeing 747-436	British Airways/Heathrow	
G-BNLT	Boeing 747-436	British Airways/Heathrow	
G-BNLU	—	—	
G-BNLV	—	—	
G-BNLW	—	—	
G-BNLX	—	—	
G-BNLY	—	—	
G-BNLZ	—	—	
G-BNMA	Cameron O-77 balloon	Flying Colours Balloon Group	
G-BNMB	PA-28-151 Warrior	Angelchain Ltd/Manchester	
G-BNMC	Cessna 152	D. M. Leonard/Teesside	
G-BNMD	Cessna 152	T. M. Jones	
G-BNME	Cessna 152	G. C. Winter & G. Hopkins/Leeds	
G-BNMF	Cessna 152	RJS Aviation Ltd/Halfpenny Green	
G-BNMG	Cameron V-77 balloon	Windsor Life Assurance Co Ltd	
G-BNMH	Pietenpol Aircamper	N. M. Hitchman	
G-BNMI	Colt Flying Fantasy SS balloon	Thunder & Colt Ltd	
G-BNMK	Dornier Do.27A-1	G. Machie	
G-BNML	Rand KR-2	R. J. Smyth	
G-BNMM	Bell 206B JetRanger	Veritair Ltd	
G-BNMN	PA-28R-201 Arrow III	Sandford Aviation Ltd	
G-BNMO	Cessna R.182RG	Avionics Research Ltd/Cambridge	
G-BNMP	Cessna R.182RG	Avionics Research Ltd/Cambridge	
G-BNMX	Thunder Ax7-77 balloon	S. A. D. Beard	
G-BNMZ	Isaacs Fury II	T. E. G. Buckett	
G-BNNA	Stolp SA.300 Starduster Too	D. F. Simpson & M. A. P. Thompson	
G-BNNB	PA-34-200 Seneca II	Helicopter Crop Spraying Services Ltd	
G-BNNC	Cameron N-77 balloon	West Country Business Machines Ltd	
G-BNND	BAe 146-200	British Aerospace PLC/Hatfield	
G-BNNE	Cameron N-77 balloon	The Balloon Stable Ltd	
G-BNNF	SA.315B Alouette III Lama	London & Sheffield Industrial Finance Co Ltd	
G-BNNG	Cessna T.337D	Somet Ltd (G-COLD)	
G-BNNI	Boeing 727-276	Dan-Air Services Ltd/Gatwick	
G-BNNJ	Boeing 737-3Q8	Dan-Air Services Ltd/Gatwick	
G-BNNK	Boeing 737-4Q8	Dan-Air Services Ltd/Gatwick	
G-BNNL	Boeing 737-4Q8	Dan-Air Services Ltd/Gatwick	
G-BNNO	PA-28-161 Warrior II	W. Lancs Aero Club Ltd/Woodvale	
G-BNNP	PA-28-181 Archer II	Flairhire Ltd/Redhill	
G-BNNR	Cessna 152	Interair (Aviation) Ltd/Bournemouth	
G-BNNS	PA-28-161 Warrior II	Seal Executive Aircraft Ltd	
G-BNNT	PA-28-151 Warrior	T. Miller	
G-BNNU	PA-38-112 Tomahawk	Seal Executive Aircraft Ltd	
G-BNNV	Enstrom 280C-UK Shark	Southern Air Ltd/Shoreham	
G-BNNX	PA-28R-201T Turbo Arrow III	C. Dugard Ltd/Shoreham	
G-BNNY	PA-28-161 Warrior II	Holmes Rentals	
G-BNNZ	PA-28-161 Warrior II	P. J. & A. J. Batten/Shoreham	
G-BNOA	PA-38-112 Tomahawk	Halsmith (Aircraft Sales) Ltd	
G-BNOB	Wittman W.8 Tailwind	M. Robson-Robinson	
G-BNOC	EMB-110P1 Bandeirante	National Airways/Southend	
G-BNOD	PA-28-161 Warrior II	BAe Flying College/Prestwick	
G-BNOE	PA-28-161 Warrior II	BAe Flying College/Prestwick	
G-BNOF	PA-28-161 Warrior II	BAe Flying College/Prestwick	
G-BNOG	PA-28-161 Warrior II	BAe Flying College/Prestwick	
G-BNOH	PA-28-161 Warrior II	BAe Flying College/Prestwick	
G-BNOI	PA-28-161 Warrior II	BAe Flying College/Prestwick	
G-BNOJ	PA-28-161 Warrior II	BAe Flying College/Prestwick	
G-BNOK	PA-28-161 Warrior II	BAe Flying College/Prestwick	
G-BNOL	PA-28-161 Warrior II	BAe Flying College/Prestwick	
G-BNOM	PA-28-161 Warrior II	BAe Flying College/Prestwick	
G-BNON	PA-28-161 Warrior II	BAe Flying College/Prestwick	
G-BNOO	PA-28-161 Warrior II	BAe Flying College/Prestwick	
G-BNOP	PA-28-161 Warrior II	BAe Flying College/Prestwick	
G-BNOR	PA-28-161 Warrior II	BAe Flying College/Prestwick	
G-BNOS	PA-28-161 Warrior II	BAe Flying College/Prestwick	
G-BNOT	PA-28-161 Warrior II	BAe Flying College/Prestwick	
G-BNOU	PA-28-161 Warrior II	BAe Flying College/Prestwick	
G-BNOV	PA-28-161 Warrior II	BAe Flying College/Prestwick	
G-BNOW	PA-28-161 Warrior II	BAe Flying College/Prestwick	
G-BNOX	Cessna R.182	G-Air Ltd	
G-BNOY	Colt 90A balloon	Thunder & Colt Ltd	
G-BNOZ	Cessna 152	Merrett Aviation Ltd	
G-BNPA	Boeing 737-3S3	Air Europe Ltd/Gatwick	

113

Notes	Reg.	Type	Owner or Operator
	G-BNPB	Boeing 737-3S3	Air Europe Ltd/Gatwick
	G-BNPC	Boeing 737-3S3	Air Europe Ltd/Gatwick
	G-BNPD	PA-23 Aztec 250E	Cormack (Aircraft Services) Ltd/ Glasgow
	G-BNPE	Cameron N-77 balloon	Kent Garden Centres Ltd
	G-BNPF	Slingsby T.31M	S. Luck & ptnrs
	G-BNPH	P.66 Pembroke C.1	J. S. Allison
	G-BNPI	Colt 21A balloon	Virgin Atlantic Airways Ltd
	G-BNPK	Cameron DP-70 airship	Cameron Balloons Ltd
	G-BNPL	PA-38-112 Tomahawk	Tomahawk Aviation Ltd/Leavesden
	G-BNPM	PA-38-112 Tomahawk	Leavesden Flight Centre Ltd
	G-BNPN	PA-28-181 Archer II	Archer Aviation Ltd
	G-BNPO	PA-28-181 Archer II	Leavesden Flight Centre Ltd
	G-BNPP	Colt 90A balloon	Thunder & Colt Ltd
	G-BNPR	Colt 90A balloon	Thunder & Colt Ltd
	G-BNPS	MBB Bo105CBS/4	Helicopters UK Ltd
	G-BNPT	PA-38-112 Tomahawk II	Atlantic Aviation Ltd
	G-BNPU	P.66 Pembroke C.1 (XL929) ★	Chelsea College/Shoreham
	G-BNPV	Bowers Flybaby 1A	J. G. Day
	G-BNPY	Cessna 152	GNJ Engineering Ltd
	G-BNPZ	Cessna 152	Bristol Flying Centre Ltd
	G-BNRA	SOCATA TB.10 Tobago	D. Marriott
	G-BNRB	Robin DR.400/180R	Soaring (Oxford) Ltd/Booker
	G-BNRC	AB-206A JetRanger	Coventry Helicopters
	G-BNRD	AB-206A JetRanger	Coventry Helicopters
	G-BNRE	AB-206A JetRanger	Aqua Glass Ltd
	G-BNRF	PA-28-181 Archer II	G-Air Ltd/Goodwood
	G-BNRG	PA-28-161 Warrior II	B. E. Simpson/Booker
	G-BNRH	Beech 95-E55 Baron	National Airways/Southend
	G-BNRI	Cessna U.206G	Flying Tigers Ltd
	G-BNRK	Cessna 152	Redhill Flying Club
	G-BNRL	Cessna 152	J. R. Nicholls/Sibson
	G-BNRM	—	—
	G-BNRP	PA-28-181 Archer II	Atomchoice Ltd/Goodwood
	G-BNRR	Cessna 172P	J. M. Hoblyn
	G-BNRS	MBB Bo 105DBS	Helicopters UK Ltd
	G-BNRT	Boeing 737-3T5	Orion/Britannia Airways/Luton
	G-BNRU	Cameron V-77 balloon	M. A. Mueller
	G-BNRV	Thunder Ax7-77 balloon	R. & R. Edgar-Dimmack
	G-BNRW	Colt 69A balloon	Callers Pegasus Travel Service Ltd
	G-BNRX	PA-34-200T Seneca II	Orkney Property Services
	G-BNRY	Cessna 182Q	Reefly Ltd
	G-BNRZ	Robinson R-22B	W. Jorden-Millers Ltd
	G-BNSA	Douglas DC-9-83	British Island Airways Ltd/Gatwick
	G-BNSB	Douglas DC-9-83	British Island Airways Ltd Island Equinox/Gatwick
	G-BNSC	Cessna 550 Citation II	Oceanair (CI) Ltd
	G-BNSD	Boeing 757-236	Air Europe/Air Europa (EC-.....)
	G-BNSE	Boeing 757-236	Air Europe Ltd/Gatwick
	G-BNSF	Boeing 757-236	Air Europ/Air Europa (EC-.....)
	G-BNSG	PA-28R-201 Arrow III	Ewdec Technology Ltd
	G-BNSH	Sikorsky S-76A	Bond Helicopters Ltd/Bourn
	G-BNSI	Cessna 152	Interair (Aviation) Ltd
	G-BNSL	PA-38-112 Tomahawk II	M. H. Kleiser
	G-BNSM	Cessna 152	Propwash Investments/Swansea
	G-BNSN	Cessna 152	M. K. Barnes & G. N. Olson/Bristol
	G-BNSO	Slingsby T.67M Mk II	Slingsby Aviation Ltd/Kirkbymoorside
	G-BNSP	Slingsby T.67M	Slingsby Aviation Ltd/Kirkbymoorside
	G-BNSR	Slingsby T.67M	Slingsby Aviation Ltd/Kirkbymoorside
	G-BNSS	Cessna 150M	Erafan Ltd/Bournemouth
	G-BNST	Cessna 172N	E. J. H. Morgan
	G-BNSU	Cessna 152	Channel Aviation Ltd
	G-BNSV	Cessna 152	Channel Aviation Ltd
	G-BNSW	Cessna 152	S. V. R. Williamson
	G-BNSY	PA-28-161 Warrior II	E. P. C. Rabson
	G-BNSZ	PA-28-161 Warrior II	Carill Aviation Ltd
	G-BNTB	F.27 Friendship Mk 600	Air UK Ltd/Norwich
	G-BNTC	PA-28RT-201T Turbo Arrow IV	Techspan Aviation Ltd/Booker
	G-BNTD	PA-28-161 Warrior II	Davair Ltd
	G-BNTE	FFA AS.202/184A Wren	BAe Flying College Ltd/Prestwick
	G-BNTF	FFA AS.202/184A Wren	BAe Flying College Ltd/Prestwick
	G-BNTG	FFA AS.202/184A Wren	BAe Flying College Ltd/Prestwick
	G-BNTH	FFA AS.202/184A Wren	BAe Flying College Ltd/Prestwick
	G-BNTI	FFA AS.202/184A Wren	BAe Flying College Ltd/Prestwick

Reg.	Type	Owner or Operator	Notes
G-BNTJ	FFA AS.202/184A Wren	BAe Flying College Ltd/Prestwick	
G-BNTK	FFA AS.202/184A Wren	BAe Flying College Ltd/Prestwick	
G-BNTL	FFA AS.202/184A Wren	BAe Flying College Ltd/Prestwick	
G-BNTM	FFA AS.202/184A Wren	BAe Flying College Ltd/Prestwick	
G-BNTN	FFA AS.202/184A Wren	BAe Flying College Ltd/Prestwick	
G-BNTO	FFA AS.202/184A Wren	BAe Flying College Ltd/Prestwick	
G-BNTP	Cessna 172N	Aerojet Ltd/Barton	
G-BNTS	PA-28RT-201T Turbo Arrow IV	EJWB Aviation Ltd	
G-BNTT	Beech 76 Duchess	L. & J. Donne	
G-BNTU	Cessna 152	Seal Executive Aviation Ltd	
G-BNTV	Cessna 172N	M. O. O'Nions	
G-BNTW	Cameron V-77 balloon	P. R. S. Briault	
G-BNTX	Short SD3-30 Variant 100	Fairflight Ltd (G-BKDN)/Biggin Hill	
G-BNTY	Short SD3-30 Variant 100	Fairflight Ltd (G-BKDO)/Biggin Hill	
G-BNTZ	Cameron N-77 balloon	Nationwide Anglia Building Soc	
G-BNUB	—	—	
G-BNUC	Cameron O-77 balloon	Bridges Van Hire Ltd	
G-BNUE	Thunder Ax8-105Z balloon	Thunder & Colt Ltd	
G-BNUF	Thunder Ax8-105Z balloon	Thunder & Colt Ltd	
G-BNUG	Cameron O-105 balloon	Thunder & Colt Ltd	
G-BNUH	Cameron O-105 balloon	Thunder & Colt Ltd	
G-BNUI	Rutan Vari-Eze	T. N. F. Skead	
G-BNUJ	Thunder Ax8-105Z balloon	Thunder & Colt Ltd	
G-BNUK	Cameron O-84 balloon	Thunder & Colt Ltd	
G-BNUL	Cessna 152	Osprey Air Services Ltd	
G-BNUN	Beech 95-58P Baron	British Midland Airways Ltd/E. Midlands	
G-BNUO	Beech 76 Duchess	B. & W. Aircraft Ltd	
G-BNUR	Cessna 172E	Orviston Ltd	
G-BNUS	Cessna 152	Stapleford Flying Club Ltd	
G-BNUT	Cessna 152 Turbo	Stapleford Flying Club Ltd	
G-BNUU	PA-44-180T Turbo Seminole	Morgan Laboratories Ltd/Elstree	
G-BNUV	PA-23 Aztec 250F	J. Williams	
G-BNUW	Bell 206B JetRanger	Hewitts of Cranleigh Ltd	
G-BNUX	Hoffmann H-36 Dimona	Soaring (Oxford) Ltd/Booker	
G-BNUY	PA-38-112 Tomahawk II	AT Aviation Ltd/Cardiff	
G-BNUZ	Robinson R-22B	J. L. E. Smith	
G-BNVB	AA-5A Cheetah	E. P. C. Rabson	
G-BNVD	PA-38-112 Tomahawk	Channel Aviation Ltd	
G-BNVE	PA-28-181 Archer II	Janair Services Ltd/Stapleford	
G-BNVF	Robinson R-22B	Jetbury Ltd	
G-BNVG	ARV Super 2	ARV Aviation Ltd/Sandown	
G-BNVH	ARV Super 2	ARV Aviation Ltd/Sandown	
G-BNVI	ARV Super 2	ARV Aviation Ltd/Sandown	
G-BNVJ	ARV Super 2	ARV Aviation Ltd/Sandown	
G-BNVK	ARV Super 2	reservation	
G-BNVL	ARV Super 2	reservation	
G-BNVM	ARV Super 2	reservation	
G-BNVN	ARV Super 2	reservation	
G-BNVO	ARV Super 2	reservation	
G-BNVP	ARV Super 2	reservation	
G-BNVR	ARV Super 2	reservation	
G-BNVT	PA-28R-201T Turbo Arrow III	Commercial Coachbuilders (Strathclyde) Ltd	
G-BNVV	Cameron DG-19 airship	US Skyship (UK) Ltd	
G-BNVW	Dornier Do.28A-1	Wessex Aviation & Transport Ltd	
G-BNVX	Dornier Do.27A-4	Wessex Aviation & Transport Ltd	
G-BNVZ	Beech 95-B55 Baron	C. A. Breeze/Barton	
G-BNWA	Boeing 767-336ER	British Airways Severn Bridge/Heathrow	
G-BNWB	Boeing 767-336ER	British Airways Forth Bridge/Heathrow	
G-BNWC	Boeing 767-336ER	British Airways Clifton Bridge/Heathrow	
G-BNWD	Boeing 767-336ER	British Airways Humber Bridge/Heathrow	
G-BNWE	Boeing 767-336ER	British Airways Tower Bridge/Heathrow	
G-BNWF	Boeing 767-336ER	British Airways London Bridge/Heathrow	
G-BNWG	Boeing 767-336ER	British Airways Chelsea Bridge/Heathrow	
G-BNWH	Boeing 767-336ER	British Airways Brig O'Doon/Heathrow	
G-BNWI	Boeing 767-336ER	British Airways Iron Bridge/Heathrow	

G-BNWJ — G-BNZR

Notes	Reg.	Type	Owner or Operator
	G-BNWJ	Boeing 767-336ER	British Airways *Southwark Bridge*/Heathrow
	G-BNWK	Boeing 767-336ER	British Airways *Kew Bridge*/Heathrow
	G-BNWL	—	—
	G-BNWM	—	—
	G-BNWN	—	—
	G-BNWO	—	—
	G-BNWP	—	—
	G-BNWR	—	—
	G-BNWS	—	—
	G-BNWT	—	—
	G-BNWU	—	—
	G-BNWV	—	—
	G-BNWW	—	—
	G-BNWX	—	—
	G-BNWY	—	—
	G-BNWZ	—	—
	G-BNXA	BN-2A Islander	Atlantic Air Transport Ltd/Coventry
	G-BNXB	BN-2A Islander	Atlantic Air Transport Ltd/Coventry
	G-BNXC	Cessna 152	Sir W. G. Armstrong-Whitworth Flying Group/Coventry
	G-BNXD	Cessna 172N	B. W. Wells & Burbage Farms Ltd
	G-BNXE	PA-28-161 Warrior II	Rugby Autobody Repairs
	G-BNXF	Bell 206B JetRanger	P. Pilkington & K. M. Armitage
	G-BNXG	Cameron DP-70 airship	Rexstyle Ltd
	G-BNXH	Cessna T.210N	Wilson Feeds Ltd
	G-BNXI	Robin DR.400-180R	London Gliding Club Ltd/Dunstable
	G-BNXJ	Robinson R-22B	J. D. Marsh
	G-BNXK	Nott-Cameron ULD-3 balloon	J. R. P. Nott
	G-BNXL	Glaser-Dirks DG.400	B. A. Eastwell
	G-BNXM	PA-18 Super Cub 95	D. M. Jagger
	G-BNXN	Partenavia P.68B	Connector Technology Ltd/Elstree
	G-BNXO	Colt 21A balloon	Thunder & Colt Ltd
	G-BNXP	Boeing 737-3S3	Air Europe/Air Europa (EC-ECM)
	G-BNXR	Cameron O-84 balloon	J. A. & N. J. Ballard Gray
	G-BNXS	Cessna 404	Turnbull Associates
	G-BNXT	PA-28-161 Warrior II	S. P. Donoghue/Leavesden
	G-BNXU	PA-28-161 Warrior II	S. P. Donoghue/Leavesden
	G-BNXV	PA-38-112 Tomahawk	Falcon Flying Services/Biggin Hill
	G-BNXX	SOCATA TB.20 Trinidad	EAC Components Ltd
	G-BNXY	Cessna 172M	Dewest Ltd/Biggin Hill
	G-BNXZ	Thunder Ax7-77 balloon	Hale Hot Air Balloon Group
	G-BNYA	Short SD3-30	Fairflight Ltd (G-BKSU)
	G-BNYB	PA-28-201T Turbo Dakota	B. W. Wells & Burbage Farms Ltd
	G-BNYD	Bell 206B JetRanger	M & H Plastics Ltd
	G-BNYJ	Cessna 421B	Charles Robertson (Developments) Ltd
	G-BNYK	PA-38-112 Tomahawk	Seal Executive Aircraft Ltd
	G-BNYL	Cessna 152	Seal Executive Aircraft Ltd
	G-BNYM	Cessna 172N	Decoy Engineering Projects Ltd
	G-BNYN	Cessna 152	Redhill Flying Club
	G-BNYO	Beech 76 Duchess	Skyhawk Ltd
	G-BNYP	PA-28-181 Archer II	Janair Services Ltd
	G-BNYR	Cameron N-105 balloon	Cameron Balloons Ltd
	G-BNYS	Boeing 767-204	Britannia Airways Ltd/Luton
	G-BNYU	Faithfull Ax7-61A balloon	M. L. Faithfull
	G-BNYV	PA-38-112 Tomahawk	Falcon Flying Services/Biggin Hill
	G-BNYX	Denney Aerocraft Kitfox	R. W. Husband
	G-BNYY	PA-28RT-201T Turbo Arrow IV	MM & G Aviation/Liverpool
	G-BNYZ	SNCAN Stampe SV-4E	Tapestry Colour Ltd
	G-BNZA	Beech 300LW Super King Air	British Airways/Heathrow
	G-BNZB	PA-28-161 Warrior II	Hillvine Ltd
	G-BNZC	D.H.C.1 Chipmunk 22	British Aerial Museum (G-ROYS)/Duxford
	G-BNZF	Grob G.109B	N. Adam
	G-BNZG	PA-28RT-201T Turbo Arrow IV	Trinity Garage (Gainsborough) Ltd
	G-BNZH	Beech 200 Super King Air	A. F. Budge (Aviation) Ltd/Gamston
	G-BNZI	PA-31-350 Navjo Chieftain	Airstar (Air Transport) Ltd
	G-BNZJ	Colt 21A balloon	Thunder & Colt Ltd
	G-BNZK	Thunder Ax7-77 balloon	Wye Valley Aviation Ltd
	G-BNZL	Rotorway Scorpion 133	G. Snook
	G-BNZM	Cessna T.210N	Stansted Fluid Power (Products) Ltd
	G-BNZN	Cameron N-56 balloon	Cameron Balloons Ltd
	G-BNZO	Rotorway Executive	M. G. Wiltshire
	G-BNZR	FRED Srs 2	R. M. Waugh

Reg.	Type	Owner or Operator	Notes
G-BNZS	Mooney M.20K	P. E. Sandy	
G-BNZU	—	—	
G-BNZV	PA-25 Pawnee 235	Northumbria Soaring Co Ltd	
G-BNZX	—	—	
G-BNZY	SA.365N Dauphin 2	McAlpine Helicopters Ltd/Hayes	
G-BNZZ	PA-28-161 Warrior II	J. P. Alexander/Denham	
G-BOAA	Concorde 102	British Airways (G-N94AA)/Heathrow	
G-BOAB	Concorde 102	British Airways (G-N94AB)/Heathrow	
G-BOAC	Concorde 102	British Airways (G-N81AC)/Heathrow	
G-BOAD	Concorde 102	British Airways (G-N94AD)/Heathrow	
G-BOAE	Concorde 102	British Airways (G-N94AE)/Heathrow	
G-BOAF	Concorde 102	British Airways (G-N94AF/G-BFKX)/ Heathrow	
G-BOAG	Concorde 102	British Airways (G-BFKW)/Heathrow	
G-BOAH	PA-28-161 Warrior II	Garrick Aviation/Denham	
G-BOAI	Cessna 152	G. Duncan	
G-BOAJ	—	—	
G-BOAK	PA-22 Caribbean 150	I. B. Grace & ptnrs	
G-BOAL	Cameron V-65 balloon	A. Lindsay	
G-BOAM	Robinson R-22B	Cinnamond Ltd	
G-BOAN	PA-30 Twin Comanche 160B	R. L. C. Appleton	
G-BOAO	Thunder Ax7-77 balloon	D. V. Fowler	
G-BOAP	Colt 160A balloon	Thunder & Colt Ltd	
G-BOAS	Air Command 503 Commander	R. Robinson	
G-BOAU	Cameron V-77 balloon	J. Smallwood	
G-BOAW	D.H.C.7-110 Dash Seven	London City Airways Ltd	
G-BOAX	D.H.C.7-110 Dash Seven	London City Airways Ltd	
G-BOAY	D.H.C.7-110 Dash Seven	London City Airways Ltd	
G-BOAZ	D.H.C.7-110 Dash Seven	London City Airways Ltd	
G-BOBA	PA-28R-201 Arrow III	Lyndon Scaffolding Hire Ltd	
G-BOBB	Cameron O-120 balloon	J. M. Albury	
G-BOBC	BN-2T Islander	Rhine Army Parachute Association (G-BJYZ)	
G-BOBD	Cameron O-160 balloon	Heart of England Balloon Club	
G-BOBE	Cameron O-160 balloon	Heart of England Balloon Club	
G-BOBF	Brugger MB.2 Colibri	R. Bennett	
G-BOBG	Jodel D.150	C. A. Laycock	
G-BOBH	Airtour AH-77 balloon	Airtour Balloon Co Ltd	
G-BOBI	Cessna 152	R. M. Seath (G-BHJD)/Sherburn	
G-BOBJ	PA-38-112 Tomahawk	Surrey & Kent Flying Club (1982) Ltd/ Biggin Hill	
G-BOBK	PA-38-112 Tomahawk	Surrey & Kent Flying Club (1982) Ltd/ Biggin Hill	
G-BOBL	PA-38-112 Tomahawk	Surrey & Kent Flying Club (1982) Ltd/ Biggin Hill	
G-BOBN	Cessna 310R	Auxili-Air Aviation Ltd	
G-BOBO	Robinson R-22	M. E. Mortlock	
G-BOBP	Cameron A-250 balloon	W. A. Q. McGill	
G-BOBR	Cameron N-77 balloon	Loganair Ltd	
G-BOBS	Quickie Q.2	R. R. Stevens/Denham	
G-BOBT	Stolp SA.300 Starduster Too	I. G. Anderson	
G-BOBU	Colt 90A balloon	Thunder & Colt Ltd	
G-BOBV	Cessna F.150M	Osprey Air Services Ltd/Cranfield	
G-BOBW	Air & Space 18A gyroplane	M. A. Schumann/Shipdham	
G-BOBX	G.159 Gulfstream 1	Birmingham Executive Airways PLC	
G-BOBY	Monnet Sonerai II	R. G. Hallam (stored)/Sleap	
G-BOBZ	PA-28-181 Archer II	Trustcomms International Ltd	
G-BOCA	PA-38-112 Tomahawk	Goodwood Terrena Ltd	
G-BOCB	H.S.125 Srs 1B/522	McAlpine Aviation Ltd (G-OMCA/ G-DJMJ/G-AWUF)/Luton	
G-BOCC	PA-38-112 Tomahawk	Goodwood Terrena Ltd	
G-BOCD	Grob G.115	Soaring (Oxford) Ltd	
G-BOCF	Colt 77A balloon	P. S. J. Mason	
G-BOCG	PA-34-200T Seneca II	Preston Contractors Ltd	
G-BOCH	PA-32 Cherokee Six 300	Basic Vale Ltd	
G-BOCI	Cessna 140A	D. Nieman	
G-BOCK	Sopwith Triplane replica	Shuttleworth Trust/O. Warden	
G-BOCL	Slingsby T.67C	C.S.E. Aviaton Ltd/Kidlington	
G-BOCM	Slingsby T.67C	C.S.E. Aviation Ltd/Kidlington	
G-BOCN	Robinson R-22B	J. Bignall	
G-BOCO	Schweizer 269C	C.S.E. Aviation Ltd/Kidlington	
G-BOCP	PA-34-220T Seneca III	BAe Flying College Ltd/Prestwick	
G-BOCR	PA-34-220T Seneca III	BAe Flying College Ltd/Prestwick	
G-BOCS	PA-34-220T Seneca III	BAe Flying College Ltd/Prestwick	

Notes	Reg.	Type	Owner or Operator
	G-BOCT	PA-34-220T Seneca III	BAe Flying College Ltd/Prestwick
	G-BOCU	PA-34-220T Seneca III	BAe Flying College Ltd/Prestwick
	G-BOCV	PA-34-220T Seneca III	BAe Flying College Ltd/Prestwick
	G-BOCW	PA-34-220T Seneca III	BAe Flying College Ltd/Prestwick
	G-BOCX	PA-34-220T Seneca III	BAe Flying College Ltd/Prestwick
	G-BOCY	PA-34-220T Seneca III	BAe Flying College Ltd/Prestwick
	G-BOCZ	PA-34-220T Seneca III	BAe Flying College Ltd/Prestwick
	G-BODA	PA-28-161 Warrior II	C.S.E. Aviation Ltd/Kidlington
	G-BODB	PA-28-161 Warrior II	C.S.E. Aviation Ltd/Kidlington
	G-BODC	PA-28-161 Warrior II	C.S.E. Aviation Ltd/Kidlington
	G-BODD	PA-28-161 Warrior II	C.S.E. Aviation Ltd/Kidlington
	G-BODE	PA-28-161 Warrior II	C.S.E. Aviation Ltd/Kidlington
	G-BODF	PA-28-161 Warrior II	C.S.E. Aviation Ltd/Kidlington
	G-BODG	Slingsby T.31 Cadet III	H. P. Vox
	G-BODH	Slingsby T.31 Cadet III	C. D. Denham
	G-BODI	—	—
	G-BODK	Rotorway Scorpion 133	J. Brannigan
	G-BODL	Steen Skybolt	K. E. Armstrong
	G-BODM	PA-28 Cherokee 180	Bristol & Wessex Aeroplane Club Ltd
	G-BODN	PA-28R-201 Arrow III	N. M. G. Pearson/Bristol
	G-BODO	Cessna 152	P. A. Lancaster
	G-BODP	PA-38-112 Tomahawk	N. C. Gray
	G-BODR	PA-28-161 Warrior II	Airways Aero Associations Ltd/Booker
	G-BODS	PA-38-112 Tomahawk	B. E. Simpson/Booker
	G-BODT	Jodel D.18	R. A. Jarvis
	G-BODU	Scheibe SF.25C	Soaring Equipment Ltd
	G-BODW	Bell 206B JetRanger	Heli-Flair Ltd
	G-BODX	Beech 76 Duchess	Hubert C. Leach (Overseas) Ltd/Elstree
	G-BODY	Cessna 310R	Atlantic Air Transport Ltd/Coventry
	G-BODZ	Robinson R-22B	A. J. Langley Group Ltd
	G-BOEB	PA-38-112 Tomahawk	Botsford & Willard Ltd/Panshanger
	G-BOEC	PA-38-112 Tomahawk	Botsford & Willard Ltd/Panshanger
	G-BOED	Cameron Opera House SS balloon	Cameron Balloons Ltd
	G-BOEE	PA-28-181 Archer II	T. B. Parmenter
	G-BOEH	Jodel DR.340	E. J. Horsfall/Blackpool
	G-BOEI	Short SD3-60	Short Bros PLC/Sydenham
	G-BOEK	Cameron V-77 balloon	A. J. E. Jones
	G-BOEM	Aerotek-Pitts S-2A	Walsh Bros (Tunneling) Ltd
	G-BOEN	Cessna 172M	P. N. Herold
	G-BOEP	Bell 212	Bristow Helicopters Ltd
	G-BOER	PA-28-161 Warrior II	Ridgway Aviation Services Ltd/Booker
	G-BOES	Cessna FA.152	Royalair Services Ltd (G-FLIP)/Tollerton
	G-BOET	PA-28RT-201 Arrow IV	K. Phillips Ltd
	G-BOEV	Robinson R-22B	Bristow Helicopters Ltd
	G-BOEW	Robinson R-22B	Bristow Helicopters Ltd
	G-BOEX	Robinson R-22B	Bristow Helicopters Ltd
	G-BOEY	Robinson R-22B	Bristow Helicopters Ltd
	G-BOEZ	Robinson R-22B	Bristow Helicopters Ltd
	G-BOFA	Robinson R-22	RM Aviation Ltd
	G-BOFB	Sikorsky S-76A	Bond Helicopters Ltd/Bourn
	G-BOFC	Beech 76 Duchess	Wickenby Aviation Ltd
	G-BOFD	Cessna U.206G	R. M. McCarthy/Norwich
	G-BOFE	PA-34-200T Seneca II	E. C. English
	G-BOFF	Cameron N-77 balloon	Systems-80 Double Glazing Ltd
	G-BOFL	Cessna 152	Coventry (Civil) Aviation Ltd
	G-BOFM	Cessna 152	Coventry (Civil) Aviation Ltd
	G-BOFN	Beech 100 King Air	Essex Leasing/Southend
	G-BOFO	Ultimate 10-200	D. F. Lea
	G-BOFV	PA-44-180 Seminole	K. A. Summers
	G-BOFW	Cessna A.150M	J. Whiting
	G-BOFX	Cessna A.150M	Thirsk Aero Services Ltd
	G-BOFY	PA-28 Cherokee 140	Bristol & Wessex Aeroplane Club Ltd
	G-BOFZ	PA-28-161 Warrior II	Bristol & Wessex Aeroplane Club Ltd
	G-BOGA	Cessna 500 Citation	World Carrier Aviation Ltd/Leavesden
	G-BOGB	Hawker Tempest II replica	D. L. Riley
	G-BOGC	Cessna 152	Skyviews & General Ltd/Leeds
	G-BOGF	—	—
	G-BOGG	Cessna 152	C. D. Brack
	G-BOGI	Robin DR.400/180	B. Hodge
	G-BOGJ	PA-28RT-201T Turbo Arrow IV	J. McW. Henderson
	G-BOGK	ARV Super 2	S. W. Ward
	G-BOGL	Thunder Ax7-77 balloon	Thunder & Colt Ltd
	G-BOGM	PA-28RT-201T Turbo Arrow IV	C. Moore/Stapleford

Reg.	Type	Owner or Operator	Notes
G-BOGO	PA-32R-301T Saratoga SP	C. Moore/Stapleford	
G-BOGP	Cameron V-77 balloon	The Wealden Balloon Group	
G-BOGR	Colt 180A balloon	The Balloon Club of Great Britain Ltd	
G-BOGS	PA-34-200T Seneca II	Airways Flight Training (Exeter) Ltd	
G-BOGT	Colt 77A balloon	The Hot Air Balloon Co Ltd	
G-BOGU	—	—	
G-BOGV	Air Command 532 Elite	Deandell Productions Ltd	
G-BOGW	Air Command 532 Elite	Skyrider Aviation Ltd	
G-BOGX	AS.355F-2 Twin Squirrel	McAlpine Helicopters Ltd	
G-BOGY	Cameron V-77 balloon	P. J. Bish	
G-BOHA	PA-28-161 Warrior II	London Flight Centre (Stansted) Ltd	
G-BOHB	Cessna 152	London Flight Centre (Stansted) Ltd	
G-BOHC	Boeing 757-236	Air Europe Ltd/Air Europa (EC-ELA)	
G-BOHD	Colt 77A balloon	County Garage Ltd	
G-BOHE	Cameron O-120 balloon	H. R. Evans	
G-BOHF	Thunder Ax8-84 balloon	Slater Hogg & Howison Ltd	
G-BOHG	Air Command 532 Elite	T. E. McDonald	
G-BOHH	Cessna 172N	P. G. Fearon	
G-BOHI	Cessna 152	F. E. P. Holmes	
G-BOHJ	Cessna 152	F. E. P. Holmes	
G-BOHL	Cameron A-120 balloon	The Balloon Stable Ltd	
G-BOHM	PA-28 Cherokee 180	M. C. Wroe	
G-BOHN	PA-38-112 Tomahawk	AT Aviation Ltd	
G-BOHO	PA-28-161 Warrior II	Air Navigation & Trading Ltd/Blackpool	
G-BOHP	PA-28-161 Warrior II	Victor Air Services Ltd/Leavesden	
G-BOHR	PA-28-151 Warrior	L. T. Evans	
G-BOHS	PA-38-112 Tomahawk	Falcon Flying Services/Biggin Hill	
G-BOHT	PA-38-112 Tomahawk	Falcon Flying Services/Biggin Hill	
G-BOHU	PA-38-112 Tomahawk	Falcon Flying Services/Biggin Hill	
G-BOHV	Wittman W.8 Tailwind	R. A. Povall	
G-BOHW	Van's RV-4	R. W. H. Cole & D. Frapple	
G-BOHX	PA-44-180 Seminole	B. Walker & Co (Dursley) Ltd	
G-BOHY	H.S.748 Srs 2B	British Airways/Glasgow	
G-BOHZ	H.S.748 Srs 2B	British Airways/Glasgow	
G-BOIA	Cessna 180K	A. W. Kennedy	
G-BOIB	Wittman W.10 Tailwind	P. H. Lewis	
G-BOIC	PA-28R-201T Turbo Arrow III	Yorkclose Ltd	
G-BOID	Bellanca 7ECA Citabria	Chemtech Ltd	
G-BOIE	Beech 95-B58P Baron	Atlantic Craft International Ltd	
G-BOIF	Beech 95-B55 Baron	B. W. Wells & Burbage Farms Ltd	
G-BOIG	PA-28-161 Warrior II	D. W. Higgins	
G-BOIH	Pitts S-1E Special	S. L. Goldspink	
G-BOII	Cessna 172N	Trevair Group/Bournemouth	
G-BOIJ	Thunder Ax7-77 balloon	Oswestry Balloon Club	
G-BOIK	Air Command 503 Commander	G. R. Horner	
G-BOIL	Cessna 172N	Upperstack Ltd	
G-BOIM	Cessna 150M	Clacton Aero Club (1988) Ltd	
G-BOIN	Bellanca 7ECA Citabria	AV Aviation Ltd	
G-BOIO	Cessna 152	AV Aviation Ltd	
G-BOIP	Cessna 152	AV Aviation Ltd	
G-BOIR	Cessna 152	Shropshire Aero Club Ltd/Shobdon	
G-BOIS	PA-31 Turbo Navajo	G. Grenall (G-AYNB)/Bristol	
G-BOIT	SOCATA TB.10 Tobago	Air Touring Services Ltd/Biggin Hill	
G-BOIU	SOCATA TB.10 Tobago	Air Touring Services Ltd/Biggin Hill	
G-BOIV	Cesna 150M	F. E. P. Holmes	
G-BOIW	Cessna 152	London Flight Centre (Stansted) Ltd	
G-BOIX	Cessna 172N	JR Flying Ltd	
G-BOIY	Cessna 172N	London Flight Centre (Stansted) Ltd	
G-BOIZ	PA-34-200T Seneca II	T. I. Dale-Harris & KNC (One) Ltd	
G-BOJB	Cameron V-77 balloon	P. Nandi	
G-BOJD	Cameron V-77 balloon	The Independent Balloon Co Ltd	
G-BOJE	PA-28-236 Dakota	Pathrace Ltd/Biggin Hill	
G-BOJF	Air Command 532 Elite	P. J. Davies	
G-BOJG	Air Command 532 Elite	B. F. Muldowney	
G-BOJH	PA-28R Cherokee Arrow 200	M. J. Horton	
G-BOJI	PA-28RT-201 Arrow IV	K. W. Felton	
G-BOJJ	—	—	
G-BOJK	PA-34-220T Seneca III	Technical Flight Services Ltd (G-BRUF)	
G-BOJL	M.S.885 Super Rallye	J. Rees	
G-BOJM	PA-28-181 Archer II	H. Skelton	
G-BOJN	Fairchild SA227AC Metro III	Air Metro Ltd/Bournemouth	
G-BOJO	Colt 120A balloon	Airbureau Ltd	
G-BOJR	Cessna 172P	Exeter Flying Club Ltd	
G-BOJS	Cessna 172P	Eggesford Flying	

Notes	Reg.	Type	Owner or Operator
	G-BOJT	Beech 76 Duchess	Aviation Services (UK) Ltd
	G-BOJU	Cameron N-77 balloon	The Hot Air Balloon Co Ltd
	G-BOJV	Bell 206B JetRanger 2	George Barlow & Sons Ltd
	G-BOJW	PA-28-161 Warrior II	T. Miller
	G-BOJX	PA-28-181 Archer II	Southern Air Ltd/Shoreham
	G-BOJY	PA-28-161 Warrior II	Southern Air Ltd/Shoreham
	G-BOJZ	PA-28-161 Warrior II	Southern Air Ltd/Shoreham
	G-BOKA	PA-28-201T Turbo Dakota	CBG Aviation Ltd/Biggin Hill
	G-BOKB	PA-28-161 Warrior II	Southern Air Ltd/Shoreham
	G-BOKE	PA-34-200T Seneca II	Tayflite Ltd
	G-BOKF	Air Command 532 Elite	Nobles Motors (Mainbest) Ltd
	G-BOKG	Slingsby Cadet III Motor Glider	A. M. Witt
	G-BOKH	Whittaker MW.7	M. W. J. Whittaker
	G-BOKI	Whittaker MW.7	R. K. Willcox
	G-BOKJ	Whittaker MW.7	M. N. Gauntlett
	G-BOKK	PA-28-161 Warrior II	Biblio Aviation Ltd/Denham
	G-BOKL	PA-28-161 Warrior II	BAe Flying College Ltd/Prestwick
	G-BOKM	PA-28-161 Warrior II	BAe Flying College Ltd/Prestwick
	G-BOKN	PA-28-161 Warrior II	BAe Flying College Ltd/Prestwick
	G-BOKO	PA-28-161 Warrior II	BAe Flying College Ltd/Prestwick
	G-BOKP	PA-28-161 Warrior II	BAe Flying College Ltd/Prestwick
	G-BOKR	PA-28-161 Warrior II	BAe Flying College Ltd/Prestwick
	G-BOKS	PA-28-161 Warrior II	BAe Flying College Ltd/Prestwick
	G-BOKT	PA-28-161 Warrior II	BAe Flying College Ltd/Prestwick
	G-BOKU	PA-28-161 Warrior II	BAe Flying College Ltd/Prestwick
	G-BOKW	Bo 208C Junior	R. A. Farrington (G-BiTT)
	G-BOKX	PA-28-161 Warrior II	W. P. J. Jackson
	G-BOKY	Cessna 152	London Flight Centre (Stansted) Ltd
	G-BOLA	Agusta A.109A II	Fizzle Ltd
	G-BOLB	Taylorcraft BC-12-65	A. D. Pearce
	G-BOLC	Fournier RF-6B-100	S. G. Kwiecien
	G-BOLD	PA-38-112 Tomahawk	B. R. Pearson & B. F. Fraser-Smith
	G-BOLE	PA-38-112 Tomahawk	B. R. Pearson & B. F. Fraser-Smith
	G-BOLF	PA-38-112 Tomahawk	B. R. Pearson & B. F. Fraser-Smith
	G-BOLG	Bellanca 7KCAB Citabria	B. R. Pearson
	G-BOLH	Cessna 172P	Herefordshire Aero Club Ltd/Shobdon
	G-BOLI	Cessna 172P	Denham School of Flying Ltd
	G-BOLJ	GA-7 Cougar	Gemcircle Ltd/Biggin Hill
	G-BOLK	PA-28-161 Warrior II	Leo Air Ltd/Biggin Hill
	G-BOLL	Lake LA-4 Skimmer	T. M. Kidd
	G-BOLM	Boeing 737-3T0	Orion/Britannia Airways/Luton
	G-BOLN	Colt 21A balloon	Airship & Balloon Co Ltd
	G-BOLO	Bell 206B JetRanger	Hargreaves Construction Co Ltd/Shoreham
	G-BOLP	Colt 21A balloon	Airship & Balloon Co Ltd
	G-BOLR	Colt 21A balloon	Airship & Balloon Co Ltd
	G-BOLS	FRED Srs 2	R. G. Goodburn
	G-BOLT	R. Commander 114	Hooper & Jones Ltd/Kidlington
	G-BOLU	Robin R.3000/120	Lydair Ltd/Lydd
	G-BOLV	Cessna 152	London Flight Centre (Stansted) Ltd
	G-BOLW	Cessna 152	Seawing Flying Club Ltd/Southend
	G-BOLX	Cessna 172N	London Flight Centre (Stansted) Ltd
	G-BOLY	Cessna 172N	London Flight Centre (Headcorn) Ltd
	G-BOLZ	Rand KR-2	B. Normington
	G-BOMB	Cussutt Racer	R. W. L. Breckell
	G-BOMC	BN-2B Islander	Pilatus BN Ltd/Bembridge
	G-BOMD	BN-2B Islander	Pilatus BN Ltd/Bembridge
	G-BOME	BN-2B Islander	Pilatus BN Ltd/Bembridge
	G-BOMF	BN-2B Islander	Pilatus BN Ltd/Bembridge
	G-BOMG	BN-2B Islander	Pilatus BN Ltd/Bembridge
	G-BOML	Hispano HA.1112MIL	E. N. Grace/Goodwood
	G-BOMM	Beech 200 Super King Air	Asda Group PLC
	G-BOMN	—	—
	G-BOMO	PA-38-112 Tomahawk	Gloucester & Cheltenham School of Flying/Staverton
	G-BOMP	PA-28-181 Archer II	Halsmith (Aircraft Sales) Ltd
	G-BOMR	PA-28-151 Warrior	Halsmith (Aircraft Sales) Ltd
	G-BOMS	Cessna 172N	Osprey Air Services Ltd
	G-BOMT	Cessna 172N	Halsmith (Aircraft Sales) Ltd
	G-BOMU	PA-28-181 Archer II	E. D. Rees/Swansea
	G-BOMY	PA-28-161 Warrior II	B. E. Simpson/Booker
	G-BOMZ	PA-38-112 Tomahawk	B. E. Simpson/Booker
	G-BONA	Cessna 172RG	A. Garner
	G-BONC	PA-28RT-201 Arrow IV	J. Lloyd

Reg.	Type	Owner or Operator	Notes
G-BOND	Sikorsky S-76A	Bond Helicopters Ltd/Bourn	
G-BONE	Pilatus P2-06 (U-142)	D. C. R. Writer	
G-BONG	Enstrom F-28A	Blades Helicopters Ltd	
G-BONH	Enstrom F-28A	Blades Helicopters Ltd	
G-BONK	Colt 180A balloon	Wye Valley Aviation Ltd	
G-BONL	Bell 206B JetRanger 2	Dollar Air Services Ltd	
G-BONO	Cessna 172N	C. D. Brack	
G-BONP	CFM Streak Shadow	CFM Metal-Fax Ltd	
G-BONR	Cessna 172N	Micro Installation Services Ltd	
G-BONS	Cessna 172N	N. P. Bendle	
G-BONT	Slingsby T.67M Mk II	Slingsby Aviation Ltd/Kirkbymoorside	
G-BONU	Slingsby T.67B	Slingsby Aviation Ltd/Kirkbymoorside	
G-BONV	Colt 17A balloon	Airship & Balloon Co Ltd	
G-BONW	Cessna 152	Lincoln Aero Club Ltd/Sturgate	
G-BONX	Robinson R-22B	Rightbest Ltd	
G-BONY	Denney Aerocraft Kitfox	Penny Hydraulics Ltd	
G-BONZ	Beech V35B Bonanza	P. M. Coulten	
G-BOOB	Cameron N-65 balloon	I. J. Sadler	
G-BOOC	PA-18 Super Cub 150	R. R. & S. A. Marriott	
G-BOOD	Slingsby T.31M Cadet III	P. J. Titherington	
G-BOOE	GA-7 Cougar	G. L. Cailes	
G-BOOF	PA-28-181 Archer II	Golf Boof Group	
G-BOOG	PA-28RT-201T Turbo Arrow IV	TEL (IoM) Ltd/Ronaldsway	
G-BOOH	Jodel D.112	D. F. Madams	
G-BOOI	Cessna 152	Stapleford Flying Club Ltd	
G-BOOJ	Air Command 532 Elite	H. P. Barlow	
G-BOOK	Pitts S-1S Special	A. N. R. Houghton	
G-BOOL	Cessna 172N	Butler Associates (Aviation) Ltd	
G-BOOM	Hunter T.7	Berowell Management Ltd	
G-BOON	PA-32RT-300 Lance II	G-BOON Ltd	
G-BOOO	Brugger MB .2 Colibri	D. G. Cole	
G-BOOP	Cameron N-90 balloon	The Hot Air Balloon Co Ltd	
G-BOOS	Colt 240A balloon	Thunder & Colt Ltd	
G-BOOT	Colt 240A balloon	Thunder & Colt Ltd	
G-BOOU	Cameron N-77 balloon	Aqualisa Products Ltd	
G-BOOV	AS.355F-2 Twin Squirrel	McAlpine Helicopters Ltd/Hayes	
G-BOOW	Aerosport Scamp	B. I. Turner	
G-BOOX	Rutan LongEz	I. R. Thomas & I. R. Wilde	
G-BOOZ	Cameron N-77 balloon	T. M. Donnelly	
G-BOPA	PA-28-181 Archer II	Premier Flight Services Ltd	
G-BOPB	Boeing 767-204ER	Britannia Airways Ltd *Captain Sir Ross Smith*/Luton	
G-BOPC	PA-28-161 Warrior II	Channel Aviation Ltd	
G-BOPD	Bede BD-4	S. T. Dauncey	
G-BOPE	Hiller UH-12E	T. J. Clarke	
G-BOPG	Cessna 182Q	Donington Aviation Ltd/E. Midlands	
G-BOPH	Cessna TR.182RG	E. A. L. Sturmer	
G-BOPJ	Boeing 737-46B	Novair Ltd/Gatwick	
G-BOPK	Boeing 737-46B	Novair Ltd/Gatwick	
G-BOPL	PA-28-161 Warrior II	Cambrian Flying Club/Swansea	
G-BOPM	Brooklands OA.7 Optica	Brooklands Aerospace Group PLC/ Old Sarum	
G-BOPN	Brooklands OA.7 Optica	Brooklands Aerospace Group PLC/ Old Sarum	
G-BOPO	Brooklands OA.7 Optica	Brooklands Aerospace Group PLC/ Old Sarum	
G-BOPP	Brooklands OA.7 Optica	Brooklands Aerospace Group PLC/ Old Sarum	
G-BOPR	Brooklands OA.7 Optica	Brooklands Aerospace Group PLC/ Old Sarum	
G-BOPS	AS.355F-1 Twin Squirrel	Walsh Aviation	
G-BOPT	Grob G.115	Light Planes Lancashire Ltd/Barton	
G-BOPU	Grob G.115	Light Planes Lancashire Ltd/Barton	
G-BOPV	PA-34-200T Seneca II	Gwent Plant Sales	
G-BOPW	Cessna A.152	Halsmith (Aircraft Sales) Ltd	
G-BOPX	Cessna A.152	Halsmith (Aircraft Sales) Ltd	
G-BOPY	Putzer Elster C	D. M. Fenton	
G-BOPZ	Cameron DP-70 airship	The Hot-Air Balloon Co Ltd	
G-BORA	Colt 77A balloon	Cala Homes (Southern) Ltd	
G-BORB	Cameron V-77 balloon	P. Allwork	
G-BORC	Colt 180A balloon	Airship & Balloon Co Ltd	
G-BORD	Thunder Ax7-77 balloon	D. D. Owen	
G-BORE	Colt 77A balloon	Thunder & Colt Ltd	
G-BORF	Colt AS-80 Mk II airship	Thunder & Colt Ltd	

Notes	Reg.	Type	Owner or Operator
	G-BORG	Campbell Cricket	N. G. Bailey
	G-BORH	PA-34-200T Seneca II	E. Woods
	G-BORI	Cessna 152	R. D. Ward
	G-BORJ	Cessna 152	Antler Enterprises Ltd
	G-BORK	PA-28-161 Warrior II	Avalon Aviation Ltd
	G-BORL	PA-28-161 Warrior II	D. C. Harry
	G-BORM	H.S.748 Srs 2B	Sean T. Hully (Sales) Ltd
	G-BORN	Cameron N-77 balloon	Laing Homes Ltd
	G-BORO	Cessna 152	Seal Executive Aircraft Ltd
	G-BORP	PA-46-310P Malibu	SMC Aviation Ltd/Southend
	G-BORR	Thunder Ax8-90 balloon	W. J. Harris
	G-BORS	PA-28-181 Archer II	G. D. Shaw/Elstree
	G-BORT	Colt 77A balloon	M. J. Low Builders Ltd
	G-BORU	PA-28RT-201 Arrow IV	R. J. Browne
	G-BORV	Bell 206B JetRanger 2	Helicopters UK Ltd
	G-BORW	Cessna 172P	Briter Aviation Ltd/Coventry
	G-BORX	Bell 206B JetRanger 2	Helicopters UK Ltd
	G-BORY	Cessna 150L	Seal Executive Aircraft Ltd
	G-BOSA	Boeing 737-204ADV	Paramount Airways Ltd (G-BAZI)
	G-BOSB	Thunder Ax7-77 balloon	M. Gallagher
	G-BOSC	Cessna U.206G	Bob Crowe Aircraft Sales Ltd/Cranfield
	G-BOSD	PA-34-200T Seneca II	Sunny Sky Aviation Ltd/Jersey
	G-BOSE	PA-28-181 Archer II	A. P. Bath
	G-BOSF	Colt 69A balloon	Airship & Balloon Co Ltd
	G-BOSG	Colt 17A balloon	Airship & Balloon Co Ltd
	G-BOSH	Thunder Ax8-84 balloon	Ace Balloons (Bath) Ltd
	G-BOSI	Cessna 172M	W. Rennie-Roberts
	G-BOSJ	Nord 3400	M. F. W. Boyd-Maunsell
	G-BOSK	AS.355F-1 Twin Squirrel	McAlpine Helicopters Ltd/Hayes
	G-BOSM	Jodel DR.253B	S. R. Winder
	G-BOSN	AS.355F Twin Squirrel	T. W. Walker
	G-BOSO	Cessna A.152	Redhill Flying Club
	G-BOSP	PA-28-151 Warrior	F. E. P. Holmes/Andrewsfield
	G-BOSR	PA-28 Cherokee 140	F. E. P. Holmes/Andrewsfield
	G-BOSU	PA-28 Cherokee 140	M. A. Roberts
	G-BOSV	Cameron V-77 balloon	K. H. Greenaway
	G-BOSW	Bell 206B JetRanger	Air Hanson Aircraft Sales Ltd/ Blackbushe
	G-BOSY	Robinson R-22B	Cross Lane Properties (Builders) Ltd
	G-BOSZ	—	—
	G-BOTA	—	—
	G-BOTB	Cessna 152	Stapleford Flying Club Ltd
	G-BOTC	Cessna 152	Stapleford Flying Club Ltd
	G-BOTD	Cameron O-105 balloon	P. J. D. Kerr
	G-BOTE	Thunder Ax8-90 balloon	R. S. Hunjan
	G-BOTF	PA-28-151 Warrior	R. E. Pettit/Southend
	G-BOTG	Cessna 152	Donington Aviation Ltd/E. Midlands
	G-BOTH	Cessna 182Q	Donington Aviation Ltd/E. Midlands
	G-BOTI	PA-28-151 Warrior	R. E. Pettit/Southend
	G-BOTJ	BAe Jetstream 3200	British Aerospace PLC
	G-BOTK	Cameron O-105 balloon	S. J. Fensome
	G-BOTL	Colt 42R balloon	Colt Balloons Ltd
	G-BOTM	Bell 206B JetRanger 2	SMC Aviation Ltd
	G-BOTN	PA-28-161 Warrior II	G. E. E. Hunter-Jones/White Waltham
	G-BOTO	Bellanca 7ECA Citabria	P. D. Smith & D. K. Oakeley
	G-BOTP	Cessna 150J	J. W. Sharman
	G-BOTR	—	—
	G-BOTS	Hughes 269C	Horizon Helicopters
	G-BOTT	Rand KR-2	M. D. Ott & M. R. Hutchins
	G-BOTU	Piper J-3C-65 Cub	B. G. Ell
	G-BOTV	PA-32RT-300 Lance II	Sunny Sky Aviation Ltd
	G-BOTW	Cameron V-77 balloon	D. N. Malcolm
	G-BOTY	Cessna 150J	T. J. C. Darby & G. Webster
	G-BOTZ	Bensen B.80R	C. Jones
	G-BOUD	PA-38-112 Tomahawk	Halsmith (Aircraft Sales) Ltd
	G-BOUE	Cessna 172N	K. Ripper
	G-BOUF	Cessna 172N	R. J. Lock
	G-BOUG	—	
	G-BOUH	Cessna 172RG	M. Timmins
	G-BOUI	PA-28-236 Dakota	Solvit Software
	G-BOUJ	Cessna 150M	P. & M. O'Conner
	G-BOUK	PA-34-200T Seneca II	Wessex Air Services Ltd
	G-BOUL	PA-34-200T Seneca II	C.S.E. Aviation Ltd/Kidlington
	G-BOUM	PA-34-200T Seneca II	C.S.E. Aviation Ltd/Kidlington

Reg.	Type	Owner or Operator	Notes
G-BOUN	Rand KR-2	W. J. Allen	
G-BOUO	Thunder Ax8-105 balloon	V. D. Ling	
G-BOUP	PA-28-161 Warrior II	C.S.E. Aviation Ltd/Kidlington	
G-BOUR	PA-28-161 Warrior II	C.S.E. Aviation Ltd/Kidlington	
G-BOUS	PA-28RT-201 Arrow IV	Hamilton Compass Aviation Ltd	
G-BOUT	Colomban MC.12 Cri-Cri	A. J. Brand	
G-BOUU	—	—	
G-BOUV	Bensen B.8R	P. Wilkinson	
G-BOUW	Robinson R-22B	Stratton Motor Co (Norfolk) Ltd	
G-BOUX	—	—	
G-BOUY	Bell 206B JetRanger	Three Oaks Finance Ltd	
G-BOUZ	Cessna 150G	G. Webster & T. J. C. Darby	
G-BOVA	PA-31-310 Turbo Navajo C	Air Bristol Ltd (G-BECP)	
G-BOVB	PA-15 Vagabond	A. J. Helstrip	
G-BOVC	Everett gyroplane	M. T. Byrne	
G-BOVD	—	—	
G-BOVE	—	—	
G-BOVF	—	—	
G-BOVG	Cessna F.172H	The G-BOVG Group	
G-BOVH	PA-28-161 Warrior II	R. W. Tebby	
G-BOVJ	PA-34-220T Seneca III	Skylem Ltd	
G-BOVK	PA-28-161 Warrior II	Skylem Ltd	
G-BOVL	SNCAN Stampe SV-4C	T. A. Reed	
G-BOVN	Air Command 532 Elite	I. R. Lee	
G-BOVO	PA-28-181 Archer II	R. J. Browne	
G-BOVP	Air Command 532 Elite	C. K. Park	
G-BOVR	Robinson R-22	E. A. R. Laurensz & J. Harrison	
G-BOVS	Cessna 150M	W. Rennie-Roberts	
G-BOVT	Cessna 150M	M. A. Roberts	
G-BOVU	Stoddard-Hamilton Glasair 3	W. N. Blair-Hickman	
G-BOVV	Cameron V-77 balloon	J. P. Clifford	
G-BOVW	Colt 69A balloon	V. Hyland	
G-BOVX	Hughes 269C	March Helicopters Ltd/Sywell	
G-BOVY	Hughes 269C	R. C. Button	
G-BOVZ	Hughes 269C	TV-2 Colour Video Productions Ltd	
G-BOWA	Thunder Ax8-90 balloon	G. & L. Fitzpatrick	
G-BOWB	Cameron V-77 balloon	R. C. Stone	
G-BOWC	Cessna 150J	R. D. Cooper	
G-BOWD	Cessna F.337G	John Hewitson Ltd (G-BLSB)	
G-BOWE	PA-34-200T Seneca II	C.S.E. Aviation Ltd/Kidlington	
G-BOWK	Cameron N-90 balloon	S. R. Bridge	
G-BOWL	Cameron V-77 balloon	Matrix Computers Ltd	
G-BOWM	Cameron V-56 balloon	N. J. Harding	
G-BOWN	PA-12 Super Cruiser	F. E. P. Holmes/Andrewsfield	
G-BOWO	Cessna R.182	Sunny Sky Aviation Ltd	
G-BOWP	Jodel D.120A	G. L. Brown	
G-BOWR	Boeing 737-3Q8	Orion/Britannia Airways Ltd/Luton	
G-BOWS	Cessna 150M	Semloh Aviation Services/ Andrewsfield	
G-BOWT	Stolp SA.300 Starduster Too	F. E. P. Holmes/ Andrewsfield	
G-BOWU	Cameron O-84 balloon	Raybrake & Co Ltd	
G-BOWV	Cameron V-65 balloon	C. P. R. & S. J. Baxter	
G-BOWX	—	—	
G-BOWY	PA-28RT-201T Turbo Arrow IV	M & E Machinery Ltd/Elstree	
G-BOWZ	Benson B.80V	W. M. Day	
G-BOXA	PA-28-161 Warrior II	CI Aero Holdings Ltd	
G-BOXB	PA-28-161 Warrior II	CI Aero Holdings Ltd	
G-BOXC	PA-28-161 Warrior II	CI Aero Holdings Ltd	
G-BOXD	BAe 146-200	British Aerospace PLC/Hatfield	
G-BOXE	BAe 146-200	British Aerospace PLC/Hatfield	
G-BOXF	Cameron DP-70 airship	Cameron Balloons Ltd	
G-BOXG	Cameron O-77 balloon	S. J. Butler	
G-BOXH	Pitts S-1S Special	M. G. Jefferies	
G-BOXI	H.S. 125 Srs 700B	Tiphook Associated Finance Ltd	
G-BOXJ	Piper J-3C-65 Cub	J. L. Quick	
G-BOXK	Slingsby T.67C	Slingsby Aviation Ltd/Kirkbymoorside	
G-BOXL	Slingsby T.67M-200	Slingsby Aviation Ltd/Kirkbymoorside	
G-BOXM	Slingsby T.67M-200	Slingsby Aviation Ltd/Kirkbymoorside	
G-BOXN	Robinson R-22B	Conguess Aviation Ltd	
G-BOXO	H.S. Gnat T.1	Ruanil Investments Ltd/Cranfield	
G-BOXP	H.S. Gnat T.1	Ruanil Investments Ltd/Cranfield	
G-BOXR	GA-7 Cougar	Campbell Distribution Ltd	
G-BOXS	Hughes 269C	Ford Helicopters Ltd	

Notes	Reg.	Type	Owner or Operator
	G-BOXT	Hughes 269C	Ford Helicopters Ltd
	G-BOXU	AA-5B Tiger	South Coast Aviation Ltd/Goodwood
	G-BOXV	Pitts S-1D	D. H. Nourish
	G-BOXW	Cassutt Racer Srs IIIM	D. I. Johnson
	G-BOXX	Robinson R-22B	Highfield Developments (Yorkshire) Ltd
	G-BOXY	PA-28-181 Archer II	Halsmith (Aircraft Sales) Ltd
	G-BOXZ	PA-28-181 Archer II	Halsmith (Aircraft Sales) Ltd
	G-BOYA	Cessna A.152	Halsmith (Aircraft Sales) Ltd
	G-BOYB	Cessna A.152	Halsmith (Aircraft Sales) Ltd
	G-BOYC	Robinson R-22B	K. M. Hiley
	G-BOYD	Colt 90A balloon	United Friendly Insurance Ltd
	G-BOYE	Cessna TR.182RG	E. A. Matty
	G-BOYF	Sikorsky S-76B	Darley Steel Management Co Ltd
	G-BOYG	Cessna 421C	Leeds Aviation Ltd
	G-BOYH	PA-28-151 Warrior	W. London Aero Services Ltd/ White Waltham
	G-BOYI	PA-28-161 Warrior II	W. London Aero Services Ltd/ White Waltham
	G-BOYJ	—	—
	G-BOYK	Benson B.8	P. Crossman
	G-BOYL	Cessna 152	T. Hayseldon (Doncaster) Ltd
	G-BOYM	Cameron O-84 balloon	Frontline Distribution Ltd
	G-BOYN	Boeing 737-3S3	Air Europe Ltd/Air Europa (EC-ECQ)
	G-BOYO	Cameron V-20 balloon	Cameron Balloons Ltd
	G-BOYP	Cessna 172N	S. J. Randle & T. W. Crow
	G-BOYR	Cessna F.337G	C. M. Vlieland-Boddy
	G-BOYS	Cameron N-77 balloon	The Independent Balloon Co Ltd
	G-BOYT	PA-38-112 Tomahawk	Seal Executive Aircraft Ltd
	G-BOYU	Cessna A.150L	Seal Executive Aircraft Ltd
	G-BOYV	PA-28R-201T Turbo Arrow III	P. R. Goldsworthy
	G-BOYW	—	—
	G-BOYX	Robinson R-22B	Grill Floors Ltd
	G-BOYY	Cameron A-105 balloon	Hoyers (UK) Ltd
	G-BOYZ	Laser Z.200	M. G. Jefferies
	G-BOZA	Boeing 737-3L9	British Airways *River Lossie*/Heathrow
	G-BOZB	Boeing 737-3L9	British Airways *River Wyre*/Heathrow
	G-BOZC	—	—
	G-BOZD	—	—
	G-BOZE	—	—
	G-BOZF	—	—
	G-BOZG	—	—
	G-BOZH	—	—
	G-BOZI	PA-28-161 Warrior II	Klingair Ltd/Conington
	G-BOZJ	Thunder Ax8-105 balloon	Thunder & Colt Ltd
	G-BOZK	AS.332L Super Puma	British International Helicopters Ltd
	G-BOZL	Bell 206B JetRanger	Ernest George Aviation Ltd
	G-BOZM	PA-38-112 Tomahawk	Severn Aircraft Co
	G-BOZN	Cameron N-77 balloon	Calarel Developments Ltd
	G-BOZO	AA-5B Tiger	Becketts Honda Car Centre Ltd
	G-BOZP	Beech 76 Duchess	Wycombe Air Centre Ltd
	G-BOZR	Cessna 152	Interair (Aviation) Ltd/Bournemouth
	G-BOZS	Pitts S-1C Special	P. A. Grant/Shoreham
	G-BOZT	PA-28-181 Archer II	GT Aviation
	G-BOZU	Sparrow Hawk Mk II	R. V. Phillimore
	G-BOZV	CEA DR.340	E. H. Ellis
	G-BOZW	Benson B.8M	M. E. Wills
	G-BOZX	Robinson R-22B	M. J. Burgess
	G-BOZY	Cameron RTW-120 balloon	Pacific Television Enterprises Ltd
	G-BOZZ	AA-5B Tiger	P. R. Draper
	G-BPAA	Acro Advanced	Acro Engines & Airframes Ltd
	G-BPAB	Cessna 150M	Ark Ltd
	G-BPAC	PA-28-161 Warror II	Ark Ltd
	G-BPAD	PA-34-200T Seneca II	Channel Aviation Ltd
	G-BPAE	Cameron V-77 balloon	A. R. Peart & J. E. Astall
	G-BPAF	PA-28-161 Warrior II	Hendafern Ltd
	G-BPAG	Bellanca 8KCAB Decathlon	Aerojet Ltd
	G-BPAH	Colt 69A balloon	International Distillers & Vintners Ltd
	G-BPAI	Bell 47F-2A1	Fizzle Ltd
	G-BPAJ	B.H.82A Tiger Moth	P. A. Jackson (G-AOIX)
	G-BPAK	Air Command 532 Elite	R. Gardner
	G-BPAL	D.H.C.1 Chipmunk 22 (WG350)	D. F. Ranger (G-BCYE)
	G-BPAM	Jodel D.150A	A. J. Symes-Bullen
	G-BPAN	—	—

124

Reg.	Type	Owner or Operator	Notes
G-BPAO	Air Command 503 Commander	D. J. Sagar	
G-BPAP	Robinson R-22B	Stag Electronic Design Ltd	
G-BPAR	—	—	
G-BPAS	SOCATA TB.20 Trinidad	V. E. Denton	
G-BPAT	—	—	
G-BPAU	PA-28-161 Warrior II	Multirun Ltd	
G-BPAV	FRED Srs 2	P. A. Valentine	
G-BPAW	Cessna 150M	S. Magowan/Prestwick	
G-BPAX	Cessna 150M	S. Magowan/Prestwick	
G-BPAY	PA-28-181 Archer II	South Coast Aviation Ltd/Goodwood	
G-BPAZ	—	—	
G-BPBA	Benson B.8	M. E. Green	
G-BPBB	Evans VP-2	P. D. J. Brown	
G-BPBC	Bell 206B JetRanger	Delfino Maritime Ltd	
G-BPBD	—	—	
G-BPBE	—	—	
G-BPBF	—	—	
G-BPBG	Cessna 152	Atlantic Air Transport Ltd/Coventry	
G-BPBH	Cessna 152	Atlantic Air Transport Ltd/Coventry	
G-BPBI	Cessna 152	Atlantic Air Transport Ltd/Coventry	
G-BPBJ	Cessna 152	Atlantic Air Transport Ltd/Coventry	
G-BPBK	Cessna 152	Atlantic Air Transport Ltd/Coventry	
G-BPBL	Cessna 152	Atlantic Air Transport Ltd/Coventry	
G-BPBM	PA-28-161 Warrior II	T. Hayselden (Doncaster) Ltd	
G-BPBN	—	—	
G-BPBO	PA-28RT-201T Turbo Arrow IV	TEL (IoM) Ltd	
G-BPBP	Brugger MB.2 Colibri Mk II	M. F. Collett	
G-BPBR	PA-38-112 Tomahawk	A.T. Aviation Ltd/Cardiff	
G-BPBS	BAe 146-200	British Aerospace PLC/Hatfield	
G-BPBT	BAe 146-200	British Aerospace PLC/Hatfield	
G-BPBU	Cameron V-77 balloon	G. Illing	
G-BPBV	Cameron V-77 balloon	J. E. Smith	
G-BPBW	Cameron O-105 balloon	R. J. Mansfield	
G-BPBX	Cameron V-77 balloon	A. R. M. Hill	
G-BPBY	Cameron V-77 balloon	T. J. Brewster	
G-BPBZ	Thunder Ax7-77 balloon	B. K. Robbins	
G-BPCA	BN-2B Islander	Loganair Ltd (G-BLNX)/Glasgow	
G-BPCB	BN-2A-26 Islander	Air & General Services Ltd (G-BEXA/ G-MALI/G-DIVE)	
G-BPCC	AB-206B JetRanger	Fagins Toys Ltd	
G-BPCD	BN-2A-26 Islander	Air & General Services Ltd (G-BFNV)	
G-BPCE	Stolp SA.300 Starduster Too	R. E. Todd	
G-BPCF	—	—	
G-BPCG	Colt AS-80 airship	Thunder & Colt Ltd	
G-BPCI	Cessna R.172K	B. E. Simpson	
G-BPCJ	Cessna 150J	C. R. Hughes & B. E. Simpson	
G-BPCK	PA-28-161 Warrior II	C. R. Hughes & B. E. Simpson	
G-BPCL	SA Bulldog 120/128	J. D. Richardson	
G-BPCM	Rotorway Executive	Normans Ltd	
G-BPCN	Cameron A-160 balloon	Chard Balloon Co Ltd	
G-BPCO	Short SD3-60 variant 100	Air Europe Express (G-RMSS/G-BKKU)/ Gatwick	
G-BPCP	—	—	
G-BPCR	Mooney M.20K	T. & R. Harris	
G-BPCT	Bell 206L-1 LongRanger	Trillionair Ltd	
G-BPCV	Montgomerie Bensen MB.8R	J. Fisher	
G-BPCW	Slingsby Cadet III	P. C. Williams	
G-BPCX	PA-28-236 Dakota	Visual Phantom Ltd	
G-BPCY	PA-34-200T Seneca	R. St. Aubyn	
G-BPCZ	Bell 206B JetRanger	Sterling Side Ltd	
G-BPDA	H.S.748 Srs 2A	Scottish European Airways (G-GLAS)/ Glasgow	
G-BPDB	—	—	
G-BPDC	PA-46-310P Malibu	D. W. Clark	
G-BPDD	Colt 240A balloon	Thunder & Colt Ltd	
G-BPDE	Colt 56A balloon	J. W. Weidema	
G-BPDF	Cameron V-77 balloon	Boyson Construction Ltd	
G-BPDG	Cameron V-77 balloon	A. & M. A. Dunning	
G-BPDH	Robinson R-22B	E. Wootton	
G-BPDJ	Chris Tena Mini Coupe	Air Time Acquistion Ltd	
G-BPDK	Sorrell SNS-7 Hyperbipe	R. E. Todd	
G-BPDL	EMB-110P1 Bandeirante	Titan Airways/Stansted	
G-BPDM	C.A.S.A. 1.131E Jungmann	V. S. E. Norman	
G-BPDN	PA-28R-201 Arrow III	J. M. C. Crompton	

Notes	Reg.	Type	Owner or Operator
	G-BPDP	AS.355F-1 Twin Squirrel	European Helicopters Ltd
	G-BPDR	Schweizer 269C	C.S.E. Aviation Ltd/Kidlington
	G-BPDS	PA-28-161 Warrior II	Hendafern Ltd
	G-BPDT	PA-28-161 Warrior II	Hendafern Ltd
	G-BPDU	PA-28-161 Warrior II	Hendafern Ltd
	G-BPDV	Pitts S-1S Special	D. Clarke
	G-BPDW	—	—
	G-BPDX	D.H.C.7-102 Dash Seven	Brymon Airways Ltd/Plymouth
	G-BPDY	Westland-Bell 47G-3B1	Fairglobe Ltd
	G-BPDZ	Cessna 340A	Gwent Plant Sales
	G-BPEA	Boeing 757-236	Caledonian Airways Ltd *Loch of the Clans*/Gatwick
	G-BPEB	Boeing 757-236	Caledonian Airways Ltd *Loch Lomond*/Gatwick
	G-BPEC	—	—
	G-BPED	—	—
	G-BPEE	—	—
	G-BPEF	—	—
	G-BPEH	—	—
	G-BPEI	—	—
	G-BPEJ	—	—
	G-BPEK	—	—
	G-BPEL	PA-28-151 Warrior	M. E. Benterman
	G-BPEM	Cessna 150K	C. A. Outhwaite
	G-BPEN	—	—
	G-BPEO	Cessna 152	M. E. Benterman
	G-BPER	PA-38-112 Tomahawk	Seal Executive Aircraft Ltd
	G-BPES	PA-38-112 Tomahawk	Seal Executive Aircraft Ltd
	G-BPET	Slingsby T.67M-200	Slingsby Aviation Ltd/Kirkbymoorside
	G-BPEU	Slingsby T.67M-200	Slingsby Aviation Ltd/Kirkbymoorside
	G-BPEV	Slingsby T.67M-200	Slingsby Aviation Ltd/Kirkbymoorside
	G-BPEW	Robinson R-22B	R. B. Porch & Co (Southern) Ltd
	G-BPEX	Boeing A75N-1	D. Gardner
	G-BPEY	Bell 412	Autair Helicopters Ltd
	G-BPEZ	Colt 77A balloon	Thunder & Colt Ltd
	G-BPFA	Knight GK-2 Swallow	G. Knight & D. G. Pridham
	G-BPFB	Colt 77A balloon	S. Ingram
	G-BPFC	Mooney M.20C	Cashfield Ltd
	G-BPFD	Jodel D.112	K. Manley
	G-BPFE	Lightning T.5	Ruanil Investments Ltd/Cranfield
	G-BPFF	Cameron DP-70 airship	Cameron Balloons Ltd
	G-BPFG	SOCATA TB.20 Trinidad	F. T. Arnold
	G-BPFH	PA-28-161 Warrior II	M. H. Kleiser
	G-BPFI	PA-28-181 Archer II	Dixon Spain Estates Ltd
	G-BPFJ	Cameron 90 Club balloon	The Hot-Air Ballon Co Ltd
	G-BPFK	Bensen B.8M	S. J. Ball
	G-BPFL	Davis DA-2	C. A. Lightfoot
	G-BPFM	Aeronca 7AC Champion	R. J. Grimstead
	G-BPFP	Short SD3-60	Short Bros PLC/Sydenham
	G-BPFR	Short SD3-60	Short Bros PLC/Sydenham
	G-BPFS	Short SD3-60	Short Bros PLC/Sydenham
	G-BPFT	Cameron N-77 balloon	Cameron Balloons Ltd
	G-BPFU	H.S.748 Srs 2A	Scottish European Airways Ltd (G-EDIN)/Glasgow
	G-BPFV	Boeing 767-204ER	Britannia Airways Ltd/Luton
	G-BPFW	Air Command 532 Elite	B. A. Snell
	G-BPFX	Colt 21A balloon	The Hot-Air Balloon Co Ltd
	G-BPFY	Consolidated PBY-6A Catalina	Aces High Ltd/North Weald
	G-BPFZ	Cessna 152	J. J. Baumhardt/Southend
	G-BPGA	Mooney M.20J	M. G. Brown
	G-BPGB	Cessna 150J	Cormack (Aircraft Sales) Ltd/Glasgow
	G-BPGC	Air Command 532 Elite	R. E. Derbyshire
	G-BPGD	Cameron V-65 balloon	Gone With The Wind Ltd
	G-BPGE	Cessna U.206C	B. W. Wells & Burbage Farms Ltd
	G-BPGF	Thunder Ax7-77 balloon	Dovetail Upholstery Co Ltd
	G-BPGG	Thunder Ax6-56 balloon	Thunder & Colt Ltd
	G-BPGH	EAA AcroSport 2	Pennine Lightning Film & TV Ltd
	G-BPGI	Colt 69A balloon	Thunder & Colt Ltd
	G-BPGJ	Colt 31A balloon	Thunder & Colt Ltd
	G-BPGK	—	—
	G-BPGL	PA-28 Cherokee 180	C. N. Ellerbrook
	G-BPGM	Cessna 152	Three Counties Aero Club Ltd/Blackbushe
	G-BPGN	Cameron 90 Tractor SS balloon	Cameron Balloons Ltd

Reg.	Type	Owner or Operator	Notes
G-BPGO	—	—	
G-BPGP	—	—	
G-BPGR	H.S.125 Srs 800B	British Aerospace PLC/Hatfield	
G-BPGS	H.S.125 Srs 800B	British Aerospace PLC/Hatfield	
G-BPGT	Colt AS-80 airship	Thunder & Co Ltd	
G-BPGU	PA-28-181 Archer II	G. Underwood	
G-BPGV	Robinson R-22B	Allied Restaurants PLC	
G-BPGW	Boeing 757-236	Air Europe Ltd *Anne Marie*/Gatwick	
G-BPGX	SOCATA TB.9 Tampico	Martin Ltd/Biggin Hill	
G-BPGY	Cessna 150H	Three Counties Aero Club Ltd	
G-BPGZ	Cessna 150G	D. F. Sperring	
G-BPHA	Air Command 532 Elite	E. Kelly	
G-BPHB	PA-28-161 Warrior II	C.S.E. Aviation Ltd/Kidlington	
G-BPHC	AS.355F-1 Twin Squirrel	European Helicopters Ltd	
G-BPHD	—	—	
G-BPHE	PA-28-161 Warrior II	Seal Executive Aircraft Ltd	
G-BPHF	AB-206A JetRanger	Heliwork Services Ltd	
G-BPHG	Robin DR.400/180		
G-BPHH	Cameron V-77 balloon	C. J. Madigan	
G-BPHI	PA-38-112 Tomahawk	Gray Tuplin Ltd	
G-BPHJ	Cameron V-77 balloon	R. G. Davidson	
G-BPHK	Whittaker MW.7	J. G. Beesley	
G-BPHL	PA-28-161 Warrior II	Anglia Aviation Ltd	
G-BPHM	Beech A36 Bonanza	A. F. Budge (Aviation) Ltd	
G-BPHN	EMB-110P1 Bandeirante	National Airways/Southend	
G-BPHO	Taylorcraft BC-12D	A. Liddiard	
G-BPHP	Taylorcraft BC-12-65	A. Liddiard	
G-BPHR	D.H.82A Tiger Moth	S. M. Riseborough	
G-BPHS	Cessna 152	S. P. Donoghue	
G-BPHT	Cessna 152	S. P. Donoghue	
G-BPHU	Thunder Ax7-77 balloon	G. G. Bacon	
G-BPHV	Colt Montgolfier balloon	Thunder & Colt Ltd	
G-BPHW	Cessna 140	Ark Ltd	
G-BPHX	Cessna 140	Ark Ltd	
G-BPHY	Cameron COW-110 balloon	Cameron Balloons Ltd	
G-BPHZ	—	—	
G-BPIA	Cameron DP-90 airship	Cameron Balloons Ltd	
G-BPIB	AB-206A JetRanger	Heliwork Services Ltd	
G-BPIC	—	—	
G-BPID	—	—	
G-BPIE	Bell 206B JetRanger	R. P. Harper	
G-BPIF	Bensen 2 seat	C. Churchyard	
G-BPIG	—	—	
G-BPIH	Rand KR-2	J. R. Rowley	
G-BPII	Denney Aerocraft Kitfox	R. E. Derbyshire	
G-BPIJ	—	—	
G-BPIK	PA-38-112 Tomahawk	Cormack (Aircraft Services) Ltd	
G-BPIL	—	—	
G-BPIM	Cameron N-77 balloon	Thermalite Ltd	
G-BPIN	Glaser-Dirks DG.400	M. P. Seth-Smith	
G-BPIO	Cessna F.152	S. Harcourt	
G-BPIP	Slingsby Cadet III	J. H. Beard	
G-BPIR	Scheibe SF.25E Super Falke	M. R. Shelton	
G-BPIS	—	—	
G-BPIT	Robinson R-22B	Northern Helicopters Ltd	
G-BPIU	PA-28-161 Warrior II	I. R. Jones	
G-BPIV	—	—	
G-BPIW	H.S.748 Srs 2B	British Aerospace PLC/Woodford	
G-BPIX	AA-5A Cheetah	BLS Aviation Ltd	
G-BPIY	Cessna 152	J. J. Baumhardt	
G-BPIZ	—	—	
G-BPJA	Beech 58 Baron	Morse Computers Ltd	
G-BPJB	Schweizer 269C	J. F. Britten	
G-BPJC	Robinson R-22B	N. T. Burton	
G-BPJD	SOCATA Rallye 110ST	W. E. Taylor & Son Ltd	
G-BPJE	Cameron A-105 balloon	J. S. Eckersley	
G-BPJF	—	—	
G-BPJG	PA-18 Super Cub 150	Amcot Ltd	
G-BPJH	PA-18 Super Cub 95	P. J. Heron	
G-BPJI	—	—	
G-BPJJ	Colt 180A balloon	Airship & Balloon Co Ltd	
G-BPJK	Colt 77A balloon	Akal Ltd	
G-BPJL	Cessna 152	London Flight Centre (Headcorn) Ltd	
G-BPJM	—	—	

Notes	Reg.	Type	Owner or Operator
	G-BPJN	Jodel D.18	J. A. Nugent
	G-BPJO	PA-28-161 Warrior II	C.S.E. Aviation Ltd/Kidlington
	G-BPJP	PA-28-161 Warrior II	C.S.E. Aviation Ltd/Kidlington
	G-BPJR	PA-28-161 Warrior II	C.S.E. Aviation Ltd/Kidlington
	G-BPJS	PA-28-161 Warrior II	C.S.E. Aviation Ltd/Kidlington
	G-BPJT	PA-28-161 Warrior II	C.S.E. Aviation Ltd/Kidlington
	G-BPJU	PA-28-161 Warrior II	C.S.E. Aviation Ltd/Kidlington
	G-BPJV	Taylorcraft F-21	J. W. Heale
	G-BPJW	Cessna A.150K	Heathgrange Ltd
	G-BPJX	PA-31-350 Navajo Chieftain	UK Airways Ltd/Bournemouth
	G-BPJY	Air Command 532 Elite	T. D. Inch
	G-BPJZ	Cameron O-160 balloon	M. L. Gabb
	G-BPKA	Boeing 737-4S3	Air Europe Ltd/Gatwick
	G-BPKB	Boeing 737-4S3	Air Europe Ltd/Gatwick
	G-BPKC	Boeing 737-4S3	Air Europe Ltd/Gatwick
	G-BPKD	Boeing 737-4S3	Air Europe Ltd/Gatwick
	G-BPKE	Boeing 737-4S3	Air Europe Ltd/Gatwick
	G-BPKF	Grob G.115	Soaring (Oxford) Ltd
	G-BPKG	Grob G.115	Soaring (Oxford) Ltd
	G-BPKH	—	—
	G-BPKI	—	—
	G-BPKJ	Colt AS-80 Mk II airship	Thunder & Co Ltd
	G-BPKK	Denney Aerocraft Kitfox	M. W. Holmes
	G-BPKL	Mooney M.20J	Astraflight Ltd
	G-BPKM	PA-28-161 Warrior II	J. D. Poole
	G-BPKN	Colt AS-80 Mk II airship	Thunder & Colt Ltd
	G-BPKO	Cessna 140	I. B. Grace
	G-BPKP	—	—
	G-BPKR	—	—
	G-BPKS	—	—
	G-BPKT	—	—
	G-BPKU	—	—
	G-BPKV	Short SD3-60	Short Bros PLC/Sydenham
	G-BPKW	Short SD3-60	Short Bros PLC/Sydenham
	G-BPKX	Short SD3-60	Short Bros PLC/Sydenham
	G-BPKY	Short SD3-60	Short Bros PLC/Sydenham
	G-BPKZ	Short SD3-60	Short Bros PLC/Sydenham
	G-BPLC	Beech 200 Super King Air	Bass PLC
	G-BPLD	Thunder & Colt AS-261 airship	Thunder & Colt Ltd
	G-BPLE	Cameron A-160 balloon	Balloons & Airships International Ltd
	G-BPLF	Cameron V-77 balloon	Dalesight Ltd
	G-BPLJ	Colt 90A balloon	Thunder & Colt Ltd
	G-BPLN	BN-2B Islander	Pilatus BN Ltd/Bembridge
	G-BPLO	BN-2B Islander	Pilatus BN Ltd/Bembridge
	G-BPLP	BN-2B Islander	Pilatus BN Ltd/Bembridge
	G-BPLR	BN-2B Islander	Pilatus BN Ltd/Bembridge
	G-BPLS	BN-2B Islander	Pilatus BN Ltd/Bembridge
	G-BPLT	Bristol M.1C replica	AJD Engineering Ltd
	G-BPLU	Thunder Ax10-160 balloon	Subsearch Ltd
	G-BPLV	Cameron V-77 balloon	Jessops (Tailors) Ltd
	G-BPLW	Cessna 152	Fleetdelta Ltd
	G-BPLX	Cessna 172P	Tech Air (Cambridge) Ltd
	G-BPLY	Pitts S-2B Special	D. A. Hammant
	G-BPMA	Short SD3-30 Variant 100	Short Bros PLC (G-BIRN)/Sydenham
	G-BPMB	Maule M5-235C Lunar Rocket	P. M. Breton
	G-BPMC	Air Command 503 Commander	M. A. Cheshire
	G-BPME	Cessna 152	London Flight Centre (Headcorn) Ltd
	G-BPMG	Bensen B.8MR	P. Doherty
	G-BPMI	Colt 56A balloon	Thunder & Colt Ltd
	G-BPMJ	Colt 56A balloon	Thunder & Colt Ltd
	G-BPMN	Aerocar Sooper Coot Model A	P. Napp
	G-BPND	Boeing 727-2D3	Dan-Air Services Ltd/Gatwick
	G-BPNO	Zlin Z.326 Trener Master	J. A. S. Bailey & S. T. Logan
	G-BPNR	BAe 146-300	Dan-Air Services Ltd/Gatwick
	G-BPNT	BAe 146-300	Dan-Air Services Ltd/Gatwick
	G-BPNX	BAC One-Eleven 304AX	Dan-Air Services Ltd (G-YMRU/G-ATPH) /Gatwick
	G-BPPN	Cessna F.182Q	Hunt Norris Ltd
	G-BPPP	Cameron V-77 balloon	P. F. Smart
	G-BPPS	Mudry CAARP CAP.21	Nullmint Ltd/Booker
	G-BPRM	Cessna F.172L	Nultree Ltd (G-AZKG)
	G-BPUF	Thunder Ax6-56Z balloon	Buf-Puf Balloon Group
	G-BPYN	Piper J-3C-65 Cub	The Aquila Group/White Waltham
	G-BPZD	Nord NC.858S	A. Richards & ptnrs

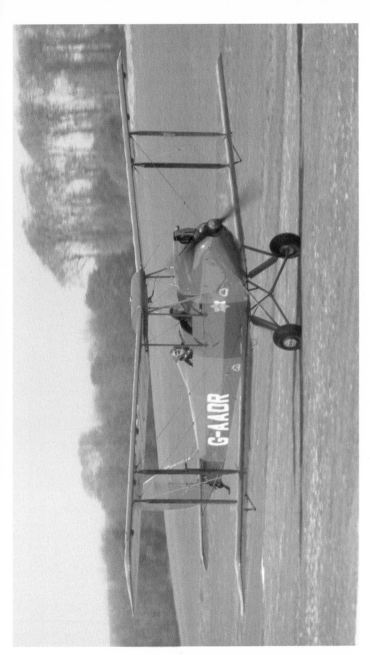

G-AADR   DH 60GM Moth.   *Alan J. Wright (AJW)*

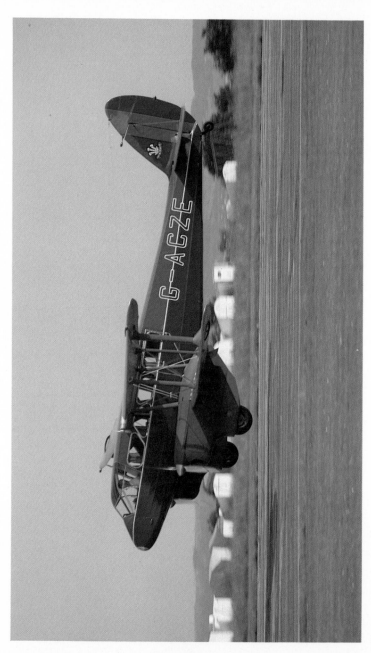

G-ACZE   DH 89A Dragon Rapide.   AJW

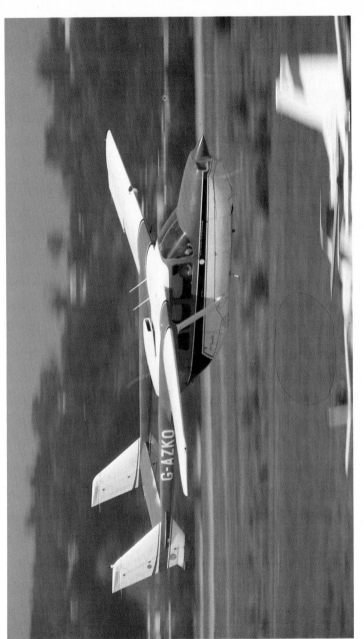

G-AZKO   Cessna F337F Super Skymaster.   AJW

G-BBAE   L-1011-385 TriStar of Caledonian Airways.   AJW

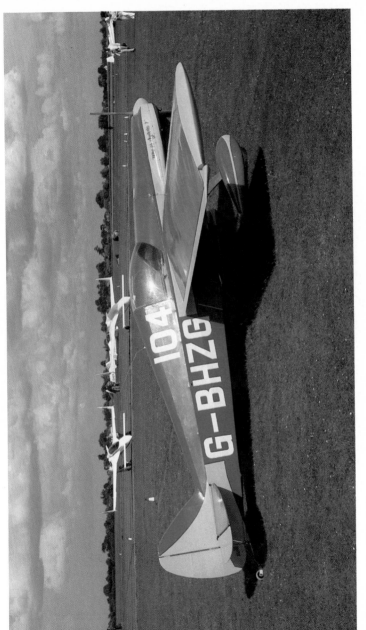

G-BHZG   Monnet Sonerai II.   AJW

G-BISI   Robinson R-22.   AJW

G-BMNB   Airbus A300B4-203 of Dan-Air Services.   AJW

G-BMYL   BAe ATP of British Midland Airways.   *A. S. Wright*

G-BNBZ   LET L200D Morava.   *Peter R. March*

G-DAJB   Boeing 757-2T7 of Monarch Airlines.   AJW

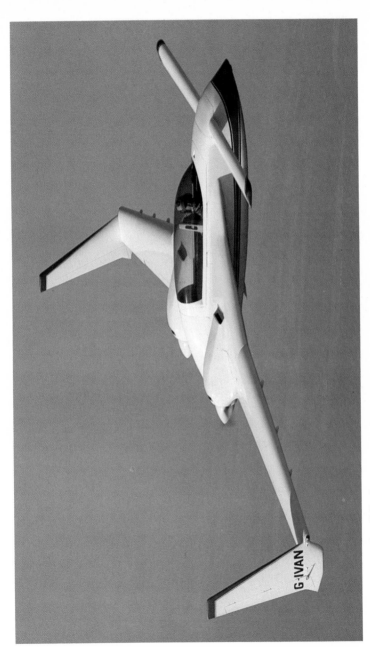

G-IVAN Shaw TwinEze. *Peter R. March*

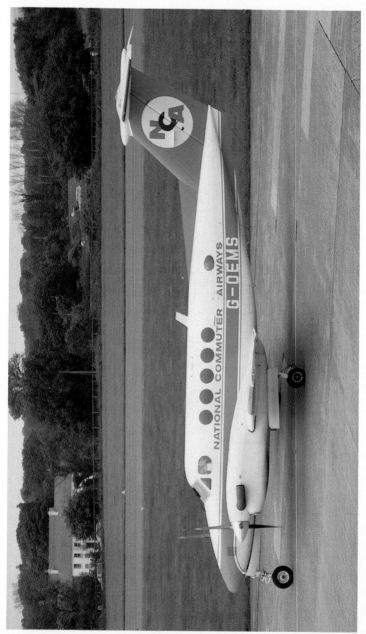

G-OEMS   Beech 200 Super King Air of National Commuter Airways.   AJW

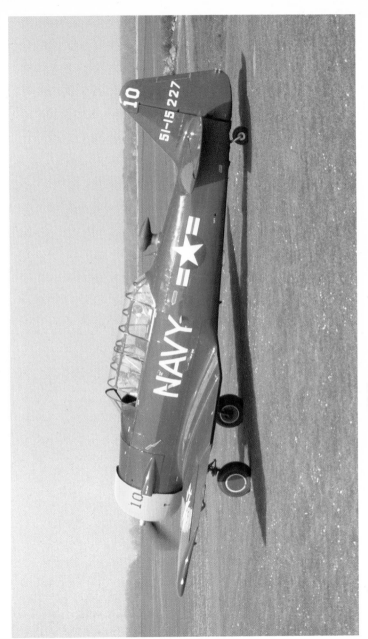

51-15227 North American T-6G Texan, civil identity G-BKRA. AJW

D-AGEB   Boeing 737-35B of Germania.   AJW

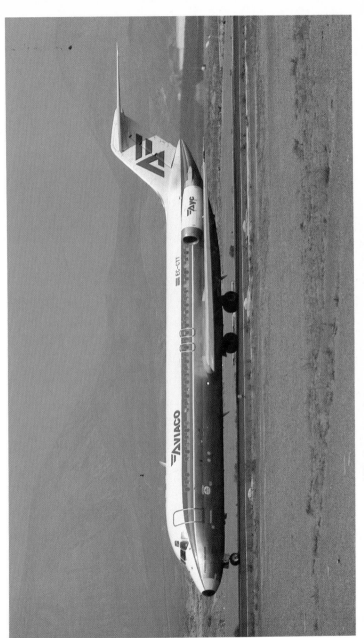

EC-CTT   Douglas DC-9-34CF of Aviaco.   AJW

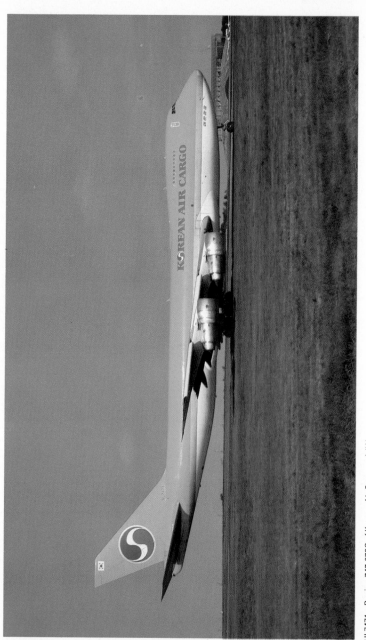

HL7471   Boeing 747-273C of Korean Air Cargo.   AJW

Out-of-Sequence Registrations

Reg.	Type	Owner or Operator	Notes
G-BRAD	Beech 95-B55 Baron	C. Walker/Perth	
G-BRAF	V. S. Spitfire XVIII (SM969)	D. W. Arnold	
G-BRAG	Taylor JT.2 Titch	A. R. Greenfield	
G-BRAK	Cessna 172N	C. D. Brack	
G-BRAL	G.159 Gulfstream 1	Ford Motor Co Ltd/Stansted	
G-BRAV	PA-23 Aztec 250	Hartfield Aviation Ltd (G-BBCM)/ Biggin Hill	
G-BRDD	Avions Mudry CAP.10B	R. D. Dickson	
G-BRDI	H.S.125 Srs 700B	Aravco Ltd (G-HHOI/G-BHTJ)/Heathrow	
G-BREW	PA-31-350 Navajo Chieftain	Whitbread & Co Ltd/Biggin Hill	
G-BRFC	P.57 Sea Prince T.1 (WP321)	Rural Naval Air Service/Bourn	
G-BRGH	FRED Srs 2	F. G. Hallam	
G-BRGN	BAe Jetstream 3102	British Aerospace PLC (G-BLHC)/ Prestwick	
G-BRGW	GY-201 Minicab	R. G. White	
G-BRID	Cessna U.206A	Emair Bridlington Ltd	
G-BRIK	T.66 Nipper 3	C. W. R. Piper	
G-BRIT	Cessna 421C	Chaseside Holdings Ltd/Exeter	
G-BRIX	PA-32-301 Saratoga SP	Taylor Maxwell & Co Ltd/Bristol	
G-BRJW	Bellanca 7GCBC Citabria	Cleanacres Ltd/Staverton	
G-BRMA	WS-51 Dragonfly Mk 5 (WG719) ★	British Rotorcraft Museum	
G-BRMB	B.192 Belvedere Mk 1 (XG452) ★	British Rotorcraft Museum	
G-BRMC	Stampe SV-4B	E. K. Coventry	
G-BRMH	Bell 206B JetRanger 2	R. M. H. Stainless Ltd (G-BBUX)	
G-BROM	ICA IS-28M2	Kent Motor Gliding & Soaring Centre	
G-BRPM	T.66 Nipper 3	M. M. H. J. Omar	
G-BRSL	Cameron N-56 balloon	S. Budd	
G-BRUM	Cessna A.152	Warwickshire Flying Training Centre Ltd	
G-BRUW	Schweizer 269C	Kendrick Construction Ltd	
G-BRUX	PA-44-180 Seminole	Hambrair Ltd/Tollerton	
G-BRWN	G.159 Gulfstream 1	Peregrine Air Services Ltd/Aberdeen	
G-BRYA	D.H.C. 7-110 Dash Seven	Brymon Aviation Ltd/Plymouth	
G-BRYB	D.H.C. 7-110 Dash Seven	Brymon Aviation Ltd/Plymouth	
G-BRYC	D.H.C. 7-110 Dash Seven	Brymon Aviation Ltd/Plymouth	
G-BRYD	D.H.C. 7-110 Dash Seven	Brymon Aviation Ltd/Plymouth	
G-BRYL	Agusta A.109A	Castle Air Charters Ltd (G-ROPE/G-OAMH)	
G-BSAN	G.1159A Gulfstream 3	Shell Aviation Ltd/Heathrow	
G-BSAT	PA-28-181 Archer II	A1 Aircraft Ltd/Biggin Hill	
G-BSBH	Short SD3-30 ★	Ulster Aviation Soc	
G-BSBS	PA-34-200 Seneca II	B. Kreisky (G-BDRI)	
G-BSDL	SOCATA TB.10 Tobago	Consort Aviation Ltd	
G-BSEL	Slingsby T.61G Super Falke	RAFGSA/Bicester	
G-BSET	B.206 Srs 1 Basset	Beagle Basset Ltd/Shoreham	
G-BSFC	PA-38-112 Tomahawk	Sherwood Flying Club Ltd/Tollerton	
G-BSFT	PA-31 Turbo Navajo	SFT Aviation Ltd (G-AXYC)/ Bournemouth	
G-BSHL	H.S.125 Srs 600B	S. H. Services Ltd (G-BBMD)/Luton	
G-BSHR	Cessna F.172N	H. Rothwell (G-BFGE)/Dundee	
G-BSIT	Robinson R-22B	M. A. Billings	
G-BSOL	PA-32R-301 Saratoga SP	B. A. Solomon	
G-BSPC	Jodel D.140C	B. E. Cotton/Headcorn	
G-BSPE	Cessna F.172P	P. & M. Jones/Denham	
G-BSSM	AS.355F-1 Twin Squirrel	Blue Star Ship Management Ltd (G-BMTC/G-BKUK)	
G-BSSS	Cessna 421C	Ten Tenths Ltd	
G-BSST	Concorde 002 ★	FAA Museum/Yeovilton	
G-BSTA	BAe 146-100	British Aerospace PLC (G-BPNP/ G-SSHH/G-OPSA/G-BIAE)/Hatfield	
G-BSUS	Taylor JT.1 Monoplane	R. Parker	
G-BSVP	PA-23 Aztec 250F	Time Electronics Ltd/Biggin Hill	
G-BTAB	H.S. 125 Srs 800B	Abbey Investment Co Ltd (G-BOOA)	
G-BTAL	Cessna F.152	TG Aviation Ltd	
G-BTAN	Thunder Ax7-65Z balloon	The BTAN Balloon Group	
G-BTAX	PA-31-350 Navajo Chieftain	Chaseside Holdings Ltd	
G-BTBT	PA-32R-301 Saratoga SP	B. Taylor/Blackpool	
G-BTCG	PA-23 Aztec 250C	Eagle Tugs Ltd (G-AVRX)/Mombasa	

Notes	Reg.	Type	Owner or Operator
	G-BTCM	Cameron N-90 balloon	Chesterfield Cold Storage Co Ltd
	G-BTDK	Cessna 421B	RK Technologies Ltd/Manchester
	G-BTEA	Cameron N-105 balloon	Southern Balloon Group
	G-BTFC	Cessna F.152 II	Tayside Aviation Ltd/Dundee
	G-BTGS	Stolp SA.300 Starduster Too	T. G. Soloman (G-AYMA)
	G-BTIE	SOCATA TB.10 Tobago	Rotaters Ltd/Manchester
	G-BTJM	Taylor JT.2 Titch	T. J. Miller/Dunkeswell
	G-BTLE	PA-31-350 Navajo Chieftain	Galecall Ltd
	G-BTLT	Colt 31A balloon	Thunder & Colt Ltd
	G-BTOM	PA-38-112 Tomahawk	C. R. Timber Ltd
	G-BTOW	SOCATA Rallye 180T	Mixamate Ltd/Biggin Hill
	G-BTPA	BAe ATP	British Airways *Strathallan*/Glasgow
	G-BTPB	Cameron N-105 balloon	British Telecom PLC
	G-BTPC	BAe ATP	British Airways *Strathblane*/Glasgow
	G-BTPD	BAe ATP	British Airways *Strathconon*/Glasgow
	G-BTPE	BAe ATP	British Airways *Strathdon*/Glasgow
	G-BTPF	BAe ATP	British Airways *Strathlarn*/Glasgow
	G-BTPG	BAe ATP	British Airways *Strathfillan*/Glasgow
	G-BTPH	BAe ATP	British Airways *Strathnaver*/Glasgow
	G-BTPJ	BAe ATP	British Airways *Strathpeffer*/Glasgow
	G-BTSC	Evans VP-2	B. P. Irish
	G-BTSG	Cessna 414A	T. S. Grimshaw Ltd (G-BTFH)
	G-BTSL	Cameron Glass SS balloon	Bass & Tennent Sales Ltd
	G-BTUC	EMB-312 Tucano	Short Bros PLC/Sydenham
	G-BTUG	SOCATA Rallye 180T	Lasham Gliding Soc Ltd
	G-BTWW	AB-206B JetRanger	Dollar Air Services Ltd/Coventry
	G-BTXL	BAe Jetstream 3102	Berlin Regional UK Ltd (G-BLDO)
	G-BUBL	Thunder Ax8-105 balloon	Moet & Chandon (London) Ltd
	G-BUBU	PA-34-220T Seneca III	Brinor (Holdings) Ltd
	G-BUCK	C.A.S.A. 1.131E Jungmann (BU+CK)	W. G. V. Hall
	G-BUDG	Cessna 421C	A. F. Budge Ltd (G-BKWX)/E. Midlands
	G-BUDS	Rand KR-2	D. W. Munday
	G-BUDY	Colt 17A balloon	Bondbaste Ltd
	G-BUEM	C.A.S.A. 1.131E Jungmann	E. K. McEntee (G-BUCC)/White Waltham
	G-BUFF	Jodel D.112	D. J. Buffham/Fenland
	G-BUKA	Fairchild SA.227AC Metro III	Air Metro/Bournemouth
	G-BULL	SA Bulldog 120/128	J. D. Richardson
	G-BUMF	Robinson R-22	Skyline Helicopters Ltd (G-BMBU)
	G-BUMP	PA-28-181 Archer II	H. McC. Clarke
	G-BUND	PA-28R-201T Turbo Arrow III	Metafin Holdings Ltd
	G-BUNY	Beech 95-B55 Baron	Gama Aviation Ltd
	G-BUPI	Cameron V-77 balloon	S. A. Masey (G-BOUC)
	G-BURD	Cessna F.172N	RJS Aviation Ltd/Halfpenny Green
	G-BURT	PA-28-161 Warrior II	A. T. Howarth/Biggin Hill
	G-BUSB	Airbus A.320-111	British Airways *Isle of Jersey*
	G-BUSC	Airbus A.320-111	British Airways *Isle of Skye*
	G-BUSD	Airbus A.320-111	British Airways *Isle of Mull*
	G-BUSE	Airbus A.320-111	British Airways *Isle of Scilly*
	G-BUSF	Airbus A.320-111	British Airways *Isle of Man*
	G-BUSG	Airbus A.320-111	British Airways *Isle of Wight*
	G-BUSH	Airbus A.320-111	British Airways *Isle of Jura*
	G-BUSI	Airbus A.320-111	British Airways *Isle of Anglesey*
	G-BUSJ	Airbus A.320-111	British Airways *Isle of Sark*
	G-BUSK	Airbus A.320-111	British Airways *Isle of Guernsey*
	G-BUSS	Cameron Bus SS balloon	A. Faulkner
	G-BUSY	Thunder Ax6-56A balloon	B. R. & Mrs M. Boyle *Busy Bodies*
	G-BUTL	PA-24 Comanche 250	D. Buttle (G-ARLB)/Blackbushe
	G-BUTT	Cessna FA.150K	P. L. Borek (G-AXSJ)
	G-BUYI	Thunder Ax7-77 balloon	Chelmsford Developments Ltd
	G-BUZZ	AB-206B JetRanger 2	ICS Worldwide Courier Ltd
	G-BVAN	M.S.892E Rallye 150	C. D. Weiswall
	G-BVAX	Colt 77A balloon	Vax Appliances Ltd
	G-BVMM	Robin HR.200/100	M. G. Owen
	G-BVMZ	Robin HR.100/210	Chiltern Handbags (London) Ltd
	G-BVPI	Evans VP-1	C. M. Gibson
	G-BVPM	Evans VP-2	P. Marigold
	G-BWAS	PA-31-350 Navajo Chieftain	BWOC Ltd/Bristol
	G-BWAY	Beech A36 Bonanza	Briway Transit Systems
	G-BWDJ	Jurca MJ.5 Sirocco	B. W. Davies
	G-BWDT	PA-34-220T Seneca II	Budleigh Estates Ltd (G-BKHS)
	G-BWEC	Cassutt-Colson Variant	N. R. Thomason & M. P. J. Hill
	G-BWFJ	Evans VP-1	W. F. Jones
	G-BWHY	Robinson R-22	Cotwell Air Services

Reg.	Type	Owner or Operator	Notes
G-BWIG	G.17S replica	K. Wigglesworth	
G-BWJB	Thunder Ax8-105 balloon	Justerini & Brooks Ltd *Whiskey J. & B.*	
G-BWKK	Auster AOP.9 (XP279)	A. Hawley	
G-BWMB	Jodel D.119	K. Jarman & N. Chapman	
G-BWMP	Gulfstream 695A	R. B. Tyler (Plant) Ltd	
G-BWOC	PA-31-350 Navajo Chieftain	BWOC Ltd	
G-BWRB	D.H.C.6 Twin Otter 310	Brymon Aviation Ltd/Plymouth	
G-BWSI	K&S SA.102.5 Cavalier	B. W. Shaw	
G-BWTX	PA-42-720 Cheyenne III	Broome & Wellington (Aviation) Ltd	
G-BWVE	Bell 206B JetRanger	Willow Vale Electronics Ltd (G-BOSX)	
G-BWWJ	Hughes 269C	B. W. W. Jones (G-BMYZ)	
G-BWWW	BAe Jetstream 3102	British Aerospace PLC/Dunsfold	
G-BXVI	V.S.361 Spitfire F.XVI	D. Arnold	
G-BXYZ	R. Turbo Commander 690C	British Airports Authority/Gatwick	
G-BYEE	Mooney M.20K	Axe & Status Ltd	
G-BYLL	F.8L Falco	N. J. Langrick	
G-BYNG	Cessna T.303	J. M. E. Byng (G-PTWB)	
G-BYRD	Mooney M.20K	V. J. Holden/Teesside	
G-BYSE	AB-206B JetRanger 2	Bewise Ltd (G-BFND)	
G-BYSL	Cameron O-56 balloon	Charles of the Ritz Ltd	
G-BZAC	Sikorsky S-76A	British International Helicopters Ltd/ Aberdeen	
G-BZBH	Thunder Ax6-65 balloon	R. S. Whittaker & P. E. Sadler	
G-BZBY	Colt 56 Buzby balloon	British Telecom	
G-BZFE	PA-23 Aztec 250E	S. E. Hobbs & Co Ltd (G-AZFE)	
G-BZKK	Cameron V-56 balloon	P. J. Green & C. Bosley *Gemini II*	
G-BZZZ	Enstrom F-28C-UK	Owners Abroad Aviation Ltd (G-BBBZ)	
G-CALL	PA-23 Aztec 250F	Woodgate Aviation Ltd/Ronaldsway	
G-CAXF	Cameron O-77 balloon	R. D. & S. J. Sarjeant	
G-CAYN	Dornier Do.228-201	Mann Aviation Sales Ltd (G-MLNR)	
G-CBEA	BAe Jetstream 3102-01	Birmingham Executive Airways Ltd	
G-CBIA	BAC One-Eleven 416	British Island Airways PLC (G-AWXJ) *Island Ensign*/Gatwick	
G-CBIL	Cessna 182K	N. Law/Manchester	
G-CBKT	Cameron O-77 balloon	Caledonian Airways Ltd	
G-CBOR	Cessna F.172N	M. Byl	
G-CCAR	Cameron N-77 balloon	A. G. E. Faulkner	
G-CCCC	Cessna 172H	B. J. Crow/Elstree	
G-CCIX	V.S.361 Spitfire LF.IX	Charles Church (Displays) Ltd (G-BIXP)	
G-CCOZ	Monnet Sonerai II	P. R. Cozens	
G-CCUB	Piper J-3C-65 Cub	Cormack (Aircraft Services) Ltd	
G-CCVV	V.S.379 Spitfire FR.XIV	Charles Church Displays Ltd	
G-CDAH	Taylor Sooper Coot A	D. A. Hood	
G-CDET	Culver LCA Cadet	H. B. Fox/Booker	
G-CDGA	Taylor JT.1 Monoplane	R. M. Larimore	
G-CDGL	Saffery S.330 balloon	C. J. Dodd & G. J. Luckett *Penny*	
G-CDON	PA-28-161 Warrior II	East Midlands Flying Club Ltd	
G-CDOS	Beech 58 Baron	Astra Aviation Ltd	
G-CEAS	HPR-7 Herald 214	Channel Express Freight (UK) Ltd (G-BEBB)/Bournemouth	
G-CEGA	PA-34-200T Seneca II	Hendefern Ltd	
G-CEGB	AS.355F1 Twin Squirrel	Central Electricity Generating Board (G-BLJL)	
G-CELL	PA-32R-301 Saratoga SP	CEL Electronics Ltd	
G-CERT	Mooney M.20K	N. Jagger	
G-CETC	Aeronca 15AC Sedan	J. W. Scale	
G-CEXP	HPR-7 Herald 209	Channel Express Air Services Ltd (G-BFRJ)/Bournemouth	
G-CEZY	Thunder Ax9-140 balloon	R. Carr/France	
G-CFBI	Colt 56A balloon	G. H. Dorrell	
G-CFLY	Cessna 172F	Cee-Fly	
G-CGHM	PA-28 Cherokee 140	CGH Managements Ltd/Elstree	
G-CHAR	Grob G.109B	RAFGSA/Bicester	
G-CHEM	PA-34-200T Seneca II	Mega Yield Ltd	
G-CHIK	Cessna F.152	Stapleford Flying Club Ltd (G-BHAZ)	
G-CHIL	Robinson R-22HP	L. M. Dresher	
G-CHIP	PA-28-181 Archer II	C. M. Hough/Fairoaks	
G-CHOK	Cameron V-77 balloon	K. W. Overton	
G-CHOP	Westland-Bell 47G-3B1	Time Choppers Ltd/Chilbolton	
G-CHRO	Thunder & Colt Flying Book SS balloon	Chronicle Communications Ltd	
G-CHSR	BAe 146-200	Air UK Ltd/Norwich	
G-CHTA	AA-5A Cheetah	Rapid Spin Ltd (G-BFRC)/Biggin Hill	

Notes	Reg.	Type	Owner or Operator
	G-CHTT	Varga 2150A Kachina	C.H.T. Trace
	G-CINE	Bell 206L-1 LongRanger	Airward Aviation Ltd
	G-CIPI	AJEP Wittman W.8 Tailwind	G. J. Z. Cipirski (G-AYDU)/Biggin Hill
	G-CITB	Boeing 747-2D3B	British Airways *City of Norwich*
	G-CITI	Cessna 501 Citation	Consultant Services Ltd
	G-CITY	PA-31-350 Navajo Chieftain	Woodgate Aviation Ltd/Ronaldsway
	G-CJBC	PA-28 Cherokee 180	J. B. Cave/Halfpenny Green
	G-CJCB	Bell 206L LongRanger	J. C. Bamford (Excavators) Ltd (G-LIII)/ E. Midlands
	G-CJCI	Pilatus P2-06	Charles Church Displays Ltd
	G-CJET	Learjet 35A	Interflight (Learjet) Ltd (G-SEBE/G-ZIPS/ G-ZONE)/Gatwick
	G-CJHI	Bell 206B JetRanger	Tudorbury (Air Services) Ltd (G-BBFB)
	G-CJIM	Taylor JT.1 Monoplane	J. Crawford
	G-CLAC	PA-28-161 Warrior II	J. D. Moonie
	G-CLAW	EMB-110P1 Bandeirante	National Airways/Southend
	G-CLEA	PA-28-161 Warrior II	Creative Logistics Enterprises & Aviation Ltd
	G-CLEM	Bo 208A2 Junior	G. Clements (G-ASWE)/Netherthorpe
	G-CLIK	PA-18 Super Cub 95	N. J. R. Empson/Ipswich
	G-CLOS	PA-34-200 Seneca II	Green Close Ltd
	G-CLUB	Cessna FRA.150M	R. C. Button
	G-CLUX	Cessna F.172N	D. Bardsley/Manchester
	G-CMMP	Boeing 737-3L9	British Airways *River Colne*/Heathrow
	G-CMMR	Boeing 737-3L9	British Airways *River Orwell*/Heathrow
	G-CNIS	Partenavia P.68B	M. R. Cross (G-BJOF/G-PAUL)
	G-CNMF	BAe 146-200	Air UK Ltd/Norwich
	G-COCO	Cessna F.172M	SEH (Ipswich) Ltd
	G-COIN	Bell 206B JetRanger 2	P. Woodward
	G-COKE	Cameron O-65 balloon	M. C. Bradley
	G-COLL	Enstrom 280C-UK-2 Shark	Estate Computer Systems Ltd
	G-COLR	Colt 69A balloon	Graeme Scaife Productions Ltd
	G-COMB	PA-30 Twin Comanche 160B	W. A. L. Mitchell (G-AVBL)/Ronaldsway
	G-COMM	PA-23 Aztec 250C	M. G. Wild (G-AZMG)
	G-COMP	Cameron N-90 balloon	Computacenter Ltd
	G-CONI	L.749A Constellation (N7777G) ★	Science Museum/Wroughton
	G-COOK	Cameron N-77 balloon	IAZ (International) Ltd
	G-COOP	Cameron N-31 balloon	Balloon Stable Ltd *Co-op*
	G-COPE	Enstrom 280C-UK-2 Shark	Vissenta Ltd
	G-COPS	Piper J-3C-65 Cub	W. T. Sproat
	G-COPY	AA-5A Cheetah	Emberden Ltd (G-BIEU)/Biggin Hill
	G-CORD	Nipper T.66 RA.45 Srs 3	B. A. Wright (G-AVTB)
	G-CORK	Air Command 532 Elite	D. N. B. McCorquodale
	G-COTT	Cameron 60 SS balloon	Nottingham Hot-Air Balloon Club
	G-COWE	Beech C90A King Air	Cowie Aviation Ltd/Newcastle
	G-COWI	Cessna 414A	Milegood Ltd (G-MLCS/G-MHGI/ G-BHKK)
	G-COWS	ARV Super 2	Bayles & Wylie Ltd (G-B ONB)
	G-COZY	Rutan Cozy	J. F. MacKay
	G-CPFC	Cessna F.152	Osprey Air Services Ltd/Cranfield
	G-CPTL	Short SD3-60	Capital Airlines Ltd (G-BOFI)/Leeds
	G-CPTS	AB-206B JetRanger 2	A. R. B. Aspinall
	G-CRAN	Robin R.1180T	Slea Aviation Ltd/Cranwell
	G-CRIC	Colomban MC.15 Cri-Cri	A. J. Maxwell
	G-CRIL	R. Commander 112B	Rockwell Aviation Group/Cardiff
	G-CRIS	Taylor JT.1 Monoplane	C. J. Bragg
	G-CRZY	Thunder Ax8-105 balloon	R. Carr (G-BDLP)/France
	G-CSBM	Cessna F.150M	Coventry (Civil) Aviation Ltd
	G-CSCS	Cessna F.172N	Conegate Ltd
	G-CSFC	Cessna 150L	Shropshire Aero Club Ltd
	G-CSFT	PA-23 Aztec 250D	SFT Aviation Ltd (G-AYKU)/ Bournemouth
	G-CSJH	BAe 146-200	Air UK Ltd/Norwich
	G-CSNA	Cessna 421C	Knightway Air Charter Ltd/Leeds
	G-CSZB	V.807B Viscount	British Air Ferries *Viscount Scotland* (G-AOXU)/Southend
	G-CTIX	V.S.509 Spitfire T.IX (PT462)	Charles Church (Displays) Ltd
	G-CTKL	CCF Harvard IV (54137)	J. A. Carr
	G-CTRN	Enstrom F-28C-UK	W. E. Taylor & Son Ltd
	G-CTRX	H.P.137 Jetstream 200	Centrax Ltd (G-BCWW/G-AXUN)/Exeter
	G-CTSI	Enstrom 280C-UK Shark	Sullivan Management Control Ltd (G-BKIO)
	G-CUBB	PA-18 Super Cub 180	G. J. Busby/Booker
	G-CUBI	PA-18 Super Cub 135	R. C. Atkinson

132

Reg.	Type	Owner or Operator	Notes
G-CUBJ	PA-18 Super Cub 150	A. K. Leasing (Jersey) Ltd	
G-CUGA	GA-7 Cougar	Frontline Aviation Ltd	
G-CUKL	Beech 200 Super King Air	Conoco (UK) Ltd (G-CNSI/G-OSKA)	
G-CVAN	Cessna F.406 Caravan 2	Bob Crowe Aircraft Sales Ltd	
G-CWOT	Currie Wot	D. A. Lord	
G-CXCX	Cameron N-90 balloon	Cathay Pacific Airways (London) Ltd	
G-CYMA	GA-7 Cougar	Cyma Petroleum Ltd (G-BKOM)/Elstree	
G-DAAH	PA-28T-201T Turbo Arrow IV	Parelarch Ltd	
G-DACA	P.57 Sea Prince T.1	Atlantic & Caribbean Aviation Ltd/ Staverton	
G-DACC	Cessna 401B	Niglon Ltd (G-AYOU)/Birmingham	
G-DAFS	Cessna 404 Titan	Dept. of Agriculture & Fisheries for Scotland (G-BHNH)/Edinburgh	
G-DAFT	AS.355F-2 Twin Squirrel	Powersense Ltd (G-BNNN)/Hayes	
G-DAJB	Boeing 757-2T7	Monarch Airlines Ltd/Luton	
G-DAJW	K & S Jungster 1	A. J. Walters	
G-DAKS	Dakota 3 (KG874)	Aces High Ltd/North Weald	
G-DAND	SOCATA TB.10 Tobago	Whitemoor Engineering Co Ltd	
G-DANN	Stampe SV-4B	I. M. White	
G-DARA	PA-34-220T Seneca III	Sunspot Investments Ltd	
G-DART	Rollason Beta B2	M. G. Ollis	
G-DASH	R. Commander 112A	Josef D. J. Jons & Co Ltd (G-BDAJ)	
G-DASI	Short SD3-60	Air UK Ltd (G-BKKW)/Norwich	
G-DAVE	Jodel D.112	D. A. Porter/Sturgate	
G-DAVY	Evans VP-2	D. Morris	
G-DBAL	H.S.125 Srs 3B	Falcon Jet Centre Ltd (G-BSAA)	
G-DBAR	Beech 200 Super King Air	Brown & Root (UK) Ltd	
G-DCAN	PA-38-112 Tomahawk	Airways Aero Associations Ltd/Booker	
G-DCCH	MBB Bo 105D	Devon & Cornwall Police Authority	
G-DCFB	Cessna 425	Foodbrokers Ltd (G-BMSH)	
G-DCIO	Douglas DC-10-30	British Airways Epping Forest/Gatwick	
G-DCKK	Cessna F.172N	C. R. Timber Ltd/Andrewsfield	
G-DCXL	Jodel D.140C	P. Underhill	
G-DDAY	PA-28-201T Turbo Arrow III	S. C. Walters (G-BPDO)	
G-DDCD	D.H.104 Dove 8	C. Daniel (G-ARUM)/Biggin Hill	
G-DDDV	Boeing 737-2S3	Caledonian/Gibair/Gatwick	
G-DEAL	Robinson R-22B	Ingamells (Machinery) Services Ltd	
G-DEBS	Colt AA-150 gas balloon	Hot-Air Balloon Co Ltd	
G-DEDE	Cessna 421C	Dick McNeil Associates Ltd	
G-DELB	Robinson R-22B	Derek Williams (Film Editors) Ltd	
G-DELI	Thunder Ax7-77 balloon	Thunder & Colt Ltd	
G-DEMO	BN-2T Islander	Pilatus BN Ltd (G-BKEA)/Bembridge	
G-DENS	CP.301S Smaragd	N. D. Russell & R. Pidcock	
G-DENW	PA-44-180 Seminole	D. A. Woodhams	
G-DERV	Cameron Truck SS balloon	The Hot Air Balloon Co Ltd	
G-DESS	Mooney M.20J	W. E. Newnes	
G-DEVN	D.H.104 Devon C.2 (WB533)	T. P. Luscombe & P. Gaston/Lympne	
G-DEVS	PA-28 Cherokee 180	H. C. Devenish (G-BGVJ)/Southend	
G-DEXI	Cessna 340A	Barons (UK) Ltd	
G-DEXP	ARV Super 2	Kintai Developments Ltd	
G-DFLY	PA-38-112 Tomahawk	Airways Aero Associations Ltd/Booker	
G-DFTS	Cessna FA.152	Tayside Aviation Ltd/Dundee	
G-DFVA	Cessna R.172K	R. A. Plowright	
G-DGDG	Glaser-Dirks DG.400/17	DG400 Flying Group/Lasham	
G-DHSW	Boeing 737-3Y0	Monarch Airlines Ltd/Luton	
G-DHTM	D.H.82A Tiger Moth replica	C. R. Hardiman	
G-DIAL	Cameron N-90 balloon	A. J. Street	
G-DIAN	Extra EA.230	D. M. Britten	
G-DICK	Thunder Ax6-56Z balloon	Bandag Tyre Co	
G-DIDI	PA-31-310 Turbo Navajo	Airstar (Air Transport) Ltd/Luton	
G-DIME	R. Commander 114	Badminton Horse Boxes Ltd	
G-DINA	AA-5B Tiger	Simon Deverall Print Ltd/ Compton Abbas	
G-DIPI	Cameron Tub SS balloon	Airship & Balloon Co Ltd	
G-DIPS	Taylor JT.1 Monoplane	B. J. Halls	
G-DIPZ	Colt 17A balloon	Airship & Balloon Co Ltd	
G-DIRK	Glaser-Dirks DG.400	D. M. Chalmers	
G-DIRT	Thunder Ax7-77Z balloon	R. J. Ngbaronye	
G-DISC	Cessna U.206A	I. A. Louttit (G-BGWR)/Exeter	
G-DISO	Jodel D.150	P. F. Craven & J. H. Shearer	
G-DIVA	Cessna R.172K XPII	R. A. Plowright & J. A. Kaye/ Biggin Hill	
G-DIXI	PA-31-350 Navajo Chieftain	Birmingham Aerocentre Ltd	

Notes	Reg.	Type	Owner or Operator
	G-DIZY	PA-28R-201T Turbo Arrow III	Precision Engineering (UK) Ltd
	G-DJBE	Cessna 550 Citation II	Fisons PLC/E. Midlands
	G-DJHB	Beech A23-19 Musketeer	R. A. Young & A. R. Mangham (G-AZZE)
	G-DJIM	MHCA-I	J. Crawford
	G-DJJA	PA-28-181 Archer II	Astro Technology Ltd
	G-DKDP	Grob G.109	Diss Aviation Ltd/Tibenham
	G-DKGF	Viking Dragonfly	K. G. Fathers
	G-DLRA	BN-2T Islander	Pilatus BN Ltd (G-BJYU)/Bembridge
	G-DLTA	Slingsby T.67M	Delta Flight (G-SFTX)
	G-DLTI	Robinson R-22B	Springfield Aviation Ltd
	G-DMCH	Hiller UH-12E	D. McK. Carnegie & ptnrs
	G-DMCS	PA-28R Cherokee Arrow 200-II	Trade Screen Processes (G-CPAC)
	G-DNLD	Cameron 97 Donald SS balloon	The Walt Disney Co Ltd
	G-DODD	Cessna F.172P-II	K. Watts/Elstree
	G-DODS	PA-46-310P Malibu	Abersoch Land & Sea Ltd
	G-DOFY	Bell 206B JetRanger	Walsh Aviation
	G-DOGS	Cessna R.182RG	Usoland Ltd
	G-DONS	PA-28RT-201T Turbo Arrow IV	Arrowone Group
	G-DOOK	Beech 60 Duke	Pan Gulf Construction (UK) Ltd (G-AXEN)
	G-DOOR	M.S.893E Rallye 180	C. Walsh
	G-DOOZ	AS.355F-1 Twin Squirrel	Lynton Aviation Ltd (G-BNSX)
	G-DOVE	Cessna 182Q	P. J. Contracting
	G-DRAY	Taylor JT.1 Monoplane	L. J. Dray
	G-DRJC	Boeing 757-2T7	Monarch Airlines Ltd/Luton
	G-DROP	Cessna U.206C	A. A. Louttit (G-UKNO/G-BAMN)
	G-DSAM	AS.350B Ecureuil	Samworth Brothers Ltd
	G-DSGN	Robinson R-22B	William Towns Ltd
	G-DTOO	PA-38-112 Tomahawk	A. Todd
	G-DUCH	Beech 76 Duchess	Carriage Communications Consultancy Ltd
	G-DUCK	Grumman G.44 Widgeon	L. E. Usher/Ipswich
	G-DUET	Wood Duet	C. Wood
	G-DUNN	Zenair CH.250	A. Dunn
	G-DUST	Stolp SA.300 Starduster Too	Chemtech Ltd
	G-DUVL	Cessna F.172N	Duval Studios Ltd/Denham
	G-DVON	D.H.104 Devon C.2 (VP955)	C. L. Thatcher
	G-DWHH	Boeing 737-2T7	Monarch Airlines Ltd/Luton
	G-DWMI	Bell 206L-1 LongRanger	Glenwood Helicopters Ltd/Fairoaks
	G-DXRG	Cameron 105 Agfa SS balloon	Cameron Balloons Ltd
	G-DYNE	Cessna 414	Commair Aviation Ltd/E. Midlands
	G-DYOU	PA-38-112 Tomahawk	Airways Aero Associations Ltd/Booker
	G-EAGL	Cessna 421C	Humberside Commercial Aviation Ltd
	G-EBJI	Hawker Cygnet Replica	A. V. Francis
	G-EBZN	D. H. 60X Moth	I. B. Grace (G-UAAP)
	G-ECAV	Beech 200 Super King Air	GEC Avionics Ltd/Rochester
	G-ECBH	Cessna F.150K	Air Fenland Ltd
	G-ECGC	Cessna F.172N-II	Leicestershire Aero Club Ltd
	G-ECHO	Enstrom 280C-UK-2 Shark	ALP Electrical (Maidenhead) Ltd (G-LONS/G-BDIB)/White Waltham
	G-ECMA	PA-31-310 Turbo Navajo	Elliot Bros (London) Ltd/Rochester
	G-ECOX	Grega GN.1 Air Camper	H. C. Cox
	G-EDEN	SOCATA TB.10 Tobago	N. I. Mandell & J. D. Wittich/ Elstree
	G-EDGE	Jodel D.150	A. D. Edge
	G-EDIF	Evans VP-2	R. Simpson
	G-EDIT	Beech B95 Travel Air	P. Tweedy (G-AXUX)
	G-EDNA	PA-38-112 Tomahawk	MSF Aviation Ltd
	G-EDRY	Cessna T.303	Pat Eddery Ltd
	G-EEEE	Slingsby T.31 Motor Glider	R. F. Selby
	G-EEGE	Robinson R-22A	Northern Helicopters Ltd (G-BKZK)
	G-EENY	GA-7 Cougar	Charles Henry Leasing/Elstree
	G-EESE	Cessna U.206G	D. M. Penny
	G-EEUP	SNCAN Stampe SV-4C	Minrealm Ltd
	G-EEZE	Rutan Vari-Eze	A. J. Nurse
	G-EGAP	Sequoia F.8L Falco	E. G. A. Prance
	G-EGEE	Cessna 310Q	A. J. Fuller & ptnrs (G-AZVY)
	G-EGGS	Robin DR.400/180	R. Foot
	G-EGLE	Christen Eagle II	Myrick Aviation Services Ltd
	G-EHAP	Sportavia-Pützer RF.7	M. J. Revill/Exeter
	G-EHIL	Westland-Agusta EH.101	Westland Helicopters Ltd/Yeovil
	G-EHMM	Robin DR.400/180R	Booker Gliding Club Ltd
	G-EIIO	EMB-110P2 Bandeirante	National Airways Ltd (G-DATA/G-BGNK) /Southend

Reg.	Type	Owner or Operator	Notes
G-EIIR	Cameron N-77 balloon	Major C. J. T. Davey *Silver Jubilee*	
G-EIST	Robinson R-22B	T. N. Moores	
G-EITE	Luscombe 8A Silvaire	D. L. Eite	
G-EIWT	Cessna FR.182RG	P. P. D. Howard-Johnston/Edinburgh	
G-EJCB	Agusta A.109A Mk2	J. C. Bamford Excavators Ltd	
G-EJGO	Z.226HE Trener	N. J. Radford	
G-ELEC	Westland WG.30 Srs 200	Westland Helicopters Ltd (G-BKNV)/ Yeovil	
G-ELOT	Cessna 550 Citation II	Elliotts Brick Ltd	
G-EMAK	PA-28R-201 Arrow III	Arrow Aircraft Group/E. Midlands	
G-EMKM	Jodel D.120A	Cawdor Flying Group/Inverness	
G-EMMA	Cessna F.182Q	Watkiss Group Aviation	
G-EMMS	PA-38-112 Tomahawk	G. C. J. Moffatt & Co Ltd/Cardiff	
G-EMMY	Rutan Vari-Eze	M. J. Tooze	
G-ENAM	Cessna 340A	Benham & Wilcox Ltd	
G-ENCE	Partenavia P.68B	P. A. de Courcy-Swoffe & D. S. Innes (G-OROY/G-BFSU)	
G-ENIE	T.66 Nipper 3	G. Weale/Shoreham	
G-ENII	Cessna F.172M	Keenair North West Ltd/Liverpool	
G-ENIU	PA-24 Comanche 260	A. F. Warnell (G-AVJU)/Stapleford	
G-ENNY	Cameron V-77 balloon	B. G. Jones	
G-ENOA	Cessna F.172F	M. Konstantinovic (G-ASZW)/ Stapleford	
G-ENSI	Beech F33A Bonanza	Nesstra Services (UK) Ltd	
G-EOFF	Taylor JT.2 Titch	G. H. Wylde	
G-EORG	PA-38-112 Tomahawc	Airways Aero Association/Booker	
G-EPDI	Cameron N-77 balloon	R. Moss & Pegasus Aviation Ltd	
G-ERIC	R. Commander 112TC	P. P. Patterson/Newcastle	
G-ERIK	Cameron N-77 balloon	Cultural Resource Management Ltd	
G-ERIX	Boeing-Stearman A75N-1	E. E. Rix	
G-ERMO	ARV Super 2	M. J. Holdsworth Ltd (G-BMWK)	
G-ERMS	Thunder AS-33 airship	B. R. & M. Boyle	
G-ERRY	AA-5B Tiger	P. D. Cullen (G-BFMJ)	
G-ERTY	D.H.82A Tiger Moth	J. A. Thomas & R. F. Tolhurst (G-ANDC)	
G-ESSX	PA-28-161 Warrior II	S. Harcourt (G-BHYY)/Shoreham	
G-ESTE	AA-5A Cheetah	McGeoghan Plant Hire & Excavations Ltd (G-GHNC)	
G-ETCD	Colt 77A balloon	Philips Electronics Ltd	
G-ETDA	PA-28-161 Warrior II	P. D. Foster	
G-ETDB	PA-38-112 Tomahawk	Gloucester & Cheltenham School of Flying/Staverton	
G-ETDC	Cessna 172P	Osprey Air Services Ltd	
G-ETIN	Robinson R-22B	Lullingstone Water Ltd	
G-ETON	Maule M5-235C Lunar Rocket	J. R. Heaton (G-BHDB)	
G-EURA	Agusta-Bell 47J-2	E. W. Schnedlitz (G-ASNV)	
G-EURP	Boeing 737-35B	Berlin European UK/Monarch Airlines/ Euroberlin	
G-EVAN	Taylor JT.2 Titch	E. Evans	
G-EWBJ	SOCATA TB.10 Tobago	Lydd Air Training Centre Ltd	
G-EWIZ	Pitts S-2E Special	R. H. Jago	
G-EWUD	Cessna F.172F	Viewmoor Ltd (G-ATBK)	
G-EXEC	PA-34-200 Seneca	C. R. Lord/Coventry	
G-EXEX	Cessna 404	Atlantic Air Transport Ltd/Coventry	
G-EXIT	M.S.893E Rallye 180GT	G-Exit Ltd/Rochester	
G-EXPR	Colt 90A balloon	Air Canada Ltd	
G-EYEI	Bell 206A JetRanger	Clyde Helicopters Ltd	
G-EZEE	Rutan Vari-Eze	D. & M. Schwier	
G-EZIO	EMB-120RT Brasilia	National Commuter Airways/Southend	
G-EZOS	Rutan Vari-Eze	O. Smith/Tees-side	
G-FAGN	Robinson R-22B	Fagins Toys Ltd	
G-FAIR	SOCATA TB.10 Tobago	Sally Marine Ltd/Guernsey	
G-FALC	Aeromere F.8L Falco	P. W. Hunter (G-AROT)/Elstree	
G-FALK	Sequoia F.8L Falco 4	I. Chancellor	
G-FANG	AA-5A Cheetah	George Cross Services Ltd	
G-FANL	Cessna FR.172K XP-II	J. Woodhouse & Co/Staverton	
G-FARM	SOCATA Rallye 235GT	Bristol Cars Ltd	
G-FARR	Jodel D.150	G. H. Farr	
G-FAST	Cessna 337G	Continental Acquisitions Ltd	
G-FAYE	Cessna F.150M	Cheshire Air Training School Ltd/ Liverpool	
G-FBWH	PA-28R Cherokee Arrow 180	Servicecentre Systems (Cambs) Ltd	
G-FCHJ	Cessna 340A	P. L. & M. J. E. Builder (G-BJLS)	
G-FDGM	Beech B60 Duke	Parissi Air Ltd/Perth	

Notes	Reg.	Type	Owner or Operator
	G-FEBE	Cessna 340A	C. J. Chapman
	G-FEDL	Hughes 369D	Federal Aviation Ltd
	G-FELT	Cameron N-77 balloon	Allan Industries Ltd
	G-FENI	Robinson R-22B	I. Fenwick
	G-FESL	PA-28R-201T Turbo Arrow III	Fire Engineering Services Ltd (G-BNRN)
	G-FFBR	Thunder Ax8-105 balloon	Fuji Photo Film (UK) Ltd
	G-FFEN	Cessna F.150M	Suffolk Aero Club Ltd/Ipswich
	G-FFLT	H.S.125 Srs 600B	Fairflight Ltd/Biggin Hill
	G-FFOR	Cessna 310R	G. W. Carruthers (G-BMGF)
	G-FFTN	Bell 206B JetRanger	Fountain Forestry Ltd
	G-FHAS	Scheibe SF.25E Super Falke	Tatenhill Aviation
	G-FIFI	SOCATA TB.20 Trinidad	D. J. & M. Gower (G-BMWS)
	G-FIGA	Cessna 152	Relstage Trading Ltd
	G-FIGB	Cessna 152	Fujair Flight (UK) Ltd
	G-FILE	PA-34-200T Seneca	Filemart Ltd
	G-FIMI	Bell 206L-1 LongRanger	Lynton Aviation Ltd
	G-FINN	Cameron 90 Reindeer SS balloon	Forbes Europe Inc
	G-FINS	AB-206B JetRanger 2	Willow Vale Electronics Ltd (G-FSCL)
	G-FIRE	V.S.379 Spitfire XIVc	Classic Air Displays Ltd/Kidlington
	G-FISH	Cessna 310R-II	Boston Deep Sea Fisheries Ltd/ Humberside
	G-FISK	Pazmany PL-4A	K. S. Woodard
	G-FIST	Fieseler Fi.156C Storch	Spoils Kitchen Reject Shops Ltd
	G-FIZZ	PA-28-161 Warrior II	N. C. L. & J. E. Wright
	G-FKKM	PA-28RT-201T Turbo Arrow IV	Hubert C. Leach (Overseas) Ltd
	G-FLCO	Sequoia F.8L Falco	J. B. Mowforth
	G-FLEA	SOCATA TB.10 Tobago	Fleair Trading Co/Biggin Hill
	G-FLEN	PA-28-161 Warrior II	Flentri Aircraft Leasing/Fairoaks
	G-FLIK	Pitts S.1S Special	R. P. Millinship
	G-FLIX	Cessna E.310P	C Air Ltd (G-AZFL)
	G-FLMS	Colt 600A balloon	Thunder & Colt Ltd
	G-FLPI	R. Commander 112A	Tuscany Ltd/Leicester
	G-FLYI	PA-34-200 Seneca	G. W. Plowman & Sons Ltd (G-BHVO)/ Elstree
	G-FLYV	Slingsby T.67M-200	Firefly Aerial Promotions Ltd
	G-FMUS	Robinson R-22	C. W. Cayzer (G-BJBT)
	G-FNLD	Cessna 172N	Papa Hotel Flying Group
	G-FOAL	PA-31 Turbo Navajo	W. R. C. M. Foyle (G-RMAE/G-BAEG)/ Luton
	G-FOCK	WAR Focke-Wulf Fw.190-A	P. R. Underhill
	G-FOEL	PA-31-350 Navajo Chieftain	W. R. C. M. Foyle (G-BBXR)/Luton
	G-FOGG	Cameron N-90 balloon	Derwent Valley Foods Ltd
	G-FONE	Colt Cityman SS balloon	Thunder & Colt Ltd
	G-FOOD	Beech B200 Super King Air	Specbridge Ltd/Gamston
	G-FORC	SNCAN Stampe SV-4A	J. A. Sykes
	G-FORD	SNCAN Stampe SV-4B	P. Meeson & R. A. J. Spurrell/ White Waltham
	G-FOTO	PA-E23 Aztec F	Davis Gibson Advertising Ltd (G-BJDH/ G-BDXV)/Denham
	G-FOWL	Colt 90A balloon	Chesterfield Cold Storage Ltd
	G-FRAA	Dassault Falcon 20F	FR Finances Ltd/Bournemouth
	G-FRAB	Dassault Falcon 20F	FR Finances Ltd/Bournemouth
	G-FRAC	Dassault Falcon 20F	FR Finances Ltd/Bournemouth
	G-FRAD	Dassault Falcon 20E	FR Finances Ltd (G-BCYF)/Bournemouth
	G-FRAE	Dassault Falcon 20E	FR Finances Ltd/Bournemouth
	G-FRAF	Dassault Falcon 20E	FR Finances Ltd/Bournemouth
	G-FRAG	PA-32-300 Cherokee Six	R. Goodwin & Co Ltd/Southend
	G-FRAN	Piper J-3C-90 Cub (480321)	D. E. Blaxford & ptnrs (G-BIXY)
	G-FRAX	Cessna 441	FR Finances Ltd (G-BMTZ)/ Bournemouth
	G-FRAZ	Cessna 441	FR Finances Ltd/Bournemouth
	G-FRED	FRED Srs 2	R. Cox
	G-FREE	Pitts S-2A Special	Pegasus Flying Group/Fairoaks
	G-FRJB	Britten Sheriff SA-1 ★	Aeropark/E. Midlands
	G-FROZ	Cessna 421C	Mashmor Investments Ltd
	G-FRST	PA-44-180T Turbo Seminole	Frost & Frost/Kidlington
	G-FRYS	Christen Eagle II	R. W. J. Foster
	G-FSDA	AB-206B JetRanger 2	Heli-Flair Ltd (G-AWJW)
	G-FSDC	Enstrom 280C-UK Shark	Heli-Flair Ltd (G-BKTG)
	G-FSDG	AB-206B JetRanger	Flair (Soft Drinks) Ltd (G-ROOT/G-JETR)
	G-FSDH	Hughes 269A	Heli-Flair Ltd/Shoreham
	G-FSDT	Hughes 269A	Heli-Flair Ltd/Shoreham
	G-FSPL	PA-32R-300 Lance	P. J. Withinshaw/Conington
	G-FTAX	Cessna 421C	Chaseside Holdings Ltd/Exeter

Reg.	Type	Owner or Operator	Notes
G-FTFT	Colt Financial Times SS balloon	Financial Times Ltd	
G-FTIL	Robin DR.400/180R	Flight Training International Ltd	
G-FTIM	Robin DR.400/100	Flight Training International Ltd	
G-FTIN	Robin DR.400/100	Flight Training International Ltd	
G-FTIO	Robin DR.400/100	Flight Training International Ltd	
G-FUEL	Robin DR.400/180	R. Darch/Compton Abbas	
G-FUJI	Fuji FA.200-180	G. H. Willson & ptnrs	
G-FULL	PA-28R Cherokee Arrow 200-II	Fuller Aviation (G-HWAY/G-JULI)	
G-FUND	Thunder Ax7-65Z balloon	Schroder Life Assurance Ltd	
G-FUZY	Cameron N-77 balloon	Allan Industries Ltd	
G-FUZZ	PA-18 Super Cub 95	G. W. Cline	
G-FVEE	Monnet Sonerai I	D. R. Sparke	
G-FWPW	PA-28-236 Dakota	P. A. & F. C. Winters	
G-FWRP	Cessna 421C	Vange Scaffolding & Engineering Co Ltd	
G-FXIV	V.S.379 Spitfire FR.XIV (MV370)	R. Lamplough	
G-FZZY	Colt 69A balloon	Hot-Air Balloon Co Ltd	
G-FZZZ	Colt 56A balloon	Hot-Air Balloon Co Ltd	
G-GABD	GA-7 Cougar	J. Bett/Glasgow	
G-GACA	P.57 Sea Prince T.1	Atlantic & Caribbean Aviation Ltd/Staverton	
G-GAFG	Slingsby T.67C	S. J. Donkin (G-BODJ)	
G-GAGA	AA-5B Tiger	BLS Aviation Ltd (G-BGPG)	
G-GAIR	PA-60 Aerostar 601P	Avionics Research Ltd	
G-GAJB	AA-5B Tiger	G. A. J. Bowles (G-BHZN)	
G-GALE	PA-34-200T Seneca II	Gale Construction Co Ltd/Norwich	
G-GAMA	Beech B58 Baron	Gama Aviation Ltd (G-BBSD)/Fairoaks	
G-GAME	Cessna T.303	Ripley Aviation Ltd	
G-GANE	Sequoia F.8L Falco	S. J. Gane	
G-GANJ	Fournier RF-6B-100	Soaring Equipment Ltd/Coventry	
G-GASC	Hughes 369HS	Charles Clowes (Estates) Co Ltd (G-WELD/G-FROG)	
G-GAYL	Learjet 35A	Automobile Association Developments Ltd (G-ZING)/Coventry	
G-GAZE	Robinson R-22A	G. Clarke/Stapleford	
G-GBAO	Robin R.1180TD	J. Kay-Movat	
G-GBLR	Cessna F.150L	Peter Collier Aviation Ltd	
G-GBSL	Beech 76 Duchess	Water Management Services Ltd (G-BGVG)	
G-GCAA	PA-28R Cherokee Arrow 200	Southern Air Ltd/Shoreham	
G-GCAB	PA-30 Twin Comanche 180	Southern Air Ltd/Shoreham	
G-GCAL	Douglas DC-10-10	Novair Ltd (G-BELO)/Gatwick	
G-GCAT	PA-28 Cherokee 140B	G. S. B. Large (G-BFRH)/Denham	
G-GCCL	Beech 76 Duchess	Golden Castle Caravans Ltd	
G-GCKI	Mooney M.20K	G. C. Kent/Tollerton	
G-GCNZ	Cessna 150M	Heathgrange Ltd	
G-GDAM	PA-18 Super Cub 135	G. D. A. Martin	
G-GDAY	Robinson R-22B	G. A. Watchorn	
G-GEAR	Cessna FR.182Q	Ashcombe Distributors/Sywell	
G-GEEP	Robin R.1180T	Organic Concentrates Ltd/Booker	
G-GEES	Cameron N-77 balloon	Mark Jarvis Ltd *Mark Jarvis*	
G-GEEZ	Cameron N-77 balloon	Charnwood Forest Turf Accountants Ltd	
G-GEIL	H.S.125 Srs 800B	Heron Management Ltd	
G-GEOF	Pereira Osprey 2	G. Crossley	
G-GEUP	Cameron N-77 balloon	D. P. & B. O. Turner	
G-GFLY	Cessna F.150L	W. Lancashire Aero Club Ltd/Woodvale	
G-GGGG	Thunder Ax7-77A balloon	T. A. Gilmour	
G-GHRW	PA-28RT-201 Arrow IV	Leavesden Flight Centre Ltd (G-ONAB/G-BHAK)	
G-GIGI	M.S.893A Rallye Commodore	P. J. C. Phillips (G-AYVX)	
G-GILY	Robinson R-22B	Reynard Racing Cars Ltd	
G-GINA	AS.350B Ecureuil	Endeavour Aviation Ltd	
G-GIRO	Schweizer 269C	F. J. Barnett	
G-GJCB	H.S.125 Srs 800B	J. C. Bamford Excavators Ltd	
G-GLAW	Cameron N-90 balloon	George Law Ltd	
G-GLEN	Bell 212	Autair International Ltd/Panshanger	
G-GLOR	Cessna 425	Real Estate Consultancy Services (CI) Ltd	
G-GLOS	H.P.137 Jetstream 200	British Aerospace (G-BCGU/G-AXRI)	
G-GLUE	Cameron N-65 balloon	L. J. M. Muir & G. D. Hallett	
G-GLYN	Boeing 747-211B	British Airways *City of Perth*	
G-GMAX	SNCAN Stampe SV-4C	Glidegold Ltd (G-BXNW)	

Notes	Reg.	Type	Owner or Operator
	G-GMSI	SOCATA TB.9 Tampico	Subtec Aviation Ltd
	G-GNAT	H.S. Gnat T.1 (XS101)	Ruanil Investments Ltd/Cranfield
	G-GNSY	HPR-7 Herald 209	Channel Express Air Services Ltd (G-BFRK)/Bournemouth
	G-GOGO	Hughes 369D	A. W. Alloys Ltd
	G-GOLD	Thunder Ax6-56A balloon	Joseph Terry & Sons Ltd
	G-GOLF	SOCATA TB.10 Tobago	E. H. Scamell
	G-GOMM	PA-32R-300 Lance	A. Kazaz/Leicester
	G-GONE	D.H.112 Venom FB.50	P. Meeson/Bournemouth
	G-GOOS	Cessna F.182Q	Roger Clark (Air Transport) Ltd
	G-GOSS	Jodel DR.221	M. I. Goss
	G-GOZO	Cessna R.182	Transmatic Fyllan Ltd (G-BJZO)/Cranfield
	G-GRAC	GA-7 Cougar	B. W. Wells & Burbage Farms Ltd
	G-GRAY	Cessna 172N	Truman Aviation Ltd/Tollerton
	G-GREG	Jodel DR.220 2+2	G. G. L. Thomas/Swansea
	G-GRIF	R. Commander 112TCA	International Motors Ltd (G-BHXC)
	G-GROB	Grob G.109	G-GROB Ltd
	G-GROW	Cameron N-77 balloon	Derbyshire Building Society
	G-GRUB	PA-28 Cherokee 180	E. W. Lyon (G-AYAS)
	G-GSAM	H.S.125 Srs 800B	BSM Holdings Ltd
	G-GSFC	Robinson R-22B	Stenoak Fencing & Construction Co Ltd
	G-GTAX	PA-31-350 Navajo Chieftain	Chaseside Holdings Ltd (G-OIAS)
	G-GTHM	PA-38-112 Tomahawk	Merrett Aviation Ltd
	G-GTPL	Mooney M.20K	E. G. Nash & Partners Ltd (G-BHOS)
	G-GUNN	Cessna F.172H	J. G. Gunn (G-AWGC)
	G-GUYI	PA-28-181 Archer II	B. Butler
	G-GUYS	PA-34-200T Seneca	H. Jowett & Co Ltd (G-BMWT)
	G-GWEN	Cessna F.172M	R. E. Youngsworth (G-GBLP)
	G-GWHH	AS.355F Twin Squirrel	Wimpey Homes Holdings Ltd (G-BKUL)
	G-GWIL	AS.350B Ecureuil	Talan Ltd
	G-GWIT	Cameron O-84 balloon	M. Pearce & V. J. Thorne
	G-GWYN	Cessna F.172M	C. Bosher
	G-GYAV	Cessna 172N	Fletcher Bros (Car Hire) Ltd
	G-GYRO	Bensen B.8	N. A. Pitcher & A. L. Howell
	G-GZDO	Cessna 172N	Firecrest Aviation Ltd
	G-HAEC	Commonwealth Mustang 22	R. G. Hanna/Duxford
	G-HAGS	Bensen B.8	R. H. Harry
	G-HAIG	Rutan LongEz	P. N. Haigh
	G-HAJJ	Glaser-Dirks DG.400	P. W. Endean
	G-HALK	H.S.125 Srs 600B	Chelsea Girl Ltd (G-PJWB/G-DMAN)
	G-HALL	PA-22 Tri-Pacer 160	F. P. Hall (G-ARAH)
	G-HALP	SOCATA TB.10 Tobago	D. Halpera (G-BITD)/Elstree
	G-HAMA	Beech 200 Super King Air	Gama Aviation Ltd/Fairoaks
	G-HAMP	Bellanca 7ACA Champ	R. J. Grimstead
	G-HANS	Robin DR.400 2+2	Headcorn Flying School Ltd
	G-HAPR	B.171 Sycamore HR.14 (XG547) ★	British Rotorcraft Museum
	G-HARE	Cameron N-77 balloon	M. F. Glue
	G-HASL	AA-5A Cheetah	D.B.G. Ltd (G-BGSL)/(stored)
	G-HAUL	Westland WG.30 Srs 300	Westland Helicopters PLC/Yeovil
	G-HAWK	H.S.1182 Hawk	British Aerospace/Dunsfold
	G-HAZE	Thunder Ax8-90 balloon	H. A. Ingham
	G-HBCA	Agusta A.109A-II	British Car Auctions (Aviation) Ltd
	G-HBCO	PA-31-325 Navajo C/R	Holding & Barnes Ltd
	G-HBUS	Bell 206L-1 LongRanger	Foreman Group Holdings Ltd
	G-HDBA	H.S.748 Srs 2B	British Airways Glen Esk/Glasgow
	G-HDBB	H.S.748 Srs 2B	British Airways Glen Clova/Glasgow
	G-HDBC	H.S.748 Srs 2B	British Airways/Glasgow
	G-HEAD	Colt 56 balloon	Colt Balloons Ltd
	G-HELI	Saro Skeeter Mk 12 (XM556) ★	British Rotorcraft Museum
	G-HELN	PA-18 Super Cub 95	J. J. Anziani (G-BKDG)/Booker
	G-HELO	Bell 206B JetRanger 2	Surrey Helicopter Hire Ltd (G-BAZN)
	G-HELP	Colt 17A balloon	Ligher-Than-Air Ltd
	G-HELX	Cameron N-31 balloon	Hot-Air Balloon Co Ltd
	G-HELY	Agusta 109A	Castle Air Charters Ltd
	G-HEMS	SA.365N Dauphin 2	Express Newspapers PLC
	G-HENS	Cameron N-65 balloon	Horrells Dairies Ltd
	G-HERB	PA-28R-201 Arrow III	Woodgate Aviation Services Ltd
	G-HERO	PA-32RT-300 Lance II	C. Moore (G-BOGN)
	G-HEWI	Piper J-3C-90 Cub	Denham Grasshopper Group (G-BLEN)
	G-HEWT	Hughes 369D	A. H. Canvin
	G-HEYY	Cameron 77 Bear SS balloon	Hot-Air Balloon Co Ltd George

Reg.	Type	Owner or Operator	Notes
G-HFCB	Cessna F.150L	Horizon Flying Club Ltd (G-AZVR)/ Ipswich	
G-HFCI	Cessna F.150L	Horizon Flying Club Ltd/Ipswich	
G-HFCL	Cessna F.152	Horizon Flying Club Ltd (G-BGLR)/ Ipswich	
G-HFCT	Cessna F.152	P. Ratcliffe	
G-HFGP	Beech 200 Super King Air	Hughes Food Group PLC	
G-HFTG	PA-23 Aztec 250E	Field Aircraft Services (Heathrow) Ltd (G-BSOB/G-BCJR)	
G-HGPC	BN-2A-27 Islander	Para-Freight Ltd (G-FANS)/Halfpenny Green	
G-HGPI	SOCATA TB.20 Trinidad	K. Piggott	
G-HIGG	Beech 200 Super King Air	National Airways (G-BLKN)/Southend	
G-HIGS	Cessna 404 Titan	Artac Airchartering Services Ltd (G-ODAS)/Southend	
G-HIHI	PA-32R-301 Saratoga SP	N. M. Jagger	
G-HILR	Hiller UH-12E	G. & S. G. Neal (Helicopters) Ltd	
G-HILS	Cessna F.172H	Heathfield Investments Ltd (G-AWCH)	
G-HILT	SOCATA TB.10 Tobago	A. Castell	
G-HINT	Cameron N-90 balloon	Hinton Garage Bath Ltd	
G-HIRE	GA-7 Cougar	London Aerial Tours Ltd (G-BGSZ)/ Biggin Hill	
G-HIVA	Cessna 337A	High Voltage Applications Ltd (G-BAES)	
G-HIVE	Cessna F.150M	M. P. Lynn (G-BCXT)/Sibson	
G-HJET	AS.355F-1 Twin Squirrel	BAC Ltd	
G-HLFT	SC.5 Belfast 2	HeavyLift Cargo Airlines Ltd/Stansted	
G-HLIX	Cameron 80 Oil Can balloon	Hot-Air Balloon Co Ltd	
G-HMAN	AS.305B Ecureuil	Direct Produce Supplies Ltd (G-SKIM/ G-BIVP)	
G-HMMM	Cameron N-65 balloon	S. Moss	
G-HMPH	Bell 206B JetRanger2	Mightycraft Ltd (G-BBUY)	
G-HOCK	PA-28 Cherokee 180	C. Hampshire & B. Allan (G-AVSH)	
G-HOFM	Cameron N-56 balloon	Hot-Air Balloon Co Ltd	
G-HOLL	Cessna 500 Citation	Albion Aviation Ltd	
G-HOLT	Taylor JT.1 Monoplane	K. D. Holt	
G-HOME	Colt 77A balloon	Anglia Balloon School *Tardis*	
G-HONK	Cameron O-105 balloon	T. F. W. Dixon & Son Ltd	
G-HOOV	Cameron N-56 balloon	H. R. Evans	
G-HOPE	Beech F33A Bonanza	Eurohaul Ltd/Southampton	
G-HOPS	Thunder Ax8-90 balloon	A. Ahlstrom	
G-HORN	Cameron V-77 balloon	Travel Gas (Midlands) Ltd	
G-HOST	Cameron N-77 balloon	D. Grimshaw	
G-HOTI	Colt 77A balloon	R. Ollier	
G-HOTL	Cessna 550 Citation II	Queens Moat Houses PLC	
G-HOTS	Thunder Colt AS-80 airship	Island Airship Ltd	
G-HOUL	FRED Srs 2	D. M. M. Richardson	
G-HOUS	Colt 31A balloon	Anglia Balloons Ltd	
G-HOVR	Robinson R-22B	Tukair Aircraft Charter	
G-HPVC	Partenavia P.68B	Airtime (Hampshire) Ltd	
G-HRAY	AB-206B JetRanger 3	Hecray Co Ltd (G-VANG/G-BIZA)	
G-HRIO	Robin HR.100/120	Moto Baldet (Northampton) Ltd/Sywell	
G-HRIS	Cessna P210N	Birmingham Aviation Ltd	
G-HRLM	Brugger MB.2 Colibri	R. A. Harris	
G-HRZN	Colt 77A balloon	D. Gaze	
G-HSDW	Bell 206B JetRanger	Winfield Shoe Co Ltd	
G-HTAX	PA-31-350 Navajo Chieftain	Chaseside Holdings Ltd	
G-HUBB	Partenavia P.68B	Hubbardair Ltd/Norwich	
G-HUEY	Bell UH-1H	RAF Benevolent Fund/Odiham	
G-HUFF	Cessna 182P	J. R. W. Keates/Biggin Hill	
G-HUGE	Boeing 747-2D3B	British Airways *City of Exeter*	
G-HULL	Cessna F.150M	A. D. McLeod	
G-HUMF	Robinson R-22B	Hands Technical Services Ltd	
G-HUMP	Beech 95-B55 Baron	J. H. Humphreys (G-BAMI)/Guernsey	
G-HUMT	Bell 206B JetRanger	H. J. Walters	
G-HUNN	Hispano HA.1112MIL	Charles Church Displays Ltd (G-BJZZ)	
G-HUNY	Cessna F.150G	T. J. Lynn (G-AVGL)	
G-HURI	CCF Hawker Hurricane IIB	B. J. S. Grey	
G-HVRD	PA-31-350 Navajo Chieftain	Biggin Hill Executive Aviation Ltd (G-BEZU)	
G-HWBK	Agusta A.109A	Camlet Helicopters Ltd	
G-HWKN	PA-31P Pressurised Navajo	Earlyexact Ltd	
G-HYGA	H.S.125 Srs 800B	York Aviation Ltd	
G-HYLT	PA-32R-301 Saratoga	G-Air Ltd/Goodwood	

Notes	Reg.	Type	Owner or Operator
	G-IBAC	Beech 95-58 Baron	BAC Aviation Ltd/Southend
	G-IBAK	Cessna 421C	Middle East Business Club Ltd
	G-IBET	Cameron 70 Can SS balloon	Bass & Tennent Sales Ltd
	G-IBFW	PA-28R-201 Arrow III	B. Walker & Co (Dursley) Ltd & J. & C. Ward (Holdings) Ltd/ Staverton
	G-IBLW	BAe Jetstream 3109	Aliblu Airways (Italy)
	G-IBLX	BAe Jetstream 3109	Aliblu Airways (Italy)
	G-IBTY	Boeing 737-2E3	British Airways/GB Airways (G-BNZT)
	G-IBTZ	Boeing 737-2U4	British Airways (G-OSLA)
	G-ICED	Cessna 501 Citation	Iceland Frozen Foods PLC/Manchester
	G-IDDY	D.H.C.1 Super Chipmunk	A. J. E. Ditheridge (G-BBMS)
	G-IDEA	AA.5A Cheetah	P. W. Spencer (G-BGNO)/Biggin Hill
	G-IDJB	Cessna 150L	R. J. Browne
	G-IDWR	Hughes 369HS	Ryburn Air Ltd (G-AXEJ)
	G-IEPF	Robinson R-22B	Airmarch Ltd
	G-IESA	Cessna 421C	Primerent Ltd
	G-IESH	D.H.82A Tiger Moth	I. E. S. Huddleston (G-ANPE)
	G-IFIT	PA-31-350 Navajo Chieftain	Walsh Aviation (G-NABI/G-MARG)
	G-IFLI	AA.5A Cheetah	Biggin Hill School of Flying
	G-IFLP	PA-34-200T Seneca II	Golf-Sala Ltd
	G-IFTA	PA-31-350 Navajo Chieftain	Interflight (Air Charters) Ltd (G-BAVM)/ Gatwick
	G-IFTD	Cessna 404	Interflight (Air Charters) Ltd (G-BKUN)/ Gatwick
	G-IGAR	PA-31-310 Turbo Navajo C	BWOC Ltd
	G-IGON	PA-31-310 Turbo Navajo	Air Charter (Scotland) Ltd/Glasgow
	G-IIRR	G.1159 Gulfstream 2	Rolls-Royce PLC/Filton
	G-IJET	H.S.125 Srs 700B	Yeates of Leicester Ltd (G-RACL)
	G-IKIS	Cessna 210M	A. C. Davison
	G-ILEG	Robin HR.100/200B	S. V. Swallow (G-AZHK)
	G-ILLY	PA-28-181 Archer II	A. G. & K. M. Spiers
	G-ILSE	Corby CJ-1 Starlet	S. Stride
	G-IMBE	PA-31 Turbo Navajo	Ambrion Aviation Ltd (G-BXYB/ G-AXYB)/Leavesden
	G-IMLH	Bell 206A JetRanger 3	Subaru (UK) Ltd
	G-IMLI	Cessna 310Q	Michael Leonard Interiors Ltd (G-AZYK)/ Blackbushe
	G-IMPW	PA-32R-301 Saratoga SP	Bellman Investments Ltd
	G-INAV	Aviation Composites Mercury	Aviation Composites Co Ltd
	G-INCA	Glaser-Dirks DG.400	H. W. Ober
	G-INDC	Cessna T.303	Howarth Timber (Aircharters) Ltd
	G-INGB	Robinson R-22B	Filemart Ltd
	G-INMO	PA-31-310 Turbo Navajo	Subaru (UK) Ltd/Coventry
	G-INNY	SE-5A Replica (F5459)	R. M. Ordish/Old Sarum
	G-INOW	Monnet Moni	T. W. Clark
	G-IOOI	Robin DR.400/160	Ten Tenths Ltd
	G-IOSI	Jodel DR.1051	R. G. E. Simpson & A. M. Alexander
	G-IPEC	SIAI-Marchetti S.205-18F	P. J. Annard & G. Hunter (G-AVEG)
	G-IPPM	SA.102-5 Cavalier	I. D. Perry & P. S. Murfitt
	G-IPRA	Beech A200 Super King Air	IPRA Ltd (G-BGRD)/Stansted
	G-IPSI	Grob G.109B	J. Statham (G-BMLO)
	G-IPSY	Rutan Vari-Eze	R. A. Fairclough/Biggin Hill
	G-IRIS	AA-5B Tiger	E. I. Bett (G-BIXU)
	G-IRLS	Cessna FR.172J	Starvillas Ltd/Luton
	G-ISIS	D.H.82A Tiger Moth	D. R. & M. Wood (G-AODR)
	G-ISLE	Short SD3-60	Manx Airlines Ltd/Loganair Ltd (G-BLEG)
	G-ISMO	Robinson R-22B	Alphameric Systems Ltd
	G-ITTU	PA-23 Aztec 250E	London Flight Centre (Stansted) Ltd & A. F. Aviation Ltd (G-BCSW)
	G-ITUP	Hughes 369D	David Richards Autosport Ltd (G-KSBF/ G-BMJH)
	G-IVAN	Shaw TwinEze	I. Shaw
	G-IVOR	Aeronca 11AC Chief	E. T. Wicks
	G-IWPL	Cessna F.172M	Reedy Supplies Ltd/Exeter
	G-IXCC	V.S.361 Spitfire LF.IXe	Charles Church Displays Ltd
	G-IZMO	Thunder Ax8-90 balloon	Landrell Fabric Engineering Ltd
	G-JACT	Partenavia P.68C	JCT 600 Ltd (G-NVIA)/Leeds
	G-JADE	Beech 95-58 Baron	Myrick Aviation Services Ltd
	G-JAJV	Partenavia P.68C	Galecall Ltd
	G-JAKE	D.H.C.1 Chipmunk 22	J. M. W. Henstock (G-BBMY)/ Netherthorpe

Reg.	Type	Owner or Operator	Notes
G-JAKY	PA-31-325 Turbo Navajo C/R	Ace Aviation Ltd/Glasgow	
G-JANA	PA-28-181 Archer II	Janair Services Ltd/Stapleford	
G-JANE	Cessna 340A	Bumbles Ltd/Jersey	
G-JANS	Cessna FR.172J	I. G. Aizlewood/Luton	
G-JANT	PA-28-181 Archer II	Janair Services Ltd/Stapleford	
G-JASM	Robinson R-22A	J. L. Lawrence & ptnrs	
G-JASP	PA-23 Turbo Aztec 250E	Landsurcon (Air Survey) Ltd/Staverton	
G-JAZZ	AA-5A Cheetah	Falcon Flying Services/Biggin Hill	
G-JBET	Beech F33A Bonanza	Air Hanson Aircraft Sales Ltd/ Blackbushe	
G-JBJB	Colt 69A balloon	Justerini & Brooks Ltd	
G-JBUS	FRED Srs 2	R. V. Joyce	
G-JCUB	PA-18 Super Cub 135	Piper Cub Consortium Ltd/Jersey	
G-JDEE	SOCATA TB.20 Trinidad	John Dee Transport Ltd (G-BKLA)	
G-JDHI	Enstrom F-28C-UK	Valiant Press Ltd (G-BCOT)	
G-JDIX	Mooney M.20B	J. E. Dixon (G-ARTB)	
G-JDTI	Cessna 421C	Eastfield Air Ltd/Sturgate	
G-JEAA	F.27 Friendship Mk 500F	Jersey European Airways Ltd	
G-JEAB	F.27 Friendship Mk 500F	Jersey European Airways Ltd	
G-JEAC	D.H.C.6 Twin Otter 310	Guide Leasing Ltd (G-BGMC)	
G-JEAN	Cessna 500 Citation	Foster Associates Ltd	
G-JEET	Cessna FA.152	Falcon Flying Services (G-BHMF)/ Biggin Hill	
G-JEFF	PA-38-112 Tomahawk	R. J. Alford	
G-JENA	Mooney M.20K	P. Leverkuehn/Biggin Hill	
G-JENI	Cessna R.182	Datamart (Scotland) Ltd/Edinburgh	
G-JENN	AA-5B Tiger	R. P. Coyle & R. Shearwood	
G-JENS	SOCATA Rallye 100ST	Palmer Pastoral Co Ltd (G-BDEG)	
G-JENY	Baby Great Lakes	J. M. C. Pothecary	
G-JERY	AB-206B JetRanger 2	Heliwork Services Ltd (G-BDBR)/ Thruxton	
G-JEST	PA-22 Tri-Pacer 160	Saltair Ltd (G-ARGY)	
G-JETA	Cessna 550 Citation II	IDS Aircraft Ltd/Heathrow	
G-JETC	Cessna 550 Citation II	IDS Aircraft Ltd/Heathrow	
G-JETE	Cessna 500 Citation	IDS Aircraft Ltd (G-BCKM)/Heathrow	
G-JETH	Hawker Sea Hawk FGA.6 ★	P. G. Vallence Ltd/Charlwood	
G-JETI	H.S.125 Srs 800B	Yeates of Leicester Ltd	
G-JETM	Gloster Meteor T.7	Aces High Ltd/North Weald	
G-JETP	Hunting Jet Provost T.54A	LGH Aviation Ltd/Cranfield	
G-JETS	A.61 Terrier 2	J. E. Tootell (G-ASOM)	
G-JETX	Bell 206B JetRanger	Tripgate Ltd	
G-JFRS	Cessna 550 Citation II	Paramount Executive Ltd/Birmingham	
G-JFWI	Cessna F.172N	Fleetair Ltd/Goodwood	
G-JGAL	Beech E90 King Air	Vaux (Aviation) Ltd/Newcastle	
G-JGCL	Cessna 414A	Westair Flying Services Ltd/Blackpool	
G-JGFF	AB-206B JetRanger 3	S.W. Electricity Board/Lulsgate	
G-JHEW	Robinson R-22B	Burbage Farms Ltd	
G-JILL	R. Commander 112TCA	Hanover Aviation/Elstree	
G-JIMS	Cessna 340A-II	Granpack Ltd (G-PETE)/Leavesden	
G-JJAN	PA-28-181 Archer II	J. A. Powell	
G-JJSG	Learjet 35A	Smurfit Ltd	
G-JLBZ	Bell 222	Air Hanson Sales Ltd (G-BNDB)	
G-JLEE	AB-206B JetRanger	Lee Aviation Ltd (G-JOKE/G-CSKY/ G-TALY)	
G-JLMW	Cameron V-77 balloon	J. L. M. Watkins	
G-JLRW	Beech 76 Duchess	B. Walker & Co (Dursley) Ltd	
G-JMDD	Cessna 340A	Thoroughbred Technology Ltd	
G-JMFW	Taylor JT.1 Monoplane	G. J. M. F. Winder	
G-JMTT	PA-28R-201T Turbo Arrow III	Thoroughbred Technology Ltd (G-BMHM)	
G-JMWT	SOCATA TB.10 Tobago	Halton Communications Ltd/Liverpool	
G-JODL	Jodel DR.1050M	S. R. Winder	
G-JOEY	BN-2A Mk III-2 Trislander	Aurigny Air Services (G-BDGG)/ Guernsey	
G-JOIN	Cameron V-65 balloon	Derbyshire Building Society	
G-JOLY	Cessna 120	J. D. Tarrant/Bristol	
G-JONE	Cessna 172M	A. Pierce	
G-JONI	Cessna FA.152	Luton Flight Training Ltd (G-BFTU)	
G-JONO	Colt 77A balloon	The Sandcliffe Motor Group	
G-JONS	PA-31-350 Navajo Chieftain	Riordan Group Ltd	
G-JORR	AS.350B Ecureuil	Helicopters UK Ltd (G-BJMY)	
G-JOSH	Cameron N-105 balloon	Duskytone Ltd	
G-JRBI	AS.350B Ecureuil	Berkeley Leisure Group Ltd (G-BKJY)	
G-JSSD	SA. Jetstream 3001	British Aerospace (G-AXJZ)/Prestwick	

Notes	Reg.	Type	Owner or Operator
	G-JTCA	PA-23 Aztec 250E	J. D. Tighe (G-BBCU)/Sturgate
	G-JUDE	CEA DR.400/180	L. R. Marks
	G-JUDI	AT-6D Harvard II (FX301)	A. Haig-Thomas
	G-JUDY	AA-5A Cheetah	Biggin Hill School of Flying
	G-JUIN	Cessna 303	Michael Newman Aviation Ltd/Denham
	G-JUNG	C.A.S.A. 1.131E Jungmann	M. Q. Connor
	G-JURG	R. Commander 114A	Jurgair Ltd
	G-JVAJ	PA-31T1 Cheyenne	Jacques Vert PLC
	G-JVJA	Partenavia P.68C	Twinflite Aviation Ltd (G-BMEI)
	G-JVMR	Partenavia P.68B	Sonardyne Ltd (G-JCTI/G-OJOE)/ Blackbushe
	G-JWDS	Cessna F.150G	London Aerial Tours Ltd (G-AVNB)
	G-JWIV	Jodel DR.1051	R. A. Bragger
	G-JWSD	Robinson R-22B	J. W. Sparrow Developments Ltd
	G-KADY	Rutan Long Ez	M. W. Caddy
	G-KAFE	Cameron N-65 balloon	Hot-Air Balloon Co Ltd
	G-KAIR	PA-28-181 Archer II	Academy Lithoplates Ltd/Aldergrove
	G-KARI	Fuji FA.200-160	C. J. Zetter (G-BBRE)
	G-KATE	Westland WG.30 Srs 100	Helicopter Hire Ltd/Southend
	G-KATH	Cessna P.210N	Wilson-Air Ltd
	G-KATS	PA-28 Cherokee 140	R. K. Buckle (G-BIRC)/Booker
	G-KBCA	Beech 200 Super King Air	British Car Auctions (Aviation) Ltd
	G-KBPI	PA-28-161 Warrior II	K. B. Page (Aviation) Ltd (G-BFSZ)/ Shoreham
	G-KCAS	Beech 95-B55 Baron	KC Air Services Ltd
	G-KCIG	Sportavia RF-5B	Exeter Sperber Syndicate Ltd
	G-KDFF	Scheibe SF.25E Super Falke	Deeside Super Falke Group
	G-KDIX	Jodel D.9 Bebe	D. J. Wells
	G-KEAA	Beech 65-70 Queenair	Kent Executive Aviation Ltd (G-REXP/ G-AYPC)
	G-KEAB	Beech 65-B80 Queen Air	Kent Executive Aviation Ltd (G-BSSL/ G-BFEP)
	G-KEAC	Beech 65-A80 Queen Air	Kent Executive Aviation Ltd (G-REXY/ G-AVNG)
	G-KEEN	Stolp SA.300 Starduster Too	L. V. B. van Groenou
	G-KEMC	Grob G.109	Eye-Fly Ltd
	G-KENN	Robinson R-22B	Thetford Compactors Finance Ltd
	G-KERC	Nord NC.854S	Kirk Aviation
	G-KERR	Cessna FR.172K-XP	A. G. Chrismas Ltd/Shoreham
	G-KERY	PA-28 Cherokee 180	Kerrytype Ltd (G-ATWO)/Goodwood
	G-KEYB	Cameron O-84 balloon	B. P. Key
	G-KEYS	PA-23 Aztec 250F	Wards Aviation Ltd
	G-KEYY	Cameron N-77 balloon	Business Design Group Ltd (G-BORZ)
	G-KFDF	Bell 206B JetRanger 2	Hecray Ltd
	G-KFIT	Beech F90 King Air	Kwik Fit Euro Ltd (G-BHUS)/Edinburgh
	G-KFOX	Denney Aerocraft Kitfox	J. Hannibal
	G-KHRE	M.S.893E Rallye 150SV	Kenlyn Enterprises Ltd/Shoreham
	G-KIAM	Grob G.109B	D. T. Hulme
	G-KIDS	PA-34-220T Seneca III	BWOC Ltd
	G-KILY	Robinson R-22A	Julians Supermarket Ltd
	G-KINE	AA-5A Cheetah	G. W. Plowman Ltd
	G-KING	PA-38-112 Tomahawk	M. Hunter
	G-KIRK	Piper J-3C-65 Cub	M. J. Kirk
	G-KISS	Rand KR-2	A. J. Barthwick
	G-KITE	PA-28-181 Archer II	World Business Publications Ltd/Elstree
	G-KJET	Beech B90 King Air	Hawk Aviation Ltd (G-AXFE)
	G-KKUH	Boeing 737-3Q8	Air 2000 Ltd/Manchester
	G-KLAY	Enstrom 280C Shark	Daron Motors Ltd (G-BGZD)
	G-KMAC	Bell 206B JetRanger	Specbridge Ltd
	G-KNOW	PA-32 Cherokee Six 300	P. H. Knowland
	G-KODA	Cameron O-77 balloon	United Photofinishers Ltd
	G-KOOL	D.H.104 Devon C.2 ★	E. Surrey Technical College/nr Redhill
	G-KORN	Cameron 70 Brentzen SS balloon	Cameron Balloons Ltd
	G-KOTA	PA-28-236 Dakota	Klingair Ltd/Conington
	G-KRIS	Maule M5-235C Lunar Rocket	Lord Howard de Walden
	G-KUKU	Pfalzkuku (BS676)	A. D. Lawrence
	G-KUTU	Quickie Q2	J. Parkinson & ptnrs
	G-KWAX	Cessna 182E Skylane	A. R. Carrillo/Bournemouth
	G-KWIK	Partenavia P.68B	Birchwood Aviation Ltd
	G-KYAK	Yakolev C-11 (00)	R. Lamplough/Duxford
	G-LADE	PA-32 Cherokee Six 300E	Freshcode Ltd/White Waltham
	G-LAGR	Cameron N-90 balloon	Bass & Tennent Sales Ltd

Reg.	Type	Owner or Operator	Notes
G-LAKE	Lake LA.250	Stanford Ltd	
G-LAKI	Jodel DR.1050	V. Panteli	
G-LAMB	Beech C90 King Air	Lambson Group Ltd	
G-LAMS	Cessna F.152	J. J. Baumhardt/Southend	
G-LANA	SOCATA TB.10 Tobago	Pektron Ltd	
G-LANC	Avro 683 Lancaster X ★	Imperial War Museum/Duxford	
G-LAND	Robinson R-22B	Charter Group PLC	
G-LANE	Cessna F.172N	Bantin & Kingman Ltd	
G-LARK	Helton Lark 95	J. Fox	
G-LASH	Monnet Sonerai II	A. Lawson	
G-LASS	Rutan Vari-Eze	G. Lewis/Liverpool	
G-LATC	EMB-110P1 Bandeirante	National Airways/Business Air	
G-LAZE	Jodel DR.1050	N. B. Holmes	
G-LBAT	Pitts S-1S Special	C. J. D. Hackett (G-UCCI/G-BIYN)	
G-LBRC	PA-28RT-201 Arrow IV	R. Chown	
G-LCOK	Colt 69A balloon	Hot-Air Balloon Co Ltd (G-BLWI)	
G-LDYS	Colt 56A balloon	A. Green	
G-LEAM	PA-28-236 Dakota	Ritair Ltd (G-BHLS)	
G-LEAN	Cessna FR.182	J. G. Hogg (G-BGAP)	
G-LEAP	BN-2B Islander	Army Parachute Association (G-BLND)/Netheravon	
G-LEAR	Learjet 35A	Northern Executive Aviation Ltd/Manchester	
G-LEAU	Cameron N-31 balloon	Balloon Stable Ltd	
G-LECA	AS.355F-1 Twin Squirrel	S. W. Electricity Board (G-BNBK)/Bristol	
G-LEEM	PA-28R Cherokee Arrow 200-II	B. J. Mounce (G-BJXW)	
G-LEES	Glaser-Dirks DG.400	I. C. Lees	
G-LEGS	Short SD3-60	Manx Airlines Ltd (G-BLEF)/Ronaldsway	
G-LEIC	Cessna FA.152	Leicestershire Aero Club Ltd	
G-LEIS	Bell 206-1 LongRanger	Leisure & Retail Consultants Ltd	
G-LENN	Cameron V-56 balloon	Anglia Balloon School Ltd	
G-LENS	Thunder Ax7-77Z balloon	Big Yellow Balloon Group	
G-LEON	PA-31-350 Navajo Chieftain	Chauffair Ltd/Blackbushe	
G-LEOS	Robin DR.400/120	Aeromarine Ltd	
G-LEPF	Fairchild 24R-46A Argus III	J. M. Greenland	
G-LEPI	Colt 16A balloon	Thunder & Colt Ltd	
G-LEXI	Cameron N-77 balloon	R. H. Welch	
G-LEZE	Rutan Long Ez	K. G. M. Loyal & ptnrs	
G-LFCA	Cessna F.152	Midland Aircraft Leasing Ltd	
G-LFIX	V.S.509 Spitfire T.IX (ML407)	C. P. B. Horsley & E. N. Grace/Goodwood	
G-LIBS	Hughes 369HS	Satinclass Ltd	
G-LICK	Cessna 172N	Dacebow Ltd (G-BNTR)	
G-LIDE	PA-31-350 Navajo Chieftain	Oxford Aero Charter Ltd/Kidlington	
G-LIFE	Thunder Ax6-56Z balloon	Schroder Life Assurance Ltd	
G-LIGG	Cessna F.182Q	Navair Ltd (G-THAM)	
G-LIMA	R. Commander 114	P. E. Williams	
G-LINC	Hughes 369HS	John Holborn (Helicopters) Ltd	
G-LING	Thunder Ax7-65 balloon	C. W. G. Rigby	
G-LIOA	Lockheed 10A Electra ★ (NC5171N)	Science Museum/Wroughton	
G-LION	PA-18 Super Cub 135 (542457)	A. W. Kennedy	
G-LIPP	BN-2T Turbine Islander	Rhine Army Parachute Association (G-BKJG)	
G-LISA	Steen Skybolt	T. C. Humphreys	
G-LITE	R. Commander 112A	Rhoburt Ltd/Manchester	
G-LIZY	Westland Lysander III	G. A. Warner/Duxford	
G-LJET	Learjet 35A	Atlantic Learjet Sales Ltd	
G-LLAI	Colt 21A balloon	Lighter-Than-Air Ltd	
G-LOAG	Cameron N-77 balloon	Matthew Gloag & Son Ltd	
G-LOAN	Cameron N-77 balloon	Newbury Building Soc	
G-LOCH	Piper J-3C-90 Cub	J. M. Greenland	
G-LOND	V.806 Viscount	Calcos International Airways Ltd (G-AOYI)	
G-LONG	Bell 206L LongRanger	Air Hanson Ltd/Brooklands	
G-LOOP	Pitts S-1C Special	R. I. Warman	
G-LORD	PA-34-200T Seneca II	C. R. Lord	
G-LORI	H.S.125 Srs 403B	Re-Enforce Trading Co Ltd (G-AYOJ)	
G-LORY	Thunder Ax4-31Z balloon	A. J. Moore	
G-LOSM	Gloster Meteor NF.11 (WM167)	LGH Aviation Ltd	
G-LOSS	Cameron N-77 balloon	J. A. Kershaw	
G-LOTI	Bleriot XI (replica)	M. L. Beach	
G-LOVX	Cessna 441 Conquest	Lovaux Ltd (G-BLCJ)	
G-LOWE	Monnet Sonerai II	P. Fabish	

143

Notes	Reg.	Type	Owner or Operator
	G-LOYD	SA.341G Gazelle Srs 1	Appollo Manufacturing (Derby) Ltd (G-SFTC)
	G-LRII	Bell 206L LongRanger	Carroll Industries Leasing Ltd
	G-LSFI	AA-5A Cheetah	BLS Aviation Ltd (G-BGSK)/Elstree
	G-LSHI	Colt 77A balloon	Lambert Smith Hampton Ltd
	G-LSMI	Cessna F.152	Andrewsfield Flying Club Ltd
	G-LUAR	SOCATA TB.10 Tobago	L. R. & L. M. Marks/Southampton
	G-LUBE	Cameron N-77 balloon	A. C. K. Rawson
	G-LUCA	Thunder Ax7-77Z balloon	Lucas Aerospace Ltd
	G-LUCK	Cessna F.150M	T. J. C. Darby
	G-LUKE	Rutan LongEz	S. G. Busby
	G-LULU	Grob G.109	Strathtay Flying Group
	G-LUNA	PA-32RT-300T Turbo Lance II	Martin Brundle (Overseas) Ltd/ Shipdham
	G-LUSC	Luscombe 8E Silvaire	M. Fowler
	G-LUXE	BAe 146-300	British Aerospace PLC (G-SSSH)/ Hatfield
	G-LYNN	PA-32RT-300 Lance II	Neilson Leisure Group Ltd (G-BGNY)/ Leeds
	G-LYNX	Westland WG.13 Lynx	Westland Helicopters Ltd/Yeovil
	G-LYTE	Thunder Ax7-77 balloon	A. S. Morton
	G-MABI	Cessna F.150L	Anglian Flight Training Ltd (G-BGOJ)/ Norwich
	G-MACH	SIAI-Marchetti SF.260	Cheyne Motors Ltd/Popham
	G-MACK	PA-28R Cherokee Arrow 200	Grumman Travel (Surrey) Ltd
	G-MAFF	BN-2T Islander	FR Aviation Ltd/(G-BJEO)/Bournemouth
	G-MAFI	Dornier Do.228-200	FR Finances Ltd/Bournemouth
	G-MAGG	Pitts S-1SE Special	C. A. Boardman
	G-MAGS	Cessna 340A	Tunstall Group PLC
	G-MAGY	AS.350B Ecureuil	Quantel Ltd (G-BIYC)
	G-MALA	PA-28-181 Archer II	H. Burtwhistle & Son (G-BIIU)
	G-MALC	AA-5 Traveler	C. B. Drew (G-BCPM)
	G-MALK	Cessna F.172N	R. R. & M. Mackay/Liverpool
	G-MALS	Mooney M.20K-231	P. B. Lewis
	G-MAMA	Cessna 550 Citation II	McCarthy & Stone (Group Services) Ltd
	G-MAMO	Cameron V-77 balloon	The Marble Mosaic Co Ltd
	G-MANN	SA.341G Gazelle	Robert Fraser & Partners Ltd (G-BKLW)
	G-MANT	Cessna 210L	B. W. Wells & Burbage Farms Ltd (G-MAXY)
	G-MANX	FRED Srs 2	T. A. Timms
	G-MARC	AS.350B Ecureuil	Denis Ferranti Hoverknights Ltd (G-BKHU)
	G-MARE	Schweizer 269C	The Earl of Caledon
	G-MARI	PA-32R-301 Saratoga SP	A. Somverville
	G-MARR	Cessna 421C	Jacmil Ltd (G-JTIE/G-RBBE)
	G-MARY	Cassutt Special 1	J. Chadwick/Redhill
	G-MATI	Stolp SA.200 Starduster Too	M. R. Clarke
	G-MATP	BAe 748ATP	British Aerospace PLC/Woodford
	G-MATS	Colt GA-42 balloon	Thunder & Colt Ltd
	G-MATT	Robin R.2160	Sierra Flying Group (G-BKRC)/ Newcastle
	G-MAUK	Colt 77A balloon	Lighter-Than-Air Ltd
	G-MAWL	Maule M4-210C Rocket	D. Group
	G-MAXI	PA-34-200T Seneca II	C. W. Middlemass
	G-MAYO	PA-28-161 Warrior II	Jermyk Engineering/Fairoaks
	G-MCAR	PA-32 Cherokee Six 300D	Miller Aerial Spraying Ltd (G-LADA/G-AYWK)/Wickenby
	G-MCOX	Fuji FA.200-180AO	W. Surrey Engineering (Shepperton) Ltd
	G-MDAC	PA-28-181 Archer II	Chalkfarm Productions Ltd
	G-MDAS	PA-31-310 Turbo Navajo C	Warwickshire Flying Training Centre Ltd (G-BCJZ)/Birmingham
	G-MEBC	Cessna 310-1	P. H. Johnson (G-ROGA/G-ASVV)
	G-MEGA	PA-28R-201T Turbo Arrow III	Travelworth Ltd
	G-MELD	AA-5A Cheetah	Judgeshire Ltd (G-BHCB)/Biggin Hill
	G-MELT	Cessna F.172H	Alvair Aviation (Sales) Ltd (G-AWTI)/ Coventry
	G-MELV	SOCATA Rallye 235E	M. G. Sanders Co Ltd (G-BIND)/Sywell
	G-MERC	Colt 56A balloon	Castles Northgate Ltd
	G-MERI	PA-28-181 Archer II	Scotia Safari Ltd/Glasgow
	G-MERL	PA-28RT-201 Arrow IV	M. Giles
	G-META	Bell 222	The Metropolitan Police/Lippitts Hill
	G-METB	Bell 222	The Metropolitan Police/Lippitts Hill
	G-METC	Bell 222	The Metropolitan Police (G-JAMC)/ Lippitts Hill

Reg.	Type	Owner or Operator	Notes
G-METP	Short SD3-30	National Airways (G-METO/G-BKIE)/ Southend	
G-MFHL	Robinson R-22B	MFH Ltd	
G-MFMF	Bell 206B JetRanger 3	S.W. Electricity Board (G-BJNJ)/Bristol	
G-MHBD	Cameron O-105 balloon	K. Hull	
G-MHIH	H.S. 125 Srs 700B	Queens Moat Houses PLC (G-BKAA)	
G-MICH	Robinson R-22B	T. D. Mitchell (G-BNKY)	
G-MICK	Cessna F.172N	S. Grant & ptnrs	
G-MIKE	Hornet Gyroplane	M. H. J. Goldring	
G-MIKY	Cameron 90 Mickey SS balloon	The Walt Disney Co Ltd	
G-MILK	SOCATA TB.10 Tobago	G. Whincup	
G-MILL	PA-32-301T Turbo Saratoga	A. J. L. Levitt-Cooke/Sibson	
G-MINI	Currie Wot	D. Collinson	
G-MINT	Pitts S-1S Special	T. G. Anderson/Tollerton	
G-MIOO	Miles GM.100 Student 2	M. Woodley (G-APLK)/(stored) N. Weald	
G-MISS	Taylor JT.2 Titch	A. Brennan	
G-MIST	Cessna T.210K	Allzones Travel Ltd (G-AYGM)/ Biggin Hill	
G-MITS	Cameron N-77 balloon	Colt Car Co Ltd	
G-MITZ	Cameron N-77 balloon	Colt Car Co Ltd	
G-MKAY	Cessna 172N	Limbros Demolition Ltd	
G-MKEE	EAA Acro Sport	G. M. McKee	
G-MKIX	V.S.361 Spitfire F.IX (NH238)	D. W. Arnold	
G-MKVC	V.S.349 Spitfire F.Vc★	Charles Church Displays Ltd	
G-MLAS	Cessna 182E (EE606)	Parachute jump trainer/St Merryn	
G-MLBU	PA-46-310P Malibu	Northern Scaffold Group Ltd	
G-MLEE	Cessna 650 Citation III	Mountleigh Air Services Ltd	
G-MLGL	Colt 21A balloon	Colt Balloons Ltd	
G-MLWI	Thunder Ax7-77 balloon	M. L. & L. P. Willoughby	
G-MOAT	Beech 200 Super King Air	Queens Moat Houses PLC	
G-MOBL	EMB-110P2 Bandeirante	National Airways/Business Air	
G-MOGG	Cessna F.172N	J. G. James (G-BHDY)	
G-MOGI	AA-5A Cheetah	BLS Aviation Ltd (G-BFMU)/Elstree	
G-MOGY	Robinson R-22B	Reachmain Ltd	
G-MOHR	Cameron 105 Sarotti balloon	Cameron Balloons Ltd	
G-MOLE	Taylor JT.2 Titch	S. R. Mowle	
G-MOLY	PA-23 Apache 160	A. H. Hunt & ptnrs (G-APFV)/ St Just	
G-MONA	M.S.880B Rallye Club	G. L. Thomas	
G-MONB	Boeing 757-2T7	Monarch Airlines Ltd/Luton	
G-MONC	Boeing 757-2T7	Monarch Airlines Ltd/Luton	
G-MOND	Boeing 757-2T7	Monarch Airlines Ltd/Luton	
G-MONE	Boeing 757-2T7	Monarch Airlines Ltd/Luton	
G-MONF	Boeing 737-3Y0	Monarch Airlines Ltd/Luton	
G-MONG	Boeing 737-3Y0	Monarch Airlines Ltd/Luton	
G-MONH	Boeing 737-3Y0	Monarch Airlines Ltd/Luton	
G-MONI	Monnet Moni	R. J. Baron	
G-MONJ	Boeing 757-2T7	Monarch Airlines Ltd/Luton	
G-MONK	Boeing 757-2T7	Monarch Airlines Ltd/Luton	
G-MONL	Boeing 737-3Y0	Monarch Airlines Ltd/Euro Berlin	
G-MONM	Boeing 737-3Y0	Monarch Airlines Ltd/Euro Berlin	
G-MONN	Boeing 737-33A	Monarch Airlines Ltd/Euro Berlin	
G-MONO	Taylor JT.1 Monoplane	A. J. Holmes	
G-MONP	Boeing 737-33A	Monarch Airlines Ltd/Euro Berlin	
G-MOON	Mooney M.20K	M. A. Eccles	
G-MOTH	D.H.82A Tiger Moth (K2567)	M. C. Russell/Duxford	
G-MOTO	PA-24 Comanche 160	Baythorn Ltd (G-EDHE/G-ASFH)/ Fairoaks	
G-MOUS	Cameron 90 Mickey SS balloon	The Walt Disney Co Ltd	
G-MOVE	Aerostar 601P	Red Dragon Travel Ltd/Cardiff	
G-MOZY	D.H.98 (replica)	J. Beck & G. L. Kemp	
G-MPBH	Cessna FA.152	R. W. Restorick (G-FLIC/G-BILV)	
G-MPCU	Cessna 402B	Atlantic Air Transport Ltd/Coventry	
G-MPWI	Robin HR.100/210	Propwash Investments Ltd/Swansea	
G-MPWT	PA-34-220T Seneca III	MPW Aviation Ltd	
G-MRFB	H.S.125 Srs 3B	RCR Aviation Ltd (G-AZVS)	
G-MRST	PA-28RT-201 Arrow IV	Winchfield Enterprises Ltd	
G-MRTY	Cameron N-77 balloon	R. A. & P. G. Vale	
G-MSFY	H.S.125 Srs 700B	Mohamed Said Fakhry/Heathrow	
G-MSLY	Cessna 550 Citation II	Moseley Group (PSV) Ltd (G-FERY/ G-JDBI)	
G-MTLE	Cessna 501 Citation	Talan Ltd (G-GENE)	
G-MUFF	AS.355F-1 Twin Squirrel	Lynton Aviation Ltd (G-CORR)	
G-MULL	Douglas DC-10-30	British Airways/Gatwick	

Notes	Reg.	Type	Owner or Operator
	G-MURF	AA-5B Tiger	D. Murphy (G-JOAN/G-BFML)
	G-MUSI	Robinson R-22B	F. M. Usher-Smith
	G-MUSO	Rutan LongEz	M. Moran
	G-MUSS	Robinson R-22B	Mussett Engineering Ltd
	G-NACA	Norman NAC.2 Freelance 180	The Norman Aeroplane Co Ltd/Cardiff
	G-NACI	Norman NAC.1 Srs 100	The Norman Aeroplane Co Ltd/Cardiff
	G-NACL	Norman NAC.6 Fieldmaster	Legistshelfco Ltd (G-BNEG)/Cardiff
	G-NACM	Norman NAC.6 Fieldmaster	Legistshelfco Ltd/Cardiff
	G-NACN	Norman NAC.6 Fieldmaster	Legistshelfco Ltd/Cardiff
	G-NACO	Norman NAC.6 Fieldmaster	Legistshelfco Ltd/Cardiff
	G-NACP	Norman NAC.6 Fieldmaster	Legistshelfco Ltd/Cardiff
	G-NASH	AA-5A Cheetah	Sky Rambler Ltd/Southampton
	G-NATO	AB-206B JetRanger 3	Defence Products Ltd (G-FLCH/G-BGGX)
	G-NATT	R. Commander 114A	Northgleant Ltd
	G-NATX	Cameron O-65 balloon	A. Faulkner
	G-NAVY	D.H.104 Sea Devon C.20 (XJ348)	Hayward & Green Ltd (G-AMXX)/ Shoreham
	G-NAZO	PA-31-310 Navajo B	Pathway Holdings Ltd (G-AZIM)
	G-NBDD	Robin DR.400/180	D. Dufton
	G-NBSI	Cameron N-77 balloon	Nottingham Hot-Air Balloon Club
	G-NCMT	Cessna 500 Citation	Numerically Controlled Machine Tools (G-BIZZ)
	G-NCUB	Piper J-3C-65 Cub	N. Thomson (G-BGXV)/Norwich
	G-NDGC	Grob G.109	Wiltshire Aeroplane Club/Old Sarum
	G-NDNI	NDN-1 Firecracker	Norman Marsh Aircraft Ltd
	G-NEAL	PA-32 Cherokee Six 260	Midland Aircraft Maintenance Ltd (G-BFPY)
	G-NEEP	Bell 206B JetRanger	Dollar Air Services Ltd/Coventry
	G-NEGS	Thunder Ax7-77 balloon	R. Holden
	G-NEIL	Thunder Ax3 balloon	Islington Motors (Trowbridge) Ltd
	G-NELL	R. Commander 112A	Airspeed (Aircraft) Ltd
	G-NEPB	Cameron N-77 balloon	The Post Office
	G-NEUS	Brugger MB.2 Colibri	G. E. Smeaton
	G-NEWR	PA-31-350 Navajo Chieftain	Eastern Air Executive Ltd/Sturgate
	G-NEWS	Bell 206B JetRanger 3	Peter Press Ltd
	G-NEXT	AS.355F-1 Twin Squirrel	Next PLC (G-OMAV)
	G-NGBI	AA-5B Tiger	Filemart Ltd (G-JAKK/G-BHWI)/ Biggin Hill
	G-NHRH	PA-28 Cherokee 140	H. Dodd
	G-NHVH	Maule M5-235C Lunar Rocket	Commercial Go-Karts Ltd/Exeter
	G-NICK	PA-18 Super Cub 95	J. G. O'Donnell & I. Woolacott
	G-NIFR	Beech 76 Duchess	J. J. Baumhardt
	G-NIGB	Boeing 747-211B	British Airways City of Gloucester
	G-NIKY	PA-31-350 Navajo Chieftain	Stanton Aircraft Management Ltd G-BPAR)/Biggin Hill
	G-NINA	PA-28-161 Warrior II	Bailey Aviation Ltd (G-BEUC)
	G-NIPU	Beech 58P Baron	J. A. Sheehan
	G-NISR	R. Commander 690A	Z. I. Bilbeisi
	G-NITA	PA-28 Cherokee 180	J. Staite (G-AVVG)/Coventry
	G-NIUK	Douglas DC-10-30	British Airways Cairn Edward Forest/ Gatwick
	G-NJAG	Cessna 207	G. H. Nolan Ltd
	G-NJSH	Robinson R-22B	T. F. Hawes
	G-NNAC	PA-18 Super Cub 135	P. A. Wilde
	G-NOBY	Rand KR-2	N. P. Rieser
	G-NODE	AA-5B Tiger	Curd & Green Ltd/Elstree
	G-NONI	AA-5 Traveler	M. S. Harvell (G-BBDA)
	G-NORD	Nord NC.854	R. G. E. Simpson & A. M. Alexander/ (stored)
	G-NORS	Cessna 425	D. C. Cook Holdings PLC
	G-NOTT	Nott ULD-2 balloon	J. R. P. Nott
	G-NOVO	Colt AS-56 airship	Rowntree Mackintosh Confectionery Ltd
	G-NRDC	NDN-6 Fieldmaster	The Norman Aeroplane Co Ltd/Cardiff
	G-NROA	Boeing 727-217	Dan-Air Services Ltd (G-BKNG)/Gatwick
	G-NUIG	Beech C90-1 King Air	Norwich Union Fire Insurance Soc (G-BKIP)
	G-NUTS	Cameron 35 SS balloon	The Balloon Stable Ltd
	G-NUTZ	AS.355F-1 Twin Squirrel	McAlpine Helicopters Ltd (G-BLRI)/ Hayes
	G-NWPB	Thunder Ax7-77Z balloon	Lighter-Than-Air Ltd
	G-NWPR	Cameron N-77 balloon	Post Office N.W. Postal Board
	G-NYTE	Cessna F.337G	Nite Signs Ltd (G-BATH)
	G-NZGL	Cameron O-105 balloon	P. G. & P. M. Vale

Reg.	Type	Owner or Operator	Notes
G-OAAC	Airtour AH-77B balloon	Army Air Corps	
G-OAAL	PA-38-112 Tomahawk	Atlantic Aviation Ltd	
G-OABC	Colt 69A balloon	Airship & Balloon Co Ltd	
G-OABG	Hughes 369E	A. B. Gee of Ripley	
G-OABI	Cessna 421C	Blue Star Ship Management Ltd	
G-OACE	Valentin Taifun 17E	Aero Club Enstone	
G-OADE	Cessna F.177RG	R. Windley (G-AZKH)	
G-OADS	Cessna 401	Automated Data Systems Ltd (G-OROG/ G-ZEUS/G-ODJS/G-BSIX/G-CAFE/ G-AWXM)	
G-OADY	Beech B76 Duchess	Adcliffe Engineers Ltd	
G-OAFB	Beech 200 Super King Air	A. F. Budge Ltd	
G-OAFT	Cessna 152	Fleetdelta Ltd (G-BNKM)	
G-OAIM	Hughes 369HS	J. E. Clarke (G-BDFP)/Bournemouth	
G-OAJF	BAe 146-300	British Aerospace PLC/Hatfield	
G-OAJH	AA-5A Cheetah	Garrick Aviation (G-KILT/G-BJFA)/ Elstree	
G-OAKL	Beech 200 Super King Air	Air Kilroe Ltd (G-BJZG)/Manchester	
G-OAKM	Beech 200 Super King Air	Air Kilroe Ltd (G-BCUZ)/Manchester	
G-OAKS	Cessna 421C	Barratt Developments Ltd/Newcastle	
G-OAKZ	Beech C90A King Air	Barratt Developments Ltd	
G-OALD	SOCATA TB.20 Trinidad	D. A. Williamson	
G-OALF	Dornier Do.228-201K	Region Airways Ltd (G-MLDO)/ Southend	
G-OAMG	Bell 206B JetRanger 3	Camlet Helicopters Ltd (G-COAL)	
G-OAMY	Cessna 152	Warwickshire Flying Training Centre Ltd/Birmingham	
G-OANC	PA-28-161 Warrior II	ANC (Tyne & Wear) Ltd (G-BFAD)	
G-OARV	ARV Super 2	ARV Aviation Ltd/Sandown	
G-OASH	Robinson R-22B	A. S. Hawkridge	
G-OATP	BAe ATP	Manx Airlines Ltd (G-BZWW)/ Ronaldsway	
G-OATS	PA-38-112 Tomahawk	Truman Aviation Ltd/Tollerton	
G-OAUS	Sikorsky S-76A	Ashton Upthorpe Stud & Farms Ltd	
G-OAVX	Beech 200 Super King Air	AVX Ltd (G-IBCA/G-BMCA)/Blackbushe	
G-OAWY	Cessna 340A	Industrial Alum Ltd	
G-OBAL	Mooney M.20J	Britannia Airways Ltd/Luton	
G-OBAT	Cessna F.152	J. J. Baumhardt	
G-OBEA	BAe Jetstream 3102-01	Birmingham Executive Airways Ltd	
G-OBED	PA-34-200T Seneca II	V. J. Holden/Newcastle	
G-OBEY	PA-23 Aztec 250C	Creaton Aircraft Services (G-BAAJ)	
G-OBHD	Short SD3-60	Jersey European Airways (G-BNDK)	
G-OBHX	Cessna F.172H	Jones Aviation Sales Ltd (G-AWMU)	
G-OBIL	Robinson R-22B	W. G. W. Samuelson	
G-OBLC	Beech 76 Duchess	Lydd Air Training Centre Ltd	
G-OBLD	AB-206B JetRanger	Bartlett Land Developments Ltd	
G-OBLK	Short SD3-60	Jersey European Airways (G-BNDI)	
G-OBMA	Boeing 737-33A	British Midland Airways Ltd/E. Midlands	
G-OBMB	Boeing 737-33A	British Midland Airways Ltd/E. Midlands	
G-OBMC	Boeing 737-33A	British Midland Airways Ltd/E. Midlands	
G-OBMD	Boeing 737-33A	British Midland Airways Ltd/E. Midlands	
G-OBMF	Boeing 737-4Y0	British Midland Airways Ltd/E. Midlands	
G-OBMS	Cessna F.172N	BMS Electrical Services Ltd/ Birmingham	
G-OBMW	AA-5 Traveler	Fretcourt Ltd (G-BDPV)	
G-OBOH	Short SD3-60	Jersey European Airways (G-BNDJ)	
G-OBPG	Brantly B.2B	A. C. Dent (G-AWIO)	
G-OBSF	AA-5A Cheetah	Blackbushe School of Flying Ltd (G-ODSF/G-BEUW)	
G-OBSV	Partenavia P.68B Observer	Galecall Ltd	
G-OBUD	Colt 69A balloon	Hot-Air Balloon Co Ltd	
G-OBUS	PA-28-181 Archer II	Oldbus Ltd (G-BMTT)	
G-OCAL	Partenavia P.68B	Grosvenor Aviation Services Ltd (G-BGMY)/Manchester	
G-OCAP	Bell 206B JetRanger 3	Capital Computers (G-OACS)	
G-OCAR	Colt 77A balloon	Toyota (UK) Ltd	
G-OCAT	Eiri PIK-20E	W. A. D. Thorp/Doncaster	
G-OCCC	H.S.125 Srs 800B	Consolidated Contractors International	
G-OCDS	Aviamilano F.8L Falco II	D. I. Simpson & Computer Diskdrive Services ltd (G-VEGL)	
G-OCFS	PA-23 Aztec 250E	B. Butler (G-BBFU)	
G-OCHD	Beech 300 Super King Air	Cameron Hall Developments Ltd	
G-OCHL	Bell 206B JetRanger 2	Interactive Skills Ltd	
G-OCJK	Schweizer 269C	M. D. Thorpe	

Notes	Reg.	Type	Owner or Operator
	G-OCME	BN-2A Mk III-1 Trislander	Avon Aviation Services Ltd (G-AYWI)
	G-OCND	Cameron O-77 balloon	D. P. H. Smith & Dalby
	G-OCPC	Cessna FA.152	Westward Airways (Lands End) Ltd/ St Just
	G-OCTA	BN-2A Mk III-2 Trislander	Galecall Ltd (G-BCXW)
	G-OCTI	PA-32 Cherokee Six 260	M. H. Bishop (G-BGZX)/Netherthorpe
	G-OCUB	Piper J-3C-90 Cub	C. A. Foss & P. A. Brook/Shoreham
	G-OCWC	AA-5A Cheetah	Canonbury Wine Ltd (G-WULL)
	G-ODAH	Aerotek-Pitts S.2A Special	PDQ Computer Graphics Ltd (G-BDKS)
	G-ODAM	AA-5A Cheetah	Biblio Aviation Ltd (G-FOUX)
	G-ODAY	Cameron N-56 balloon	C. O. Day (Estate Agents)
	G-ODEL	Falconar F-11-3	R. H. Ford
	G-ODER	Cameron O-77 balloon	W. H. Morgan
	G-ODHL	Cameron N-77 balloon	DHL International (UK) Ltd
	G-ODIL	Bell 206B JetRanger	Assetglobal Ltd
	G-ODJP	Robinson R-22	D. J. Powell
	G-ODLY	Cessna 310J	W. H. Reeves (G-TUBY/G-ASZZ)
	G-ODMM	PA-31-350 Navajo Chieftain	DMM Ltd
	G-OEAC	Mooney M.20J	Trifik Services Ltd
	G-OEMS	Beech 200 Super King Air	National Commuter Airways Ltd/ Southend
	G-OESX	PA-23 Aztec 250E	J. J. Baumhardt (G-BAJX)
	G-OEZE	Rutan Vari-Eze	S. Stride & ptnrs
	G-OFAB	Bell 206B JetRanger	Findon Air Services
	G-OFBL	Beech C90 King Air	Thurston Aviation Ltd (G-MEDI)/ Stansted
	G-OFCM	Cessna F172L	F. C. M Aviation Ltd (G-AZUN)/Guernsey
	G-OFHJ	Cessna 441	Tilling Associates Ltd (G-HSON)
	G-OFLI	Colt 105A balloon	Virgin Atlantic Airways Ltd
	G-OFLY	Cessna 210L	A. P. Mothew/Stapleford
	G-OFOR	Thunder Ax3 balloon	A. Walker
	G-OFRB	Everett gyroplane	F. R. Blennerhassett
	G-OFRH	Cessna 421C	Rogers Aviation Sales Ltd (G-NORX)/ Cranfield
	G-OFUN	Valentin Taifun 17E	J. A. Sangster/Booker
	G-OGAS	Westland WG.30 Srs 100	Bristol Helicopters Ltd (G-BKNW)
	G-OGDN	Beech A200 Super King Air	A. Ogden & Sons Ltd/Leeds
	G-OGEM	PA-28-181 Archer II	GEM Rewinds Ltd
	G-OGET	PA-39 Twin Comanche 160	P. G. Kitchingman (G-AYXY)
	G-OGOS	Everett Autogyro	L. W. Sampson
	G-OGRV	PA-31-350 Navajo Chieftain	Grosvenor Aviation Services Ltd (G-BMPX)
	G-OGTS	Air Command 532 Elite	GTS Engineering (Coventry) Ltd
	G-OHCA	SC.5 Belfast (XR363)	HeavyLift Cargo Airlines Ltd/Southend
	G-OHEA	H.S.125 Srs 3B/RA	Rogers Aviation Sales Ltd (G-AVRG)/ Cranfield
	G-OHLA	Cessna 501 Citation	Havelet Leasing Ltd
	G-OHTL	Sikorsky S-76A	Air Hanson Ltd/Brooklands
	G-OHUB	Cessna 404 Titan	Hubbardair Ltd/Norwich
	G-OIAN	M.S.880B Rallye Club	Ian Richard Transport Services Ltd
	G-OIBM	R. Commander 114	South Coast Computers Ltd (G-BLVZ)
	G-OIBO	PA-28 Cherokee 180	P. D. Bruce (G-AVAZ)/Biggin Hill
	G-OICI	Quickie Q.2	Quickie Aircraft (Europe) Ltd (G-OGKN)
	G-OIFR	Cessna 172RG	J. J. Baumhardt (G-BHJG) (stored)
	G-OIMC	Cessna 152	E. Midlands Flying School Ltd
	G-OING	AA-5A Cheetah ★	Abraxas Aviation Ltd (G-BFPD)/Denham
	G-OINK	Piper J-3C-65 Cub	A. R. Harding (G-BILD/G-KERK)
	G-OIOI	Westland EH.101	Westland Helicopters Ltd/Yeovil
	G-OJCB	AB-206B JetRanger 2	Air Hanson Ltd/Blackbushe
	G-OJCW	PA-32RT-300 Lance II	M. J. Metham/Blackbushe
	G-OJEE	Bede BD-4	G. Hodges
	G-OJET	BAe 146-100	Manx Airlines Ltd (G-BRJS/G-OBAF/ G-SCHH)/Ronaldsway
	G-OJFR	Bell 206B JetRanger	Huntingdon Enterprises Ltd
	G-OJGA	Beech 200 Super King Air	Gulliver Associates Ltd
	G-OJIM	PA-28R-201T Turbo Arrow III	J. J. McVey
	G-OJJB	Mooney M.20K	Jeff Brown (Aviation Services)
	G-OJON	Taylor JT.2 Titch	J. H. Fell
	G-OJOR	AS.355-2 Twin Squirrel	Daniel Martin Plant Ltd (G-FTWO/ G-BMUS)
	G-OJPI	Robinson R-22B	John Battleday at Kirton Farms Ltd
	G-OJPW	PA-31-310 Turbo Navajo C	Walsh Aviation (G-BGCC)
	G-OJSY	Short SD3-60	Jersey European Airways Ltd (G-BKKT)
	G-OJVC	J/1N Alpha	R. W. J. Holland (G-AHCL)/Sywell

Reg.	Type	Owner or Operator	Notes
G-OJVH	Cessna F.150H	Yorkshire Light Aircraft Ltd (G-AWJZ)/ Leeds	
G-OJVI	Robinson R-22B	JV Investments Ltd (G-OJVJ)	
G-OJWS	PA-28-161 Warrior II	J. W. Sharman	
G-OKAG	PA-28R Cherokee Arrow 180	Panorama Design Consultants Ltd	
G-OKAT	AS.350B Ecureuil	Tom Walkinshaw Racing Ltd (G-BGIM)	
G-OKAY	Pitts S-1E Special	Aerial & Aerobatic Service/Booker	
G-OKCC	Cameron N-90 balloon	Kerridge Computer Co Ltd	
G-OKEN	PA-28R-201T Turbo Arrow III	K. Hassall	
G-OKIT	Rotorway Executive	C. W. Thomas	
G-OKSP	Cessna 500 Citation	Osiwel Ltd/Leavesden	
G-OKYA	Cameron V-77 balloon	14/20 Kings Hussars	
G-OKYM	PA-28 Cherokee 140	D. Hotham (G-AVLS)	
G-OLAF	Beech C90 King Air	Merak Aviation Ltd (G-BFVX)	
G-OLBA	Short SD3-60 Variant 100	Capital Airlines Ltd (G-BOFG/Leeds	
G-OLCA	BAe 146-200	Loganair Ltd/Glasgow	
G-OLCB	BAe 146-200	Loganair Ltd/British Aerospace	
G-OLCC	BAe ATP	Loganair Ltd/Glasgow	
G-OLCD	BAe ATP	Loganair Ltd/Glasgow	
G-OLDN	Bell 206L LongRanger	Autoklenz (UK) Ltd (G-TBCA/G-BFAL)	
G-OLDS	Colt AS-105 airship	Hot-Air Balloon Co Ltd	
G-OLDY	Luton LA-5 Major	M. P. & A. P. Sargent	
G-OLEE	Cessna F.152	Warwickshire Flying Training Centre Ltd/Birmingham	
G-OLFC	PA-38-112 Tomahawk	Leavesden Flight Centre (G-BGZG)	
G-OLFS	M.S.880B Rallye Club	A. G. Martlew (G-AYYZ)	
G-OLFT	R. Commander 114	W. R. M. C. Foyle (G-WJMN)/Luton	
G-OLGW	Short SD3-60	Capital Airlines Ltd (G-BOFK)/Leeds	
G-OLIE	Robinson R-22B	Optionbuild Ltd	
G-OLIZ	Robinson R-22B	H. Pelham	
G-OLLE	Cameron O-84 balloon	N. A. Robertson	
G-OLLI	Cameron O-31 SS balloon	N. A. Robertson	
G-OLLY	PA-31-350 Navajo Chieftain	G. Greenall (G-BCES)/Bristol	
G-OLMA	Partenavia P.68B	Landell Mills Associates Ltd (G-BGBT)	
G-OLSC	Cessna 182A	London Skydiving Centre Ltd (G-ATNU)/Cranfield	
G-OLTN	Short SD3-60	Capital Airlines Ltd (G-BOFH)/Leeds	
G-OLVR	FRED Srs 2	A. R. Oliver	
G-OMAC	Cessna FR.172E	R. G. & M. W. Warwick	
G-OMAF	Dornier Do.228-200	FR Aviation Ltd/Bournemouth	
G-OMAR	PA-34-220T Seneca III	Redhill Flying Club	
G-OMAT	PA-28 Cherokee 140	Midland Air Training School (G-JIMY/ G-AYUG)/Coventry	
G-OMAX	Brantly B.2B	P. D. Benmax (G-AVJN)	
G-OMCL	Cessna 550 Citation II	Quantel Ltd/Biggin Hill	
G-OMCP	Enstrom 280C-UK-2 Shark	Midland City Partnership PLC (G-KENY/ G-BJFG)	
G-OMDH	Hughes 369E	Southern Air Ltd/Shoreham	
G-OMED	AA-5B Tiger	Caslon Ltd (G-BERL)/Elstree	
G-OMEG	PA-31-325 Navajo C/R	AEW Engineering Ltd (G-BFBH)	
G-OMHC	PA-28RT-201 Arrow IV	M. H. Cundley/Redhill	
G-OMJD	Robinson R-22B	M. I. Davis (Building Contractor) Ltd	
G-OMMC	Mooney M.20J	A. D. Russell	
G-OMNI	PA-28R Cherokee Arrow 200D	G. Walsh & ptnrs/Barton	
G-OMOB	Robinson R-22B	Triple Oak Ltd/Booker	
G-OMOG	AA-5A Cheetah	K. Robinson (G-BHWR)/Biggin Hill	
G-OMRG	Hoffmann H.36 Dimona	MRG Systems Ltd (G-BLHG)	
G-ONCA	Beech 200 Super King Air	National Airways/Southend	
G-ONEA	Beech 200 Super King Air	Northern Executive Aviation Ltd/ Manchester	
G-ONOR	Cessna 425	Rockville Investments (Jersey) Ltd (G-BKSA)	
G-ONOW	Bell 206A JetRanger 2	Hadley Green Garage Ltd (G-AYMX)	
G-ONTA	Hughes 369D	Cosworth Engineering Ltd/Sywell	
G-ONTB	Bell 206B JetRanger	Looporder Ltd	
G-ONZO	Cameron N-77 balloon	J. A. Kershaw	
G-OOAG	Beech E90 King Air	Owners Abroad Group PLC (G-BAVG)	
G-OODE	SNCAN Stampe SV-4C (G)	The Biplane Co Ltd (G-AZNN)	
G-OODI	Pitts S-1D Special	R. N. Goode (G-BBBU)/White Waltham	
G-OODS	Extra EA.230	R. N. Goode	
G-OODW	PA-28-181 Archer II	Goodwood Terrena Ltd	
G-OOFI	Cameron N-77 balloon	I. Fishwick	
G-OOFY	Rollason Beta	G. Staples	
G-OOGA	GA-7 Cougar	Trent Air Services Ltd/Cranfield	

149

Notes	Reg.	Type	Owner or Operator
	G-OOLY	Everett Gyroplane	N. A. Brandish/Southend
	G-OONE	Mooney M.20J	N. Skipworth/Booker
	G-OOOA	Boeing 757-28A	Air 2000 Ltd/Manchester
	G-OOOB	Boeing 757-28A	Air 2000 Ltd/Manchester
	G-OOOC	Boeing 757-28A	Air 2000 Ltd/Manchester
	G-OOOD	Boeing 757-28A	Air 2000 Ltd/Manchester
	G-OOOO	Mooney M.20J	Kyrstle Aviation/Southampton
	G-OOSE	Rutan Vari-Eze	J. A. Towers
	G-OPAL	Robinson R-22B	Property Associates Ltd
	G-OPAM	Cessna F.152	Stapleford Flying Club Ltd (G-BFZS)
	G-OPAT	Beech 76 Duchess	Ray Holt (Land Drainage) Ltd/(G-BHAO)
	G-OPED	Partenavia P.68B	Pedley Woodwork Ltd/(G-BFKP)
	G-OPEE	Cessna 421C	Activewear Ltd (G-OSSH)
	G-OPIG	ARV Super 2	Airtime (Hampshire) Ltd (G-BMSJ)
	G-OPIK	Eiri PIK-20E	K. & S. C. A. Dudley
	G-OPJC	Cessna 152	PJC Leasing Ltd/Stapleford
	G-OPMB	Cessna P.201N	Policy Master Ltd
	G-OPOL	H.S.125 Srs F3B/RA	McAlpine Aviation Ltd (G-BXPU/ G-IBIS/G-AXPU)
	G-OPOP	Enstrom 280C-UK-2 Shark	J. C. Elmer (G-OFED)/Shoreham
	G-OPPL	AA-5A Cheetah	London School of Flying Ltd (G-BGNN)/ Elstree
	G-OPSF	PA-38-112 Tomahawk	Panshanger School of Flying (G-BGZI)
	G-OPST	Cessna 182R	Lota Ltd/Shoreham
	G-OPUP	B.121 Pup 2	P. W. Hunter (G-AXEU)
	G-ORAY	Cessna F.182Q II	C. Robinson (G-BHDN)/Blackpool
	G-ORCE	Cessna 550 Citation II	Oracle Corporation UK Ltd (G-MINE)
	G-ORCL	Cessna 421C	Oracle Corporation UK Ltd
	G-ORED	BN-2T Islander	The Red Devils (G-BJYW)/Farnborough
	G-OREG	BN-2A Mk III-1 Trislander	Regency Aviation Services Ltd (G-OAVW/G-AZLJ)
	G-ORFC	Jurca MJ.5 Sirocco	RFC Flying Group/Popham
	G-ORGE	SA.341G Gazelle Srs 1	Xanadu Aviation Ltd (G-BBHU)
	G-ORJW	Laverda F.8L Falco Srs 4	L. V. Broese van Groenou
	G-ORME	Bell 206B JetRanger	Dollar Air Services Ltd/Coventry
	G-ORON	Cameron 77A balloon	A. M. Rocliffe
	G-ORTM	Glaser-Dirks DG.400	I. M. Stromberg/Barton
	G-OSAL	Cessna 421C	Ultraseal International Ltd
	G-OSCC	PA-32 Cherokee Six 300	Plant Aviation Ltd (G-BGFD)/Elstree
	G-OSDI	Beech 95-58 Baron	Systems Designers Aviation Ltd (G-BHFY)
	G-OSEA	BN-2B-26 Islander	Pilatus BN/Loganair (G-BKOL)
	G-OSEB	Bell 222	Air Hanson Sales Ltd (G-BNDA)
	G-OSFC	Cessna F.152	Stapleford Flying Club (G-BIVJ)
	G-OSIX	PA-32 Cherokee Six 260	Strata Surveys Ltd (G-AZMO)
	G-OSKY	Cessna 172M	Waygrand Ltd
	G-OSND	Cessna FRA.150M	J. J. Baumhardt (G-BDOU)/Southend
	G-OSPI	Robinson R-22B	IMM Ltd
	G-OSRF	Cessna 421C	Marginslot Ltd/Elstree
	G-OSST	Colt 77A balloon	British Airways PLC
	G-OSSY	PA-28-181 Archer II	Bryan Goss Motorcycles Ltd/ Bournemouth
	G-OSUE	Bell 206B JetRanger 3	British Car Auctions (Aviation) Ltd (G-BKBY)
	G-OTAL	ARV Super 2	Taurus Aviation Ltd (G-BNGZ)
	G-OTAX	PA-31-350 Navajo Chieftain	Chaseside Holdings Ltd
	G-OTHE	Enstrom 280C-UK Shark	The Engineering Co Ltd (G-OPJT/ G-BKCO)
	G-OTOW	Cessna 175BX	Sywell Air Services (G-AROC)
	G-OTRG	Cessna TR.182RG	A. Hopper
	G-OTSB	BN-2A Mk III-2 Trislander	Aurigny Air Services Ltd (G-BDTO)
	G-OTSL	Agusta A.109A Srs 11	Direct Smooth Ltd
	G-OTTA	Colt 1.5 MCB balloon	Colt Balloons Ltd
	G-OTUG	PA-18 Super Cub 150	B. Walker & Co (Dursley) Ltd
	G-OTVS	BN-2T Islander	Headcorn Parachute Club Ltd (G-BPNG/ G-BCMY)
	G-OTWO	Rutan Defiant	D. G. Foreman
	G-OULD	Gould Mk I balloon	C. A. Gould
	G-OUSA	Colt 105A balloon	Continental Airlines Inc
	G-OVAN	SC.7 Skyvan 3 Variant 100	Peterborough Parachute Centre (G-AYZA)/Sibson
	G-OVER	PA-28-161 Warrior II	D. W. Overbeck (G-BKNE)
	G-OVFM	Cessna 120	Storyteller Cassettes Ltd
	G-OVFR	Cessna F.172N	Sunningdale Aviation Services Ltd

Reg.	Type	Owner or Operator	Notes
G-OVIP	G.1159 Gulfstream 2	VIP Marine & Aviation Ltd (G-AYMI)	
G-OVMC	Cessna F.152 II	Staverton Flying Services Ltd	
G-OVNE	Cessna 401A	Bearing Supplies Ltd/Norwich	
G-OWAC	Cessna F.152	George Cross Services Ltd (G-BHEB)	
G-OWAK	Cessna F.152	George Cross Services Ltd (G-BHEA)	
G-OWAR	PA-28-161 Warrior II	Biblio Aviation Ltd/Denham	
G-OWEB	H.S.125 Srs 700B	Rapid 3451 Ltd/Luton	
G-OWEN	K & S Jungster	R. C. Owen	
G-OWIN	BN-2A-8 Islander	UK Parachute Services Ltd (G-AYXE)	
G-OWNR	Beech 200 Super King Air	Owners Abroad Group PLC/Luton	
G-OWVA	PA-28 Cherokee 140	Woodvale Aviation Co Ltd	
G-OWYN	Aviamilano F.14 Nibbio	J. R. Wynn	
G-OYAK	Yakovlev C-11	E. K. Coventry	
G-OZOI	Cessna R.182	Velcourt (East) Ltd (G-ROBK)	
G-OZUP	Colt 77A balloon	Yanin International Ltd	
G-PACE	Robin R.1180T	Millicron Instruments Ltd/Coventry	
G-PACY	Rutan Vari-Viggen	E. Pace	
G-PADI	Cameron V-77 balloon	T. R. Duffell	
G-PAGE	Cessna F.150L	E. Shipley/Clacton	
G-PALS	Enstrom 280C-UK-2 Shark	Acme Jewellery Ltd	
G-PAMI	AS.355F-1 Twin Squirrel	Airzed Ltd (G-BUSA)/Southampton	
G-PAPA	AS.355F-1 Twin Squirrel	McCarthy & Stone (Group Services) Ltd (G-MCAH/G-CNET)	
G-PARA	Cessna 207	Paraski/Swansea	
G-PARI	Cessna 172RG Cutlass	Applied Signs Ltd	
G-PARS	Evans VP-2	A. Parsfield	
G-PART	Partenavia P.68B	Highway Windscreens Ltd/Stapleford	
G-PATA	Douglas DC-9-83	Paramount Airways Ltd	
G-PATB	Douglas DC-9-83	Paramount Airways Ltd	
G-PATC	Douglas DC-9-83	Paramount Airways Ltd	
G-PATD	Douglas DC-9-83	Paramount Airways Ltd	
G-PATT	Cessna 404 Titan	Casair Aviation Ltd (G-BHGL)/ Teesside	
G-PATY	Colt Flying Sausage balloon	Colt Balloons Ltd	
G-PAWL	PA-28 Cherokee 140	A. M. & D. Fitton (G-AWEU)	
G-PAWS	AA-5A Cheetah	George Cross Services Ltd	
G-PAXX	PA-20 Pacer 135	D. W. & M. R. Grace	
G-PBBT	Cameron N-56 balloon	British Telecom PLC	
G-PBHF	Robinson R-22B	Broughton-Hall Security Fencing	
G-PCUB	PA-18 Super Cub 135 (54-2474)	M. J. Wilson/Redhill	
G-PDES	SA.365N Dauphin 2	Land Leisure PLC (G-BKXK)	
G-PDHJ	Cessna T.182R	G. P. Grant-Suttie	
G-PDOC	PA-44-180 Seminole	Medicare (G-PVAF)	
G-PDON	WMB.2 Windtracker balloon	P. Donnellan	
G-PDSI	Cessna 172N	Quick Logic Ltd	
G-PEAL	Aerotek Pitts S-2A	S. M. Trickey	
G-PEAT	Cessna 421B	Forest Aviation Ltd (G-BBIJ)/ Manchester	
G-PEET	Cessna 401A	Villotel Ltd	
G-PELE	Cameron 80 Pele SS balloon	Cameron Balloons Ltd	
G-PENN	AA-5B Tiger	Compair	
G-PENY	Sopwith LC-IT Triplane	J. S. Penny	
G-PERL	Robinson R-22B	R. Fawcett	
G-PERR	Cameron 60 bottle balloon	The Balloon Stable Ltd	
G-PERS	Colt Soapbox SS balloon	Thunder & Colt Ltd	
G-PETR	PA-28 Cherokee 140	E. W. Keeble/Ipswich (G-BCJL)	
G-PFAA	EAA Model P biplane	P. E. Barker	
G-PFAB	Colomban MC.15 Cri-Cri	P. Fabish	
G-PFAC	FRED Srs 2	M. J. Hayman	
G-PFAD	Wittman W.8 Tailwind	M. R. Stamp	
G-PFAE	Taylor JT.1 Monoplane	G. Johnson	
G-PFAF	FRED Srs 2	M. S. Perkins	
G-PFAG	Evans VP-1	P. A. Evans	
G-PFAH	Evans VP-1	J. A. Scott	
G-PFAI	Clutton EC.2 Easy Too	G. W. Cartledge	
G-PFAL	FRED Srs 2	J. McD. Robinson	
G-PFAM	FRED Srs 2	W. C. Rigby	
G-PFAN	Avro 558 (replica)	N. P. Harrison	
G-PFAO	Evans VP-1	P. W. Price	
G-PFAP	Currie Wot/SE-5A (C1904)	P. G. Abbey	
G-PFAR	Isaacs Fury II (K2059)	C. J. Repik	
G-PFAS	GY-20 Minicab	J. Sproston & F. W. Speed	

Notes	Reg.	Type	Owner or Operator
	G-PFAT	Monnet Sonerai II	H. B. Carter
	G-PFAU	Rand KR-2	D. E. Peace
	G-PFAV	D.31 Turbulent	B. A. Luckins
	G-PFAW	Evans VP-1	R. F. Shingler
	G-PFAX	FRED Srs 2	A. J. Dunston
	G-PFAY	EAA Biplane	A. K. Lang & A. L. Young
	G-PFAZ	Evans VP-1	B. Kylo
	G-PHIL	Hornet Gyroplane	A. J. Philpotts
	G-PICS	Cessna 182F	Astral Aerial Surveys Ltd (G-ASHO)
	G-PIEL	Piel CP.301A Emeraude	P. R. Thorne (G-BARY)
	G-PIES	Thunder Ax7-77Z balloon	Pork Farms Ltd
	G-PIGS	SOCATA Rallye 150ST	Boonhill Flying Group (G-BDWB)
	G-PIKK	PA-28 Cherokee 140	L. P. & I. Keegan (G-AVLA)
	G-PIKN	Extra EA.230	Van Bosch Ltd
	G-PINT	Cameron 65 SS balloon	Charles Wells Ltd
	G-PIPE	Cameron N-56 SS balloon	Carreras Rothmans Ltd
	G-PITS	Pitts S-2AE	D. Rolfe
	G-PITZ	Pitts S.2A Special	Swift 1673 Ltd
	G-PIXS	Cessna 336	Astral Aerial Surveys Ltd
	G-PKBD	Douglas DC-9-32	British Midland Airways Ltd *Jubilee Diamond*/E. Midlands
	G-PKBE	Douglas DC-9-32	British Midland Airways Ltd *Excelsior Diamond*/E. Midlands
	G-PKBM	Douglas DC-9-32	British Midland Airways Ltd *The Tiffany Diamond*/E. Midlands
	G-PLAN	Cessna F.150L	Phoenix Aviation (Bedford) Ltd/Cranfield
	G-PLAS	GA-7 Cougar	S. J. A. Smith (G-BGHL)/Biggin Hill
	G-PLAY	Robin R.2100A	Cotswold Aero Club Ltd/Staverton
	G-PLEE	Cessna 182Q	Sunderland Parachute Centre Ltd
	G-PLEV	Cessna 340	KJ Bill Aviation Ltd/Halfpenny Green
	G-PLIV	Pazmany PL.4	B. P. North
	G-PLMA	AS.350B Ecureuil	PLM Helicopters Ltd (G-BMMA)
	G-PLMB	AS.350B Ecureuil	PLM Helicopters Ltd (G-BMMB)
	G-PLMC	AS.350B Ecureuil	PLM Helicopters Ltd (G-BKUM)
	G-PLMD	AS.350B Ecureuil	Hope Sixteen (No 107) Ltd (G-NIAL)
	G-PLME	AS.350B-1 Ecureuil	PLM Helicopters Ltd (G-BONN)
	G-PLOW	Hughes 269B	March Helicopters Ltd (G-AVUM)/Sywell
	G-PLUS	PA-34-200T Seneca II	C. G. Strasser/Jersey
	G-PMAM	Cameron V-65 balloon	P. A. Meecham
	G-PMCN	Monnet Sonerai II	P. J. McNamee
	G-PMNL	Extra EA.230	Aerobatic Displays Ltd
	G-PNAV	PA-31P Pressurised Navajo	Tech Air (Cambridge) Ltd
	G-POAV	SA.365N1 Dauphin 2	The Peninsular & Oriental Steamship Co Ltd (G-BOPI)
	G-POLE	Rutan LongEz	A. M. Dutton
	G-POLO	PA-31-350 Navajo Chieftain	Grosvenor Aviation Services Ltd/Manchester
	G-POLY	Cameron N-77 balloon	Empty Wallets Balloon Group
	G-PONY	Colt 31A balloon	Ace Balloons (Bath) Ltd
	G-POOH	Piper J-3C-65 Cub	P. & H. Robinson
	G-POOL	ARV Super 2	Falstaff Finance Ltd (G-BNHA)
	G-POPE	Eiri PIK-20E-1	C. J. Hadley
	G-PORK	AA-5B Tiger	P. H. Johnson (G-BFHS)
	G-POSH	Colt 56A balloon	Thunder & Colt Ltd (G-BMPT)
	G-POSN	H.S.125 Srs 800B	P&O Containers (Assets) Ltd
	G-POST	EMB-110P1 Bandeirante	National Airways/Southend
	G-POWL	Cessna 182R	J. & B. Powell (Printers) Ltd
	G-PPLI	Pazmany PL.1	G. Anderson
	G-PRAG	Brugger MB.2 Colibri	R. J. Hodder & ptnrs
	G-PRIM	PA-38-112 Tomahawk	Nultree Ltd
	G-PRIT	Cameron N-90 balloon	Henkel Chemicals Ltd
	G-PRMC	H.S.125 Srs 700B	RMC Group Services Ltd (G-BFSP)/Biggin Hill
	G-PROP	AA-5A Cheetah	Falcon Flying Services Ltd (G-BHKU)/Biggin Hill
	G-PROV	Hunting Jet Provost T.54A	LGH Aviation Ltd/Cranfield
	G-PRTT	Cameron N-31 balloon	Henkel Chemicals Ltd
	G-PRUE	Cameron O-84 balloon	Lalondes Residential Ltd
	G-PRXI	V.S.365 Spitfire PR.XI (PL983)	D. W. Arnold/Biggin Hill
	G-PSVS	Beech 58 Baron	Astra Aviation Ltd/Guernsey
	G-PTER	Beech C90 King Air	Moseley Group (PSV) Ltd (G-BIEE)
	G-PTRE	SOCATA TB.20	Beechair Ltd (G-BNKU)

Reg.	Type	Owner or Operator	Notes
G-PTWO	Pilatus P2-05 (RF+16)	C. M. Lee	
G-PUBS	Colt 56 SS balloon	The Balloonatics	
G-PUDD	Robinson R-22B	Pique Holdings PLC	
G-PUFF	Thunder Ax7-77A balloon	Intervarsity Balloon Club *Puffin II*	
G-PULP	Colt Orangina balloon	The Balloon Stable Ltd	
G-PUMA	AS.332L Super Puma	Bond Helicopters Ltd/Bourn	
G-PUMB	AS.332L Super Puma	Bond Helicopters Ltd/Bourn	
G-PUMD	AS.332L Super Puma	Bond Helicopters Ltd/Bourn	
G-PUME	AS.332L Super Puma	Bond Helicopters Ltd/Bourn	
G-PUMG	AS.332L Super Puma	Bond Helicopters Ltd/Bourn	
G-PUMH	AS.332L Super Puma	Bond Helicopters Ltd/Bourn	
G-PUMI	AS.332L Super Puma	Bond Helicopters Ltd/Bourn	
G-PURR	AA-5A Cheetah	Blackbushe School of Flying Ltd (G-BJDN)	
G-PUSH	Rutan LongEz	E. G. Peterson	
G-PUSI	Cessna T.303	Avisford Park Hotel Ltd	
G-PUSS	Cameron N-77 balloon	London Life Association Ltd	
G-PVAM	Port Victoria 7 Grain Kitten replica	A. J. Manning	
G-PYRO	Cameron N-65 balloon	P. S. Wheeler	
G-RAAD	Mooney M.20L	A. A. Aljamali	
G-RACA	P.57 Sea Prince T.1	Atlantic & Caribbean Aviation Ltd/Staverton	
G-RACH	Robinson R-22B	T. C. Barry	
G-RADE	Cessna 210L	R. J. Herbert (G-CENT)	
G-RAEM	Rutan LongEz	G. F. H. Singleton	
G-RAFC	Robin R.2112	RAF Cranwell Flying Club	
G-RAFE	Thunder Ax7-77 balloon	A. J. W. Rose	
G-RAFF	Learjet 35A	Graff Aviation Ltd/Heathrow	
G-RAFT	Rutan LongEz	D. G. Foreman	
G-RAFW	Mooney M.20E	G. C. Smith (G-ATHW)/Southend	
G-RAIN	Maule M5-235C Lunar Rocket	J. S. Mehew	
G-RALE	SA.341G Gazelle Srs 1	Malcolm Wilson (Motorsport) Ltd (G-SFTG)	
G-RALI	Hughes 369HS	David Richards Autosport Ltd (G-BLKO)	
G-RAMS	PA-32R-301 Saratoga SP	Peacock & Archer Ltd/Manchester	
G-RAND	Rand KR-2	R. L. Wharmby	
G-RANY	Cessna 421C	McCarthy & Stone (Developments) Ltd (G-BHLA)	
G-RAPA	BN-2T Islander	Joint Services Parachute Centre	
G-RAPE	Colt 300A balloon	O. T. Holmes & R. J. Barr	
G-RAPH	Cameron O-77 balloon	P. H. Jenkins	
G-RARE	Thunder Ax5-42 SS balloon	International Distillers & Vintners Ltd	
G-RASC	Evans VP-2	R. A. Codling	
G-RASS	Bell 206L-1 LongRanger 1	Arlington Securities Ltd (G-JLBI)	
G-RATE	AA-5A Cheetah	J. P. Alexander (G-BIFF)/Denham	
G-RAVL	H.P.137 Jetstream Srs 200	Racal Avionics Ltd (G-AWVK)	
G-RAVY	Cessna 500 Citation	Aerospace Finance Corporate Aircraft Ltd	
G-RAYS	Zenair CH.250	R. E. Delves	
G-RBIN	Robin DR.400/2+2	Headcorn Flying School Ltd	
G-RBOS	Colt AS-105 airship ★	Science Museum/Wroughton	
G-RCGI	Robinson R-22B	Norwich Aviation Ltd	
G-RCMF	Cameron V-77 balloon	Mouldform Ltd	
G-RCPW	AA-5A Cheetah	Walsh Aviation (G-BERM)	
G-RDCI	R. Commander 112A	A. C. Hendriksen (G-BFWG)	
G-RDON	WMB.2 Windtracker balloon	P. J. Donnellan (G-BICH)	
G-READ	Colt 77A balloon	CB Helicopters Ltd	
G-REAT	GA-7 Cougar	Autair Helicopters Ltd	
G-RECK	PA-28 Cherokee 140	L. V. Gunter (G-AXJW)	
G-REEK	AA-5A Cheetah	Velopend Ltd	
G-REEN	Cessna 340	Ernest Green International Ltd (G-AZYR)	
G-REES	Jodel D.140C	M. D. S. Hood/Redhill	
G-REGA	EMB-110P1 Bandeirante	Region Airways Ltd/Southend	
G-REID	Rotorway Scorpion 133	J. Reid (G-BGAW)	
G-REIS	PA-28R-201T Turbo Arrow III	H. Reis (Hard Chrome) Ltd/Halfpenny Green	
G-RENO	SOCATA TB.10 Tobago	Lascar Electronics Ltd/Old Sarum	
G-RENT	Robinson R-22B	Rentatruck Self Drive Ltd	
G-REPM	PA-38-112 Tomahawk	Nultree Ltd	
G-REST	Beech P35 Bonanza	C. R. Taylor (G-ASFJ)	
G-RETA	C.A.S.A. 1.131 Jungmann	J. S. Allison/Denham	
G-REXS	PA-28-181 Archer II	Channel Islands Aero Holdings (Jersey) Ltd	

Notes	Reg.	Type	Owner or Operator
	G-RFSB	Sportavia RF-5B	S. W. Brown
	G-RGUS	Fairchild 24R-46A Argus 3 (44-83184)	A. E. Poulson
	G-RHCC	PA-31-350 Navajo Chieftain	Delta Commerical Ltd
	G-RHCN	Cessna FR.182RG	R. H. C. Neville
	G-RHHT	PA-32RT-300 Lance II	Penny (Mechanical Services) Ltd
	G-RIAN	AB-206A JetRanger	Autoklass (South Shields) Ltd (G-BHSG)
	G-RICH	Cessna F.152	Stanton Aircraft Management Ltd
	G-RICK	Beech 95-B55 Baron	R. M. S. Holland (G-BAAG)
	G-RIDE	Stephens Akro	R. Mitchell/Coventry
	G-RIFF	SA.341G Gazelle 1	Griffair Ltd (G-BLAN)
	G-RIGB	Thunder Ax7-77 balloon	Antrum & Andrews Ltd
	G-RIGS	Aerostar 601P	Rigs Design Services Ltd/Fairoaks
	G-RILL	Cessna 421C	Maxwell Restaurants Ltd (G-BGZM)/ Elstree
	G-RILY	Monnet Sonerai II	J. T. Taylor
	G-RIND	Cessna 335	ATA Grinding Processes/Leavesden
	G-RING	Cessna FR.182RG	Oxford Aviation Co Ltd
	G-RINO	Thunder Ax7-77 balloon	S. P. Davis
	G-RIOO	Beech B200 Super King Air	Belaire Factoring Ltd
	G-RIST	Cessna 310R-II	Air Service Training Ltd (G-DATS)/Perth
	G-RITA	Cessna 340A	C. Good
	G-RJMI	AA-5A Cheetah	R. J. Mole
	G-RJMS	PA-28R-201 Arrow III	Robin James Ltd
	G-RJRI	H.S. 125 Srs 700B	Field Aircraft Services (Heathrow) Ltd (G-BNVU/G-CCAA/G-DBBI)
	G-RJWW	Maule M5-235C Lunar Rocket	R. J. W. Wood (G-BRWG)
	G-RLMC	Cessna 421C	Richard Lawson Motor Co Ltd
	G-RMAM	Musselwhite MAM.1	M. A. Musselwhite
	G-RMGN	AS.355F-1 Twin Squirrel	VIP Marine & Aviation Ltd (G-BMCY)
	G-RNAS	D.H.104 Sea Devon C.20 (XK896)	D. W. Hermiston-Hooper/Sandown
	G-RNCO	R. Commander 690C	Ranco Europe Ltd/Plymouth
	G-RNMO	Short SD3-30	Fairflight Ltd/Gill Air (G-BFZW)/ Newcastle
	G-RNRM	Cessna A.185F	G-Air Ltd/Goodwood
	G-RNTV	PA-30 Twin Comanche 160C	Amcan Electronic Developments Ltd (G-AXDL)
	G-ROAN	Boeing E.75N-1 Stearman ★	R. Windley (stored)
	G-ROAR	Cessna 401	Cleanacres Ltd (G-BZFL/G-AWSF)/ Staverton
	G-ROBB	Grob G.109B	A. P. Mayne
	G-ROBE	Grob G.109B	Corbett Farms Ltd/Shobdon
	G-ROBI	Grob G.109B	A. W. McGarrigle/Cardiff
	G-ROBN	Robin R.1180T	J. G. Beaumont
	G-ROBO	Robinson R-22B	C. Henry
	G-ROBY	Colt 17A balloon	Lighter-Than-Air Ltd
	G-ROCK	Thunder Ax7-77 balloon	The Long Rake Spar Co Ltd
	G-RODI	Isaacs Fury (K3731)	D. C. J. Summerfield
	G-RODS	A-Bell 206B JetRanger 2	Crook & Son (G-NOEL/G-BCWN)
	G-ROGR	Bell 206A JetRanger	Crook & Son (G-AXMM(
	G-ROLA	PA-34-200T Seneca	Highsteeple Ltd
	G-ROLF	PA-32R-301 Saratoga SP	R. W. Burchardt
	G-ROLL	Pitts S-2A Special	RPM Aviation Ltd/Guernsey
	G-RONT	Enstrom F-28A	R. Thomas (G-BDAW)
	G-RONW	FRED Srs 2	P. J. D. Granow
	G-ROOF	Brantly B.2B	S. Lee (G-AXSR)
	G-ROOK	Cessna F.172P	Crop Aviation (UK) Ltd
	G-ROOM	Short SD3-60	Short Bros Ltd (G-BSBL)/Sydenham
	G-ROPI	Hughes 369HS	C. J. M. Greenwood (G-ROMA/G-ONPP)
	G-RORO	Cessna 337B	C. Keane (G-AVIX)
	G-RORY	Piaggio FW P.149D	R. McCarthy (G-TOWN)/Booker
	G-ROSE	Evans VP-1	W. K. Rose
	G-ROSI	Thunder Ax7-77 balloon	Scotia Balloons Ltd
	G-ROSS	Practavia Pilot Sprite	F. M. T. Ross
	G-ROTA	Bensen B.8	D. Ellerton
	G-ROUP	Cessna F.172M	George Cross Services Ltd (G-BDPH)
	G-ROUS	PA-34-200T Seneca II	C.S.E. Aviation Ltd/Kidlington
	G-ROVE	PA-18 Super Cub 135	Cormack (Aircraft Services) Ltd/ Glasgow
	G-ROVI	Aviamilano F.8L Falco Srs 2	J. B. McBride
	G-ROWL	AA-5B Tiger	Aviation Simulation/Biggin Hill
	G-ROWN	Beech 200 Super King Air	Gatebar Ltd (G-BHLC)
	G-ROWS	PA-28-151 Warrior	P. G. Lee

Reg.	Type	Owner or Operator	Notes
G-ROYI	PA-32R-301 Saratoga	R. L. West (G-BMEY)	
G-ROYL	Taylor JT.1 Monoplane	R. L. Wharmby	
G-ROYW	PA-28RT-201 Arrow IV	R. L. West (G-CRTI)	
G-ROYY	Robinson R-22B	Tudor Motorcycles	
G-ROZY	Cameron R.36 balloon	Jacques W. Soukup Ltd	
G-RPAH	Rutan Vari-Eze	B. Hanson	
G-RPEZ	Rutan LongEz	B. A. Fairston & D. Richardson	
G-RRRR	Privateer Motor Glider	R. F. Selby	
G-RRSG	Thunder Ax7-77 balloon	J. N. Harley	
G-RRTM	Sikorsky S-70C	Rolls-Royce PLC/Filton	
G-RSUL	Cessna T.303	Sulair Services Ltd/Gamston	
G-RTHL	Leivers Special	R. Leivers	
G-RUBB	AA-5B Tiger	J. M. Summerfield/Elstree	
G-RUBI	Thunder Ax7-77 balloon	Anglia Balloon School Ltd	
G-RUDD	Cameron V-65 balloon	N. A. Apsey	
G-RUIA	Cessna F.172M	F. Daly	
G-RUMN	AA-1A Trainer	L. J. Smith	
G-RUNT	Cassutt Racer IIIM	A. L. Hall-Carpenter	
G-RUSH	Cessna 404 Titan	Kondair (G-BEMX)/Stansted	
G-RUSS	Cessna 172N	Leisure Lease/Southend	
G-RYAN	PA-28R-201T Turbo Arrow III	M. Collins & P. J. Tallant (G-BFMN)	
G-RYOB	Bell 206B JetRanger 2	Oastdane Ltd (G-BLWU)	
G-SAAB	R. Commander 112TC	S. Richmen (G-BEFS)	
G-SAAM	Cessna T.182R	Hopstop Ltd (G-TAGL)/Elstree	
G-SABA	PA-28R-201T Turbo Arrow III	G. I. Cooper (G-BFEN)	
G-SACA	Cessna 152 II	Graham Cook Aviation Ltd (G-HOSE)/ Shoreham	
G-SACB	Cessna F.152 II	Westward Airways (Land's End) Ltd (G-BFRB)/St Just	
G-SACD	Cessna F.172H	Graham Cook Aviation Ltd (G-AVCD)/ Shoreham	
G-SACE	Cessna F.150L	Graham Cook Aviation Ltd (G-AZLK)/ Shoreham	
G-SACF	Cessna 152 II	Graham Cook Aviation Ltd (G-BHSZ)/ Shoreham	
G-SAFE	Cameron N-77 balloon	Nottingham Hot Air Balloon Club	
G-SAHI	Trago Mills SAH-1	Trago Mills Ltd/Bodmin	
G-SAIR	Cessna 421C	Essair Ltd (G-OBCA)	
G-SALA	PA-32-300 Cherokee Six	Golf-Sala Ltd/Elstree	
G-SALI	Cessna 421C	Rapid 3864 Ltd/Luton	
G-SALL	Cessna F.150L (Tailwheel)	Lubair (Transport Services) Ltd/ E. Midlands	
G-SALT	PA-23 Aztec 250F	Scotia Safari Ltd (G-BGTH)/Prestwick	
G-SALU	Short SD3-60	Manx Airlines Ltd (G-BKZR)/ Ronaldsway	
G-SALV	Beech C90 King Air	Christian Salvensen Ltd (G-BIXM)/ Edinburgh	
G-SALY	Hawker Sea Fury FB.11 (WJ288)	T. P. Luscombe & ptnrs/Lympne	
G-SAMA	PA-31-350 Navajo Chieftain	Asseman Ltd	
G-SAMG	Grob G.109B	RAFGSA/Bicester	
G-SAMM	Cessna 340A	Messenger Newspapers Ltd	
G-SAMS	M.S.880B Rallye Club	D. L. Johns/Sibson	
G-SAMZ	Cessna 150D	N. E. Sames (G-ASSO)	
G-SANB	Beech E90 King Air	Scottish & Newcastle Breweries PLC (G-BGNU)	
G-SARA	PA-28-181 Archer II	R. H. Ford/Elstree	
G-SARN	BN-2A Mk III-2 Trislander	Air Sarnia Ltd (G-BEFO)/Guernsey	
G-SARO	Saro Skeeter Mk 12	F. F. Chamberlain/Inverness	
G-SATI	Cameron 105 Sphere balloon	Cameron Balloons Ltd	
G-SATO	PA-23 Aztec 250E	J. J. Baumhardt (G-BCXP)/Southend	
G-SAVE	PA-31-350 Navajo Chieftain	Skyguard Ltd/Birmingham	
G-SBEC	Cessna 501 Citation	Sibec Aldershot Two Ltd/Manchester	
G-SBUS	BN-2A-26 Islander	Isles of Scilly Skybus Ltd (G-BMMH)/St Just	
G-SCAH	Cameron V-77 balloon	S. C. A. Howarth	
G-SCAN	Vinten-Wallis WA-116/100	W. Vinten Ltd	
G-SCAT	Cessna F.150F	Cheshire Air Training School (G-ATRN)/ Liverpool	
G-SCFO	Cameron O-77 balloon	D. V. Fowler	
G-SCHH	BAe 146-100	Dan-Air Services Ltd/Gatwick	
G-SCOT	PA-31-350 Navajo Chieftain	David Martin Couriers Ltd	
G-SCTT	HPR-7 Herald 210	Channel Express Air Services Ltd (G-ASPJ)/Bournemouth	

Notes	Reg.	Type	Owner or Operator
	G-SCUB	PA-18 Super Cub 135 (542447)	N. D. Needham Farms
	G-SCUH	Boeing 737-3Q8	Dan-Air Services Ltd/Gatwick
	G-SEAB	Republic RC-3 Seabee	G. Cormack/Glasgow
	G-SEAH	Hawker Sea Hawk FB.3	Sark International Airways Ltd
	G-SEAT	Colt 42 balloon	Virgin Atlantic Airways
	G-SEBB	Brugger MB.2 Colibri	M. Riddin
	G-SEED	Piper J-3C-65 Cub	J. H. Seed
	G-SEEK	Cessna T.210N	3M United Kingdom PLC
	G-SEGO	Robinson R-22B	G. Seago
	G-SEJW	PA-28-161 Warrior II	Truman Aviation Ltd/Tollerton
	G-SELL	Robin DR.400/180	Sellair
	G-SEPT	Cameron N-105 balloon	Deproco UK Ltd
	G-SEVA	SE-5A replica (F141)	I. D. Gregory
	G-SEWL	PA-28-151 Warrior	A. R. Sewell & Sons/Andrewsfield
	G-SEXY	AA-1 Yankee	W. Davies (G-AYLM)/Cardiff
	G-SFHR	PA-23 Aztec 250F	E. L. Becker & J. Harper (G-BHSO)
	G-SFTD	SA.341G Gazelle Srs 1	Blades Helicopters Ltd/Goodwood
	G-SFTH	SA.341G Gazelle	Sarum Aviation Ltd (G-BLAP)
	G-SFTR	NDN-1T Turbo Firecracker	Specialist Flying Training Ltd/Cardiff
	G-SFTS	NDN-1T Turbo Firecracker	Marinco Ltd
	G-SFTZ	Slingsby T.67M Firefly	Specialist Flying Training Ltd/Carlisle
	G-SHAA	Enstrom 280-UK	Manchester Helicopter Centre/Barton
	G-SHAW	PA-30 Twin Comanche 160B	Micro Metalsmiths Ltd
	G-SHCC	AB-206B JetRanger	Starline Helicopters Ltd
	G-SHDD	Enstrom F-28C	Malthouse Securities Ltd (G-BNBS)
	G-SHEL	Cameron O-56 balloon	The Shell Company of Hong Kong Ltd
	G-SHIP	PA-23 Aztec 250F ★	Midland Air Museum/Coventry
	G-SHIV	GA-7 Cougar	G. L. Cailes & Robin Hood Aviation Ltd/ Southampton
	G-SHJJ	Bell 206B JetRanger	Starline Helicopters Ltd
	G-SHOT	Cameron V-77 balloon	Bucks Hot-Air Balloon Group
	G-SHOW	M.S.733 Alycon	Vintage Aircraft Team/Cranfield
	G-SHST	Colt 180A balloon	G. V. Beckwith
	G-SHUG	PA-28R-201T Turbo Arrow III	N. E. Rennie
	G-SIGN	PA-39 Twin Comanche 160 C/R	Liontravel Ltd/Elstree
	G-SILV	Cessna 340A	Middle East Business Club/Guernsey
	G-SING	Beech B60 Duke	Sasha Fashions International Ltd/ Leavesden
	G-SIPA	SIPA 903	M. Collins (G-BGBM)
	G-SITU	Partenavia P.68C	Air Sarnia Ltd (G-NEWU/G-BHJX)/ Guernsey
	G-SIXC	Douglas DC-6B	Atlantic Air Transport Ltd/Coventry
	G-SIXX	Colt 77A balloon	G. E. Harris & S. C. Kinsey
	G-SJAB	PA-39 Twin Comanche 160 C/R	Foyle Flyers Ltd
	G-SJGM	Cessna 182R	Crystal Air Ltd
	G-SKAN	Cessna F.172M	Aircraft Rentals Humberside Ltd (G-BFKT)
	G-SKIP	Cameron N-77 balloon	Skipton Building Soc
	G-SKSA	Airship Industries SKS.500	Airship Industries Ltd/Cardington
	G-SKSB	Airship Industries SKS.500	Airship Industries Ltd/Cardington
	G-SKSC	Airship Industries SKS.600	Airship Industries Ltd/Cardington
	G-SKSG	Airship Industries SKS.600/03	Airship Industries Ltd/Cardington
	G-SKSH	Airship Industries SKS.600/06	Airship Industries Ltd/Cardington
	G-SKSJ	Airship Industries SKS.600/05	Airship Industries Ltd/Cardington
	G-SKSL	Airship Industries SKS.600	Airship Industries (UK) Ltd
	G-SKSN	Airship Industries SKS.600	Airship Industries (UK) Ltd
	G-SKYE	Cessna TU.206G	RAF Sport Parachute Association
	G-SKYH	Cessna 172N	Elgor Hire Purchase & Credit Ltd/ Southend
	G-SKYI	Air Command 532 Elite	Skyrider Aviation Ltd
	G-SKYM	Cessna F.337E	Bencray Ltd (G-AYHW) (stored)/ Blackpool
	G-SKYS	Cameron O-84 balloon	J. R. Christopher
	G-SLEA	Mudry/CAARP CAP.10B	P. D. Southerington/Sturgate
	G-SLIK	Taylor JT.2 Titch	J. A. Jennings
	G-SLIM	Colt 56A balloon	Hot-Air Balloon Co Ltd
	G-SLOT	Cessna 340A	Ace Coin Equipment Ltd
	G-SMAF	Sikorsky S-76A	Fayair (Jersey) 1984 Ltd
	G-SMCI	Bell 206B JetRanger	SMC Aviation Ltd
	G-SMHK	Cameron D-38 airship	San Miguel Brewery Ltd
	G-SMIG	Cameron O-65 balloon	Hong Kong Balloon & Airship Club
	G-SMJJ	Cessna 414A	Gull Air Ltd/Guernsey
	G-SMUJ	Enstrom F-28C-UK	Rotorchamp Ltd (G-BHTF)

156

Reg.	Type	Owner or Operator	Notes
G-SNAP	Cameron V-77 balloon	N. A. Apsey	
G-SNIP	Cessna F.172H	Anglian Flight Training Ltd (G-AXSI)/ Norwich	
G-SNOB	Beech A.36 Bonanza	R. I. Craddock (G-BEIK)	
G-SNOW	Cameron V-77 balloon	M. J. Snow	
G-SOAR	Eiri PIK-20E	P. Rees	
G-SOFA	Cameron N-65 balloon	Northern Upholstery Ltd	
G-SOFE	Cessna 441	Imbergem Ltd/Goodwood	
G-SOFI	PA-60 Aerostar 601P (Machen Superstar II)	Allzones Travel Ltd/Biggin Hill	
G-SOFS	F.27 Friendship Mk 200	Secretary of State for Scotland & Department of Agriculture and Fisheries (G-BLML)/Edinburgh	
G-SOFT	Thunder Ax7-77 balloon	Bristol Software Factory Ltd	
G-SOLA	Star-Lite SL.1	P. Clifton & A. Clarke	
G-SOLD	Robinson R-22A	Travel Management Ltd	
G-SOLO	Pitts S-2S Special	Fyat Ltd/Booker	
G-SONA	SOCATA TB.10 Tobago	J. Greenwood (G-BIBI)	
G-SONY	Aero Commander 200D	General Airline Ltd (G-BGPS)	
G-SOOE	Hughes 369E	Manchester Air Charter Ltd	
G-SOOS	Colt 21A balloon	The Independent Balloon Co Ltd	
G-SOOT	PA-28 Cherokee 180	Streamline Aviation (G-AVNM)/ E. Midlands	
G-SOUL	Cessna 310R	Atlantic Air Transport Ltd/Coventry	
G-SPAR	Cameron N-77 balloon	Nicholas Sanders Ltd	
G-SPBA	Bell 412	Bristow Helicopters Ltd	
G-SPEY	AB-206B JetRanger 3	Castle Air Charters Ltd (G-BIGO)	
G-SPIN	Pitts S-2A Special	R. N. Goode/White Waltham	
G-SPIT	V.S.379 Spitfire XIV (MV293)	B. J. S. Grey (G-BGHB)/Duxford	
G-SRES	Beech 300 Super King Air	Vernair Transport Services Ltd Liverpool	
G-SSBS	Colting Ax77 balloon	K. J. & M. E. Gregory	
G-SSFT	PA-28-161 Warrior II	SFT Aviation Ltd (G-BHIL)/Bournemouth	
G-STAG	Cameron O-65 balloon	Holker Estates Ltd	
G-STAN	F.27 Friendship Mk.200	Air UK/Norwich	
G-STAP	Cessna FA.152	Stapleford Flying Club Ltd	
G-STAT	Cessna U.206F	SMK Engineers Ltd	
G-STEF	Hughes 369HS	D. J. L. Wood (G-BKTK)	
G-STEV	Jodel DR.221	S. W. Talbot/Long Marston	
G-STMP	SNCAN Stampe SV-4A	W. R. Partridge	
G-STOI	Robinson R-22B	Tickstop Ltd	
G-STOY	Robinson R-22B	Tickstop Ltd	
G-STST	Bell 206B JetRanger 3	Petrochemical Supplies Ltd	
G-STVE	AS.355F-1 Twin Squirrel	James Wilkes PLC (G-TOFF/G-BKJX)	
G-STVI	Bell 206L-1 LongRanger	Clyde Helicopters Ltd	
G-STVN	HPR-7 Herald 210	Channel Express Air Services Ltd/ Bournemouth	
G-STWO	ARV Super 2	ARV Aviation Ltd	
G-STYL	Pitts S-1S Special	B. MacMillan	
G-SULL	PA-32R-301 Saratoga SP	B. R. Chaplin	
G-SULY	Monnet Moni	M. J. Sullivan	
G-SUPA	PA-18 Super Cub 150	Yorkshire Gliding Club (Pty) Ltd	
G-SUSI	Cameron V-77 balloon	H. S. & C. J. Dryden	
G-SUSY	P-51D-25-NA Mustang	Charles Church Displays Ltd	
G-SUTT	Hughes 369E	Southern Air Ltd (G-OEPF/G-OMJH)/ Shoreham	
G-SUZI	Beech 95-B55 Baron	M. Joy (G-BAXR)	
G-SUZY	Taylor JT.1 Monoplane	E. J. Blackoe	
G-SVHA	Partenavia P.68B	D. Martin Couriers Ltd	
G-SWFT	Beech 200 Super King Air	Airswift Ltd (G-SIBE/G-MCEO/G-BILY)	
G-SWOT	Currie Super Wot	R. A. Bowes	
G-SWPR	Cameron N-56 balloon	Balloon Stable Ltd	
G-SXVI	V.S.361 Spitfire F.XVI	D. Arnold	
G-SYFW	Focke-Wulf Fw.190 replica (2+1)	M. R. Parr	
G-SYKS	Cessna 550 Citation II	Paul Sykes (Aviation) Ltd	
G-TACA	P.57 Sea Prince T.1	Atlantic & Caribbean Aviation Ltd/ Staverton	
G-TACE	H.S.125 Srs 403B	Lynx Aviation Ltd (G-AYIZ)/Cranfield	
G-TACK	Grob G.109B	Oval (275) Ltd/Bristol	
G-TAFF	CASA 1.131 Jungmann	Custompac Ltd (G-BFNE)	
G-TAFY	Piper J-3F-65 Cub	C. Evans	
G-TAGS	PA-28-161 Warrior II	Tophart Ltd	
G-TAIR	PA-34-200T Seneca II	Wessex Mouldings Ltd	

Notes	Reg.	Type	Owner or Operator
	G-TALI	AS.355F-1 Twin Squirrel	The Duke of Westminster
	G-TAMY	Cessna 421B	Abbergail Ltd/Luton
	G-TAPE	PA-23 Aztec 250D	Merlix Ltd (G-AWVW)
	G-TARA	Christen Eagle II	F. E. P. Holmes
	G-TATT	GY-20 Minicab	L. Tattershall
	G-TAXI	PA-23 Aztec 250E	Northern Executive Aviation Ltd/ Manchester
	G-TBIO	SOCATA TB.10 Tobago	H. M. Fenn & J. E. Hailes
	G-TBXX	SOCATA TB.20 Trinidad	JDM Electrical & Mechanical Services Ltd/Denham
	G-TBZO	SOCATA TB.20 Trinidad	M. Barnett/Elstree
	G-TCAR	Robin HR.100/210	Gibad Aviation Ltd
	G-TCMP	Robinson R-22B	T. C. M. Porter
	G-TCUB	Piper J-3C-65 Cub	M. & J. McGachy
	G-TDFS	IMCO Callair A.9	Dollarhigh Ltd (G-AVZA)
	G-TEAC	AT-6C Harvard IIA (EX280)	E. C. English/Bourn
	G-TECH	R. Commander 114	P. A. Reed (G-BEDH)/Denham
	G-TECK	Cameron V-77 balloon	G. M. N. Spencer
	G-TEDD	Cessna 310R	Birchwood Boat International Ltd (G-MADI)
	G-TEDS	SOCATA TB.10 Tobago	Redhill Flying Club (G-BHCO)
	G-TEES	Cessna F.152	Cleveland Flying School Ltd (G-BIUI)/ Teesside
	G-TEFC	PA-28 Cherokee 140	A. J. Cornish
	G-TEFH	Cessna 500 Citation	Birmingham Aviation Ltd (G-BCII)
	G-TELE	Partenavia P.68C	Aerocharter (Midlands) Ltd (G-DORE)
	G-TEMI	BN-2T Islander	Pilatus BN Ltd (G-BJYX)/Bembridge
	G-TESS	Quickie Q.2	D. Evans
	G-TEWS	PA-28 Cherokee 140	M. J. & M. J. Tew (G-KEAN/G-AWTM)
	G-TFCI	Cessna FA.152	Tayside Aviation Ltd/Dundee
	G-TFUN	Valentin Taifun 17E	P. J. Evans/Biggin Hill
	G-TGAS	Cameron O-160 balloon	Travel Gas (Midlands) Ltd
	G-TGER	AA-5B Tiger	A. Wuensche (G-BFZP)
	G-THCL	Cessna 550 Citation II	Tower House Consultants Ltd
	G-THEA	Boeing E75 Stearman	L. M. Walton
	G-THOM	Thunder Ax6-56 balloon	T. H. Wilson
	G-THOR	Thunder Ax8-105 balloon	N. C. Faithful *Turncoat*
	G-THOS	Thunder Ax7-77 balloon	Thos Wood & Son (Builders) Ltd
	G-THSL	PA-28R-201 Arrow III	G. Fearnley/Southend
	G-TICK	Cameron V-77 balloon	T. J. Tickler
	G-TIDS	Jodel D.150	R. A. Locke
	G-TIGA	D.H.82A Tiger Moth	Truman Aviation Ltd (G-AOEG)
	G-TIGB	AS.332L Super Puma	Bristow Helicopters Ltd (G-BJXC)
	G-TIGC	AS.332L Super Puma	Bristow Helicopters Ltd (G-BJYH)
	G-TIGE	AS.332L Super Puma	Bristow Helicopters Ltd (G-BJYJ)
	G-TIGF	AS.332L Super Puma	Bristow Helicopters Ltd
	G-TIGG	AS.332L Super Puma	Bristow Helicopters Ltd
	G-TIGH	AS.332L Super Puma	Bristow Helicopters Ltd
	G-TIGI	AS.332L Super Puma	Bristow Helicopters Ltd
	G-TIGJ	AS.332L Super Puma	Bristow Helicopters Ltd
	G-TIGK	AS.332L Super Puma	Bristow Helicopters Ltd
	G-TIGL	AS.332L Super Puma	Bristow Helicopters Ltd
	G-TIGM	AS.332L Super Puma	Bristow Helicopters Ltd
	G-TIGN	AS.332L Super Puma	Bristow Helicopters Ltd
	G-TIGO	AS.332L Super Puma	Bristow Helicopters Ltd
	G-TIGP	AS.332L Super Puma	Bristow Helicopters Ltd
	G-TIGR	AS.332L Super Puma	Bristow Helicopters Ltd
	G-TIGS	AS.332L Super Puma	Bristow Helicopters Ltd
	G-TIGT	AS.332L Super Puma	Bristow Helicopters Ltd
	G-TIGU	AS.332L Super Puma	Bristow Helicopters Ltd
	G-TIGV	AS.332L Super Puma	Bristow Helicopters Ltd
	G-TIGW	AS.332L Super Puma	Bristow Helicopters Ltd
	G-TIGZ	AS.332L Super Puma	British International Helicopters Ltd
	G-TIKI	Colt 105A balloon	Lighter-Than-Air Ltd (G-BKWV)
	G-TIMB	Rutan Vari-Eze	T. M. Bailey (G-BKXJ)
	G-TIME	Aerostar 601P	J. J. Donn
	G-TIMJ	Rand KR-2	G. Griffith
	G-TIMK	PA-28-181 Archer II	T. Baker
	G-TIMW	PA-28 Cherokee 140C	W. H. Sanders (G-AXSH)
	G-TINA	SOCATA TB.10 Tobago	A. Lister
	G-TINS	Cameron N-90 balloon	Bass & Tennent Sales Ltd
	G-TIRE	Colt Flying Tyre balloon	Bandag Tyres Ltd
	G-TISH	PA-31-310 Turbo Navajo	Subtec Aviation Ltd (G-BFKJ)
	G-TJET	Lockheed T-33A-1-LO	Aces High Ltd/North Weald

Reg.	Type	Owner or Operator	Notes
G-TLOL	Cessna 421C	Littlewoods Organisation Ltd/ Liverpool	
G-TMAS	H.S.125 Srs 600B	Jetlease Ltd (G-MFEU)	
G-TMJH	Hughes 369E	Annoville Ltd	
G-TMMC	AS.355F-1 Twin Squirrel	The Colt Car Co Ltd (G-JLCO)	
G-TNTA	BAe 146-200QT	TNT Roadfreight (UK) Ltd/Birmingham	
G-TNTB	BAe 146-200QT	TNT Roadfreight (UK) Ltd/Birmingham	
G-TNTH	BAe 146-200QT	TNT Express (UK) Ltd (G-BNYC)	
G-TNTJ	BAe 146-200QT	TNT Express (UK) Ltd (G-BOHK)	
G-TOAD	Jodel D.140B	Mothballs Ltd	
G-TOBE	PA-28R Cherokee Arrow 200	J. Bradley & Barry Ltd (G-BNRO)	
G-TOBI	Cessna F.172K	I. Addy (G-AYVB)	
G-TOBY	Cessna 172B	J. A. Kelman (G-ARCM)/Elstree	
G-TODD	ICA IS-28M2A	C. I. Roberts & C. D. King	
G-TOGA	PA-32-301 Saratoga	W. H. Carson/Elstree	
G-TOMI	H.S.125 Srs 600B	Falcon Jet Centre Ltd (G-BBEP/G-BJOY)/Heathrow	
G-TOMO	BAC One-Eleven 487GK	Anglo Cargo Airlines Ltd/Manston	
G-TOMS	PA-38-112 Tomahawk	R. J. Alford	
G-TOMY	Mitsubishi Mu.300 Diamond	Lynton Aviation Ltd	
G-TONE	Pazmany PL.4	J. A. Walmsley	
G-TONI	Cessna 421C	Broomsleigh Construction Ltd/ Biggin Hill	
G-TOUR	Robin R.2112	Barnes Martin Ltd	
G-TOYS	Enstrom 280C-UK-2 Shark	Southern Air Ltd (G-BISE)/Shoreham	
G-TPII	Colt 21A balloon	Airship & Balloon Co Ltd	
G-TPTR	AB-206B JetRanger 3	Mann Aviation Ltd (G-LOCK)/Fairoaks	
G-TRAF	SA.365N Dauphin 2	Trans World Leasing Ltd (G-BLDR)	
G-TRAK	Edgley EA.7 Optica	Entertainment Film Productions Ltd (G-BLFC)	
G-TREE	Bell 206B JetRanger	LGH Aviation Ltd	
G-TRFM	PA-23 Aztec 250F	R. E. Coldham/Biggin Hill	
G-TRIK	Bell 206B JetRanger 2	Annabelle Casion Ltd (G-BMWY)	
G-TRIM	Monnet Moni	J. E. Bennell	
G-TRIP	PA-32R-301 Saratoga SP	A. P. J. Lavelle & I. Fabini (G-HOSK)	
G-TRIV	Colt Trivial Pursuit SS balloon	Airship & Balloon Co Ltd	
G-TRIX	V.S.509 Spitfire T.IX	R. J. F. Parker	
G-TROP	Cessna 310R	Tropair Cooling and Heating Ltd	
G-TRUK	Stoddard Hamilton Glasair RG	Archer Engineering (Leeds) Ltd	
G-TSAM	H.S.125 Srs 800B	BSM Holdings Ltd/Heathrow	
G-TSGJ	PA-28-181 Archer II	B. R. Sedgeman	
G-TSIX	AT-6C Harvard IIA	D. Taylor/E. Midlands	
G-TTAM	Taylor JT.2 Titch	A. J. Manning	
G-TTEL	PA-E23 Aztec 250D	G-Air Ltd (G-BBXE)/Lydd	
G-TTWO	Colt 56A balloon	P. N. Tilney	
G-TUBS	Beech 65-80 Queen Air	A. H. Bowers (G-ASKM)/Staverton	
G-TUDR	Cameron V-77 balloon	Jacques W. Soukup Ltd	
G-TUGG	PA-18 Super Cub 150	Ulster Gliding Club Ltd	
G-TUKE	Robin DR.400/160	Tukair/Headcorn	
G-TURB	D.31 Turbulent	A. Ryan-Fecitt	
G-TURK	Cameron 80 Sultan SS balloon	Forbes Europe Inc	
G-TURN	Steen Skybolt	W. B. & C. J. Hosie	
G-TURP	SA.341G Gazelle 1	Lenval Essex Ltd (G-BKLS)	
G-TVKE	Cessna 310R	Ewart & Co (Studio) Ltd (G-EURO)/ Elstree	
G-TVMM	Cessna 310Q	Enterprise Television Ltd (G-CETA/ G-BBIM)	
G-TVSA	R. Commander 690B	Technical Flight Services Ltd (G-JRMM)	
G-TVSI	Campbell Cricket	W. H. Beevers (G-AYHH)	
G-TWEL	PA-28-181 Archer II	Universal Salvage (Holdings) Ltd	
G-TWEY	Colt 69A balloon	British Telecom Thameswey	
G-TWIN	PA-44-180 Seminole	Leavesden Flight Centre Ltd	
G-TWOB	BN-2B-26 Islander	Pilatus BN Ltd (G-BKJJ)/Bembridge	
G-TYGA	AA-5B Tiger	Hovemere Ltd (G-BHNZ)/Biggin Hill	
G-TYME	R. Commander 690B	Marlborough (London) Ltd	
G-TYRE	Cessna F.172M	Staverton Flying Services Ltd	
G-UARD	Sequoia F.8L Falco	A. J. Baggarley	
G-UBSH	Beech 300 Super King Air	United Biscuits (UK) Ltd/Denham	
G-UERN	BN-2B-26 Islander	Air Sarnia Ltd (G-BHXI)/Guernsey	
G-UIDE	Jodel D.120	S. T. Gilbert/Popham	
G-UIET	BAe ATP	Manx Airlines Ltd/Ronaldsway	
G-UILD	Grob G.109B	Runnymede Consultants Ltd	
G-UKCA	H.S.125 Srs 700B	McAlpine Aviation Ltd/Luton	

Notes	Reg.	Type	Owner or Operator
	G-UKHP	BAe 146-300	Air UK Ltd/Norwich
	G-UKLA	Boeing 737-4Y0	Air UK Leisure Ltd *Flagship St Andrew*/Stansted
	G-UKLB	Boeing 737-4Y0	Air UK Leisure Ltd *Flagship St Francis*/Stansted
	G-UKLC	Boeing 737-42C	Air UK Leisure Ltd *Flagship St David*/Stansted
	G-UKLD	Boeing 737-42C	Air UK Leisure Ltd *Flagship St Patrick*/Stansted
	G-UKLE	Boeing 737-4Y0	Air UK Leisure Ltd *Flagship St George*/Stansted
	G-UKSC	BAe 146-300	Air UK Ltd/Norwich
	G-UMBO	Thunder Ax7-77A balloon	Virgin Atlantic Airways Ltd
	G-UNIC	AS.350B Ecureuil	Winterbourne Construction Ltd (G-COLN/G-BHIV)
	G-UNIK	AB-206B JetRanger 2	Winterbourne Construction Ltd (G-TPPH/G-BCYP)
	G-UPDN	Cameron V-65 balloon	R. J. O. Evans
	G-UPPP	Colt 77A balloon	M. Williams
	G-USAF	NA T-28C Trojan	M. B. Walker
	G-USAM	Cameron Uncle Sam balloon	Jacques W. Soukup Ltd
	G-USGB	Colt 105A balloon	Thunder & Colt Ltd
	G-USSY	PA-28-181 Archer II	H. J. Pelham
	G-USTY	FRED Srs 2	K. Jones
	G-UTSY	PA-28R-201 Arrow III	D. G. Perry/Stapleford
	G-UTZY	SA.341G Gazelle 1	Davinci Aviation Ltd (G-BKLV)
	G-VAGA	PA-15 Vagabond	E. J. McEntee/White Waltham
	G-VARG	Varga 2150A Kachina	J. Hannibal/Halfpenny Green
	G-VAUK	PA-31-350 Navajo Chieftain	C. Evans & Sons Ltd (G-GWEA)
	G-VAUN	Cessna 340	F. E. Peacock & Son (Thorney) Ltd
	G-VENI	D.H.112 Venom FB.50	Source Premium & Promotional Consultants Ltd
	G-VEZE	Rutan Vari-Eze	P. J. Henderson
	G-VGIN	Boeing 747-243B	Virgin Atlantic Airways Ltd *Scarlet Lady*/Gatwick
	G-VICK	PA-31 Turbo Navajo	Howard Richard & Co Ltd (G-AWED)/Elstree
	G-VIDI	D.H.112 Venom FB.50	Source Premium & Promotional Consultants Ltd
	G-VIEW	Vinten-Wallis WA-116/100	W. Vinten Ltd
	G-VIII	V. S. Spitfire F.VIII (MT719)	—
	G-VIKE	Bellanca 1730A Viking	Modular Business Computers Ltd/Elstree
	G-VIRG	Boeing 747-287B	Virgin Atlantic Airways Ltd *Maiden Voyager*/Gatwick
	G-VIST	PA-30 Twin Comanche 160B	A. R. Taylor (G-AVHZ)
	G-VITE	Robin R.1180T	Trans Global Aviation Supply Co Ltd/Booker
	G-VIVA	Thunder Ax7-65 balloon	J. G. Spearing
	G-VIXN	D.H.110 Sea Vixen FAW.2	Brencham Historic Aircraft Ltd/Bournemouth
	G-VIZZ	Sportavia RS.180 Sportsman	Executive Air Sport Ltd/Exeter
	G-VJAI	GA-7 Cougar	United Breweries (International) Ltd (G-OCAB/G-BICF)/Elstree
	G-VJCB	Agusta A.109A II	J. C. Bamford Excavators Ltd (G-BOUA)
	G-VJCT	Partenavia P.68C	Montrose Leasing Ltd
	G-VJET	Avro 698 Vulcan B.2 (XL426)	R. E. Jacobsen
	G-VLAD	Yakolev Yak-50	R. Goode
	G-VMAX	Mooney M.20K	Glidegold Ltd
	G-VMDE	Cessna P.210N	V. S. Evans & Horne & Sutton Ltd/Cranfield
	G-VNOM	D.H.112 Venom FB.50	A. Topen/Cranfield
	G-VOID	PA-28RT-201 Arrow IV	R. B. H. Vetch
	G-VPII	Evans VP-2	V. D. J. Hitchings
	G-VPLC	Beech 200 Super King Air	Vickers Shipbuilding & Engineering Ltd
	G-VPTO	Evans VP-2	J. Cater
	G-VRES	Beech A200 Super King Air	Northern Executive Aviation Ltd/Manchester
	G-VSEL	Beech 200 Super King Air	Vickers Shipbuilding & Engineering Ltd (G-SONG/G-BKTI)/Barrow
	G-VSOP	Cameron 60 SS balloon	J. R. Parkington & Co Ltd
	G-VTAX	PA-31-350 Navajo Chieftain	Chaseside Holdings Ltd
	G-VTEN	Vinten-Wallis WA-117	W. Vinten Ltd

Reg.	Type	Owner or Operator	Notes
G-VTII	D.H.115 Vampire T.11 (WZ507)	J. Turnbull & ptnrs/Cranfield	
G-VTOL	H.S. Harrier T52	British Aerospace/Dunsfold	
G-VULC	Avro 698 Vulcan B.2	R. E. Jacobsen	
G-WAAC	Cameron N-56 balloon	Advertising Balloon Co	
G-WACA	Cessna F.152	Wycombe Air Centre Ltd	
G-WACB	Cessna F.152	Wycombe Air Centre Ltd	
G-WACC	Cessna F.152	Wycombe Air Centre Ltd	
G-WACD	Cessna F.152	Wycombe Air Centre Ltd	
G-WACE	Cessna F.152	Wycombe Air Centre Ltd	
G-WACF	Cessna 152	Wycombe Air Centre Ltd	
G-WACG	Cessna F.152	Wycombe Air Centre Ltd	
G-WACH	Cessna FA.152	Wycombe Air Centre Ltd	
G-WACI	Beech 76 Duchess	Wycombe Air Centre Ltd	
G-WACK	Short SD3-60 Variant 100	Loganair Ltd (G-BMAJ)/Glasgow	
G-WACO	Waco UPF.7	Ray Holt (Land Drainage) Ltd	
G-WACR	PA-28 Cherokee 180	Wycombe Air Centre Ltd (G-BCZF)	
G-WACS	Cessna F.152	Hartmann Ltd/Booker	
G-WACT	Cessna F.152 II	Hartmann Ltd (G-BKFT)/Booker	
G-WACU	Cessna FA.152	Hartmann Ltd (G-BJZU)/Booker	
G-WACV	Cessna 182N	Hartmann Ltd (G-AZEA)/Booker	
G-WACW	Cessna 172P	Wycombe Air Centre Ltd	
G-WACX	Cessna F.172M	Wycombe Air Centre Ltd (G-BAEX)	
G-WACY	Cessna F.172P	Wycombe Air Centre Ltd	
G-WACZ	Cessna F.172M	Wycombe Air Centre Ltd (G-BCUK)	
G-WAGI	Robinson R-22B	J. Wagstaff	
G-WAGY	Cessna F.172N	J. B. Wagstaff/E. Midlands	
G-WALK	Cessna F.182Q	Walk-Air Ltd (G-BEZM)/Leeds	
G-WALL	Beech 95-58P Baron	C. D. Weiswall/Elstree	
G-WALS	Cessna A.152	Wallis & Son Ltd	
G-WARD	Taylor JT.1 Monoplane	G. & G. D. Ward	
G-WARI	PA-28-161 Warrior II	Denham School of Flying Ltd	
G-WARR	PA-28-161 Warrior II	M. Rumbol	
G-WARI	PA-28-161 Warrior II	Denham School of Flying Ltd	
G-WASH	Noble 1250 balloon	Noble Adventures Ltd	
G-WASP	Brantly B.2B	W. C. Evans & M. L. Morris (G-ASXE)	
G-WBPR	H.S.125 Srs 800B	Trusthouse Forte PLC/Heathrow	
G-WCEI	M.S.894E Rallye 220GT	R. C. Holmes (G-BAOC)	
G-WEBB	PA-23 Aztec 250E	Brands Hatch Circuit Ltd (G-BJBU)	
G-WELI	Cameron N-77 balloon	N. J. Tovey	
G-WELL	Beech E90 King Air	CEGA Aviation Ltd/Goodwood	
G-WELS	Cameron N-65 balloon	Charles Wells Ltd	
G-WEND	PA-28RT-201 Arrow IV	Trent Insulations Ltd/Birmingham	
G-WERY	SOCATA TB.20 Trinidad	G. J. Werry/Manston	
G-WEST	Agusta A.109A	Westland Helicopters Ltd/Yeovil	
G-WETI	Cameron N-31 balloon	C. A. Butter	
G-WGCS	PA-18 Super Cub 95	T. M. Storey/Shoreham	
G-WGEL	Boeing 737-2U4	Dan-Air Services Ltd (G-ILFC/G-BOSL)/Gatwick	
G-WHIZ	Pitts S-1 Special	K. M. McLeod	
G-WHIZ†	V.701 Viscount ★	Saltwell Park (G-AMOE)/Gateshead	
G-WHIZ†	V.732 Viscount (fuselage only) ★	Wales Aircraft Museum (G-ANRS)/Cardiff	
G-WHYZ	Hughes 369HS	N. C. B. Cheyney & M. Wells	
G-WICH	FRED Srs 2	R. H. Hearn	
G-WICK	Partenavia P.68B	Strix Ltd (G-BGFZ)	
G-WILD	Pitts S-1T Special	B. K. Lecomber	
G-WILI	PA-32R-301 Saratoga SP	Minster Enterprises Ltd	
G-WILK	Beech B200 Super King Air	A. F. Budge (Aviation) Ltd (G-BOBM)/Gamston	
G-WILO	Bell 206B JetRanger	Candyfleet Ltd	
G-WILY	Rutan LongEz	W. S. Allen	
G-WIMP	Colt 56A balloon	C. Wolstenholme *Wimp*	
G-WINE	Thunder Ax7-77Z balloon	R. Brooker	
G-WIRL	Robinson R-22B	Northern Helicopters Ltd	
G-WITE	Cessna 414A	City Flight Ltd (G-LOVO/G-KENT)	
G-WIZO	PA-34-220T Seneca III	Market Vision Ltd	
G-WIZZ	AB-206B JetRanger 2	Triple Oak Ltd	
G-WLAD	BAC One-Eleven 304AX	— (G-ATPI)	
G-WMCC	BAe Jetstream 3102-01	Birmingham Executive Airways PLC (G-TALL)	
G-WOLD	Scheibe SF.25E Falke	Wolds Gliding Club Ltd (G-BOVM)	
G-WOLF	PA-28 Cherokee 140	E. Ford	
G-WOOD	Beech 95-B55 Baron	Gama Aviation Ltd (G-AYID)/Fairoaks	

Notes	Reg.	Type	Owner or Operator
	G-WOSP	Bell 206B JetRanger 3	Gleneagles Helicopter Services (Scotland) Ltd
	G-WOTG	BN-2T Islander	Secretary of State for Defence (G-BJYT)/Bicester
	G-WRCF	Beech 200 Super King Air	W. R. C. M. Foyle/Luton
	G-WREN	Pitts S-2A Special	P. Meeson/Booker
	G-WRIT	Thunder Ax7-77A balloon	J. Edge
	G-WRMN	Glaser-Dirks DG-400	W. R. McNair
	G-WRIT	Thunder Ax7-77A balloon	J. Edge
	G-WSEC	Enstrom F-28C	Guardwell Security Ltd (G-BONF)
	G-WSFT	PA-23 Aztec 250F	SFT Aviation Ltd (G-BTHS)/ Bournemouth
	G-WSKY	Enstrom 280C-UK-2 Shark	Footlea Ltd (G-BEEK)
	G-WSSC	PA-31-350 Navajo Chieftain	Air Kilroe Ltd/Manchester
	G-WSSL	PA-31-350 Navajo Chieftain	Foster Yeoman Ltd
	G-WTFA	Cessna F.182P	WTFA Ltd
	G-WULF	WAR Focke-Wulf Fw.190 (08)	R. C. & R. C. Dean/Biggin Hill
	G-WWII	V.S. 379 Spitfire XIV	B. S. J. Grey/Duxford
	G-WWUK	Enstrom F-28A-UK	Shimfoam Ltd (G-BFFN)
	G-WWWW	AS.355F-2 Twin Squirrel	Chivas Bros Ltd
	G-WYCH	Cameron 90 Witch balloon	Jacques W. Soukup Enterprises Ltd
	G-WYNN	Rand KR-2	W. Thomas
	G-WYNT	Cameron N-56 balloon	Jacques W. Soukup Enterprises Ltd
	G-WYTE	Bell 47G-2A-1	CKS Air Ltd/Southend
	G-WZZZ	Colt AS-56 airship	Hot-Air Balloon Co Ltd
	G-XALP	Schweizer 269C	Danbank Developments Ltd
	G-XCUB	PA-18 Super Cub 150	W. G. Fisher/Sandown
	G-XIIX	Robinson R-22B	Defence Products Ltd
	G-XITD	Cessna 310G	ITD Aviation Ltd (G-ASYV)
	G-XMAF	G.1159A Gulfstream 3	Fayair (Jersey) 1984 Ltd
	G-XRAY	Rand KR-2	R. S. Smith
	G-XSFT	PA-23 Aztec 250F	SFT Aviation Ltd (G-CPPC/G-BGBH)/ Bournemouth
	G-XTRA	Extra EA.230	B. K. Lecomber
	G-YBAA	Cessna FR.172J	J. Blackburn
	G-YIII	Cessna F.150L	Sherburn Aero Club Ltd
	G-YLAN	PA-31-350 Navajo Chieftain	J. J. Baumhardt/Southend
	G-YNOT	D.62B Condor	T. Littlefair (G-AYFH)
	G-YOGI	Robin DR.400/140B	R. M. Gosling (G-BDME)
	G-YORK	Cessna F.172M	Sherburn Aero Club Ltd
	G-YOTT	Cessna 425	Tarquin Boat Company Ltd (G-NORC)
	G-YPSY	Andreasson BA-4B	H. P. Burrill
	G-YROI	Air Command Commander 532	W. B. Lumb
	G-YROS	Bensen B.80-D	J. M. Montgomerie
	G-YSFT	PA-23 Aztec 250F	SFT Aviation Ltd (G-BEJT)/ Bournemouth
	G-YSKY	PA-31-350 Navajo Chieftain	J. J. Baumhardt/Southend
	G-YTWO	Cessna F.172M	Sherburn Aero Club Ltd
	G-YUGO	H.S.125 Srs 1B/R-522	Burtonwood Development Ltd (G-ATWH)
	G-YULL	PA-28 Cherokee 180E	Lansdowne Chemical Co (G-BEAJ)/ Kidlington
	G-YUPI	Cameron N-90 balloon	West Country Marketing & Advertising Ltd
	G-ZARI	AA-5B Tiger	Zarina Husein-Ellis (G-BHVY)
	G-ZAZA	PA-18 Super Cub 95	M. C. Barraclough
	G-ZBAC	AS.350B Ecureuil	BAC Ltd (G-SEBI/G-BMCU)
	G-ZBCA	Colt 77A balloon	British Car Auctions Ltd
	G-ZERO	AA-5B Tiger	Snowadem Ltd/Luton
	G-ZIPI	Robin DR.400/180	Stahl Engineering Co Ltd/Headcorn
	G-ZIPP	Cessna E.310Q	Bank Farm Ltd (G-BAYU)
	G-ZLIN	Z.526 Trener Master	V. S. E. Norman
	G-ZSOL	Zlin Z.50L	V. S. E. Norman/Kemble
	G-ZULU	PA-28-161 Warrior II	Denham School of Flying Ltd
	G-ZUMP	Cameron N-77 balloon	M. J. Allen *Gazump*

Toy Balloons

Reg.	Type	Owner or Operator	Notes
G-FYAK	European E.21	J. E. Christopher	
G-FYAN	Williams	M. D. Williams	
G-FYAO	Williams	M. D. Williams	
G-FYAR	Williams Mk 2	S. T. Wallbank	
G-FYAT	Osprey Mk 4D	S. D. Templeman	
G-FYAU	Williams MK 2	P. Bowater	
G-FYAV	Osprey Mk 4E2	C. D. Egan & C. Stiles	
G-FYAZ	Osprey Mk 4D2	M. A. Roblett	
G-FYBA	Portswood Mk XVI	C. R. Rundle	
G-FYBD	Osprey Mk 1E	M. Vincent	
G-FYBE	Osprey Mk 4D	M. Vincent	
G-FYBF	Osprey Mk V	M. Vincent	
G-FYBG	Osprey Mk 4G2	M. Vincent	
G-FYBH	Osprey Mk 4G	M. Vincent	
G-FYBI	Osprey Mk 4H	M. Vincent	
G-FYBP	European E.84PW	D. Eaves	
G-FYBR	Osprey Mk 4G2	A. J. Pugh	
G-FYBU	Portswood Mk XVI	M. A. Roblett	
G-FYBX	Portswood Mk XVI	I. Chadwick	
G-FYCA	Osprey Mk 4D	R. G. Crewe	
G-FYCC	Osprey Mk 4G2	A. Russell	
G-FYCF	Portswood Mk XVI	R. S. Joste	
G-FYCG	Portswood Mk XVI	R. S. Joste	
G-FYCH	Swan Mk 1	R. S. Joste	
G-FYCL	Osprey Mk 4G	P. J. Rogers	
G-FYCN	Osprey Mk 4D	C. F. Chipping	
G-FYCO	Osprey Mk 4B	C. F. Chipping	
G-FYCP	Osprey Mk 1E	C. F. Chipping	
G-FYCR	Osprey MK 4D	C. F. Chipping	
G-FYCT	Osprey Mk 4D	S. T. Wallbank	
G-FYCU	Osprey Mk 4D	G. M. Smith	
G-FYCV	Osprey Mk 4D	M. Thomson	
G-FYCW	Osprey Mk 4D	M. L. Partridge	
G-FYCZ	Osprey Mk 4D2	P. Middleton	
G-FYDC	European EDH-1	D. Eaves & H. Goddard	
G-FYDD	Osprey Mk 4D	A. C. Mitchell	
G-FYDF	Osprey Mk 4D	K. A. Jones	
G-FYDI	Williams Westwind Two	M. D. Williams	
G-FYDK	Williams Westwind Two	M. D. Williams	
G-FYDM	Williams Westwind Four	M. D. Williams	
G-FYDN	European 8C	P. D. Ridout	
G-FYDO	Osprey Mk 4D	N. L. Scallan	
G-FYDP	Williams Westwind Three	M. D. Williams	
G-FYDS	Osprey Mk 4D	N. L. Scallan	
G-FYDW	Osprey Mk 4B	R. A. Balfre	
G-FYEB	Rango Rega	N. H. Ponsford	
G-FYEG	Osprey Mk 1C	P. E. Prime	
G-FYEI	Portswood Mk XVI	A. Russell	
G-FYEJ	Rango NA.24	N. H. Ponsford	
G-FYEK	Unicorn UE.1C	D. & D. Eaves	
G-FYEL	European E.84Z	D. Eaves	
G-FYEO	Eagle Mk 1	M. E. Scallon	
G-FYEV	Osprey Mk 1C	M. E. Scallen	
G-FYEZ	Firefly Mk 1	M. E. & N. L. Scallan	
G-FYFA	European E.84LD	D. Goddard & D. Eaves	
G-FYFG	European E.84DE	D. Eaves	
G-FYFH	European E.84DS	D. Eaves	
G-FYFI	European E.84DS	M. Stelling	
G-FYFJ	Williams Westland 2	P. Feasey	
G-FYFK	Williams Westland 2	D. Feasey	
G-FYFN	Osprey Saturn 2	J. & M. Woods	
G-FYFT	Rango NA-32BC	Rango Kite & Balloon Co	
G-FYFV	Saffrey Grand Edinburgh	I. G. & G. M. McIntosh	
G-FYFW	Rango NA-55	Rango Kite & Balloon Co	
G-FYFY	Rango NA-55RC	A. M. Lindsay	
G-FYFZ	Booth C-141D	N. R. Booth	
G-FYGA	Rango NA-50RC	Rango Kite & Balloon Co	
G-FYGB	Rango NA-105RC	Rango Kite & Balloon Co	
G-FYGC	Rango NA-42B	L. J. Wardle	
G-FYGG	Buz-B20	D. P. Busby & S. Spink	

Microlights

Notes	Reg.	Type	Owner or Operator
	G-MBAA	Hiway Skytrike Mk 2	Hiway Hang Gliders Ltd
	G-MBAB	Hovey Whing-Ding II	R. F. Morton
	G-MBAD	Weedhopper JC-24A	M. Stott
	G-MBAE	Lazair	H. A. Leek
	G-MBAF	R. J. Swift 3	C. G. Wrzesien
	G-MBAG	Skycraft Scout	B. D. Jones
	G-MBAI	Typhoon Tripacer 250	C. J. & K. Yarrow
	G-MBAJ	Chargus T.250	V. F. Potter
	G-MBAK	Eurowing Spirit	J. S. Potts
	G-MBAL	Hiway Demon	I. M. Munster
	G-MBAM	Skycraft Scout 2	J. P. & C. J. Carney
	G-MBAN	American Aerolights Eagle	R. W. Millward
	G-MBAP	Rotec Rally 2B	P. D. Lucas
	G-MBAR	Skycraft Scout	L. Chiappi
	G-MBAS	Typhoon Tripacer 250	T. J. Birkbeck
	G-MBAU	Hiway Skytrike	R. E. Tallack
	G-MBAV	Weedhopper	L. F. Smith
	G-MBAW	Pterodactyl Ptraveller	J. C. K. Soardifield
	G-MBAX	Hiway Skytrike	D. Clarke
	G-MBAZ	Rotec Rally 2B	Western Skysports Ltd
	G-MBBA	Ultraflight Lazair	P. Roberts
	G-MBBB	Skycraft Scout 2	A. J. & B. Chalkley
	G-MBBD	Pterodactyl Ptraveller	R. N. Greenshields
	G-MBBE	Striplin Skyranger	A. S. Coombes
	G-MBBF	Chargus Titan 38	Chargus Gliding Co
	G-MBBG	Weedhopper JC-24B	A. J. Plumbridge & G. E. Kershaw
	G-MBBH	Flexiform Sealander 160	D. A. Campbell
	G-MBBI	Ultraflight Mirage	G. A. Squires
	G-MBBJ	Hiway Demon Trike	E. B. Jones
	G-MBBL	Lightning Microlight	I. M. Grayland
	G-MBBM	Eipper Quicksilver MX	J. Brown
	G-MBBN	Eagle Microlight	S. Taylor & D. Williams
	G-MBBO	Rotec Rally 2B	P. T. Dawson
	G-MBBP	Chotia Weedhopper	G. L. Moon
	G-MBBR	Weedhopper JC-24B	J. G. Wallers
	G-MBBS	Chargus T.250	P. R. De Fraine
	G-MBBT	Ultrasports Tripacer 330	The Post Office
	G-MBBU	Southdown Savage	D. Ward & B. J. Holloway
	G-MBBV	Rotec Rally 2B	Blois Aviation Ltd
	G-MBBW	Flexiform Hilander	R. J. Hamilton & W. J. Shaw
	G-MBBX	Chargus Skytrike	D. A. Bradley
	G-MBBY	Flexiform Sealander	P. M. Fidell & H. M. Johnson
	G-MBBZ	Volmer Jensen VJ-24W	D. G. Cook
	G-MBCA	Chargus Cyclone T.250	E. M. Jelonek
	G-MBCD	La Mouette Atlas	M. G. Dean
	G-MBCE	American Aerolights Eagle	I. H. Lewis
	G-MBCF	Pterodactyl Ptraveler	T. C. N. Carroll
	G-MBCG	Ultrasports Tripacer T.250	A. G. Parkinson
	G-MBCI	Hiway Skytrike	J. R. Bridge
	G-MBCJ	Mainair Sports Tri-Flyer	R. A. Smith
	G-MBCK	Eipper Quicksilver MX	G. W. Rowbotham
	G-MBCL	Hiway Demon Triflyer	B. R. Underwood & P. J. Challis
	G-MBCM	Hiway Demon 175	G. M. R. & D. M. Walters
	G-MBCN	Hiway Super Scorpion	M. J. Hadland
	G-MBCO	Flexiform Sealander Buggy	P. G. Kavanagh
	G-MBCP	Mainair Tri-Flyer 250	J. B. Wincott
	G-MBCR	Ultraflight Mirage	B. N. Bower
	G-MBCS	American Aerolights Eagle	Pleasurecraft Ltd
	G-MBCT	American Aerolights Eagle	Pleasurecraft Ltd
	G-MBCU	American Aerolights Eagle	J. L. May
	G-MBCV	Hiway Skytrike	C. J. Greasley
	G-MBCW	Hiway Demon 175	C. Foster & S. B. Elwis
	G-MBCX	Airwave Nimrod 165	M. J. Ashley-Rogers
	G-MBCY	American Aerolights Eagle	C. J. Blundell
	G-MBCZ	Chargus Skytrike 160	R. M. Sheppard
	G-MBDA	Rotec Rally 2B	Blois Aviation Ltd
	G-MBDB	Solar Wings Typhoon	D. J. Smith
	G-MBDC	Skyhook Cutlass	R. M. Tunstall
	G-MBDD	Skyhook Skytrike	D. Hancock
	G-MBDE	Flexiform Skytrike	F. P. Latham
	G-MBDF	Rotec Rally 2B	J. R. & B. T. Jordan
	G-MBDG	Eurowing Goldwing	N. W. Beadle & ptnrs

Reg.	Type	Owner or Operator	Notes
G-MBDH	Hiway Demon Triflyer	A. T. Delaney	
G-MBDI	Flexiform Sealander	K. Bryan	
G-MBDJ	Flexiform Sealander Triflyer	J. W. F. Hargrave	
G-MBDK	Solar Wings Typhoon	A. O'Brien	
G-MBDL	Lone Ranger Microlight	Aero & Engineering Services Ltd	
G-MBDM	Southdown Sigma Trike	A. R. Prentice	
G-MBDN	Hornet Atlas	P. J. Kidson	
G-MBDO	Flexiform Sealander Trike	K. Kerr	
G-MBDP	Flexiform Sealander Skytrike	D. Mackillop	
G-MBDR	U.A.S. Stormbuggy	R. V. Hoss	
G-MBDT	American Aerolights Eagle	I. D. Stokes	
G-MBDU	Chargus Titan 38	Property Associates Ltd	
G-MBDW	Ultrasports Tripacer Skytrike A	J. T. Meager	
G-MBDX	Electraflyer Eagle	Ardenco Ltd	
G-MBDY	Weedhopper 2	G. N. Mayes	
G-MBDZ	Eipper Quicksilver MX	H. Glover	
G-MBEA	Hornet Nimrod	M. Holling	
G-MBEB	Hiway Skytrike 250 Mk II	K. D. Napier & ptnrs	
G-MBEC	Hiway Super Scorpion	C. S. Wates	
G-MBED	Chargus Titan 38	G. G. Foster	
G-MBEE	Hiway Super Scorpion Skytrike 160	J. N. Horner	
G-MBEG	Eipper Quicksilver MX	T. V. Wood	
G-MBEJ	Electraflyer Eagle	D. J. Royce & C. R. Gale	
G-MBEL	Electraflyer Eagle	J. R. Fairweather	
G-MBEN	Eipper Quicksilver MX	A. A. McKenzie	
G-MBEO	Flexiform Sealander	H. W. Williams	
G-MBEP	American Aerolights Eagle	R. W. Lavender	
G-MBES	Skyhook Cutlass	Skyhook Sailwings Ltd	
G-MBET	MEA Mistral Trainer	B. H. Stephens	
G-MBEU	Hiway Demon T.250	R. C. Smith	
G-MBEV	Chargus Titan 38	N. Hooper	
G-MBEW	UAS Solar Buggy	A. G. Davies	
G-MBEZ	Pterodactyl Ptraveller II	M. P. Bywater	
G-MBFA	Hiway Skytrike 250	P. S. Jones	
G-MBFD	Gemini Hummingbird	Micro Aviation Ltd	
G-MBFE	American Aerolights Eagle	P. W. Cole	
G-MBFF	Southern Aerosports Scorpion	H. Redwin	
G-MBFG	Skyhook Sabre	M. Williamson	
G-MBFH	Hiway Skytrike	P. Baldwin	
G-MBFI	Hiway Skytrike II	J. R. Brabbs	
G-MBFJ	Chargus Typhoon T.250	R. J. B. Perry	
G-MBFK	Hiway Demon	D. W. Stamp	
G-MBFL	Hiway Demon	J. C. Houghton	
G-MBFM	Hiway Hang Glider	G. P. Kimmons & T. V. O. Mahony	
G-MBFN	Hiway Skytrike II	R. Williamson	
G-MBFO	Eipper Quicksilver MX	F. G. Shepherd	
G-MBFR	American Aerolights Eagle	W. G. Bradley	
G-MBFS	American Aerolights Eagle	R. Fox	
G-MBFT	Southdown Sigma 12 Meter	D. P. Watts	
G-MBFU	Ultrasports Tripacer	T. H. J. Prowse	
G-MBFV	Comet Skytrike	R. Willis	
G-MBFX	Hiway Skytrike 250	D. A. Robinson	
G-MBFY	Mirage II	J. P. Metcalf	
G-MBFZ	M. S. S. Goldwing	I. T. Barr	
G-MBGA	Solar Wings Typhoon	A. D. Fennell	
G-MBGB	American Aerolights Eagle	J. C. Miles	
G-MBGD	Pterodactyl 430C Replica	C. Wilkinson	
G-MBGE	Hiway Scorpion Trike	J. A. Rudd	
G-MBGF	Twamley Trike	T. B. Woolley	
G-MBGG	Chargus Titan 38	Solar Wings Ltd	
G-MBGH	Chargus T.250	A. G. Doubtfire	
G-MBGI	Chargus Titan 38	A. G. Doubtfire	
G-MBGJ	Hiway Skytrike Mk 2	B. C. Norris & J. R. Edwards	
G-MBGK	Electra Flyer Eagle	R. J. Osbourne	
G-MBGM	Eipper Quicksilver MX	G. G. Johnson	
G-MBGN	Weedhopper Model A	D. Roberts	
G-MBGO	American Aerolights Eagle	J. E. Bennison	
G-MBGP	Solar Wings Typhoon Skytrike	C. A. Mitchell	
G-MBGR	Eurowing Goldwing	G. A. J. Salter	
G-MBGS	Rotec Rally 2B	P. C. Bell	
G-MBGT	American Aerolights Eagle	D. C. Lloyd	
G-MBGV	Skyhook Cutlass	D. M. Parsons	
G-MBGW	Hiway Skytrike	G. W. R. Cooke	
G-MBGX	Southdown Lightning	T. Knight	
G-MBGY	Hiway Demon Skytrike	W. Hopkins	
G-MBGZ	American Aerolights Eagle	Flying Machine (Circa 1910) Ltd	

Notes	Reg.	Type	Owner or Operator
	G-MBHA	Trident Trike	P. Jackson
	G-MBHB	Cenrair Moto Delta G-11	Moto Baldet (Northampton) Ltd
	G-MBHC	Chargus Lightning T.250	R. E. Worth
	G-MBHD	Hiway Vulcan Trike	D. Kiddy
	G-MBHE	American Aerolights Eagle	D. J. Lewis
	G-MBHF	Pterodactyl Ptraveller	D. B. Girry
	G-MBHH	Flexiform Sealander Skytrike	S. Adams
	G-MBHI	Ultrasports Tripacer 250	P. T. Anstey
	G-MBHJ	Hornet Skyhook Cutlass	D. Shakelton
	G-MBHK	Flexiform Skytrike	E. Barfoot
	G-MBHL	Skyhook Skytrike	C. R. Brewitt
	G-MBHM	Weedhopper	J. Hopkinson
	G-MBHN	Weedhopper	S. Hopkinson
	G-MBHO	Skyhook Super Sabre Trike	E. Smith
	G-MBHP	American Aerolights Eagle II	P. V. Trollope & H. Caldwell
	G-MBHR	Flexiform Skytrike	Y. P. Osbourne
	G-MBHT	Chargus T.250	S. F. Dawe
	G-MBHU	Flexiform Hilander Skytrike	R. Bridgstock
	G-MBHW	American Aerolights Eagle	M. A. Alker
	G-MBHX	Pterodactyl Ptraveller	F. D. C. Luddington & P. J. Dunmore
	G-MBHZ	Pterodactyl Ptraveller	J. C. K. Scardfield
	G-MBIA	Flexiform Sealander Skytrike	I. P. Cook
	G-MBIB	Mainair Flexiform Sealander	A. D. Pearson
	G-MBIC	Maxair Hummer	G. C. Calow
	G-MBID	American Aerolights Eagle	D. A. Campbell
	G-MBIE	Flexiform Striker	Flying Machine (Circa 1910) Ltd
	G-MBIF	American Aerolights Eagle	Flying Machine (Circa 1910) Ltd
	G-MBIG	American Aerolights Eagle	H. G. I. Goodheart
	G-MBIH	Flexiform Skytrike	M. Hurtley
	G-MBII	Hiway Skytrike	K. D. Beeton
	G-MBIK	Wheeler Scout	J. R. Keen
	G-MBIM	American Aerolights Sea Eagle	A. J. Sheardown
	G-MBIN	Wheeler Sea Scout	I. F. Kerr
	G-MBIO	American Aerolights Eagle Z Drive	B. J. C. Hill
	G-MBIP	Gemini Hummingbird	Micro Aviation Ltd
	G-MBIR	Gemini Hummingbird	Micro Aviation Ltd
	G-MBIS	American Aerolights Eagle	I. R. Bendall
	G-MBIT	Hiway Demon Skytrike	Kuernaland (UK) Ltd
	G-MBIU	Hiway Super Scorpion	M. E. Wills
	G-MBIV	Flexiform Skytrike	M. D. Knowlson & R. A. Pendleton
	G-MBIW	Hiway Demon Tri-Flyer Skytrike	Computer Mart Ltd
	G-MBIX	Ultra Sports	S. A. V. Smith
	G-MBIY	Ultra Sports	J. C. Beatham
	G-MBIZ	Mainair Tri-Flyer	E. F. Clapham & ptnrs
	G-MBJA	Eurowing Goldwing	W. D. Gordon
	G-MBJC	American Aerolights Eagle	R. Jenkins
	G-MBJD	American Aerolights Eagle	R. W. F. Boarder
	G-MBJE	Airwave Nimrod	M. E. Glanvill
	G-MBJF	Hiway Skytrike Mk II	C. H. Bestwick
	G-MBJG	Airwave Nimrod	D. H. George
	G-MBJI	Southern Aerosports Scorpion	Robert Montgomery Ltd
	G-MBJJ	Mirage Mk II	H. Glover
	G-MBJK	American Aerolights Eagle	B. W. Olley
	G-MBJL	Airwave Nimrod	A. G. Lowe
	G-MBJM	Striplin Lone Ranger	C. K. Brown
	G-MBJN	Electraflyer Eagle	M. M. Wallace
	G-MBJO	Birdman Cherokee	T. A. Hinton
	G-MBJP	Hiway Skytrike	R. C. Crowley
	G-MBJR	American Aerolights Eagle	M. P. Skelding
	G-MBJS	Mainair Tri-Flyer	T. W. Taylor
	G-MBJT	Hiway Skytrike II	R. A. Kennedy
	G-MBJU	American Aerolights Eagle	J. Basford
	G-MBJV	Rotec Rally 2B	S. Wilson
	G-MBJW	Hiway Demon Mk II	M. J. Grace
	G-MBJX	Hiway Super Scorpion	D. G. Hughes
	G-MBJY	Rotec Rally 2B	C. R. V. Hitch
	G-MBJZ	Eurowing Catto CP.16	Neville Chamberlain Ltd
	G-MBKA	Mistral Trainer	G. H. Liddle
	G-MBKB	Pterodactyl Ptraveller	W. H. Foddy
	G-MBKC	Southdown Lightning	D. Bradbury
	G-MBKD	Chargus T.250	P. Kerr
	G-MBKE	Eurowing Catto CP.16	R. S. Tuberville
	G-MBKF	Striplin Skyranger	R. Towle

Reg.	Type	Owner or Operator	Notes
G-MBKG	Batchelor-Hunt Skytrike	M. J. Batchelor & ptnrs	
G-MBKH	Southdown Skytrike	S. T. D. Hands	
G-MBKI	Solar Wings Typhoon	S. T. Jones	
G-MBKJ	Chargus TS.440 Titan 38	Westair Microlights	
G-MBKK	Pterodactyl Ascender	T. D. Baker	
G-MBKN	Chargus TS.440 Titan	Solar Wings Ltd	
G-MBKO	Chargus TS.440 Titan	Solar Wings Ltd	
G-MBKP	Hiway Skytrike 160	R. A. Davies	
G-MBKR	Hiway Skytrike	C. J. Macey	
G-MBKS	Hiway Skytrike 160	J. Dilks	
G-MBKT	Mitchell Wing B.10	T. Beckett	
G-MBKU	Hiway Demon Skytrike	K. Lowery	
G-MBKV	Eurowing Goldwing	Entertainment Film Productions Ltd	
G-MBKW	Pterodactyl Ptraveller	A. J. Glynn	
G-MBKY	American Aerolights Eagle	S. M. Beddin	
G-MBKZ	Hiway Skytrike	S. I. Harding	
G-MBLA	Flexiform Skytrike	R. Wilding	
G-MBLB	Eipper Quicksilver MX	Southern Microlight Centre Ltd	
G-MBLD	Flexiform Striker	F. A. Craig	
G-MBLE	Hiway Demon Skytrike II	R. E. Harvey	
G-MBLF	Hiway Demon 195 Tri Pacer	A. P. Rostron	
G-MBLG	Chargus Titan T.38	P. R. F. Glenville	
G-MBLH	Flexwing Tri-Flyer 330	N. S. Davison	
G-MBLJ	Eipper Quicksilver MX	Flylight South East	
G-MBLK	Southdown Puma	P. Davies	
G-MBLM	Hiway Skytrike	W. N. Natson	
G-MBLN	Pterodactyl Ptraveller	W. F. Tremayne	
G-MBLO	Sealander Skytrike	A. R. Fawkes	
G-MBLP	Pterodactyl Ptraveller	R. N. Greenshields	
G-MBLR	Ultrasports Tripacer	M. N. Asquith	
G-MBLS	MEA Mistral	I. D. Stokes	
G-MBLT	Chargus TS.440 Titan	P. J. Harvey	
G-MBLU	Southdown Lightning L.195	C. R. Franklin	
G-MBLV	Ultrasports Hybrid	L. A. Hendrick	
G-MBLX	Eurowing Goldwing	W. B. Thomas	
G-MBLY	Flexiform Sealander Trike	J. Clithero	
G-MBLZ	Southern Aerosports Scorpion	J. P. Bennett-Snewin	
G-MBMA	Eipper Quicksilver MX	M. Maxwell	
G-MBMC	Waspair Tomcat	F. D. Buckle	
G-MBMD	Eurowing CP.16	S. Dorrance	
G-MBME	American Aerolights Eagle Z Drive	Perme Westcott Flying Club	
G-MBMF	Rotec Rally 2B	J. G. Woods	
G-MBMG	Rotec Rally 2B	J. R. Pyper	
G-MBMH	American Aerolights Eagle	M. S. Scott	
G-MBMI	Chargus T.440	G. Durbin	
G-MBMJ	Mainair Tri-Flyer	P. A. Gardner	
G-MBMK	Weedhopper Model B	P. W. Grange	
G-MBML	American Aerolights Zenoah Eagle	R. C. Jones	
G-MBMN	Skyhook Silhouette	A. D. F. Clifford	
G-MBMO	Hiway Skytrike 160	S. G. Isaac	
G-MBMP	Mitchell Wing B.10	J. Pavelin	
G-MBMR	Ultrasports Tripacer Typhoon	L. Mills	
G-MBMS	Hornet	R. L. Smith	
G-MBMT	Mainair Tri-Flyer	T. R. Yeomans	
G-MBMU	Eurowing Goldwing	P. R. Wason	
G-MBMV	Chargus TS.440 Titan 38	K. Brogden	
G-MBMW	Solar Wings Typhoon	R. Harrison	
G-MBMY	Pterodactyl Fledge	C. J. Blundell	
G-MBMZ	Sealander Tripacer	T. D. Otho-Briggs	
G-MBNA	American Aerolights Eagle	N. D. Hall	
G-MBNC	Southdown Sailwings Puma	Southern Airsports Ltd	
G-MBND	Skyhook Sailwings SK TR.2	Eastern Microlight Aircraft Centre Ltd	
G-MBNF	American Aerolights Eagle	D. Read	
G-MBNG	Hiway Demon Skytrike	C. J. Clayson	
G-MBNH	Southern Airsports Scorpion	R. F. Thomas	
G-MBNJ	Eipper Quicksilver MX	C. Lamb	
G-MBNK	American Aerolights Eagle	R. Moss	
G-MBNL	Hiway Skytrike C.2	K. V. Shail & H. W. Preston	
G-MBNM	American Aerolights Eagle	D. W. J. Orchard	
G-MBNN	Southern Microlight Gazelle P.160N	N. A. Pitcher	
G-MBNP	Eurowing Catto CP.16	M. H. C. Bishop	

Notes	Reg.	Type	Owner or Operator
	G-MBNS	Chargus Titan 38	P. N. Lynch
	G-MBNT	American Aerolights Eagle	M. D. O'Brien
	G-MBNV	Sheffield Aircraft Skytrike	D. L. Buckley
	G-MBNW	Meagher Flexwing	P. R. Collier
	G-MBNX	Solar Storm	F. Kratky
	G-MBNY	Steer Terror Fledge II	M. J. Steer
	G-MBNZ	Hiway Skytrike Demon	J. E. Brown
	G-MBOA	Flexiform Hilander	A. F. Stafford
	G-MBOB	American Aerolights Eagle	K. A. C. Black
	G-MBOD	American Aerolights Eagle	M. A. Ford & ptnrs
	G-MBOE	Solar Wing Typhoon Trike	W. Turner & C. Ferrie
	G-MBOF	Pakes Jackdaw	L. G. Pakes
	G-MBOG	Flexiform Sealander	M. J. B. Knapp
	G-MBOH	Microlight Engineering Mistral	N. A. Bell
	G-MBOI	Ultralight Flight Mirage II	H. I. Jones
	G-MBOJ	Pterodactyl Pfledgling	S. P. Dewhurst
	G-MBOK	Dunstable Microlight	W. E. Brooks
	G-MBOL	Pterodactyl Pfledgling 360	W. J. Neath
	G-MBOM	Hiway Hilander	P. H. Beaumont
	G-MBON	Eurowing Goldwing Canard	A. H. Dunlop
	G-MBOR	Chotia 460B Weedhopper	D. J. Whysall
	G-MBOS	Hiway Super Scorpion	C. Montgomery
	G-MBOT	Hiway 250 Skytrike	I. C. Campbell
	G-MBOU	Wheeler Scout	P. Stark
	G-MBOV	Southdown Lightning Trike	J. Messenger
	G-MBOW	Solar Wing Typhoon	R. Luke
	G-MBOX	American Aerolights Eagle	J. S. Paine
	G-MBPA	Weedhopper Srs 2	C. H. & P. B. Smith
	G-MBPB	Pterodactyl Ptraveller	P. E. Bailey
	G-MBPC	American Aerolights Eagle	Aerial Imaging Systems Ltd
	G-MBPD	American Aerolights Eagle	R. G. Harris & K. Hall
	G-MBPE	Ultrasports Trike	K. L. Turner
	G-MBPG	Hunt Skytrike	W. Shaw
	G-MBPI	MEA Mistral Trainer	M. J. Kenniston
	G-MBPJ	Moto-Delta	J. B. Jackson
	G-MBPL	Hiway Demon	B. J. Merrett
	G-MBPM	Eurowing Goldwing	F. W. McCann
	G-MBPN	American Aerolights Eagle	N. O. G. & P. C. Wooler
	G-MBPO	Volnik Arrow	N. A. Seymour
	G-MBPP	American Aerolights Eagle	R. C. Colbeck
	G-MBPR	American Aerolights Eagle	P. Kift
	G-MBPS	Gryphon Willpower	J. T. Meager
	G-MBPT	Hiway Demon	K. M. Simpson
	G-MBPU	Hiway Demon	N. Shaw
	G-MBPW	Weedhopper	P. G. Walton
	G-MBPX	Eurowing Goldwing	W. R. Haworth & V. C. Cannon
	G-MBPY	Ultrasports Tripacer 330	P. J. Sutton
	G-MBPZ	Flexiform Striker	C. Harris
	G-MBRA	Eurowing Catto CP.16	J. Brown
	G-MBRB	Electraflyer Eagle 1	R. C. Bott
	G-MBRC	Wheeler Scout Mk 3A	Skycraft (UK) Ltd
	G-MBRD	American Aerolights Eagle	D. G. Fisher
	G-MBRE	Wheeler Scout	R. G. Buck
	G-MBRF	Weedhopper 460C	L. R. Smith
	G-MBRH	Ultraflight Mirage Mk II	R. W. F. Boarder
	G-MBRK	Huntair Pathfinder	F. M. Sharland
	G-MBRM	Hiway Demon	T. M. Clarke
	G-MBRN	Hiway Demon 175	G. J. Dunn
	G-MBRO	Hiway Skytrike 160	P. F. Bett
	G-MBRP	American Aerolights Eagle	F. G. Rainbow
	G-MBRS	American Aerolights Eagle	R. W. Chatterton
	G-MBRU	Skyhook Cutlass	T. J. McLauchlan
	G-MBRV	Eurowing Goldwing	J. H. G. Lywood & A. A. Boyle
	G-MBRZ	Hiway Vulcan 250	D. J. Jackson
	G-MBSA	Ultraflight Mirage II	M. J. Laxton
	G-MBSB	Ultraflight Mirage II	Windsports Centre
	G-MBSC	Ultraflight Mirage II	R. P. Warren
	G-MBSD	Southdown Puma DS	D. J. Whysall
	G-MBSF	Ultraflight Mirage II	A. J. Horne
	G-MBSG	Ultraflight Mirage II	P. E. Owen
	G-MBSI	American Aerolights Eagle	M. Day
	G-MBSN	American Aerolights Eagle	D. Duckworth
	G-MBSR	Southdown Puma DS	J. G. H. Featherstone
	G-MBSS	Ultrasports Puma DS	W. G. Lindsay & Air Westward Co Ltd

Reg.	Type	Owner or Operator	Notes
G-MBST	Mainair Gemini Sprint	D. F. Coles	
G-MBSU	Ultraflight Mirage II	R. Lynn	
G-MBSW	Ultraflight Mirage II	G. Clare	
G-MBTA	UAS Storm Buggy 5 Mk 2	N. & D. McEwan	
G-MBTB	Davies Tri-Flyer S	R. J. Wilson	
G-MBTC	Weedhopper	P. C. Lovegrove	
G-MBTD	Solar Wings Cherokee 250 Trike	R. D. Yaxley	
G-MBTE	Hornet Dual Trainer Trike	A. R. Glenn	
G-MBTF	Mainair Tri-Flyer Skytrike	C. Fox	
G-MBTG	Mainair Gemini	A. J. Smith	
G-MBTH	Whittaker MW.4	MWA Flying Group	
G-MBTI	Hovey Whing Ding	A. Carr & R. Saddington	
G-MBTJ	Solar Wings Microlight	J. Swingler	
G-MBTL	Hiway Super Scorpion	C. S. Beer	
G-MBTN	Mitchell Wing B.10	N. F. James	
G-MBTO	Mainair Tri-Flyer 250	P. G. Griffin	
G-MBTP	Hiway Demon	E. M. Jelonek	
G-MBTR	Skyhook Sailwings	R. Smith	
G-MBTS	Hovey WD-II Whing-Ding	T. G. Solomon	
G-MBTV	Ultraflight Tomcat	M. C. Latham	
G-MBTW	Raven Vector 600	W. I. Fuller	
G-MBTY	American Aerolights Eagle	Southall College of Technology	
G-MBTZ	Huntair Pathfinder	G. M. Hayden	
G-MBUA	Hiway Demon	R. J. Nicholson	
G-MBUB	Horne Sigma Skytrike	L. G. Horne	
G-MBUC	Huntair Pathfinder	Huntair Ltd	
G-MBUD	Wheeler Scout Mk III	R. J. Adams	
G-MBUE	MBA Tiger Cub 440	N. M. Cuthbertson	
G-MBUH	Hiway Skytrike	G. T. Cairns	
G-MBUI	Wheeler Scout Mk I	G. C. Martin	
G-MBUJ	Rotec Rally 2B	L. T. Swallham	
G-MBUK	Mainair 330 Tri Pacer	D. G. Matthews	
G-MBUL	American Aerolights Eagle	Nottingham Offshore Marine	
G-MBUO	Southern Aerosports Scorpion	I. C. Vanner	
G-MBUP	Hiway Skytrike	P. Hamilton	
G-MBUT	UAS Storm Buggy	J. N. Wrigley	
G-MBUV	Huntair Pathfinder	G. H. Cork	
G-MBUW	Skyhook Sabre Trike	D. F. Soul	
G-MBUX	Pterodactyl Ptraveller	J. J. Harris	
G-MBUY	American Aerolights Eagle	Nottingham Offshore Marine	
G-MBUZ	Wheeler Scout Mk II	A. B. Cameron	
G-MBVA	Volmer Jensen VJ-23E	D. P. Eichorn	
G-MBVC	American Aerolights Eagle	E. M. Salt	
G-MBVE	Hiway 160 Valmet	T. J. Daly	
G-MBVF	Hornet	P. D. Hopkins	
G-MBVG	American Aerolights Eagle	Cipher Systems Ltd	
G-MBVH	Mainair Triflyer Striker	S. Wigham	
G-MBVI	Hiway 250 Skytrike	D. L. B. Holliday	
G-MBVJ	Skyhook Trike	A. H. Milne	
G-MBVK	Ultraflight Mirage II	C. W. Grant	
G-MBVL	Southern Aerosports Scorpion	R. H. Wentham	
G-MBVM	Ultraflight Mirage II	Normalair Garrett Ltd	
G-MBVP	Mainair Triflyer 330 Striker	S. M. C. Kenton	
G-MBVR	Rotec Rally 2B	A. C. W. Day	
G-MBVS	Hiway Skytrike	M. A. Brown	
G-MBVT	American Aerolights Eagle	D. Cracknell	
G-MBVU	Flexiform Sealander Triflyer	D. Laverick	
G-MBVV	Hiway Skytrike	G. Hayton	
G-MBVW	Skyhook TR.2	M. Jobling	
G-MBVX	Tigair Power Fledge	D. G. Tigwell	
G-MBVY	Eipper Quicksilver MX	J. Moss	
G-MBVZ	Hornet Trike 250	R. F. Southcott	
G-MBWA	American Aerolights Eagle	S. Pizzey	
G-MBWB	Hiway Skytrike	C. K. Board	
G-MBWD	Rotec Rally 2B	A. Craw	
G-MBWE	American Aerolights Eagle	R. H. Tombs	
G-MBWF	Mainair Triflyer Striker	J. B. Brierley	
G-MBWG	Huntair Pathfinder	S. M. Pascoe	
G-MBWH	Designability Duet I	Designability Ltd	
G-MBWI	Microlight Lafayette Mk 1	F. W. Harrington	
G-MBWK	Mainair Triflyer	G. C. Weighwell	
G-MBWL	Huntair Pathfinder	D. A. Izod & R. C. Wright	
G-MBWM	American Aerolights Eagle	J. N. B. Mourant	
G-MBWN	American Aerolights Eagle	J. N. B. Mourant	

Notes	Reg.	Type	Owner or Operator
	G-MBWO	Hiway Demon Skytrike	J. T. W. J. Edwards
	G-MBWP	Ultrasports Trike	C. Riley
	G-MBWR	Hornet	G. Edwards
	G-MBWT	Huntair Pathfinder	D. G. Gibson
	G-MBWU	Hiway Demon Skytrike	R. M. Lister
	G-MBWW	Southern Aerosports Scorpion	D. Batters
	G-MBWX	Southern Aerosports Scorpion	Twinflight Ltd
	G-MBWY	American Aerolights Eagle	J. P. Donovan
	G-MBWZ	American Aerolights Eagle	B. Busby
	G-MBXB	Southdown Sailwings Puma	B. P. Barker
	G-MBXC	Eurowing Goldwing	A. J. J. Bartak
	G-MBXD	Huntair Pathfinder	Border Aviation Ltd
	G-MBXE	Hiway Skytrike	T. A. Harlow
	G-MBXF	Hiway Skytrike	R. Ford
	G-MBXH	Southdown Sailwings Puma	M. Sorbie
	G-MBXI	Hiway Skytrike	P. J. Davis
	G-MBXJ	Hiway Demon Skytrike	D. C. & J. M. Read
	G-MBXK	Ultrasports Puma	P. J. Brookman
	G-MBXL	Eipper Quicksilver MX2	Flying Machines (Circa 1910) Ltd
	G-MBXM	American Aerolights Eagle	P. D. Schramm
	G-MBXN	Southdown Sailwings Lighting	T. W. Robinson
	G-MBXO	Sheffield Trident	M. I. Watson
	G-MBXP	Hornet Skytrike	G. Little
	G-MBXR	Hiway Skytrike 150	C. Shutt
	G-MBXT	Eipper Quicksilver MX2	B. J. Gordon
	G-MBXW	Hiway Skytrike	R. M. Hydes
	G-MBXX	Ultraflight Mirage II	Westward Airways (Lands End) Ltd
	G-MBXY	Hornet	C. Leach
	G-MBYD	American Aerolights Eagle	J. M. Hutchinson
	G-MBYE	Eipper Quicksilver MX	M. J. Beeby
	G-MBYF	Skyhook TR2	E. J. Larnder
	G-MBYH	Maxair Hummer	A. Edwards
	G-MBYI	Ultraflight Lazair	A. M. Fleming
	G-MBYJ	Hiway Super Scorpion IIC	R. Flaum
	G-MBYK	Huntair Pathfinder	W. E. Lambert
	G-MBYL	Huntair Pathfinder 330	J. S. S. Calder & R. Tyler
	G-MBYM	Eipper Quicksilver MX	J. Wibberley
	G-MBYN	Livesey Super-Fly	D. M. Livesey
	G-MBYO	American Aerolights Eagle	B. J. & M. G. Ferguson
	G-MBYP	Hornet 440cc Flexwing Cutlass	T. J. B. Daly
	G-MBYR	American Aerolights Eagle	F. Green & G. McCready
	G-MBYS	Ultraflight Mirage II	I. M. Willsher
	G-MBYT	Ultraflight Mirage II	L. J. Perring
	G-MBYU	American Aerolights Eagle	F. L. Wiseman
	G-MBYV	Mainair Tri-Flyer 330	I. T. Ferguson
	G-MBYW	Levi Magpie	R. Levi
	G-MBYX	American Aerolights Eagle	N. P. Austen
	G-MBYY	Southern Aerosports Scorpion	D. J. Lovell
	G-MBZA	Ultrasports Tripacer 330	C. R. Thorne
	G-MBZB	Hiway Skytrike	M. W. Hurst & B. Emery
	G-MBZF	American Aerolights Eagle	G. Calder & A. C. Bernard
	G-MBZG	Twinflight Scorpion 2 seat	H. T. Edwards
	G-MBZH	Eurowing Goldwing	J. Spavins
	G-MBZI	Eurowing Goldwing	G. M. Hayden
	G-MBZJ	Ultrasports Puma	G. A. Burridge
	G-MBZK	Ultrasports Tripacer 250	M. T. Pearce
	G-MBZL	Weedhopper	A. R. Prior
	G-MBZM	UAS Storm Buggy	S. Comber & A. Crabtree
	G-MBZN	Ultrasports Puma	A. Brown
	G-MBZO	Mainair Triflyer 330	J. Baxendale
	G-MBZP	Skyhook TR2	Army Hang Gliding School
	G-MBZR	Eipper Quicksilver MX	R. Gill
	G-MBZS	Ultrasports Puma	T. Coughlan
	G-MBZT	Solarwings Skytrike	S. Hetherton
	G-MBZU	Skyhook Sabre C	G. N. Beyer-Kay
	G-MBZV	American Aerolights Eagle	M. H. & G. C. Davies
	G-MBZW	American Aerolights Eagle	M. J. Pugh
	G-MBZX	American Aerolights Eagle	D. W. Roberts
	G-MBZY	Waspair Tom Cat HM.81	A. C. Wendelken
	G-MBZZ	Southern Aerosports Scorpion	P. J. Harlow
	G-MGUY	CFM Shadow Srs BD	Aerolite Flight Parks Ltd
	G-MJAA	Ultrasports Tripacer	M. P. Carr & D. Baker

Reg.	Type	Owner or Operator	Notes
G-MJAB	Ultrasports Skytrike	I. W. Kemsley	
G-MJAC	American Aerolights Eagle 3	P. R. Fellden	
G-MJAD	Eipper Quicksilver MX	J. McCullough	
G-MJAE	American Aerolights Eagle	T. B. Wooley	
G-MJAF	Ultrasports Puma 440	M. A. Hodgson	
G-MJAG	Skyhook TR1	D. J. Wright & L. Florence	
G-MJAH	American Aerolights Eagle	R. L. Arscott	
G-MJAI	American Aerolights Eagle	D. J. Gardner	
G-MJAJ	Eurowing Goldwing	J. S. R. Moodie	
G-MJAK	Hiway Demon	F. C. Potter	
G-MJAL	Wheeler Scout 3	G. W. Wickington	
G-MJAM	Eipper Quicksilver MX	J. C. Larkin	
G-MJAN	Hiway Skytrike	G. M. Sutcliffe	
G-MJAO	Hiway Skytrike	T. Le Gassicke	
G-MJAP	Hiway 160	F. Naylor	
G-MJAR	Chargus Titan	Quest Air Ltd	
G-MJAT	Hiway Demon Skytrike	P. H. Howell	
G-MJAU	Hiway Skytrike 244cc	A. P. Cross	
G-MJAV	Hiway Demon Skytrike 244cc	M. P. Bloomfield	
G-MJAW	Solar Wings Typhoon	M. R. Nicholls	
G-MJAX	American Aerolights Eagle	J. P. Simpson & C. W. Mellard	
G-MJAY	Eurowing Goldwing	C. Tuxworth	
G-MJAZ	Aerodyne Vector 610	B. Fussell	
G-MJBA	Raven Vector 610	Raven Leisure Industries Ltd	
G-MJBB	Raven Vector 610	Raven Leisure Industries Ltd	
G-MJBC	Raven Vector 610	Raven Leisure Industries Ltd	
G-MJBD	Raven Vector 610	Raven Leisure Industries Ltd	
G-MJBE	Wheeler Scout X	Newell Aircraft & Tool Co Ltd	
G-MJBF	Southdown Puma 330	C. Jacobs	
G-MJBG	Mainair Solarwings Typhoon	N. J. Mackay	
G-MJBH	American Aerolights Eagle	P. Smith	
G-MJBI	Eipper Quicksilver MX	J. I. Visser	
G-MJBK	Swallow AeroPlane Swallow B	B. J. Towers	
G-MJBL	American Aerolights Eagle	B. W. Olley	
G-MJBM	Eurowing CP.16	A. H. Milne	
G-MJBN	American Aerolights Eagle	D. Darke	
G-MJBO	Bell Microlight Type A	G. Bell	
G-MJBP	Eurowing Catto CP.16	I. Wilson	
G-MJBS	Ultralight Stormbuggy	G. I. Sargeant	
G-MJBT	Eipper Quicksilver MX	G. A. Barclay	
G-MJBV	American Aerolights Eagle	B. H. Stephens	
G-MJBW	American Aerolights Eagle	J. D. Penman	
G-MJBX	Pterodactyl Ptraveller	R. E. Hawkes	
G-MJBY	Rotec Rally 2B	B. Eastwood	
G-MJBZ	Huntair Pathfinder	J. C. Rose	
G-MJCA	Skyhook Sabre	B. G. Axworthy	
G-MJCB	Hornet 330	A. C. Aspden & ptnrs	
G-MJCC	Ultrasports Puma	S. Hudson	
G-MJCD	Sigma Tetley Skytrike	N. L. Betts & B. Tetley	
G-MJCE	Ultrasports Tripacer	Charter Systems	
G-MJCF	Maxair Hummer	J. G. Bussell & A. G. Hazlewood	
G-MJCG	S.M.C. Flyer Mk 1	E. N. Skinner	
G-MJCH	Ultraflight Mirage II	R. Sherwin	
G-MJCI	Kruchek Firefly 440	E. Kepka	
G-MJCJ	Hiway Spectrum	J. F. Mayes	
G-MJCK	Southern Aerosports Scorpion	S. L. Moss	
G-MJCL	Eipper Quicksilver MX	R. F. Witt	
G-MJCM	S.M.C. Flyer Mk 1	P. L. Gooch	
G-MJCN	S.M.C. Flyer Mk 1	C. W. Merriam	
G-MJCO	Striplin Lone Ranger	J. G. Wellans	
G-MJCP	Huntair Pathfinder	R. C. Wright	
G-MJCR	American Aerolights Eagle	R. F. Hinton	
G-MJCS	EFS Pterodactyl	D. W. Evans	
G-MJCT	Hiway Skytrike	E. W. Barker	
G-MJCU	Tarjani	T. A. Sayer	
G-MJCV	Southern Flyer Mk 1	G. N. Harris	
G-MJCW	Hiway Super Scorpion	M. G. Sheppard	
G-MJCX	American Aerolights Eagle	S. C. Weston	
G-MJCY	Eurowing Goldwing	A. E. Dewdeswell	
G-MJCZ	Southern Aerosports Scorpion 2	C. Baldwin	
G-MJDA	Hornet Trike Executive	J. Hainsworth	
G-MJDB	Birdman Cherokee	W. G. Farr	
G-MJDC	Mainair Tri-Flyer Dual	A. C. Dommett	
G-MJDE	Huntair Pathfinder	E. H. Gould	

Notes	Reg.	Type	Owner or Operator
	G-MJDF	Tripacer 250cc Striker	F. R. Loft
	G-MJDG	Hornet Supertrike	I. Roy
	G-MJDH	Huntair Pathfinder	J. P. Harding
	G-MJDI	Southern Flyer Mk 1	N. P. Day
	G-MJDJ	Hiway Skytrike Demon	A. J. Cowan
	G-MJDK	American Aerolights Eagle	P. A. McPherson & ptnrs
	G-MJDM	Wheeler Scout Mk III	Skycraft (UK) Ltd
	G-MJDN	Skyhook Single Seat	G. Morgan
	G-MJDO	Southdown Puma 440	M. J. Knight
	G-MJDP	Eurowing Goldwing	J. R. Ledbrook & F. C. James
	G-MJDR	Hiway Demon Skytrike	J. M. MacDonald
	G-MJDU	Eipper Quicksilver MX2	Microlight Airsport Services Ltd
	G-MJDV	Skyhook TR-1	R. Mason
	G-MJDW	Eipper Quicksilver MX	Remus International Ltd
	G-MJDX	Moyes Mega II	P. H. Davies
	G-MJDY	Ultrasports Solarwings	S. A. Barnes
	G-MJEA	Flexiform Striker	S. J. O'Neill
	G-MJEC	Ultrasports Puma	M. C. Gardner
	G-MJED	Eipper Quicksilver MX	R. Haslam
	G-MJEE	Mainair Triflyer Trike	M. F. Eddington
	G-MJEF	Gryphon 180	F. C. Coulson
	G-MJEG	Eurowing Goldwing	G. J. Stamper
	G-MJEH	Rotec Rally 2B	J. G. Lindley
	G-MJEI	American Aerolights Eagle	A. Moss
	G-MJEJ	American Aerolights Eagle	J. Cole
	G-MJEK	Hiway Demon 330 Skytrike	J. Grant
	G-MJEL	GMD-01 Trike	G. M. Drinkell
	G-MJEN	Eurowing Catto CP.16	A. D. G. Wright
	G-MJEO	American Aerolights Eagle	A. M. Shaw
	G-MJEP	Pterodactyl Ptraveller	G. H. Liddle
	G-MJER	Flexiform Striker	D. S. Simpson
	G-MJES	Stratos Prototype 3 Axis 1	Stratos Aviation Ltd
	G-MJET	Stratos Prototype 3 Axis 1	Stratos Aviation Ltd
	G-MJEU	Hiway Skytrike	P. Best
	G-MJEV	Flexiform Striker	C. Scoble
	G-MJEX	Eipper Quicksilver MX	M. J. Sundaram
	G-MJEY	Southdown Lightning	P. M. Coppola
	G-MJEZ	Raven Vector 600	D. H. Handley
	G-MJFB	Flexiform Striker	B. Tetley
	G-MJFD	Ultrasports Tripacer	R. N. O. Kingsbury
	G-MJFE	Hiway Scorpion	N. A. Fisher
	G-MJFF	Huntair Pathfinder	F. E. Hardy
	G-MJFG	Eurowing Goldwing	J. G. Aspinall & H. R. Marsden
	G-MJFH	Eipper Quicksilver MX	I. Waldram
	G-MJFI	Flexiform Striker	A. L. Virgoe
	G-MJFJ	Hiway Skytrike 250	J. S. Woollatt
	G-MJFK	Flexiform Skytrike Dual	J. J. Woollen
	G-MJFL	Mainair Tri-Flyer 440	J. Phillips
	G-MJFM	Huntair Pathfinder	J. T. Houghton
	G-MJFN	Huntair Pathfinder	Times Newspapers Ltd
	G-MJFP	American Aerolights Eagle	R. C. Colbeck
	G-MJFR	American Aerolights Eagle	Southall College of Technology
	G-MJFS	American Aerolights Eagle	P. R. A. Elliston
	G-MJFT	American Aerolights Eagle	D. S. McMullen
	G-MJFV	Ultrasports Tripacer	Hatfield Polytechnic Students Union
	G-MJFW	Ultrasports Puma	J. McCarthy
	G-MJFX	Skyhook TR-1	M. R. Dean
	G-MJFY	Hornet 250	H. Lang
	G-MJFZ	Hiway Demon Skytrike	J. A. Lowie
	G-MJGA	Hiway Skytrike 160	J. H. Wadsworth
	G-MJGB	American Aerolights Eagle	N. P. Day
	G-MJGC	Hornet	P. C. & S. J. Turnbull
	G-MJGD	Huntair Pathfinder	A. Carling
	G-MJGE	Eipper Quicksilver MX	D. Brown
	G-MJGF	Poisestar Aeolus Mk 1	Poisestar Ltd
	G-MJGG	Skyhook TR-1	R. Pritchard
	G-MJGH	Flexiform Skytrike	P. Newman
	G-MJGI	Eipper Quicksilver MX	J. M. Hayer & J. R. Wilman
	G-MJGJ	American Aerolights Eagle	B. J. Houlihan
	G-MJGK	Eurowing Goldwing	P. E. P. Shephard
	G-MJGL	Chargus Titan 38	J. Houston & J. R. Appleton
	G-MJGM	Hiway Demon 195 Skytrike	J. M. Creasey
	G-MJGN	Greenslade Monotrike	P. G. Greenslade
	G-MJGO	Barnes Avon Skytrike	B. R. Barnes

Reg.	Type	Owner or Operator	Notes
G-MJGP	Hiway Demon Skytrike	G. I. J. Thompson	
G-MJGR	Hiway Demon Skytrike	L. V. Strickland & P. H. Howell	
G-MJGS	American Aerolights Eagle	P. D. Griffiths	
G-MJGT	Skyhook Cutlass Trike	T. Silvester	
G-MJGU	Pterodactyl Mk 1	J. Pemberton	
G-MJGV	Eipper Quicksilver MX2	D. Beer	
G-MJGW	Solar Wings Trike	D. J. D. Beck	
G-MJGX	Ultrasports Puma 250	TDJ Flying Club	
G-MJGZ	Mainair Triflyer 330	A. Holt	
G-MJHA	Hiway Skytrike 250 Mk II	R. J. Perry	
G-MJHB	AES Sky Ranger	J. H. L. B. Wijsmuller	
G-MJHC	Ultrasports Tripacer 330	S. Galley	
G-MJHD	Campbell-Jones Ladybird	M. A. Campbell-Jones	
G-MJHE	Hiway Demon Skytrike	S. Pickering	
G-MJHF	Skyhook Sailwing Trike	R. A. Watering	
G-MJHG	Huntair Pathfinder 330	A. Nice	
G-MJHH	Soleair Dactyl	C. N. Giddings	
G-MJHI	Soleair Dactyl	S. B. Giddings	
G-MJHJ	Redwing G.W.W.1	N. J. Mackay	
G-MJHK	Hiway Demon 195	J. C. Bowden	
G-MJHL	Mainair Triflyer Mk II	D. G. Jones	
G-MJHM	Ultrasports Trike	D. B. Markham	
G-MJHN	American Aerolights Eagle	P. K. Ewens	
G-MJHO	Shilling Bumble Bee Srs 1	C. R. Shilling	
G-MJHP	American Aerolights Eagle	K. Garnett & ptnrs	
G-MJHR	Southdown Lightning	B. R. Barnes	
G-MJHS	American Aerolights Eagle	R. M. Bacon	
G-MJHT	Eurowing Goldwing	J. D. Penman	
G-MJHU	Eipper Quicksilver MX	P. J. Hawcock & ptnrs	
G-MJHV	Hiway Demon 250	A. G. Griffiths	
G-MJHW	Ultrasports Puma 1	R. C. Barnett	
G-MJHX	Eipper Quicksilver MX	P. D. Lucas	
G-MJHY	American Aerolights Eagle	S. Hardy	
G-MJHZ	Southdown Sailwings	T. L. Dean	
G-MJIA	Flexiform Striker	R. M. Jamison	
G-MJIB	Hornet 250	S. H. Williams	
G-MJIC	Ultrasports Puma 330	C. R. Marriott	
G-MJID	Southdown Sailwings Puma DS	P. Jarman	
G-MJIE	Hornet 330	C. J. Dalby	
G-MJIF	Mainair Triflyer	R. J. Payne	
G-MJIG	Hiway Demon Skytrike	E. Dauncey	
G-MJIH	Ultrasports Tripacer	J. L. Bakewell	
G-MJII	American Aerolights Eagle	M. Flitman	
G-MJIJ	Ultrasports Tripacer 250	D. H. Targett	
G-MJIK	Southdown Sailwings Lightning	J. F. Chithalan	
G-MJIL	Bremner Mitchell B.10	D. S. & R. M. Bremner	
G-MJIM	Skyhook Cutlass	P. Rayner	
G-MJIN	Hiway Skytrike	P. W. Harding	
G-MJIO	American Aerolights Eagle	R. Apps & J. Marshall	
G-MJIP	Wheeler Scout Mk 33A	A. V. Wilson	
G-MJIR	Eipper Quicksilver MX	H. Feeney	
G-MJIS	American Aerolights Eagle	E. Gee	
G-MJIT	Hiway Skytrike	F. A. Mileham & D. W. B. Hatch	
G-MJIU	Eipper Quicksilver MX	O. W. A. Church	
G-MJIV	Pterodactyl Ptraveller	G. E. Fowles	
G-MJIX	Flexiform Hilander	D. Beer	
G-MJIY	Flexiform Voyage	R. J. Sims	
G-MJIZ	Southdown Lightning	J. J. Crudington	
G-MJJA	Huntair Pathfinder	J. B. & J. M. Watkins	
G-MJJB	Eipper Quicksilver MX	T. V. Thorp	
G-MJJC	Eipper Quicksilver MX2	R. G. Pickard	
G-MJJD	Birdman Cherokee	B. J. Sanderson	
G-MJJE	Douglas Type 1	R. A. Douglas	
G-MJJF	Sealey	L. G. Thomas & R. D. Thomasson	
G-MJJI	Mackinder Skyrider	R. H. Mackinder	
G-MJJJ	Moyes Knight	R. J. Broomfield	
G-MJJK	Eipper Quicksilver MX2	M. J. O'Malley	
G-MJJL	Solar Wings Storm	P. Wharton	
G-MJJM	Birdman Cherokee Mk 1	R. J. Wilson	
G-MJJN	Ultrasports Puma	J. E. Gooch	
G-MJJO	Flexiform Skytrike Dual	Kington Mead Flying Group	
G-MJJP	American Aerolights Eagle	Flying Machines (Circa 1910) Ltd	
G-MJJR	Huntair Pathfinder 330	R. D. Beavan	
G-MJJS	Swallow AeroPlane Swallow B	D. Corrigan	

Notes	Reg.	Type	Owner or Operator
	G-MJJT	Huntair Pathfinder	Macpara Ltd
	G-MJJU	Hiway Demon	I. C. Willetts
	G-MJJV	Wheeler Scout	C. G. Johes
	G-MJJW	Chargus Kilmarnock	J. S. Potts
	G-MJJX	Hiway Skytrike	P. C. Millward
	G-MJJY	Tirith Firefly	Tirith Microplane Ltd
	G-MJJZ	Hiway Demon 175 Skytrike	B. C. Williams
	G-MJKA	Skyhook Sabre Trike	J. Petter & J. Armstrong
	G-MJKB	Striplin Skyranger	A. P. Booth
	G-MJKC	Mainair Triflyer 330 Striker	W. H. Prince
	G-MJKE	Mainair Triflyer 330	R. E. D. Bailey
	G-MJKF	Hiway Demon	S. D. Hill
	G-MJKG	John Ivor Skytrike	R. C. Wright
	G-MJKH	Eipper Quicksilver MX II	E. H. E. Nunn
	G-MJKI	Eipper Quicksilver MX	D. R. Gibbons
	G-MJKJ	Eipper Quicksilver MX	Aerolite Aviation Co Ltd
	G-MJKL	Ultrasports Puma	D. P. McHenry
	G-MJKM	Chargus Titan TS.440/38	Hiway Flight Services Ltd
	G-MJKN	Hiway Demon	Hiway Flight Services Ltd
	G-MJKO	Goldmarque 250 Skytrike	M. J. Barry
	G-MJKP	Hiway Super Scorpion	M. Horsfall
	G-MJKR	Rotec Rally 2B	J. R. Darlow & J. D. Whitcock
	G-MJKS	Mainair Triflyer	A. R. R. Williams
	G-MJKT	Hiway Super Scorpion	K. J. Morris
	G-MJKU	Hiway Demon 175	M. R. Taylor
	G-MJKV	Hornet	D. A. Robinson
	G-MJKW	Maxair Hummer TX	D. Roberts
	G-MJKX	Ultralight Skyrider Phantom	L. K. Fowler
	G-MJKY	Hiway Skytrike	J. P. Wild
	G-MJLA	Ultrasports Puma 2	G. F. Cutler
	G-MJLB	Ultrasports Puma 2	Breen Aviation Ltd
	G-MJLC	American Aerolights Double Eagle	Ardenco Ltd
	G-MJLD	Wheeler Scout Mk III	M. Buchanan-Jones
	G-MJLE	Lightwing Rooster 2 Type 5	J. Lee
	G-MJLF	Southern Microlight Trike	P. A. Grimes
	G-MJLG	Hiway Skytrike Mk II	R. E. Neilson
	G-MJLH	American Aerolights Eagle 2	A. Cussins
	G-MJLI	Hiway Demon Skytrike	A. J. P. Farmer
	G-MJLJ	Flexiform Sealander	Questair Ltd
	G-MJLK	Dragonfly 250-II	G. Carter
	G-MJLL	Hiway Demon Skytrike	D. Hines
	G-MJLM	Mainair Triflyer 250	C. Wong
	G-MJLN	Southern Microlight Gazelle	R. Rossiter
	G-MJLO	Goldmarque Skytrike	K. G. Steer
	G-MJLR	Skyhook SK-1	T. Moore
	G-MJLS	Rotec Rally 2B	G. Messenger
	G-MJLT	American Aerolights Eagle	P. de Vere Hunt
	G-MJLU	Skyhook	C. A. Shayes
	G-MJLV	Eipper Quicksilver MX	W. Wade-Gery
	G-MJLW	Chargus Titan	C. Ellison
	G-MJLX	Rotec Rally 2B	J. Houldenshaw
	G-MJLY	American Aerolights Eagle	A. H. Read
	G-MJLZ	Hiway Demon Skytrike	K. Pickering
	G-MJMA	Hiway Demon	R. I. Simpson
	G-MJMB	Weedhopper	J. E. Brown
	G-MJMC	Huntair Pathfinder	R. Griffiths
	G-MJMD	Hiway Demon Skytrike	D. Cussen
	G-MJME	Ultrasports Tripacer Mega II	A. D. Cranfield
	G-MJMG	Weedhopper	S. Reynolds
	G-MJMH	American Aerolights Eagle	D. Crowson
	G-MJMI	Skyhook Sabre	W. P. Klotz
	G-MJMJ	Wheeler Scout III	R. Mitchell
	G-MJMK	Ultrasports Tripacer	M. F. J. Shipp
	G-MJML	Weedhopper D	V. Dixon
	G-MJMM	Chargus Vortex	R. J. Gray
	G-MJMN	Mainair Trike	D. Harrison
	G-MJMO	Lancashire Microlight Striker	N. Heap
	G-MJMP	Eipper Quicksilver MX	S. A. S. McCulloch
	G-MJMR	Mainair Trike	T. Anderson
	G-MJMS	Hiway Skytrike	G. J. Foard
	G-MJMT	Hiway Demon Skytrike	N. J. Brunskill
	G-MJMU	Hiway Demon	J. Hall
	G-MJMV	Vulcan 2	R. Rawcliffe

Reg.	Type	Owner or Operator	Notes
G-MJMW	Eipper Quicksilver MX2	S. E. Borrow	
G-MJMX	Ultrasports Tripacer	D. Myles	
G-MJMZ	Robertson Ultralight B1-RD	Southwest Aviation	
G-MJNA	Mainair Triflyer	M. T. Byrne	
G-MJNB	Hiway Skytrike	G. Hammond	
G-MJNC	Hiway Demon Skytrike	T. Gdaniec	
G-MJNE	Hornet Supreme Dual Trike	Hornet Microlights	
G-MJNG	Eipper Quicksilver MX	R. Briggs-Price	
G-MJNH	Skyhook Cutlass Trike	M. E. James	
G-MJNI	Hornet Sabre	N. J. Kipling	
G-MJNJ	Gregory Typhoon	M. R. Gregory	
G-MJNK	Hiway Skytrike	E. J. Blyth	
G-MJNL	American Aerolights Eagle	W. A. H. Vick	
G-MJNM	American Aerolights Double Eagle	E. G. Cullen	
G-MJNN	Ultraflight Mirage II	Breen Aviation Ltd	
G-MJNO	American Aerolights Double Eagle	R. S. Martin & J. L. May	
G-MJNP	American Aerolights Eagle	D. J. Jackson	
G-MJNR	Ultralight Solar Buggy	D. J. Smith	
G-MJNS	Swallow AeroPlane Swallow B	S. M. Pickard	
G-MJNT	Hiway Skytrike	J. W. Richardson	
G-MJNU	Skyhook Cutlass	D. M. Camm	
G-MJNV	Eipper Quicksilver MX	W. Toulmin	
G-MJNW	Skyhook Silhouette	R. Hamilton	
G-MJNX	Eipper Quicksilver MX	R. Hurley	
G-MJNY	Skyhook Sabre Trike	P. Ratcliffe	
G-MJNZ	Skyhook Sabre Trike	R. Huthison	
G-MJOA	Chargus T.250 Vortex	S. F. Chave	
G-MJOB	Skyhook Cutlass CD Trike	J. M. Oliver	
G-MJOC	Huntair Pathfinder	R. Bowring	
G-MJOD	Rotec Rally 2B	A. J. Capel & K. D. Halsey	
G-MJOE	Eurowing Goldwing	R. J. Osbourne	
G-MJOF	Eipper Quicksilver MX	S. M. Wellband	
G-MJOG	American Aerolights Eagle	J. B. Rush	
G-MJOI	Hiway Demon	S. J. Walker	
G-MJOJ	Flexiform Skytrike	D. Haynes	
G-MJOK	Mainair Triflyer 250	S. Pike & K. Fagan	
G-MJOL	Skyhook Cutlass	G. Singh	
G-MJOM	Southdown Puma 40F	J. G. Crawford	
G-MJON	Southdown Puma 40F	Peninsula Flight Ltd	
G-MJOO	Southdown Puma 40F	D. J. England	
G-MJOP	Southdown Puma 40F	Peninsula Flight Ltd	
G-MJOR	Solair Phoenix	T. V. Wood	
G-MJOS	Southdown Lightning 170	A. Faiers	
G-MJOT	Airwave Nimrod	W. G. Lamyman	
G-MJOU	Hiway Demon 175	H. Phipps	
G-MJOV	Solar Wings Typhoon	I. R. Hoad	
G-MJOW	Eipper Quicksilver MX	P. N. Haigh	
G-MJOX	Solar Wings Typhoon	L. Johnston	
G-MJOY	Eurowing CP.16	J. P. B. Chilton	
G-MJPA	Rotec Rally 2B	G. S. Adams	
G-MJPB	Manuel Ladybird	W. L. Manuel	
G-MJPC	American Aerolights Double Eagle	D. M. Jackson	
G-MJPD	Hiway Demon Skytrike	K. A. Stewart	
G-MJPE	Hiway Demon Skytrike	D. Hill	
G-MJPF	American Aerolights Eagle 430R	A. E. F. McClintock	
G-MJPG	American Aerolights Eagle 430R	N. R. Macrae	
G-MJPH	Huntair Pathfinder	A. J. Lambert	
G-MJPI	Flexiform Striker	D. A. Watkins	
G-MJPJ	Flexiform Dual Trike 440	M. D. Phillips & ptnrs	
G-MJPK	Hiway Vulcan	R. G. Darcy	
G-MJPL	Birdman Cherokee	P. A. Leach	
G-MJPM	Huntair Pathfinder	Swift Systems Ltd	
G-MJPN	Mitchell B10	T. Willford	
G-MJPO	Eurowing Goldwing	M. Merryman	
G-MJPP	Hiway Super Scorpion	K. L. Mercer	
G-MJPR	Birdman Cherokee 250	G. A. Webb	
G-MJPS	American Aerolights Eagle 430R	Peter Symonds & Co	
G-MJPT	Dragon	Fly-In Ltd	

Notes	Reg.	Type	Owner or Operator
	G-MJPU	Solar Wings Typhoon	B. G. Birkett
	G-MJPV	Eipper Quicksilver MX	N. G. Jagger
	G-MJPW	Mainair Merlin	G. Deegan
	G-MJPX	Hiway Demon	R. Todd
	G-MJPY	American Aerolights Eagle	N. G. Jagger
	G-MJPZ	American Aerolights Eagle	A. T. Croy
	G-MJRA	Hiway Demon	P. Richardson & J. Martin
	G-MJRC	Eipper Quicksilver MX	R. W. Bunting
	G-MJRE	Hiway Demon	P. A. Smith
	G-MJRG	Ultrasports Puma	J. Lakin
	G-MJRH	Hiway Skytrike	N. C. Hopwood
	G-MJRI	American Aerolights Eagle	N. N. Brown
	G-MJRJ	Hiway Demon 175 Skytrike	M. Tomlinson
	G-MJRK	Flexiform Striker	P. J. & G. Long
	G-MJRL	Eurowing Goldwing	L. S. Nicholson
	G-MJRM	Dragon 150	Fly-In Ltd
	G-MJRN	Flexiform Striker	K. Handley
	G-MJRO	Eurowing Goldwing	S. P. Reeve
	G-MJRP	Mainair Triflyer 330	A. Hulme
	G-MJRR	Striplin Skyranger Srs 1	J. R. Reece
	G-MJRS	Eurowing Goldwing	R. V. Hogg
	G-MJRT	Southdown Lightning DS	R. J. Perry
	G-MJRU	MBA Tiger Cub 440	D. V. Short
	G-MJRV	Eurowing Goldwing	D. N. Williams
	G-MJRX	Ultrasports Puma II	E. M. Woods
	G-MJRY	MBA Super Tiger Cub 440	Vintage Displays & Training Services Ltd
	G-MJRZ	MBA Super Tiger Cub 440	Vintage Displays & Training Services Ltd
	G-MJSA	Mainair 2-Seat Trike	D. Verdon
	G-MJSB	Eurowing Catto CP.16	Independent Business Forms (Scotland) Ltd
	G-MJSC	American Aerolights Eagle	E. McGuiness
	G-MJSD	Rotec Rally 2B Srs 1	K. J. Dickson
	G-MJSE	Skyrider Airsports Phantom	S. Montandon
	G-MJSF	Skyrider Airsports Phantom	Skyrider Airsports
	G-MJSH	American Aerolights Eagle	J. Walsom
	G-MJSI	Huntair Pathfinder	Huntair Ltd
	G-MJSK	Skyhook Sabre	G. E. Coole
	G-MJSL	Dragon 200	S. C. Weston
	G-MJSM	Weedhopper B	J. R. Bancroft
	G-MJSO	Hiway Skytrike	G. A. Ede
	G-MJSP	MBA Super Tiger Cub 440	J. W. E. Romain
	G-MJSR	Flexiform Micro-Trike II	R. J. S. Galley
	G-MJSS	American Aerolights Eagle	G. N. S. Farrant
	G-MJST	Pterodactyl Ptraveler	C. H. J. Goodwin
	G-MJSU	MBA Tiger Cub	R. J. Adams
	G-MJSV	MBA Tiger Cub	D. A. Izod
	G-MJSX	Simplicity Microlight	N. Smith
	G-MJSY	Eurowing Goldwing	A. J. Rex
	G-MJSZ	D.H. Wasp	P. S. Cotterell
	G-MJTA	Flexiform Striker	K. J. Regan
	G-MJTB	Eipper Quicksilver MX	R. F. G. King
	G-MJTC	Solar Wings Typhoon	D. W. Foreman & J. A. Iszard
	G-MJTD	Gardner T-M Scout	D. Gardner
	G-MJTE	Skyrider Airsports Phantom	A. L. Hastings
	G-MJTF	Gryphon Wing	A. T. Armstrong
	G-MJTG	AES Sky Ranger	Aero & Engineering Services Ltd
	G-MJTH	S.M.D. Gazelle	D. Marsh
	G-MJTI	Huntair Pathfinder II	B. Gunn
	G-MJTJ	Weedhopper	M. J. Blanchard
	G-MJTK	American Aerolights Eagle	N. R. MacRae
	G-MJTL	Aerostructure Pipistrelle 2B	J. McD. Robinson & C. G. McCrae
	G-MJTM	Aerostructure Pipistrelle 2B	Southdown Aero Services Ltd
	G-MJTN	Eipper Quicksilver MX	N. F. Cuthbert
	G-MJTO	Jordan Duet Srs 1	J. R. Jordan
	G-MJTP	Flexiform Striker	R. D. A. Henderson
	G-MJTR	Southdown Puma DS Mk 1	P. Soanes
	G-MJTU	Skyhook Cutlass 185	P. D. Wade
	G-MJTW	Eurowing Trike	W. G. Lindsay
	G-MJTX	Skyrider Phantom	Haywood Design
	G-MJTY	Huntair Pathfinder	C. H. Smith
	G-MJTZ	Skyrider Airsports Phantom	A. I. Stott
	G-MJUA	MBA Super Tiger Cub	M. Ward

Reg.	Type	Owner or Operator	Notes
G-MJUB	MBA Tiger Cub 440	C. C. Butt	
G-MJUC	MBA Tiger Cub 440	G. A. Costelloe	
G-MJUD	Southdown Puma 440	R. S. W. Jones	
G-MJUE	Southdown Wild Cat ll	W. M. A. Alladin	
G-MJUF	MBA Super Tiger Cub 440	J. A. Robinson	
G-MJUH	MBA Tiger Cub 440	J. E. Carr	
G-MJUI	Flexiform Striker	L. M. & R. E. Bailey	
G-MJUJ	Eipper Quicksilver MX II	P. J. McEvoy	
G-MJUK	Eipper Quicksilver MX II	J. C. M. Haigh	
G-MJUL	Southdown Puma Sprint	M. L. Harris	
G-MJUM	Flexiform Striker	M. J. W. Holding	
G-MJUN	Hiway Skytrike	A. Donohue	
G-MJUO	Eipper Quicksilver MX II	Border Aviation Ltd	
G-MJUP	Weedhopper B	R. A. P. Cox	
G-MJUR	Skyrider Airsports Phantom	J. Hannibal	
G-MJUS	MBA Tiger Cub 440	B. Jenks	
G-MJUT	Eurowing Goldwing	D. L. Eite	
G-MJUU	Eurowing Goldwing	B. Brown	
G-MJUV	Huntair Pathfinder	B. E. Francis	
G-MJUW	MBA Tiger Cub 440	H. F. Robertson & R. J. Anderson	
G-MJUX	Skyrider Airsports Phantom	C. M. Tomkins	
G-MJUY	Eurowing Goldwing	J. E. M. Barnatt-Millns	
G-MJUZ	Dragon Srs 150	J. R. Fairweather	
G-MJVA	Skyrider Airsports Phantom	Skyrider Airsports	
G-MJVC	Hiway Skytrike	J. H. Stage	
G-MJVE	Hybred Skytrike	S. F. Carey	
G-MJVF	CFM Shadow	D. G. Cook	
G-MJVG	Hiway Skytrike	D. Bridges	
G-MJVH	American Aerolights Eagle	R. G. Glenister	
G-MJVI	Lightwing Rooster 1 Srs 4	J. M. Lee	
G-MJVJ	Flexiform Striker	Hornet Microlights	
G-MJVL	Flexiform Striker	H. Phipps	
G-MJVM	Dragon 150	A. Fairweather	
G-MJVN	Ultrasports Puma 440	O. R. Pluck	
G-MJVP	Eipper Quicksilver MX II	R. F. Witt	
G-MJVR	Flexiforn Striker	D. R. Sutton	
G-MJVS	Hiway Super Scorpion	T. C. Harrold	
G-MJVT	Eipper Quicksilver MX	A. M. Reid	
G-MJVU	Eipper Quicksilver MX II	F. J. Griffith	
G-MJVV	Hornet Supreme Dual	P. M. Gilfoyle	
G-MJVW	Airwave Nimrod	T. P. Mason	
G-MJVX	Skyrider Airsports Phantom	J. A. Grindley	
G-MJVY	Dragon Srs 150	J. C. Craddock	
G-MJVZ	Hiway Demon Tripacer	M. G. & M. L. Sadler	
G-MJWA	Birdman Cherokee	R. Jakeway	
G-MJWB	Eurowing Goldwing	R. A. Davies	
G-MJWC	Paraglide Fabric Self Inflating Wing	O. W. Neumark	
G-MJWD	Solar Wings Typhoon XL	I. Cummins	
G-MJWE	Hiway Demon	S. R. Loomes	
G-MJWF	MBA Tiger Cub 440	B. R. Hunter	
G-MJWG	MBA Tiger Cub 440	D. H. Carter	
G-MJWI	Flexiform Striker	R. W. Twamley	
G-MJWJ	MBA Tiger Cub 440	H. A. Bromiley	
G-MJWK	Huntair Pathfinder	M. R. Swaffield & J. E. Bogart	
G-MJWL	Chargus Vortex T250	Solar Wings Ltd	
G-MJWM	Chargus Vortex T250	Solar Wings Ltd	
G-MJWN	Flexiform Striker	A. C. Rowlands	
G-MJWO	Hiway Skytrike	M. J. Gillespie	
G-MJWR	MBA Tiger Cub 440	M. G. &. M. W. Sadler	
G-MJWS	Eurowing Goldwing	J. W. Salter & R. J. Bell	
G-MJWT	American Aerolights Eagle	D. S. Baber	
G-MJWU	Maxair Hummer TX	J. Bagnall	
G-MJWV	Southdown Puma MS	D. E. Gwehih	
G-MJWW	MBA Super Tiger Cub 440	P. J. Ward	
G-MJWX	Flexiform Striker	W. A. Bibby	
G-MJWY	Flexiform Striker	M. B. Horan	
G-MJWZ	Ultrasports Panther XL	T. V. Ward	
G-MJXA	Flexiform Striker	C. A. Palmer	
G-MJXB	Eurowing Goldwing	A. W. Odell	
G-MJXD	MBA Tiger Cub 440	W. L. Rogers	
G-MJXE	Hiway Demon	H. Sykes	
G-MJXF	MBA Tiger Cub 440	N. P. Day	
G-MJXG	Flexiform Striker	D. W. Barnes	

Notes	Reg.	Type	Owner or Operator
	G-MJXH	Mitchell Wing B10	M. M. Ruck
	G-MJXI	Flexiform Striker	A. P. Pearson
	G-MJXJ	MBA Tiger Cub 440	J. E. Carr
	G-MJXL	MBA Tiger Cub 440	M. J. Lister
	G-MJXM	Hiway Skytrike	G. S. & P. W. G. Carter
	G-MJXN	American Aerolights Eagle	C. H. Middleton
	G-MJXO	Middleton CM.5	C. H. Middleton
	G-MJXR	Huntair Pathfinder II	J. F. H. James
	G-MJXS	Huntair Pathfinder II	A. E. Sawyer
	G-MJXT	Phoenix Falcon 1	Phoenix Aircraft Co
	G-MJXU	MBA Tiger Cub 440	Radio West Ltd
	G-MJXV	Flexiform Striker	E. T. Mapes
	G-MJXW	Southdown Sigma	C. J. Tansley
	G-MJXX	Flexiform Striker Dual	H. A. Ward
	G-MJXY	Hiway Demon Skytrike	P. E. A. Dook
	G-MJXZ	Hiway Demon	O. Wood
	G-MJYA	Huntair Pathfinder	Ultrasports Ltd
	G-MJYB	Eurowing Goldwing	D. A. Farnworth
	G-MJYC	Ultrasports Panther XL Dual 440	D. D. Boy
	G-MJYD	MBA Tiger Cub 440	R. Lumb
	G-MJYE	Southdown Lightning Trike	J. A. Hindley
	G-MJYF	Mainair Gemini Flash	R. Young
	G-MJYG	Skyhook Orion Canard	Skyhook Sailwings Ltd
	G-MJYI	Mainair Triflyer	R. A. Rawes
	G-MJYJ	MBA Tiger Cub 440	M. F. Collett
	G-MJYL	Airwave Nimrod	M. P. Dale
	G-MJYM	Southdown Puma Sprint	Breen Aviation Ltd
	G-MJYN	Mainair Triflyer 440	A. J. Girling
	G-MJYO	Mainair Triflyer 330	P. Best
	G-MJYP	Mainair Triflyer 440	Mainair Sports Ltd
	G-MJYR	Catto CP.16	M. Hindley
	G-MJYS	Southdown Puma Sprint	G. Breen
	G-MJYT	Southdown Puma Sprint	G. Breen
	G-MJYV	Mainair Triflyer 2 Seat	D. A. McFadyean
	G-MJYW	Wasp Gryphon III	P. D. Lawrence
	G-MJYX	Mainair Triflyer	R. K. Birlison
	G-MJYY	Hiway Demon	N. Smith
	G-MJYZ	Flexiform Striker	S. C. Beesley
	G-MJZA	MBA Tiger Cub	D. W. Bedford
	G-MJZB	Flexiform Striker Dual	A. Faiers
	G-MJZC	MBA Tiger Cub 440	P. G. Walton
	G-MJZD	Mainair Gemini Flash	A. R. Gaivoto
	G-MJZE	MBA Tiger Cub 440	D. Ridley & ptnrs
	G-MJZF	La Mouette Atlas 16	W. R. Crew
	G-MJZG	Mainair Triflyer 440	K. C. Bennett
	G-MJZH	Southdown Lightning 195	P. H. Risdale
	G-MJZI	Eurowing Goldwing	A. J. Sharpe
	G-MJZJ	Hiway Cutlass Skytrike	G. D. H. Sandlin
	G-MJZK	Southdown Puma Sprint 440	K. B. Tolley
	G-MJZL	Eipper Quicksilver MX II	S. R. Jackson
	G-MJZM	MBA Tiger Cub 440	F. M. Ward
	G-MJZN	Pterodactyl	C. J. Blundell
	G-MJZO	Flexiform Striker	M. G. Rawsthorne
	G-MJZP	MBA Tiger Cub 440	Herts & Cambs Biplanes Ltd
	G-MJZR	Eurowing Zephyr 1	I. M. Vass
	G-MJZT	Flexiform Striker	J. Whitehouse
	G-MJZU	Flexiform Striker	R. G. Hooker
	G-MJZV	Livesey Micro 5	D. M. Livesey
	G-MJZW	Eipper Quicksilver MX II	W. Smith & ptnrs
	G-MJZX	Maxair Hummer TX	R. J. Folwell
	G-MJZZ	Skyhook Cutlass	P. E. Penrose
	G-MMAC	Dragon Srs 150	R. W. Sage
	G-MMAE	Dragon Srs 150	I. Fleming
	G-MMAG	MBA Tiger Cub 440	W. R. Tull
	G-MMAH	Eipper Quicksilver MX II	J. C. Larkin
	G-MMAI	Dragon Srs 150	T. W. Dukes
	G-MMAJ	Mainair Tri-Flyer 440	D. A. Frank & M. J. Moon
	G-MMAK	MBA Tiger Cub 440	G. E. Heritage
	G-MMAL	Flexiform Striker Dual	D. J. Hand
	G-MMAM	MBA Tiger Cub 440	I. M. Bartlett
	G-MMAN	Flexiform Striker	E. Dean
	G-MMAO	Southdown Puma Sprint	R. A. Downham
	G-MMAP	Hummer TX	J. S. Millard

Reg.	Type	Owner or Operator	Notes
G-MMAR	Southdown Puma Sprint MS	J. R. North	
G-MMAT	Southdown Puma Sprint MS	Mainair Sports Ltd	
G-MMAU	Flexiform Rapier	R. Hemsworth	
G-MMAV	American Aerolights Eagle	Aeri-Visual Ltd	
G-MMAW	Mainair Rapier	T. Green	
G-MMAX	Flexiform Striker	G. P. Jones	
G-MMAY	Airwave Magic Nimrod	R. E. Patterson	
G-MMAZ	Southdown Puma Sprint	A. R. Smith	
G-MMBA	Hiway Super Scorpion	B. J. Hampshire	
G-MMBB	American Aerolights Eagle	M. R. Starling	
G-MMBC	Hiway Super Scorpion	A. T. Grain	
G-MMBD	Spectrum 330	J. Hollings	
G-MMBE	MBA Tiger Cub 440	R. J. B. Jordan & R. W. Pearce	
G-MMBF	American Aerolights Eagle	N. V. Middleton	
G-MMBG	Chargus Cyclone	P. N. Long	
G-MMBH	MBA Super Tiger Cub 440	C. H. Jennings & J. F. Howesman	
G-MMBJ	Solar Wings Typhoon	D. W. Beach	
G-MMBK	American Aerolights Eagle	B. M. Quinn	
G-MMBL	Southdown Puma	A. J. M. Berry	
G-MMBM	La Mouette Azure	A. Christian	
G-MMBN	Eurowing Goldwing	M. R. Grunwell	
G-MMBR	Hiway Demon 175	S. S. M. Turner	
G-MMBS	Flexiform Striker	P. Thompson	
G-MMBT	MBA Tiger Cub 440	F. F. Chamberlain	
G-MMBU	Eipper Quicksilver MX II	R. Barrow	
G-MMBV	Huntair Pathfinder	M. P. Phillippe	
G-MMBW	MBA Tiger Cub 440	J. C. Miles	
G-MMBX	MBA Tiger Cub 440	Fox Brothers Blackpool Ltd	
G-MMBY	Solar Wings Storm	R. M. Clarke	
G-MMCA	Solar Wings Storm	P. B. Currell	
G-MMCC	American Aerolights Eagle	Microlight Aviation (UK) Ltd	
G-MMCD	Southdown Lightning DS	I. K. Wilson	
G-MMCE	MBA Tiger Cub 440	M. K. Dring	
G-MMCF	Solar Wings Panther 330	N. Birkin	
G-MMCG	Eipper Quicksilver MX I	L. W. Farrow	
G-MMCH	Southdown Lightning Phase II	R. S. Andrew	
G-MMCI	Southdown Puma Sprint	R. J. Webb	
G-MMCJ	Flexiform Striker	P. Hayes	
G-MMCK	Stewkie Aer-O-Ship LTA	K. Stewart	
G-MMCL	Stewkie Aer-O-Ship HAA	K. Stewart	
G-MMCM	Southdown Puma Sprint	J. G. Kane	
G-MMCN	Solar Wings Storm	A. P. S. Presland	
G-MMCO	Southdown Sprint	D. J. Smith	
G-MMCP	Southdown Lightning	J. McAlpine	
G-MMCR	Eipper Quicksilver MX	T. L. & B. L. Holland	
G-MMCS	Southdown Puma Sprint	R. G. Calvert	
G-MMCT	Hiway Demon	R. G. Gray	
G-MMCV	Solar Wings Typhoon III	G. W. Doswell	
G-MMCW	Southdown Puma Sprint	S. Grant	
G-MMCX	MBA Super Tiger Cub 440	D. Harkin	
G-MMCY	Flexiform Striker	K. E. Preston	
G-MMCZ	Flexiform Striker	T. D. Adamson	
G-MMDA	Mitchell Wing B-10	H. F. French	
G-MMDB	La Mouette Atlas	K. A. Martin	
G-MMDC	Eipper Quicksilver MXII	M. Risdale & C. Lamb	
G-MMDD	Huntair Pathfinder	M. R. Starling	
G-MMDE	Solar Wings Typhoon	D. E. Smith	
G-MMDF	Southdown Lightning Phase II	P. Kelly	
G-MMDG	Eurowing Goldwing	Edgim Ltd	
G-MMDH	Manta Fledge 2B	C. R. Brewitt	
G-MMDI	Hiway Super Scorpion	R. E. Hodge	
G-MMDJ	Solar Wings Typhoon	D. Johnson	
G-MMDK	Flexiform Striker	P. D. Blyth	
G-MMDL	Dragon Srs 150	Dragon Light Aircraft Co Ltd	
G-MMDM	MBA Tiger Cub 440	D. Marsh	
G-MMDN	Flexiform Striker	M. G. Griffiths	
G-MMDO	Southdown Sprint	S. Stevens	
G-MMDP	Southdown Sprint	R. M. Strange	
G-MMDR	Huntair Pathfinder II	M. Shapland	
G-MMDS	Ultrasports Panther XLS	L. A. Bastin	
G-MMDT	Flexiform Striker	A. Pauline	
G-MMDU	MBA Tiger Cub 440	G. Perlmutter	
G-MMDV	Ultrasports Panther	M. C. Druce	
G-MMDW	Pterodactyl Pfledgling	J. Fletcher	

Notes	Reg.	Type	Owner or Operator
	G-MMDX	Solar Wings Typhoon	E. J. Lloyd
	G-MMDY	Southdown Puma Sprint	A. J. Perry
	G-MMDZ	Flexiform Dual Strike	D. C. Seager-Thomas
	G-MMEA	MBA Tiger Cub 440	Border Aviation Ltd
	G-MMEB	Hiway Super Scorpion	A. A. Ridgway
	G-MMEC	Southdown Puma DS	A. E. Wilson
	G-MMED	Aeolus Mk 1	Aeolus Aviation
	G-MMEE	American Aerolights Eagle	G. R. Bell & J. D. Bailey
	G-MMEF	Hiway Super Scorpion	J. H. Cooling
	G-MMEG	Eipper Quicksilver MX	W. K. Harris
	G-MMEH	Ultrasports Panther	P. A. Harris
	G-MMEI	Hiway Demon	W. H. Shakeshaft
	G-MMEJ	Flexiform Striker	J. E. Chisholm
	G-MMEK	Solar Wings Typhoon XL2	T. A. Baker
	G-MMEL	Solar Wings Typhoon XL2	D. Rigden
	G-MMEM	Solar Wings Typhoon XL2	Wyndham Wade Ltd
	G-MMEN	Solar Wings Typhoon XL2	I. M. Rapley
	G-MMEP	MBA Tiger Cub 440	P. M. Yeoman & D. Freestone-Barks
	G-MMES	Southdown Puma Sprint	B. J. Sanderson
	G-MMET	Skyhook Sabre TR-1 Mk II	A. B. Greenbank
	G-MMEU	MBS Tiger Cub 440	R. Taylor
	G-MMEV	American Aerolights Eagle	J. G. Jennings
	G-MMEW	MBA Tiger Cub 440	V. N. Baker
	G-MMEX	Solar Wings Sprint	E. Bayliss
	G-MMEY	MBA Tiger Cub 440	M. G. Selley
	G-MMEZ	Southdown Puma Sprint	Southdown Sailwings
	G-MMFB	Flexiform Striker	P. N. Bailey
	G-MMFC	Flexiform Striker	D. Haynes
	G-MMFD	Flexiform Striker	M. E. & W. L. Chapman
	G-MMFE	Flexiform Striker	W. Camm
	G-MMFF	Flexiform Striker	D. S. Simpson
	G-MMFG	Flexiform Striker	D. L. Aspinall
	G-MMFH	Flexiform Striker	Flexiform Sky Sails
	G-MMFI	Flexiform Striker	A. J. Wood
	G-MMFJ	Flexiform Striker	A. W. Abraham
	G-MMFK	Flexiform Striker	S. W. England
	G-MMFL	Flexiform Striker	I. D. Evans
	G-MMFM	Piranha Srs 200	D. E. Richards
	G-MMFN	MBA Tiger Cub 440	R. L. Barnett
	G-MMFP	MBA Tiger Cub 440	R. J. Adams
	G-MMFR	MBA Tiger Cub 440	R. J. Adams
	G-MMFS	MBA Tiger Cub 440	P. J. Hodgkinson
	G-MMFT	MBA Tiger Cub 440	E. Barfoot
	G-MMFV	Flexiform Dual Striker	R. A. Walton
	G-MMFW	Skyhook Cutlass	W. Chapel
	G-MMFX	MBA Tiger Cub 440	J. W. E. Romain
	G-MMFY	Flexiform Dual Striker	P. J. Anderson
	G-MMFZ	AES Sky Ranger	H. A. Ward
	G-MMGA	Bass Gosling	G. J. Bass
	G-MMGB	Southdown Puma Sprint	G. Breen
	G-MMGC	Southdown Puma Sprint	Innovative Air Services Ltd
	G-MMGD	Southdown Puma Sprint	I. Hughes
	G-MMGE	Hiway Super Scorpion	P. Gregory
	G-MMGF	MBA Tiger Cub 440	L. P. Durrant
	G-MMGG	Southdown Puma	J. D. Penman
	G-MMGH	Flexiform Dual Striker	J. Whitehouse
	G-MMGI	Flexiform Dual Striker	M. Hurtley
	G-MMGJ	MBA Tiger Cub 440	J. Laidler
	G-MMGK	Skyhook Silhouette	N. E. Smith
	G-MMGL	MBA Tiger Cub 440	A. R. Cornelius
	G-MMGN	Southdown Puma Sprint	H. Stieker
	G-MMGO	MBA Tiger Cub 440	T. J. Court
	G-MMGP	Southdown Puma Sprint	M. D. Morris
	G-MMGR	Flexiform Dual Striker	E. J. Richards
	G-MMGS	Solar Wings Panther Dual	G. D. Featherstone
	G-MMGT	Solar Wings Typhoon	J. A. Hunt
	G-MMGU	Flexiform Sealander	C. J. Meadows
	G-MMGV	Whittaker MW.5 Sorcerer Srs A	G. N. Haffey & G. M. Hislop
	G-MMGW	Whittaker MW.5 Sorcerer Srs B	Microknight Aviation Ltd
	G-MMGX	Southdown Puma	G. S. Mitchell
	G-MMGY	Dean Piranha 1000	M. G. Dean
	G-MMHA	Skyhook TR-1 Pixie	P. J. & A. St J. Hollis
	G-MMHB	Skyhook TR-1 Pixie	D. M. Pollard
	G-MMHC	American Aerolights Eagle	G. Davies

Reg.	Type	Owner or Operator	Notes
G-MMHD	Hiway Demon 175	F. L. Allatt	
G-MMHE	Southdown Puma Sprint MS	J. Mayer	
G-MMHF	Southdown Puma Sprint	B. R. Claughton	
G-MMHG	Solar Wings Storm	W. T. Price	
G-MMHH	Solar Wings Panther Dual	D. R. Beaumont	
G-MMHI	MBA Tiger Cub 440	R. W. Iddon	
G-MMHJ	Flexiform Hilander	E. J. Binch & J. B. Wilkinson	
G-MMHK	Hiway Super Scorpion	R. Pearson	
G-MMHL	Hiway Super Scorpion	G. Ross	
G-MMHM	Goldmarque Gyr	G. J. Foard	
G-MMHN	MBA Tiger Cub 440	Gt Consall Copper Mines Co Ltd	
G-MMHO	MBA Tiger Cub 440	C. R. Perfect	
G-MMHP	Hiway Demon	P. Bedford	
G-MMHR	Southdown Puma Sprint DS	C. A. Eagles	
G-MMHS	SMD Viper	C. Scoble	
G-MMHT	Flexiform Striker	T. G. F. Trenchard	
G-MMHU	Flexiform Striker	P. R. Farnell	
G-MMHV	Chargus Vortex 120/T225	P. D. Larkin	
G-MMHW	Chargus Vortex 120/T225	P. D. Larkin	
G-MMHX	Hornet Invader 440	Hornet Microlights	
G-MMHY	Hornet Invader 440	W. Finlay	
G-MMHZ	Solar Wings Typhoon XL	S. J. Pain	
G-MMIA	Westwind Phoenix XP-3	Westwind Corporation Ltd	
G-MMIB	MEA Mistral	D. Hines	
G-MMIC	Luscombe Vitality	Luscombe Aircraft Ltd	
G-MMID	Flexiform Dual Striker	D. C. North	
G-MMIE	MBA Tiger Cub 440	M. L. Philpott	
G-MMIF	Wasp Gryphon	F. Coulson	
G-MMIG	MBA Tiger Cub 440	R. F. Witt	
G-MMIH	MBA Tiger Cub 440	W. A. Taylor	
G-MMII	Southdown Puma Sprint 440	T. C. Harrold	
G-MMIJ	Ultrasports Tripacer	R. W. Evans	
G-MMIK	Eipper Quicksilver MX II	Microlight Airsport Services Ltd	
G-MMIL	Eipper Quicksilver MX II	C. K. Brown	
G-MMIM	MBA Tiger Cub 440	D. A. Small	
G-MMIN	Luscombe Vitality	Luscombe Aircraft Ltd	
G-MMIO	Huntair Pathfinder II	C. Slater	
G-MMIP	Hiway Vulcan	A. A. Cale	
G-MMIR	Mainair Tri-Flyer 440	F. A. Prescott	
G-MMIS	Hiway Demon	M. P. Wing	
G-MMIT	Hiway Demon	S. R. Grant	
G-MMIU	Southdown Puma Sprint	P. J. Bullock	
G-MMIV	Southdown Puma Sprint	J. S. Walton	
G-MMIW	Southdown Puma Sprint	A. Twedell	
G-MMIX	MBA Tiger Cub 440	M. J. Butler & C. Bell	
G-MMIY	Eurowing Goldwing	R. J. Wood	
G-MMIZ	Southdown Lightning II	M. A. Cooper	
G-MMJA	Mitchell Wing B.10	J. Abbott	
G-MMJC	Southdown Sprint	P. G. Marshall	
G-MMJD	Southdown Puma Sprint	N. G. Tibbenham	
G-MMJE	Southdown Puma Sprint	F. N. M. Sergeant	
G-MMJF	Ultrasports Panther Dual 440	D. H. Stokes	
G-MMJG	Mainair Tri-Flyer 440	A. D. Stewart	
G-MMJH	Southdown Puma Sprint	A. R. Lawrence & T. J. Weston	
G-MMJI	Southdown Puma Sprint	R. Jenkins	
G-MMJJ	Solar Wings Typhoon	R. J. Wood	
G-MMJK	Hiway Demon	J. B. C. Brown & M. L. Jones	
G-MMJL	Flexiform 1+1 Sealander	K. Wade	
G-MMJM	Southdown Puma Sprint	R. J. Sanger	
G-MMJN	Eipper Quicksilver MX II	R. M. Gunn	
G-MMJO	MBA Tiger Cub 440	R. J. Adams	
G-MMJP	Southdown Lightning II	A. Slaghekke	
G-MMJR	MBA Tiger Cub 440	J. F. Ratcliffe	
G-MMJS	MBA Tiger Cub	Woodgate Air Services Ltd	
G-MMJT	Southdown Puma Sprint MS	Aircare Compressor Services	
G-MMJU	Hiway Demon	D. Whiteside	
G-MMJV	MBA Tiger Cub 440	K. Bannister	
G-MMJW	Southdown Puma Sprint	C. L. S. Boswell	
G-MMJX	Teman Mono-Fly	B. F. J. Hope	
G-MMJY	MBA Tiger Cub 440	Peterson Clarke Sports Ltd	
G-MMJZ	Skyhook Pixie	P. J. McNamee	
G-MMKA	Ultrasports Panther Dual	R. S. Wood	
G-MMKB	Ultralight Flight Mirage II	K. G. Wigley	
G-MMKC	Southdown Puma Sprint MS	J. Potts	

Notes	Reg.	Type	Owner or Operator
	G-MMKD	Southdown Puma Sprint	J. T. Wilson
	G-MMKE	Birdman Chinook WT-11	C. R. Gale & D. J. Royce
	G-MMKF	Ultrasports Panther Dual 440	G. H. Cork
	G-MMKG	Solar Wings Typhoon XL	P. G. Valentine
	G-MMKH	Solar Wings Typhoon XL	D. E. Home & M. Baylis
	G-MMKI	Ultasports Panther 330	Lightflight Aviation
	G-MMKJ	Ultrasports Panther 330	L. G. Horne
	G-MMKK	Mainair Flash	J. R. Brabbs
	G-MMKL	Mainair Flash	Mainair Sports Ltd
	G-MMKM	Flexiform Dual Striker	M. R. Starling
	G-MMKN	Mitchell Wing B-10	R. A. Rumney
	G-MMKO	Southdown Puma Sprint	G. Breen
	G-MMKP	MBA Tiger Cub 440	G. G. J. Derrick
	G-MMKR	Southdown Lightning DS	R. I. Lowe
	G-MMKS	Southdown Lightning 195	B. J. Marshall
	G-MMKT	MBA Tiger Cub 440	K. N. Townsend
	G-MMKU	Southdown Puma Sprint MS	J. S. Yates
	G-MMKV	Southdown Puma Sprint	J. Walsom
	G-MMKW	Solar Wings Storm	P. M. & R. Dewhurst
	G-MMKY	Jordan Duet	C. H. Smith
	G-MMKZ	Ultrasports Puma 440	M. G. Edwards
	G-MMLA	American Aerolights Eagle	Ardenco Ltd
	G-MMLB	MBA Tiger Cub 440	A. Newton
	G-MMLD	Solar Wings Typhoon S	N. P. Moran
	G-MMLE	Eurowing Goldwing SP	D. Lamberty
	G-MMLF	MBA Tiger Cub 440	J. R. Chichester-Constable
	G-MMLG	Solar Wings Typhoon S4 XL	R. M. Cornwell
	G-MMLH	Hiway Demon	P. M. Hendry & D. J. Lukery
	G-MMLI	Solar Wings Typhoon S	J. D. Grey
	G-MMLJ	—	—
	G-MMLK	MBA Tiger Cub 440	P. Flynn
	G-MMLL	Midland Ultralights Sirocco	Midland Ultralights Ltd
	G-MMLM	MBA Tiger Cub 440	D. R. G. Whitelaw
	G-MMLN	Skyhook Pixie	P. G. G. Taylor
	G-MMLO	Skyhook Pixie	T. G. Hilton
	G-MMLP	Southdown Sprint	Aactron Equipment Co Ltd
	G-MMLR	Ultrasports Panther 330	Lightflight Aviation
	G-MMLU	—	—
	G-MMLV	Southdown Puma 330	P. K. Dean
	G-MMLW	—	—
	G-MMLX	Ultrasports Panther	D. R. Crook
	G-MMLY	—	—
	G-MMLZ	Mainair Tri-Flyer	D. A. Whiteside
	G-MMMA	Flexiform Dual Striker	N. P. Heap
	G-MMMB	Mainair Tri-Flyer	D. M. Rusbridge
	G-MMMC	Southdown Puma SS	M. E. Hollis
	G-MMMD	Flexiform Dual Striker	K. P. Southwell & ptnr
	G-MMME	American Aerolights Eagle	G. Davies
	G-MMMF	American Aerolights Eagle	Aeronautical Logistics Ltd
	G-MMMG	Eipper Quicksilver MXL	W. Murphy
	G-MMMH	Hadland Willow	M. J. Hadland
	G-MMMI	Southdown Lightning	J. N. Whelan
	G-MMMJ	Southdown Sprint	R. R. Wolfenden
	G-MMMK	Hornet Invader	R. R. Wolfenden
	G-MMML	Dragon 150	R. G. Huntley
	G-MMMN	Ultrasports Panther Dual 440	T. L. Travis
	G-MMMO	Solar Wings Typhoon	B. R. Underwood
	G-MMMP	Flexiform Dual Striker	K. P. Southwell
	G-MMMR	Flexiform Striker	M. A. Rigler
	G-MMMS	MBA Tiger Cub 440	M. H. D. Soltau
	G-MMMT	Hornet Sigma	B. O'Connell
	G-MMMU	Skyhook Cutlass CD	F. J. Lightburn
	G-MMMV	Skyhook Cutlass Dual	R. R. Wolfenden
	G-MMMW	Flexiform Striker	K. & M. Spedding
	G-MMMX	Hornet Nimrod	R. Patrick
	G-MMMY	Hornet Nimrod	Bradford Motorcycle Ltd
	G-MMMZ	Southdown Puma Sprint MS	J. S. Potts
	G-MMNA	Eipper Quicksilver MX II	R. W. Payne
	G-MMNB	Eipper Quicksilver MX	J. T. Lindop
	G-MMNC	Eipper Quicksilver MX	K. R. Daly
	G-MMND	Eipper Quicksilver MX II-Q2	J. E. Holloway
	G-MMNF	Hornet	C. Hudson
	G-MMNG	Solar Wings Typhoon XL	R. Simpson
	G-MMNH	Dragon 150	J. S. Millard

Reg.	Type	Owner or Operator	Notes
G-MMNJ	Hiway Skytrike	A. Helliwell	
G-MMNK	Solar Wings Typhoon S4	P. Jackson	
G-MMNL	Solar Wings Typhoon S4	P. Jackson	
G-MMNM	Hornet 330	J. M. Elvy	
G-MMNN	Buzzard	E. W. Sherry	
G-MMNO	American Aerolights Eagle	P. J. Pentreath	
G-MMNP	Ultrasports Panther 250	R. Richardson	
G-MMNR	Dove	A. D. Wright	
G-MMNS	Mitchell U-2 Super Wing	D. J. Baldwin	
G-MMNT	Flexiform Striker	A. C. Coutts	
G-MMNU	Ultrasports Panther	S. J. Baker	
G-MMNV	Weedhopper	N. L. Rice	
G-MMNW	Mainair Tri-Flyer 330	T. Jackson	
G-MMNX	Solar Wings Panther XL	B. Montsern	
G-MMNY	Skyhook TR-1	N. H. Morley	
G-MMNZ	—	—	
G-MMOA	—	—	
G-MMOB	Southdown Sprint	D. Woolcock	
G-MMOC	Huntair Pathfinder II	E. H. Gould	
G-MMOD	MBA Tiger Cub 440	G. W. de Lancey Aitchison	
G-MMOE	Mitchell Wing B-10	T. Boyd	
G-MMOF	MBA Tiger Cub 440	Sunderland Microlights	
G-MMOG	Huntair Pathfinder	R. G. Maguire	
G-MMOH	Solar Wings Typhoon XL	T. H. Scott	
G-MMOI	MBA Tiger Cub 440	J. S. Smith & P. R. Talbot	
G-MMOJ	—	—	
G-MMOK	Solar Wings Panther XL	R. F. Foster	
G-MMOL	Skycraft Scout R3	P. D. G. Weller	
G-MMOM	Flexiform Striker	D. Haynes	
G-MMOO	Southdown Storm	S. Bourne	
G-MMOP	Solar Wings Panther Dual 440	J. Murphy	
G-MMOR	American Aerolights Eagle Cuyana	Southwest Air Sports Ltd	
G-MMOU	American Aerolights Eagle	T. Crispin	
G-MMOV	Mainair Gemini Flash	R. C. Coles	
G-MMOW	Mainair Gemini Flash	T. Rankin	
G-MMOX	Mainair Gemini Flash	K. Handley	
G-MMOY	Mainair Gemini Sprint	Mainair Sports Ltd	
G-MMPB	Solar Wings Typhoon S	P. T. F. Bowden	
G-MMPC	Skyhook TR-1	J. S. Garvey	
G-MMPD	Mainair Tri-Flyer	A. R. J. Dorling	
G-MMPE	Eurowing Goldwing	J. Cuff	
G-MMPF	Eurowing Goldwing	T. J. Ambler	
G-MMPG	Southdown Puma	B. R. Shepherd	
G-MMPH	Southdown Puma Sprint	A. Tristram	
G-MMPI	Pterodactyl Ptraveller	Goodwins of Hanley Ltd	
G-MMPJ	Mainair Tri-Flyer 440	K. R. Pickering	
G-MMPK	Solar Wings Typhoon 1	P. J. D. Kerr	
G-MMPL	Flexiform Dual Striker	P. D. Lawrence	
G-MMPM	Ultrasports Puma 330	C. G. Veitch	
G-MMPN	Chargus T250	S. M. Powrie	
G-MMPO	Mainair Gemini Flash	H. B. Baker	
G-MMPP	ParaPlane	GQ Defence Equipment Ltd	
G-MMPR	Dragon 150	P. N. B. Rosenfeld	
G-MMPS	American Aerolights Eagle	J. M. Tingle	
G-MMPT	SMD Gazelle	R. J. Humphries & I. J. Drake	
G-MMPU	Ultrasports Tripacer 250	B. D. W. Steen	
G-MMPV	MBA Tiger Cub 440	R. Felton	
G-MMPW	Airwave Nimrod	D. A. Smith	
G-MMPX	Ultrasports Panther Dual 440	M. T. Jones	
G-MMPY	Solar Wings Typhoon	A. W. Read	
G-MMPZ	Teman Mono-Fly	J. W. Highton	
G-MMRA	Mainair Tri-Flyer 250	S. R. Criddle	
G-MMRB	Hiway Skytrike 250	E. Garbutt	
G-MMRC	Southdown Lightning	J. C. Dodin & L. A. Ithier	
G-MMRD	Skyhook Cutlass CD	C. & R. A. White	
G-MMRE	Maxair Hummer	G. W. Doswell	
G-MMRF	MBA Tiger Cub 440	R. Gardner	
G-MMRG	Eipper Quicksilver MX	L. P. Diede	
G-MMRH	Hiway Demon	J. S. McCaig	
G-MMRI	Skyhook Sabre	G. M. Wrigley	
G-MMRJ	Solar Wings Panther XL	E. W. P. van Zeller	
G-MMRK	Ultrasports Panther XL	Enstone Microlight Centre	
G-MMRL	Solar Wings Panther XL	R. G. Thomas & H. A. Griffiths	

Notes	Reg.	Type	Owner or Operator
	G-MMRM	—	—
	G-MMRN	Southdown Puma Sprint	C. F. Bloyce
	G-MMRO	Mainair Gemini 440	P. R. Grady
	G-MMRP	Mainair Gemini	M. A. Pugh
	G-MMRR	Southdown Panther 250	D. D. & A. R. Young
	G-MMRS	Dragon 150	R. H. W. Strange
	G-MMRT	Southdown Puma Sprint	V. Brierley
	G-MMRU	Tirith Firebird FB-2	Tirith Microplane Ltd
	G-MMRV	MBA Tiger Cub 440	C. J. R. V. Baker
	G-MMRW	Flexiform Dual Striker	M. D. Hinge
	G-MMRX	Willmot J.W.1	N. J. Willmot
	G-MMRY	Chargus T.250	D. L. Edwards ⅛ ptnrs
	G-MMRZ	Ultrasports Panther Dual 440	Lancaster Partners (Holdings) Ltd
	G-MMSA	Ultrasports Panther XL	D. W. Taylor
	G-MMSB	Huntair Pathfinder II	S. R. Baugh
	G-MMSC	Mainair Gemini	A. B. Jones
	G-MMSD	—	—
	G-MMSE	Eipper Quicksilver MX	S. Bateman
	G-MMSF	—	—
	G-MMSG	Solar Wings Typhoon XL	R. Simpson
	G-MMSH	Solar Wings Panther XL	I. J. Drake
	G-MMSI	ParaPlane	International Fund for Animal Welfare
	G-MMSJ	ParaPlane	International Fund for Animal Welfare
	G-MMSK	—	—
	G-MMSL	Ultrasports Panther XLS	G. J. Slater
	G-MMSM	Mainair Gemini Flash	A. W. Birchley
	G-MMSN	Mainair Gemini	P. M. Feasey
	G-MMSO	Mainair Tri-Flyer 440	D. Morley
	G-MMSP	Mainair Gemini Flash	B. J. Robe
	G-MMSR	MBA Tiger Cub 440	G. Quarendon
	G-MMSS	Solar Wings Panther 330	S. J. Baker
	G-MMST	Southdown Puma Sprint	I. Davis
	G-MMSU	American Aerolights Eagle B	C. Bilham
	G-MMSV	Southdown Puma Sprint	M. P. Bloomfield
	G-MMSW	MBA Tiger Cub 440	D. R. Hemmings
	G-MMSX	Ultrasports Panther	M. J. Linford
	G-MMSZ	Medway Half Pint	Lancaster Partners (Holdings) Ltd
	G-MMTA	Ultrasports Panther XL	J. W. Wall
	G-MMTB	—	—
	G-MMTC	Ultrasports Panther Dual	J. M. Butler
	G-MMTD	Mainair Tri-Flyer 330	E. I. Armstrong
	G-MMTE	Mainair Gemini	B. F. Crick
	G-MMTF	Southdown Puma Sprint	P. J. K. Scriven
	G-MMTG	Mainair Gemini	R. P. W. Johnstone
	G-MMTH	Southdown Puma Sprint	R. G. Tomlinson
	G-MMTI	Southdown Puma Sprint	M. A. Baldwin
	G-MMTJ	Southdown Puma Sprint	M. R. Pearce
	G-MMTK	Medway Hybred	J. F. Nicholls
	G-MMTL	Mainair Gemini	M. R. Bailey
	G-MMTM	Mainair Tri-Flyer 440	Medi-Cine Productions Ltd
	G-MMTN	Hiway Skytrike	A. J. Blake
	G-MMTO	Mainair Tri-Flyer	R. G. Swales
	G-MMTP	Eurowing Goldwing	T. Crispin
	G-MMTR	Ultrasports Panther	R. A. Youngs
	G-MMTS	Solar Wings Panther XL	C. N. Bond
	G-MMTT	Ultrasports Panther XL	W. Levinson
	G-MMTU	Flylite Super Scout	M. C. Drew
	G-MMTV	American Aerolights Eagle	P. J. Scott
	G-MMTW	American Aerolights Eagle	K. R. Gillett
	G-MMTX	Mainair Gemini 440	R. L. Mann
	G-MMTY	Fisher FP.202U	B. E. Maggs
	G-MMTZ	Eurowing Goldwing	R. B. D. Baker
	G-MMUA	Southdown Puma Sprint	J. T. Houghton
	G-MMUB	Ultrasports Tripacer 250	P. G. Thompson
	G-MMUC	Mainair Gemini 440	H. Edwards
	G-MMUD	Willmot Junior Cub	N. J. Willmot
	G-MMUE	Mainair Gemini Flash	Motor Services (Manchester) Ltd
	G-MMUF	Mainair Gemini	C. J. Ellison
	G-MMUG	Mainair Tri-Flyer	K. C. Rutland
	G-MMUH	Mainair Tri-Flyer	J. P. Nicklin
	G-MMUI	—	—
	G-MMUJ	Southdown Puma Sprint 440	T. A. Hinton
	G-MMUK	Mainair Tri-Flyer	B. R. Kirk
	G-MMUL	Ward Elf E.47	M. Ward

Reg.	Type	Owner or Operator	Notes
G-MMUM	MBA Tiger Cub 440	N. C. Butcher	
G-MMUN	Ultrasports Panther Dual XL	K. S. Smith	
G-MMUO	Mainair Gemini Flash	Cloudbase	
G-MMUP	Airwave Nimrod 140	R. J. Bickham	
G-MMUR	Hiway Skytrike 250	W. J. Clayton	
G-MMUS	Mainair Gemini	R. M. Findlay	
G-MMUU	ParaPlane PM-1	Colt Balloons Ltd	
G-MMUV	Southdown Puma Sprint	D. C. Read	
G-MMUW	Mainair Gemini Flash	J. C. K. Scardifield	
G-MMUX	Mainair Gemini	D. C. North	
G-MMUY	Mainair Gemini Flash	W. A. Bibby	
G-MMUZ	American Aerolights Eagle	A. C. Lowings	
G-MMVA	Southdown Puma Sprint	N. W. O'Brien	
G-MMVB	Skyhook Pixie	G. A. Breen	
G-MMVC	Ultrasports Panther XL	E. R. Holton	
G-MMVE	—	—	
G-MMVF	Ultrasports Panther XL	Microlight Tuition & Sales Ltd	
G-MMVG	MBA Tiger Cub 440	C. W. Grant	
G-MMVH	Southdown Raven	A. Reynolds	
G-MMVI	Southdown Puma Sprint	C. F. Boyton	
G-MMVJ	Southdown Puma Sprint	S. L. Robbins	
G-MMVK	Sigh Wing ParaPlane	M. T. Byrne	
G-MMVL	Ultrasports Panther XL-S	B. Milton	
G-MMVM	Whiteley Orion 1	P. N. Whiteley	
G-MMVN	Solar Wings Typhoon	D. C. Davies	
G-MMVO	Southdown Puma Sprint	R. W. Jennings	
G-MMVP	Mainair Gemini Flash	G. P. Shepherd	
G-MMVR	Hiway Skytrike 1	F. Naylor	
G-MMVS	Skyhook Pixie	G. Bilham	
G-MMVT	Mainair Gemini Flash	Aircraft Microlight Services	
G-MMVU	Mainair Gemini Flash	R. Wheeler	
G-MMVW	Skyhook Pixie	R. Keighley	
G-MMVX	Southdown Puma Sprint	D. J. Reynolds	
G-MMVY	American Aerolights Eagle	R. Savva	
G-MMVZ	Southdown Puma Sprint	M. R. Bayliss	
G-MMWA	Mainair Gemini Flash	K. Akister	
G-MMWB	Huntair Pathfinder II	Brinhan Ltd	
G-MMWC	Eipper Quicksilver MXII	P. W. Cole & L. R. Mudge	
G-MMWE	Hiway Skytrike 250	R. Bailey	
G-MMWF	Hiway Skytrike 250	J. R. Du Plessis	
G-MMWG	Greenslade Mono-Trike	P. A. Leach	
G-MMWH	Southdown Puma Sprint 440	G. Nightingale	
G-MMWI	Southdown Lightning	A. W. Cove	
G-MMWJ	Pterodactyl Ptraveler	P. Careless	
G-MMWK	Hiway Demon	L. Bennett	
G-MMWL	Eurowing Goldwing	D. J. White	
G-MMWM	—	—	
G-MMWN	Ultrasports Tripacer	J. M. Balfe	
G-MMWO	Ultrasports Panther XL	P. F. J. Rogers	
G-MMWP	American Aerolights Eagle	C. E. Tait	
G-MMWR	—	—	
G-MMWS	Mainair Tri-Flyer	I. G. Cole	
G-MMWT	CFM Shadow	K. H. Abel	
G-MMWU	Ultrasports Tripacer 250	J. A. Clare	
G-MMWV	Flight Research Nomad 425F	R. J. B. S. Escott	
G-MMWX	Southdown Puma Sprint	D. O. Lewis & ptnrs	
G-MMWY	Skyhook Pixie	N. M. Cuthbertson	
G-MMWZ	Southdown Puma Sprint	R. J. J. Wesson	
G-MMXA	Mainair Gemini Flash	L. Bennett & J. A. Robinson	
G-MMXB	—	—	
G-MMXC	Mainair Gemini Flash	M. R. Coultas	
G-MMXD	Mainair Gemini Flash	D. Lund	
G-MMXE	Mainair Gemini Flash	Aircraft Microlight Services	
G-MMXF	Mainair Gemini Flash	D. Hughes	
G-MMXG	Mainair Gemini Flash	Allied Electrical	
G-MMXH	Mainair Gemini Flash	M. J. Starling	
G-MMXI	Horizon Prototype	Horizon Aerosails Ltd	
G-MMXJ	Mainair Gemini Flash	R. Meredith-Hardy	
G-MMXK	Mainair Gemini Flash	N. S. Brown	
G-MMXL	Mainair Gemini Flash	D. Yates	
G-MMXM	Mainair Gemini Flash	R. Perrett	
G-MMXN	Southdown Puma Sprint	R. J. Grainger	
G-MMXO	Southdown Puma Sprint	D. J. Tasker	
G-MMXP	Southdown Puma Sprint	D. M. Humphreys	

Notes	Reg.	Type	Owner or Operator
	G-MMXR	Southdown Puma DS	J. S. Freestone
	G-MMXT	Mainair Gemini Flash	S. J. Basey-Fisher
	G-MMXU	Mainair Gemini Flash	T. J. Franklin
	G-MMXV	Mainair Gemini Flash	A. V. Szolin
	G-MMXW	Mainair Gemini	A. Hodgson
	G-MMXX	Mainair Gemini	S. & S. Warburton-Pitt
	G-MMXY	—	—
	G-MMXZ	Eipper Quicksilver MXII	D. T. Clarke & B. J. O'Brien
	G-MMYA	Solar Wings Pegasus XL	Solar Wings Ltd
	G-MMYB	Solar Wings Pegasus XL	Solar Wings Ltd
	G-MMYD	CFM Shadow Srs B	CFM Metal-Fax Ltd
	G-MMYE	—	—
	G-MMYF	Southdown Puma Sprint	D. O. Crane
	G-MMYG	—	—
	G-MMYH	—	—
	G-MMYI	Southdown Puma Sprint	L. A. J. Parren
	G-MMYJ	Southdown Puma Sprint	J. C. Longmore
	G-MMYK	Southdown Puma Sprint	I. Hawes
	G-MMYL	Cyclone 70	J. T. Halford
	G-MMYM	—	—
	G-MMYN	Ultrasports Panther XL	G. M. R. Walters & H. Clarke
	G-MMYO	Southdown Puma Sprint	K. J. Taylor
	G-MMYP	—	—
	G-MMYR	Eipper Quicksilver MXII	M. Reed
	G-MMYS	Southdown Puma Sprint	Enstone Microlight Centre
	G-MMYT	Southdown Puma Sprint	I. S. Stamp
	G-MMYU	Southdown Puma Sprint	I. Parr
	G-MMYV	Webb Trike	A. P. Fenn
	G-MMYX	Mitchell U-2	R. A. Codling
	G-MMYY	Southdown Puma Sprint	J. C. & A. M. Rose
	G-MMYZ	Southdown Puma Sprint	N. Crisp
	G-MMZA	Mainair Gemini Flash	G. W. Peacock
	G-MMZB	Mainair Gemini Flash	M. A. Nolan
	G-MMZC	Mainair Gemini Flash	G. T. Johnston
	G-MMZD	Mainair Gemini Flash	R. Clegg
	G-MMZE	Mainair Gemini Flash	S. Saul
	G-MMZF	Mainair Gemini Flash	A. R. Rhodes
	G-MMZG	Ultrasports Panther XL-S	G. D. Fogg
	G-MMZH	Ultrasports Tripacer	R. Bacon
	G-MMZI	Medway 130SX	P. M. Lang
	G-MMZJ	Mainair Gemini Flash	D. J. Griffiths
	G-MMZK	Mainair Gemini Flash	J. D. O. Gill
	G-MMZL	Mainair Gemini Flash	P. R. Sexton
	G-MMZM	Mainair Gemini Flash	R. W. Bunting
	G-MMZN	Mainair Gemini Flash	K. C. Wigley
	G-MMZO	Microflight Spectrum	Microflight Aircraft Ltd
	G-MMZP	Ultrasports Panther XL	H. Phipps
	G-MMZR	Southdown Puea Sprint	A. McDermid
	G-MMZS	Eipper Quicksilver MX1	J. T. Halford
	G-MMZT	Ultrasports Tripacer	J. Bell
	G-MMZU	Southdown Puma DS	E. Clark
	G-MMZV	Mainair Gemini Flash	J. F. Bishop
	G-MMZW	Southdown Puma Sprint	T. & M. Bowyer
	G-MMZX	Southdown Puma Sprint	D. P. G. Sarll
	G-MMZY	Ultrasports Tripacer 330	G. P. Gibson
	G-MMZZ	Maxair Hummer	Microflight Ltd
	G-MNAA	Striplin Sky Ranger	Ingleby Microlight Flying Club
	G-MNAC	Mainair Gemini Flash	D. Holliday
	G-MNAD	Mainair Gemini Flash	P. G. Moore
	G-MNAE	Mainair Gemini Flash	A. D. Gilbert
	G-MNAF	Solar Wings Panther XL	D. T. Smith
	G-MNAG	Hiway Skytrike 1	R. J. Grogan
	G-MNAH	Solar Wings Panther XL	B. S. Buddery
	G-MNAI	Ultrasports Panther XL-S	J. C. Johnson
	G-MNAJ	Solar Wings Panther XL-S	C. Laverty
	G-MNAK	Solar Wings Panther XL-S	E. R. WIlson
	G-MNAL	MBA Tiger Cub 440	Ace Aero Ltd
	G-MNAM	Solar Wings Panther XL-S	J. Batchelor
	G-MNAN	Solar Wings Panther XL-S	B. Clough
	G-MNAO	Solar Wings Panther XL-S	D. K. Fuller
	G-MNAP	—	—
	G-MNAR	Solar Wings Panther XL-S	B. R. Cannon
	G-MNAS	Solar Wings Pegasus XL-R	N. S. Payne

Reg.	Type	Owner or Operator	Notes
G-MNAT	Solar Wings Pegasus XL-R	Solar Wings Ltd	
G-MNAU	Solar Wings Pegasus XL-R	L. G. Taylor	
G-MNAV	Southdown Puma Sprint	M. Ward	
G-MNAW	Solar Wings Pegasus XL-R	A. W. Kowles	
G-MNAX	Solar Wings Pegasus XL-R	D. R. Gazey	
G-MNAY	Ultrasports Panther XL-S	N. Baumber	
G-MNAZ	Solar Wings Pegasus XL-R	S. J. Baker	
G-MNBA	Solar Wings Pegasus XL-R	S. F. Buckingham-Smart	
G-MNBB	Solar Wings Pegasus XL-R	M. Sims	
G-MNBC	Solar Wings Pegasus XL-R	M. N. Hudson	
G-MNBD	Mainair Gemini Flash	G. J. & G. G. Norris	
G-MNBE	Southdown Puma Sprint	J. P. Bleakley & J. M. Travers	
G-MNBF	Mainair Gemini Flash	J. C. Duncan	
G-MNBG	Mainair Gemini Flash	D. A. Riggs & A. B. Shepherd	
G-MNBH	Southdown Puma Sprint	M. N. Cowley	
G-MNBI	Ultrasports Panther XL	Microflight Tuition & Sales Ltd	
G-MNBJ	Skyhook Pixie	G. M. Mansfield	
G-MNBK	Hiway Skytrike	J. D. Swinbank	
G-MNBL	American Aerolights Z Eagle	J. H. Telford	
G-MNBM	Southdown Puma Sprint	M. W. Hurst	
G-MNBN	Mainair Gemini Flash	J. L. Eden	
G-MNBP	Mainair Gemini Flash	R. Whitby	
G-MNBR	Mainair Gemini Flash	M. R. Haines	
G-MNBS	Mainair Gemini Flash	J. G. Crawford	
G-MNBT	Mainair Gemini Flash	D. W. Barnes	
G-MNBU	Mainair Gemini Flash	K. L. Turner	
G-MNBV	Mainair Gemini Flash	S. B. Jones	
G-MNBW	Mainair Gemini Flash	S. W. Shackleford	
G-MNBX	—	—	
G-MNBY	Mainair Gemini	G. Popplewell	
G-MNBZ	Medway Half Pint	C. J. Draper	
G-MNCB	Mainair Gemini Flash	K. B. O'Regan	
G-MNCC	Mainair Gemini	P. Browne	
G-MNCD	Harmsworth Trike	A. D. Cranfield	
G-MNCE	Skyhook Pixie	C. F. Corke	
G-MNCF	Mainair Gemini Flash	A. W. Abraham	
G-MNCG	Mainair Gemini Flash	J. K. Cross	
G-MNCH	Lancashire Micro Trike 330	C. F. Horsall	
G-MNCI	Southdown Puma Sprint	R. Blamires	
G-MNCJ	Mainair Gemini Flash	C. J. Hall	
G-MNCK	Southdown Puma Sprint	D. J. Gibbs	
G-MNCL	Southdown Puma Sprint	N. M. Lassman	
G-MNCM	CFM Shadow Srs B	P. B. Merritt	
G-MNCN	Hiway Skytrike 250	N. J. Clemens	
G-MNCO	Eipper Quicksilver MXII	S. Lawton	
G-MNCP	Southdown Puma Sprint	J. G. Sealey	
G-MNCR	Flexiform Striker	I. M. Stamp	
G-MNCS	Skyrider Airsports	E. A. Matty	
G-MNCT	—	—	
G-MNCU	Medway Hybred	K. L. Fenn	
G-MNCV	Medway Typhoon XL	M. Pryke	
G-MNCW	Hornet Dual Trainer	D. L. Bowtell & J. B. Harper	
G-MNCX	Mainair Gemini Flash	A. Hardwick	
G-MNCY	Skyhook Pixie	B. F. Johnson	
G-MNCZ	Solar Wings Pegasus XL-T	Solar Wings Ltd	
G-MNDA	Thruster TST	Thruster Aircraft (UK) Ltd	
G-MNDB	Southdown Puma Sprint	J. C. Neale	
G-MNDC	Mainair Gemini Flash	P. J. Hepburn	
G-MNDD	Mainair Scorcher Solo	M. R. Middleton	
G-MNDE	Medway Half Pint	A. A. Houghton	
G-MNDF	Mainair Gemini Flash	R. Meredith-Hardy	
G-MNDG	Southdown Puma Sprint	M. Cox	
G-MNDH	Hiway Skytrike	N. R. Holloway	
G-MNDI	MBA Tiger Cub 440	F. Clarke	
G-MNDJ	—	—	
G-MNDK	Mainair Tri-Flyer 440	D. Kerr	
G-MNDM	Mainair Gemini Flash	J. H. Bradbury	
G-MNDN	Southdown Puma Sprint	C. H. Middleton	
G-MNDO	Mainair Flash	C. L. Salter & C. Squibbs	
G-MNDP	Southdown Puma Sprint	K. O'Connell	
G-MNDR	NIB II Vertigo	S. J. Sharley	
G-MNDS	—	—	
G-MNDT	—		
G-MNDU	Midland Sirocco 377GB	R. F. Bridgeland	

Notes	Reg.	Type	Owner or Operator
	G-MNDV	Midland Sirocco 377GB	V. H. Spencer
	G-MNDW	Midland Sirocco 377GB	G. van der Gaag
	G-MNDX	—	—
	G-MNDY	Southdown Puma Sprint	M. A. Ford
	G-MNDZ	Southdown Puma Sprint	M. F. Belbin
	G-MNEA	Southern Airwolf	Southdown International Ltd
	G-MNEB	Southern Airwolf	Southdown International Ltd
	G-MNEC	Southern Airwolf	Southdown International Ltd
	G-MNED	Skyhook Pixie	O. McCullogh
	G-MNEE	—	—
	G-MNEF	Mainair Gemini Flash	C. Parkinson
	G-MNEG	Mainair Gemini Flash	D. P. Moxon
	G-MNEH	Mainair Gemini Flash	I. Rawson
	G-MNEI	Medway Hybred 440	R. F. Miller
	G-MNEK	Medway Half Pint	M. I. Dougall
	G-MNEL	Medway Half Pint	D. R. Young
	G-MNEM	Solar Wings Pegasus Dual	C. Smith
	G-MNEN	Southdown Puma Sprint	A. J. Mann
	G-MNEO	Southdown Raven	Lawlor Car Service
	G-MNEP	Aerostructure Pipstrelle P.2B	M. R. Guerard
	G-MNER	CFM Shadow Srs B	D. Roberts
	G-MNET	Mainair Gemini Flash	S. W. Barker
	G-MNEU	—	—
	G-MNEV	Mainair Gemini Flash	Alfasound Ltd
	G-MNEW	Mainair Tri-Flyer	D. C. Hibbitt
	G-MNEX	Mainair Gemini Flash	A. Holc
	G-MNEY	Mainair Gemini Flash	R. H. Faux
	G-MNEZ	Skyhook TR1 Mk 2	H. Lang
	G-MNFA	Solar Wings Typhoon	D. R. Joint
	G-MNFB	Southdown Puma Sprint	C. Lawrence
	G-MNFC	Midland Ultralights Sirocco 377GB	D. J. Cole
	G-MNFD	Southdown Raven	F. Dorsett
	G-MNFE	Mainair Gemini Flash	C. H. Spencer
	G-MNFF	Mainair Gemini Flash	C. H. Spencer
	G-MNFG	Southdown Puma Sprint	K. D. Beeton
	G-MNFH	Mainair Gemini Flash	W. D. Holmes
	G-MNFI	Medway Half Pint	M. I. J. Hewett
	G-MNFJ	Mainair Gemini Flash	M. R. Moore
	G-MNFK	Mainair Gemini Flash	A. Konieczek
	G-MNFL	AMF Chevron	P. W. Wright
	G-MNFM	Mainair Gemini Flash	J. W. Teesdale
	G-MNFN	Mainair Gemini Flash	J. R. Martin
	G-MNFP	Mainair Gemini Flash	S. Farnsworth & P. Howarth
	G-MNFR	Wright Tri-Flyer	R. L. Arscott
	G-MNFS	Ikarus Sherpa Dopplesitzer	U. Silvan
	G-MNFT	Mainair Gemini Flash	P. Brewster
	G-MNFU	—	—
	G-MNFV	Ultrasports Trike	R. G. Grundy
	G-MNFW	Medway Hybred 44XL	R. L. Wadley
	G-MNFX	Southdown Puma Sprint	A. M. Shaw
	G-MNFY	Hornet 250	M. O'Hearne
	G-MNFZ	Southdown Puma Sprint	R. C. Colbeck
	G-MNGA	Aerial Arts Chaser 110SX	J. F. Chitalan
	G-MNGB	Mainair Gemini Flash	R. Harrison
	G-MNGC	CFM Shadow Srs B	C. R. Garner
	G-MNGD	Quest Air Services	P. R. Davey
	G-MNGF	Solar Wings Pegasus	E. A. Wrathall
	G-MNGG	Solar Wings Pegasus XL-R	R. Carson
	G-MNGH	Skyhook Pixie	A. R. Smith
	G-MNGI	—	—
	G-MNGJ	Skyhook Zipper	Skyhook Sailwings Ltd
	G-MNGK	Mainair Gemini Flash	J. A. Shepherdson
	G-MNGL	Mainair Gemini Flash	C. C. Mercer
	G-MNGM	Mainair Gemini Flash	M. A. Hayward
	G-MNGN	Mainair Gemini Flash	M. A. Dobson
	G-MNGO	Solar Wings Storm	S. Adams
	G-MNGP	—	—
	G-MNGR	Southdown Puma Sprint	H. L. Dyson
	G-MNGS	Southdown Puma 330	C. R. Mortlock & B. P. Cooke
	G-MNGT	Mainair Gemini Flash	G. A. Brown
	G-MNGU	Mainair Gemini Flash	C. S. Purdy
	G-MNGV	—	—
	G-MNGW	Mainair Gemini Flash	E. H. E. Nunn

Reg.	Type	Owner or Operator	Notes
G-MNGX	Southdown Puma Sprint	R. J. Morris	
G-MNGY	Hiway Skytrike 160	D. Braddick	
G-MNGZ	Mainair Gemini Flash	G. T. Snoddon	
G-MNHA	Noble Hardman Snowbird	Noble Hardman Aviation Ltd	
G-MNHB	Solar Wings Pegasus XL-R	P. Jarman	
G-MNHC	Solar Wings Pegasus XL-R	W. R. Pryce	
G-MNHD	Solar Wings Pegasus XL-R	P. D. Stiles	
G-MNHE	Solar Wings Pegasus XL-R	C. Kay	
G-MNHF	Solar Wings Pegasus XL-R	J. Cox	
G-MNHG	Solar Wings Pegasus XL-R	Sure Chemicals Ltd	
G-MNHH	Solar Wings Panther XL-S	D. J. Hampson	
G-MNHI	Solar Wings Pegasus XL-R	P. G. Pickett	
G-MNHJ	Solar Wings Pegasus XL-R	S. J. Wood	
G-MNHK	Solar Wings Pegasus XL-R	Battalion Grenadier Guards Microlight Group	
G-MNHL	Solar Wings Pegasus XL-R	Agro Exports Ltd	
G-MNHM	Solar Wings Pegasus XL-R	M. P. Tyson	
G-MNHN	Solar Wings Pegasus XL-R	G. W. Scarborough	
G-MNHO	—	—	
G-MNHP	Solar Wings Pegasus XL-R	A. D. & G. P. Leslie	
G-MNHR	Solar Wings Pegasus XL-R	M. F. Eddington	
G-MNHS	Solar Wings Pegasus XL-R	M. S. Henson	
G-MNHT	Solar Wings Pegasus XL-R	P. E. England	
G-MNHU	Solar Wings Pegasus XL-R	C. Pidler	
G-MNHV	Solar Wings Pegasus XL-R	P. R. Gapper	
G-MNHW	Medway Half Pint	A. R. Morrison	
G-MNHX	Solar Wings Typhoon S4	R. Blackwell	
G-MNHY	Mainair Tri-Flyer 440	K. Wright	
G-MNHZ	Mainair Gemini Flash	J. R. Hewson	
G-MNIA	Mainair Gemini Flash	A. E. Dix	
G-MNIB	American Aerolights Eagle 215B	C. R. Cattell	
G-MNIC	MBA Tiger Cub 440	N. B. Kirby	
G-MNID	Mainair Gemini Flash	G. Penson	
G-MNIE	Mainair Gemini Flash	P. Eden & B. Weinrabe	
G-MNIF	Mainair Gemini Flash	D. Yarr	
G-MNIG	Mainair Gemini Flash	S. J. Bennett & I. S. Everett	
G-MNIH	Mainair Gemini Flash	I. C. Lomax	
G-MNII	Mainair Gemini Flash	R. F. Finnis	
G-MNIL	Southdown Puma Sprint	C. D. West	
G-MNIM	Maxair Hummer	P. J. Brookman	
G-MNIN	Designability Duet	S. Osmond	
G-MNIO	Mainair Gemini Flash	M. A. Hayward	
G-MNIP	Mainair Gemini Flash	G. S. Bulpitt	
G-MNIR	Skyhook Pixie 130	I. G. Cole	
G-MNIS	CFM Shadow Srs B	R. W. Payne	
G-MNIT	Aerial Arts 130SX	G. R. Baker	
G-MNIU	Solar Wings Pegasus Photon	K. Roberts	
G-MNIV	Solar Wings Typhoon	D. Tipping	
G-MNIW	Airwave Nimrod 165	J. A. McIntosh & R. W. Mitchell	
G-MNIX	Mainair Gemini Flash	M. R. Clucas	
G-MNIY	Skyhook Pixie Zipper	Skyhook Sailwings Ltd	
G-MNIZ	Mainair Gemini Flash	B. Cowburn	
G-MNJA	Southdown Lightning Skytrike	D. M. Travers	
G-MNJB	Southdown Raven	D. Millar	
G-MNJC	MBA Tiger Cub 440	J. G. Carpenter	
G-MNJD	Southdown Puma Sprint	J. B. Duffus	
G-MNJE	Southdown Puma Sprint	T. Powell	
G-MNJF	Dragon 150	L. R. Jillings	
G-MNJG	Mainair Tri-Flyer	C. R. Read	
G-MNJH	Solar Wings Pegasus Flash	D. Gandle	
G-MNJI	Solar Wings Pegasus Flash	M. J. O'Connor	
G-MNJJ	Solar Wings Pegasus Flash	B. P. Peissel	
G-MNJK	Solar Wings Pegasus Flash	C. Green	
G-MNJL	Solar Wings Pegasus Flash	G. H. Cork	
G-MNJM	Solar Wings Pegasus Flash	N. Jefferson	
G-MNJN	Solar Wings Pegasus Flash	D. J. Pay	
G-MNJO	Solar Wings Pegasus Flash	S. J. Farrant & Sons Ltd	
G-MNJP	Solar Wings Pegasus Flash	R. J. Butler	
G-MNJR	Solar Wings Pegasus Flash	J. Stokes	
G-MNJS	Southdown Puma Sprint	C. E. Bates	
G-MNJT	Southdown Raven	W. G. Reynolds	
G-MNJU	Mainair Gemini Flash	N. V. Wnekowski	
G-MNJV	Medway Half Pint	C. C. W. Mates	
G-MNJW	Mitchell Wing B10	J. D. Webb	

Notes	Reg.	Type	Owner or Operator
	G-MNJX	Medway Hybred 44XL	H. A. Stewart
	G-MNJY	Medway Half Pint	P. M. Stoney
	G-MNJZ	Aerial Arts Alpha 130SX	I. M. Grayland
	G-MNKA	Solar Wings Pegasus Photon	T. E. Edmond
	G-MNKB	Solar Wings Pegasus Photon	M. E. Gilbert
	G-MNKC	Solar Wings Pegasus Photon	H. C. Mowthorpe
	G-MNKD	Solar Wings Pegasus Photon	R. Colquhoun
	G-MNKE	Solar Wings Pegasus Photon	T. M. Edmond
	G-MNKG	Solar Wings Pegasus Photon	P. D. Atkinson
	G-MNKH	Solar Wings Pegasus Photon	A. G. Drury
	G-MNKI	Solar Wings Pegasus Photon	Solar Wings Ltd
	G-MNKJ	Solar Wings Pegasus Photon	G. Townshend
	G-MNKK	Solar Wings Pegasus Photon	K. S. Marine
	G-MNKL	Mainair Gemini Flash	R. Thorpe
	G-MNKM	MBA Tiger Cub 440	L. J. Forinton
	G-MNKN	Skycraft Scout Mk III	E. A. Diamond
	G-MNKO	Solar Wings Pegasus Flash	D. M. Law
	G-MNKP	Solar Wings Pegasus Flash	M. West
	G-MNKR	Solar Wings Pegasus Flash	C. Broadley
	G-MNKS	Solar Wings Pegasus Flash	A. D. Langtree
	G-MNKT	Solar Wings Typhoon S4	C. R. Sykes
	G-MNKU	Southdown Puma Sprint	R. W. Jones
	G-MNKV	Solar Wings Pegasus Flash	J. H. Kempton
	G-MNKW	Solar Wings Pegasus Flash	P. Ridout
	G-MNKX	Solar Wings Pegasus Flash	P. Samal
	G-MNKY	Southdown Raven	G. A. Harman
	G-MNKZ	Southdown Raven	A. E. Silvey
	G-MNLA	Solar Wings Typhoon	J. A. Havers
	G-MNLB	Southdown Raven X	N. E. Smith
	G-MNLC	Southdown Raven	P. M. Coppola
	G-MNLE	Southdown Raven X	N. J. Stoneman
	G-MNLF	Southdown Puma	K. Brunnekant
	G-MNLG	Southdown Lightning	D. J. Edwards
	G-MNLH	Romain Cobra Biplane	J. W. E. Romain
	G-MNLI	Mainair Gemini Flash	F. M. Pearce
	G-MNLJ	—	—
	G-MNLK	Southdown Raven	G. C. Weighell
	G-MNLL	Southdown Raven	M. R. Wilson
	G-MNLM	Southdown Raven	A. P. White
	G-MNLN	Southdown Raven	S. J. M. Morling
	G-MNLO	Southdown Raven	D. Kiddy
	G-MNLP	Southdown Raven	G. M. Mansfield
	G-MNLR	Solar Wings Typhoon	B. J. Farrell
	G-MNLS	Southdown Raven	L. P. Geer
	G-MNLU	Southdown Raven	I. E. Spencer
	G-MNLV	Southdown Raven	J. Murphy
	G-MNLW	Medway Half Pint	C. F. Medgett
	G-MNLX	Mainair Gemini Flash	B. J. Cook
	G-MNLY	Mainair Gemini Flash	P. Orritt & ptnrs
	G-MNLZ	Southdown Raven	D. M. Punnett
	G-MNMA	Solar Wings Pegasus Flash	J. C. B. Halford
	G-MNMB	Solar Wings Pegasus Flash	M. Wells
	G-MNMC	Southdown Puma MS	R. E. Symonds
	G-MNMD	Southdown Raven	E. M. Woods & D. Little
	G-MNME	Hiway Skytrike	W. T. Church
	G-MNMF	Maxair Hummer TX	M. I. Smith
	G-MNMG	Mainair Gemini Flash	N. A. M. Beyer-Kay
	G-MNMH	Mainair Gemini Flash	R. St John Harrison
	G-MNMI	Mainair Gemini Flash	T. E. McDonald
	G-MNMJ	Mainair Gemini Flash	H. N. Houghton
	G-MNMK	Solar Wings Pegasus XL-R	Knowles Transport Ltd
	G-MNML	Southdown Puma Sprint	M. J. Hammond
	G-MNMM	Aerotech MW.5 Sorcerer	Aerotech International Ltd
	G-MNMN	Medway Microlights Hybred 44	R. Skene
	G-MNMO	Mainair Gemini Flash	M. W. Walsh
	G-MNMP	Pritchard Experimental Mk 1	M. H. Pritchard
	G-MNMR	Solar Wings Typhoon 180	B. D. Jackson
	G-MNMS	Wheeler Scout	M. I. Smith
	G-MNMT	Southdown Raven	Hornet Microlights
	G-MNMU	Southdown Raven	P. A. Winfield
	G-MNMV	Mainair Gemini Flash	D. Sutherland
	G-MNMW	Aerotech MW.6 Merlin	E. F. Clapham & ptnrs
	G-MNMX	Sigh-Wing Paraplane	Sigh-Wing Ltd
	G-MNMY	Cyclone 70	Cyclone Hovercraft Ltd

Reg.	Type	Owner or Operator	Notes
G-MNMZ	—	—	
G-MNNA	Southdown Raven	D. & G. D. Palfrey	
G-MNNB	Southdown Raven	P. C. Knight	
G-MNNC	Southdown Raven	J. G. Beesley	
G-MNND	Solar Wings Pegasus Flash	W. R. Davis-Smith	
G-MNNE	Mainair Gemini Flash	B. L. Benson	
G-MNNF	Mainair Gemini Flash	P. J. Jenson	
G-MNNG	Squires Lightfly	P. G. Angus	
G-MNNH	Medway 130SX Export	Chris Taylor Racing Preparations	
G-MNNI	Mainair Gemini Flash	A. Anderson	
G-MNNJ	Mainair Gemini Flash	M. J. W. Thake	
G-MNNK	Mainair Gemini Flash	S. B. Hodgson	
G-MNNL	Mainair Gemini Flash	D. Wilson & A. Bielawski	
G-MNNM	Mainair Scorcher Solo	M. R. Parr	
G-MNNN	Southdown Raven	F. Byford & S. Hooker	
G-MNNO	Southdown Raven	J. R. Poolman	
G-MNNP	Mainair Gemini Flash	K. J. Regan	
G-MNNR	Mainair Gemini Flash	Milequip Computer Systems	
G-MNNS	Eurowing Goldwing	D. Johnstone & R. J. Wood	
G-MNNT	Medway Microlights Hybred	J. R. A. Dickinson & D. J. Cropper	
G-MNNU	Mainair Gemini Flash	D. J. Dawson	
G-MNNV	Mainair Gemini Flash	Ardrossan Auto Spares	
G-MNNX	—	—	
G-MNNY	Solar Wings Pegasus Flash	C. M. Blanchard	
G-MNNZ	Solar Wings Pegasus Flash	P. A. R. Hicks	
G-MNPA	Solar Wings Pegasus Flash	E. J. Blyth	
G-MNPB	Solar Wings Pegasus Flash	G. E. Jewitt	
G-MNPC	Mainair Gemini Flash	B. F. Crick	
G-MNPD	Midland Ultralights 130SX	C. Jones	
G-MNPF	Mainair Gemini Flash	M. G. A. Wood	
G-MNPG	Mainair Gemini Flash	P. Kirton	
G-MNPH	Flexiform Dual Striker	D. L. Aspinall	
G-MNPI	Southdown Pipistrelle 2C	D. M. White	
G-MNPJ	Southdown Pipistrelle 2C	D. A. Gleason	
G-MNPK	Southdown Pipistrelle 2C	Southdown Aerostructure Ltd	
G-MNPL	Ultrasports Panther 330	P. N. Long	
G-MNPM	Southdown Pipistrelle 2C	Southdown Aerostructure Ltd	
G-MNPN	Southdown Pipistrelle 2C	Southdown Aerostructure Ltd	
G-MNPO	Romain Cobra Biplane	D. Stott	
G-MNPP	Romain Cobra Biplane	J. W. E. Romain	
G-MNPR	Hiway Demon 175	S. Jodrell	
G-MNPS	Skyhook Pixie	Skyhook Sailwings Ltd	
G-MNPU	Skyhook Pixie	Skyhook Sailwings Ltd	
G-MNPV	Mainair Scorcher Solo	G. W. Doswell	
G-MNPW	AMF Chevron	AMF Microlight Ltd	
G-MNPX	Mainair Gemini Flash	T. A. Cockerell	
G-MNPY	Mainair Scorcher Solo	R. N. O. Kingsbury	
G-MNPZ	Mainair Scorcher Solo	Mainair Sports Ltd	
G-MNRA	CFM Shadow Srs B	CFM Metal-Fax Ltd	
G-MNRB	Southdown Puma	Aerotech Africa Ltd	
G-MNRD	Ultraflight Lazair	D. W. & M. F. Briggs	
G-MNRE	Mainair Scorcher Solo	G. A. Archer	
G-MNRF	Mainair Scorcher Solo	W. C. Yates	
G-MNRG	Mainair Scorcher Solo	M. E. Jarman	
G-MNRH	Mainair Scorcher Solo	Mainair Sports Ltd	
G-MNRI	Hornet Dual Trainer	R. L. Manby	
G-MNRJ	Hornet Dual Trainer	A. J. Maclachlan	
G-MNRK	Hornet Dual Trainer	D. J. Walter	
G-MNRL	Hornet Dual Trainer	Hornet Microlights	
G-MNRM	Hornet Dual Trainer	R. I. Cannon	
G-MNRN	Hornet Dual Trainer	Hornet Microlights	
G-MNRO	Southdown Raven	Mosaic King (UK) Ltd	
G-MNRP	Southdown Raven	C. Moore	
G-MNRR	Southdown Raven X	J. G. Jennings	
G-MNRS	Southdown Raven	P. H. E. Woodliffe-Thomas	
G-MNRT	Midland Ultralights Sirocco	R. F. Hinton	
G-MNRU	Midland Ultralights Sirocco	Midland Ultralights Ltd	
G-MNRV	American Aerolights Eagle	P. J. Buckner	
G-MNRW	Mainair Gemini Flash II	L. A. Maynard	
G-MNRX	Mainair Gemini Flash II	J. Greenhalgh	
G-MNRY	Mainair Gemini Flash	M. A. Lomas	
G-MNRZ	Mainair Scorcher Solo	J. J. Naughton	
G-MNSA	Mainair Gemini Flash	L. M. Retallick	
G-MNSB	Southdown Puma Sprint	C. J. Whittaker	

Notes	Reg.	Type	Owner or Operator
	G-MNSC	Flexiform Hi-Line	J. F. Holdsworth
	G-MNSD	Solar Wings Typhoon	W. Read & A. J. Lloyd
	G-MNSE	Mainair Gemini Flash	J. S. Mather
	G-MNSF	Hornet Dual Trainer	R. Pattrick
	G-MNSG	Hornet Dual Trainer	R. R. Wolfenden
	G-MNSH	Solar Wings Pegasus Flash II	P. A. Lee
	G-MNSI	Mainair Gemini Flash	J. L. Wakefield
	G-MNSJ	Mainair Gemini Flash	M. L. Plant Insulations Ltd
	G-MNSK	Hiway Skytrike	E. B. Jones
	G-MNSL	Southdown Raven X	P. B. Robinson
	G-MNSM	Hornet Demon	A. R. Glenn
	G-MNSN	Solar Wings Pegasus Flash II	P. R. Waite
	G-MNSO	Solar Wings Pegasus Flash II	P. W. Giesler
	G-MNSP	Aerial Arts 130SX	C. J. Upton-Taylor
	G-MNSR	Mainair Gemini Flash	J. Brown
	G-MNSS	American Aerolights Eagle	G. P. Jones
	G-MNST	Vector 600	M. Quigley
	G-MNSU	Aerial Arts 130SX	I. M. Grayland & ptnrs
	G-MNSV	CFM Shadow Srs B	P. J. W. Rowell
	G-MNSW	Southdown Raven X	P. J. Barton
	G-MNSX	Southdown Raven X	J. D. Thompson
	G-MNSY	Southdown Raven X	R. Stoner
	G-MNSZ	Noble Hardman Snowbird	Noble Hardman Aviation Ltd
	G-MNTA	—	—
	G-MNTB	Solar Wings Typhoon S4	A. H. Trapp
	G-MNTC	Southdown Raven X	R. B. D. Baker
	G-MNTD	Aerial Arts Chaser 110SX	H. Phipps
	G-MNTE	Southdown Raven X	D. Kiddy
	G-MNTF	Southdown Raven X	J. S. Freestone
	G-MNTG	Southdown Raven X	D. Thorpe
	G-MNTH	Mainair Gemini Flash	B. A. Phillips
	G-MNTI	Mainair Gemini Flash	R. T. Strathie
	G-MNTJ	American Aerolights Eagle	D. S. J. Boston
	G-MNTK	CFM Shadow Srs B	M. I. M. Smith
	G-MNTL	Arbee Wasp Gryphon	D. K. Liddard
	G-MNTM	Southdown Raven X	M. W. Hurst
	G-MNTN	Southdown Raven X	J. Hall
	G-MNTO	Southdown Raven X	J. T. Nunn
	G-MNTP	CFM Shadow Srs B	G. E. Gould
	G-MNTR	—	—
	G-MNTS	Mainair Gemini Flash II	K. J. & G. E. Cole
	G-MNTT	Medway Half Pint	Lancaster Partners (Holdings) Ltd
	G-MNTU	Mainair Gemini Flash II	M. A. E. Harris
	G-MNTV	Mainair Gemini Flash II	K. L. Turner
	G-MNTW	Mainair Gemini Flash II	A. Dix & S. Clarke
	G-MNTX	Mainair Gemini Flash II	C. W. Thomas
	G-MNTY	Southdown Raven X	T. E. Baxter
	G-MNTZ	Mainair Gemini Flash II	Weston Furnishers
	G-MNUA	Mainair Gemini Flash II	R. T. R. Morwood
	G-MNUB	Mainair Gemini Flash II	R. V. Emerson
	G-MNUC	Solar Wings Pegasus Flash II	K. D. Calvert
	G-MNUD	Solar Wings Pegasus Flash II	J. D. R. Broadbent
	G-MNUE	Solar Wings Pegasus Flash II	S. Rands
	G-MNUF	Mainair Gemini Flash II	E. Marsh
	G-MNUG	Mainair Gemini Flash II	A. F. Stafford
	G-MNUH	Southdown Raven X	R. Fyson
	G-MNUI	Skyhook Cutlass Dual	M. Holling
	G-MNUJ	Solar Wings Pegasus Photon	W. G. Farr
	G-MNUK	Midland Ultralights SX130	B. G. Colvin
	G-MNUL	Midland Ultralights SX130	B. D. W. Steen
	G-MNUM	Southdown Puma Sprint MS	B. Rawlance
	G-MNUN	—	—
	G-MNUO	Mainair Gemini Flash II	P. Cooper
	G-MNUP	Mainair Gemini Flash II	S. Fairweather
	G-MNUR	Mainair Gemini Flash II	J. C. Lucas
	G-MNUS	Mainair Gemini Flash II	Containerway Ltd
	G-MNUT	Southdown Raven X	J. C. Goodchild
	G-MNUU	Southdown Raven X	M. J. W. Holding
	G-MNUV	Southdown Raven X	D. Houghton
	G-MNUW	Southdown Raven X	B. A. McDonald
	G-MNUX	Solar Wings Pegasus XL-R	N. Smith
	G-MNUY	Mainair Gemini Flash II	W. J. Dufour & P. S. Pontin
	G-MNUZ	Mainair Gemini Flash II	G. Brunton
	G-MNVA	Solar Wings Pegasus XL-R	P. M. Aslin

Reg.	Type	Owner or Operator	Notes
G-MNVB	Solar Wings Pegasus XL-R	J. R. Deverell	
G-MNVC	Solar Wings Pegasus XL-R	T. Davies	
G-MNVE	Solar Wings Pegasus XL-R	M. Aris	
G-MNVF	Solar Wings Pegasus Flash II	A. Rooker	
G-MNVG	Solar Wings Pegasus Flash II	M. A. Farr	
G-MNVH	Solar Wings Pegasus Flash II	S. G. Murray	
G-MNVI	CFM Shadow Srs B	D. R. C. Pugh	
G-MNVJ	CFM Shadow Srs B	B. F. Hill	
G-MNVK	CFM Shadow Srs B	G. W. Sisson	
G-MNVL	Medway Half Pint	K. M. Taylor	
G-MNVM	Southdown Raven X	R. Turnbull	
G-MNVN	Southdown Raven X	M. D. & S. M. North	
G-MNVO	Hovey Whing-Ding II	C. Wilson	
G-MNVP	Southdown Raven X	R. A. Keene	
G-MNVR	Mainair Gemini Flash II	Multiscope Ltd	
G-MNVS	Mainair Gemini Flash II	D. P. Ballard & W. G. Prout	
G-MNVT	Mainair Gemini Flash II	ACB Hydraulics	
G-MNVU	Mainair Gemini Flash II	W. R. Marsh	
G-MNVV	Mainair Gemini Flash II	P. T. Stamer	
G-MNVW	Mainair Gemini Flash II	L. M. Westwood	
G-MNVX	Solar Wings Pegasus Flash II	Pegasus Flight Training Ltd	
G-MNVY	Solar Wings Pegasus Photon	J. R. Charlton	
G-MNVZ	Solar Wings Pegasus Photon	J. J. Russ	
G-MNWA	Southdown Raven X	A. Reynolds	
G-MNWB	Thruster TST	H. E. Hewitt	
G-MNWC	Mainair Gemini Flash II	B. Dungworth	
G-MNWD	Mainair Gemini Flash	P. Crossman	
G-MNWE	—	—	
G-MNWF	Southdown Raven X	Southdown International Ltd	
G-MNWG	Southdown Raven X	B. J. Marshall	
G-MNWH	Aerial Arts 130SX	P. N. & A. M. Keohane	
G-MNWI	Mainair Gemini Flash II	B. Bennison	
G-MNWJ	Mainair Gemini Flash II	A. J. Brown	
G-MNWK	CFM Shadow Srs B	T. Green	
G-MNWL	Aerial Arts 130SX	Arbiter Services Ltd	
G-MNWM	CFM Shadow Srs B	J. E. Laidler	
G-MNWN	Mainair Gemini Flash II	Airbourne Aviation Ltd	
G-MNWO	Mainair Gemini Flash II	P. B. Kerr	
G-MNWP	Solar Wings Pegasus Flash II	G. Ferguson	
G-MNWR	Medway Hybred 44LR	C. J. Draper	
G-MNWT	Southdown Raven	M. T. Tongne	
G-MNWU	Solar Wings Pegasus Flash II	F. J. E. Browshill & W. Parkin	
G-MNWV	Solar Wings Pegasus Flash II	A. G. & P. J. Dover	
G-MNWW	Solar Wings Pegasus XL-R	K. S. Wright	
G-MNWX	Solar Wings Pegasus XL-R	B. N. Thresher	
G-MNWY	CFM Shadown Srs B	M. H. Player	
G-MNWZ	Mainair Gemini Flash II	J. McDowall	
G-MNXA	Southdown Raven X	D. Coging	
G-MNXB	Solar Wings Photon	F. S. Ogden	
G-MNXC	Aerial Arts 110SX	J. E. Sweetingham	
G-MNXD	Southdown Raven	J. C. O'Donnell	
G-MNXE	Southdown Raven X	A. K. Pomroy	
G-MNXF	Southdown Raven	D. R. Cox	
G-MNXG	Southdown Raven X	M. A. & E. M. Miller	
G-MNXH	La Mouette Azure	D. S. Bremner	
G-MNXI	Southdown Raven X	I. R. & A. J. Lilburne	
G-MNXJ	Medway Half Pint	M. Dougall	
G-MNXK	Medway Half Pint	E. W. P. van Zeller	
G-MNXL	Medway Half Pint	M. Evanson	
G-MNXM	Medway Hybred 44XLR	C. J. Draper	
G-MNXN	Medway Hybred 44XLR	J. Rodger & J. Dinwoodey	
G-MNXO	Medway Hybred 44XLR	S. R. Grant	
G-MNXP	Solar Wings Pegasus Flash II	T. J. Walsh	
G-MNXR	Mainair Gemini Flash II	B. J. Crockett	
G-MNXS	Mainair Gemini Flash II	F. T. Rawlings	
G-MNXT	Mainair Gemini Flash II	N. W. Barnett	
G-MNXU	Mainair Gemini Flash II	F. R. Curtis	
G-MNXV	—	—	
G-MNXW	Mainair Gemini Flash II	R. Mason	
G-MNXX	CFM Shadow Srs BD	F. J. Luckhurst	
G-MNXY	Whittaker MW.5 Sorcerer	Cyclone Hovercraft Ltd	
G-MNXZ	Whittaker MW.5 Sorcerer	M. N. Gauntlett	
G-MNYA	Solar Wings Pegasus Flash II	B. O. Dowsett	
G-MNYB	Solar Wings Pegasus XL-R	J. G. Robinson	

Notes	Reg.	Type	Owner or Operator
	G-MNYC	Solar Wings Pegasus XL-R	I. D. Cosh
	G-MNYD	Aerial Arts 110SX Chaser	H. Phipps
	G-MNYE	Aerial Arts 110SX Chaser	J. R. Charlton
	G-MNYF	Aerial Arts 110SX Chaser	B. Richardson
	G-MNYG	Southdown Raven	D. V. Brunt
	G-MNYH	Southdown Puma Sprint	E. K. Battersea
	G-MNYI	Southdown Raven X	Industrial Foam Systems Ltd
	G-MNYJ	Mainair Gemini Flash II	J. G. Jones
	G-MNYK	Mainair Gemini Flash II	S. J. Matthews
	G-MNYL	Southdown Raven X	R. W. Tompkins
	G-MNYM	Southdown Raven X	M. Timwey
	G-MNYN	Southdown Raven X	Aerotech International Ltd
	G-MNYO	Southdown Raven X	Aerotech International Ltd
	G-MNYP	Southdown Raven X	A. G. Davies
	G-MNYR	—	—
	G-MNYS	Southdown Raven X	M. R. Dickens
	G-MNYT	Solar Wings Pegasus XL-R	M. P. Johnson
	G-MNYU	Solar Wings Pegasus XL-R	P. D. Bethal & R. M. Lusty
	G-MNYV	Solar Wings Pegasus XL-R	G. R. Oscroft
	G-MNYW	Solar Wings Pegasus XL-R	M. P. Waldock
	G-MNYX	Solar Wings Pegasus XL-R	Dartsprint Ltd
	G-MNYY	Solar Wings Pegasus Flash II	S. A. Jaques
	G-MNYZ	Solar Wings Pegasus Flash	F. C. Claydon
	G-MNZA	Solar Wings Pegasus Flash II	A. D. Fennell & S. P. Cholmondeley
	G-MNZB	Mainair Gemini Flash II	C. J. Millership
	G-MNZC	Mainair Gemini Flash II	A. R. Lawrence
	G-MNZD	Mainair Gemini Flash II	G. R. Maclean
	G-MNZE	Mainair Gemini Flash II	A. I. Grant
	G-MNZF	Mainair Gemini Flash II	C. B. White
	G-MNZG	Aerial Arts 110SX	C. F. Grainger
	G-MNZH	AMF Chevron 2-32	AMF Microlight Ltd
	G-MNZI	Prone Power Typhoon 2	R. J. Folwell
	G-MNZJ	CFM Shadow Srs BD	B. D. Godden
	G-MNZK	Solar Wings Pegasus XL-R	G. Twomlow
	G-MNZL	Solar Wings Pegasus XL-R	M. A. Concannon
	G-MNZM	Solar Wings Pegasus XL-R	Solar Wings Ltd
	G-MNZN	Solar Wings Pegasus Flash II	Solar Wings Ltd
	G-MNZO	Solar Wings Pegasus Flash II	D. Johnson & K. B. Woods
	G-MNZP	CFM Shadow Srs B	S. N. Freestone & J. G. Wakefield
	G-MNZR	CFM Shadown Srs BD	CFM Metal-Fax Ltd
	G-MNZS	Aerial Arts 130SX	C. P. Vandenberghe
	G-MNZU	Eurowing Goldwing	H. B. Baker
	G-MNZV	Southdown Raven X	P. J. Walker
	G-MNZW	Southdown Raven X	P. G. Greenslade
	G-MNZX	Southdown Raven X	M. D. Phillips
	G-MNZY	Striker Tri-Flyer 330	P. W. Fieldman
	G-MNZZ	CFM Shadow Srs B	Lancaster Partners (Holdings) Ltd
	G-MTAA	Solar Wings Pegasus XL-R	B. Dossett
	G-MTAB	Mainair Gemini Flash II	J. P. Leigh
	G-MTAC	Mainair Gemini Flash II	F. Credland
	G-MTAD	Mainair Gemini Skyflash	Mainair Sports Ltd
	G-MTAE	Mainair Gemini Flash II	B. J. Scott
	G-MTAF	Mainair Gemini Flash II	C. Johnson
	G-MTAG	Mainair Gemini Flash II	R. G. Verdon-Roe
	G-MTAH	Mainair Gemini Flash II	P. & J. B. Hay
	G-MTAI	Solar Wings Pegasus XL-R	M. E. Bates Engineering
	G-MTAJ	Solar Wings Pegasus XL-R	N. R. Holloway
	G-MTAK	Solar Wings Pegasus XL-R	T. A. Sayer
	G-MTAL	Solar Wings Photon	I. Munro
	G-MTAM	Solar Wings Pegasus Flash	J. P. Scales
	G-MTAN	Bragg Dual Seat	I. Ellithorn
	G-MTAO	Solar Wings Pegasus XL-R	B. Bond
	G-MTAP	Southdown Raven X	J. B. Rutland
	G-MTAR	Mainair Gemini Flash II	J. Sharman
	G-MTAS	Whittaker MW.5 Sorcerer	E. A. Henman
	G-MTAT	Solar Wings Pegasus XL-R	M. J. Kimber
	G-MTAU	Solar Wings Pegasus XL-R	R. K. Parry
	G-MTAV	Solar Wings Pegasus XL-R	D. B. Ash
	G-MTAW	Solar Wings Pegasus XL-R	T. Cameron
	G-MTAX	Solar Wings Pegasus XL-R	M. D. Haynes
	G-MTAY	Solar Wings Pegasus XL-R	S. A. McLatchie
	G-MTAZ	Solar Wings Pegasus XL-R	H. W. Banham
	G-MTBA	Solar Wings Pegasus XL-R	J. Kinson

Reg.	Type	Owner or Operator	Notes
G-MTBB	Southdown Raven X	C. M. Raven	
G-MTBC	Mainair Gemini Flash II	M. J. Coomber	
G-MTBD	Mainair Gemini Flash II	A. M. Smyth	
G-MTBE	CFM Shadow Srs BD	S. Delia	
G-MTBF	Mirage Mk II	I. M. Willeher	
G-MTBG	Mainair Gemini Flash II	N. Spencer-Baryn	
G-MTBH	Mainair Gemini Flash II	G. E. Cole	
G-MTBI	Mainair Gemini Flash II	D. J. Bowie	
G-MTBJ	Mainair Gemini Flash II	P. K. Bishop	
G-MTBK	Southdown Raven X	R. C. Barnett	
G-MTBL	Solar Wings Pegasus XL-R	R. N. Whiting	
G-MTBM	Airwave Nimrod	B. R. Beer	
G-MTBN	Southdown Raven X	A. J. Crosby-Jones	
G-MTBO	Southdown Raven X	A. Miller	
G-MTBP	Aerotech MW.5 Sorcerer	A. A. Heseldine	
G-MTBR	Aerotech MW.5 Sorcerer	C. D. Hatcher	
G-MTBS	Aerotech MW.5 Sorcerer	S. Solley	
G-MTBT	Aerotech MW.5 Sorcerer	I. D. G. Forbes	
G-MTBU	Solar Wings Pegasus XL-R	Building Profiles Ltd	
G-MTBV	Solar Wings Pegasus XL-R	G. E. Etheridge	
G-MTBW	Mainair Gemini Flash II	R. Nicklin	
G-MTBX	Mainair Gemini Flash II	R. H. Bambury	
G-MTBY	Mainair Gemini Flash II	A. R. Hawkins	
G-MTBZ	Southdown Raven X	R. J. Henney	
G-MTCA	CFM Shadow Srs B	J. B. T. Christie	
G-MTCB	Snowbird Mk III	Noble Hardman Aviation Ltd	
G-MTCC	Mainair Gemini Flash II	R. C. Barker	
G-MTCD	Southdown Raven X	D. J. Smith	
G-MTCE	Mainair Gemini Flash II	Konfax Ltd	
G-MTCF	Farnell Flexwing	P. R. Farnell	
G-MTCG	Solar Wings Pegasus XL-R	R. W. Allen	
G-MTCH	Solar Wings Pegasus XL-R	R. E. H. Harris	
G-MTCJ	Aerial Arts Avenger	I. M. Grayland	
G-MTCK	Solar Wings Pegasus Flash	Richard Daniels Homes Ltd	
G-MTCL	Southdown Raven X	W. Nonforth	
G-MTCM	Southdown Raven X	J. J. Lancaster	
G-MTCN	Solar Wings Pegasus XL-R	R. W. H. de Serville	
G-MTCO	Solar Wings Pegasus XL-R	D. M. Savage	
G-MTCP	Aerial Arts Chaser 110SX	D. Cannon	
G-MTCR	Solar Wings Pegasus XL-R	K. Pratt	
G-MTCT	CFM Shadow Srs BD	J. W. Lang	
G-MTCU	Mainair Gemini Flash II	P. Kneeshaw	
G-MTCV	Microflight Spectrum	Microflight Aircraft Ltd	
G-MTCW	Mainair Gemini Flash	M. R. Starling	
G-MTCX	Solar Wings Pegasus XL-R	N. B. Morley	
G-MTCY	Southdown Raven X	Airbourne Aviation Ltd	
G-MTCZ	Ultrasports Tripacer 250	R. Parkin	
G-MTDA	Hornet Dual Trainer	R. Nay	
G-MTDB	Owen Pola Mk 1	P. E. Owen	
G-MTDC	Owen Pola Mk 1	P. E. Owen	
G-MTDD	Aerial Arts Chaser 110SX	R. Bacon	
G-MTDE	American Aerolights 110SX	E. K. Jupp	
G-MTDF	Mainair Gemini Flash II	K. M. Pinkard	
G-MTDG	Solar Wings Pegasus XL-R	P. Bradshaw	
G-MTDH	Solar Wings Pegasus XL-R	D. B. Casley-Smith	
G-MTDI	Solar Wings Pegasus XL-R	P. M. Wisniewski	
G-MTDJ	Medway Hybred 44XL	J. A. Slocombe & C. D. Gates	
G-MTDK	Aerotech MW.5 Sorcerer	A. J. Edwards	
G-MTDL	Solar Wings Pegasus XL-R	R. W. Wotton	
G-MTDM	Mainair Gemini Flash II	J. F. Cawley	
G-MTDN	Ultraflight Lazair IIIE	R. D. Good	
G-MTDO	Eipper Quicksilver MXII	D. L. Ham	
G-MTDP	Solar Wings Pegasus XL-R	S. P. Mcandy	
G-MTDR	Mainair Gemini Flash II	K. Dale	
G-MTDS	Solar Wings Photon	A. J. Macfie	
G-MTDT	Solar Wings Pegasus XL-R	M. T. Jones	
G-MTDU	CFM Shadow Srs BD	M. Jones	
G-MTDV	Solar Wings Pegasus XL-R	B. Curtis	
G-MTDW	Mainair Gemini Flash II	S. R. Leeper	
G-MTDX	CFM Shadow Srs BD	M. P. Chetwynd-Talbot	
G-MTDY	Mainair Gemini Flash II	S. Penoyre	
G-MTDZ	Eipper Quicksilver MXII	Survival Anglia Ltd	
G-MTEA	Solar Wings Pegasus XL-R	F. H. Shaw	
G-MTEB	Solar Wings Pegasus XL-R	T. R. Grief	

Notes	Reg.	Type	Owner or Operator
	G-MTEC	Solar Wings Pegasus XL-R	R. W. Glover
	G-MTED	Solar Wings Pegasus XL-R	D. Marsh
	G-MTEE	Solar Wings Pegasus XL-R	S. M. Dewson
	G-MTEF	Solar Wings Pegasus XL-R	B. D. Waller
	G-MTEG	Mainair Gemini Flash II	HRH Sheikh Omar Bin Saqr Al Qassimi Ras Al Khaimah
	G-MTEH	Mainair Gemini Flash II	E. P. Howard & P. G. Peal
	G-MTEJ	Mainair Gemini Flash II	C. H. Booth
	G-MTEK	Mainair Gemini Flash II	A. Carter
	G-MTEL	Mainair Gemini Flash II	J. W. Townsend
	G-MTEM	Mainair Gemini Flash II	S. J. Pullan
	G-MTEN	Mainair Gemini Flash II	S. Mersay
	G-MTEO	Midland Ultralight Sirocco 337	J. Brown
	G-MTER	Solar Wings Pegasus XL-R	W. G. Bond
	G-MTES	Solar Wings Pegasus XL-R	I. Callaghan
	G-MTET	Solar Wings Pegasus XL-R	D. A. Slater
	G-MTEU	Solar Wings Pegasus XL-R	E. J. Blyth
	G-MTEV	Solar Wings Pegasus XL-R	J. S. & M. R. Fuller
	G-MTEW	Solar Wings Pegasus XL-R	M. J. Lancey & B. Bott
	G-MTEX	Solar Wings Pegasus XL-R	A. L. Flude
	G-MTEY	Mainair Gemini Flash II	S. A. Rennison
	G-MTEZ	Ultraflight Lazair IIIE	M. J. Ford
	G-MTFA	Solar Wings Pegasus XL-R	W. J. M. Lowe
	G-MTFB	Solar Wings Pegasus XL-R	A. A. Craig
	G-MTFC	Medway Hybred 44XLR	Speed Couriers Ltd
	G-MTFD	Hiway Demon	M. A. Hodgson
	G-MTFE	Solar Wings Pegasus XL-R	M. P. Lewis
	G-MTFF	Mainair Gemini Flash II	T. N. Taylor
	G-MTFG	AMF Chevvron 232	AMF Microflight Ltd
	G-MTFH	Aerotech MW.5B Sorcerer	R. C. H. Russell
	G-MTFI	Mainair Gemini Flash II	R. A. P. Swainston
	G-MTFJ	Mainair Gemini Flash II	G. Souch & M. D. Peacock
	G-MTFK	Flexiform Striker	D. I. Moult
	G-MTFL	AMF Lazair IIIE	P. J. Turrell
	G-MTFM	Solar Wings Pegasus XL-R	D. J. Still & A. J. Hickey
	G-MTFN	Aerotech MW.5 Sorcerer	A. G. Dyer
	G-MTFO	Solar Wings Pegasus XL-R	E. Findley
	G-MTFP	Solar Wings Pegasus XL-R	F. R. Hart
	G-MTFR	Solar Wings Pegasus XL-R	V. & D. Concannon
	G-MTFS	Solar Wings Pegasus XL-R	T. J. Acton
	G-MTFT	Solar Wings Pegasus XL-R	A. C. Tyler
	G-MTFU	CFM Shadow Series BD	G. R. Eastwood
	G-MTFW	Mainair Gemini Flash	M. T. G. Pope
	G-MTFX	Mainair Gemini Flash	S. G. A. Heward
	G-MTFY	CFM Shadow Srs BD	CFM Metal-Fax Ltd
	G-MTFZ	CFM Shadow Srs BD	Target Technology Ltd
	G-MTGA	Mainair Gemini Flash	H. R. Bethune & S. P. Watkins
	G-MTGB	Thruster TST Mk 1	G. Arthur
	G-MTGC	Thruster TST Mk 1	D. K. Frampton
	G-MTGD	Thruster TST Mk 1	Cumbria Microlights
	G-MTGE	Thruster TST Mk 1	R. Gowler
	G-MTGF	Thruster TST Mk 1	S. R. Swallow
	G-MTGH	Mainair Gemini Flash IIA	D. Shackleton
	G-MTGI	Solar Wings Pegasus XL-R	P. D. Myer & T. P. Bee
	G-MTGJ	Solar Wings Pegasus XL-R	C. M. Council
	G-MTGK	Solar Wings Pegasus XL-R	I. A. Smith
	G-MTGL	Solar Wings Pegasus XL-R	R. T. Curant
	G-MTGM	Solar Wings Pegasus XL-R	B. M. Marsh
	G-MTGO	Mainair Gemini Flash	D. W. Smith
	G-MTGP	Thruster TST Mk 1	G. J. Pill
	G-MTGR	Thruster TST Mk 1	S. A. Wood
	G-MTGS	Thruster TST Mk 1	G. & G. E. F. Warren
	G-MTGT	Thruster TST Mk 1	P. J. Ladd
	G-MTGU	Thruster TST Mk 1	AV Aviation Ltd
	G-MTGV	CFM Shadow Srs BD	S. A. Wood
	G-MTGX	Hornet Dual Trainer	A. R. Wells
	G-MTGY	Southdown Lightning	P. J. S. Ritchie
	G-MTHB	Aerotech MW.5B Sorcerer	D. B. White
	G-MTHC	Raven X	N. G. Souter
	G-MTHD	Hiway Demon 195	J. M. Spatchert
	G-MTHF	Solar Wings Pegasus XL-R	W. R. Keene
	G-MTHG	Solar Wings Pegasus XL-R	P. M. Gosney
	G-MTHH	Solar Wings Pegasus XL-R	A. E. Goodwin
	G-MTHI	Solar Wings Pegasus XL-R	J. F. Walker

Reg.	Type	Owner or Operator	Notes
G-MTHJ	Solar Wings Pegasus XL-R	B. R. Ward & P. A. Simpson	
G-MTHK	Solar Wings Pegasus XL-R	B. P. Somerville-Large	
G-MTHL	Solar Wings Pegasus XL-R	S. R. S. Evans	
G-MTHM	Solar Wings Pegasus XL-R	D. Cameron	
G-MTHN	Solar Wings Pegasus XL-R	M. J. Mawle	
G-MTHO	Solar Wings Pegasus XL-R	P. Cotton	
G-MTHP	Solar Wings Pegasus XL-R	J. S. Wright	
G-MTHS	CFM Shadow Srs BD	R. Clegg	
G-MTHT	CFM Shadow Srs BD	N. F. L. Agar	
G-MTHU	Hornet Dual Trainer	D. M. Couling & P. Myers	
G-MTHV	CFM Shadow Srs BD	P. Walker	
G-MTHW	Mainair Gemini Flash II	G. C. Brown	
G-MTHX	Mainair Gemini Flash IIA	L. G. G. Faulkner	
G-MTHY	Mainair Gemini Flash IIA	M. Stevenson	
G-MTHZ	Mainair Gemini Flash IIA	G. J. Stallard	
G-MTIA	Mainair Gemini Flash IIA	M. Callum	
G-MTIB	Mainair Gemini Flash IIA	D. Esau	
G-MTIC	Mainair Gemini Flash IIA	P. Whitney	
G-MTID	Southdown Raven X	R. G. Feathersby	
G-MTIE	Solar Wings Pegasus XL-R	A. G. Sayers	
G-MTIF	Solar Wings Pegasus XL-R	A. J. Westcott	
G-MTIG	Solar Wings Pegasus XL-R	A. R. Gouge	
G-MTIH	Solar Wings Pegasus XL-R	J. A. Iszard	
G-MTII	Solar Wings Pegasus XL-R	W. G. McKinnon	
G-MTIJ	Solar Wings Pegasus XL-R	D. O'Gorman	
G-MTIK	Southdown Raven X	B. W. Atkinson	
G-MTIL	Mainair Gemini Flash IIA	J. L. Hamer	
G-MTIM	Mainair Gemini Flash IIA	C. E. D. Smith	
G-MTIN	Mainair Gemini Flash IIA	B. J. Avery	
G-MTIO	Solar Wings Pegasus XL-R	M. A. Coe	
G-MTIP	Solar Wings Pegasus XL-R	L. F. Banham	
G-MTIR	Solar Wings Pegasus XL-R	D. C. Britton	
G-MTIS	Solar Wings Pegasus XL-R	T. M. Stiles	
G-MTIT	Solar Wings Pegasus XL-R	Solar Wings Ltd	
G-MTIU	Solar Wings Pegasus XL-R	J. W. Teesdale	
G-MTIV	Solar Wings Pegasus XL-R	K. S. Kelso	
G-MTIW	Solar Wings Pegasus XL-R	A. Holmes	
G-MTIX	Solar Wings Pegasus XL-R	H. J. & R. M. Page	
G-MTIY	Solar Wings Pegasus XL-R	I. R. Banbury	
G-MTIZ	Solar Wings Pegasus XL-R	H. R. Block	
G-MTJA	Mainair Gemini Flash IIA	J. A. Cuthbertson	
G-MTJB	Mainair Gemini Flash IIA	J. K. Cross	
G-MTJC	Mainair Gemini Flash IIA	S. M. Vickers	
G-MTJD	Mainair Gemini Flash IIA	Vinmar Holdings Ltd	
G-MTJE	Mainair Gemini Flash IIA	D. S. Worman	
G-MTJF	Mainair Gemini Flash IIA	J. H. Hambleton	
G-MTJG	Medway Hybred 44XLR	M. Anthony	
G-MTJH	Solar Wings Pegasus Flash	C. L. Parker	
G-MTJI	Raven X	L. E. Frank	
G-MTJK	Mainair Gemini Flash IIA	R. C. White	
G-MTJL	Mainair Gemini Flash IIA	R. L. Crowe	
G-MTJM	Mainair Gemini Flash IIA	J. Wilson	
G-MTJN	Midland Ultralights Sirocco 377GB	R. Harris	
G-MTJO	Mainair Gemini Flash II	G. Dalgarno	
G-MTJP	Medway Hybred 44XLR	J. R. Wells	
G-MTJR	Solar Wings Pegasus XL-R	Pegasus Skylink Ltd	
G-MTJS	Solar Wings Pegasus XL-Q	J. C. W. Smith	
G-MTJT	Mainair Gemini Flash IIA	R. G. Morris	
G-MTJU	MBA Tiger Cub	N. P. Thomson	
G-MTJV	Mainair Gemini Flash IIA	N. Charles & J. Richards	
G-MTJW	Mainair Gemini Flash IIA	J. D. Smith	
G-MTJX	Hornet Dual Trainer	R. J. Perrin	
G-MTJY	Mainair Gemini Flash IIA	S. J. Smith	
G-MTJZ	Mainair Gemini Flash IIA	A. R. Max	
G-MTKA	Thruster TST Mk 1	S. McKenzie & S. Cordova	
G-MTKB	Thruster TST Mk 1	A. Troughton	
G-MTKD	Thruster TST Mk 1	I. K. Ratcliffe	
G-MTKE	Thruster TST Mk 1	M. P. Allinson	
G-MTKF	Solar Wings Pegasus XL-R	Pegasus Skylink Ltd	
G-MTKG	Solar Wings Pegasus XL-R	S. J. Beecroft	
G-MTKH	Solar Wings Pegasus XL-R	R. J. Kelly	
G-MTKI	Solar Wings Pegasus XL-R	M. J. Calnan	
G-MTKJ	Solar Wings Pegasus XL-R	I. K. Donkin	

Notes	Reg.	Type	Owner or Operator
	G-MTKK	Solar Wings Pegasus XL-R	J. L. Rawlings
	G-MTKL	—	
	G-MTKM	Gardner T-M Scout S.2	D. Gardner
	G-MTKN	Mainair Gemini Flash IIA	A. J. Taylor
	G-MTKO	Mainair Gemini Flash IIA	Microflight Sales Ltd
	G-MTKP	Solar Wings Pegasus XL-R	E. J. Blyth
	G-MTKS	CFM Shadow Srs BD	R. B. Milton
	G-MTKU	CFM Shadow Srs BD	R. D. & A. C. Hill
	G-MTKV	Mainair Gemini Flash	J. P. Harmer
	G-MTKW	Mainair Gemini Flash IIA	K. E. Wedl
	G-MTKX	Mainair Gemini Flash IIA	W. P. Garrod
	G-MTKY	Mainair Gemini Flash IIA	A. J. Haworth
	G-MTKZ	Mainair Gemini Flash IIA	D. Naylor
	G-MTLA	Mainair Gemini Flash IIA	J. M. Thornton
	G-MTLB	Mainair Gemini Flash IIA	M. Richardson
	G-MTLC	Mainair Gemini Flash IIA	R. J. Alston
	G-MTLD	Mainair Gemini Flash IIA	D. J. Wood
	G-MTLE	See main Register	—
	G-MTLF	Solar Wings Pegasus XL-R	G. A. Harman
	G-MTLG	Solar Wings Pegasus XL-R	C. J. Dodwell
	G-MTLH	Solar Wings Pegasus XL-R	B. S. Waite
	G-MTLI	Solar Wings Pegasus XL-R	Metropolitan Ambulance Services Co Ltd
	G-MTLJ	Solar Wings Pegasus XL-R	T. D. P. Gates
	G-MTLK	Raven X	Raven Aircraft International Ltd
	G-MTLL	Mainair Gemini Flash IIA	M. F. Shaw & M. J. Bird
	G-MTLM	Thruster TST Mk 1	D. Roberts
	G-MTLN	Thruster TST Mk 1	Bode Laboratories (UK)
	G-MTLO	Thruster TST Mk 1	M. Rudd
	G-MTLP	Thruster TST Mk 1	D. S. Worman
	G-MTLR	Thruster TST Mk 1	I. Bartlett
	G-MTLS	Solar Wings Pegasus XL-R	K. M. Simmons
	G-MTLT	Solar Wings Pegasus XL-R	L. A. Humphreys
	G-MTLU	Solar Wings Pegasus XL-R	S. M. Hall
	G-MTLV	Solar Wings Pegasus XL-R	B. J. Gordon
	G-MTLW	Solar Wings Pegasus XL-R	S. R. Sutch
	G-MTLX	Medway Hybred 44XLR	S. P. Baines
	G-MTLY	Solar Wings Pegasus XL-R	G. P. Wilkins
	G-MTLZ	Whittaker MW.5 Sorceror	E. H. Gould
	G-MTMA	Mainair Gemini Flash IIA	H. Grindrod & G. C. Hobson
	G-MTMB	Mainair Gemini Flash IIA	E. J. Archer
	G-MTMC	Mainair Gemini Flash IIA	R. Lloyd
	G-MTMD	Whittaker MW.6 Merlin	F. A. Letcher & J. G. Beesley
	G-MTME	Solar Wings Pegasus XL-R	M. T. Finch
	G-MTMF	Solar Wings Pegasus XL-R	J. T. M. Smith
	G-MTMG	Solar Wings Pegasus XL-R	C. W. & P. E. F. Suckling
	G-MTMH	Solar Wings Pegasus XL-R	V. E. J. Smith
	G-MTMI	Solar Wings Pegasus XL-R	T. D. Barrass
	G-MTMJ	Maxair Hummer	M. J. Makin
	G-MTMK	Raven X	R. G. Padfield
	G-MTML	Mainair Gemini Flash IIA	S. M. Cawthra
	G-MTMM	CFM Shadow Srs BD	W. Friend
	G-MTMO	Raven X	T. A. Saunderson
	G-MTMP	Hornet Dual Trainer/Raven	P. Thompson
	G-MTMR	Hornet Dual Trainer/Raven	J. G. Teague
	G-MTMT	Mainair Gemini Flash IIA	C. Briggs
	G-MTMU	Mainair Gemini Flash IIA	B. Kirkland
	G-MTMV	Mainair Gemini Flash IIA	J. Clarke
	G-MTMW	Mainair Gemini Flash IIA	D. M. Law
	G-MTMX	CFM Shadow Srs BD	Thorndon Aviation
	G-MTMY	CFM Shadow Srs BD	P. A. James
	G-MTMZ	CFM Shadow Srs BD	C. A. Keens
	G-MTNA	CFM Shadow Srs BD	Allders International Ltd
	G-MTNB	Raven X	R. Coar
	G-MTNC	Mainair Gemini Flash IIA	R. Handley
	G-MNTD	Medway Hybred 44XLR	R. A. Clarke
	G-MTNE	Medway Hybred 44XLR	P. Sawday
	G-MTNF	Medway Hybred 44XLR	R. Heathcote
	G-MTNG	Mainair Gemini Flash IIA	S. Lichtenstein
	G-MTNH	Mainair Gemini Flash IIA	E. A. Butler
	G-MTNI	Mainair Gemini Flash IIA	K. P. Widdowson
	G-MTNJ	Mainair Gemini Flash IIA	R. H. Hunt
	G-MTNK	Weedhopper JC-24B	K. J. Tomlinson
	G-MTNL	Mainair Gemini Flash IIA	Microflight Sales Ltd

Reg.	Type	Owner or Operator	Notes
G-MTNM	Mainair Gemini Flash IIA	Microflight Sales Ltd	
G-MTNN	Mainair Gemini Flash IIA	M. Byl	
G-MTNO	Solar Wings Pegasus XL-Q	A. F. Batchelor	
G-MTNP	Solar Wings Pegasus XL-Q	G. G. Roberts	
G-MTNR	Thruster TST Mk 1	S. McCaffery	
G-MTNS	Thruster TST Mk 1	Airbourne Aviation Ltd	
G-MTNT	Thruster TST Mk 1	Microflight Tuition & Sales Ltd	
G-MTNU	Thruster TST Mk 1	D. G. Marwick	
G-MTNV	Thruster TST Mk 1	J. B. Russell	
G-MTNW	Thruster TST Mk 1	P. J. Ward & ptnrs	
G-MTNX	Mainair Gemini Flash II	P. J. Corker	
G-MTNY	Mainair Gemini Flash IIA	S. J. Ives	
G-MTNZ	Solar Wings Pegasus XL-Q	R. C. Crowley	
G-MTOA	Solar Wings Pegasus XL-R	R. A. Bird	
G-MTOB	Solar Wings Pegasus XL-R	R. F. Walbank	
G-MTOC	Solar Wings Pegasus XL-R	D. Jordan	
G-MTOD	Solar Wings Pegasus XL-R	G. G. Clayton	
G-MTOE	Solar Wings Pegasus XL-R	A. J. Prince	
G-MTOF	Solar Wings Pegasus XL-R	C. Stebbings	
G-MTOG	Solar Wings Pegasus XL-R	J. C. Owens	
G-MTOH	Solar Wings Pegasus XL-R	H. Cook	
G-MTOI	Solar Wings Pegasus XL-R	J. Grotian	
G-MTOJ	Solar Wings Pegasus XL-R	T. J. Bax	
G-MTOK	Solar Wings Pegasus XL-R	D. G. Hall	
G-MTOL	Solar Wings Pegasus XL-R	I. Colborn	
G-MTOM	Solar Wings Pegasus XL-R	A. J. Macfie	
G-MTON	Solar Wings Pegasus XL-R	J. K. Henderson	
G-MTOO	Solar Wings Pegasus XL-R	P. Devlin	
G-MTOP	Solar Wings Pegasus XL-R	Solar Wings Ltd	
G-MTOR	Solar Wings Pegasus XL-R	Solar Wings Ltd	
G-MTOS	Solar Wings Pegasus XL-R	N. A. Summerbell	
G-MTOT	Solar Wings Pegasus XL-R	J. H. Sparks	
G-MTOU	Solar Wings Pegasus XL-R	W. A. Emmerson	
G-MTOV	Solar Wings Pegasus XL-R	K. F. Baker	
G-MTOW	Solar Wings Pegasus XL-R	Solar Wings Ltd	
G-MTOX	Solar Wings Pegasus XL-R	Solar Wings Ltd	
G-MTOY	Solar Wings Pegasus XL-R	N. B. Morley & P. M. Humphris	
G-MTOZ	Solar Wings Pegasus XL-R	K. Wright	
G-MTPA	Mainair Gemini Flash IIA	W. H. Smith	
G-MTPB	Mainair Gemini Flash IIA	M. P. Middleton	
G-MTPC	Raven X	R. L. Cross	
G-MTPD	Solar Wings Pegasus XL-Q	P. Devlin	
G-MTPE	Solar Wings Pegasus XL-R	D. G. Benson	
G-MTPF	Solar Wings Pegasus XL-R	P. A. West	
G-MTPG	Solar Wings Pegasus XL-R	E. K. Battersea	
G-MTPH	Solar Wings Pegasus XL-R	G. R. Hall	
G-MTPI	Solar Wings Pegasus XL-R	I. J. Alexander	
G-MTPJ	Solar Wings Pegasus XL-R	E. J. Larnder	
G-MTPK	Solar Wings Pegasus XL-R	M. K. McCall & A. Garwood	
G-MTPL	Solar Wings Pegasus XL-R	D. Stott	
G-MTPM	Solar Wings Pegasus XL-R	E. K. Battersea	
G-MTPN	Solar Wings Pegasus XL-Q	M. G. Welch	
G-MTPO	Solar Wings Pegasus XL-Q	F. R. Hart	
G-MTPP	Solar Wings Pegasus XL-R	D. Corke	
G-MTPR	Solar Wings Pegasus XL-R	M. Castle	
G-MTPS	Solar Wings Pegasus XL-Q	P. R. Snowden	
G-MTPT	Thruster TST Mk Mk 1	G. S. Langdon	
G-MTPU	Thruster TST Mk 1	E. B. Landsler	
G-MTPV	Thruster TST Mk 1	R. E. D. Bailey	
G-MTPW	Thruster TST Mk 1	L. Mullin	
G-MTPX	Thruster TST Mk 1	B. J. Gordon	
G-MTPY	Thruster TST Mk 1	A. N. Wicks	
G-MTPZ	Solar Wings Pegasus XL-R	M. R. P. McCarthy	
G-MTRA	Mainair Gemini Flash IIA	A. Bulling	
G-MTRB	Mainair Gemini Flash IIA	Microflight Sales Ltd	
G-MTRC	Midlands Ultralights Sirocco 377GB	J. Bagnall	
G-MTRD	Midlands Ultralights Sirocco 377GB	J. R. North	
G-MTRE	Whittaker MW.6 Merlin	M. J. Batchelor	
G-MTRF	Mainair Gemini Flash IIA	J. McGaughran	
G-MTRG	Mainair Gemini Flash IIA	D. C. Harrison	
G-MTRH	Hiway Demon	D. C. P. Cardey	
G-MTRI	Hiway Demon	S. D. Pain	

Notes	Reg.	Type	Owner or Operator
	G-MTRJ	AMF Chevvron 232	Chartersteps Ltd
	G-MTRK	Hornet Dual Trainer	K. W. E. Brunnenkant
	G-MTRL	Hornet Dual Trainer	A. Ascroft
	G-MTRM	Solar Wings Pegasus XL-R	D. Dugdale
	G-MTRN	Solar Wings Pegasus XL-R	T. G. M. White
	G-MTRO	Solar Wings Pegasus XL-R	D. G. Burrows
	G-MTRP	Solar Wings Pegasus XL-R	D. W. Cardy
	G-MTRR	Solar Wings Pegasus XL-R	D. T. Hutchinson
	G-MTRS	Solar Wings Pegasus XL-R	R. H. Braithwaite
	G-MTRT	Raven X	R. J. Henney
	G-MTRU	Solar Wings Pegasus XL-Q	A. Barnish
	G-MTRV	Solar Wings Pegasus XL-Q	C. Leighton-Thomas
	G-MTRW	Raven X	P. R. A. & S. Elliston
	G-MTRX	Whittaker MW.5 Sorceror	W. Turner
	G-MTRY	Noble Hardman Snowbird IV	E. J. Blyth
	G-MTRZ	Mainair Gemini Flash IIA	B. L. Benson
	G-MTSA	Mainair Gemini Flash IIA	N. P. A. & W. R. J. Wallis
	G-MTSB	Mainair Gemini Flash IIA	C. E. Walley
	G-MTSC	Mainair Gemini Flash IIA	E. G. Astin
	G-MTSD	Raven X	I. D. Forsdike
	G-MTSE	Flexiform Striker	D. Dixon
	G-MTSF	Aerial Arts Chaser 110SX	D. Dixon
	G-MTSG	CFM Shadow Srs BD	J. W. E. Pearson
	G-MTSH	Thruster TST Mk 1	M. Hanna
	G-MTSI	Thruster TST Mk 1	G. H. Cork
	G-MTSJ	Thruster TST Mk 1	A. Kingston
	G-MTSK	Thruster TST Mk 1	E. K. Battersea
	G-MTSL	Thruster TST Mk 1	J. R. Hammett
	G-MTSM	Thruster TST Mk 1	H. Smith & ptnrs
	G-MTSN	Solar Wings Pegasus XL-R	A. J. Blackwell
	G-MTSO	Solar Wings Pegasus XL-R	P. A. Mercer
	G-MTSP	Solar Wings Pegasus XL-R	S. P. Christian
	G-MTSR	Solar Wings Pegasus XL-R	N. H. Dyer
	G-MTSS	Solar Wings Pegasus XL-R	H. T. Edmonds
	G-MTSU	Solar Wings Pegasus XL-R	S. M. Saint
	G-MTSV	Solar Wings Pegasus XL-R	D. A. Carter
	G-MTSW	Solar Wings Pegasus XL-R	J. Devine
	G-MTSX	Solar Wings Pegasus XL-R	Midland Airsports Ltd
	G-MTSY	Solar Wings Pegasus XL-R	B. Alexander
	G-MTSZ	Solar Wings Pegasus XL-R	S. Beeson
	G-MTTA	Solar Wings Pegasus XL-R	M. Greene
	G-MTTB	Solar Wings Pegasus XL-R	D. V. Lawrence
	G-MTTC	Solar Wings Pegasus XL-R	C. J. Jakes
	G-MTTD	Solar Wings Pegasus XL-R	Southwest Airsports Ltd
	G-MTTE	Solar Wings Pegasus XL-R	Solar Wings Ltd
	G-MTTF	Aerotech MW.6 Merlin	V. E. Booth
	G-MTTG	Excalibur TriPacer 250	S. C. Goozee
	G-MTTH	CFM Shadow Srs BD	C. T. H. Pattison
	G-MTTI	Mainair Gemini Flash IIA	D. Houghton
	G-MTTK	Southdown Lightning DS	D. E. Oakley
	G-MTTL	Hiway Sky-Trike	S. P. Hayes
	G-MTTM	Mainair Gemini Flash IIA	Milequip Computer Systems
	G-MTTN	Ultralight Flight Phantom	H. R. Duggins
	G-MTTO	Mainair Gemini Flash IIA	R. Painter
	G-MTTP	Mainair Gemini Flash IIA	J. Windmill
	G-MTTR	Mainair Gemini Flash IIA	M. Richardson
	G-MTTS	Mainair Gemini Flash IIA	M. J. Aubrey
	G-MTTT	—	—
	G-MTTU	Solar Wings Pegasus XL-R	B. C. Allen
	G-MTTV	Solar Wings Pegasus XL-Q	Pegasus Skylink Ltd
	G-MTTW	Mainair Gemini Flash IIA	R. M. Shipp
	G-MTTX	Solar Wings Pegasus XL-Q	P. G. Moss
	G-MTTY	Solar Wings Pegasus XL-Q	D. R. Lever
	G-MTTZ	Solar Wings Pegasus XL-Q	J. Haskett
	G-MTUA	Solar Wings Pegasus XL-R	D. W. Suttill
	G-MTUB	Thruster TST Mk 1	Thruster Aircraft (UK) Ltd
	G-MTUC	Thruster TST Mk 1	C. B. Price
	G-MTUD	Thruster TST Mk 1	K. J. Lywood
	G-MTUE	Thruster TST Mk 1	A. Troughton
	G-MTUF	Thruster TST Mk 1	Oban Divers Ltd
	G-MTUG	Thruster TST Mk 1	A. G. Procter
	G-MTUH	Solar Wings Pegasus XL-R	Solar Wings Ltd
	G-MTUI	Solar Wings Pegasus XL-R	B. J. Keylock
	G-MTUJ	Solar Wings Pegasus XL-R	R. C. Taplin

Reg.	Type	Owner or Operator	Notes
G-MTUK	Solar Wings Pegasus XL-R	D. J. Binnie	
G-MTUL	Solar Wings Pegasus XL-R	S. H. James	
G-MTUM	Solar Wings Pegasus XL-R	Solar Wings Ltd	
G-MTUN	Solar Wings Pegasus XL-Q	B. J. Gordon & D. L. Smith	
G-MTUO	Solar Wings Pegasus XL-Q	D. J. Gardner	
G-MTUP	Solar Wings Pegasus XL-Q	G. T. Gooch & T. A. Patricot	
G-MTUR	Solar Wings Pegasus XL-Q	Solar Wings Ltd	
G-MTUS	Solar Wings Pegasus XL-Q	D. G. Mayling	
G-MTUT	Solar Wings Pegasus XL-Q	R. P. Tinsley	
G-MTUU	Mainair Gemini Flash IIA	W. Myers	
G-MTUV	Mainair Gemini Flash IIA	P. A. Lee	
G-MTUW	Mainair Gemini Flash IIA	Mainair Sports Ltd	
G-MTUX	Medway Hybred 44XLR	M. Preston	
G-MTUY	Solar Wings Pegasus XL-Q	Viscount Lowther	
G-MTUZ	Hornet Dual Trainer	Pegasus Skylink Ltd	
G-MTVA	Solar Wings Pegasus XL-R	Solar Wings Ltd	
G-MTVB	Solar Wings Pegasus XL-R	Solar Wings Ltd	
G-MTVC	Solar Wings Pegasus XL-R	T. A. Earley	
G-MTVE	Solar Wings Pegasus XL-R	Solar Wings Ltd	
G-MTVF	Solar Wings Pegasus XL-R	Solar Wings Ltd	
G-MTVG	Mainair Gemini Flash IIA	D. Clarke	
G-MTVH	Mainair Gemini Flash IIA	P. I. Frost	
G-MTVI	Mainair Gemini Flash IIA	S. A. Jaques	
G-MTVJ	Mainair Gemini Flash IIA	D. C. Scully	
G-MTVK	Solar Wings Pegasus XL-R	A. S. Wason	
G-MTVL	Solar Wings Pegasus XL-R	D. M. Smith	
G-MTVM	Solar Wings Pegasus XL-R	P. M. Harrison	
G-MTVN	Solar Wings Pegasus XL-R	R. A. Benson	
G-MTVO	Solar Wings Pegasus XL-R	W. I. Burnet	
G-MTVP	Thruster TST Mk 1	B. Bayley	
G-MTVR	Thruster TST Mk 1	S. F. Vint & ptnrs	
G-MTVS	Thruster TST Mk 1	K. Fletcher	
G-MTVT	Thruster TST Mk 1	C. E. Brown	
G-MTVU	Thruster TST Mk 1	I. D. Stokes	
G-MTVV	Thruster TST Mk 1	A. Hipkin	
G-MTVW	Southdown Lightning	B. Dixon	
G-MTVX	Solar Wings Pegasus XL-Q	A. W. Buchan	
G-MTVY	Solar Wings Pegasus XL-Q	K. Handley	
G-MTVZ	Powerchute Raider	Powerchute Systems International Ltd	
G-MTWA	Solar Wings Pegasus XL-R	Data Pacific Systems Ltd	
G-MTWB	Solar Wings Pegasus XL-R	J. E. Glendinning	
G-MTWC	Solar Wings Pegasus XL-R	D. H. Griffin	
G-MTWD	Solar Wings Pegasus XL-R	R. H. Evans	
G-MTWE	Solar Wings Pegasus XL-R	Southern Microlight Training Centre Ltd	
G-MTWF	Mainair Gemini Flash IIA	Microflight Tuition & Sales Ltd	
G-MTWG	Mainair Gemini Flash IIA	R. E. D. Bailey	
G-MTWH	CFM Shadow Srs BD	V. A. Hutchinson	
G-MTWI	—	—	
G-MTWJ	—		
G-MTWK	CFM Shadow Srs BD	CFM Metal-Fax Ltd	
G-MTWL	CFM Shadow Srs BD	K. J. Cadman	
G-MTWM	CFM Shadow Srs BD	B. R. Johnson	
G-MTWN	CFM Shadow Srs BD	R. K. Waddams	
G-MTWO	Weedhopper JC-24B	A. J. Glynn	
G-MTWP	CFM Shadow Srs BD	L. J. Chapman	
G-MTWR	Mainair Gemini Flash IIA	C. Foster	
G-MTWS	Mainair Gemini Flash IIA	G. V. Nash & J. G. Lees	
G-MTWW	Solar Wings Typhoon	C. W. Payne	
G-MTWX	Mainair Gemini Flash IIA	P. B. Nicholas	
G-MTWY	Thruster TST Mk 1	J. F. Bickerstaffe	
G-MTWZ	Thruster TST Mk 1	G. F. Beabey	
G-MTXA	Thruster TST Mk 1	R. J. Bowering	
G-MTXB	Thruster TST Mk 1	M. Watson	
G-MTXC	Thruster TST Mk 1	Southwest Airsports Ltd	
G-MTXD	Thruster TST Mk 1	R. D. Chiles	
G-MTXE	Hornet Dual Trainer	B. Berry	
G-MTXF	Hornet Dual Trainer	Pegasus Skylink Ltd	
G-MTXG	Solar Wings Pegasus XL-Q	P. Wright	
G-MTXH	Solar Wings Pegasus XL-Q	D. J. Moseley	
G-MTXI	Solar Wings Pegasus XL-Q	R. B. Best	
G-MTXJ	Solar Wings Pegasus XL-Q	A. R. Brough & ptnrs	
G-MTXK	Solar Wings Pegasus XL-Q	J. McConnachie	
G-MTXL	Noble Hardman Snowbird Mk IV	W. Murphy	
G-MTXM	Mainair Gemini Flash IIA	W. Thorne	

Notes	Reg.	Type	Owner or Operator
	G-MTXN	MBA Tiger Cub 440	E. Barfoot
	G-MTXO	Whittaker MW.6	J. G. Vaughan
	G-MTXP	Mainair Gemini Flash IIA	L. D. Esposti
	G-MTXR	CFM Shadow Srs BD	J. C. Carpenter
	G-MTXS	Mainair Gemini Flash IIA	D. J. Francis
	G-MTXT	MBA Tiger Cub 440	A. F. Stafford
	G-MTXU	Noble Hardman Snowbird Mk IV	Davlin Microlights Ltd
	G-MTXV	Noble Hardman Snowbird Mk IV	Skyrider Aviation Ltd
	G-MTXW	Noble Hardman Snowbird Mk IV	Skyrider Aviation Ltd
	G-MTXX	Hornet Dual Trainer	Pegasus Skylink Ltd
	G-MTXY	Hornet Dual Trainer	Hornet Microlights
	G-MTXZ	Mainair Gemini Flash IIA	W. T. J. Bridgwater
	G-MTYA	Solar Wings Pegasus XL-Q	D. Christy
	G-MTYB	Solar Wings Pegasus XL-Q	Solar Wings Ltd
	G-MTYC	Solar Wings Pegasus XL-Q	Timeshare Bourse Ltd
	G-MTYD	Solar Wings Pegasus XL-Q	H. J. Aldridge
	G-MTYE	Solar Wings Pegasus XL-Q	G. C. Weighell
	G-MTYF	Solar Wings Pegasus XL-Q	J. Hyde
	G-MTYG	Solar Wings Pegasus XL-Q	D. C. Fellows
	G-MTYH	Solar Wings Pegasus XL-Q	DSG Aviation Sales
	G-MTYI	Solar Wings Pegasus XL-Q	K. J. Berrisford
	G-MTYJ	Solar Wings Pegasus XL-Q	Solar Wings Ltd
	G-MTYK	Solar Wings Pegasus XL-Q	G. H. Watts
	G-MTYL	Solar Wings Pegasus XL-Q	T. P. Roche
	G-MTYM	Solar Wings Pegasus XL-Q	D. R. Cowieson
	G-MTYN	Solar Wings Pegasus XL-Q	K. Hann
	G-MTYO	Solar Wings Pegasus XL-Q	G. P. Wilkins
	G-MTYP	Solar Wings Pegasus XL-Q	C. Stallard
	G-MTYR	Solar Wings Pegasus XL-Q	Airplay (UK) Ltd
	G-MTYS	Solar Wings Pegasus XL-Q	Airplay (UK) Ltd
	G-MTYT	Solar Wings Pegasus XL-Q	S. R. Giles
	G-MTYU	Solar Wings Pegasus XL-Q	G. J. Parker
	G-MTYV	Raven X	A. Reynolds
	G-MTYW	Raven X	The Hon J. Nivison
	G-MTYX	—	
	G-MTYY	Solar Wings Pegasus XL-R	I. P. Harris
	G-MTYZ	Mainair Gemini Flash IIA	R. Findlow
	G-MTZA	Thruster TST Mk 1	M. W. Stevens
	G-MTZB	Thruster TST Mk 1	P. Milne
	G-MTZC	Thruster TST Mk 1	P. J. Gribben
	G-MTZD	Thruster TST Mk 1	P. V. Valenti
	G-MTZE	Thruster TST Mk 1	J. L. Phipps
	G-MTZF	Thruster TST Mk 1	B. J. Gordon
	G-MTZG	Mainair Gemini Flash IIA	A. Arnold & C. D. Stokes
	G-MTZH	Mainair Gemini Flash IIA	K. N. Dickinson
	G-MTZI	Solar Wings Pegasus XL-R	G. A. Breen
	G-MTZJ	Solar Wings Pegasus XL-R	P. J. Burns
	G-MTZK	Solar Wings Pegasus XL-R	P. R. Claridge
	G-MTZL	Mainair Gemini Flash IIA	M. L. Smith
	G-MTZM	Mainair Gemini Flash IIA	Brend Design Ltd
	G-MTZN	Mainair Gemini Flash IIA	R. Almond
	G-MTZO	Mainair Gemini Flash IIA	Pegasus Building Preservation
	G-MTZP	Solar Wings Pegasus XL-Q	J. E. Gooch
	G-MTZR	Solar Wings Pegasus XL-Q	S. S. Dixon
	G-MTZS	Solar Wings Pegasus XL-Q	R. J. Bottrell
	G-MTZT	Solar Wings Pegasus XL-Q	S. Solley
	G-MTZU	Solar Wings Pegasus XL-Q	Solar Wings Ltd
	G-MTZV	Mainair Gemini Flash IIA	S. G. Hampson
	G-MTZW	Mainair Gemini Flash IIA	R. Mason
	G-MTZX	Mainair Gemini Flash IIA	R. E. D. Bailey
	G-MTZY	Mainair Gemini Flash IIA	F. D. Bennett
	G-MTZZ	Mainair Gemini Flash IIA	R. E. D. Bailey
	G-MVAA	Mainair Gemini Flash IIA	N. S. Payne
	G-MVAB	Mainair Gemini Flash IIA	M. J. Burton
	G-MVAC	CFM Shadow Srs BD	J. V. Thompson
	G-MVAD	Mainair Gemini Flash IIA	K. A. Lindley
	G-MVAE	—	
	G-MVAF	Southdown Puma Sprint	W. G. Harling
	G-MVAG	Thruster TST Mk 1	N. P. Thomson
	G-MVAH	Thruster TST Mk 1	D. C. Mant
	G-MVAI	Thruster TST Mk 1	P. J. Cave
	G-MVAJ	Thruster TST Mk 1	T. S. Mangat
	G-MVAK	Thruster TST Mk 1	M. L. Smith

Reg.	Type	Owner or Operator	Notes
G-MVAL	Thruster TST Mk 1	Altec Syndicate	
G-MVAM	CFM Shadow Srs BD	H. Grindrod & ptnrs	
G-MVAN	CFM Shadow Srs BD	A. M. C. Batten	
G-MVAO	Mainair Gemini Flash IIA	T. Gate	
G-MVAP	Mainair Gemini Flash IIA	A. Buck	
G-MVAR	Solar Wings Pegasus XL-R	K. H. Creeo	
G-MVAS	Solar Wings Pegasus XL-R	G. A. Breen	
G-MVAT	Solar Wings Pegasus XL-R	T. D. Grieve	
G-MVAU	Solar Wings Pegasus XL-R	R. & J. A. Rhodes	
G-MVAV	Solar Wings Pegasus XL-R	P. G. Gardner	
G-MVAW	Solar Wings Pegasus XL-Q	Solar Wings Ltd	
G-MVAX	Solar Wings Pegasus XL-Q	Solar Wings Ltd	
G-MVAY	Solar Wings Pegasus XL-Q	Solar Wings Ltd	
G-MVAZ	Solar Wings Pegasus XL-Q	Solar Wings Ltd	
G-MVBA	Solar Wings Pegasus XL-Q	Solar Wings Ltd	
G-MVBB	CFM Shadow Srs BD	A. Dale	
G-MVBC	Aerial Arts Tri-Flyer 130SX	D. Beer	
G-MVBD	Mainair Gemini Flash IIA	A. L. Ruben	
G-MVBE	Mainair Scorcher	K S. Woodard	
G-MVBF	Mainair Gemini Flash IIA	A. K. Rupai	
G-MVBG	Mainair Gemini Flash IIA	A. P. Sherrott	
G-MVBH	Mainair Gemini Flash IIA	D. K. Ross	
G-MVBI	Mainair Gemini Flash IIA	G. C. Hobson	
G-MVBJ	Solar Wings Pegasus XL-R	C. Montgomery	
G-MVBK	Mainair Gemini Flash IIA	J. R. Holloway	
G-MVBL	Mainair Gemini Flash IIA	J. P. Fitzmaurice	
G-MVBM	Mainair Gemini Flash IIA	D. &. S. Jackson	
G-MVBN	Mainair Gemini Flash IIA	J. A. C. Terry	
G-MVBO	Mainair Gemini Flash IIA	A. B. French	
G-MVBP	Thruster TST Mk 1	N. O. G. Wooler	
G-MVBR	Thruster TST Mk 1	Thruster Aircraft (UK) Ltd	
G-MVBS	Thruster TST Mk 1	J. K. Cross	
G-MVBT	Thruster TST Mk 1	Thruster Aircraft (UK) Ltd	
G-MVBU	Thruster TST Mk 1	W. H. J. Knowles	
G-MVBV	Thruster TST Mk 1	Thruster Aircraft (UK) Ltd	
G-MVBW	CFM Shadow Srs BD	J. K. England Ltd	
G-MVBX	Solar Wings Pegasus XL-R	A. J. B. Winter	
G-MVBY	Solar Wings Pegasus XL-R	J. D. Sings	
G-MVBZ	Solar Wings Pegasus XL-R	Midland Airsports Ltd	
G-MVCA	Solar Wings Pegasus XL-R	C. P. Gray	
G-MVCB	Solar Wings Pegasus XL-R	G. T. Clipstone	
G-MVCC	CFM Shadow Srs BD	J. E. Pratt	
G-MVCD	Medway Hybred 44XLR	M. Filmer	
G-MVCE	Mainair Gemini Flash IIA	J. H. Stothert	
G-MVCF	Mainair Gemini Flash IIA	J. L. Hamer	
G-MVCG	Skyhook Cutlas	J. D. Garrett	
G-MVCH	Noble Hardman Snowbird Mk IV	M. L. Smith	
G-MVCI	Noble Hardman Snowbird Mk IV	A. R. Wells	
G-MVCJ	Noble Hardman Snowbird Mk IV	D. Golding & ptnrs	
G-MVCK	La Mouette Profil 19	S. D. Alsop	
G-MVCL	Solar Wings Pegasus XL-Q	D. J. Hill	
G-MVCM	Solar Wings Pegasus XL-Q	S. Vassiliades	
G-MVCN	Solar Wings Pegasus XL-Q	M. L. Smith	
G-MVCO	Solar Wings Pegasus XL-Q	B. H. Ashman	
G-MVCP	Solar Wings Pegasus XL-Q	P. E. Leicester	
G-MVCR	Solar Wings Pegasus XL-Q	H. D. J. Niece	
G-MVCS	Solar Wings Pegasus XL-Q	Solar Wings Ltd	
G-MVCT	Solar Wings Pegasus XL-Q	Solar Wings Ltd	
G-MVCU	Solar Wings Pegasus XL-Q	A. D. Stewart	
G-MVCV	Solar Wings Pegasus XL-Q	G. Bye	
G-MVCW	CFM Shadow Srs BD	R. A. Smith	
G-MVCX	Chargus Vortex	T. Farrell	
G-MVCY	Mainair Gemini Flash IIA	T. D. Neal	
G-MVCZ	Mainair Gemini Flash IIA	Microflight Tuition & Sales Ltd	
G-MVDA	Mainair Gemini Flash IIA	Mainair Sports Ltd	
G-MVDB	Medway Hybred 44XLR	R. M. Summers	
G-MVDC	Medway Hybred 44XLR	M. Kaye	
G-MVDD	Thruster TST Mk 1	Thruster Aircraft (UK) Ltd	
G-MVDE	Thruster TST Mk 1	R. H. Davis	
G-MVDF	Thruster TST Mk 1	Thruster Aircraft (UK) Ltd	
G-MVDG	Thruster TST Mk 1	R. T. Laking	
G-MVDH	Thruster TST Mk 1	M. L. Roberts	
G-MVDI	Thruster TST Mk 1	Thruster Aircraft (UK) Ltd	

Notes	Reg.	Type	Owner or Operator
	G-MVDJ	Medway Hybred 44XLR	A. Dring
	G-MVDK	Aerial Arts Chaser S	Aerial Arts Ltd
	G-MVDL	Aerial Arts Chaser S	S. J. Walker
	G-MVDM	Aerial Arts Chaser S	P. A. R. Hicks
	G-MVDN	Aerial Arts Chaser S	R. Riley
	G-MVDO	Aerial Arts Chaser S	J. Riley
	G-MVDP	Aerial Arts Chaser S	Airplay (UK) Ltd
	G-MVDR	Aerial Arts Chaser S	W. H. Sherlock
	G-MVDS	Hiway Skytrike	P. Butler
	G-MVDT	Mainair Gemini Flash IIA	D. C. Stephens
	G-MVDU	Solar Wings Pegasus XL-R	T. B. Jenkins
	G-MVDV	Solar Wings Pegasus XL-R	D. A. Preston
	G-MVDW	Solar Wings Pegasus XL-R	R. Hoddinott
	G-MVDX	Solar Wings Pegasus XL-R	J. A. Haggie
	G-MVDY	Solar Wings Pegasus XL-R	H. M. Read
	G-MVDZ	Solar Wings Pegasus XL-R	A. J. Tillman
	G-MVEA	Solar Wings Pegasus XL-R	R. F. Wood
	G-MVEB	Solar Wings Pegasus XL-R	Solar Wings Ltd
	G-MVEC	Solar Wings Pegasus XL-R	G. C. Weighell
	G-MVED	Solar Wings Pegasus XL-R	D. R. Piggott
	G-MVEE	Medway Hybred 44XLR	D. Evans
	G-MVEF	Solar Wings Pegasus XL-R	E. J. Blyth
	G-MVEG	Solar Wings Pegasus XL-R	J. M. Wassmer
	G-MVEH	Mainair Gemini Flash IIA	J. I. Greenshields
	G-MVEI	CFM Shadow Srs BD	Atlantic Aviation Ltd
	G-MVEJ	Mainair Gemini Flash IIA	M. G. Jones
	G-MVEK	Mainair Gemini Flash IIA	J. R. Spinks
	G-MVEL	Mainair Gemini Flash IIA	L. R. H. D'Eath
	G-MVEM	Mainair Gemini Flash IIA	Mainair Sports Ltd
	G-MVEN	CFM Shadow Srs BD	T. J. T. Dorricott
	G-MVEO	Mainair Gemini Flash IIA	J. C. R. Gubbins
	G-MVEP	Mainair Gemini Flash IIA	E. Marsh
	G-MVER	Mainair Gemini Flash IIA	G. K. Hoult
	G-MVES	Mainair Gemini Flash IIA	A. Anderson
	G-MVET	Mainair Gemini Flash IIA	Microlight Tuition & Sales Ltd
	G-MVEU	Hornet Dual Trainer	Pegasus Skylink Ltd
	G-MVEV	Mainair Gemini Flash IIA	M. T. Hill
	G-MVEW	Mainair Gemini Flash IIA	N. A. Dye
	G-MVEX	Solar Wings Pegasus XL-Q	J. S. Hamilton
	G-MVEY	Solar Wings Pegasus XL-Q	Airplay (UK) Ltd
	G-MVEZ	Solar Wings Pegasus XL-Q	P. W. Millar
	G-MVFA	Solar Wings Pegasus XL-Q	I. R. Banbury
	G-MVFB	Solar Wings Pegasus XL-Q	A. G. Drury
	G-MVFC	Solar Wings Pegasus XL-Q	J. K. Turner
	G-MVFD	Solar Wings Pegasus XL-Q	Solar Wings Ltd
	G-MVFE	Solar Wings Pegasus XL-Q	D. Young
	G-MVFF	Solar Wings Pegasus XL-Q	P. E. Maxwell
	G-MVFG	Solar Wings Pegasus XL-Q	Solar Wings Ltd
	G-MVFH	CFM Shadow Srs BD	CFM Metal-Fax Ltd
	G-MVFI	Ultrasports Panther XL	A. P. White
	G-MVFJ	Thruster TST Mk 1	A. R. James
	G-MVFK	Thruster TST Mk 1	J. E. L. Goodall
	G-MVFL	Thruster TST Mk 1	Thruster Aircraft (UK) Ltd
	G-MVFM	Thruster TST Mk 1	J. D. Wainwright
	G-MVFN	Thruster TST Mk 1	Thruster Aircraft (UK) Ltd
	G-MVFO	Thruster TST Mk 1	Thruster Aircraft (UK) Ltd
	G-MVFP	Solar Wings Pegasus XL-R	P. Woodcock
	G-MVFR	Solar Wings Pegasus XL-R	T. G. Jackson
	G-MVFS	Solar Wings Pegasus XL-R	Solar Wings Ltd
	G-MVFT	Solar Wings Pegasus XL-R	J. E. Halsall
	G-MVFU	Solar Wings Pegasus XL-R	Solar Wings Ltd
	G-MVFV	Solar Wings Pegasus XL-R	Solar Wings Ltd
	G-MVFW	Solar Wings Pegasus XL-R	Solar Wings Ltd
	G-MVFX	Solar Wings Pegasus XL-R	Solar Wings Ltd
	G-MVFY	Solar Wings Pegasus XL-R	Solar Wings Ltd
	G-MVFZ	Solar Wings Pegasus XL-R	Solar Wings Ltd
	G-MVGA	Aerial Arts Chaser S	Cyclone Hovercraft Ltd
	G-MVGB	Medway Hybred 44XLR	D. Coward
	G-MVGC	AMF Chevvron 232	C. J. L. Hunt
	G-MVGD	AMF Chevvron 232	Calvert Holdings Ltd
	G-MVGE	AMF Chevvron 232	K. G. Baker
	G-MVGF	Aerial Arts Chaser S	I. D. Baxter
	G-MVGG	Aerial Arts Chaser S	M. I. Hubbard
	G-MVGH	Aerial Arts Chaser S	M. M. Christian

Reg.	Type	Owner or Operator	Notes
G-MVGI	Aerial Arts Chaser S	M. D. Phillips	
G-MVGJ	Aerial Arts Chaser S	P. J. McNamee	
G-MVGK	Aerial Arts Chaser S	C. F. Grainger	
G-MVGL	Medway Hybred 44XLR	S. Tensch	
G-MVGM	Mainair Gemini Flash IIA	J. Cunliffe	
G-MVGN	Solar Wings Pegasus XL-R	Solar Wings Ltd	
G-MVGO	Solar Wings Pegasus XL-R	Solar Wings Ltd	
G-MVGP	Solar Wings Pegasus XL-R	Solar Wings Ltd	
G-MVGR	Solar Wings Pegasus XL-R	Solar Wings Ltd	
G-MVGS	Solar Wings Pegasus XL-R	Solar Wings Ltd	
G-MVGT	Solar Wings Pegasus XL-Q	Cloudbase Airsports Ltd	
G-MVGU	Solar Wings Pegasus XL-Q	Solar Wings Ltd	
G-MVGV	Solar Wings Pegasus XL-Q	Solar Wings Ltd	
G-MVGW	Solar Wings Pegasus XL-Q	Solar Wings Ltd	
G-MVGX	Solar Wings Pegasus XL-Q	Solar Wings Ltd	
G-MVGY	Medway Hybred 44XL	Medway Microlights	
G-MVGZ	Ultraflight Lazair IIIE	M. F. Briggs	
G-MVHA	Aerial Arts Chaser S	R. Meredith-Hardy	
G-MVHB	Powerchute Raider	Powerchute Systems International Ltd	
G-MVHC	Powerchute Raider	Powerchute Systems International Ltd	
G-MVHD	CFM Shadow Srs BD	T. B. McDermott	
G-MVHE	Mainair Gemini Flash IIA	S. A. Clarehugh	
G-MVHF	Mainair Gemini Flash IIA	D. Haslam	
G-MVHG	Mainair Gemini Flash IIA	R. S. Jordan	
G-MVHH	Mainair Gemini Flash IIA	Microflight Tuition & Sales Ltd	
G-MVHI	Thruster TST Mk 1	Thruster Aircraft (UK) Ltd	
G-MVHJ	Thruster TST Mk 1	Thruster Aircraft (UK) Ltd	
G-MVHK	Thruster TST Mk 1	Thruster Aircraft (UK) Ltd	
G-MVHL	Thruster TST Mk 1	Thruster Aircraft (UK) Ltd	
G-MVHM	Whittaker MW.5 Sorcerer	J. F. Bakewell	
G-MVHN	Aerial Arts Chaser S	K. J. Regan	
G-MVHO	Solar Wings Pegasus XL-Q	Solar Wings Ltd	
G-MVHP	Solar Wings Pegasus XL-Q	V. E. J. Smith	
G-MVHR	Solar Wings Pegasus XL-Q	A. W. Reed	
G-MVHS	Solar Wings Pegasus XL-Q	H. R. Block	
G-MVHT	Solar Wings Pegasus XL-Q	O. J. J. Rogers	
G-MVHU	Solar Wings Pegasus XL-Q	Solar Wings Ltd	
G-MVHV	Solar Wings Pegasus XL-Q	R. Jenkins	
G-MVHW	Solar Wings Pegasus XL-Q	Solar Wings Ltd	
G-MVHX	Solar Wings Pegasus XL-Q	Solar Wings Ltd	
G-MVHY	Solar Wings Pegasus XL-Q	Solar Wings Ltd	
G-MVHZ	Hornet Dual Trainer	A. R. Hogg	
G-MVIA	Solar Wings Pegasus XL-R	S. C. Wintle	
G-MVIB	Mainair Gemini Flash IIA	LSA Systems Ltd	
G-MVIC	Mainair Gemini Flash IIA	W. A. Emmerson	
G-MVID	Aerial Arts Chaser S	D. W. Foreman	
G-MVIE	Aerial Arts Chaser S	T. M. Stiles	
G-MVIF	Medway Hybred 44XLR	E. Watson	
G-MVIG	CFM Shadow Srs B	M. P. & P. A. G. Harper	
G-MVIH	Mainair Gemini Flash IIA	J. H. Tope	
G-MVII	Hornet Dual Trainer	L. Mullin	
G-MVIJ	Hornet Dual Trainer	Templeward Ltd	
G-MVIK	Hornet Dual Trainer	Templeward Ltd	
G-MVIL	—	—	
G-MVIM	—	—	
G-MVIN	—	—	
G-MVIO	—	—	
G-MVIP	AMF Chevvron 232	Chilbolton Flying Club	
G-MVIR	Thruster TST Mk 1	Thruster Aircraft (UK) Ltd	
G-MVIS	Thruster TST Mk 1	Thruster Aircraft (UK) Ltd	
G-MVIT	Thruster TST Mk 1	Thruster Aircraft (UK) Ltd	
G-MVIU	Thruster TST Mk 1	Thruster Aircraft (UK) Ltd	
G-MVIV	Thruster TST Mk 1	Thruster Aircraft (UK) Ltd	
G-MVIW	Thruster TST Mk 1	Thruster Aircraft (UK) Ltd	
G-MVIX	Mainair Gemini Flash IIA	C. Laverty	
G-MVIY	Mainair Gemini Flash IIA	G. Brown	
G-MVIZ	Mainair Gemini Flash IIA	B. D. Godden	
G-MVJA	Mainair Gemini Flash IIA	Microflight Tuition & Sales Ltd	
G-MVJB	Mainair Gemini Flash IIA	M. M. Mason	
G-MVJC	Mainair Gemini Flash IIA	D. Clarke	
G-MVJD	Solar Wings Pegasus XL-R	A. Nichols	
G-MVJE	Mainair Gemini Flash IIA	S. J. Whistance	
G-MVJF	Aerial Arts Chaser S	B. R. Underwood	
G-MVJG	Aerial Arts Chaser S	P. Johnson	

Notes	Reg.	Type	Owner or Operator
	G-MVJH	Aerial Arts Chaser S	J. P. Wild
	G-MVJI	Aerial Arts Chaser S	P. M. Dewhurst
	G-MVJJ	Aerial Arts Chaser S	Aerotech International Ltd
	G-MVJK	Aerial Arts Chaser S	Aerotech International Ltd
	G-MVJL	Mainair Gemini Flash IIA	P. G. Woodcock
	G-MVJM	Microflight Spectrum	Microflight Aircraft Ltd
	G-MVJN	Solar Wings Pegasus XL-Q	J. W. Wall
	G-MVJO	Solar Wings Pegasus XL-Q	Solar Wings Ltd
	G-MVJP	Solar Wings Pegasus XL-Q	Solar Wings Ltd
	G-MVJR	Solar Wings Pegasus XL-Q	I. D. Rutherford
	G-MVJS	Solar Wings Pegasus XL-Q	Solar Wings Ltd
	G-MVJT	Solar Wings Pegasus XL-Q	Solar Wings Ltd
	G-MVJU	Solar Wings Pegasus XL-Q	Solar Wings Ltd
	G-MVJV	Solar Wings Pegasus XL-Q	Solar Wings Ltd
	G-MVJW	Solar Wings Pegasus XL-Q	Solar Wings Ltd
	G-MVJX	Solar Wings Pegasus XL-Q	Solar Wings Ltd
	G-MVJY	Hornet Dual Trainer	Templeward Ltd
	G-MVJZ	Birdman Cherokee	N. E. Birch
	G-MVKA	Medway Hybred 44XLR	A. R. Wells
	G-MVKB	—	
	G-MVKC	Mainair Gemini Flash IIA	M. J. Trevillion
	G-MVKD	Solar Wings Pegasus XL-R	Solar Wings Ltd
	G-MVKE	Solar Wings Pegasus XL-R	Solar Wings Ltd
	G-MVKF	Solar Wings Pegasus XL-R	Solar Wings Ltd
	G-MVKG	Solar Wings Pegasus XL-R	Solar Wings Ltd
	G-MVKH	Solar Wings Pegasus XL-R	Solar Wings Ltd
	G-MVKI	Solar Wings Pegasus XL-R	Solar Wings Ltd
	G-MVKJ	Solar Wings Pegasus XL-R	Solar Wings Ltd
	G-MVKK	Solar Wings Pegasus XL-R	Solar Wings Ltd
	G-MVKL	Solar Wings Pegasus XL-R	Solar Wings Ltd
	G-MVKM	Solar Wings Pegasus XL-R	Solar Wings Ltd
	G-MVKN	Solar Wings Pegasus XL-Q	Solar Wings Ltd
	G-MVKO	Solar Wings Pegasus XL-Q	Solar Wings Ltd
	G-MVKP	Solar Wings Pegasus XL-Q	Solar Wings Ltd
	G-MVKR	Solar Wings Pegasus XL-Q	Solar Wings Ltd
	G-MVKS	Solar Wings Pegasus XL-Q	Solar Wings Ltd
	G-MVKT	Solar Wings Pegasus XL-Q	Solar Wings Ltd
	G-MVKU	Solar Wings Pegasus XL-Q	Solar Wings Ltd
	G-MVKV	Solar Wings Pegasus XL-Q	Solar Wings Ltd
	G-MVKW	Solar Wings Pegasus XL-Q	Solar Wings Ltd
	G-MVKX	Solar Wings Pegasus XL-Q	Solar Wings Ltd
	G-MVKY	Aerial Arts Chaser S	A. L. Rogers
	G-MVKZ	Aerial Arts Chaser S	R. J. Garland
	G-MVLA	Aerial Arts Chaser S	R. Thorpe
	G-MVLB	Aerial Arts Chaser S	C. R. Read
	G-MVLC	Aerial Arts Chaser S	B. R. Barnes
	G-MVLD	Aerial Arts Chaser S	T. G. Elmhirst
	G-MVLE	Aerial Arts Chaser S	D. G. Hill
	G-MVLF	—	
	G-MVLG	Aerial Arts Chaser S	D. Little
	G-MVLH	Aerial Arts Chaser S	P. J. D. Kerr
	G-MVLI	—	—
	G-MVLJ	—	—
	G-MVLK	Hornet RS	Templeward Ltd
	G-MVLL	Mainair Gemini Flash IIA	L. E. Comben
	G-MVLM	Solar Wings Pegasus Bandit	Solar Wings Ltd
	G-MVLN	CFM Shadow Srs BD	CFM Metal-Fax Ltd
	G-MVLO	CFM Shadow Srs BD	CFM Metal-Fax Ltd
	G-MVLP	CFM Shadow Srs BD	CFM Metal-Fax Ltd
	G-MVLR	Mainair Gemini Flash IIA	K. Akister
	G-MVLS	—	—
	G-MVLT	Aerial Arts Chaser S	C. R. Thorne
	G-MVLU	Aerial Arts Chaser S	M. J. Aubrey
	G-MVLV	—	—
	G-MVLW	Aerial Arts Chaser S	J. C. Goodchild
	G-MVLX	Solar Wings Pegasus XL-Q	Solar Wings Ltd
	G-MVLY	Solar Wings Pegasus XL-Q	Solar Wings Ltd
	G-MVLZ	Solar Wings Pegasus XL-Q	Solar Wings Ltd
	G-MVMA	Solar Wings Pegasus XL-Q	Solar Wings Ltd
	G-MVMB	Solar Wings Pegasus XL-Q	Solar Wings Ltd
	G-MVMC	Solar Wings Pegasus XL-Q	Solar Wings Ltd
	G-MVMD	Powerchute Raider	Powerchute Systems International Ltd
	G-MVME	Thruster TST Mk 1	Thruster Aircraft (UK) Ltd
	G-MVMF	—	—

Reg.	Type	Owner or Operator	Notes
G-MVMG	Thruster TST Mk 1	Thruster Aircraft (UK) Ltd	
G-MVMH	Thruster TST Mk 1	Thruster Aircraft (UK) Ltd	
G-MVMI	Thruster TST Mk 1	Thruster Aircraft (UK) Ltd	
G-MVMJ	Thruster TST Mk 1	Thruster Aircraft (UK) Ltd	
G-MVMK	Medway Hybred 44XLR	D. J. Lewis	
G-MVML	Aerial Arts Chaser S	P. R. Leach	
G-MVMM	—	—	
G-MVMN	—	—	
G-MVMO	Mainair Gemini Flash IIA	R. C. Colclough	
G-MVMP	Eipper Quicksilver MXII	R. Daltrey	
G-MVMR	—	—	
G-MVMS	Mainair Razor	Mainair Sports Ltd	
G-MVMT	Mainair Gemini Flash IIA	Microflight Tuition & Sales Ltd	
G-MVMU	Mainair Gemini Flash IIA	Microflight Tuition & Sales Ltd	
G-MVMV	Mainair Gemini Flash IIA	Microflight Tuition & Sales Ltd	
G-MVMW	—	—	
G-MVMX	Mainair Gemini Flash IIA	F. L. James	
G-MVMY	Mainair Gemini Flash IIA	J. B. Hay	
G-MVMZ	Mainair Gemini Flash IIA	Microflight Tuition & Sales Ltd	
G-MWCR	Southdown Puma Sprint	P. N. Cruise	
G-MWEE	Solar Wings Pegasus XL-Q	Solar Wings Ltd	
G-MWFT	MBA Tiger Cub 440	W. F. Tremayne	
G-MWIZ	CFM Shadow Srs BD	CFM Metal-Fax Ltd	
G-MWOW	CFM Shadow Srs B	Global Aviation Projects Ltd	
G-MWPL	MBA Tiger Cub 440	P. A. Lee	
G-MWRS	Ultravia Super Pelican	Embermere Ltd	
G-MWTF	Mainair Gemini	G. D. C. Buyers	
G-MYKE	CFM Shadow Srs BD	M. Hughes	
G-MYNA	CFM Shadow Srs BD	N. H. Martin	
G-MYTH	CFM Shadow Srs BD	E. G. Shimmin	

Serial carried	Civil identity	Serial carried	Civil identity
2+1 (Luftwaffe)	G-SYFW	51-15227 (USN)	G-BKRA
8 (Luftwaffe)	G-WULF	607327 (09-L USAAF)	G-ARAO
14 (Luftwaffe)	G-BJAX	A16-199 (SF-R RAAF)	G-BEOX
17 (Luftwaffe)	G-ATBG	A8226	G-BIDW
26 (US)	G-BAVO	B1807	G-EAVX
45 (Aeronavale)	G-BHFG	B4863	G-BLXT
75	G-AFDX	B6401	G-AWYY
88 (USN)	G-BKCK	B7270	G-BFCZ
92 (Moroccan AF)	G-BJGW	C4912	G-BLWM
120 (Fr AF)	G-AZGC	D88	G-AWXZ
152/17	G-ATJM	D5397/17	G-BFXL
164 (USN)	G-BKGL	C1904	G-PFAP
168	G-BFDE	D7889	G-AANM
177 (Irish AC)	G-BLIW	D8096 (D)	G-AEPH
178 (Irish AC)	G-BKOS	E-15 (RNethAF)	G-BIYU
385 (RCAF)	G-BGPB	E449	G-EBJE
422-15	G-AVJO	EM-01 (Spanish AF)	G-AAOR
425/17	G-BEFR	E6452	G-AXNW
1076	G-AVEB	F141	G-SEVA
2345	G-ATVP	F235	G-BMDB
2807 (VE-111 USN)	G-BHTH	F904	G-EBIA
3066	G-AETA	F938	G-EBIC
4253/18	G-BFPL	F939 (6)	G-EBIB
5964	G-BFVH	F943	G-BIHF
7198/18	G-AANJ	F943	G-BKDT
7797 (USAAF)	G-BFAF	F1425 (17)	G-BEFR
8449M	G-ASWJ	F5447 (N)	G-BKER
18393 (C.A.F.)	G-BCYK	F5459	G-INNY
30210	N9455Z	F8010	G-BDWJ
54137 (USN)	G-CTKL	F8614	G-AWAU
56321 (U-AB RNorAF)	G-BKPY	G-48-1 (Class B)	G-ALSX
88297	N8297	H2311	G-ABAA
115042 (TA-042 USAF)	G-BGHU	H5199	G-ADEV
115302 (TP USAAF)	G-BJTP	J9941 (57)	G-ABMR
18-2001 (USAAF)	G-BIZV	— (K-33 USAAF)	G-BJLH
121714	NX700HL	K1786	G-AFTA
133722	NX1337A	K1930	G-BKBB
226671 (USAAF)	N47DD	K2050	G-ASCM
231983 (USAAF)	F-BDRS	K2059	G-PFAR
236800 (A-44 USAAF)	G-BHPK	K2060	G-BKZM
315509 (USAAF)	G-BHUB	K2567	G-MOTH
329417 (USAAF)	G-BDHK	K2568	G-APMM
329471 (F-44 USAAF)	G-BGXA	K2572	G-AOZH
329601 (D-44 USAAF)	G-AXHR	K3215	G-AHSA
329854 (A-72 USAAF)	G-BMKC	K3731	G-RODI
329934 (B-72 USAAF)	G-BCPH	K4235	G-AHMJ
330485 (C-44 USAAF)	G-AJES	K5414	G-AENP
413048 (E-39 USAAF)	G-BCXJ	L2301	G-AIZG
429366 (USAAF)	N9115Z	L8032	G-AMRK
430823	N1042B	N1854	G-AIBE
454537 (J-04 USAAF)	G-BFDL	N3788	G-AKPF
454467 (J-44 USAAF)	G-BILI	N4877 (VX-F)	G-AMDA
461748	G-BHDK	N5180	G-EBKY
463221 (G4-5 USAAF)	N51JJ	N5182	G-APUP
472216 HO-L USAAF)	G-BIXL	N5195	G-ABOX
479766 (USAAF)	G-BKHG	N6452	G-BIAU
480015 (USAAF)	G-AKIB	N6466	G-ANKZ
480133 (B-44 USAAF)	G-BDCD	N6532	G-ANTS
480321 (H-44 USAAF)	G-FRAN	N6847	G-APAL
480480 (USAAF)	G-BECN	N6848	G-BALX
485784 (YB-E)	G-BEDF	N6985	G-AHMN
44-73149	NL314BG	N9191	G-ALND
44-79609 (PR USAAF)	G-BHXY	N9238	G-ANEL
44-80594 (USAAF)	G-BEDJ	N9389	G-ANJA
44-83184	G-RGUS	N9510	G-AOEL
511371 (USAAF VF-S)	NL1051S	P6382	G-AJRS
542447	G-SCUB	R-163 (RNethAF)	G-BIRH
542457	G-LION	R1914	G-AHUJ
542474 (R-184)	G-PCUB	R4907	G-ANCS

Serial carried	Civil Identity	Serial carried	Civil Identity
R4959	G-ARAZ	MV154	G-BKMI
R5086	G-APIH	MV293	G-SPIT
S1287	G-BEYB	MV370 (AV-L)	G-FXIV
S3398 (2)	G-BFYO	MW100	G-AGNV
T5424	G-AJOA	NF875 (603/CH)	G-AGTM
T5493	G-ANEF	NH238 (D-A)	G-MKIX
T5672	G-ALRI	NJ695	G-AJXV
T5854	G-ANKK	NJ703	G-AKPI
T5879	G-AXBW	NP181	G-AOAR
T6099	G-AOGR	NP184	G-ANYP
T6313	G-AHVU	NP303	G-ANZJ
T6645	G-AIIZ	NX611	G-ASXX
T6818	G-ANKT	PG617	G-AYVY
T7281	G-ARTL	PL983	G-PRXI
T7404	G-ANMV	PT462	G-CTIX
T7909	G-ANON	RG333	G-AIEK
T7997	G-AOBH	RG333	G-AKEZ
T9707	G-AKKR	RH377	G-ALAH
T9738	G-AKAT	RL962	G-AHED
U-0247	G-AGOY	RM221	G-ANXR
U-142 (Swiss AF)	G-BONE	RM689 (MN-E)	G-ALGT
V3388	G-AHTW	RR299 (HT-E)	G-ASKH
V9281 (RU-M)	G-BCWL	RT486	G-AJGJ
V9441 (AR-A)	G-AZWT	RT520	G-ALYB
W5856	G-BMGC	SM832	G-WWII
Z2033	G-ASTL	SM969	G-BRAF
Z7015	G-BKTH	TA634	G-AWJV
Z7197	G-AKZN	TA719	G-ASKC
Z7258	G-AHGD	TE566	G-BLCK
AP507 (KX-P)	G-ACWP	TJ569	G-AKOW
AR213 (PR-D)	G-AIST	TW439	G-ANRP
AR501 (NN-D)	G-AWII	TW467	G-ANIE
BS676 (K-U)	G-KUKU	TW536	G-BNGE
DE208	G-AGYU	TW591	G-ARIH
DE363	G-ANFC	TW641	G-ATDN
DE623	G-ANFI	VF516	G-ASMZ
DE992	G-AXXV	VF548	G-ASEG
DF128 (RCO-U)	G-AOJJ	VI-3 (Finnish AF)	G-BAAY
DF155	G-ANFV	VL348	G-AVVO
DF198	G-BBRB	VL349	G-AWSA
DG590	G-ADMW	VM360	G-APHV
DR613	G-AFJB	VP955	G-DVON
EE606	G-MKVC	VP962	G-BLRB
EM903	G-APBI	VR192	G-APIT
EX280	G-TEAC	VR249	G-APIY
EZ259	G-BMJW	VS356	G-AOLU
FE992	G-BDAM	VS610	G-AOKL
FH153	G-BBHK	VS623	G-AOKZ
FR870	NL1009N	VX118	G-ASNB
FS728	G-BAFM	VZ728	G-AGOS
FT239	G-BIWX	WA576	G-ALSS
FT391	G-AZBN	WA577	G-ALST
FX301 (FD-NQ)	G-JUDI	WB533	G-DEVN
HB275	N5063N	WB585 (RCU-X)	G-AOSY
HB751	G-BCBL	WB588 (D)	G-AOTD
HD368 (VO-A)	G-BKXW	WB660	G-ARMB
JV928 (Y)	G-BLSC	WB763	G-BBMR
KB976 (LQ-K)	G-BCOH	WD305	G-ARGG
KG874 (YS-L)	G-DAKS	WD363 (5)	G-BCIH
KL161	N88972	WD379 (K)	G-APLO
LB294	G-AHWJ	WD413	G-BFIR
LB312	G-AHXE	WE569	G-ASAJ
LB375	G-AHGW	WG307	G-BCYJ
LF858	G-BLUZ	WG316	G-BCAH
LZ766	G-ALCK	WG348	G-BBMV
MD497	G-ANLW	WG350	G-BPAL
MH434	G-ASJV	WG422 (16)	G-BFAX
MJ627	G-BMSB	WG719	G-BRMA
MJ730 (GN-F)	G-BLAS	WJ237 (113/O)	G-BLTG
ML407 (OU-V)	G-LFIX	WJ288 (029)	G-SALY
ML417 (2I-T)	G-BJSG	WJ358	G-ARYD
MP425	G-AITB		
MT438	G-AREI		
MT719	G-VIII		

Serial carried	Civil Identity	Serial carried	Civil Identity
WJ945	G-BEDV	XL426	G-VJET
WK522	G-BCOU	XL502	G-BMYP
WK611	G-ARWB	XL717	G-AOXG
WK622	G-BCZH	XL809	G-BLIX
WL626	G-BHDD	XL929	G-BNPU
WM167	G-LOSM	XM553	G-AWSV
WP321 (750/CU)	G-BRFC	XM556	G-HELI
WP788	G-BCHL	XM575	G-BLMC
WP790	G-BBNC	XM655	G-VULC
WP808	G-BDEU	XM685	G-AYZJ
WP857 (24)	G-BDRJ	XN351	G-BKSC
WP903	G-BCGC	XN435	G-BGBU
WP971	G-ATHD	XN437	G-AXWA
WP977	G-BHRD	XN441	G-BGKT
WR410	G-BLKA	XN637	G-BKOU
WT933	G-ALSW	XP279	G-BWKK
WV198	G-BJWY	XP282	G-BGTC
WV493	G-BDYG	XP328	G-BKHC
WV686	G-BLFT	XP355	G-BEBC
WV783	G-ALSP	XR240	G-BDFH
WW397 (N-E)	G-BKHP	XR241	G-AXRR
WZ507	G-VTII	XR267	G-BJXR
WZ662	G-BKVK	XR269	G-BDXY
WZ711	G-AVHT	XR363	G-OHCA
WZ868 (H)	G-BCIW	XR944	G-ATTB
XB733	G-ATBF	XS101	G-GNAT
XF690	G-BGKA	XT788 (442)	G-BMIR
XF785	G-ALBN	A1+BT	G-APRR
XF836 (J-G)	G-AWRY	F+IS (Luftwaffe)	G-BIRW
XF877 (JX)	G-AWVF	BU+CK (Luftwaffe)	G-BUCK
XG452	G-BRMB	1Z+EK (Luftwaffe)	N9012P
XG547	G-HAPR	RF+16 (Luftwaffe)	G-PTWO
XJ348	G-NAVY	N7+AA (Luftwaffe)	G-BFHF
XJ389	G-AJJP	ZA+WN (Luftwaffe)	G-AZMH
XJ763	G-BKHA	00 (Russian AF)	G-KYAK
XK417	G-AVXY	CE (USAAF)	G-BICE
XK896	G-RNAS		

Overseas Airliner Registrations

(Aircraft included in this section are those most likely to be seen at UK and major European airports on scheduled or charter services.)

A6 (United Arab Emirates)

Reg.	Type	Owner or Operator	Notes
A6-EKA	Airbus A.310-304	Emirate Airlines	
A6-EKB	Airbus A.310-304	Emirate Airlines	
A6-EKC	Airbus A.300-603R	Emirate Airlines	
A6-	Airbus A.300-603R	Emirate Airlines	

A40 (Oman)

A40-TP	L-1011-385 TriStar 100 (110)	Gulf Air	
A40-TR	L-1011-385 TriStar 100 (111)	Gulf Air	
A40-TS	L-1011-385 TriStar 100 (109)	Gulf Air	
A40-TT	L-1011-385 TriStar 200 (107)	Gulf Air	
A40-TV	L-1011-385 TriStar 200 (108)	Gulf Air	
A40-TW	L-1011-385 TriStar 200 (101)	Gulf Air	
A40-TX	L-1011-385 TriStar 200 (102)	Gulf Air	
A40-TY	L-1011-385 TriStar 200 (103)	Gulf Air	
A40-TZ	L-1011-385 TriStar 200 (104)	Gulf Air	
A40-GF	Boeing 767-3P6ER (601)	Gulf Air	
A40-GG	Boeing 767-3P6ER (602)	Gulf Air	
A40-GH	Boeing 767-3P6ER	Gulf Air	
A40-GI	Boeing 767-3P6ER	Gulf Air	
A40-GJ	Boeing 767-3P6ER	Gulf Air	
A40-GK	Boeing 767-3P6ER	Gulf Air	

Note: Gulf Air also operates TriStar 200s N92TA (105) and N92TB (106).

AP (Pakistan)

AP-AXA	Boeing 707-340C	Pakistan International Airlines	
AP-AXG	Boeing 707-340C	Pakistan International Airlines	
AP-AYV	Boeing 747-282B	Pakistan International Airlines	
AP-AYW	Boeing 747-282B	Pakistan International Airlines	
AP-AZW	Boeing 707-351B	Pakistan International Airlines	
AP-BAA	Boeing 707-351B	Pakistan International Airlines	
AP-BAK	Boeing 747-240B (SCD)	Pakistan International Airlines	
AP-BAT	Boeing 747-240B (SCD)	Pakistan International Airlines	
AP-BBK	Boeing 707-323C	Pakistan International Airlines	
AP-BCL	Boeing 747-217B	Pakistan International Airlines	
AP-BCM	Boeing 747-217B	Pakistan International Airlines	
AP-BCN	Boeing 747-217B	Pakistan International Airlines	
AP-BCO	Boeing 747-217B	Pakistan International Airlines	

B (China/Taiwan)

B-160	Boeing 747-209F	China Airlines	
B-198	Boeing 747-2R7F (SCD)	China Airlines	
B-1862	Boeing 747SP-09	China Airlines	
B-1864	Boeing 747-209B (SCD)	China Airlines	
B-1866	Boeing 747-209B	China Airlines	
B-1880	Boeing 747SP-09	China Airlines	
B-1886	Boeing 747-209B	China Airlines	
B-1888	Boeing 747-209B	China Airlines	
B-1894	Boeing 747-209F (SCD)	China Airlines	

Notes	Reg.	Type	Owner or Operator
	B-	Boeing 747-409	China Airlines
	B-	Boeing 747-409	China Airlines
	B-	Boeing 747-409	China Airlines
	B-2402	Boeing 707-3J6B	CAAC
	B-2404	Boeing 707-3J6B	CAAC
	B-2406	Boeing 707-3J6B	CAAC
	B-2408	Boeing 707-3J6B	CAAC
	B-2410	Boeing 707-3J6C	CAAC
	B-2412	Boeing 707-3J6C	CAAC
	B-2414	Boeing 707-3J6C	CAAC
	B-2416	Boeing 707-3J6C	CAAC
	B-2418	Boeing 707-3J6C	CAAC
	B-2420	Boeing 707-3J6C	CAAC
	B-2442	Boeing 747SP-J6	CAAC
	B-2444	Boeing 747SP-J6	CAAC
	B-2446	Boeing 747-2J6B (SCD)	CAAC
	B-2448	Boeing 747-2J6B (SCD)	CAAC
	B-2450	Boeing 747-2J6B	CAAC
	B-2452	Boeing 747SP-J6	CAAC
	B-2456	Boeing 747-4J6	CAAC
	B-2458	Boeing 747-4J6	CAAC
	B-2460	Boeing 747-4J6	CAAC

Note: CAAC also operates Boeing 747SP N1301E. China Airlines operates N4508H and N4522V, both Boeing 747SP-09s.

C5 (Gambia)

Note: Gambia Airways operates one Boeing 707 on lease.

C9 (Mozambique)

Note: Lineas Aereas de Mocambique (LAM) operates DC-10-30 F-GDJK on lease from UTA.

C-F and C-G (Canada)

	C-FBEF	Boeing 767-233ER (617)	Air Canada
	C-FBEG	Boeing 767-233ER (618)	Air Canada
	C-FBEM	Boeing 767-233ER (619)	Air Canada
	C-F	Boeing 767-233ER	Air Canada
	C-F	Boeing 767-233ER	Air Canada
	C-F	Boeing 767-233ER	Air Canada
	C-FCMV	Douglas DC-8-53	Minerve Canada (F-GEDM leased)
	C-FCPO	Douglas DC-8-63 (801)	Worldways Canada
	C-FCPP	Douglas DC-8-63 (802)	Worldways Canada
	C-FCPQ	Douglas DC-8-63 (803)	Worldways Canada
	C-FCPS	Douglas DC-8-63 (804)	Worldways Canada
	C-FCRA	Douglas DC-10-30 (909)	Canadian Airlines International Empress of Hong Kong
	C-FCRB	Douglas DC-10-30 (910)	Canadian Airlines International Empress of Tokyo
	C-FCRD	Douglas DC-10-30 (912)	Canadian Airlines International Empress of Lisbon
	C-FCRE	Douglas DC-10-30 (911)	Canadian Airlines International Empress of Canada
	C-FDJC	Boeing 747-1D1 (399)	Wardair Canada Phil Garrett
	C-FFUN	Boeing 747-1D1 (398)	Wardair Canada Romeo Vachan
	C-FGWD	Airbus A.310-304 (803)	Wardair Canada G. Lewie Leigh
	C-FHWD	Airbus A.310-304 (804)	Wardair Canada Don C. Braun
	C-FNWD	Airbus A.310-304 (805)	Wardair Canada Jack Moar
	C-FPCA	Boeing 767-357ER	Canadian Airlines International
	C-FSWD	Airbus A.310-304 (801)	Wardair Canada A. M. 'Matt' Berry
	C-FTCA	Boeing 767-357ER	Canadian Airlines International
	C-FTIK	Douglas DC-8-73AF (867)	Air Canada
	C-FTIO	Douglas DC-8-73AF (871)	Air Canada
	C-FTIP	Douglas DC-8-73AF (872)	Air Canada
	C-FTIQ	Douglas DC-8-73AF (873)	Air Canada
	C-FTIR	Douglas DC-8-73AF (874)	Air Canada

Reg.	Type	Owner or Operator	Notes
C-FTIS	Douglas DC-8-73AF (875)	Air Canada	
C-FTIU	Douglas DC-8-73AF (876)	Air Canada	
C-FTIV	Douglas DC-8-73AF (877)	Air Canada	
C-FTNA	L.1011-385 TriStar 1	Air Transat	
C-FTNC	L.1011-385 TriStar 1	Air Transat	
C-FTNH	L.1011-385 TriStar 1 (508)	Air Canada	
C-FTNI	L.1011-385 TriStar 100 (509)	Air Canada	
C-FTNJ	L.1011-385 TriStar 100 (510)	Air Canada	
C-FTNK	L.1011-385 TriStar 100 (511)	Air Canada	
C-FTNL	L.1011-385 TriStar 100 (512)	Air Canada	
C-FTOB	Boeing 747-133 (302)	Wardair Canada H. A. 'Doc' Oakes	
C-FTOC	Boeing 747-133 (303)	Air Canada	
C-FTOD	Boeing 747-133 (304)	Air Canada	
C-FTOE	Boeing 747-133 (305)	Air Canada	
C-FWDX	Airbus A.310-304 (802)	Wardair Canada H. W. 'Harry' Hayter	
C-FZWD	Airbus A.310-304 (813)	Wardair Canada Herbert Hollick-Kenyon	
C-GAGA	Boeing 747-233B (306)	Air Canada	
C-GAGB	Boeing 747-233B (307)	Air Canada	
C-GAGC	Boeing 747-238B (308)	Air Canada	
C-GAGF	L.1011-385 TriStar 500 (551)	Air Canada	
C-GAGG	L.1011-385 TriStar 500 (552)	Air Canada	
C-GAGH	L.1011-385 TriStar 500 (553)	Air Canada	
C-GAGI	L.1011-385 TriStar 500 (554)	Air Canada	
C-GAGJ	L.1011-385 TriStar 500 (555)	Air Canada	
C-GAGK	L.1011-385 TriStar 500 (556)	Air Canada	
C-GAUY	Boeing 767-233 (609)	Air Canada	
C-GAVC	Boeing 767-233ER (611)	Air Canada	
C-GAVF	Boeing 767-233ER (612)	Air Canada	
C-GBWD	Airbus A.310-304 (806)	Wardair Canada C. C. 'Carl' Agar	
C-GCPC	Douglas DC-10-30 (901)	Canadian Airlines International Empress of Amsterdam	
C-GCPD	Douglas DC-10-30 (902)	Canadian Airlines International Empress of British Colombia	
C-GCPE	Douglas DC-10-30ER (903)	Canadian Airlines International Empress of Buenos Aires	
C-GCPF	Douglas DC-10-30ER (904)	Canadian Airlines International Empress of Santiago	
C-GCPG	Douglas DC-10-30ER (905)	Canadian Airlines International Empress of Fiji	
C-GCPH	Douglas DC-10-30ER (906)	Canadian Airlines International Empress of Lima	
C-GCPI	Douglas DC-10-30ER (907)	Canadian Airlines International Empress of Auckland	
C-GCPJ	Douglas DC-10-30 (908)	Canadian Airlines International Empress of Rome	
C-GCWD	Airbus A.310-304 (807)	Wardair Canada G. W. C. 'Grant' McConachie	
C-GDSP	Boeing 767-233ER (613)	Air Canada	
C-GDSS	Boeing 767-233ER (614)	Air Canada	
C-GDSU	Boeing 767-233ER (615)	Air Canada	
C-GDSY	Boeing 767-233ER (616)	Air Canada	
C-GDWD	Airbus A.310-304 (808)	Wardair Canada T. 'Rusty' Baker	
C-GFHX	Douglas DC-10-30 (914)	Canadian Airlines International	
C-GIES	L.1011-385 TriStar 50 (101)	Worldways Canada	
C-GIFE	L.1011-385 TriStar 50 (102)	Worldways Canada	
C-GIWD	Airbus A.310-304 (809)	Wardair Canada S. R. 'Stan' McMillan	
C-GJWD	Airbus A.310-304 (810)	Wardair Canada Sheldon Luck	
C-GKWD	Airbus A.310-304 (811)	Wardair Canada W. R. 'Wop' May	
C-GLWD	Airbus A.310-304 (812)	Wardair Canada C. H. 'Punch' Dickens	
C-GMXB	Douglas DC-8-61 (801)	Nationair	
C-GMXD	Douglas DC-8-61 (805)	Nationair	
C-GMXL	Douglas DC-8-61	Nationair	
C-GMXQ	Douglas DC-8-61 (802)	Nationair	
C-GMXR	Douglas DC-8-62 (803)	Nationair	
C-GMXY	Douglas DC-8-62 (804)	Nationair	
C-GPWD	Airbus A.310-304 (814)	Wardair Canada Cy Becker	
C-GQBA	Douglas DC-8-63	Nationair	
C-GQBF	Douglas DC-8-63	Nationair	
C-G	Boeing 757-200	Odyssey International	
C-G	Boeing 757-200	Odyssey International	

Note: Airline fleet number carried on aircraft is shown in parenthesis.

213

CCCP (Russia)

All aircraft listed are operated by Aeroflot. The registrations are prefixed by CCCP in each case.

Notes	Reg.	Type	Notes	Reg.	Type
	65020	Tu-134A		65652	Tu-134A
	65024	Tu-134A		65653	Tu-134A
	65027	Tu-134A		65654	Tu-134A
	65028	Tu-134A		65655	Tu-134A
	65035	Tu-134A		65656	Tu-134A
	65036	Tu-134A		65657	Tu-134A
	65038	Tu-134A		65658	Tu-134A
	65040	Tu-134A		65659	Tu-134A
	65042	Tu-134A		65660	Tu-134A
	65044	Tu-134A		65661	Tu-134A
	65048	Tu-134A		65662	Tu-134A
	65050	Tu-134A		65663	Tu-134A
	65051	Tu-134A		65664	Tu-134A
	65076	Tu-134A		65665	Tu-134A
	65077	Tu-134A		65666	Tu-134A
	65087	Tu-134A		65667	Tu-134A
	65089	Tu-134A		65669	Tu-134A
	65107	Tu-134A		65681	Tu-134A
	65119	Tu-134A		65697	Tu-134A
	65134	Tu-134A		65717	Tu-134A-3
	65135	Tu-134A		65739	Tu-134A
	65145	Tu-134A		65757	Tu-134A
	65550	Tu-134A		65758	Tu-134A
	65551	Tu-134A		65765	Tu-134A
	65555	Tu-134A		65769	Tu-134A-3
	65601	Tu-134		65770	Tu-134A-3
	65602	Tu-134		65772	Tu-134A
	65603	Tu-134		65777	Tu-134A-3
	65604	Tu-134		65780	Tu-134A
	65605	Tu-134		65781	Tu-134A-3
	65606	Tu-134		65782	Tu-134A
	65607	Tu-134		65783	Tu-134A-3
	65608	Tu-134		65784	Tu-134A-3
	65609	Tu-134		65785	Tu-134A-3
	65610	Tu-134		65786	Tu-134A-3
	65611	Tu-134		65790	Tu-134A-3
	65612	Tu-134		65791	Tu-134A
	65613	Tu-134		65794	Tu-134A
	65614	Tu-134		65801	Tu-134A
	65615	Tu-134		65802	Tu-134A
	65616	Tu-134		65803	Tu-134A
	65617	Tu-134		65815	Tu-134A
	65618	Tu-134		65837	Tu-134A
	65619	Tu-134		65851	Tu-134A
	65620	Tu-134		65854	Tu-134A
	65621	Tu-134		65862	Tu-134A
	65625	Tu-134		65864	Tu-134A
	65627	Tu-134		65872	Tu-134A
	65628	Tu-134		65888	Tu-134A
	65629	Tu-134		65892	Tu-134A
	65630	Tu-134M		65894	Tu-134A
	65631	Tu-134		65904	Tu-134A
	65632	Tu-134M		65911	Tu-134A
	65633	Tu-134M		65912	Tu-134A-3
	65634	Tu-134		65915	Tu-134A
	65635	Tu-134M		65916	Tu-134A
	65636	Tu-134		65919	Tu-134A
	65637	Tu-134		65951	Tu-134A
	65639	Tu-134		65953	Tu-134A
	65642	Tu-134		65954	Tu-134A
	65643	Tu-134		65955	Tu-134A
	65644	Tu-134M		65965	Tu-134A
	65645	Tu-134A		65967	Tu-134A
	65646	Tu-134M		65971	Tu-134A
	65647	Tu-134M		65972	Tu-134A
	65648	Tu-134M		65973	Tu-134A
	65649	Tu-134M		65974	Tu-134A
	65650	Tu-134A		65976	Tu-134A
	65651	Tu-134A		85001	Tu-154

Reg.	Type	Notes	Reg.	Type	Notes
85002	Tu-154		85090	Tu-154A	
85003	Tu-154		85091	Tu-154A	
85004	Tu-154		85092	Tu-154B-1	
85005	Tu-154		85093	Tu-154A	
85006	Tu-154		85094	Tu-154A	
85007	Tu-154		85096	Tu-154B-2	
85008	Tu-154		85097	Tu-154B-1	
85009	Tu-154		85098	Tu-154A	
85010	Tu-154		85099	Tu-154A	
85011	Tu-154		85100	Tu-154A	
85012	Tu-154		85101	Tu-154A	
85013	Tu-154		85102	Tu-154A	
85014	Tu-154		85103	Tu-154A	
85015	Tu-154		85104	Tu-154A	
85016	Tu-154		85105	Tu-154A	
85017	Tu-154		85106	Tu-154B-2	
85018	Tu-154		85107	Tu-154A	
85019	Tu-154		85108	Tu-154A	
85020	Tu-154		85109	Tu-154B-1	
85021	Tu-154		85110	Tu-154A	
85022	Tu-154		85111	Tu-154A	
85024	Tu-154		85112	Tu-154A	
85025	Tu-154		85113	Tu-154A	
85028	Tu-154		85114	Tu-154A	
85029	Tu-154		85115	Tu-154A	
85030	Tu-154		85116	Tu-154A	
85031	Tu-154		85117	Tu-154A	
85032	Tu-154		85118	Tu-154B	
85033	Tu-154		85119	Tu-154A	
85034	Tu-154		85120	Tu-154B	
85037	Tu-154		85121	Tu-154B	
85038	Tu-154		85122	Tu-154B	
85039	Tu-154		85123	Tu-154B	
85040	Tu-154		85124	Tu-154B	
85041	Tu-154		85125	Tu-154B	
85042	Tu-154		85129	Tu-154B	
85043	Tu-154		85130	Tu-154B	
85044	Tu-154		85131	Tu-154B	
85049	Tu-154		85132	Tu-154B	
85050	Tu-154		85133	Tu-154B	
85051	Tu-154		85134	Tu-154B	
85052	Tu-154		85135	Tu-154B	
85055	Tu-154		85136	Tu-154B	
85056	Tu-154		85137	Tu-154B	
85057	Tu-154		85138	Tu-154B	
85059	Tu-154A		85139	Tu-154B	
85060	Tu-154A		85140	Tu-154B	
85061	Tu-154A		85141	Tu-154B	
85062	Tu-154C		85142	Tu-154B	
85063	Tu-154C		85143	Tu-154B	
85064	Tu-154A		85145	Tu-154B	
85065	Tu-154A		85146	Tu-154B	
85066	Tu-154A		85147	Tu-154B	
85067	Tu-154C		85148	Tu-154B	
85068	Tu-154B		85149	Tu-154B	
85069	Tu-154A		85150	Tu-154B	
85070	Tu-154A		85151	Tu-154B	
85071	Tu-154A		85152	Tu-154B	
85072	Tu-154A		85153	Tu-154B	
85074	Tu-154A		85154	Tu-154B	
85075	Tu-154B		85155	Tu-154B	
85076	Tu-154A		85156	Tu-154B	
85078	Tu-154A		85157	Tu-154B	
85079	Tu-154A		85158	Tu-154B	
85080	Tu-154A		85160	Tu-154B	
85081	Tu-154C		85162	Tu-154B	
85082	Tu-154A		85163	Tu-154B	
85083	Tu-154A		85164	Tu-154B	
85084	Tu-154A		85165	Tu-154B	
85085	Tu-154A		85166	Tu-154B	
85086	Tu-154A		85167	Tu-154B	
85087	Tu-154A		85168	Tu-154B	
85088	Tu-154A		85169	Tu-154B	
85089	Tu-154A		85170	Tu-154B	

Notes	Reg.	Type	Notes	Reg.	Type
	85171	Tu-154B		85251	Tu-154B-1
	85172	Tu-154B		85252	Tu-154B-1
	85173	Tu-154B		85253	Tu-154B-1
	85174	Tu-154B		85255	Tu-154B-1
	85176	Tu-154B		85256	Tu-154B-1
	85177	Tu-154B		85257	Tu-154B-1
	85178	Tu-154B		85259	Tu-154B-1
	85179	Tu-154B		85260	Tu-154B-1
	85180	Tu-154B		85261	Tu-154B-1
	85181	Tu-154B		85263	Tu-154B-1
	85182	Tu-154B		85264	Tu-154B-1
	85183	Tu-154B		85265	Tu-154B-1
	85184	Tu-154B		85266	Tu-154B-1
	85185	Tu-154B		85267	Tu-154B-1
	85186	Tu-154B		85268	Tu-154B-1
	85187	Tu-154B		85269	Tu-154B-1
	85188	Tu-154B		85270	Tu-154B-1
	85189	Tu-154B		85271	Tu-154B-1
	85190	Tu-154B		85272	Tu-154B-1
	85191	Tu-154B		85273	Tu-154B-1
	85192	Tu-154B		85274	Tu-154B-1
	85193	Tu-154B		85275	Tu-154B-1
	85194	Tu-154B		85276	Tu-154B-1
	85195	Tu-154B		85277	Tu-154B-1
	85196	Tu-154B		85279	Tu-154B-1
	85197	Tu-154B		85280	Tu-154B-1
	85198	Tu-154B		85281	Tu-154B-1
	85199	Tu-154B		85282	Tu-154B-1
	85200	Tu-154B		85283	Tu-154B-1
	85201	Tu-154B		85284	Tu-154B-1
	85202	Tu-154B		85285	Tu-154B-1
	85203	Tu-154B		85286	Tu-154B-1
	85204	Tu-154B		85287	Tu-154B-1
	85205	Tu-154B		85288	Tu-154B-1
	85206	Tu-154B		85289	Tu-154B-1
	85207	Tu-154B		85290	Tu-154B-1
	85210	Tu-154B		85291	Tu-154B-1
	85211	Tu-154B		85292	Tu-154B-1
	85212	Tu-154B		85293	Tu-154B-1
	85213	Tu-154B		85294	Tu-154B-1
	85214	Tu-154B		85295	Tu-154B-1
	85215	Tu-154B		85296	Tu-154B-1
	85216	Tu-154B		85297	Tu-154B-1
	85217	Tu-154B		85298	Tu-154B-1
	85218	Tu-154B		85299	Tu-154B-1
	85219	Tu-154B		85300	Tu-154B-2
	85220	Tu-154B		85301	Tu-154B-2
	85221	Tu-154B		85302	Tu-154B-2
	85222	Tu-154B		85303	Tu-154B-2
	85223	Tu-154B		85304	Tu-154B-2
	85226	Tu-154B		85305	Tu-154B-2
	85227	Tu-154B		85306	Tu-154B-2
	85228	Tu-154B		85307	Tu-154B-2
	85229	Tu-154B-1		85308	Tu-154B-2
	85230	Tu-154B-1		85309	Tu-154B-2
	85231	Tu-154B-1		85310	Tu-154B-2
	85232	Tu-154B-1		85311	Tu-154B-2
	85233	Tu-154B-1		85312	Tu-154B-2
	85234	Tu-154B-1		85313	Tu-154B-2
	85235	Tu-154B-1		85314	Tu-154B-2
	85236	Tu-154B-1		85315	Tu-154B-2
	85237	Tu-154B-1		85316	Tu-154B-2
	85238	Tu-154B-1		85317	Tu-154M
	85240	Tu-154B-1		85318	Tu-154B-2
	85241	Tu-154B-1		85319	Tu-154B-2
	85242	Tu-154B-1		85321	Tu-154B-2
	85243	Tu-154B-1		85322	Tu-154B-2
	85244	Tu-154B-1		85323	Tu-154B-2
	85245	Tu-154B-1		85324	Tu-154B-2
	85246	Tu-154B-1		85327	Tu-154B-2
	85247	Tu-154B-1		85328	Tu-154B-2
	85248	Tu-154B-1		85329	Tu-154B-2
	85249	Tu-154B-1		85330	Tu-154B-2
	85250	Tu-1543-1		85331	Tu-154B-2

Reg.	Type	Notes	Reg.	Type	Notes
85332	Tu-154B-2		85409	Tu-154B-2	
85333	Tu-154B-2		85410	Tu-154B-2	
85334	Tu-154B-2		85411	Tu-154B-2	
85335	Tu-154B-2		85412	Tu-154B-2	
85336	Tu-154B-2		85414	Tu-154B-2	
85337	Tu-154B-2		85416	Tu-154B-2	
85338	Tu-154B-2		85417	Tu-154B-2	
85339	Tu-154B-2		85418	Tu-154B-2	
85340	Tu-154B-2		85419	Tu-154B-2	
85341	Tu-154B-2		85421	Tu-154B-2	
85343	Tu-154B-2		85423	Tu-154B-2	
85344	Tu-154B-2		85424	Tu-154B-2	
85346	Tu-154B-2		85425	Tu-154B-2	
85347	Tu-154B-2		85426	Tu-154B-2	
85348	Tu-154B-2		85427	Tu-154B-2	
85349	Tu-154B-2		85429	Tu-154B-2	
85350	Tu-154B-2		85430	Tu-154B-2	
85351	Tu-154B-2		85431	Tu-154B-2	
85352	Tu-154B-2		85432	Tu-154B-2	
85353	Tu-154B-2		85433	Tu-154B-2	
85354	Tu-154B-2		85434	Tu-154B-2	
85355	Tu-154B-2		85435	Tu-154B-2	
85356	Tu-154B-2		85436	Tu-154B-2	
85357	Tu-154B-2		85437	Tu-154B-2	
85358	Tu-154B-2		85438	Tu-154B-2	
85359	Tu-154B-2		85439	Tu-154B-2	
85360	Tu-154B-2		85440	Tu-154B-2	
85361	Tu-154B-2		85441	Tu-154B-2	
85362	Tu-154B-2		85442	Tu-154B-2	
85363	Tu-154B-2		85443	Tu-154B-2	
85364	Tu-154B-2		85444	Tu-154B-2	
85365	Tu-154B-2		85445	Tu-154B-2	
85366	Tu-154B-2		85446	Tu-154B-2	
85367	Tu-154B-2		85448	Tu-154B-2	
85368	Tu-154B-2		85449	Tu-154B-2	
85369	Tu-154B-2		85450	Tu-154B-2	
85370	Tu-154B-2		85451	Tu-154B-2	
85371	Tu-154B-2		85452	Tu-154B-2	
85372	Tu-154B-2		85453	Tu-154B-2	
85373	Tu-154B-2		85454	Tu-154B-2	
85374	Tu-154B-2		85455	Tu-154B-2	
85375	Tu-154B-2		85456	Tu-154B-2	
85376	Tu-154B-2		85457	Tu-154B-2	
85377	Tu-154B-2		85458	Tu-154B-2	
85378	Tu-154B-2		85459	Tu-154B-2	
85379	Tu-154B-2		85460	Tu-154B-2	
85380	Tu-154B-2		85461	Tu-154B-2	
85381	Tu-154B-2		85462	Tu-154B-2	
85382	Tu-154B-2		85463	Tu-154B-2	
85383	Tu-154B-2		85464	Tu-154B-2	
85384	Tu-154B-2		85465	Tu-154B-2	
85385	Tu-154B-2		85466	Tu-154B-2	
85386	Tu-154B-2		85467	Tu-154B-2	
85387	Tu-154B-2		85468	Tu-154B-2	
85388	Tu-154B-2		85469	Tu-154B-2	
85389	Tu-154B-2		85470	Tu-154B-2	
85390	Tu-154B-2		85471	Tu-154B-2	
85391	Tu-154B-2		85472	Tu-154B-2	
85392	Tu-154B-2		85475	Tu-154B-2	
85393	Tu-154B-2		85476	Tu-154B-2	
85394	Tu-154B-2		85477	Tu-154B-2	
85395	Tu-154B-2		85478	Tu-154B-2	
85396	Tu-154B-2		85479	Tu-154B-2	
85397	Tu-154B-2		85480	Tu-154B-2	
85398	Tu-154B-2		85481	Tu-154B-2	
85399	Tu-154B-2		85482	Tu-154B-2	
85400	Tu-154B-2		85485	Tu-154B-2	
85401	Tu-154B-2		85486	Tu-154B-2	
85402	Tu-154B-2		85487	Tu-154B-2	
85403	Tu-154B-2		85489	Tu-154B-2	
85404	Tu-154B-2		85490	Tu-154B-2	
85405	Tu-154B-2		85491	Tu-154B-2	
85406	Tu-154B-2		85492	Tu-154B-2	
85407	Tu-154B-2		85494	Tu-154B-2	

Notes	Reg.	Type	Notes	Reg.	Type
	85495	Tu-154B-2		85577	Tu-154B-2
	85496	Tu-154B-2		85578	Tu-154B-2
	85497	Tu-154B-2		85579	Tu-154B-2
	85498	Tu-154B-2		85580	Tu-154B-2
	85499	Tu-154B-2		85581	Tu-154B-2
	85500	Tu-154B-2		85582	Tu-154B-2
	85501	Tu-154B-2		85583	Tu-154B-2
	85502	Tu-154B-2		85584	Tu-154B-2
	85503	Tu-154B-2		85585	Tu-154B-2
	85504	Tu-154B-2		85586	Tu-154B-2
	85505	Tu-154B-2		85587	Tu-154B-2
	85506	Tu-154B-2		85588	Tu-154B-2
	85507	Tu-154B-2		85589	Tu-154B-2
	85508	Tu-154B-2		85590	Tu-154B-2
	85509	Tu-154B-2		85592	Tu-154B-2
	85510	Tu-154B-2		85594	Tu-154B-2
	85511	Tu-154B-2		85595	Tu-154B-2
	85512	Tu-154B-2		85596	Tu-154B-2
	85513	Tu-154B-2		85597	Tu-154B-2
	85514	Tu-154B-2		85598	Tu-154B-2
	85515	Tu-154B-2		85600	Tu-154B-2
	85516	Tu-154B-2		85601	Tu-154B-2
	85518	Tu-154B-2		85602	Tu-154B-2
	85519	Tu-154B-2		85604	Tu-154B-2
	85520	Tu-154B-2		85605	Tu-154B-2
	85521	Tu-154B-2		85606	Tu-154B-2
	85522	Tu-154B-2		85607	Tu-154B-2
	85523	Tu-154B-2		85608	Tu-154B-2
	85524	Tu-154B-2		85609	Tu-154M-2
	85525	Tu-154C-2		85610	Tu-154M
	85526	Tu-154B-2		85611	Tu-154M
	85527	Tu-154B-2		85612	Tu-154M
	85528	Tu-154B-2		85613	Tu-154M
	85529	Tu-154B-2		85614	Tu-154M
	85530	Tu-154B-2		85615	Tu-154M
	85532	Tu-154B-2		85616	Tu-154M
	85533	Tu-154B-2		85617	Tu-154M
	85534	Tu-154B-2		85618	Tu-154M
	85535	Tu-154B-2		85619	Tu-154M
	85536	Tu-154B-2		85620	Tu-154M
	85537	Tu-154B-2		85621	Tu-154M
	85538	Tu-154B-2		85622	Tu-154M
	85539	Tu-154B-2		85623	Tu-154M
	85540	Tu-154B-2		85624	Tu-154M
	85542	Tu-154B-2		85625	Tu-154M
	85545	Tu-154B-2		85626	Tu-154M
	85546	Tu-154B-2		85627	Tu-154M
	85547	Tu-154B-2		85628	Tu-154M
	85548	Tu-154B-2		85629	Tu-154M
	85549	Tu-154B-2		85630	Tu-154M
	85550	Tu-154B-2		85631	Tu-154M
	85551	Tu-154B-2		85632	Tu-154M
	85552	Tu-154B-2		85633	Tu-154M
	85553	Tu-154B-2		85634	Tu-154M
	85554	Tu-154B-2		85635	Tu-154M
	85555	Tu-154B-2		85636	Tu-154M
	85556	Tu-154B-2		85637	Tu-154M
	85557	Tu-154B-2		85638	Tu-154M
	85558	Tu-154B-2		85639	Tu-154M
	85559	Tu-154B-2		85640	Tu-154M
	85560	Tu-154B-2		85641	Tu-154M
	85561	Tu-154B-2		85642	Tu-154M
	85562	Tu-154B-2		85643	Tu-154M
	85563	Tu-154B-2		85644	Tu-154M
	85565	Tu-154B-2		85645	Tu-154M
	85566	Tu-154B-2		85646	Tu-154M
	85567	Tu-154B-2		85647	Tu-154M
	85568	Tu-154B-2		85648	Tu-154M
	85570	Tu-154B-2		85649	Tu-154M
	85571	Tu-154B-2		85650	Tu-154M
	85572	Tu-154B-2		85651	Tu-154M
	85573	Tu-154B-2		85652	Tu-154M
	85574	Tu-154B-2		85653	Tu-154M
	85575	Tu-154B-2		85654	Tu-154M

Reg.	Type	Notes	Reg.	Type	Notes
85655	Tu-154M		86090	IL-86	
85656	Tu-154M		86091	IL-86	
85657	Tu-154M		86092	IL-86	
85658	Tu-154M		86093	IL-86	
85659	Tu-154M		86094	IL-86	
85660	Tu-154M		86095	IL-86	
85661	Tu-154M		86096	IL-86	
85662	Tu-154M		86450	IL-62	
85663	Tu-154M		86451	IL-62	
85664	Tu-154M		86452	IL-62M	
85665	Tu-154M		86453	IL-62M	
85666	Tu-154M		86454	IL-62M	
85667	Tu-154M		86455	IL-62M	
85668	Tu-154M		86456	IL-62M	
85669	Tu-154M		86457	IL-62M	
85670	Tu-154M		86458	IL-62M	
86000	IL-86		86459	IL-62M	
86002	IL-86		86460	IL-62	
86003	IL-86		86461	IL-62	
86004	IL-86		86462	IL-62M	
86005	IL-86		86463	IL-62M	
86006	IL-86		86464	IL-62M	
86007	IL-86		86465	IL-62M	
86008	IL-86		86466	IL-62MK	
86009	IL-86		86467	IL-62M	
86010	IL-86		86469	IL-62M	
86011	IL-86		86471	IL-62M	
86012	IL-86		86472	IL-62M	
86013	IL-86		86473	IL-62M	
86014	IL-86		86474	IL-62M	
86015	IL-86		86475	IL-62M	
86016	IL-86		86476	IL-62M	
86017	IL-86		86477	IL-62M	
86018	IL-86		86478	IL-62M	
86050	IL-86		86479	IL-62M	
86051	IL-86		86480	IL-62M	
86052	IL-86		86481	IL-62M	
86053	IL-86		86482	IL-62M	
86054	IL-86		86483	IL-62M	
86055	IL-86		86484	IL-62M	
86056	IL-86		86485	IL-62M	
86057	IL-86		86486	IL-62M	
86058	IL-86		86487	IL-62M	
86059	IL-86		86488	IL-62M	
86060	IL-86		86489	IL-62M	
86061	IL-86		86490	IL-62M	
86062	IL-86		86491	IL-62M	
86063	IL-86		86492	IL-62M	
86064	IL-86		86493	IL-62M	
86065	IL-86		86494	IL-62M	
86066	IL-86		86495	IL-62M	
86067	IL-86		86496	IL-62M	
86068	IL-86		86497	IL-62M	
86069	IL-86		86498	IL-62M	
86070	IL-86		86499	IL-62M	
86071	IL-86		86500	IL-62M	
86072	IL-86		86501	IL-62M	
86073	IL-86		86502	IL-62M	
86074	IL-86		86503	IL-62M	
86075	IL-86		86504	IL-62M	
86076	IL-86		86505	IL-62M	
86077	IL-86		86506	IL-62M	
86078	IL-86		86507	IL-62M	
86079	IL-86		86508	IL-62M	
86080	IL-86		86509	IL-62M	
86081	IL-86		86510	IL-62M	
86082	IL-86		86511	IL-62M	
86083	IL-86		86512	IL-62M	
86084	IL-86		86513	IL-62M	
86085	IL-86		86514	IL-62M	
86086	IL-86		86516	IL-62M	
86087	IL-86		86517	IL-62MK	
86088	IL-86		86518	IL-62M	
86089	IL-86		86519	IL-62M	

Notes	Reg.	Type	Notes	Reg.	Type
	86520	IL-62MK		86662	IL-62
	86521	IL-62M		86663	IL-62
	86522	IL-62M		86664	IL-62
	86523	IL-62M		86665	IL-62
	86524	IL-62M		86666	IL-62
	86528	IL-62MK		86667	IL-62
	86530	IL-62MK		86668	IL-62
	86531	IL-62M		86669	IL-62
	86532	IL-62MK		86670	IL-62
	86533	IL-62M		86672	IL-62
	86534	IL-62MK		86673	IL-62M
	86535	IL-62M		86674	IL-62
	86536	IL-62M		86675	IL-62
	86537	IL-62M (VIP)		86676	IL-62
	86538	IL-62M (VIP)		86677	IL-62
	86540	IL-62M		86678	IL-62
	86555	IL-62M (VIP)		86679	IL-62
	86605	IL-62		86680	IL-62
	86606	IL-62		86681	IL-62
	86607	IL-62M		86682	IL-62
	86608	IL-62		86683	IL-62
	86609	IL-62		86684	IL-62
	86610	IL-62		86685	IL-62
	86611	IL-62		86686	IL-62
	86612	IL-62		86687	IL-62
	86613	IL-62		86688	IL-62
	86615	IL-62		86689	IL-62
	86616	IL-62		86690	IL-62
	86617	IL-62		86691	IL-62
	86618	IL-62M		86692	IL-62M
	86619	IL-62M		86693	IL-62M
	86620	IL-62M		86694	IL-62
	86621	IL-62M		86695	IL-62
	86622	IL-62M		86696	IL-62
	86623	IL-62M		86697	IL-62
	86624	IL-62		86698	IL-62
	86648	IL-62		86699	IL-62
	86649	IL-62		86700	IL-62M
	86650	IL-62		86701	IL-62M
	86652	IL-62		86702	IL-62M
	86653	IL-62		86703	IL-62
	86654	IL-62		86704	IL-62
	86655	IL-62		86705	IL-62M
	86656	IL-62M		86706	IL-62M
	86657	IL-62		86710	IL-62MK
	86658	IL-62M		86711	IL-62M
	86661	IL-62		86712	IL-62M

CN (Morocco)

Notes	Reg.	Type	Owner or Operator
	CN-CCF	Boeing 727-2B6	Royal Air Maroc *Fez*
	CN-CCG	Boeing 727-2B6	Royal Air Maroc *L'Oiseau de la Providence*
	CN-CCH	Boeing 727-2B6	Royal Air Maroc *Marrakech*
	CN-CCW	Boeing 727-2B6	Royal Air Maroc *Agadir*
	CN-RMB	Boeing 707-351C	Royal Air Maroc *Tangier*
	CN-RMC	Boeing 707-351C	Royal Air Maroc *Casablanca*
	CN-RME	Boeing 747-2B6B (SCD)	Royal Air Maroc
	CN-RMH	Boeing 737-2T5	Royal Air Maroc
	CN-RMI	Boeing 737-2B6	Royal Air Maroc *El Ayounne*
	CN-RMJ	Boeing 737-2B6	Royal Air Maroc *Oujda*
	CN-RMK	Boeing 737-2B6	Royal Air Maroc *Smara*
	CN-RML	Boeing 737-2B6	Royal Air Maroc
	CN-RMM	Boeing 737-2B6C	Royal Air Maroc
	CN-RMN	Boeing 737-2B6C	Royal Air Maroc
	CN-RMO	Boeing 727-2B6	Royal Air Maroc
	CN-RMP	Boeing 727-2B6	Royal Air Maroc
	CN-RMQ	Boeing 727-2B6	Royal Air Maroc
	CN-RMR	Boeing 727-2B6	Royal Air Maroc
	CN-RMS	Boeing 747SP-44	Royal Air Maroc
	CN-RMT	Boeing 757-2B6	Royal Air Maroc
	CN-RMZ	Boeing 757-2B6	Royal Air Maroc

CS (Portugal)

Reg.	Type	Owner or Operator	Notes
CS-TBK	Boeing 727-82	TAP — Air Portugal *Acores*	
CS-TBL	Boeing 727-82	TAP — Air Portugal *Madeira*	
CS-TBM	Boeing 727-82	TAP — Air Portugal *Algarve*	
CS-TBS	Boeing 727-282	TAP — Air Portugal *Lisboa*	
CS-TBW	Boeing 727-282	TAP — Air Portugal *Coimbra*	
CS-TBX	Boeing 727-282	TAP — Air Portugal *Faro*	
CS-TBY	Boeing 727-282	TAP — Air Portugal *Amadora*	
CS-TCH	Boeing 727-232	TAP — Air Atlantis *Ponta de Sagres*	
CS-TCI	Boeing 727-232	TAP — Air Atlantis *Praia da Rocha*	
CS-TCJ	Boeing 727-232	TAP — Air Atlantis *Monte Gordo*	
CS-TEA	L.1011-385 TriStar 500	TAP — Air Portugal *Luis de Camoes*	
CS-TEB	L.1011-385 TriStar 500	TAP — Air Portugal *Infante D. Henrique*	
CS-TEC	L.1011-385 TriStar 500	TAP — Air Portugal *Gago Coutinho*	
CS-TED	L.1011-385 TriStar 500	TAP — Air Portugal *Bartolomeu de Gusmao*	
CS-TEE	L.1011-385 TriStar 500	TAP — Air Portugal *St Antonio de Lisboa*	
CS-TEF	L.1011-385 TriStar 500	TAP — Air Portugal *Fernando Pessoa*	
CS-TEG	L.1011-385 TriStar 500	TAP — Air Portugal	
CS-TEH	Airbus A.310-304	TAP — Air Portugal	
CS-TEI	Airbus A.310-304	TAP — Air Portugal	
CS-TEJ	Airbus A.310-304	TAP — Air Portugal	
CS-TEK	Boeing 737-282	TAP — Air Portugal *Ponta Delgada*	
CS-TEL	Boeing 737-282	TAP — Air Portugal *Funchal*	
CS-TEM	Boeing 737-282	TAP — Air Portugal *Setubal*	
CS-TEN	Boeing 737-282	TAP — Air Portugal *Braga*	
CS-TEO	Boeing 737-282	TAP — Air Portugal *Evora*	
CS-TEP	Boeing 737-282	TAP — Air Portugal *Oporto*	
CS-TEQ	Boeing 737-282C	TAP — Air Portugal *Vila Real*	
CS-TER	Boeing 737-230	TAP — Air Portugal *Aveiro*	
CS-TES	Boeing 737-230	TAP — Air Portugal *Viana do Castelo*	
CS-TET	Boeing 737-2K9	Air Atlantis	
CS-TEU	Boeing 737-2K9	Air Atlantis	
CS-TEV	Boeing 737-230	TAP — Air Atlantis	
CS-T	Boeing 737-230	TAP — Air Portugal	
CS-TIA	Boeing 737-382	TAP — Air Portugal	
CS-TIB	Boeing 737-382	TAP — Air Portugal	
CS-TIC	Boeing 737-382	TAP — Air Portugal	
CS-TID	Boeing 737-382	TAP — Air Portugal	
CS-TIE	Boeing 737-382	TAP — Air Portugal	
CS-TIF	Boeing 737-3K9	TAP — Air Portugal	

CU (Cuba)

CU-T1208	Ilyushin IL-62M	Cubana *Capt Wifredo Perez*	
CU-T1209	Ilyushin IL-62M	Cubana	
CU-T1215	Ilyushin IL-62M	Cubana	
CU-T1216	Ilyushin IL-62M	Cubana	
CU-T1217	Ilyushin IL-62M	Cubana	
CU-T1218	Ilyushin IL-62M	Cubana	
CU-T1225	Ilyushin IL-62M	Cubana	
CU-T1226	Ilyushin IL-62M	Cubana	
CU-T1252	Ilyushin IL-62M	Cubana	
CU-T1259	Ilyushin IL-62M	Cubana	
CU-T1280	Ilyushin IL-62M	Cubana	

D (German Federal Republic)

D-AAST	S.E.210 Caravelle 10R	Aero Lloyd	
D-ABAK	S.E.210 Caravelle 10R	Aero Lloyd	
D-ABEA	Boeing 737-330	Lufthansa	
D-ABFA	Boeing 737-230	Lufthansa *Regensburg*	
D-ABFB	Boeing 737-230	Lufthansa *Flensburg*	
D-ABFC	Boeing 737-230	Lufthansa *Würzburg*	
D-ABFD	Boeing 737-230	Lufthansa *Bamberg*	
D-ABFF	Boeing 737-230	Lufthansa *Gelsenkirchen*	
D-ABFH	Boeing 737-230	Lufthansa *Pforzheim*	

Notes	Reg.	Type	Owner or Operator
	D-ABFK	Boeing 737-230	Lufthansa *Wuppertal*
	D-ABFL	Boeing 737-230	Lufthansa *Coburg*
	D-ABFM	Boeing 737-230	Lufthansa *Osnabrück*
	D-ABFN	Boeing 737-230	Lufthansa *Kempten*
	D-ABFP	Boeing 737-230	Lufthansa *Offenbach*
	D-ABFR	Boeing 737-230	Lufthansa *Solingen*
	D-ABFS	Boeing 737-230	Lufthansa *Oldenburg*
	D-ABFU	Boeing 737-230	Lufthansa *Mülheim a.d.R*
	D-ABFW	Boeing 737-230	Lufthansa *Wolfsburg*
	D-ABFX	Boeing 737-230	Lufthansa *Tübingen*
	D-ABFY	Boeing 737-230	Lufthansa *Göttingen*
	D-ABFZ	Boeing 737-230	Lufthansa *Wilhelmshaven*
	D-ABGE	Boeing 737-230C	Lufthansa
	D-ABHA	Boeing 737-230	Lufthansa *Koblenz*
	D-ABHB	Boeing 737-230	Lufthansa *Goslar*
	D-ABHC	Boeing 737-230	Lufthansa *Friedrichshafen*
	D-ABHE	Boeing 737-230C	Lufthansa
	D-ABHF	Boeing 737-230	Lufthansa *Heilbronn*
	D-ABHH	Boeing 737-230	Lufthansa *Marburg*
	D-ABHI	Boeing 727-230	Lufthansa *Mönchengladbach*
	D-ABHK	Boeing 737-230	Lufthansa *Bayreuth*
	D-ABHL	Boeing 737-230	Lufthansa *Worms*
	D-ABHM	Boeing 737-230	Lufthansa *Landshut*
	D-ABHN	Boeing 737-230	Lufthansa *Trier*
	D-ABHP	Boeing 737-230	Lufthansa *Erlangen*
	D-ABHR	Boeing 737-230	Lufthansa *Darmstadt*
	D-ABHS	Boeing 737-230	Lufthansa *Remscheid*
	D-ABHU	Boeing 737-230	Lufthansa *Konstanz*
	D-ABHW	Boeing 737-230	Lufthansa *Baden Baden*
	D-ABKA	Boeing 727-230	Lufthansa *Heidelberg*
	D-ABKB	Boeing 727-230	Lufthansa *Augsburg*
	D-ABKC	Boeing 727-230	Lufthansa *Braunschweig*
	D-ABKD	Boeing 727-230	Lufthansa *Freiburg*
	D-ABKE	Boeing 727-230	Lufthansa *Mannheim*
	D-ABKF	Boeing 727-230	Lufthansa *Saarbrücken*
	D-ABKG	Boeing 727-230	Lufthansa *Kassel*
	D-ABKH	Boeing 727-230	Lufthansa *Karlsruhe*
	D-ABKI	Boeing 727-230	Lufthansa *Bremerhaven*
	D-ABKJ	Boeing 727-230	Lufthansa *Wiesbaden*
	D-ABKK	Boeing 727-230	Condor Flugdienst
	D-ABKL	Boeing 727-230	Condor Flugdienst
	D-ABKM	Boeing 727-230	Lufthansa *Hagen*
	D-ABKN	Boeing 727-230	Lufthansa *Ulm*
	D-ABKP	Boeing 727-230	Lufthansa *Krefeld*
	D-ABKQ	Boeing 727-230	Lufthansa *Mainz*
	D-ABKR	Boeing 727-230	Lufthansa *Bielefeld*
	D-ABKS	Boeing 727-230	Lufthansa *Oberhausen*
	D-ABKT	Boeing 727-230	Lufthansa *Aachen*
	D-ABLI	Boeing 727-230	Lufthansa *Ludwigshafen a.Rh.*
	D-ABMA	Boeing 737-230	Lufthansa *Idar-Oberstein*
	D-ABMB	Boeing 737-230	Lufthansa *Ingolstadt*
	D-ABMC	Boeing 737-230	Lufthansa *Norderstedt*
	D-ABMD	Boeing 737-230	Lufthansa *Paderborn*
	D-ABME	Boeing 737-230	Lufthansa *Schweinfurt*
	D-ABMF	Boeing 737-230	Lufthansa *Verden*
	D-ABNI	Boeing 727-230	Lufthansa
	D-ABPI	Boeing 727-230	Lufthansa
	D-ABQI	Boeing 727-230	Lufthansa *Hildesheim*
	D-ABRI	Boeing 727-230	Lufthansa *Esslingen*
	D-ABSI	Boeing 727-230	Lufthansa *Hof*
	D-ABTA	Boeing 747-430 (SCD)	Lufthansa
	D-ABTB	Boeing 747-430 (SCD)	Lufthansa
	D-ABTC	Bogine 747-430 (SCD)	Lufthansa
	D-ABTI	Boeing 727-230	Condor Flugdienst
	D-ABVA	Boeing 747-430	Lufthansa
	D-ABVB	Boeing 747-430	Lufthansa
	D-ABVC	Boeing 747-430	Lufthansa
	D-ABVD	Boeing 747-430	Lufthansa
	D-ABVE	Boeing 747-430	Lufthansa
	D-ABVF	Boeing 747-430	Lufthansa
	D-ABVG	Boeing 747-430	Lufthansa
	D-ABVI	Boeing 727-230	Condor Flugdienst
	D-ABWA	Boeing 737-330	Condor Flugdienst *Claus Gillmann*
	D-ABWB	Boeing 737-330	Condor Flugdienst

Reg.	Type	Owner or Operator	Notes
D-ABWC	Boeing 737-330	Condor Flugdienst	
D-ABWD	Boeing 737-330	Condor Flugdienst	
D-ABWE	Boeing 737-330	Condor Flugdienst	
D-ABWF	Boeing 737-330	Condor Flugdienst	
D-ABWH	Boeing 737-330	Condor Flugdienst	
D-ABWI	Boeing 727-230	Condor Flugdienst	
D-ABXA	Boeing 737-330	Lufthansa *Giessen*	
D-ABXB	Boeing 737-330	Lufthansa *Passau*	
D-ABXC	Boeing 737-330	Lufthansa *Delmenhorst*	
D-ABXD	Boeing 737-330	Lufthansa *Siegen*	
D-ABXE	Boeing 737-330	Lufthansa *Hamm*	
D-ABXF	Boeing 737-330	Lufthansa *Minden*	
D-ABXH	Boeing 737-330	Lufthansa *Cuxhaven*	
D-ABXI	Boeing 737-330	Lufthansa *Berchtesgaden*	
D-ABXK	Boeing 737-330	Lufthansa *Ludwigsburg*	
D-ABXL	Boeing 737-330	Lufthansa *Neuss*	
D-ABXM	Boeing 737-330	Lufthansa *Herten*	
D-ABXN	Boeing 737-330	Lufthansa *Böblingen*	
D-ABXO	Boeing 737-330	Lufthansa *Schwäbisch-Gmünd*	
D-ABXP	Boeing 737-330	Lufthansa *Fulda*	
D-ABXR	Boeing 737-330	Lufthansa *Celle*	
D-ABXS	Boeing 737-330	Lufthansa	
D-ABXT	Boeing 737-330	Lufthansa	
D-ABXU	Boeing 737-330	Lufthansa	
D-ABXW	Boeing 737-330	Lufthansa	
D-ABXX	Boeing 737-330	Lufthansa	
D-ABXY	Boeing 737-330	Lufthansa	
D-ABXZ	Boeing 737-330	Lufthansa	
D-ABYJ	Boeing 747-230B (SCD)	Lufthansa *Hessen*	
D-ABYK	Boeing 747-230B (SCD)	Lufthansa *Rheinland-Pfalz*	
D-ABYL	Boeing 747-230B (SCD)	Lufthansa *Saarland*	
D-ABYM	Boeing 747-230B (SCD)	Lufthansa *Schleswig-Holstein*	
D-ABYN	Boeing 747-230B	Lufthansa *Baden-Wurttemberg*	
D-ABYO	Boeing 747-230F (SCD)	Lufthansa *America*	
D-ABYP	Boeing 747-230B	Lufthansa *Niedersachen*	
D-ABYQ	Boeing 747-230B	Lufthansa *Bremen*	
D-ABYR	Boeing 747-230B (SCD)	Lufthansa *Nordrhein-Westfalen*	
D-ABYS	Boeing 747-230B (SCD)	Lufthansa *Bayern*	
D-ABYT	Boeing 747-230B (SCD)	Lufthansa *Hamburg*	
D-ABYU	Boeing 747-230F (SCD)	Lufthansa *Asia*	
D-ABYW	Boeing 747-230B (SCD)	Lufthansa *Berlin*	
D-ABYX	Boeing 747-230B (SCD)	Lufthansa *Köln*	
D-ABYY	Boeing 747-230B (SCD)	Lufthansa *München*	
D-ABYZ	Boeing 747-230B (SCD)	Lufthansa *Frankfurt*	
D-ABZA	Boeing 747-230B (SCD)	Lufthansa *Dusseldorf*	
D-ABZB	Boeing 747-230F (SCD)	Lufthansa *Europa*	
D-ABZC	Boeing 747-230B (SCD)	Lufthansa *Hannover*	
D-ABZD	Boeing 747-230B	Lufthansa *Kiel*	
D-ABZE	Boeing 747-230B (SCD)	Lufthansa *Stuttgart*	
D-ABZF	Boeing 747-230F (SCD)	Lufthansa *Africa*	
D-ABZH	Boeing 747-230B	Lufthansa *Bonn*	
D-ABZI	Boeing 747-230F (SCD)	Lufthansa	
D-ACVK	S.E.210 Caravelle 10R	Aero Lloyd *Otto Trump*	
D-ADAO	Douglas DC-10-30	Lufthansa *Leverkusen*	
D-ADBO	Douglas DC-10-30	Lufthansa *Bochum*	
D-ADCO	Douglas DC-10-30	Lufthansa	
D-ADDO	Douglas DC-10-30	Lufthansa *Duisburg*	
D-ADFO	Douglas DC-10-30	Lufthansa *Fürth*	
D-ADGO	Douglas DC-10-30	Lufthansa	
D-ADHO	Douglas DC-10-30	Lufthansa	
D-ADJO	Douglas DC-10-30	Lufthansa *Essen*	
D-ADKO	Douglas DC-10-30	Lufthansa	
D-ADLO	Douglas DC-10-30	Lufthansa *Nurnberg*	
D-ADMO	Douglas DC-10-30	Lufthansa *Dortmund*	
D-ADPO	Douglas DC-10-30	Condor Flugdienst	
D-ADQO	Douglas DC-10-30	Condor Flugdienst	
D-ADSO	Douglas DC-10-30	Lufthansa	
D-ADUA	Douglas DC-8-73AF	German Cargo	
D-ADUC	Douglas DC-8-73AF	German Cargo	
D-ADUE	Douglas DC-8-73AF	German Cargo	
D-ADUI	Douglas DC-8-73CF	German Cargo	
D-ADUO	Douglas DC-8-73CF	German Cargo	
D-AELB	F.27 Friendship Mk 600	WDL	
D-AERE	L.1011-385 TriStar 1	LTU	

D

Notes	Reg.	Type	Owner or Operator
	D-AERI	L.1011-385 TriStar 1	LTU
	D-AERL	L.1011-385 TriStar 500	LTU
	D-AERM	L.1011-385 TriStar 1	LTU
	D-AERN	L.1011-385-15 TriStar 200	LTU
	D-AERP	L.1011-385 TriStar 1	LTU
	D-AERT	L.1011-385 TriStar 500	LTU
	D-AERU	L.1011-385-15 TriStar 100	LTU
	D-AERY	L.1011-385 TriStar 1	LTU
	D-AFKA	Fokker 50	D.L.T.
	D-AFKB	Fokker 50	D.L.T.
	D-AFKC	Fokker 50	D.L.T.
	D-AFKD	Fokker 50	D.L.T.
	D-AFKE	Fokker 50	D.L.T.
	D-AFKF	Fokker 50	D.L.T.
	D-AFKG	Fokker 50	D.L.T.
	D-AGEA	Boeing 737-35B	Germania
	D-AGEB	Boeing 737-35B	Germania
	D-AGEC	Boeing 737-35B	Germania
	D-AGED	Boeing 737-35B	Germania
	D-AGEE	Boeing 737-35B	Germania
	D-AHLD	Boeing 737-2K5	Hapag-Lloyd
	D-AHLG	Boeing 737-2K5	Hapag-Lloyd
	D-AHLH	Boeing 737-2K5	Hapag-Lloyd
	D-AHLI	Boeing 737-2K5	Hapag-Lloyd
	D-AHLJ	Boeing 737-4K5	Hapag-Lloyd
	D-AHLK	Boeing 737-4K5	Hapag-Lloyd
	D-AHLL	Boeing 737-4K5	Hapag-Lloyd
	D-AHLM	Boeing 727-81	Hapag-Lloyd
	D-AHLO	Boeing 737-4K5	Hapag-Lloyd
	D-AHLP	Boeing 737-4K5	Hapag-Lloyd
	D-AHLQ	Boeing 737-4K5	Hapag-Lloyd
	D-AHLS	Boeing 727-89	Hapag-Lloyd
	D-AHLT	Boeing 727-2K5	Hapag-Lloyd
	D-AHLU	Boeing 727-2K5	Hapag-Lloyd
	D-AHLV	Airbus A.310-204	Hapag-Lloyd
	D-AHLW	Airbus A.310-204	Hapag-Lloyd
	D-AHLX	Airbus A.310-204	Hapag-Lloyd
	D-AHLY	Airbus A.310-204	Hapag-Lloyd
	D-AHLZ	Airbus A.310-204	Hapag-Lloyd
	D-AHSE	H.S.748 Srs 2B	D.L.T.
	D-AHSF	H.S.748 Srs 2B	D.L.T.
	D-AIAH	Airbus A.300-603	Lufthansa *Lindau/Bodenzee*
	D-AIAI	Airbus A.300-603	Lufthansa *Erbach/Odenwald*
	D-AIAK	Airbus A.300-603	Lufthansa *Kronberg im Taunus*
	D-AIAL	Airbus A.300-603	Lufthansa *Stade*
	D-AIAM	Airbus A.300-603	Lufthansa *Rosenheim*
	D-AIAN	Airbus A.300-603	Lufthansa *Nördlingen*
	D-AIAP	Airbus A.300-603	Lufthansa *Bingen*
	D-AIAR	Airbus A.300-603R	Lufthansa
	D-AIAS	Airbus A.300-603R	Lufthansa
	D-AICA	Airbus A.310-203	Lufthansa *Neustadt an der Weinstrausse*
	D-AICB	Airbus A.310-203	Lufthansa *Garmisch-Partenkirchen*
	D-AICC	Airbus A.310-203	Lufthansa *Kaiserslauten*
	D-AICD	Airbus A.310-203	Lufthansa *Detmold*
	D-AICF	Airbus A.310-203	Lufthansa *Rüdesheim am Rhein*
	D-AICH	Airbus A.310-203	Lufthansa *Lüneburg*
	D-AICK	Airbus A.310-203	Lufthansa *Westerland-Sylt*
	D-AICL	Airbus A.310-203	Lufthansa *Rothenburg ob der Tauber*
	D-AICM	Airbus A.310-203	Condor Flugdienst
	D-AICN	Airbus A.310-203	Condor Flugdienst
	D-AICP	Airbus A.310-203	Condor Flugdienst
	D-AICR	Airbus A.310-203	Condor Flugdienst
	D-AICS	Airbus A.310-203	Lufthansa *Recklinghausen*
	D-AICT	Airbus A.310-203	Lufthansa
	D-AICU	Airbus A.310-203	Lufthansa
	D-AICW	Airbus A.310-203	Lufthansa
	D-AICX	Airbus A.310-203	Lufthansa
	D-AICY	Airbus A.310-203	Lufthansa
	D-AICZ	Airbus A.310-203	Lufthansa
	D-AIDA	Airbus A.310-304	Condor Flugdienst
	D-AIDB	Airbus A.310-304	Lufthansa
	D-AIDC	Airbus A.310-304	Condor Flugdienst
	D-AIDD	Airbus A.310-304	Lufthansa

Reg.	Type	Owner or Operator	Notes
D-AIDE	Airbus A.310-304	Lufthansa	
D-AIDF	Airbus A.310-304	Lufthansa	
D-AIDH	Airbus A.310-304	Lufthansa	
D-AIPA	Airbus A.320-210	Lufthansa	
D-AIPB	Airbus A.320-210	Lufthansa	
D-AIPC	Airbus A.320-210	Lufthansa	
D-AIPD	Airbus A.320-210	Lufthansa	
D-AIPE	Airbus A.320-210	Lufthansa	
D-AIPF	Airbus A.320-210	Lufthansa	
D-AIPH	Airbus A.320-210	Lufthansa	
D-AIPK	Airbus A.320-210	Lufthansa	
D-AIPL	Airbus A.320-210	Lufthansa	
D-AIPM	Airbus A.320-210	Lufthansa	
D-AIPN	Airbus A.320-210	Lufthansa	
D-ALLA	Douglas DC-9-32	Aero Lloyd	
D-ALLB	Douglas DC-9-32	Aero Lloyd	
D-ALLC	Douglas DC-9-32	Aero Lloyd	
D-ALLD	Douglas DC-9-83	Aero Lloyd	
D-ALLE	Douglas DC-9-83	Aero Lloyd	
D-ALLF	Douglas DC-9-83	Aero Lloyd	
D-ALLG	Douglas DC-9-87	Aero Lloyd	
D-ALLH	Douglas DC-9-87	Aero Lloyd	
D-ALLI	Douglas DC-9-87	Aero Lloyd	
D-ALLJ	Douglas DC-9-87	Aero Lloyd	
D-ALLK	Douglas DC-9-83	Aero Lloyd	
D-AL	Douglas DC-9-83	Aero Lloyd	
D-AMUN	Boeing 767-3G5	LTU-Sud	
D-	Boeing 767-3G5	LTU-Sud	
D-	Boeing 767-3G5	LTU-Sud	
D-AMUR	Boeing 757-2G5	LTU-Sud (*leased LTE as EC-EFX*)	
D-AMUS	Boeing 757-2G5	LTU-Sud (*leased LTE as EC-EGH*)	
D-AMUT	Boeing 757-2G5	LTU-Sud (*leased LTE as EC-.....*)	
D-AMUV	Boeing 757-2G5	LTU-Sud	
D-AMUW	Boeing 757-2G5	LTU-Sud	
D-AMUX	Boeing 757-2G5	LTU-Sud	
D-AM	Boeing 757-2G5	LTU-Sud	
D-AM	Boeing 757-2G5	LTU-Sud	
D-AM	Boeing 757-2G5	LTU-Sud	
D-AM	Boeing 757-2G5	LTU-Sud	
D-AM	Boeing 757-2G5	LTU-Sud	
D-A	Douglas DC-9-83	German Wings	
D-A	Douglas DC-9-83	German Wings	
D-A	Douglas DC-9-83	German Wings	
D-A	Douglas DC-9-83	German Wings	
D-BAAA	Aerospatiale ATR-42-300	Nürnberger Flugdienst (NFD)	
D-BAKA	F.27 Friendship Mk 100	WDL	
D-BAKI	F.27 Friendship Mk 100	WDL	
D-BAKO	F.27 Friendship Mk 100	WDL	
D-BAKU	F.27 Friendship Mk 200	WDL	
D-BATA	Aerospatiale ATR-42-300	Nürnberger Flugdienst (NFD)	
D-BATB	Aerospatiale ATR-42-300	Nürnberger Flugdienst (NFD)	
D-BBBB	Aerospatiale ATR-42-300	Nürnberger Flugdienst (NFD)	
D-BCCC	Aerospatiale ATR-42-300	Nürnberger Flugdienst (NFD)	
D-BCRM	Aerospatiale ATR-42-300	R.F.G.	
D-BCRN	Aerospatiale ATR-42-300	R.F.G.	
D-BC	Aerospatiale ATR-42-300	R.F.G.	
D-BDDD	Aerospatiale ATR-42-300	Nürnberger Flugdienst (NFD)	
D-B	Aerospatiale ATR-42-300	Nürnberger Flugdienst (NED)	
D-BERT	D.H.C.8 Dash Eight	Contactair/D.L.T.	
D-BEST	D.H.C.8 Dash Eight	Contactair/D.L.T.	
D-CABA	Swearingen SA227AC Metro III	Nürnberger Flugdienst (NFD)	
D-CABD	Swearingen SA227AC Metro III	Nürnberger Flugdienst (NFD)	
D-CABE	Swearingen SA227AC Metro III	Nürnberger Flugdienst (NFD)	
D-CABF	Swearingen SA227AC Metro III	Nürnberger Flugdienst (NFD)	
D-CABG	Swearingen SA227AC Metro III	Nürnberger Flugdienst (NFD)	
D-CABH	Swearingen SA227AC Metro III	Nürnberger Flugdienst (NFD)	
D-CABI	Swearingen SA227AC Metro III	Nürnberger Flugdienst (NFD)	
D-CAPA	Beech 1900	Sudavia	
D-CCCC	Douglas DC-3	Classic Wings	
D-CDIA	Saab SF.340A	Delta Air	
D-CDIB	Saab SF.340A	Delta Air	
D-CDIC	Saab SF.340A	Delta Air	
D-CDID	Saab SF.340A	Delta Air	
D-CDIZ	Dornier Do.228-201	Delta Air	

Notes	Reg.	Type	Owner or Operator
	D-CEMB	EMB-120RT Brasilia	D.L.T.
	D-CEMC	EMB-120RT Brasilia	D.L.T.
	D-CEMD	EMB-120RT Brasilia	D.L.T.
	D-CEME	EMB-120RT Brasilia	D.L.T.
	D-CEMF	EMB-120RT Brasilia	D.L.T.
	D-CEMG	EMB-120RT Brasilia	D.L.T.
	D-CEMH	EMB-120RT Brasilia	D.L.T.
	D-CEMI	EMB-120RT Brasilia	D.L.T.
	D-CEMJ	EMB-120RT Brasilia	D.L.T.
	D-CEMK	EMB-120RT Brasilia	D.L.T.
	D-CEML	EMB-120RT Brasilia	D.L.T.
	D-CEMM	EMB-120RT Brasilia	D.L.T.
	D-CEMN	EMB-120RT Brasilia	D.L.T.
	D-CEYH	Dornier Do.228-201	Hamburg Airlines
	D-CKVW	Swearingen SA227AC Metro III	Nürnberger Flugdienst (NFD)
	D-CMUC	Dornier Do.228-201	Hamburg Airlines
	D-CONA	BAe Jetstream 3102	Contactair
	D-CONE	BAe Jetstream 3102	Contactair
	D-CONI	BAe Jetstream 3102	Contactair
	D-CONU	BAe Jetstream 3102	Contactair
	D-ICFB	Swearingen SA226AT Merlin IV	R.F.G.
	D-ICRJ	Swearingen SA226TC Metro II	R.F.G.
	D-ICRK	Swearingen SA226TC Metro II	R.F.G.
	D-ICRL	Swearingen SA226TC Metro II	R.F.G.
	D-IHCW	Swearingen SA226TC Metro II	R.F.G.
	D-INWK	Swearingen SA226AT Merlin IV	Naske Air

DDR (German Democratic Republic)

Notes	Reg.	Type	Owner or Operator
	DDR-SCI	Tupolev Tu-134A	Interflug
	DDR-SCK	Tupolev Tu-134A	Interflug
	DDR-SCL	Tupolev Tu-134A	Interflug
	DDR-SCN	Tupolev Tu-134A	Interflug
	DDR-SCO	Tupolev Tu-134A	Interflug
	DDR-SCP	Tupolev Tu-134A	Interflug
	DDR-SCR	Tupolev Tu-134A	Interflug
	DDR-SCS	Tupolev Tu-134A	Interflug
	DDR-SCT	Tupolev Tu-134A	Interflug
	DDR-SCU	Tupolev Tu-134A	Interflug
	DDR-SCV	Tupolev Tu-134A	Interflug
	DDR-SCW	Tupolev Tu-134A	Interflug
	DDR-SCX	Tupolev Tu-134A	Interflug
	DDR-SCY	Tupolev Tu-134A	Interflug
	DDR-SDC	Tupolev Tu-134A	Interflug
	DDR-SDE	Tupolev Tu-134A	Interflug
	DDR-SDF	Tupolev Tu-134A	Interflug
	DDR-SEF	Ilyushin IL-62	Interflug
	DDR-SEG	Ilyushin IL-62	Interflug
	DDR-SEH	Ilyushin IL-62	Interflug
	DDR-SEI	Ilyushin IL-62M	Interflug
	DDR-SEK	Ilyushin IL-62M	Interflug
	DDR-SEL	Ilyushin IL-62M	Interflug
	DDR-SEM	Ilyushin IL-62M	Interflug
	DDR-SEN	Ilyushin IL-62M	Interflug
	DDR-SEO	Ilyushin IL-62M	Interflug
	DDR-SEP	Ilyushin IL-62M	Interflug
	DDR-SER	Ilyushin IL-62M	Interflug
	DDR-SES	Ilyushin IL-62M	Interflug
	DDR-SET	Ilyushin IL-62M	Interflug
	DDR-SEU	Ilyushin IL-62M	Interflug
	DDR-SEV	Ilyushin IL-62MK	Interflug
	DDR-SEW	Ilyushin IL-62M	Interflug
	DDR-STA	Ilyushin IL-18D	Interflug
	DDR-STD	Ilyushin IL-18D	Interflug
	DDR-STE	Ilyushin IL-18D	Interflug
	DDR-STF	Ilyushin IL-18D	Interflug
	DDR-STG	Ilyushin IL-18D	Interflug
	DDR-STH	Ilyushin IL-18D	Interflug
	DDR-STI	Ilyushin IL-18D	Interflug
	DDR-STK	Ilyushin IL-18D	Interflug
	DDR-STM	Ilyushin IL-18D	Interflug

Reg.	Type	Owner or Operator	Notes
DDR-STN	Ilyushin IL-18D	Interflug	
DDR-STO	Ilyushin IL-18D	Interflug	
DDR-STP	Ilyushin IL-18D	Interflug	
DDR-SZA	Airbus A.310-304	Interflug	
DDR-SZB	Airbus A.310-304	Interflug	
DDR-SZC	Airbus A.310-304	Interflug	

EC (Spain)

Reg.	Type	Owner or Operator
EC-BIG	Douglas DC-9-32	Iberia *Villa de Madrid*
EC-BIH	Douglas DC-9-32	Aviaco *Ciudad de Barcelona*
EC-BIJ	Douglas DC-9-32	Iberia *Santa Cruz de Tenerife*
EC-BIK	Douglas DC-9-32	Aviaco *Castillo de Guanapa*
EC-BIL	Douglas DC-9-32	Iberia *Ciudad de Zaragoza*
EC-BIM	Douglas DC-9-32	Iberia *Ciudad de Santander*
EC-BIN	Douglas DC-9-32	Iberia *Palma de Mallorca*
EC-BIO	Douglas DC-9-32	Iberia *Villa de Bilbao*
EC-BIP	Douglas DC-9-32	Aviaco *Castillo de Monteagudo*
EC-BIQ	Douglas DC-9-32	Aviaco *Castillo de Argueso*
EC-BIR	Douglas DC-9-32	Iberia *Ciudad de Valencia*
EC-BIS	Douglas DC-9-32	Iberia *Ciudad de Alicante*
EC-BIT	Douglas DC-9-32	Iberia *Ciudad de San Sebastian*
EC-BIU	Douglas DC-9-32	Iberia *Ciudad de Oviedo*
EC-BPF	Douglas DC-9-32	Iberia *Ciudad de Almeria*
EC-BPG	Douglas DC-9-32	Iberia *Ciudad de Vigo*
EC-BPH	Douglas DC-9-32	Iberia *Ciudad de Gerona*
EC-BQA	CV-990A Coronado	*(stored/Palma)*
EC-BQQ	CV-990A Coronado	*(stored/Palma)*
EC-BQT	Douglas DC-9-32	Iberia *Ciudad de Murcia*
EC-BQU	Douglas DC-9-32	Iberia *Ciudad de La Coruna*
EC-BQV	Douglas DC-9-32	Iberia *Ciudad de Ibiza*
EC-BQX	Douglas DC-9-32	Iberia *Ciudad de Valladolid*
EC-BQY	Douglas DC-9-32	Aviaco *Ciudad de Cordoba*
EC-BQZ	Douglas DC-9-32	Iberia *Ciudad de Santa Cruz de La Palma*
EC-BYD	Douglas DC-9-32	Iberia *Ciudad de Arrecife de Lanzarote*
EC-BYE	Douglas DC-9-32	Iberia *Ciudad de Mahon*
EC-BYF	Douglas DC-9-32	Iberia *Ciudad de Granada*
EC-BYG	Douglas DC-9-32	Iberia *Ciudad de Pamplona*
EC-BYH	Douglas DC-9-32	Aviaco *Castillo de Buton*
EC-BYI	Douglas DC-9-32	Iberia *Ciudad de Vitoria*
EC-BYJ	Douglas DC-9-32	Iberia *Ciudad de Salamanca*
EC-BYK	Douglas DC-9-33RC	Iberia *Ciudad de Badajoz*
EC-BYL	Douglas DC-9-33RC	Iberia *Cuidad de Albacete*
EC-BYM	Douglas DC-9-33RC	Iberia *Ciudad de Cangas de Onis*
EC-BYN	Douglas DC-9-33RC	Iberia *Ciudad de Caceres*
EC-BZO	CV-990A Coronado	*(stored/Palma)*
EC-BZP	CV-990A Coronado	*(stored/Palma)*
EC-CAI	Boeing 727-256	Iberia *Castilla la Neuva*
EC-CAJ	Boeing 727-256	Iberia *Cataluna*
EC-CAK	Boeing 727-256	Iberia *Aragon*
EC-CBA	Boeing 727-256	Iberia *Vascongadas*
EC-CBB	Boeing 727-256	Iberia *Valencia*
EC-CBC	Boeing 727-256	Iberia *Navarra*
EC-CBD	Boeing 727-256	Iberia *Murcia*
EC-CBE	Boeing 727-256	Iberia *Leon*
EC-CBF	Boeing 727-256	Iberia *Gran Canaria*
EC-CBG	Boeing 727-256	Iberia *Extremadura*
EC-CBH	Boeing 727-256	Iberia *Galicia*
EC-CBI	Boeing 727-256	Iberia *Asturias*
EC-CBJ	Boeing 727-256	Iberia *Andalucia*
EC-CBK	Boeing 727-256	Iberia *Baleares*
EC-CBL	Boeing 727-256	Iberia *Tenerife*
EC-CBM	Boeing 727-256	Iberia *Castilla La Vieja*
EC-CBO	Douglas DC-10-30	Iberia *Costa del Sol*
EC-CBP	Douglas DC-10-30	Iberia *Costa Dorada*
EC-CEZ	Douglas DC-10-30	Iberia *Costa del Azahar*
EC-CFA	Boeing 727-256	Iberia *Jerez Xeres Sherry*
EC-CFB	Boeing 727-256	Iberia *Rioja*
EC-CFC	Boeing 727-256	Iberia *Tarragona*

EC

Notes	Reg.	Type	Owner or Operator
	EC-CFD	Boeing 727-256	Iberia *Montilla-Moriles*
	EC-CFE	Boeing 727-256	Iberia *Penedes*
	EC-CFF	Boeing 727-256	Iberia *Valdepenas*
	EC-CFG	Boeing 727-256	Iberia *La Mancha*
	EC-CFH	Boeing 727-256	Iberia *Priorato*
	EC-CFI	Boeing 727-256	Iberia *Carinena*
	EC-CFK	Boeing 727-256	Iberia *Riberio*
	EC-CGN	Douglas DC-9-32	Aviaco *Martin Alonso Pinzon*
	EC-CGO	Douglas DC-9-32	Aviaco *Pedro Alonso Nino*
	EC-CGP	Douglas DC-9-32	Aviaco *Juan Sebastian Elcano*
	EC-CGQ	Douglas DC-9-32	Aviaco *Alonso de Ojeda*
	EC-CGR	Douglas DC-9-32	Aviaco *Francisco de Orellana*
	EC-CID	Boeing 727-256	Iberia *Malaga*
	EC-CIE	Boeing 727-256	Iberia *Esparragosa*
	EC-CLB	Douglas DC-10-30	Iberia *Costa Blanca*
	EC-CLD	Douglas DC-9-32	Aviaco *Hernando de Soto*
	EC-CLE	Douglas DC-9-32	Aviaco *Jaun Ponce de Leon*
	EC-CNH	CV-990A Coronado	(stored/Palma)
	EC-CSJ	Douglas DC-10-30	Iberia *Costa de la Luz*
	EC-CSK	Douglas DC-10-30	Iberia *Cornisa Cantabrica*
	EC-CTR	Douglas DC-9-34CF	Aviaco *Hernan Cortes*
	EC-CTS	Douglas DC-9-34CF	Aviaco *Francisco Pizarro*
	EC-CTT	Douglas DC-9-34CF	Aviaco *Pedro de Valdivia*
	EC-CTU	Douglas DC-9-34CF	Aviaco *Pedro de Alvarado*
	EC-DCC	Boeing 727-256	Iberia *Albarino*
	EC-DCD	Boeing 727-256	Iberia *Chacoli*
	EC-DCE	Boeing 727-256	Iberia *Mentrida*
	EC-DDV	Boeing 727-256	Iberia *Acueducto de Segovia*
	EC-DDX	Boeing 727-256	Iberia *Monasterio de Poblet*
	EC-DDY	Boeing 727-256	Iberia *Cuevas de Altamira*
	EC-DDZ	Boeing 727-256	Iberia *Murallas de Avila*
	EC-DEA	Douglas DC-10-30	Iberia *Rias Gallegas*
	EC-DGB	Douglas DC-9-34	Aviaco *Castillo de Javier*
	EC-DGC	Douglas DC-9-34	Aviaco *Castillo de Sotomayor*
	EC-DGD	Douglas DC-9-34	Aviaco *Castillo de Arcos*
	EC-DGE	Douglas DC-9-34	Aviaco *Castillo de Bellver*
	EC-DHZ	Douglas DC-10-30	Iberia *Costas Canarias*
	EC-DIA	Boeing 747-256B	Iberia *Tirso de Molina*
	EC-DIB	Boeing 747-256B	Iberia *Cervantes*
	EC-DLC	Boeing 747-256B SCD	Iberia *Francisco de Quevedo*
	EC-DLD	Boeing 747-256B SCD	Iberia *Lupe de Vega*
	EC-DLE	Airbus A.300B4-120	Iberia *Doana*
	EC-DLF	Airbus A.300B4-120	Iberia *Canadas del Teide*
	EC-DLG	Airbus A.300B4-120	Iberia *Tablas de Daimiel*
	EC-DLH	Airbus A.300B4-120	Iberia *Aigues Tortes*
	EC-DNP	Boeing 747-256B	Iberia *Juan Ramon Jimenez*
	EC-DNQ	Airbus A.300B4-120	Iberia *Islas Cies*
	EC-DNR	Airbus A.300B4-120	Iberia *Ordesa*
	EC-EAK	Boeing 737-3Q8	Air Europa/Iberia
	EC-EBX	Boeing 737-3Y0	Hispania
	EC-EBY	Boeing 737-3Y0	Hispania
	EC-ECM	Boeing 737-3S3	Air Europa/Air Europe (G-BNXP)
	EC-ECN	Douglas DC-9-83	Air Sur/Iberia
	EC-ECO	Douglas DC-9-83	Air Sur
	EC-ECQ	Boeing 737-3S3	Air Europa/Air Europe (G-BOYN)
	EC-ECR	Boeing 737-3Y0	Air Europa
	EC-ECS	Boeing 737-375	Air Europa
	EC-ECU	Douglas DC-9-32	Iberia
	EC-EDM	Boeing 737-3Q8	Universair
	EC-EEK	Boeing 747-256B (SCD)	Iberia *Garcia Lorca*
	EC-EFU	Douglas DC-9-83	Lineas Aereas Canarias *Isla de Lanzarote*
	EC-E	Douglas DC-9-83	Lineas Aereas Canarias
	EC-EFX	Boeing 757-2G5	LTE/LTU-Sud (D-AMUR)
	EC-EGH	Boeing 757-2G5	LTE/LTU-Sud (D-AMUS)
	EC-EGI	Boeing 757-236	Air Europa/Air Europe (G-BKRM)
	EC-EGQ	Boeing 737-3Q8	Universair
	EC-EHA	Boeing 737-3L9	Air Europa
	EC-EHJ	Boeing 737-33A	Hispania
	EC-EHK	Boeing 737-33A	Hispania
	EC-EHM	Boeing 737-3Q8	Air Europa/Iberia
	EC-EHT	Douglas DC-9-83	Spanair

Reg.	Type	Owner or Operator	Notes
EC-EHX	Boeing 737-3A4	Viva Air	
EC-EHY	Boeing 757-236	Air Europa	
EC-EHZ	Boeing 737-3Y0	Hispania	
EC-EIA	Boeing 737-3Y0	Hispania	
EC-EID	Boeing 737-3T0	Universair	
EC-EIG	Douglas DC-9-83	Spanair	
EC-EII	Boeing 737-3Q8	Viva Air	
EC-EIK	Douglas DC-9-83	Oasis	
EC-EIR	Boeing 737-3Q8	Viva Air	
EC-	Boeing 737-3Q8	Viva Air	
EC-	Douglas DC-9-83	Oasis	
EC-EJQ	Douglas DC-9-83	Spanair *Sunshine*	
EC-EJU	Douglas DC-9-83	Spanair *Sunbird*	
EC-EJZ	Douglas DC-9-83	Lineas Aereas Canarias	
EC-EKM	Douglas DC-9-83	Oasis	
EC-ELA	Boeing 757-236	Air Europa/Air Europe (G-BOHC)	
EC-	Boeing 737-4Y0	Nortjet	
EC-	Boeing 737-4Y0	Nortjet	
EC-	Boeing 737-4Y0	Nortjet	
EC-	Boeing 757-200	Hispania	
EC-	Boeing 757-200	Hispania	
EC-	Douglas DC-10-30	Lineas Aereas Canarias	
EC-	BAe 146-200QT	Panair/TNT	
EC-	Boeing 757-236	Air Europa/Air Europe (G-BNSD)	
EC-	Boeing 757-236	Air Europa/Air Europe (G-BNSF)	

EI (Republic of Ireland)

Including complete current Irish Civil Register

Reg.	Type	Owner or Operator	Notes
EI-ABI	D.H.84 Dragon	Aer Lingus *Iolar* (EI-AFK)	
EI-ADV	PA-12 Super Cruiser	R. E. Levis	
EI-AFF	B.A. Swallow 2 ★	J. McCarthy	
EI-AFN	B.A. Swallow 2 ★	J. McCarthy	
EI-AGB	Miles M.38 Messenger 4 ★	J. McLoughlin	
EI-AGD	Taylorcraft Plus D ★	H. Wolf	
EI-AGJ	J/1 Autocrat	W. G. Rafter	
EI-AHA	D.H.82A Tiger Moth ★	J. H. Maher	
EI-AHR	D.H.C.1 Chipmunk 22 ★	C. Lane	
EI-AKM	Piper J-3C-65 Cub	Setanta Flying Group	
EI-ALH	Taylorcraft Plus D	N. Reilly	
EI-ALP	Avro 643 Cadet	J. C. O'Loughlin	
EI-ALU	Avro 631 Cadet	M. P. Cahill (*stored*)	
EI-AMK	J/1 Autocrat	Irish Aero Club	
EI-AMO	J/1B Aiglet	R. Hassett (*stored*)	
EI-AND	Cessna 175A	Jack Braithwaite (Ireland) Ltd	
EI-ANE	BAC One-Eleven 208AL	Aer Lingus *St Mel*	
EI-ANF	BAC One-Eleven 208AL	Aer Lingus *St Malachy*	
EI-ANG	BAC One-Eleven 208AL	Aer Lingus *St Declan*	
EI-ANH	BAC One-Eleven 208AL	Aer Lingus *St Ronan*	
EI-ANT	Champion 7ECA Citabria	P. Ryan	
EI-ANY	PA-18 Super Cub 95	The Bogavia Group	
EI-AOB	PA-28 Cherokee 140	J. Surdival & ptnrs	
EI-AOK	Cessna F.172G	R. J. Cloughley & N. J. Simpson	
EI-AOO	Cessna 150E	R. Hassett (*stored*)	
EI-AOP	D.H.82A Tiger Moth ★	Institute of Technology/Dublin	
EI-AOS	Cessna 310B	Joyce Aviation Ltd	
EI-APF	Cessna F.150F	L. O. Kennedy	
EI-APS	Schleicher ASK 14	G. W. Connolly & M. Slazenger	
EI-ARH	Currie Wot/S.E.5 Replica	L. Garrison	
EI-ARM	Currie Wot/S.E.5 Replica	L. Garrison	
EI-ARW	Jodel D.R.1050	P. Walsh & P. Ryan	
EI-ASA	Boeing 737-248	Aer Lingus *St Jarlath*	
EI-ASD	Boeing 737-248C	Aer Lingus *St Ide*	
EI-ASE	Boeing 737-248C	Aer Lingus *St Fachtna*	
EI-ASF	Boeing 737-248	Aer Lingus *St Nathy*	
EI-ASG	Boeing 737-248	Aer Lingus *St Cormack*	
EI-ASH	Boeing 737-248	Aer Lingus *St Eugene*	
EI-ASI	Boeing 747-148	Aer Lingus *St Colmcille*	
EI-ASJ	Boeing 747-148	Aer Lingus *St Patrick*	
EI-ASL	Boeing 737-248C	Aer Lingus *St Killian*	

Notes	Reg.	Type	Owner or Operator
	EI-AST	Cessna F.150H	Liberty Flying Group
	EI-ATC	Cessna 310G	Iona National Airways Ltd
	EI-ATJ	B.121 Pup 1	Wexford Aero Club
	EI-ATK	PA-28 Cherokee 140	Mayo Flying Club Ltd
	EI-ATS	M.S.880B Rallye Club	O. Bruton & G. Farrar
	EI-AUC	Cessna FA.150K Aerobat	Twentieth Air Training Co Ltd
	EI-AUE	M.S.880B Rallye Club	Kilkenny Flying Club Ltd
	EI-AUG	M.S.894 Rallye Minerva 220	Weston Ltd
	EI-AUJ	M.S.880B Rallye Club	P. Mulhall
	EI-AUM	J/1 Autocrat	J. G. Rafter
	EI-AUO	Cessna FA.150K Aerobat	Kerry Aero Club
	EI-AUS	J/5F Aiglet Trainer	T. Stephens & T. Lennon
	EI-AUT	Forney F-1A Aircoupe	Joyce Aviation Ltd
	EI-AUV	PA-23 Aztec 250C	Shannon Executive Aviation
	EI-AUY	Morane-Saulnier M.S.502	G. Warner
	EI-AVB	Aeronca 7AC Champion	G. G. Bracken
	EI-AVC	Cessna F.337F	337 Flying Group
	EI-AVM	Cessna F.150L	P. Kearney
	EI-AVN	Hughes 369HM	Helicopter Maintenance Ltd
	EI-AWE	Cessna F.150M	Third Flight Group
	EI-AWH	Cessna 210J	Southern Air Ltd
	EI-AWP	D.H.82A Tiger Moth	A. Lyons
	EI-AWR	Malmo MFI-9 Junior	M. R. Nesbitt & S. Duignan
	EI-AWU	M.S.880B Rallye Club	Longford Aviation Ltd
	EI-AWW	Cessna 414	Ace Coin (Ireland) Ltd (stored)
	EI-AYA	M.S.880B Rallye Club	D. Bothwell & ptnrs
	EI-AYB	GY-80 Horizon 180	Westwing Flying Group
	EI-AYD	AA-5 Traveler	P. Howick & ptnrs
	EI-AYF	Cessna FRA.150L	Garda Flying Club
	EI-AYI	M.S.880B Rallye Club	J. McNamara
	EI-AYK	Cessna F.172M	S. T. Scully
	EI-AYL	A.109 Airedale	J. Ronan
	EI-AYN	BN-2A Islander	Aer Arran
	EI-AYO	Douglas DC-3A ★	Science Museum, Wroughton
	EI-AYR	Schleicher ASK-16	Kilkenny Airport Ltd
	EI-AYS	PA-22 Colt 108	M. Skelly & R. Hall
	EI-AYT	M.S.894A Rallye Minerva	K. A. O'Connor
	EI-AYV	M.S.892A Rallye Commodore 150	P. Murtagh
	EI-AYW	PA-23 Aztec 250	Chutehall International Ltd
	EI-AYY	Evans VP-1	M. Donoghue
	EI-BAF	Thunder Ax6-56 balloon	W. G. Woollett
	EI-BAJ	SNCAN Stampe SV-4C	Dublin Tiger Group
	EI-BAO	Cessna F.172G	Kingdom Air Ltd
	EI-BAR	Thunder Ax8-105 balloon	J. Burke & V. Hourihane
	EI-BAS	Cessna F.172M	Falcon Aviation Ltd
	EI-BAT	Cessna F.150M	J. Barrow
	EI-BAV	PA-22 Colt 108	J. P. Montcalm
	EI-BAY	Cameron V-77 balloon	F. N. Lewis
	EI-BBC	PA-28 Cherokee 180C	B. Healy
	EI-BBD	Evans VP-1	Volksplane Group
	EI-BBE	Champion 7FC Tri-Traveler (tailwheel)	R. Sharpe
	EI-BBF	EAA P-2 Biplane	B. Feeley
	EI-BBG	M.S.880B Rallye Club	Weston Ltd
	EI-BBI	M.S.892 Rallye Commodore	Kilkenny Airport Ltd
	EI-BBJ	M.S.880B Rallye Club	Weston Ltd
	EI-BBK	A.109 Airedale	H. S. Igoe
	EI-BBL	R. Commander 690A	Earl of Granard
	EI-BBM	Cameron O-65 balloon	Dublin Ballooning Club
	EI-BBN	Cessna F.150M	Sligo N.W. Aero Club
	EI-BBO	M.S.893E Rallye 180GT	J. G. Lacey & ptnrs
	EI-BBV	Piper J-3C-65 Cub	F. Cronin
	EI-BBW	M.S.894A Rallye Minerva	J. J. Ladbrook
	EI-BCE	BN-2A-26 Islander	Aer Arran
	EI-BCF	Bensen B.8M	T. A. Brennan
	EI-BCH	M.S.892A Rallye Commodore 150	The Condor Group
	EI-BCJ	F.8L Falco 1 Srs 3	D. Kelly
	EI-BCK	Cessna F.172K	H. Caulfield
	EI-BCL	Cessna 182P	Iona National Airways
	EI-BCM	Piper J-3C-65 Cub	Kilmoon Flying Group

Reg.	Type	Owner or Operator	Notes
EI-BCN	Piper J-3C-65 Cub	Snowflake Flying Group	
EI-BCO	Piper J-3C-65 Cub	J. Molloy	
EI-BCP	D.628 Condor	A. Delaney	
EI-BCR	Boeing 737-281	Aer Lingus St Oliver Plunkett	
EI-BCS	M.S.880B Rallye Club	J. Murphy	
EI-BCT	Cessna 411A	Avmark (Ireland) Ltd	
EI-BCU	M.S.880B Rallye Club	Weston Ltd	
EI-BCW	M.S.880B Rallye Club	H. Clarke & D. Lodge	
EI-BCY	Beech 200 Super King Air (232)	Minister of Defence	
EI-BDH	M.S.880B Rallye Club	Munster Wings Ltd	
EI-BDK	M.S.880B Rallye Club	Limerick Flying Club Ltd	
EI-BDL	Evans VP-2	J. Duggan	
EI-BDM	PA-23 Aztec 250D ★	Industrial Training School	
EI-BDP	Cessna 182P	172 Flying Group	
EI-BDR	PA-28 Cherokee 180	Cork Flying Club	
EI-BDY	Boeing 737-2E1	Aer Lingus Teo	
EI-BEA	M.S.880B Rallye 100ST	Weston Ltd	
EI-BEB	Boeing 737-248	Aer Lingus Teo St Eunan	
EI-BEC	Boeing 737-248	Aer Lingus Teo St Fiacre	
EI-BED	Boeing 747-130	Aer Linte Eireann Teo St Kieran	
EI-BEE	Boeing 737-281	Aer Lingus Teo St Cronin	
EI-BEI	—	Aer Lingus Teo	
EI-BEJ	—	Aer Lingus Teo	
EI-BEK	Short SD3-60	Aer Lingus Commuter Ltd St Eithne	
EI-BEL	Short SD3-60	Aer Lingus Commuter Ltd St Aoife	
EI-BEN	Piper J-3C-65 Cub	J. J. Sullivan	
EI-BEO	Cessna 310Q	Iona National Airways	
EI-BEP	M.S.892A Rallye Commodore 150	H. Lynch & J. O'Leary	
EI-BEY	Naval N3N-3 ★	Huntley & Huntley Ltd	
EI-BFF	Beech A.23 Musketeer	E. Hopkins	
EI-BFH	Bell 212	Irish Helicopters Ltd	
EI-BFI	M.S.880B Rallye 100ST	J. O'Neill	
EI-BFJ	Beech A.200 Super King Air (234)	Minister of Defence	
EI-BFM	M.S.893E Rallye 235GT	NDM Aviation	
EI-BFO	Piper J-3C-90 Cub	M. Slattery	
EI-BFP	M.S.800B Rallye 100ST	Weston Ltd	
EI-BFR	M.S.880B Rallye 100ST	P. Rogers & K. Cox	
EI-BFS	FRED Srs 2	G. J. McGlennon	
EI-BFV	M.S.880B Rallye 100T	Ormond Flying Club	
EI-BGA	SOCATA Rallye 100ST	J. J. Frew	
EI-BGB	M.S.880B Rallye Club	G. N. Atkinson	
EI-BGD	M.S.880B Rallye Club	N. Kavanagh	
EI-BGG	M.S.892E Rallye 150GT	C. Weldon	
EI-BGH	Cessna F.172N	Iona National Airways	
EI-BGJ	Cessna F.152	Hibernian Flying Club	
EI-BGK	Cessna P206D	Press 22 Aviation Ltd	
EI-BGO	Canadair CL-44D-4J ★	Irish Airports Authority/Dublin	
EI-BGP	Cessna 414A	Iona National Airways	
EI-BGS	M.S.893E Rallye 180GT	M. Farrelly	
EI-BGT	Colt 77A balloon	K. Haugh	
EI-BGU	M.S.880B Rallye Club	M. F. Neary	
EI-BGV	AA-5 Traveler	J. Crowe	
EI-BHB	M.S.887 Rallye 125	Hotel Bravo Flying Club	
EI-BHC	Cessna F.177RG	P. V. Maguire	
EI-BHD	M.S.893E Rallye 180GT	Epic Flying Group	
EI-BHF	M.S.892A Rallye Commodore 150	B. Mullen	
EI-BHI	Bell 206B JetRanger 2	J. Mansfield	
EI-BHK	M.S.880B Rallye Club	J. Lawlor & B. Lyons	
EI-BHL	Beech E90 King Air	Stewart Singlam Fabrics Ltd	
EI-BHM	Cessna 337E	The Ross Flying Group	
EI-BHN	M.S.893A Rallye Commodore 180	K. O'Driscoll & ptnrs	
EI-BHO	Sikorsky S-61N	Irish Helicopters Ltd	
EI-BHP	M.S.893A Rallye Commodore 180	G. Atkinson	
EI-BHT	Beech 77 Skipper	Waterford Aero Club	
EI-BHV	Champion 7EC Traveler	Condor Group	
EI-BHW	Cessna F.150F	Shannon Executive Aviation	
EI-BHY	SOCATA Rallye 150ST	D. Killian	

EI

Notes	Reg.	Type	Owner or Operator
	EI-BIB	Cessna F.152	Galway Flying Club
	EI-BIC	Cessna F.172N	Oriel Flying Group Ltd
	EI-BID	PA-18 Super Cub 95	D. MacCarthy
	EI-BIF	SOCATA Rallye 235E	Empire Enterprises Ltd
	EI-BIG	Zlin 526	P. von Lonkhuyzen
	EI-BIJ	AB-206B JetRanger 2	Celtic Helicopters Ltd
	EI-BIK	PA-18 Super Cub 180	Dublin Gliding Club
	EI-BIM	M.S.880B Rallye Club	D. Millar
	EI-BIO	Piper J-3C-65 Cub	Monasterevin Flying Club
	EI-BIR	Cessna F.172M	V. O'Reilly
	EI-BIS	Robin R.1180TD	Robin Aiglon Group
	EI-BIT	M.S.887 Rallye 125	City Aviation Ltd
	EI-BIU	Robin R.2112A	Wicklow Flying Group
	EI-BIV	Bellanca 8KCAB Citabria	Aerocrats Flying Group
	EI-BIW	M.S.880B Rallye Club	E. J. Barr
	EI-BJA	Cessna FRA.150L	Blackwater Flying Group
	EI-BJC	Aeronca 7AC Champion	R. J. Bentley
	EI-BJG	Robin R.1180	N. Hanley
	EI-BJJ	Aeronca 15AC Sedan	A. A. Alderdice & S. H. Boyd
	EI-BJK	M.S.880B Rallye 110ST	P. Slazenger
	EI-BJL	Cessna 550 Citation II	Helicopter Maintenance Ltd
	EI-BJM	Cessna A.152	Leinster Aero Club
	EI-BJN	Cessna 500 Citation	Tool & Mould Steel (Ireland) Ltd
	EI-BJO	Cessna R.172K	P. Hogan & G. Ryder
	EI-BJS	AA-5B Tiger	P. Morrisey
	EI-BJT	PA-38-112 Tomahawk	Shannon Executive Aviation
	EI-BJW	D.H.104 Dove 6 ★	Waterford Museum
	EI-BKC	Aeronca 115AC Sedan	G. Treacy
	EI-BKD	Mooney M.20J	Limerick Warehousing Ltd
	EI-BKF	Cessna F.172H	M. & M. C. Veale
	EI-BKK	Taylor JT.1 Monoplane	Waterford Aero Club
	EI-BKM	Zenith CH.200	B. McGann
	EI-BKN	M.S.880B Rallye 100ST	Weston Ltd
	EI-BKP	Zenith CH.200	L. McEntegart
	EI-BKS	Eipper Quicksilver	Irish Microlight Ltd
	EI-BKT	AB-206B JetRanger 3	Irish Helicopters Ltd
	EI-BKU	M.S.892A Rallye Commodore 150	Limerick Flying Club
	EI-BLB	Stampe SV-4C	J. E. Hutchinson & R. A. Stafford
	EI-BLD	Bolkow Bo 105C	Irish Helicopters Ltd
	EI-BLE	Eipper Microlight	R. P. St George-Smith
	EI-BLG	AB-206B JetRanger 3	Anglo Irish Meat Co Ltd
	EI-BLN	Eipper Quicksilver MX	O. J. Conway & B. Daffy
	EI-BLO	Catto CP.16	R. W. Hall
	EI-BLR	PA-34-200T Seneca II	R. Paris
	EI-BLU	Evans VP-1	S. Pallister
	EI-BLW	PA-23 Aztec 250C	Shannon Executive Aviation
	EI-BLY	Sikorsky S-61N	Irish Helicopters Ltd
	EI-BMA	M.S.880B Rallye Club	Trinity Aviation Ltd
	EI-BMB	M.S.880B Rallye 100T	Clyde Court Development Ltd
	EI-BMC	Hiway Demon Skytrike	S. Pallister
	EI-BMF	Laverda F.8L Falco	M. Slazenger & H. McCann
	EI-BMH	M.S.880B Rallye Club	N. J. Bracken
	EI-BMI	SOCATA TB.9 Tampico	Weston Ltd
	EI-BMJ	M.S.880B Rallye 100T	Weston Ltd
	EI-BMK	Cessna 310Q	Iona National Airways Ltd
	EI-BML	PA-23 Aztec 250	Bruton Aircraft Engineering Ltd
	EI-BMM	Cessna F.152 II	Iona National Airways Ltd
	EI-BMN	Cessna F.152 II	Iona National Airways Ltd
	EI-BMO	Robin R.2160	L. Gavin & ptnrs
	EI-BMS	Cessna F.177RG	A. M. Smyth
	EI-BMU	Monnet Sonerai II	P. Forde & D. Connaire
	EI-BMV	AA-5 Traveler	R. C. Cunningham
	EI-BMW	Vulcan Air Trike	L. Maddock
	EI-BNA	Douglas DC-8-63CF	Aer Turas
	EI-BNB	Lake LA-4-200 Buccaneer	L. McNamara & M. Ledwith
	EI-BNC	Cessna F.152	Iona National Airlines
	EI-BND	Conroy CL-44-0	HeavyLift Cargo Airlines Ltd/Stansted
	EI-BNF	Goldwing Canard	T. Morelli
	EI-BNG	M.S.892A Rallye Commodore 150	Shannon Executive Aviation

232

Reg.	Type	Owner or Operator	Notes
EI-BNH	Hiway Skytrike	M. Martin	
EI-BNJ	Evans VP-2	G. A. Cashman	
EI-BNK	Cessna U.206F	Irish Parachute Club Ltd	
EI-BNL	Rand KR-2	K. Hayes	
EI-BNN	SC.7 Skyvan	Shannon Executive Aviation	
EI-BNP	Rotorway 133	R. L. Renfroe	
EI-BNT	Cvjetkovic CA-65	B. Tobin & P. G. Ryan	
EI-BNU	M.S.880B Rallye Club	P. A. Doyle	
EI-BOA	Pterodactyl Ptraveller	A. Murphy	
EI-BOE	SOCATA TB.10 Tobago	P. Byron & ptnrs	
EI-BOH	Eipper Quicksilver	J. Leech	
EI-BOK	PA-23 Aztec 250E	K. A. O'Connor	
EI-BOM	Boeing 737-2T4	Air Tara Ltd (leased in US)	
EI-BON	Boeing 737-2T4	Air Tara Ltd (leased in US)	
EI-BOO	PA-23 Aztec 250C	P. Mercer	
EI-BOR	Bell 222	M. V. O'Brien	
EI-BOT	AS.350B Ecureuil	J. J. Kelly	
EI-BOV	Rand KR-2	G. O'Hara & G. Callan	
EI-BOX	Duet	K. Riccius	
EI-BPB	PA-28R Cherokee Arrow 200	Rathcoole Flying Club	
EI-BPD	Short SD3-60	Aer Lingus Commuter Ltd St Finbarr	
EI-BPE	Viking Dragonfly	G. Bracken	
EI-BPI	EMB-110P1 Bandeirante	Ryanair Ltd	
EI-BPJ	Cessna 182A	J. Matthews & V. McCarthy	
EI-BPL	Cessna F.172K	Phoenix Flying	
EI-BPM	AS.350B Ecureuil	Helicopter Maintenance Ltd	
EI-BPO	Puma Skytrike	A. Morelli	
EI-BPP	Quicksilver MX	J. A. Smith	
EI-BPR	Boeing 737-2S3	Air Tara Ltd (Air UK Leisure as G-BMOR to 7/89)	
EI-BPS	PA-30 Twin Comanche 160	Group Air	
EI-BPT	Skyhook Sabre	T. McGrath	
EI-BPU	Hiway Demon	A. Channing	
EI-BRG	H.S.125 Srs 600	Ven Air (UK) LTd	
EI-BRH	Mainair Gemini Flash	F. Warren & T. McGrath	
EI-BRK	Flexiform Trike	L. Maddock	
EI-BRM	Cessna 172Q	Iona National Airways	
EI-BRO	Cessna F.152	Iona National Airways	
EI-BRP	Canadair CL-44J	Aer Turas	
EI-BRS	Cessna P.172D	D. & M. Hillery	
EI-BRT	Flexwing M17727	M. J. McCrystal	
EI-BRU	Evans VP-1	C. Quinn	
EI-BRV	Hiway Demon	M. Garvey & C. Tully	
EI-BRW	Ultralight Deltabird	A. & E. Aerosports	
EI-BRX	Cessna FRA.150L	P. O'Donnell	
EI-BSC	Cessna F.172N	Colby Investments Ltd	
EI-BSD	Enstrom F-28A	R. Moffet	
EI-BSE	H.S.748 Srs 1	Ryanair Ltd (withdrawn)	
EI-BSF	H.S.748 Srs 1	Ryanair Ltd (withdrawn)	
EI-BSG	Bensen B.80	J. Todd	
EI-BSH	Colt 77A balloon	T. McCormack	
EI-BSI	Douglas C-47B	Apple Air Services Ltd (stored)	
EI-BSK	SOCATA TB.9 Tampico	Weston Ltd	
EI-BSL	PA-34-220T Seneca	E. L. Symons	
EI-BSN	Cameron O-65 balloon	W. Woollett	
EI-BSO	PA-28 Cherokee 140B	D. Rooney	
EI-BSP	Short SD3-60	Aer Lingus Commuter Ltd St Senan	
EI-BSQ	Thundercolt Ax6-56Z balloon	D. Hooper	
EI-BSR	Lake LA.4-200 Buccaneer	Avmark Ltd	
EI-BSS	RomBac One-Eleven 561RC	Ryanair Ltd Spirit of Ireland	
EI-BST	Bell 206B JetRanger	Celtic Helicopters Ltd	
EI-BSU	Champion 7KCAB	R. Bentley	
EI-BSV	SOCATA TB.20 Trinidad	J. Condron	
EI-BSW	Solar Wings Pegasus XL-R	E. Fitzgerald	
EI-BSX	Piper J-3C-65 Cub	J. & T. O'Dwyer	
EI-BSY	BAC One-Eleven 525T	Ryanair Ltd Spirit of Tipperary	
EI-BSZ	BAC One-Eleven 525T	Ryanair Ltd Spirit of Dublin	
EI-BTC	Douglas DC-9-82	Irish Aerospace Ltd (leased in US)	
EI-BTD	Douglas DC-9-82	Irish Aerospace Ltd (leased in US)	
EI-BTF	Boeing 737-3Y0	Air Tara Ltd (leased to Corse Air)	
EI-BTN	L.1101-385 TriStar 1	Air Tara Ltd (leased to Air America)	
EI-BTS	Boeing 747-283B	Air Tara Ltd	
EI-BTT	Boeing 737-3Y0	Air Tara Ltd	
EI-BTU	Douglas DC-9-82	Air Tara Ltd (leased to Unifly)	

Notes	Reg.	Type	Owner or Operator
	EI-BTV	Douglas DC-9-82	Air Tara Ltd (leased to Unifly)
	EI-BTW	Boeing 737-2Q8	Air Tara Ltd
	EI-BTX	Douglas DC-9-82	Air Tara Ltd (leased to Unifly)
	EI-BTY	Douglas DC-9-82	Air Tara Ltd
	EI-BTZ	Boeing 737-2U4	Air Tara Ltd
	EI-BUA	Cessna 172M	B. Norton
	EI-BUC	Jodel D.9 Bebe	L. Maddock
	EI-BUD	Boeing 737-348	Aer Lingus St Lawrance O'Toole
	EI-BUE	Boeing 737-348	Aer Lingus St Ciara
	EI-BUF	Cessna 210N	210 Group
	EI-BUG	SOCATA ST.10 Diplomate	Diplomatic Flying Group
	EI-BUH	Lake LA.4-200 Buccaneer	Translift Ltd
	EI-BUJ	M.S.892A Rallye Commodore 150	S. Bruton
	EI-BUK	Cessna 402B	D. & M. Hillary
	EI-BUL	MW-5 Sorcerer	J. Green
	EI-BUM	Cessna 404	Iona National Airways Ltd
	EI-BUN	Beech 76 Duchess	S. Ryle
	EI-BUO	Lavery Sea Hawker	C. Lavery & C. Donaldson
	EI-BUR	PA-38-112 Tomahawk	Avmark Ltd
	EI-BUS	PA-38-112 Tomahawk	Avmark Ltd
	EI-BUT	M.S.893A Commodore 180	T. Keating
	EI-BUU	Solar Wings Pegasus XL-R	R. L. T. Hudson
	EI-BUV	Cessna 172RG	J. J. Spollen
	EI-BUW	Noble Hardman Snowbird IIIA	Weston Ltd
	EI-BUX	Agusta A.109A	Orring Ltd
	EI-BUY	Cessna 551 Citation 2	Tool & Mould Steel (Ireland) Ltd
	EI-BUZ	Robinson R-22	Avmark Ltd
	EI-BVA	Cessna 404 Titan	Iona National Airways Ltd
	EI-BVB	Whittaker MW.6 Merlin	R. England
	EI-BVC	Cameron N-65 balloon	E. Shepherd
	EI-BVD	Boeing 707	Club Air
	EI-BVE	Jodel D.9 Bebe	J. Greene
	EI-BVF	Cessna F.172N	Ryanair Ltd
	EI-BVG	BAC One-Eleven 525FT	Ryanair Ltd
	EI-BVH	RomBac One-Eleven 561RC	Ryanair Ltd The Spirit of Tara
	EI-BVI	RomBac One-Eleven 561RC	Ryanair Ltd
	EI-BVJ	AMF Chevvron 232	W. T. King & S. G. Dunne
	EI-BVK	PA-38 Tomahawk	Shannon Executive Aviation
	EI-BVL	Bell 412	Vellore Ltd
	EI-BVM	Short SD3-60	Aer Lingus Commuter Ltd St Maeve
	EI-BVN	Bell 206B Jet Ranger	Helicopter Hire (Ireland) Ltd
	EI-BVP	Cessna T.303	Iona National Airways Ltd
	EI-BVQ	Hot Air Free balloon	T. McCormack
	EI-BVR	Robinson R-22A	Robinson Group
	EI-BVS	Cessna 172RG	Thermo Logic
	EI-BVT	Evans VP-2	J. J. Sullivan
	EI-BVU	Cessna 152	Iona National Airways Ltd
	EI-BVW	Cessna 152	Iona National Airways Ltd
	EI-BVX	EMB-110P1 Bandeirante	Iona National Airways Ltd
	EI-BVY	Zenith 200AA-RW	J. Matthews & ptnrs
	EI-BVZ	Scheibe SF.25B Falke	D. Lamb & ptnrs
	EI-BWB	Douglas DC-9-82	Air Tara Ltd
	EI-BWC	Douglas DC-9-82	Air Tara Ltd
	EI-BWD	Douglas DC-9-83	Air Tara Ltd
	EI-BWE	Douglas DC-9-83	Air Tara Ltd (leased in France)
	EI-BWF	Boeing 747-283B	Air Tara Ltd (leased)
	EI-BWG	Douglas DC-8-71	Air Tara Ltd (leased to Kenya Airways)
	EI-BWH	Partenavia P.68C	K. Buckley
	EI-BWI	BAC One-Eleven 201AC	Air Tara Ltd (leased Braniff Express)
	EI-BWJ	BAC One-Eleven 210AC	Air Tara Ltd (leased Braniff Express)
	EI-BWK	BAC One-Eleven 201AC	Air Tara Ltd (leased Braniff Express)
	EI-BWL	BAC One-Eleven 201AC	Air Tara Ltd (leased Braniff Express)
	EI-BWM	BAC One-Eleven 201AC	Air Tara Ltd (leased Braniff Express)
	EI-BWN	BAC One-Eleven 203AE	Air Tara Ltd (leased Braniff Express)
	EI-BWO	BAC One-Eleven 203AE	Air Tara Ltd (leased Braniff Express)
	EI-BWP	BAC One-Eleven 203AE	Air Tara Ltd (leased Braniff Express)
	EI-BWQ	BAC One-Eleven 401AK	Air Tara Ltd (leased Braniff Express)
	EI-BWR	BAC One-Eleven 401AK	Air Tara Ltd (leased Braniff Express)
	EI-BWS	BAC One-Eleven 201AC	Air Tara Ltd (leased Braniff Express)
	EI-BWT	BAC One-Eleven 414ED	Air Tara Ltd (leased Braniff Express)
	EI-BWU	Swearingen SA227AC Metro III	Air Tara Ltd (leased Air Kentucky)
	EI-BWV	Swearingen SA227AC Metro III	Air Tara Ltd (leased Air Kentucky)
	EI-BWW	Swearingen SA227AC Metro III	Air Tara Ltd (leased Air Kentucky)
	-BWX	D.H.C.8-102 Dash Eight	Air Tara Ltd (leased Hamburg Airlines)

Reg.	Type	Owner or Operator	Notes
EI-BWY	Boeing 737-291	Air Tara Ltd (*leased Indian Airlines*)	
EI-BWZ	Boeing 737-291	Air Tara Ltd (*leased Indian Airlines*)	
EI-BXA	Boeing 737-448	Aer Lingus Teo	
EI-BXB	Boeing 737-448	Aer Lingus Teo	
EI-BXC	—	Aer Lingus Teo	
EI-BXD	—	Aer Lingus Teo	
EI-BXE	—	Aer Lingus Teo	
EI-BXF	—	Aer Lingus Teo	
EI-BXG	—	Aer Lingus Teo	
EI-BXH	—	Aer Lingus Teo	
EI-BXI	—	Aer Lingus Teo	
EI-BXJ	—	Aer Lingus Teo	
EI-BXK	—	Aer Lingus Teo	
EI-BXL	—	Aer Lingus Teo	
EI-BXM	—	Aer Lingus Teo	
EI-BXN	Canadair CL.601A-3A Challenger	Ven Air (UK) Ltd	
EI-BXO	Fouga CM.170 Magister	G. W. Connolly	
EI-BXP	PA-23 Aztec 250E	Aer Arran	
EI-BXQ	Bell 206B JetRanger 2	Irish Helicopters Ltd	
EI-BXR	Aerospatiale ATR-42-300	Ryanair Ltd	
EI-BXS	Aerospatiale ATR-42-300	Ryanair Ltd	
EI-BXT	D.62B Condor	J. Sweeney	
EI-BXU	PA-28-161 Warrior II	W. T. King	
EI-BXV	Boeing 737-212	Air Tara Ltd (*leased Indian Airlines*)	
EI-BXW	Boeing 737-291	Air Tara Ltd (*leased Indian Airlines*)	
EI-BXX	—	—	
EI-BXY	—	—	
EI-BXZ	—	—	
EI-CHL	Bell 206B JetRanger 3		
EI-EDR	PA-28R Cherokee Arrow 200	E. Ryan	
EI-FDX	Cessna 208	Iona Naitonal Airways (FedEx)	
EI-FKA	Fokker 50	Aer Lingus Commuter	
EI-FKB	Fokker 50	Aer Lingus Commuter	
EI-FKC	Fokker 50	Aer Lingus Commuter	
EI-FKD	Fokker 50	Aer Lingus Commuter	
EI-GPA	Canadair CL-601S Challenger	Air Tara Ltd	
EI-XMA	Robinson R-22B	Spectra Photographic Laboratories Ltd	

EP (Iran)

EP-IAA	Boeing 747SP-86	Iran Air *Fars*	
EP-IAB	Boeing 747SP-86	Iran Air *Kurdistan*	
EP-IAC	Boeing 747SP-86	Iran Air *Khuzestan*	
EP-IAD	Boeing 747SP-86	Iran Air	
EP-IAG	Boeing 747-286B (SCD)	Iran Air *Azarabadegan*	
EP-IAH	Boeing 747-286B (SCD)	Iran Air *Khorasan*	
EP-IAM	Boeing 747-186B	Iran Air	
EP-ICA	Boeing 747-2J9F	Iran Air	
EP-ICB	Boeing 747-2J9F	Iran Air	
EP-ICC	Boeing 747-2J9F	Iran Air	
EP-IRK	Boeing 707-321C	Iran Air	
EP-IRL	Boeing 707-386C	Iran Air *Apadana*	
EP-IRM	Boeing 707-386C	Iran Air *Ekbatana*	
EP-IRN	Boeing 707-386C	Iran Air *Pasargad*	
EP-NHD	Boeing 747-131F	Iran Air	
EP-NHK	Boeing 747-131F	Iran Air	
EP-NHN	Boeing 747-2J9F	Iran Air	
EP-NHP	Boeing 747-131F	Iran Air	
EP-NHR	Boeing 747-131F	Iran Air	
EP-NHS	Boeing 747-131	Iran Air	
EP-NHT	Boeing 747-131F	Iran Air	
EP-NHV	Boeing 747-131F	Iran Air	

ET (Ethiopia)

ET-ACQ	Boeing 707-379C	Ethiopian Airlines	
ET-AIE	Boeing 767-260ER	Ethiopian Airlines	
ET-AIF	Boeing 767-260ER	Ethiopian Airlines	
ET-AIV	Boeing 707-327C	Ethiopian Airlines	
ET-AIZ	Boeing 767-260ER	Ethiopian Airlines	

F (France)

Notes	Reg.	Type	Owner or Operator
	F-BEIG	Douglas DC-3C	Stellair *Le Petit Prince*
	F-BIUK	F.27 Friendship Mk 100	Uni-Air
	F-BJEN	S.E.210 Caravelle 10B	Air Charter/Europe Aero Service
	F-BJTU	S.E.210 Caravelle 10B	Air Charter/Europe Aero Service
	F-BLHX	Nord 262A	Compagnie Air Littoral
	F-BMKS	S.E.210 Caravelle 10B	Air Charter/Europe Aero Service
	F-BNOG	S.E.210 Caravelle 12	Air Inter
	F-BNOH	S.E.210 Caravelle 12	Air Inter
	F-BOJA	Boeing 727-228	Air France
	F-BOJB	Boeing 727-228	Air France
	F-BOJC	Boeing 727-228	Air France
	F-BOJD	Boeing 727-228	Air France
	F-BOJE	Boeing 727-228	Air France
	F-BOJF	Boeing 727-228	Air France (*until October 1989*)
	F-BPJK	Boeing 727-228	Air France
	F-BPJL	Boeing 727-228	Air France
	F-BPJM	Boeing 727-228	Air France
	F-BPJN	Boeing 727-228	Air France (*until October 1989*)
	F-BPJO	Boeing 727-228	Air France
	F-BPJP	Boeing 727-228	Air France
	F-BPJQ	Boeing 727-228	Air France
	F-BPJR	Boeing 727-228	Air Charter
	F-BPJS	Boeing 727-228	Air France
	F-BPJT	Boeing 727-228	Air France
	F-BPJU	Boeing 727-214	Air Charter
	F-BPJV	Boeing 727-214	Air Charter
	F-BPNG	F.27 Friendship Mk 500	Brit Air
	F-BPNI	F.27 Friendship Mk 500	Brit Air
	F-BPPA	Aero Spacelines Super Guppy-201	Airbus Industrie *Airbus Skylink 2*
	F-BPUA	F.27 Friendship Mk 500	Air France
	F-BPUB	F.27 Friendship Mk 500	Air France
	F-BPUC	F.27 Friendship Mk 500	Air France
	F-BPUD	F.27 Friendship Mk 500	Air France
	F-BPUE	F.27 Friendship Mk 500	Air France
	F-BPUF	F.27 Friendship Mk 500	Air France
	F-BPUG	F.27 Friendship Mk 500	Air France
	F-BPUH	F.27 Friendship Mk 500	Air France
	F-BPUI	F.27 Friendship Mk 500	Air France
	F-BPUJ	F.27 Friendship Mk 500	Air France
	F-BPUK	F.27 Friendship Mk 500	Air France
	F-BPUL	F.27 Friendship Mk 500	Air France
	F-BPVA	Boeing 747-128	Air France
	F-BPVB	Boeing 747-128	Air France
	F-BPVC	Boeing 747-128	Air France
	F-BPVD	Boeing 747-128	Air France/Air Inter
	F-BPVE	Boeing 747-128	Air France
	F-BPVF	Boeing 747-128	Air France
	F-BPVG	Boeing 747-128	Air France
	F-BPVH	Boeing 747-128	Air France
	F-BPVJ	Boeing 747-128	Air France
	F-BPVK	Boeing 747-128	Air France
	F-BPVL	Boeing 747-128	Air France
	F-BPVM	Boeing 747-128	Air France
	F-BPVN	Boeing 747-128	Air France
	F-BPVO	Boeing 747-228F (SCD)	Air France
	F-BPVP	Boeing 747-128	Air France
	F-BPVQ	Boeing 747-128	Air France
	F-BPVR	Boeing 747-228F (SCD)	Air France
	F-BPVS	Boeing 747-228B (SCD)	Air France
	F-BPVT	Boeing 747-228B (SCD)	Air France
	F-BPVU	Boeing 747-228B (SCD)	Air France
	F-BPVV	Boeing 747-228F (SCD)	Air France
	F-BPVX	Boeing 747-228B (SCD)	Air France
	F-BPVY	Boeing 747-228B	Air France
	F-BPVZ	Boeing 747-228F (SCD)	Air France
	F-BRGU	S.E.210 Caravelle VI-N	Minerve
	F-BRUN	Beech 99	T.A.T.
	F-BSUM	F.27 Friendship Mk 500	Air France
	F-BSUN	F.27 Friendship Mk 500	Air France
	F-BSUO	F.27 Friendship Mk 500	Air France

Reg.	Type	Owner or Operator	Notes
F-BTDB	Douglas DC-10-30	Union de Transports Aériens (UTA)	
F-BTDC	Douglas DC-10-30	Union de Transports Aériens (UTA)	
F-BTDD	Douglas DC-10-30	Union de Transports Aériens (UTA)	
F-BTDE	Douglas DC-10-30	Union de Transports Aériens (UTA)	
F-BTDF	Douglas DC-10-30	Union de Transports Aériens (UTA)	
F-BTDG	Boeing 747-3B3 (SCD)	Union de Transports Aériens (UTA)	
F-BTDH	Boeing 747-3B3 (SCD)	Union de Transports Aériens (UTA)	
F-BTGV	Aero Spacelines Super Guppy-201	Airbus Industrie *Airbus Skylink 1*	
F-BTMA	Beech 99	T.A.T.	
F-BTMD	Mercure 100	Air Inter	
F-BTMJ	Beech 99A	T.A.T.	
F-BTMK	Beech 99A	T.A.T.	
F-BTOA	S.E.210 Caravelle 12	Air Inter	
F-BTOB	S.E.210 Caravelle 12	Air Inter	
F-BTOC	S.E.210 Caravelle 12	Air Inter	
F-BTOD	S.E.210 Caravelle 12	Air Inter	
F-BTOE	S.E.210 Caravelle 12	Air Inter	
F-BTSC	Concorde 101	Air France	
F-BTSD	Concorde 101	Air France	
F-BTTA	Mercure 100	Air Inter	
F-BTTB	Mercure 100	Air Inter	
F-BTTC	Mercure 100	Air Inter	
F-BTTD	Mercure 100	Air Inter	
F-BTTE	Mercure 100	Air Inter	
F-BTTF	Mercure 100	Air Inter	
F-BTTG	Mercure 100	Air Inter	
F-BTTH	Mercure 100	Air Inter	
F-BTTI	Mercure 100	Air Inter	
F-BTTJ	Mercure 100	Air Inter	
F-BUAE	Airbus A.300B2	Air Inter	
F-BUAF	Airbus A.300B2	Air Inter	
F-BUAG	Airbus A.300B2	Air Inter	
F-BUAH	Airbus A.300B2	Air Inter	
F-BUAI	Airbus A.300B2	Air Inter	
F-BUAJ	Airbus A.300B2	Air Inter	
F-BUAK	Airbus A.300B2	Air Inter	
F-BUAL	Airbus A.300B4	Air Inter	
F-BUAM	Airbus A.300B2	Air Inter	
F-BUAN	Airbus A.300B2	Air Inter	
F-BUAO	Airbus A.300B2	Air Inter	
F-BUAP	Airbus A.300B2	Air Inter	
F-BUAQ	Airbus A.300B4	Air Inter	
F-BVFA	Concorde 101	Air France	
F-BVFB	Concorde 101	Air France	
F-BVFC	Concorde 101	Air France *(stored)*	
F-BVFD	Concorde 101	Air France *(stored)*	
F-BVFF	Concorde 101	Air France	
F-BVFG	Nord 262A	Air Limousin *Lac de Vassivière*	
F-BVFH	Nord 262A	Air Limousin	
F-BVFI	Nord 262A	Air Limousin	
F-BVFJ	Nord 262A	Air Limousin *Val de Briance*	
F-BVGA	Airbus A.300B2	Air France	
F-BVGB	Airbus A.300B2	Air France	
F-BVGC	Airbus A.300B2	Air France	
F-BVGD	Airbus A.300B2	Air Inter	
F-BVGE	Airbus A.300B2	Air Inter	
F-BVGF	Airbus A.300B2	Air Inter	
F-BVGG	Airbus A.300B4	Air France	
F-BVGH	Airbus A.300B4	Air France	
F-BVGI	Airbus A.300B4	Air France	
F-BVGJ	Airbus A.300B4	Air France	
F-BVGL	Airbus A.300B4	Air France	
F-BVGM	Airbus A.300B4	Air France/Malaysian Airlines	
F-BVGN	Airbus A.300B4	Air France	
F-BVGO	Airbus A.300B4	Air France	
F-BVGP	Airbus A.300B4	Air France/Air Jamaica	
F-BVGQ	Airbus A.300B4	Air France	
F-BVGR	Airbus A.300B4	Air France	
F-BVGS	Airbus A.300B4	Air France	
F-BVGT	Airbus A.300B4	Air Charter	
F-BVJL	Beech 99A	T.A.T.	
F-BVSF	S.E.210 Caravelle VI-N	Corse Air *Golfe de Porto Vecchio*	
F-BYAB	F.27 Friendship Mk 600	Air Jet	

Notes	Reg.	Type	Owner or Operator
	F-BYAP	F.27 Friendship Mk 100	Uni-Air
	F-GAOT	F.27 Friendship Mk 100 (SCD)	Uni-Air
	F-GAPA	S.E.210 Caravelle VI-N	Minerve
	F-GATS	EMB-110P2 Bandeirante	Compagnie Air Littoral *Hérault*
	F-GATZ	S.E.210 Caravelle VI-N	Minerve
	F-GBBR	F.28 Fellowship 1000	T.A.T./Air France
	F-GBBS	F.28 Fellowship 1000	T.A.T./Air France
	F-GBBT	F.28 Fellowship 1000	T.A.T./Air France
	F-GBBX	F.28 Fellowship 1000	T.A.T./Air France
	F-GBEA	Airbus A.300B2	Air Inter
	F-GBEB	Airbus A.300B2	Air Inter
	F-GBEC	Airbus A.300B2	Air France
	F-GBEI	Nord 262B	Compagnie Air Littoral
	F-GBEJ	Nord 262B	Compagnie Air Littoral
	F-GBEK	Nord 262A	Compagnie Air Littoral
	F-GBGA	EMB-110P2 Bandeirante	Brit Air
	F-GBLE	EMB-110P2 Bandeirante	Brit Air
	F-GBME	EMB-110P2 Bandeirante	Compagnie Air Littoral *Aquitaine*
	F-GBMF	EMB-110P2 Bandeirante	Compagnie Air Littoral
	F-GBMG	EMB-110P2 Bandeirante	Brit Air
	F-GBOX	Boeing 747-2B3F (SCD)	Union de Transports Aériens (UTA)
	F-GBRM	EMB-110P2 Bandeirante	Brit Air
	F-GBRQ	FH.227B Friendship	T.A.T.
	F-GBRU	F.27J Friendship	T.A.T.
	F-GBRZ	FH.227B Friendship	T.A.T.
	F-GBTO	Swearingen SA.226TC Metro II	Compagnie Air Littoral
	F-GBYA	Boeing 737-228	Air France
	F-GBYB	Boeing 737-228	Air France
	F-GBYC	Boeing 737-228	Air France
	F-GBYD	Boeing 737-228	Air France
	F-GBYE	Boeing 737-228	Air France
	F-GBYF	Boeing 737-228	Air France
	F-GBYG	Boeing 737-228	Air France
	F-GBYH	Boeing 737-228	Air France
	F-GBYI	Boeing 737-228	Air France
	F-GBYJ	Boeing 737-228	Air France
	F-GBYK	Boeing 737-228	Air France
	F-GBYL	Boeing 737-228	Air France
	F-GBYM	Boeing 737-228	Air France
	F-GBYN	Boeing 737-228	Air France
	F-GBYO	Boeing 737-228	Air France
	F-GBYP	Boeing 737-228	Air France
	F-GBYQ	Boeing 737-228	Air France
	F-GCBA	Boeing 747-228B	Air France
	F-GCBD	Boeing 747-228B (SCD)	Air France
	F-GCBH	Boeing 747-228B (SCD)	Air France
	F-GCBI	Boeing 747-228B (SCD)	Air France
	F-GCBJ	Boeing 747-228B (SCD)	Air France
	F-GCBK	Boeing 747-228F (SCD)	Air France
	F-GCDA	Boeing 727-228	Air France
	F-GCDB	Boeing 727-228	Air France
	F-GCDC	Boeing 727-228	Air France
	F-GCDD	Boeing 727-228	Air France
	F-GCDE	Boeing 727-228	Air France
	F-GCDF	Boeing 727-228	Air France
	F-GCDG	Boeing 727-228	Air France
	F-GCDH	Boeing 727-228	Air France
	F-GCDI	Boeing 727-228	Air France
	F-GCFC	FH.227B Friendship	T.A.T.
	F-GCFE	Swearingen SA.226TC Metro II	Compagnie Air Littoral
	F-GCGH	FH.227B Friendship	T.A.T.
	F-GCGQ	Boeing 727-227	Europe Aero Service *Normandie*
	F-GCJL	Boeing 737-222	Euralair/Air Charter
	F-GCJO	FH.227B Friendship	ACE Transvalair
	F-GCJT	S.E.210 Caravelle 10B	Europe Aero Service *Alsace*
	F-GCJV	F.27 Friendship Mk 400	Air Jet
	F-GCLA	EMB-110P1 Bandeirante	Aigle Azur
	F-GCLL	Boeing 737-222	Euralair/Air Charter
	F-GCLM	FH.227B Friendship	T.A.T.
	F-GCLN	FH.227B Friendship	T.A.T./Air France
	F-GCLO	FH.227B Friendship	T.A.T.
	F-GCLQ	FH.227B Friendship	T.A.T.
	F-GCMQ	EMB-110P2 Bandeirante	Compagnie Air Littoral *Provence*

Reg.	Type	Owner or Operator	Notes
F-GCMV	Boeing 727-2X3	Air Charter	
F-GCMX	Boeing 727-2X3	Air Charter	
F-GCPG	Swearingen SA.226TC Metro II	Compagnie Air Littoral	
F-GCPT	FH.227B Friendship	T.A.T.	
F-GCPU	FH.227B Friendship	T.A.T.	
F-GCPV	FH.227B Friendship	T.A.T.	
F-GCPX	FH.227B Friendship	T.A.T.	
F-GCPY	FH.227B Friendship	T.A.T.	
F-GCPZ	FH.227B Friendship	T.A.T.	
F-GCSL	Boeing 737-222	Euralair/Air Charter	
F-GCVI	S.E.210 Caravelle 12	Air Inter	
F-GCVJ	S.E.210 Caravelle 12	Air Inter	
F-GCVK	S.E.210 Caravelle 12	Air Inter	
F-GCVL	S.E.210 Caravelle 12	Air Inter	
F-GCVM	S.E.210 Caravelle 12	Air Inter	
F-GDAQ	L.100-30 Hercules	Jet Fret	
F-GDCI	EMB-110P2 Bandeirante	Compagnie Air Littoral *Comté de Nice*	
F-GDFC	F.28 Fellowship 4000	T.A.T./Air France	
F-GDFD	F.28 Fellowship 4000	T.A.T./Air France	
F-GDFY	S.E.210 Caravelle 10B	Air Charter/Europe Aero Service	
F-GDFZ	S.E.210 Caravelle 10B	Air Charter/Europe Aero Service	
F-GDJK	Douglas DC-10-30	Lineas Aereas de Mocambique (LAM)	
F-GDJM	Douglas DC-8-62CF	Minerve	
F-GDJU	S.E.210 Caravelle 10B	Europe Aero Service *Lorraine*	
F-GDMR	Swearingen SA.226TC Metro II	Compagnie Air Littoral	
F-GDPM	Douglas DC-8-53	Minerve	
F-GDPP	Douglas DC-3	ACE Transvalair	
F-GDRM	Douglas DC-8-73	Minerve	
F-GDSG	UTA Super Guppy	Airbus Industrie *Airbus Skylink 3*	
F-GDSK	F.28 Fellowship 4000	T.A.T./Air France	
F-GDUS	F.28 Fellowship 2000	T.A.T.	
F-GDUT	F.28 Fellowship 2000	T.A.T./Air France	
F-GDUU	F.28 Fellowship 2000	T.A.T./Air France	
F-GDUV	F.28 Fellowship 2000	T.A.T./Air France	
F-GDUY	F.28 Fellowship 4000	T.A.T./Air France	
F-GDUZ	F.28 Fellowship 4000	T.A.T./Air France	
F-GDXL	Aerospatiale ATR-42-300	Brit Air/Air France	
F-GDXP	Douglas DC-3	ACE Transvalair	
F-GEAI	UTA Super Guppy	Airbus Industrie *Airbus Skylink 4*	
F-GEBD	Boeing 747-228B	Air France	
F-GEBU	Swearingen SA.226TC Metro II	Compagnie Air Littoral	
F-GECK	F.28 Fellowship 1000	T.A.T./Air France	
F-GEDR	EMB-110 P1 Bandeirante	Compagnie Air Littoral	
F-GEDZ	Aerospatiale ATR-42-300	Compagnie Air Littoral/Air France	
F-GEGD	Aerospatiale ATR-42-300	Compagnie Air Littoral/Air France	
F-GEGE	Aerospatiale ATR-42-300	Compagnie Air Littoral/Air France	
F-GEGF	Aerospatiale ATR-42-300	Compagnie Air Littoral/Air France	
F-GEJE	V.952F Vanguard	EAS Intercargo Service	
F-GELG	Saab SF.340A	Europe Air/Air France	
F-GELH	Saab SF.340A	Europe Air/Air France	
F-GELP	S.E.210 Caravelle	Europe Aero Service	
F-GEMA	Airbus A.310-203	Air France	
F-GEMB	Airbus A.310-203	Air France	
F-GEMC	Airbus A.310-203	Air France	
F-GEMD	Airbus A.310-203	Air France	
F-GEME	Airbus A.310-203	Air France/Air Inter	
F-GEMF	Airbus A.310-203	Air France	
F-GEMG	Airbus A.310-304	Air France	
F-GEMH	Airbus A.310-304	Air France	
F-GEOM	Douglas DC-3C	Stellair	
F-BEQJ	Aerospatiale ATR-42-300	TAT/Aeromaritime	
F-BEQK	Aerospatiale ATR-42-300	TAT	
F-GERV	Swearingen SA226TC Metro II	Air Vendee	
F-GESB	Douglas DC-3C	Stellair	
F-GESM	Douglas DC-8-73CF	Minerve	
F-GETA	Boeing 747-3B3 (SCD)	Union de Transports Aériens (UTA)	
F-GETB	Boeing 747-3B3 (SCD)	Union de Transports Aériens (UTA)	
F-GETM	Douglas DC-8-61	Minerve (*leased as C-FCMV*)	
F-GEXA	Boeing 747-4B3	Union de Transports Aeriens (UTA)	
F-GEXB	Boeing 747-4B3	Union de Transports Aeriens (UTA)	
F-GEXI	Boeing 737-2L9	Air Charter/Europe Aero Service	
F-GEXJ	Boeing 737-200	Air Charter/Europe Aero Service	
F-GEXR	Nord 2501 Noratlas	ACE Transvalair	
F-GEXS	Nord 2501 Noratlas	ACE Transvalair	

F

Reg.	Type	Owner or Operator
F-GEXU	F.28 Fellowship 1000	T.A.T./Air France
F-GEXX	F.28 Fellowship 1000	T.A.T./Air France
F-GEXZ	F.27J Friendship	Air Service Nantes
F-GFAE	D.H.C.6 Twin Otter 310	T.A.T.
F-GFAF	D.H.C.6 Twin Otter 310	T.A.T.
F-GFAG	D.H.C.6 Twin Otter 310	T.A.T.
F-GFAH	D.H.C.6 Twin Otter	T.A.T.
F-GFAJ	D.H.C.6 Twin Otter 310	T.A.T.
F-GFBA	S.E.210 Caravelle 10R	Europe Aero Service
F-GFBH	S.E.210 Caravelle 10B	Europe Aero Service
F-GFBI	S.E.210 Caravelle 10B	Europe Aero Serivce
F-GFBZ	Saab SF.340A	Brit Air
F-GFCN	Douglas DC-8-61	Minerve
F-GFEN	EMB-120 Brasilia	Compagnie Air Littoral/Air France
F-GFEO	EMB-120 Brasilia	Compagnie Air Littoral/Air France
F-GFEP	EMB-120 Brasilia	Compagnie Air Littoral/Air France
F-GFEQ	EMB-120 Brasilia	Compagnie Air Littoral/Air France
F-GFER	EMB-120 Brasilia	Compagnie Air Littoral/Air France
F-GFES	Aerospatiale ATR-42-300	Compagnie Air Littoral/Air France
F-GFGD	Swearingen SA226TC Metro II	T.A.T.
F-GFGE	Swearingen SA226TC Metro II	T.A.T./Air Limousin
F-GFGF	Swearingen SA226TC Metro II	T.A.T./Air Limousin
F-GFIJ	Swearingen SA226TC Metro II	Compagnie Air Littoral
F-GFIK	Swearingen SA226TC Metro II	Compagnie Air Littoral
F-GFIN	EMB-120 Brasilia	Compagnie Air Littoral
F-GFJH	Aerospatiale ATR-42-300	Brit Air/Air France
F-GFJP	Aerospatiale ATR-42-300	Brit Air/Air France
F-GFJS	F.27 Friendship Mk 600	Air Jet
F-GFJU	Swearingen SA226TC Metro II	Air Limousin
F-GFJV	Swearingen SA226TC Metro II	Air Limousin
F-GFJX	Swearingen SA226TC Metro II	Air Limousin
F-GFKA	Airbus A.320-110	Air France *Ville de Paris*
F-GFKB	Airbus A.320-110	Air France *Ville de Rome*
F-GFKD	Airbus A.320-110	Air France
F-GFKE	Airbus A.320-110	Air France
F-GFKF	Airbus A.320-110	Air France
F-GFKG	Airbus A.320-110	Air France
F-GFKH	Airbus A.320-110	Air France
F-GFKI	Airbus A.320-110	Air France
F-GFKJ	Airbus A.320-110	Air France
F-G	Airbus A.320-110	Air France
F-G	Airbus A.320-110	Air France
F-G	Airbus A.320-110	Air France
F-GFLV	Boeing 737-2K5	Air Charter
F-GFLX	Boeing 737-2K5	Air Charter
F-GFUA	Boeing 737-33A	Aeromaritime
F-GFUB	Boeing 737-33A	Aeromaritime
F-GFUC	Boeing 737-33A	Aeromaritime
F-GFUD	Boeing 737-33A	Aeromaritime
F-GFYL	Boeing 737-2A9C	Euralair
F-GFVS	Swearingen SA226TC Metro II	Air Limousin
F-GFXI	Boeing 737-230C	Air Charter/Intercargo Service
F-GFXJ	Boeing 737-230C	Air Charter/Intercargo Service
F-GFZB	Douglas DC-9-83	Air Liberte
F-GGAV	Dornier Do.228-201	Air Vendee
F-GGBJ	Saab SF.340A	Air Limousin
F-GGBV	Saab SF.340A	Air Limousin
F-GGDM	FH.227B Friendship	Uni-Air
F-GGEA	Airbus A.320-110	Air Inter
F-GGEB	Airbus A.320-110	Air Inter
F-GGEC	Airbus A.320-110	Air Inter
F-GGED	Airbus A.320-110	Air Inter
F-GGEE	Airbus A.320-110	Air Inter
F-GGEF	Airbus A.320-110	Air Inter
F-GGEG	Airbus A.320-110	Air Inter
F-GGEH	Airbus A.320-110	Air Inter
F-GGEI	Airbus A.320-110	Air Inter
F-GGEJ	Airbus A.320-110	Air Inter
F-GGEK	Airbus A.320-110	Air Inter
F-GGEL	Airbus A.320-110	Air Inter
F-G	Airbus A.320-110	Air Inter
F-GGGR	Boeing 727-2H3	Europe Aero Service
F-GGGV	Dornier Do.228-201	Air Vendee
F-GGKC	F.28 Fellowship 1000	T.A.T.

Reg.	Type	Owner or Operator	Notes
F-GGLR	Aerospatiale ATR-42-300	Brit Air/Air France	
F-GGMA	Douglas DC-9-83	Minerve	
F-GGMB	Douglas DC-9-83	Minerve	
F-GGMC	Douglas DC-9-83	Minerve	
F-GGPN	FH.227B Friendship	Uni-Air	
F-G	Boeing 737-300	Corse Air	
F-GGSV	Swearingen SA226TC Metro II	Air Vendee	
F-GHBM	Boeing 747-283B	Minerve	
F-GHDB	Saab SF.340A	Brit Air/Air France	
F-GHEB	Douglas DC-9-83	Air Liberte	
F-GHPC	Boeing 747-256B	Corse Air	
F-GHXA	F.27J Friendship	Air Service Nantes	
F-GHXB	F.27J Friendship	Air Service Nantes	
F-GHXK	Boeing 737-2A1	Europe Aero Service *Lorraine*	
F-GIHR	F.27J Friendship	Uni-Air *La Mongié*	
F-GIPD	F.27J Friendship	Uni-Air	
F-GMOL	F.28 Fellowship 1000	T.A.T.	
F-GPAN	Boeing 747-2B3F (SCD)	Air France	
F-GTNT	BAe 146-200QT	Euralair (TNT)	
F-ODJG	Boeing 747-2Q2B	Air Gabon	
F-ODVD	Airbus A.310-304	Royal Jordanian Airline *Prince Hasham*	
F-ODVE	Airbus A.310-304	Royal Jordanian Airline *Princess Iman*	
F-ODVF	Airbus A.310-304	Royal Jordanian Airline *Princess Raiyah*	
F-OGQC	Douglas DC-10-30	Air Zaire	

Note: Air France also operates four more Boeing 747s which retain the US registrations N1289E, N4506H, N4508E and N4544F. UTA also operates one DC-10-30 registered N54649.

HA (Hungary)

HA-LBE	Tupolev Tu-134	Malev	
HA-LBF	Tupolev Tu-134	Malev	
HA-LBG	Tupolev Tu-134	Malev	
HA-LBH	Tupolev Tu-134	Malev	
HA-LBI	Tupolev Tu-134A-3	Malev	
HA-LBK	Tupolev Tu-134A-3	Malev	
HA-LBN	Tupolev Tu-134A-3	Malev	
HA-LBO	Tupolev Tu-134A-3	Malev	
HA-LBP	Tupolev Tu-134A-3	Malev	
HA-LBR	Tupolev Tu-134A-3	Malev	
HA-LCA	Tupolev Tu-154B-2	Malev	
HA-LCB	Tupolev Tu-154B-2	Malev	
HA-LCE	Tupolev Tu-154B-2	Malev	
HA-LCG	Tupolev Tu-154B-2	Malev	
HA-LCH	Tupolev Tu-154B-2	Malev	
HA-LCM	Tupolev Tu-154B-2	Malev	
HA-LCN	Tupolev Tu-154B-2	Malev	
HA-LCO	Tupolev Tu-154B-2	Malev	
HA-LCP	Tupolev Tu-154B-2	Malev	
HA-LCR	Tupolev Tu-154B-2	Malev	
HA-LCS	Tupolev Tu-154B-2	Malev	
HA-LCT	Tupolev Tu-154B-2	Malev	
HA-LCU	Tupolev Tu-154B-2	Malev	
HA-LCV	Tupolev Tu-154B-2	Malev	
HA-LEA	Boeing 737-2Q8	Malev	
HA-LEB	Boeing 737-2M8	Malev	
HA-LEC	Boeing 737-2T5	Malev	
HA-TAB	BAe 146-200QT	TNT/Malev	

HB (Switzerland)

HB-AHA	Saab SF.340A	Crossair	
HB-AHB	Saab SF.340A	Crossair	
HB-AHC	Saab SF.340A	Crossair	
HB-AHD	Saab SF.340A	Crossair	
HB-AHE	Saab SF.340A	Crossair	
HB-AHF	Saab SF.340A	Crossair	
HB-AHG	Saab SF.340A	Crossair	

Notes	Reg.	Type	Owner or Operator
	HB-AHH	Saab SF.340A	Crossair
	HB-AHI	Saab SF.340A	Crossair
	HB-AHK	Saab SF.340A	Crossair
	HB-AHL	Saab SF.340A	Crossair
	HB-AHM	Saab SF.340A	Crossair
	HB-AHN	Saab SF.340A	Crossair
	HB-AHO	Saab SF.340A	Crossair
	HB-AHP	Saab SF.340A	Crossair
	HB-AHQ	Saab SF.340A	Crossair
	HB-AHR	Saab SF.340A	Crossair
	HB-AHS	Saab SF.340A	Crossair
	HB-AHT	Saab SF.340A	Crossair
	HB-	Saab SF.340B	Crossair
	HB-	Saab SF.340B	Crossair
	HB-	Saab SF.340B	Crossair
	HB-	Saab SF.340B	Crossair
	HB-	Saab SF.340B	Crossair
	HB-IBF	Douglas DC-8-63	African Safari Airways
	HB-ICI	S.E.210 Caravelle 10B1R	CTA (withdrawn)
	HB-ICJ	S.E.210 Caravelle 10B	Air City
	HB-ICO	S.E.210 Caravelle 10B1R	CTA Romandie (withdrawn)
	HB-IGC	Boeing 747-357 (SCD)	Swissair Bern
	HB-IGD	Boeing 747-357 (SCD)	Swissair Basel
	HB-IGG	Boeing 747-357 (SCD)	Swissair Ticino
	HB-IHC	Douglas DC-10-30	Swissair Obwalden
	HB-IHE	Douglas DC-10-30	Swissair Vaud
	HB-IHF	Douglas DC-10-30	Swissair Nidwalden
	HB-IHG	Douglas DC-10-30	Swissair Graubünden
	HB-IHH	Douglas DC-10-30	Swissair Schaffhausen
	HB-IHI	Douglas DC-10-30	Swissair Fribourg
	HB-IHK	Douglas DC-10-30	Balair
	HB-IHL	Douglas DC-10-30ER	Swissair Thurgau
	HB-IHM	Douglas DC-10-30ER	Swissair Valais-Wallis
	HB-IHN	Douglas DC-10-30ER	Swissair St Gallen
	HB-IHO	Douglas DC-10-30ER	Swissair Uri
	HB-IKK	Douglas DC-9-82	Alisarda (Italy)
	HB-IKL	Douglas DC-9-82	Alisarda (Italy)
	HB-ILG	L-382G Hercules	Zimex Aviation Ltd
	HB-INA	Douglas DC-9-81	Swissair Höri
	HB-INB	Douglas DC-9-82	Balair
	HB-INC	Douglas DC-9-81	Swissair Lugano
	HB-IND	Douglas DC-9-81	Swissair Bachenbülach
	HB-INE	Douglas DC-9-81	Swissair Rümlang
	HB-INF	Douglas DC-9-81	Swissair Appenzell a.Rh.
	HB-ING	Douglas DC-9-81	Swissair Winkel
	HB-INH	Douglas DC-9-81	Swissair Winterthur
	HB-INI	Douglas DC-9-81	Swissair Kloten
	HB-INK	Douglas DC-9-81	Swissair Opfikon
	HB-INL	Douglas DC-9-81	Swissair Jura
	HB-INM	Douglas DC-9-81	Swissair Lausanne
	HB-INN	Douglas DC-9-81	Swissair Bülach
	HB-INO	Douglas DC-9-81	Swissair Bellinzona
	HB-INP	Douglas DC-9-81	Swissair Oberglatt
	HB-INR	Douglas DC-9-82	Balair
	HB-INS	Douglas DC-9-81	Swissair Meyrin
	HB-INT	Douglas DC-9-81	Swissair Grand-Saconnex
	HB-INU	Douglas DC-9-81	Swissair Vernier
	HB-INV	Douglas DC-9-81	Swissair Dubendorf
	HB-INW	Douglas DC-9-82	Balair
	HB-INX	Douglas DC-9-81	Swissair Wallisellen
	HB-INY	Douglas DC-9-81	Swissair Bassersdorf
	HB-INZ	Douglas DC-9-81	Swissair Regensdorf
	HB-IPA	Airbus A.310-221	Swissair Aargau
	HB-IPB	Airbus A.310-221	Swissair Neuchatel
	HB-IPC	Airbus A.310-221	Swissair Schwyz
	HB-IPD	Airbus A.310-221	Swissair Solothurn
	HB-IPE	Airbus A.310-221	Swissair Basel-Land
	HB-IPF	Airbus A.310-322	Swissair Glarus
	HB-IPG	Airbus A.310-322	Swissair Zug
	HB-IPH	Airbus A.310-322	Swissair Appenzell i. Rh
	HB-IPI	Airbus A.310-322	Swissair Luzern
	HB-IPK	Airbus A.310-322	Balair
	HB-ISG	F.27 Friendship Mk 200	Sunshine Aviation
	HB-ISH	F.27 Friendship Mk 200	Sunshine Aviation

Reg.	Type	Owner or Operator	Notes
HB-ISX	Douglas DC-9-81	Swissair	
HB-IUA	Douglas DC-9-87	CTA	
HB-IUB	Douglas DC-9-87	CTA	
HB-IUC	Douglas DC-9-87	CTA	
HB-IUD	Douglas DC-9-87	CTA	
HB-IVA	Fokker 100	Swissair *Aarau*	
HB-IVB	Fokker 100	Swissair *Biel/Bienne*	
HB-IVC	Fokker 100	Swissair *Chur*	
HB-IVD	Fokker 100	Swissair *Dietlikon*	
HB-IVE	Fokker 100	Swissair *Baden*	
HB-IVF	Fokker 100	Swissair *Sion*	
HB-IVG	Fokker 100	Swissair *Genthod*	
HB-IVH	Fokker 100	Swissair *Binningen*	
HB-IWA	McD Douglas MD-11	Swissair	
HB-IWB	McD Douglas MD-11	Swissair	
HB-IWC	McD Douglas MD-11	Swissair	
HB-IWD	McD Douglas MD-11	Swissair	
HB-IWE	McD Douglas MD-11	Swissair	
HB-IWF	McD Douglas MD-11	Swissair	
HB-IWG	McD Douglas MD-11	Swissair	
HB-IWH	McD Douglas MD-11	Swissair	
HB-IWI	McD Douglas MD-11	Swissair	
HB-IWK	McD Douglas MD-11	Swissair	
HB-IWL	McD Douglas MD-11	Swissair	
HB-IWM	McD Douglas MD-11	Swissair	

Note: Swissair also operates two Boeing 747-357s which retain their US registrations N221GE and N221GF and are named *Genève* and *Zurich* respectively.

HK (Colombia)

HK-2980X	Boeing 747-259B	Avianca *Cartagena de Indias*	

HL (Korea)

HL7315	Douglas DC-10-30	Korean Air	
HL7316	Douglas DC-10-30	Korean Air	
HL7317	Douglas DC-10-30	Korean Air	
HL7328	Douglas DC-10-30	Korean Air	
HL7431	Boeing 707-321C	Korean Air	
HL7435	Boeing 707-321B	Korean Air	
HL7440	Boeing 747-230B	Korean Air	
HL7441	Boeing 747-230F	Korean Air	
HL7443	Boeing 747-2B5B	Korean Air	
HL7447	Boeing 747-230B	Korean Air	
HL7451	Boeing 747-2B5F (SCD)	Korean Air/Saudia	
HL7452	Boeing 747-2B5F (SCD)	Korean Air	
HL7454	Boeing 747-2B5B	Korean Air	
HL7458	Boeing 747-2B5B	Korean Air	
HL7459	Boeing 747-2B5F (SCD)	Korean Air	
HL7463	Boeing 747-2B5B	Korean Air	
HL7464	Boeing 747-2B5B	Korean Air	
HL7468	Boeing 747-3B5	Korean Air	
HL7469	Boeing 747-3B5	Korean Air	
HL7470	Boeing 747-3B5	Korean Air	
HL7471	Boeing 747-273C	Korean Air	
HL7474	Boeing 747-2S4F (SCD)	Korean Air	
HL7475	Boeing 747-2B5F	Korean Air	
HL7476	Boeing 747-2B5F	Korean Air	
HL7477	Boeing 747-4B5	Korean Air	
HL7478	Boeing 747-4B5	Korean Air	
HL7479	Boeing 747-4B5	Korean Air	

HS (Thailand)

Notes	Reg.	Type	Owner or Operator
	HS-TGA	Boeing 747-2D7B	Thai Airways International *Visuthakasatriya*
	HS-TGB	Boeing 747-2D7B	Thai Airways International *Sirisobhakya*
	HS-TGC	Boeing 747-2D7B	Thai Airways International *Dararasmi*
	HS-TGD	Boeing 747-3D7	Thai Airways International *Suchada*
	HS-TGE	Boeing 747-3D7	Thai Airways International *Chutamat*
	HS-TGF	Boeing 747-2D7B	Thai Airways International *Phimara*
	HS-TGG	Boeing 747-2D7B	Thai Airways International *Sriwanna*
	HS-TGH	Boeing 747-4D7	Thai Airways International
	HS-TGJ	Boeing 747-4D7	Thai Airways International
	HS-TGS	Boeing 747-2D7B	Thai Airways International *Chainarai*
	HS-TGV	Boeing 747-4D7	Thai Airways International
	HS-TMA	Douglas DC-10-30ER	Thai Airways International
	HS-TMB	Douglas DC-10-30ER	Thai Airways International *Thepalai*
	HS-TMC	Douglas DC-10-30ER	Thai Airways International *Sri Ubon*

HZ (Saudi Arabia)

	Reg.	Type	Owner or Operator
	HZ-AHA	L.1011-385 TriStar 200	Saudia — Saudi Arabian Airlines
	HZ-AHB	L.1011-385 TriStar 200	Saudia — Saudi Arabian Airlines
	HZ-AHC	L.1011-385 TriStar 200	Saudia — Saudi Arabian Airlines
	HZ-AHD	L.1011-385 TriStar 200	Saudia — Saudi Arabian Airlines
	HZ-AHE	L.1011-385 TriStar 200	Saudia — Saudi Arabian Airlines
	HZ-AHF	L.1011-385 TriStar 200	Saudia — Saudi Arabian Airlines
	HZ-AHG	L.1011-385 TriStar 200	Saudia — Saudi Arabian Airlines
	HZ-AHH	L.1011-385 TriStar 200	Saudia — Saudi Arabian Airlines
	HZ-AHI	L.1011-385 TriStar 200	Saudia — Saudi Arabian Airlines
	HZ-AHJ	L.1011-385 TriStar 200	Saudia — Saudi Arabian Airlines
	HZ-AHL	L.1011-385 TriStar 200	Saudia — Saudi Arabian Airlines
	HZ-AHM	L.1011-385 TriStar 200	Saudia — Saudi Arabian Airlines
	HZ-AHN	L.1011-385 TriStar 200	Saudia — Saudi Arabian Airlines
	HZ-AHO	L.1011-385 TriStar 200	Saudia — Saudi Arabian Airlines
	HZ-AHP	L.1011-385 TriStar 200	Saudia — Saudi Arabian Airlines
	HZ-AHQ	L.1011-385 TriStar 200	Saudia — Saudi Arabian Airlines
	HZ-AHR	L.1011-385 TriStar 200	Saudia — Saudi Arabian Airlines
	HZ-AIA	Boeing 747-168B	Saudia — Saudi Arabian Airlines
	HZ-AIB	Boeing 747-168B	Saudia — Saudi Arabian Airlines
	HZ-AIC	Boeing 747-168B	Saudia — Saudi Arabian Airlines
	HZ-AID	Boeing 747-168B	Saudia — Saudi Arabian Airlines
	HZ-AIE	Boeing 747-168B	Saudia — Saudi Arabian Airlines
	HZ-AIF	Boeing 747SP-68	Saudia — Saudi Arabian Airlines
	HZ-AIG	Boeing 747-168B	Saudia — Saudi Arabian Airlines
	HZ-AIH	Boeing 747-168B	Saudia — Saudi Arabian Airlines
	HZ-AII	Boeing 747-168B	Saudia — Saudi Arabian Airlines
	HZ-AIJ	Boeing 747SP-68	Saudia — Saudi Arabian Airlines
	HZ-AIK	Boeing 747-368	Saudia — Saudi Arabian Airlines
	HZ-AIL	Boeing 747-368	Saudia — Saudi Arabian Airlines
	HZ-AIM	Boeing 747-368	Saudia — Saudi Arabian Airlines
	HZ-AIN	Boeing 747-368	Saudia — Saudi Arabian Airlines
	HZ-AIO	Boeing 747-368	Saudia — Saudi Arabian Airlines
	HZ-AIP	Boeing 747-368	Saudia — Saudi Arabian Airlines
	HZ-AIQ	Boeing 747-368	Saudia — Saudi Arabian Airlines
	HZ-AIR	Boeing 747-368	Saudia — Saudi Arabian Airlines
	HZ-AIS	Boeing 747-368	Saudia — Saudi Arabian Airlines
	HZ-AIT	Boeing 747-368	Saudia — Saudi Arabian Airlines
	HZ-AIU	Boeing 747-268F	Saudia — Saudi Arabian Airlines
	HZ-AJA	Airbus A.300-620	Saudia — Saudi Arabian Airlines
	HZ-AJB	Airbus A.300-620	Saudia — Saudi Arabian Airlines
	HZ-AJC	Airbus A.300-620	Saudia — Saudi Arabian Airlines
	HZ-AJD	Airbus A.300-620	Saudia — Saudi Arabian Airlines
	HZ-AJE	Airbus A.300-620	Saudia — Saudi Arabian Airlines
	HZ-AJF	Airbus A.300-620	Saudia — Saudi Arabian Airlines
	HZ-AJG	Airbus A.300-620	Saudia — Saudi Arabian Airlines
	HZ-AJH	Airbus A.300-620	Saudia — Saudi Arabian Airlines
	HZ-AJI	Airbus A.300-620	Saudia — Saudi Arabian Airlines
	HZ-AJJ	Airbus A.300-620	Saudia — Saudi Arabian Airlines
	HZ-AJK	Airbus A.300-620	Saudia — Saudi Arabian Airlines

Note: Saudia also operates other aircraft on lease.

I (Italy)

Reg.	Type	Owner or Operator	Notes
I-ATIH	Douglas DC-9-32	Aero Trasporti Italiani (ATI) *Lido degli Estensi*	
I-ATIJ	Douglas DC-9-32	Aero Trasporti Italiani (ATI)	
I-ATIQ	Douglas DC-9-32	Aero Trasporti Italiani (ATI) *Sila*	
I-ATIU	Douglas DC-9-32	Aero Trasporti Italiani (ATI)	
I-ATIW	Douglas DC-9-32	Aero Trasporti Italiani (ATI) *Lazio*	
I-ATIY	Douglas DC-9-32	Aero Trasporti Italiani (ATI) *Lombardia*	
I-ATJA	Douglas DC-9-32	Aero Trasporti Italiani (ATI) *Sicilia*	
I-ATJB	Douglas DC-9-32	Aero Trasporti Italiani (ATI) *Riviera del Conero*	
I-BUSB	Airbus A.300B4	Alitalia *Tiziano*	
I-BUSC	Airbus A.300B4	Alitalia *Botticelli*	
I-BUSD	Airbus A.300B4	Alitalia *Caravaggio*	
I-BUSF	Airbus A.300B4	Alitalia *Tintoretto*	
I-BUSG	Airbus A.300B4	Alitalia *Canaletto*	
I-BUSH	Airbus A.300B4	Alitalia *Mantegua*	
I-BUSJ	Airbus A.300B4	Alitalia *Tiepolo*	
I-BUSL	Airbus A.300B4	Alitalia *Pinturicchia*	
I-BUSM	Airbus A.300B2	Alitalia	
I-BUSN	Airbus A.300B2	Alitalia	
I-DAVA	Douglas DC-9-82	Aero Trasporti Italiani (ATI) *Cuneo*	
I-DAVB	Douglas DC-9-82	Alitalia *Ferrara*	
I-DAVC	Douglas DC-9-82	Aero Trasporti Italiani (ATI) *Lucca*	
I-DAVD	Douglas DC-9-82	Aero Trasporti Italiani (ATI) *Mantova*	
I-DAVF	Douglas DC-9-82	Aero Trasporti Italiani (ATI) *Oristano*	
I-DAVG	Douglas DC-9-82	Aero Trasporti Italiani (ATI) *Pesaro*	
I-DAVH	Douglas DC-9-82	Aero Trasporti Italiani (ATI) *Salerno*	
I-DAVI	Douglas DC-9-82	Alitalia *Assisi*	
I-DAVJ	Douglas DC-9-82	Alitalia *Parma*	
I-DAVK	Douglas DC-9-82	Alitalia *Pompei*	
I-DAVL	Douglas DC-9-82	Alitalia	
I-DAVM	Douglas DC-9-82	Alitalia	
I-DAVN	Douglas DC-9-82	Alitalia	
I-D	Douglas DC-9-82	Alitalia	
I-D	Douglas DC-9-82	Alitalia	
I-DAWA	Douglas DC-9-82	Alitalia *Roma*	
I-DAWB	Douglas DC-9-82	Alitalia *Cagliari*	
I-DAWC	Douglas DC-9-82	Alitalia *Campobasso*	
I-DAWD	Douglas DC-9-82	Alitalia *Catanzaro*	
I-DAWE	Douglas DC-9-82	Alitalia *Milano*	
I-DAWF	Douglas DC-9-82	Alitalia *Firenze*	
I-DAWG	Douglas DC-9-82	Alitalia *L'Aquila*	
I-DAWH	Douglas DC-9-82	Alitalia *Palermo*	
I-DAWI	Douglas DC-9-82	Alitalia *Ancona*	
I-DAWJ	Douglas DC-9-82	Alitalia *Genova*	
I-DAWL	Douglas DC-9-82	Alitalia *Perugia*	
I-DAWM	Douglas DC-9-82	Alitalia *Potenza*	
I-DAWO	Douglas DC-9-82	Alitalia *Bari*	
I-DAWP	Douglas DC-9-82	Alitalia *Torino*	
I-DAWQ	Douglas DC-9-82	Alitalia *Trieste*	
I-DAWR	Douglas DC-9-82	Alitalia *Venezia*	
I-DAWS	Douglas DC-9-82	Alitalia *Aosta*	
I-DAWT	Douglas DC-9-82	Aero Trasporti Italiani (ATI) *Napoli*	
I-DAWU	Douglas DC-9-82	Alitalia *Bologna*	
I-DAWV	Douglas DC-9-82	Aero Trasporti Italiani (ATI) *Trento*	
I-DAWW	Douglas DC-9-82	Aero Trasporti Italiani (ATI) *Riace*	
I-DAWY	Douglas DC-9-82	Aero Trasporti Italiani (ATI) *Agrigento*	
I-DAWZ	Douglas DC-9-82	Aero Trasporti Italiani (ATI) *Avellino*	
I-DEMC	Boeing 747-243B (SCD)	Alitalia *Taormina*	
I-DEMD	Boeing 747-243B (SCD)	Alitalia *Cortina d'Ampezzo*	
I-DEMF	Boeing 747-243B (SCD)	Alitalia *Portofino*	
I-DEMG	Boeing 747-243B	Alitalia *Cervinia*	
I-DEML	Boeing 747-243B	Alitalia *Sorrento*	
I-DEMN	Boeing 747-243B	Alitalia *Portocervo*	
I-DEMP	Boeing 747-243B	Alitalia *Capri*	
I-DEMR	Boeing 747-243F (SCD)	Alitalia *Stresa*	
I-DEMS	Boeing 747-243B	Alitalia *Monte Argentario*	
I-DEMT	Boeing 747-243B (SCD)	Alitalia *Monte Catini*	
I-DEMV	Boeing 747-243B	Alitalia *Sestriere*	

Notes	Reg.	Type	Owner or Operator
	I-DEMW	Boeing 747-243B	Alitalia *Spoleto*
	I-DIBO	Douglas DC-9-32	Aero Trasporti Italiani (ATI) *Conca d'Ora*
	I-DIBR	Douglas DC-9-32	Alitalia *Isola di Capri*
	I-DIBS	Douglas DC-9-32	Alitalia *Isola d'Elba*
	I-DIBT	Douglas DC-9-32	Alitalia *Isola di Murano*
	I-DIBU	Douglas DC-9-32	Alitalia *Isola di Pantellaria*
	I-DIBV	Douglas DC-9-32	Alitalia *Isola d'Ischia*
	I-DIBW	Douglas DC-9-32	Alitalia *Isola del Giglio*
	I-DIBX	Douglas DC-9-32	Alitalia *Isola di Giannutri*
	I-DIBY	Douglas DC-9-32	Alitalia *Isola di Panarea*
	I-DIBZ	Douglas DC-9-32	Alitalia *Isola di Lipari*
	I-DIKM	Douglas DC-9-32	Alitalia *Isola di Positano*
	I-DIKP	Douglas DC-9-32	Alitalia *Isola di Marettimo*
	I-DIKR	Douglas DC-9-32	Alitalia *Piemonte*
	I-DIKS	Douglas DC-9-32	Aero Trasporti Italiani (ATI) *Basilicata*
	I-DIKT	Douglas DC-9-32	Aero Trasporti Italiani (ATI) *Isola d'Ustica*
	I-DIKY	Douglas DC-9-32	Aero Trasporti Italiani (ATI) *Puglia*
	I-DIZC	Douglas DC-9-32	Aero Trasporti Italiani (ATI)
	I-DIZE	Douglas DC-9-32	Alitalia *Isola della Meloria*
	I-DIZF	Douglas DC-9-32	Alitalia *Isola di Spargi*
	I-DIZI	Douglas DC-9-32	Aero Trasporti Italiani (ATI)
	I-DIZO	Douglas DC-9-32	Alitalia *Isola del Tino*
	I-DIZU	Douglas DC-9-32	Aero Trasporti Italiani (ATI) *Valle d'Aosta*
	I-RIBC	Douglas DC-9-32	Alitalia *Isola di Lampedusa*
	I-RIBD	Douglas DC-9-32	Alitalia *Isola di Montecristo*
	I-RIBJ	Douglas DC-9-32	Alitalia *Isola della Capraia*
	I-RIBN	Douglas DC-9-32	Alitalia *Isola della Palmaria*
	I-RIBQ	Douglas DC-9-32	Alitalia *Isola di Pianosa*
	I-RIKV	Douglas DC-9-32	Alitalia *Isola di Vulcano*
	I-RIKZ	Douglas DC-9-32	Alitalia *Isola di Linosa*
	I-RIZA	Douglas DC-9-32	Alitalia *Isola di Palmorola*
	I-SMEA	Douglas DC-9-51	Alisarda
	I-SMEI	Douglas DC-9-51	Alisarda
	I-SMET	Douglas DC-9-82	Alisarda
	I-SMEU	Douglas DC-9-51	Alisarda
	I-SMEV	Douglas DC-9-82	Alisarda

Note: Alisarda also uses two DC-9-82s which retain their Swiss registrations HB-IKK and HB-IKL. Two of the Alitalia DC-9-32s have been re-registered N515MD and N516MD. Similarly ATI uses N871UM, N872UM and N873UM.

JA (Japan)

	Reg.	Type	Owner or Operator
	JA8071	Boeing 747-446	Japan Air Lines
	JA8072	Boeing 747-446	Japan Air Lines
	JA8073	Boeing 747-446	Japan Air Lines
	JA8074	Boeing 747-446	Japan Air Lines
	JA8075	Boeing 747-446	Japan Air Lines
	JA8101	Boeing 747-146	Japan Air Lines
	JA8104	Boeing 747-246B	Japan Air Lines
	JA8105	Boeing 747-246B	Japan Air Lines
	JA8106	Boeing 747-246B	Japan Air Lines
	JA8107	Boeing 747-146F (SCD)	Japan Air Lines
	JA8108	Boeing 747-246B	Japan Air Lines
	JA8110	Boeing 747-246B	Japan Air Lines
	JA8111	Boeing 747-246B	Japan Air Lines
	JA8112	Boeing 747-146A	Japan Air Lines
	JA8113	Boeing 747-246B	Japan Air Lines
	JA8114	Boeing 747-246B	Japan Air Lines
	JA8115	Boeing 747-146A	Japan Air Lines
	JA8116	Boeing 747-146A	Japan Air Lines
	JA8071	Boeing 747-446	Japan Air Lines
	JA8072	Boeing 747-446	Japan Air Lines
	JA8073	Boeing 747-446	Japan Air Lines
	JA8074	Boeing 747-446	Japan Air Lines
	JA8075	Boeing 747-446	Japan Air Lines
	JA8122	Boeing 747-246B	Japan Air Lines
	JA8123	Boeing 747-246F (SCD)	Japan Air Lines

Reg.	Type	Owner or Operator	Notes
JA8125	Boeing 747-246B	Japan Air Lines	
JA8127	Boeing 747-246B	Japan Air Lines	
JA8129	Boeing 747-246B	Japan Air Lines	
JA8130	Boeing 747-246B	Japan Air Lines	
JA8131	Boeing 747-246B	Japan Air Lines	
JA8132	Boeing 747-246F	Japan Air Lines	
JA8140	Boeing 747-246B	Japan Air Lines	
JA8141	Boeing 747-246B	Japan Air Lines	
JA8144	Boeing 747-246F (SCD)	Japan Air Lines	
JA8149	Boeing 747-246B	Japan Air Lines	
JA8150	Boeing 747-246B	Japan Air Lines	
JA8151	Boeing 747-246F (SCD)	Japan Air Lines	
JA8154	Boeing 747-246B	Japan Air Lines	
JA8155	Boeing 747-246B	Japan Air Lines	
JA8160	Boeing 747-221F (SCD)	Japan Air Lines	
JA8161	Boeing 747-246B	Japan Air Lines	
JA8162	Boeing 747-246B	Japan Air Lines	
JA8163	Boeing 747-346	Japan Air Lines	
JA8165	Boeing 747-221F (SCD)	Japan Air Lines	
JA8166	Boeing 747-346	Japan Air Lines	
JA8169	Boeing 747-246B	Japan Air Lines	
JA8171	Boeing 747-246F (SCD)	Japan Air Lines	
JA8173	Boeing 747-346	Japan Air Lines	
JA8177	Boeing 747-346	Japan Air Lines	
JA8178	Boeing 747-346	Japan Air Lines	
JA8179	Boeing 747-346	Japan Air Lines	
JA8180	Boeing 747-246F (SCD)	Japan Air Lines	
JA8185	Boeing 747-346	Japan Air Lines	
JA8535	Douglas DC-10-40	Japan Air Lines	
JA8538	Douglas DC-10-40	Japan Air Lines	
JA8539	Douglas DC-10-40	Japan Air Lines	
JA8541	Douglas DC-10-40	Japan Air Lines	
JA8542	Douglas DC-10-40	Japan Air Lines	
JA8543	Douglas DC-10-40	Japan Air Lines	
JA8544	Douglas DC-10-40	Japan Air Lines	
JA8545	Douglas DC-10-40	Japan Air Lines	
JA8547	Douglas DC-10-40	Japan Air Lines	

Note: Japan Air Lines also operates a Boeing 747-221F which retains its US registration N211JL and two 747-346s N212JL and N213JL.

JY (Jordan)

JY-ADP	Boeing 707-3D3C	Royal Jordanian Airline *City of Amman*	
JY-AEC	Boeing 707-384C	Royal Jordanian Airline *Um Qais*	
JY-AFA	Boeing 747-2D3B	Royal Jordanian Airline *Prince Ali*	
JY-AGA	L.1011-385 TriStar 500	Royal Jordanian Airline *Abas Ibn Firnas*	
JY-AGB	L.1011-385 TriStar 500	Royal Jordanian Airline *Ibn Battouta*	
JY-AGC	L.1011-385 TriStar 500	Royal Jordanian Airline *Al Jawaheri*	
JY-AGD	L.1011-385 TriStar 500	Royal Jordanian Airline *Ibn Sina*	
JY-AGE	L.1011-385 TriStar 500	Royal Jordanian Airline *Princess Aysha*	
JY-AGH	L.1011-385 TriStar 500	Royal Jordanian Airline/*Prince Abollah*	
JY-AGJ	L.1011-385 TriStar 500	Royal Jordanian Airline *Princess Zein*	
JY-AJK	Boeing 707-384C	Royal Jordanian Airline *City of Jerash*	
JY-CAG	Airbus A.310-304	Royal Jordanian Airline	
JY-CAH	Airbus A.310-304	Royal Jordanian Airline	
JY-CAI	Airbus A.310-304	Royal Jordanian Airline	
JY-HKJ	L.1011-385 TriStar 500	Jordan Government	

Note: Royal Jordanian also operates three A.310-304s registered F-ODVD, F-ODVE and F-ODVF.

LN (Norway)

Notes	Reg.	Type	Owner or Operator
	LN-AKA	F.27 Friendship Mk 200	Busy Bee
	LN-AKB	F.27 Friendship Mk 200	Busy Bee
	LN-AKC	F.27 Friendship Mk 200	Busy Bee
	LN-AKD	F.27 Friendship Mk 200	Busy Bee
	LN-ALN	Douglas DC-10-30	S.A.S. Yngve Viking
	LN-BBA	Fokker 50	Busy Bee
	LN-BBB	Fokker 50	Busy Bee
	LN-BBC	Fokker 50	Busy Bee
	LN-BBD	Fokker 50	Busy Bee
	LN-BBE	Fokker 50	Busy Bee
	LN-BRL	Boeing 737-296	Braathens SAFE
	LN-BSC	F.27J Friendship	Malmo Aviation
	LN-BWG	Convair 580	Partnair
	LN-BWN	Convair 580	Partnair
	LN-FOG	L-188AF Electra	Fred Olsen Airtransport
	LN-FOH	L-188AF Electra	Fred Olsen Airtransport
	LN-FOI	L-188CF Electra	Fred Olsen Airtransport
	LN-KLK	Convair 440	Norsk Metropolitan Fly Klubb
	LN-KOA	Beech 200 Super King Air	Norsk Air
	LN-KOB	Beech 200 Super King Air	Norsk Air
	LN-KOC	EMB-120RT Brasilia	Norsk Air
	LN-KOD	EMB-120RT Brasilia	Norsk Air
	LN-KOE	EMB-120RT Brasilia	Norsk Air
	LN-KOF	EMB-120RT Brasilia	Norsk Air
	LN-MOA	Cessna 441 Conquest	Morefly
	LN-MOB	Beech 200 Super King Air	Morefly
	LN-MOD	Beech 200 Super King Air	Morefly
	LN-MOF	Douglas DC-8-63	Scanair Blenda Viking
	LN-NFT	Beech 200 Super King Air	Norsk Air
	LN-NOR	Boeing 737-33A	Norway Airlines/Air Europe City of Stavanger
	LN-NOS	Boeing 737-33A	Norway Airlines (leased as G-)
	LN-NPB	Boeing 737-2R4C	Busy Bee
	LN-NPC	F-27 Friendship Mk 100	Busy Bee
	LN-NPD	F-27 Friendship Mk 100	Busy Bee
	LN-NPH	F.27 Friendship Mk 300	Busy Bee/Gambia Air Shuttle
	LN-NPI	F.27 Friendship Mk 100	Busy Bee
	LN-NPM	F.27 Friendship Mk 100	Busy Bee
	LN-NVD	Saab SF.340A	Norving Air Services
	LN-NVE	Saab SF.340A	Norving Air Services (leased as PH-KJH)
	LN-NVF	Saab SF.340A	Norving Air Services
	LN-PAA	Convair 580	Partnair
	LN-PAD	Beech 200 Super King Air	Partnair
	LN-PAE	Beech 200 Super King Air	Partnair
	LN-PAF	Beech 200 Super King Air	Partnair
	LN-PAJ	Beech 100 King Air	Partnair
	LN-RCB	Boeing 767-383ER	S.A.S.
	LN-RKA	Douglas DC-10-30	S.A.S. Olav Viking (to C- mid 1989)
	LN-RKC	Douglas DC-10-30	S.A.S. Leif Viking
	LN-RKD	Douglas DC-10-30	S.A.S. Bjarne Viking
	LN-RLA	Douglas DC-9-41	S.A.S. Are Viking
	LN-RLB	Douglas DC-9-41	S.A.S. Arne Viking
	LN-RLC	Douglas DC-9-41	S.A.S. Gunnar Viking
	LN-RLD	Douglas DC-9-41	S.A.S. Torleif Viking
	LN-RLE	Douglas DC-9-81	S.A.S. Trygve Viking
	LN-RLF	Douglas DC-9-82	S.A.S. Finn Viking
	LN-RLG	Douglas DC-9-82	S.A.S. Trond Viking
	LN-RLH	Douglas DC-9-41	S.A.S. Einar Viking
	LN-RLJ	Douglas DC-9-41	S.A.S. Stein Viking
	LN-RLK	Douglas DC-9-41	S.A.S. Erling Viking
	LN-RLL	Douglas DC-9-21	S.A.S. Guttorm Viking
	LN-RLN	Douglas DC-9-41	S.A.S. Halldor Viking
	LN-RLO	Douglas DC-9-21	S.A.S. Gunder Viking
	LN-RLP	Douglas DC-9-41	S.A.S. Froste Viking
	LN-RLR	Douglas DC-9-82	S.A.S. Kettil Viking

Reg.	Type	Owner or Operator	Notes
LN-RLS	Douglas DC-9-41	S.A.S. *Asmund Viking*	
LN-RLT	Douglas DC-9-41	S.A.S. *Audun Viking*	
LN-RLU	Douglas DC-9-41	S.A.S. *Eivind Viking*	
LN-RLX	Douglas DC-9-41	S.A.S. *Sote Viking*	
LN-RLZ	Douglas DC-9-41	S.A.S. *Bodvar Viking*	
LN-RMA	Douglas DC-9-81	S.A.S. *Hasting Viking*	
LN-RMB	Douglas DC-9-83	S.A.S. *Erik Viking*	
LN-RMD	Douglas DC-9-82	S.A.S. *Fenge Viking*	
LN-RMF	Douglas DC-9-83	S.A.S. *Torgny Viking*	
LN-RMG	Douglas DC-9-87	S.A.S. *Snorre Viking*	
LN-RMH	Douglas DC-9-87	S.A.S. *Solmund Viking*	
LN-RNX	F.27 Friendship Mk 200	S.A.S. *Vikar Viking*	
LN-RNY	F.27 Friendship Mk 600	S.A.S. *Vatnar Viking*	
LN-RNZ	F.27 Friendship Mk 600	S.A.S. *Vemund Viking*	
LN-SUA	Boeing 737-205	Braathens SAFE *Halvdan Svarte*	
LN-SUB	Boeing 737-205	Braathens SAFE *Magnus den Gode*	
LN-SUE	F.27 Friendship Mk 100	Busy Bee	
LN-SUF	F.27 Friendship Mk 100	Busy Bee	
LN-SUG	Boeing 737-205	Braathens SAFE *Harald Gille*	
LN-SUJ	Boeing 737-205	Braathens SAFE *Magnus Barfot*	
LN-SUK	Boeing 737-205	Braathens SAFE *Magnus Erlingsson*	
LN-SUL	F.27 Friendship Mk 100	Busy Bee	
LN-SUP	Boeing 737-205	Braathens SAFE *Håkon V Magnusson*	
LN-SUQ	Boeing 737-205	Braathens SAFE *Håkon Sverresson*	
LN-SUS	Boeing 737-205	Braathens SAFE *Håkon IV Hakonsson*	
LN-SUT	Boeing 737-205	Braathens SAFE *Oystein Magnusson*	
LN-SUU	Boeing 737-205	Braathens SAFE *Harald Hardrade*	
LN-SUV	Boeing 737-205	Braathens SAFE *Harald Hafagre*	
LN-SUZ	Boeing 737-205	Braathens SAFE *Olav Kyrre*	
LN-	Boeing 737-405	Braathens SAFE	
LN-	Boeing 737-405	Braathens SAFE	
LN-	Boeing 737-405	Braathens SAFE	
LN-	Boeing 737-405	Braathens SAFE	
LN-	Boeing 737-405	Braathens SAFE	

Note: Braathens also operates the Boeing 737-205s N197QQ, N197SS, N7031A and N7031F (ex LN-SUI, -SUD, -SUH and -SUM respectively) and N197JQ.

LV (Argentina)

LV-MLO	Boeing 747-287B	Flying Tiger Line	
LV-MLP	Boeing 747-287B	Aerolineas Argentinas	
LV-MLR	Boeing 747-287B	Aerolineas Argentinas	
LV-OEP	Boeing 747-287B	Aerolineas Argentinas	
LV-OHV	Boeing 747SP-27	Aerolineas Argentinas	
LV-OOZ	Boeing 747-287B	Aerolineas Argentinas	
LV-OPA	Boeing 747-287B	Aerolineas Argentinas	

Note: Services to the UK are suspended.

LX (Luxembourg)

LX-ACV	Boeing 747-271C (SCD)	Cargolux	
LX-BCV	Boeing 747-271C (SCD)	Cargolux	
LX-ECV	Boeing 747-271C (SCD)	Cargolux	
LX-FCV	Boeing 747-121	Lionair	
LX-GCV	Boeing 747-121	Lionair	
LX-LGA	F.27 Friendship Mk 100	Luxair *Prince Henri*	
LX-LGB	F.27 Friendship Mk 100	Luxair *Prince Jean*	
LX-LGH	Boeing 737-2C9	Luxair *Prince Guillaume*	
LX-LGI	Boeing 737-2C9	Luxair *Princess Marie-Astrid*	
LX-LGJ	F.27 Friendship Mk 200	Luxair	
LX-LGK	F.27 Friendship Mk 200	Luxair	
LX-LGL	Swearingen SA.227AC Metro III	Luxair	
LX-LGM	Swearingen SA.227AC Metro III	Luxair	
LX-LGN	Boeing 737-229	Luxair	

Notes	Reg.	Type	Owner or Operator
	LX-LG	Fokker 50	Luxair
	LX-LG	Fokker 50	Luxair
	LX-LG	Fokker 50	Luxair
	LX-LGX	Boeing 747SP-44	Luxair (*leased from SAA ex ZS-SPB*)

LZ (Bulgaria)

	LZ-BEA	Ilyushin IL-18D	Balkan Bulgarian Airlines
	LZ-BEK	Ilyushin IL-18V	Balkan Bulgarian Airlines
	LZ-BEL	Ilyushin IL-18V	Balkan Bulgarian Airlines
	LZ-BEO	Ilyushin IL-18D	Balkan Bulgarian Airlines
	LZ-BEU	Ilyushin IL-18V	Balkan Bulgarian Airlines
	LZ-BEV	Ilyushin IL-18V	Balkan Bulgarian Airlines
	LZ-BTA	Tupolev Tu-154B	Balkan Bulgarian Airlines
	LZ-BTC	Tupolev Tu-154B	Balkan Bulgarian Airlines
	LZ-BTD	Tupolev Tu-154B	Balkan Bulgarian Airlines
	LZ-BTE	Tupolev Tu-154B	Balkan Bulgarian Airlines
	LZ-BTF	Tupolev Tu-154B	Balkan Bulgarian Airlines
	LZ-BTG	Tupolev Tu-154B	Balkan Bulgarian Airlines
	LZ-BTH	Tupolev Tu-154M	Balkan Bulgarian Airlines
	LZ-BTI	Tupolev Tu-154M	Balkan Bulgarian Airlines
	LZ-BTJ	Tupolev Tu-154B-1	Balkan Bulgarian Airlines
	LZ-BTK	Tupolev Tu-154B	Balkan Bulgarian Airlines
	LZ-BTL	Tupolev Tu-154B	Balkan Bulgarian Airlines
	LZ-BTM	Tupolev Tu-154B	Balkan Bulgarian Airlines
	LZ-BTO	Tupolev Tu-154B-1	Balkan Bulgarian Airlines
	LZ-BTP	Tupolev Tu-154B-1	Balkan Bulgarian Airlines
	LZ-BTQ	Tupolev Tu-154M	Balkan Bulgarian Airlines
	LZ-BTR	Tupolev Tu-154B-2	Balkan Bulgarian Airlines
	LZ-BTS	Tupolev Tu-154B-2	Balkan Bulgarian Airlines
	LZ-BTT	Tupolev Tu-154B-2	Balkan Bulgarian Airlines
	LZ-BTU	Tupolev Tu-154B-2	Balkan Bulgarian Airlines
	LZ-BTV	Tupolev Tu-154B-2	Balkan Bulgarian Airlines
	LZ-BTW	Tupolev Tu-154M	Balkan Bulgarian Airlines
	LZ-BTX	Tupolev Tu-154M	Balkan Bulgarian Airlines
	LZ-TUA	Tupolev Tu-134	Balkan Bulgarian Airlines
	LZ-TUC	Tupolev Tu-134	Balkan Bulgarian Airlines
	LZ-TUD	Tupolev Tu-134	Balkan Bulgarian Airlines
	LZ-TUE	Tupolev Tu-134	Balkan Bulgarian Airlines
	LZ-TUG	Tupolev Tu-134A-3	Balkan Bulgarian Airlines
	LZ-TUK	Tupolev Tu-134A	Balkan Bulgarian Airlines
	LZ-TUL	Tupolev Tu-134A-3	Balkan Bulgarian Airlines
	LZ-TUM	Tupolev Tu-134A-3	Balkan Bulgarian Airlines
	LZ-TUN	Tupolev Tu-134A-3	Balkan Bulgarian Airlines
	LZ-TUO	Tupolev Tu-134	Balkan Bulgarian Airlines
	LZ-TUP	Tupolev Tu-134A	Balkan Bulgarian Airlines
	LZ-TUS	Tupolev Tu-134A	Balkan Bulgarian Airlines
	LZ-TUT	Tupulev Tu-134A-3	Balkan Bulgarian Airlines
	LZ-TUU	Tupolev Tu-134A-3	Balkan Bulgarian Airlines
	LZ-TUV	Tupolev Tu-134A-3	Balkan Bulgarian Airlines
	LZ-TUZ	Tupolev Tu-134A-3	Balkan Bulgarian Airlines

N (USA)

	N20UA	Douglas DC-8-61	United Aviation Services
	N22UA	Douglas DC-8-61	United Aviation Services
	N23UA	Douglas DC-8-61	United Aviation Services
	N25UA	Douglas DC-8-61	United Aviation Services
	N26UA	Douglas DC-8-61	United Aviation Services
	N27UA	Douglas DC-8-61	United Aviation Services
	N29UA	Douglas DC-8-61	United Aviation Services
	N30UA	Douglas DC-8-61	United Aviation Services
	N47UA	Douglas DC-8-61	United Aviation Services
	N48UA	Douglas DC-8-61	United Aviation Services
	N51UA	Douglas DC-8-61	United Aviation Services
	N39ST	L-100-30 Hercules	Southern Air Transport
	N67AB	Boeing 737-3Y0	Air Berlin

Reg.	Type	Owner or Operator	Notes
N92TA	L-1011-385 TriStar 200	Gulf Air	
N92TB	L-1011-385 TriStar 200	Gulf Air	
N105WA	Douglas DC-10-30CF	World Airways	
N106WA	Douglas DC-10-30CF	World Airways	
N107WA	Douglas DC-10-30CF	World Airways	
N108WA	Douglas DC-10-30CF	World Airways	
N112WA	Douglas DC-10-30CF	World Airways	
N116KB	Boeing 747-312	Singapore Airlines	
N117KC	Boeing 747-312	Singapore Airlines	
N118KD	Boeing 747-312	Singapore Airlines	
N119KE	Boeing 747-312	Singapore Airlines	
N120KF	Boeing 747-312	Singapore Airlines	
N121KG	Boeing 747-312	Singapore Airlines	
N122KH	Boeing 747-312	Singapore Airlines	
N123KJ	Boeing 747-312	Singapore Airlines	
N124KK	Boeing 747-312	Singapore Airlines	
N125KL	Boeing 747-312	Singapore Airlines	
N133JC	Douglas DC-10-40	Northwest Airlines	
N133TW	Boeing 747-156	Trans World Airlines	
N134TW	Boeing 747-156	Trans World Airlines	
N137AA	Douglas DC-10-30	American Airlines	
N138AA	Douglas DC-10-30	American Airlines	
N139AA	Douglas DC-10-30	American Airlines	
N140AA	Douglas DC-10-30	American Airlines	
N141AA	Douglas DC-10-30	American Airlines	
N141US	Douglas DC-10-40	Northwest Airlines	
N142AA	Douglas DC-10-30	American Airlines	
N143AA	Douglas DC-10-30	American Airlines	
N144AA	Douglas DC-10-30	American Airlines	
N145US	Douglas DC-10-40	Northwest Airlines	
N146US	Douglas DC-10-40	Northwest Airlines	
N147US	Douglas DC-10-40	Northwest Airlines	
N148US	Douglas DC-10-40	Northwest Airlines	
N149US	Douglas DC-10-40	Northwest Airlines	
N150US	Douglas DC-10-40	Northwest Airlines	
N151US	Douglas DC-10-40	Northwest Airlines	
N152US	Douglas DC-10-40	Northwest Airlines	
N153US	Douglas DC-10-40	Northwest Airlines	
N154US	Douglas DC-10-40	Northwest Airlines	
N155US	Douglas DC-10-40	Northwest Airlines	
N156US	Douglas DC-10-40	Northwest Airlines	
N157US	Douglas DC-10-40	Northwest Airlines	
N158US	Douglas DC-10-40	Northwest Airlines	
N159US	Douglas DC-10-40	Northwest Airlines	
N160US	Douglas DC-10-40	Northwest Airlines	
N161US	Douglas DC-10-40	Northwest Airlines	
N162US	Douglas DC-10-40	Northwest Airlines	
N163AA	Douglas DC-10-30	American Airlines	
N164AA	Douglas DC-10-30	American Airlines	
N185TZ	L-1011 TriStar 1	American Trans Air	
N186TZ	L.1011 TriStar 1	American Trans Air	
N187TZ	L.1011 TriStar 1	American Trans Air	
N188TZ	L.1011 TriStar 1	American Trans Air	
N189TZ	L.1011 TriStar 1	American Trans Air	
N190TZ	L.1011 TriStar 1	American Trans Air	
N191TZ	L.1011 TriStar 1	American Trans Air	
N192TZ	L.1011 TriStar 1	American Trans Air	
N193TZ	L.1011 TriStar 1	American Trans Air	
N195TZ	L.1011 TriStar 50	American Trans Air	
N197JQ	Boeing 737-217	Braathens SAFE	
N197QQ	Boeing 737-205	Braathens SAFE *Haakon den Gode*	
N197SS	Boeing 737-205	Braathens SAFE *Olav Tryggvason*	
N211JL	Boeing 747-221F	Japan Air Lines	
N212JL	Boeing 747-346	Japan Air Lines	
N213JL	Boeing 747-346	Japan Air Lines	
N221GE	Boeing 747-357	Swissair *Geneve*	
N221GF	Boeing 747-357	Swissair *Zurich*	
N301FE	Douglas DC-10-30CF	Federal Express	
N301TW	Boeing 747-282B	Trans World Airlines	
N302FE	Douglas DC-10-30CF	Federal Express	
N302TW	Boeing 747-282B	Trans World Airlines	
N303FE	Douglas DC-10-30CF	Federal Express	
N303TW	Boeing 747-257B	Trans World Airlines	
N304EA	L.1011 TriStar 1	Air America	

Notes	Reg.	Type	Owner or Operator
	N304FE	Douglas DC-10-30CF	Federal Express
	N304TW	Boeing 747-257B	Trans World Airlines
	N305FE	Douglas DC-10-30CF	Federal Express
	N305TW	Boeing 747-284B	Trans World Airlines
	N306FE	Douglas DC-10-30AF	Federal Express
	N307FE	Douglas DC-10-30AF	Federal Express
	N308FE	Douglas DC-10-30AF	Federal Express
	N309FE	Douglas DC-10-30AF	Federal Express
	N310FE	Douglas DC-10-30AF	Federal Express
	N311FE	Douglas DC-10-30AF	Federal Express
	N312FE	Douglas DC-10-30AF	Federal Express
	N313FE	Douglas DC-10-30AF	Federal Express
	N314FE	Douglas DC-10-30AF	Federal Express
	N315FE	Douglas DC-10-30AF	Federal Express
	N316FE	Douglas DC-10-30AF	Federal Express
	N317FE	Douglas DC-10-30AF	Federal Express
	N318FE	Douglas DC-10-30AF	Federal Express
	N	McD Douglas MD-11F	Federal Express
	N	McD Douglas MD-11F	Federal Express
	N319AA	Boeing 767-223ER	American Airlines
	N320AA	Boeing 767-223ER	American Airlines
	N321AA	Boeing 767-223ER	American Airlines
	N322AA	Boeing 767-223ER	American Airlines
	N323AA	Boeing 767-223ER	American Airlines
	N324AA	Boeing 767-223ER	American Airlines
	N325AA	Boeing 767-223ER	American Airlines
	N327AA	Boeing 767-223ER	American Airlines
	N328AA	Boeing 767-223ER	American Airlines
	N329AA	Boeing 767-223ER	American Airlines
	N330AA	Boeing 767-223ER	American Airlines
	N332AA	Boeing 767-223ER	American Airlines
	N334AA	Boeing 767-223ER	American Airlines
	N335AA	Boeing 767-223ER	American Airlines
	N336AA	Boeing 767-223ER	American Airlines
	N338AA	Boeing 767-223ER	American Airlines
	N339AA	Boeing 767-223ER	American Airlines
	N345HC	Douglas DC-10-30ER	Finnair
	N351AA	Boeing 767-323ER	American Airlines
	N352AA	Boeing 767-323ER	American Airlines
	N353AA	Boeing 767-323ER	American Airlines
	N354AA	Boeing 767-323ER	American Airlines
	N355AA	Boeing 767-323ER	American Airlines
	N356Q	L.188 Electra	Air Bridge Carriers/E. Midlands
	N357AA	Boeing 767-323ER	American Airlines
	N358AA	Boeing 767-323ER	American Airlines
	N359AA	Boeing 767-323ER	American Airlines
	N360AA	Boeing 767-323ER	American Airlines
	N361AA	Boeing 767-323ER	American Airlines
	N362AA	Boeing 767-323ER	American Airlines
	N363AA	Boeing 767-323ER	American Airlines
	N390EA	Douglas DC-10-30	Continental Airlines
	N454PC	Boeing 707-321B	Skyworld Airlines
	N457PC	Boeing 707-323B	Skyworld Airlines
	N471EV	Boeing 747-273C	Evergreen International Airlines
	N472EV	Boeing 747-131	Evergreen International Airlines
	N515MD	Douglas DC-9-32	Alitalia *Isola di Nisida*
	N516MD	Douglas DC-9-32	Alitalia *Isola di Ponza*
	N519SJ	L-100-30 Hercules	Southern Air Transport
	N521SJ	L-100-20 Hercules	Southern Air Transport
	N522SJ	L-100-20 Hercules	Southern Air Transport
	N523SJ	Boeing 707-369C	Southern Air Transport
	N524SJ	Boeing 707-311C	Southern Air Transport
	N525SJ	Boeing 707-369C	Southern Air Transport
	N526SJ	Boeing 707-338C	Southern Air Transport
	N527SJ	Boeing 707-321C	Southern Air Transport
	N528SJ	Boeing 707-369C	Southern Air Transport
	N601BN	Boeing 747-127	Tower Air *Sam*
	N601TW	Boeing 767-231ER	Trans World Airlines
	N601US	Boeing 747-151	Northwest Airlines
	N602FF	Boeing 747-124	Tower Air
	N602TW	Boeing 767-231ER	Trans World Airlines
	N602US	Boeing 747-151	Northwest Airlines
	N603FF	Boeing 747-130	Tower Air *Suzie*
	N603PE	Boeing 747-143	Continental Airlines (*to be N17010*)

Reg.	Type	Owner or Operator	Notes
N603TW	Boeing 767-231ER	Trans World Airlines	
N603US	Boeing 747-151	Northwest Airlines	
N604FF	Boeing 747-121	Tower Air	
N604PE	Boeing 747-243B	Continental Airlines (to be N16020)	
N604TW	Boeing 767-231ER	Trans World Airlines	
N604US	Boeing 747-151	Northwest Airlines	
N605PE	Boeing 747-243B	Continental Airlines (to be N33021)	
N605TW	Boeing 767-231ER	Trans World Airlines	
N605US	Boeing 747-151	Northwest Airlines	
N606PE	Boeing 747-143	Continental Airlines (to be N17011)	
N606TW	Boeing 767-231ER	Trans World Airlines	
N606US	Boeing 747-151	Northwest Airlines	
N607PE	Boeing 747-238B	Continental Airlines (to be N50022)	
N607TW	Boeing 767-231ER	Trans Wordd Airlines	
N607US	Boeing 747-151	Northwest Airlines	
N608PE	Boeing 747-238B	Continental Airlines (to be N10023)	
N608TW	Boeing 767-231ER	Trans World Airlines	
N608US	Boeing 747-151	Northwest Airlines	
N609PE	Boeing 747-238B	Continental Airlines (to be N10024)	
N609TW	Boeing 767-231ER	Trans World Airlines	
N609US	Boeing 747-151	Northwest Airlines	
N610PE	Boeing 747-238B	Continental Airlines (to be N17025)	
N610TW	Boeing 767-231ER	Trans World Airlines	
N610US	Boeing 747-151	Northwest Airlines	
N611US	Boeing 747-251B	Northwest Airlines	
N612US	Boeing 747-251B	Northwest Airlines	
N613US	Boeing 747-251B	Northwest Airlines	
N614US	Boeing 747-251B	Northwest Airlines	
N615US	Boeing 747-251B	Northwest Airlines	
N616US	Boeing 747-251F (SCD)	Northwest Airlines	
N617US	Boeing 747-251F (SCD)	Northwest Airlines	
N618US	Boeing 747-251F (SCD)	Northwest Airlines	
N619US	Boeing 747-251F (SCD)	Northwest Airlines	
N620US	Boeing 747-135	Northwest Airlines	
N621US	Boeing 747-135	Northwest Airlines	
N622US	Boeing 747-251B	Northwest Airlines	
N623US	Boeing 747-251B	Northwest Airlines	
N624US	Boeing 747-251B	Northwest Airlines	
N625US	Boeing 747-251B	Northwest Airlines	
N626US	Boeing 747-251B	Northwest Airlines	
N627US	Boeing 747-251B	Northwest Airlines	
N628US	Boeing 747-251B	Northwest Airlines	
N629US	Boeing 747-251F (SCD)	Northwest Airlines	
N630US	Boeing 747-2J9F	Northwest Airlines	
N631US	Boeing 747-251B	Northwest Airlines	
N632US	Boeing 747-251B	Northwest Airlines	
N633US	Boeing 747-227B	Northwest Airlines	
N634US	Boeing 747-227B	Northwest Airlines	
N635US	Boeing 747-227B	Northwest Airlines	
N636US	Boeing 747-251B	Northwest Airlines	
N637US	Boeing 747-251B	Northwest Airlines	
N638US	Boeing 747-251B	Northwest Airlines	
N639US	Boeing 747-251F (SCD)	Northwest Airlines	
N640US	Boeing 747-251F (SCD)	Northwest Airlines	
N645US	Boeing 767-201ER	Piedmont Airlines	
N646US	Boeing 767-201ER	Piedmont Airlines City of London	
N647US	Boeing 767-201ER	Piedmont Airlines City of Charlotte	
N648US	Boeing 767-201ER	Piedmont Airlines City of Tampa	
N649US	Boeing 767-201ER	Piedmont Airlines City of Los Angeles	
N650US	Boeing 767-201ER	Piedmont Airlines Pride of Baltimore	
N652PA	Boeing 747-121	Pan Am Clipper Pride of the Fleet	
N653PA	Boeing 747-121 (SCD)	Pan Am Clipper Pride of the Ocean	
N655PA	Boeing 747-121 (SCD)	Pan Am Clipper Sea Serpent	
N656PA	Boeing 747-121	Evergreen International Airlines	
N657PA	Boeing 747-121	Evergreen International Airlines	
N659PA	Boeing 747-121	Pan Am Clipper Voyager	
N661US	Boeing 747-451	Northwest Airlines	
N662US	Boeing 747-451	Northwest Airlines	
N663US	Boeing 747-451	Northwest Airlines	
N664US	Boeing 747-451	Northwest Airlines	
N665US	Boeing 747-451	Northwest Airlines	
N666US	Boeing 747-451	Northwest Airlines	
N667US	Boeing 747-451	Northwest Airlines	
N668US	Boeing 747-451	Northwest Airlines	

Notes	Reg.	Type	Owner or Operator
	N669US	Boeing 747-451	Northwest Airlines
	N670US	Boeing 747-451	Northwest Airlines
	N701FT	Douglas DC-8-73CF	Flying Tiger Line
	N703FT	Douglas DC-8-73CF	Flying Tiger Line
	N703TT	L.1101-385 TriStar 50	Air America
	N705FT	Douglas DC-8-73CF	Flying Tiger Line
	N705PC	Boeing 707-323C	Skyworld Airlines
	N706PC	Boeing 707-323B	Skyworld Airlines
	N708PC	Boeing 707-323B	Skyworld Airlines
	N709PC	Boeing 707-323B	Skyworld Airlines
	N711PC	Boeing 707-323B	Skyworld Airlines
	N712PC	Boeing 707-323B	Skyworld Airlines
	N723PA	Boeing 747-212B	Pan Am *Clipper Hawaii*
	N724DA	L.1011-385 TriStar 200	Delta Air Lines
	N724PA	Boeing 747-212B	Pan Am *Clipper Fairwind*
	N725PA	Boeing 747-132 (SCD)	Pan Am *Clipper Mandarin*
	N726DY	L.1011-385 TriStar 250	Delta Air Lines
	N726PA	Boeing 747-212B	Pan Am *Clipper Cathay*
	N727PA	Boeing 747-212B	Pan Am *Clipper Cathay*
	N728PA	Boeing 747-212B (SCD)	Pan Am *Clipper Water Witch*
	N729PA	Boeing 747-212B (SCD)	Pan Am *Clipper Wild Wave*
	N730PA	Boeing 747-212B (SCD)	Pan Am *Clipper Gem of the Ocean*
	N733PA	Boeing 747-121	Pan Am *Clipper Moscow Express*
	N734PA	Boeing 747-121 (SCD)	Pan Am *Clipper Champion of the Seas*
	N735PA	Boeing 747-121	Pan Am *Clipper Spark of the Ocean*
	N736DY	L.1011-385 TriStar 250	Delta Air Lines
	N737D	L.1011-385 TriStar 250	Delta Air Lines
	N737PA	Boeing 747-121	Pan Am *Clipper Ocean Herald*
	N740DA	L.1011-385 TriStar 250	Delta Air Lines
	N740PA	Boeing 747-121	Pan Am *Clipper Ocean Pearl*
	N741DA	L.1011-385 TriStar 250	Delta Air Lines
	N741PA	Boeing 747-121	Pan Am *Clipper Special Olympian*
	N741PR	Boeing 747-2F6B	Philippine Airlines
	N742PA	Boeing 747-121	Pan Am *Clipper Neptune's Car*
	N742PR	Boeing 747-2F6B	Philippine Airlines
	N743PA	Boeing 747-121 (SCD)	Pan Am *Clipper Black Sea*
	N743PR	Boeing 747-2F6B	Philippine Airlines
	N744PA	Boeing 747-121	Pan Am *Clipper Ocean Spray*
	N744PR	Boeing 747-2F6B	Philippine Airlines
	N747PA	Boeing 747-121 (SCD)	Pan Am *Clipper Juan J. Trippe*
	N748PA	Boeing 747-121	Pan Am *Clipper Crest of the Wave*
	N749PA	Boeing 747-121	Pan Am *Clipper Dashing Wave*
	N749WA	Boeing 747-273C	Flying Tiger Line
	N750PA	Boeing 747-121	Pan Am *Clipper Neptune's Fortune*
	N751DA	L-1011-385 TriStar 500	Delta Air Lines
	N751PA	Boeing 747-121	Pan Am *Clipper Gem of the Sea*
	N752DA	L-1011-385 TriStar 500	Delta Air Lines
	N753DA	L-1011-385 TriStar 500	Delta Air Lines
	N753PA	Boeing 747-121	Pan Am *Clipper Queen of the Seas*
	N754DL	L.1011-385 TriStar 500	Delta Air Lines
	N755DL	L.1011-385 TriStar 500	Delta Air Lines
	N756DR	L.1011-385 TriStar 500	Delta Air Lines
	N759DA	L.1011-385 TriStar 500	Delta Air Lines
	N760DH	L.1011-385 TriStar 500	Delta Air Lines
	N761DA	L.1011-385 TriStar 500	Delta Air Lines
	N762DA	L.1011-385 TriStar 500	Delta Air Lines
	N771CA	Douglas DC-8-62AF	Evergreen International Airlines
	N791FT	Douglas DC-8-73CF	Emery Worldwide
	N792FT	Douglas DC-8-73CF	Emery Worldwide
	N795FT	Douglas DC-8-73CF	Emery Worldwide
	N796FT	Douglas DC-8-73CF	Emery Worldwide
	N801CK	Douglas DC-8-55F	Connie Kalitta Services
	N801PA	Airbus A.310-222	Pan Am *Clipper Berlin*
	N802CK	Douglas DC-8-54F	Connie Kalitta Services
	N802PA	Airbus A.310-222	Pan Am *Clipper Frankfurt*
	N803FT	Boeing 747-132F (SCD)	Flying Tiger Line
	N803PA	Airbus A.310-222	Pan Am *Clipper Munich*
	N804FT	Boeing 747-132F (SCD)	Flying Tiger Line
	N804PA	Airbus A.310-222	Pan Am *Clipper Hamburg*
	N805FT	Boeing 747-132F (SCD)	Flying Tiger Line
	N805PA	Airbus A.310-222	Pan Am *Clipper Miles Standish*
	N806FT	Boeing 747-249F (SCD)	Flying Tiger Line *Robert W. Prescott*
	N806PA	Airbus A.310-222	Pan Am *Clipper Betsy Ross*
	N807FT	Boeing 747-249F (SCD)	Flying Tiger Line *Thomas Haywood*

Reg.	Type	Owner or Operator	Notes
N807PA	Airbus A.310-222	Pan Am *Clipper Kit Carson*	
N808CK	Douglas DC-8-55F	Connie Kalitta Services	
N808FT	Boeing 747-249F (SCD)	Flying Tiger Line *William E. Bartling*	
N809FT	Boeing 747-2R7F	Flying Tiger Line	
N810FT	Boeing 747-249F (SCD)	Flying Tiger Line *Clifford G. Groh*	
N811FT	Boeing 747-245F (SCD)	Flying Tiger Line *Houston Rehrig*	
N811PA	Airbus A.310-324	Pan Am *Clipper Constitution*	
N812FT	Boeing 747-245F (SCD)	Flying Tiger Line	
N812PA	Airbus A.310-324	Pan Am *Clipper Freedom*	
N813FT	Boeing 747-245F (SCD)	Flying Tiger Line	
N813PA	Airbus A.310-324	Pan Am *Clipper Great Republic*	
N814FT	Boeing 747-245F (SCD)	Flying Tiger Line	
N814PA	Airbus A.310-324	Pan Am *Clipper Liberty Bell*	
N815EV	Douglas DC-8-73CF	Evergreen International Airlines	
N815FT	Boeing 747-245F (SCD)	Flying Tiger Line *W. Henry Renninger*	
N815PA	Airbus A.310-324	Pan Am *Clipper Mayflower*	
N816EV	Douglas DC-8-73CF	Air India Cargo	
N816FT	Boeing 747-245F (SCD)	Flying Tiger Line *Henry L. Heguy*	
N816PA	Airbus A.310-324	Pan Am *Clipper Meteor*	
N817EV	Douglas DC-8-62AF	Evergreen International Airlines	
N817FT	Boeing 747-121F (SCD)	Flying Tiger Line	
N817PA	Airbus A.310-324	Pan Am *Clipper Midnight Sun*	
N818FT	Boeing 747-121F (SCD)	Flying Tiger Line	
N818PA	Airbus A.310-324	Pan Am *Clipper Morning Star*	
N819FT	Boeing 747-121F (SCD)	Flying Tiger Line	
N819PA	Airbus A.310-324	Pan Am *Clipper Northern Light*	
N820FT	Boeing 747-121F (SCD)	Flying Tiger Line	
N820PA	Airbus A.310-324	Pan Am *Clipper Plymouth Rock*	
N821PA	Airbus A.310-324	Pan Am *Clipper Queen of the Skies*	
N822FT	Boeing 747-124F	Flying Tiger Line	
N822PA	Airbus A.310-324	Pan Am *Clipper Victory*	
N844TW	Boeing 727-31	Trans World Airlines	
N848TW	Boeing 727-31	Trans World Airlines	
N855TW	Boeing 727-31	Trans World Airlines	
N865F	Douglas DC-8-63CF	Emery Worldwide	
N870TV	Douglas DC-8-73CF	Emery Worldwide	
N871UM	Douglas DC-9-32	Aero Transporti Italiani (ATI)	
N872UM	Douglas DC-9-32	Aero Transporti Italiani (ATI)	
N873UM	Douglas DC-9-32	Aero Transporti Italiani (ATI)	
N890FT	Boeing 747-133	Flying Tiger Line	
N901SJ	L.100-30 Hercules	Southern Air Transport	
N902R	Douglas DC-8-55F	Connie Kalitta Services	
N902PA	Boeing 747-132	Pan Am *Clipper Seaman's Bride*	
N902SJ	L.100-30 Hercules	Southern Air Transport	
N903SJ	L.100-30 Hercules	Southern Air Transport	
N906R	Douglas DC-8-63CF	Emery Worldwide	
N907SJ	L.100-30 Hercules	Southern Air Transport	
N908SJ	L.100-30 Hercules	Southern Air Transport	
N910SJ	L.100-30 Hercules	Southern Air Transport	
N911SJ	L.100-30 Hercules	Southern Air Transport	
N912SJ	L.100-30 Hercules	Southern Air Transport	
N916SJ	L.100-30 Hercules	Southern Air Transport	
N918SJ	L.100-30 Hercules	Southern Air Transport	
N919SJ	L.100-30 Hercules	Southern Air Transport	
N920SJ	L.100-30 Hercules	Southern Air Transport	
N921R	Douglas DC-8-63CF	Emery Worldwide	
N921SJ	L.100-30 Hercules	Southern Air Transport	
N923SJ	L.100-30 Hercules	Southern Air Transport	
N929R	Douglas DC-8-63AF	Emery Worldwide	
N950R	Douglas DC-8-63AF	Emery Worldwide	
N951R	Douglas DC-8-63AF	Emery Worldwide	
N952R	Douglas DC-8-63CF	Emery Worldwide	
N957R	Douglas DC-8-63CF	Emery Worldwide	
N959R	Douglas DC-8-63CF	Emery Worldwide	
N961R	Douglas DC-8-73CF	Emery Worldwide	
N964R	Douglas DC-8-63AF	Emery Worldwide	
N1289E	Boeing 747-228B	Air France	
N1295E	Boeing 747-306	K.L.M. *The Ganges*	
N1298E	Boeing 747-306	K.L.M. *The Indus*	
N1301E	Boeing 747SP-27	CAAC	
N1309E	Boeing 747-306	K.L.M. *Admiral Richard E. Byrd*	
N1738D	L.1011-385 TriStar 250	Delta Air Lines	
N1739D	L.1011-385 TriStar 250	Delta Air Lines	
N1804	Douglas DC-8-62	Rich International Airways	

Notes	Reg.	Type	Owner or Operator
	N1805	Douglas DC-8-62	Rich International Airways
	N1808E	Douglas DC-8-62	Rich International Airways
	N2674U	Douglas DC-8-73CF	Emery Worldwide
	N3016Z	Douglas DC-10-30	Zambia Airways *Nkwazi*
	N3140D	L.1011-385 TriStar 500	B.W.I.A.
	N3878P	Douglas DC-10-30	Aeromexico *Jose Marie Morelos*
	N4201G	Aerospatiale ATR-42-300	Pan Am Express
	N4202G	Aerospatiale ATR-42-300	Pan Am Express
	N4203G	Aerospatiale ATR-42-300	Pan Am Express
	N4204G	Aerospatiale ATR-42-300	Pan Am Express
	N4502R	Boeing 747-283B	Philippine Airlines
	N4506H	Boeing 747-228B	Air France
	N4508E	Boeing 747-228F	Air France
	N4508H	Boeing 747SP-09	China Airlines
	N4522V	Boeing 747SP-09	China Airlines
	N4544F	Boeing 747-228B	Air France
	N4548M	Boeing 747-306	K.L.M. *Sir Frank Whittle*
	N4551N	Boeing 747-306	K.L.M. *Sir Geoffrey de Havilland*
	N4703U	Boeing 747-122 (SCD)	Pan Am *Clipper Nautilus*
	N4704U	Boeing 747-122	Pan Am *Clipper Belle of the Sea*
	N4710U	Boeing 747-122	Pan Am *Clipper Sea Lark*
	N4711U	Boeing 747-122	Pan Am *Clipper Witch of the Waves*
	N4712U	Boeing 747-122 (SCD)	Pan Am *Clipper Tradewind*
	N4730	Boeing 727-235	Pan Am *Clipper Fidelity*
	N4731	Boeing 727-235	Pan Am *Clipper Alert*
	N4732	Boeing 727-235	Pan Am *Clipper Challenger*
	N4733	Boeing 727-235	Pan Am *Clipper Charger*
	N4734	Boeing 727-235	Pan Am *Clipper Charmer*
	N4735	Boeing 727-235	Pan Am *Clipper Daring*
	N4736	Boeing 727-235	Pan Am *Clipper Dashaway*
	N4738	Boeing 727-235	Pan Am *Clipper Electric*
	N4739	Boeing 727-235	Pan Am *Clipper Electric Spark*
	N4740	Boeing 727-235	Pan Am *Clipper Endeavour*
	N4741	Boeing 727-235	Pan Am *Clipper Defender*
	N4742	Boeing 727-235	Pan Am *Clipper Friendship Force*
	N4743	Boeing 727-235	Pan Am *Clipper Good Hope*
	N4745	Boeing 727-235	Pan Am *Clipper Invincible*
	N4746	Boeing 727-235	Pan Am *Clipper Intrepid*
	N4747	Boeing 727-235	Pan Am *Clipper Lookout*
	N4748	Boeing 727-235	Pan Am *Clipper Progressive*
	N4749	Boeing 727-235	Pan Am *Clipper Quick Step*
	N4750	Boeing 727-235	Pan Am *Clipper Royal*
	N4751	Boeing 727-235	Pan Am *Clipper Competitor*
	N4752	Boeing 727-235	Pan Am *Clipper Surprise*
	N4753	Boeing 727-235	Pan Am *Clipper Undaunted*
	N4754	Boeing 727-235	Pan Am *Clipper Resolute*
	N7031A	Boeing 737-205	Braathens SAFE *Sigurd Jorsalfar*
	N7031F	Boeing 737-205	Braathens SAFE *Magnus Lagaboter*
	N7035T	L.1011-385 TriStar 100	Trans World Airlines
	N7036T	L.1011-385 TriStar 100	Trans World Airlines
	N8034T	L.1011-385 TriStar 100	Trans World Airlines
	N9670	Boeing 747-123	Pan Am *Clipper Empress of the Skies*
	N9674	Boeing 747-123	Pan Am *Clipper Beacon Light*
	N10023	Boeing 747-238B	Continental Airlines (N608PE)
	N10024	Boeing 747-238B	Continental Airlines (N609PE)
	N10025	Boeing 747-238B	Continental Airlines (N610PE)
	N12061	Douglas DC-10-30	Continental Airlines *Richard M. Adams*
	N13066	Douglas DC-10-30	Continental Airlines
	N14062	Douglas DC-10-30	Continental Airlines
	N14063	Douglas DC-10-30	Continental Airlines
	N16020	Boeing 747-243B	Continental Airlines (N604PE)
	N17010	Boeing 747-143	Continental Airlines (N603PE)
	N17011	Boeing 747-143	Continental Airlines (N606PE)
	N17125	Boeing 747-136	Trans World Airlines
	N17126	Boeing 747-136	Trans World Airlines
	N19072	Douglas DC-10-30	Continental Airlines
	N31018	L.1011-385 TriStar 50	Trans World Airlines
	N31019	L.1011-385 TriStar 50	Trans World Airlines
	N31021	L.1011-385 TriStar 50	Trans World Airlines
	N31022	L.1011-385 TriStar 50	Trans World Airlines
	N31023	L.1011-385 TriStar 50	Trans World Airlines
	N31024	L.1011-385 TriStar 50	Trans World Airlines
	N31029	L.1011-385 TriStar 100	Trans World Airlines
	N31030	L.1011-385 TriStar 100	Trans World Airlines

Reg.	Type	Owner or Operator	Notes
N31031	L.1011-385 TriStar 100	Trans World Airlines	
N31032	L.1011-385 TriStar 100	Trans World Airlines	
N31033	L.1011-385 TriStar 100	Trans World Airlines	
N33021	Boeing 747-243B	Continental Airlines (N605PE)	
N39356	Boeing 767-323ER	American Airlines	
N39364	Boeing 767-323ER	American Airlines	
N39365	Boeing 767-323ER	American Airlines	
N41020	L.1011-385 TriStar 50	Trans World Airlines	
N46965	L-100-30 Hercules	Southern Air Transport	
N50022	Boeing 747-238B	Continental Airlines (N607PE)	
N53110	Boeing 747-131	Trans World Airlines	
N53116	Boeing 747-131	Trans World Airlines	
N54649	Douglas DC-10-30	U.T.A.	
N68060	Douglas DC-10-30	Continental Airlines *Robert F. Six*	
N68065	Douglas DC-10-30	Continental Airlines	
N81025	L.1011-385 TriStar 100	Trans World Airlines	
N81026	L.1011-385 TriStar 100	Trans World Airlines	
N81027	L.1011-385 TriStar 50	Trans World Airlines	
N81028	L.1011-385 TriStar 100	Trans World Airlines	
N93104	Boeing 747-131	Trans World Airlines	
N93105	Boeing 747-131	Trans World Airlines	
N93106	Boeing 747-131	Trans World Airlines	
N93107	Boeing 747-131	Trans World Airlines	
N93108	Boeing 747-131	Trans World Airlines	
N93109	Boeing 747-131	Trans World Airlines	
N93115	Boeing 747-131F	Evergreen International Airlines	
N93117	Boeing 747-131	Trans World Airlines/Tower Air	
N93119	Boeing 747-131	Trans World Airlines	

OD (Lebanon)

Reg.	Type	Owner or Operator	Notes
OD-AFD	Boeing 707-3B4C	Middle East Airlines	
OD-AFE	Boeing 707-3B4C	Middle East Airlines	
OD-AFM	Boeing 720-023B	Middle East Airlines	
OD-AFN	Boeing 720-023B	Middle East Airlines	
OD-AFY	Boeing 707-327C	Trans Mediterranean Airways	
OD-AFZ	Boeing 720-023B	Middle East Airlines	
OD-AGB	Boeing 720-023B	Middle East Airlines	
OD-AGD	Boeing 707-323C	Trans Mediterranean Airways	
OD-AGF	Boeing 720-047B	Middle East Airlines	
OD-AGO	Boeing 707-321C	Trans Mediterranean Airways	
OD-AGP	Boeing 707-321C	Trans Mediterranean Airways	
OD-AGS	Boeing 707-331C	Trans Mediterranean Airways	
OD-AGU	Boeing 707-347C	Middle East Airlines	
OD-AGV	Boeing 707-347C	Middle East Airlines	
OD-AGX	Boeing 707-327C	Trans Mediterranean Airways	
OD-AGY	Boeing 707-327C	Trans Mediterranean Airways	
OD-AHC	Boeing 707-323C	Middle East Airlines	
OD-AHD	Boeing 707-323C	Middle East Airlines	
OD-AHE	Boeing 707-323C	Middle East Airlines	
OD-	Boeing 707-323B	Middle East Airlines	

OE (Austria)

Reg.	Type	Owner or Operator	Notes
OE-ILF	Boeing 737-3Z9	Lauda Air *Bob Marley*	
OE-ILG	Boeing 737-3Z9	Lauda Air *John Lennon*	
OE-ILH	Boeing 737-3Z9	Lauda Air	
OE-LAA	Airbus A.310-324	Austrian Airlines	
OE-LAB	Airbus A.310-324	Austrian Airlines	
OE-	Airbus A.310-324	Austrian Airlines	
OE-LAU	Boeing 767-3Z9ER	Lauda Air	
OE-LAV	Boeing 767-3Z9ER	Lauda Air	
OE-	Boeing 767-3Z9ER	Lauda Air	
OE-LDG	Douglas DC-9-32	Austrian Airlines	
OE-LDH	Douglas DC-9-32	Austrian Airlines	

Notes	Reg.	Type	Owner or Operator
	OE-LDI	Douglas DC-9-32	Austrian Airlines *Bregenz*
	OE-LDP	Douglas DC-9-81	Austrian Airlines *Niederösterreich*
	OE-LDR	Douglas DC-9-81	Austrian Airlines *Wien*
	OE-LDS	Douglas DC-9-81	Austrian Airlines *Burgenland*
	OE-LDT	Douglas DC-9-81	Austrian Airlines *Kärnten*
	OE-LDU	Douglas DC-9-81	Austrian Airlines *Steiermark*
	OE-LDV	Douglas DC-9-81	Austrian Airlines *Oberösterreich*
	OE-LDW	Douglas DC-9-81	Austrian Airlines *Salzburg*
	OE-LDX	Douglas DC-9-81	Austrian Airlines *Tirol*
	OE-LDY	Douglas DC-9-81	Austrian Airlines *Vorarlberg*
	OE-LDZ	Douglas DC-9-81	Austrian Airlines *Graz*
	OE-LLP	D.H.C.8-103 Dash Eight	Tyrolean Airways
	OE-LLR	D.H.C.8-102 Dash Eight	Tyrolean Airways *Stadt Graz*
	OE-LLS	D.H.C.7-102 Dash Seven	Tyrolean Airways *Stadt Innsbruck*
	OE-LLT	D.H.C.7-102 Dash Seven	Tyrolean Airways *Stadt Wien*
	OE-	D.H.C.7-102 Dash Seven	Tyrolean Airways
	OE-LMA	Douglas DC-9-81	Austrian Airlines *Linz*
	OE-LMB	Douglas DC-9-81	Austrian Airlines *Eisenstadt*
	OE-LMC	Douglas DC-9-81	Austrian Airlines *Baden*
	OE-LMK	Douglas DC-9-87	Austrian Airlines *St Pölten*
	OE-LML	Douglas DC-9-87	Austrian Airlines *Stadt Salzburg*
	OE-LMM	Douglas DC-9-87	Austrian Airlines
	OE-LMN	Douglas DC-9-87	Austrian Airlines
	OE-LMO	Douglas DC-9-87	Austrian Airlines
	OE-LMP	Douglas DC-9-87	Austrian Airlines

Note: The four DC-9-32s are leased by Austrian pending delivery of the DC-9-87s.

OH (Finland)

	OH-LAA	Airbus A.300B4-203	Kar-Air
	OH-LAB	Airbus A.300B4-203	Kar-Air
	OH-LGA	McD Douglas MD-11	Finnair
	OH-LGB	McD Douglas MD-11	Finnair
	OH-LHA	Douglas DC-10-30ER	Finnair *Iso Antti*
	OH-LHB	Douglas DC-10-30ER	Finnair
	OH-LHD	Douglas DC-10-30ER	Finnair
	OH-LHE	Douglas DC-10-30ER	Finnair
	OH-LMA	Douglas DC-9-87	Finnair
	OH-LMB	Douglas DC-9-87	Finnair
	OH-LMC	Douglas DC-9-87	Finnair
	OH-	Douglas DC-9-87	Finnair
	OH-	Douglas DC-9-87	Finnair
	OH-LMG	Douglas DC-9-83	Finnair
	OH-	Douglas DC-9-82	Finnair
	OH-LMN	Douglas DC-9-82	Finnair
	OH-LMO	Douglas DC-9-82	Finnair
	OH-LMP	Douglas DC-9-82	Finnair
	OH-LMR	Douglas DC-9-83	Finnair
	OH-LMS	Douglas DC-9-83	Finnair
	OH-LMT	Douglas DC-9-82	Finnair
	OH-LMU	Douglas DC-9-83	Finnair
	OH-LMV	Douglas DC-9-83	Finnair
	OH-LMW	Douglas DC-9-82	Finnair
	OH-LMX	Douglas DC-9-82	Finnair
	OH-LNB	Douglas DC-9-41	Finnair
	OH-LNC	Douglas DC-9-41	Finnair
	OH-LND	Douglas DC-9-41	Finnair
	OH-LNE	Douglas DC-9-41	Finnair
	OH-LNF	Douglas DC-9-41	Finnair
	OH-LYN	Douglas DC-9-51	Finnair
	OH-LYO	Douglas DC-9-51	Finnair
	OH-LYP	Douglas DC-9-51	Finnair
	OH-LYR	Douglas DC-9-51	Finnair
	OH-LYS	Douglas DC-9-51	Finnair
	OH-LYT	Douglas DC-9-51	Finnair
	OH-LYU	Douglas DC-9-51	Finnair
	OH-LYV	Douglas DC-9-51	Finnair

Reg.	Type	Owner or Operator	Notes
OH-LYW	Douglas DC-9-51	Finnair	
OH-LYX	Douglas DC-9-51	Finnair	
OH-LYY	Douglas DC-9-51	Finnair	
OH-LYZ	Douglas DC-9-51	Finnair	

Note: Finnair also operates a DC-10-30ER which retains its US registration N345HC.

OK (Czechoslovakia)

OK-CFC	Tupolev Tu-134A	Ceskoslovenske Aerolinie	
OK-CFE	Tupolev Tu-134A	Ceskoslovenske Aerolinie	
OK-CFF	Tupolev Tu-134A	Ceskoslovenske Aerolinie	
OK-CFG	Tupolev Tu-134A	Ceskoslovenske Aerolinie	
OK-CFH	Tupolev Tu-134A	Ceskoslovenske Aerolinie	
OK-DBE	Ilyushin IL-62	Ceskoslovenske Aerolinie *Brno*	
OK-DFI	Tupolev Tu-134A	Ceskoslovenske Aerolinie	
OK-EBG	Ilyushin IL-62	Ceskoslovenske Aerolinie *Banska Bystrica*	
OK-EFJ	Tupolev Tu-134A	Ceskoslovenske Aerolinie	
OK-EFK	Tupolev Tu-134A	Ceskoslovenske Aerolinie	
OK-FBF	Ilyushin IL-62	Ceskoslovenske Aerolinie	
OK-GBH	Ilyushin IL-62	Ceskoslovenske Aerolinie *Usti Nad Labem*	
OK-HFL	Tupolev Tu-134A	Ceskoslovenske Aerolinie	
OK-HFM	Tupolev Tu-134A	Ceskoslovenske Aerolinie	
OK-IFN	Tupolev Tu-134A	Ceskoslovenske Aerolinie	
OK-JBI	Ilyushin IL-62M	Ceskoslovenske Aerolinie *Plzen*	
OK-JBJ	Ilyushin IL-62M	Ceskoslovenske Aerolinie *Hradec Kralové*	
OK-KBK	Ilyushin IL-62M	Ceskoslovenske Aerolinie *Ceske Budejovice*	
OK-KBN	Ilyushin Il-62M	Ceskoslovenske Aerolinie	
OK-OBL	Ilyushin IL-62M	Ceskoslovenske Aerolinie *Ostrava*	
OK-PBM	Ilyushin IL-62M	Ceskoslovenske Aerolinie	
OK-SCA	Tupolev Tu-154M	Ceskoslovenske Aerolinie *Mesto Piestany*	
OK-TCB	Tupolev Tu-154M	Ceskoslovenske Aerolinie	
OK-TCC	Tupolev Tu-154M	Ceskoslovenske Aerolinie	
OK-	Tupolev Tu-154M	Ceskoslovenske Aerolinie	
OK-	Tupolev Tu-154M	Ceskoslovenske Aerolinie	
OK-	Tupolev Tu-154M	Ceskoslovenske Aerolinie	
OK-	Tupolev Tu-154M	Ceskoslovenske Aerolinie	

OO (Belgium)

OO-CDE	Boeing 707-365C	Belgian International Air Cargo	
OO-DHB	Convair Cv.580	European Air Transport (DHL)	
OO-DHC	Convair Cv.580	European Air Transport (DHL)	
OO-DHD	Convair Cv.580	European Air Transport (DHL)	
OO-DHE	Convair Cv.580	European Air Transport (DHL)	
OO-DHL	Convair Cv.580	European Air Transport (DHL)	
OO-DJA	F.27 Fellowship 3000	Delta Air Transport	
OO-DJB	F.28 Fellowship 4000	Delta Air Transport	
OO-DTA	FH-227B Friendship	Delta Air Transport	
OO-DTB	FH-227B Friendship	Delta Air Transport	
OO-DTE	FH-227B Friendship	Delta Air Transport	
OO-DTF	EMB-120 Brasilia	Delta Air Transport	
OO-DTG	EMB-120 Brasilia	Delta Air Transport	
OO-DTH	EMB-120 Brasilia	Delta Air Transport	
OO-D	EMB-120 Brasilia	Delta Air Transport	
OO-D	EMB-120 Brasilia	Delta Air Transport	
OO-HUB	Convair Cv.580	European Air Transport (DHL)	
OO-	Convair Cv.580	European Air Transport (DHL)	
OO-ILF	Boeing 737-3Q8	Air Belgium	
OO-ILH	Boeing 737-4Q8	Air Belgium	
OO-JPA	Swearingen SA226AT Merlin IVA	European Air Transport	
OO-JPI	Swearingen SA226TC Metro II	European Air Transport	
OO-JPK	Swearingen SA226TC Metro II	European Air Transport	

Notes	Reg.	Type	Owner or Operator
	OO-JPN	Swearingen SA226AT Merlin IVA	European Air Transport
	OO-LTA	Boeing 737-3M8	Trans European Airways (*for lease*)
	OO-LTB	Boeing 737-3M8	Trans European Airways (*for lease*)
	OO-LTC	Boeing 737-3M8	Trans European Airways (*for lease*)
	OO-LTD	Boeing 737-3M8	Trans European Airways
	OO-LTE	Boeing 737-3M8	Trans European Airways
	OO-LTF	Boeing 737-3M8	Trans European Airways
	OO-LTG	Boeing 737-3M8	Trans European Airways
	OO-LTH	Boeing 737-3M8	Trans European Airways
	OO-LTI	Boeing 737-3M8	Trans European Airways
	OO-SBQ	Boeing 737-229	Sobelair
	OO-SBS	Boeing 737-229	Sobelair
	OO-SBT	Boeing 737-229	Sobelair
	OO-SBU	Boeing 707-373C	Sobelair
	OO-SBZ	Boeing 737-329	Sobelair
	OO-SCA	Airbus A.310-221	Sabena
	OO-SCB	Airbus A.310-221	Sabena
	OO-SCC	Airbus A.310-322	Sabena
	OO-SDB	Boeing 737-229	Sabena/Trans European Airways
	OO-SDC	Boeing 737-229	Sabena/Trans European Airways
	OO-SDD	Boeing 737-229	Sabena
	OO-SDE	Boeing 737-229	Sabena
	OO-SDF	Boeing 737-229	Sabena
	OO-SDG	Boeing 737-229	Sabena
	OO-SDJ	Boeing 737-229C	Sabena
	OO-SDK	Boeing 737-229C	Sabena
	OO-SDL	Boeing 737-229	Sabena
	OO-SDM	Boeing 737-229	Sabena
	OO-SDN	Boeing 737-229	Sabena
	OO-SDO	Boeing 737-229	Sabena
	OO-SDP	Boeing 737-229C	Sabena
	OO-SDR	Boeing 737-229C	Sabena
	OO-SDV	Boeing 737-329	Sabena
	OO-SDW	Boeing 737-329	Sabena
	OO-SDX	Boeing 737-329	Sabena
	OO-SDY	Boeing 737-329	Sabena
	OO-SGA	Boeing 747-129A (SCD)	Sabena
	OO-SGB	Boeing 747-129A (SCD)	Sabena
	OO-SGC	Boeing 747-329 (SCD)	Sabena
	OO-SLA	Douglas DC-10-30CF	Sabena
	OO-SLB	Douglas DC-10-30CF	Sabena
	OO-SLC	Douglas DC-10-30CF	Sabena
	OO-SLD	Douglas DC-10-30CF	Sabena
	OO-SLE	Douglas DC-10-30CF	Sabena
	OO-SQA	Boeing 737-329	Sabena
	OO-SQB	Boeing 737-329	Sabena
	OO-TEF	Airbus A.300B1	Trans European Airways *Aline*
	OO-TEH	Boeing 737-2M8	Trans European Airways
	OO-TEK	Boeing 737-2Q9	Trans European Airways
	OO-TEL	Boeing 737-2M8	Trans European Airways
	OO-TYC	Boeing 707-328B	Trans European Airways
	OO-VGC	Swearingen SA226AT Merlin IV	European Air Transport *Kristin*
	OO-VGD	Swearingen SA226AT Merlin IV	European Air Transport
	OO-VGH	Convair Cv.580	European Air Transport (DHL)
	OO-VGI	Convair Cv.580	European Air Transport (DHL)

OY (Denmark)

Notes	Reg.	Type	Owner or Operator
	OY-BDD	Nord 262A-21	Cimber Air
	OY-BPH	Swearingen SA227AC Metro III	Metro Airways
	OY-BPJ	Swearingen SA227AC Metro III	Midtfly
	OY-BVF	F.27 Friendship Mk 600	Business Flight
	OY-BYH	Swearingen SA226TC Metro II	Muk Air
	OY-BYN	Swearingen SA226TC Metro II	Muk Air
	OY-BZW	Swearingen SA226TC Metro II	Midtfly
	OY-CCK	F.27 Friendship Mk 600	Starair
	OY-CCL	F.27 Friendship Mk.600	Starair
	OY-CIB	Aerospatiale ATR-42-300	Cimber Air
	OY-CIC	Aerospatiale ATR-42-300	Cimber Air
	OY-C	Aerospatiale ATR-42-300	Cimber Air
	OY-C	Aerospatiale ATR-42-300	Cimber Air

Reg.	Type	Owner or Operator	Notes
OY-CNA	Airbus A.300-320	Conair	
OY-CNK	Airbus A.300-320	Conair	
OY-CNL	Airbus A.300-320	Conair	
OY-CTA	Douglas DC-9-51	S.A.S. *Turgeis Viking*	
OY-CTB	Douglas DC-9-51	S.A.S. *Ingvar Viking*	
OY-CTD	Douglas DC-9-51	S.A.S. *Stavar Viking*	
OY-DDA	Douglas DC-3	Danish Air Lines	
OY-KAC	F.27 Friendship Mk 600	S.A.S.	
OY-KAD	F.27 Friendship Mk 600	S.A.S.	
OY-KDA	Douglas DC-10-30	S.A.S. *Gorm Viking*	
OY-KDB	Douglas DC-10-30	S.A.S. *Frode Viking*	
OY-KDC	Douglas DC-10-30	S.A.S. *Godfred Viking*	
OY-KDH	Boeing 767-383ER	S.A.S.	
OY-KDI	Boeing 767-383ER	S.A.S.	
OY-KDK	Boeing 767-383ER	S.A.S.	
OY-KGA	Douglas DC-9-41	S.A.S. *Heming Viking*	
OY-KGB	Douglas DC-9-41	S.A.S. *Toste Viking*	
OY-KGC	Douglas DC-9-41	S.A.S. *Helge Viking*	
OY-KGD	Douglas DC-9-21	S.A.S. *Ubbe Viking*	
OY-KGE	Douglas DC-9-21	S.A.S. *Orvar Viking*	
OY-KGF	Douglas DC-9-21	S.A.S. *Rolf Viking*	
OY-KGG	Douglas DC-9-41	S.A.S. *Sune Viking*	
OY-KGH	Douglas DC-9-41	S.A.S. *Eiliv Viking*	
OY-KGI	Douglas DC-9-41	S.A.S. *Bent Viking*	
OY-KGK	Douglas DC-9-41	S.A.S. *Ebbe Viking*	
OY-KGL	Douglas DC-9-41	S.A.S. *Angantyr Viking*	
OY-KGM	Douglas DC-9-41	S.A.S. *Arnfinn Viking*	
OY-KGN	Douglas DC-9-41	S.A.S. *Gram Viking*	
OY-KGO	Douglas DC-9-41	S.A.S. *Holte Viking*	
OY-KGP	Douglas DC-9-41	S.A.S. *Torbern Viking*	
OY-KGR	Douglas DC-9-41	S.A.S. *Holger Viking*	
OY-KGS	Douglas DC-9-41	S.A.S. *Hall Viking*	
OY-KGT	Douglas DC-9-81	S.A.S. *Hake Viking*	
OY-KGY	Douglas DC-9-81	S.A.S. *Rollo Viking*	
OY-KGZ	Douglas DC-9-81	S.A.S. *Hagbard Viking*	
OY-KHC	Douglas DC-9-81	S.A.S. *Faste Viking*	
OY-KHE	Douglas DC-9-82	S.A.S. *Saxo Viking*	
OY-KHF	Douglas DC-9-87	S.A.S. *Ragnar Viking*	
OY-KHG	Douglas DC-9-81	S.A.S. *Alle Viking*	
OY-KHI	Douglas DC-9-87	S.A.S. *Roald Viking*	
OY-KHK	Douglas DC-9-87	S.A.S. *Torkel Viking*	
OY-KTF	Douglas DC-8-63	Scanair *Mette Viking*	
OY-KTG	Douglas DC-8-63	Scanair *Torodd Viking*	
OY-MBD	D.H.C.7 Dash Seven	Maersk Air	
OY-MBE	D.H.C.7 Dash Seven	Maersk Air	
OY-MBV	Boeing 737-2L9	Maersk Air	
OY-MBW	Boeing 737-2L9	Maersk Air	
OY-MBZ	Boeing 737-2L9	Maersk Air	
OY-MMG	Fokker 50	Maersk Air	
OY-MMH	Fokker 50	Maersk Air	
OY-MMI	Fokker 50	Maersk Air	
OY-MMJ	Fokker 50	Maersk Air	
OY-MML	Boeing 737-3L9	Maersk Air	
OY-MMM	Boeing 737-3L9	Maersk Air	
OY-MMS	Fokker 50	Maersk Air	
OY-MMT	Fokker 50	Maersk Air	
OY-MMU	Fokker 50	Maersk Air	
OY-MMV	Fokker 50	Maersk Air	
OY-MUF	F.27J Friendship	Muk Air	
OY-SAS	Boeing 727-2J4	Sterling Airways	
OY-SAT	Boeing 727-2J4	Sterling Airways	
OY-SAU	Boeing 727-2J4	Sterling Airways	
OY-SBE	Boeing 727-2J4	Sterling Airways	
OY-SBF	Boeing 727-2J4	Sterling Airways	
OY-SBG	Boeing 727-2J4	Sterling Airways	
OY-SBH	Boeing 727-2B7	Sterling Airways	
OY-SBI	Boeing 727-270	Sterling Airways	
OY-SBK	Douglas DC-8-63	Scanair	
OY-SBL	Douglas DC-8-63	Scanair	
OY-SBN	Boeing 727-2B7	Sterling Airways	
OY-SBO	Boeing 727-2K3	Sterling Airways	
OY-SCA	Boeing 727-2H3	Sterling Airways	
OY-SRA	F.27 Friendship Mk 600	Starair	
OY-SRR	F.27 Friendship Mk 600	Starair	

OY/PH

Notes	Reg.	Type	Owner or Operator
	OY-STC	S.E.210 Caravelle 10B	Sterling Airways
	OY-STD	S.E.210 Caravelle 10B	Sterling Airways
	OY-STF	S.E.210 Caravelle 10B	Baltic Aviation
	OY-STH	S.E.210 Caravelle 10B	Sterling Airways
	OY-STI	S.E.210 Caravelle 10B	Sterling Airways
	OY-STM	S.E.210 Caravelle 10B	Sterling Airways
	OY-TOV	Nord 262A-30	Cimber Air

PH (Netherlands)

	Reg.	Type	Owner or Operator
	PH-AGA	Airbus A.310-203	K.L.M. *Rembrandt*
	PH-AGB	Airbus A.310-203	K.L.M. *Jeroen Bosch*
	PH-AGC	Airbus A.310-203	K.L.M. *Albert Cuyp*
	PH-AGD	Airbus A.310-203	K.L.M. *Marinus Ruppert*
	PH-AGE	Airbus A.310-203	K.L.M. *Nicolaas Maes*
	PH-AGF	Airbus A.310-203	K.L.M. *Jan Steen*
	PH-AGG	Airbus A.310-203	K.L.M. *Vincent van Gogh*
	PH-AGH	Airbus A.310-203	K.L.M. *Peiter de Hoogh*
	PH-AGI	Airbus A.310-203	K.L.M. *Jan Toorop*
	PH-AGK	Airbus A.310-203	K.L.M. *Johannes Vermeer*
	PH-AHE	Boeing 757-27B	Air Holland
	PH-AHF	Boeing 757-27B	Air Holland
	PH-AHI	Boeing 757-27B	Air Holland *Majoor Alida Bosshardt*
	PH-AH	Boeing 757-27B	Air Holland
	PH-BDA	Boeing 737-306	K.L.M. *Willem Barentz*
	PH-BDB	Boeing 737-306	K.L.M. *Olivier van Noort*
	PH-BDC	Boeing 737-306	K.L.M. *Cornelis De Houteman*
	PH-BDD	Boeing 737-306	K.L.M. *Anthony van Diemen*
	PH-BDE	Boeing 737-306	K.L.M. *Abel J. Tasman*
	PH-BDG	Boeing 737-306	K.L.M. *Michiel A. D. Ruyter*
	PH-BDH	Boeing 737-306	K.L.M. *Petrus Plancius*
	PH-BDI	Boeing 737-306	K.L.M. *Maarten H. Tromp*
	PH-BDK	Boeing 737-306	K.L.M. *Jan H. van Linschoten*
	PH-BDL	Boeing 737-306	K.L.M. *Piet Heyn*
	PH-BDN	Boeing 737-306	K.L.M. *Willem van Ruysbroeck*
	PH-BDO	Boeing 737-306	K.L.M. *Jacob van Heemskerck*
	PH-BDP	Boeing 737-306	K.L.M. *Jacob Rogeveen*
	PH-BDS	Boeing 737-406	K.L.M.
	PH-BDT	Boeing 737-406	K.L.M.
	PH-B	Boeing 737-406	K.L.M.
	PH-BFA	Boeing 747-406	K.L.M. *City of Atlanta*
	PH-BFB	Boeing 747-406	K.L.M. *City of Bangkok*
	PH-BFC	Boeing 747-406	K.L.M. *City of Calgary*
	PH-BFD	Boeing 747-406	K.L.M. *City of Dubai*
	PH-BFE	Boeing 747-406	K.L.M. *City of Melbourne*
	PH-BFF	Boeing 747-406	K.L.M. *City of Freetown*
	PH-BFG	Boeing 747-406	K.L.M. *City of Guayaquil*
	PH-BFH	Boeing 747-406	K.L.M. *City of Hong Kong*
	PH-BUA	Boeing 747-206B	K.L.M. *The Mississippi*
	PH-BUB	Boeing 747-206B	K.L.M. *The Danube*
	PH-BUC	Boeing 747-206B	K.L.M. *The Amazon*
	PH-BUD	Boeing 747-206B	K.L.M. *The Nile*
	PH-BUE	Boeing 747-206B	K.L.M. *Rio de la Plata*
	PH-BUG	Boeing 747-206B	K.L.M. *The Orinoco*
	PH-BUH	Boeing 747-306	K.L.M. *Dr Albert Plesman*
	PH-BUI	Boeing 747-306	K.L.M. *Wilbur Wright*
	PH-BUK	Boeing 747-306	K.L.M. *Louis Blériot*
	PH-BUL	Boeing 747-306	K.L.M. *Charles A. Lindbergh*
	PH-BUM	Boeing 747-306	K.L.M. *Sir Charles E. Kingsford-Smith*
	PH-BUN	Boeing 747-306	K.L.M. *Anthony H. G. Fokker*
	PH-BUO	Boeing 747-306	K.L.M. *Missouri*
	PH-BUW	Boeing 747-306	K.L.M. *Leonardo da Vinci*
	PH-CHB	F.28 Fellowship 4000	N.L.M. *Birmingham*
	PH-CHD	F.28 Fellowship 4000	N.L.M. *Maastricht*
	PH-CHF	F.28 Fellowship 4000	N.L.M. *Guernsey*
	PH-CHN	F.28 Fellowship 4000	N.L.M.
	PH-DDA	Douglas DC-3	Dutch Dakota Association
	PH-DTA	Douglas DC-10-30	K.L.M. *Johann Sebastian Bach*
	PH-DTB	Douglas DC-10-30	K.L.M. *Ludwig van Beethoven*
	PH-DTC	Douglas DC-10-30	K.L.M. *Frédéric François Chopin*
	PH-DTD	Douglas DC-10-30	K.L.M. *Maurice Ravel*

Reg.	Type	Owner or Operator	Notes
PH-DTL	Douglas DC-10-30	K.L.M. *Edvard Hagerup Grieg*	
PH-FKT	F-27 Friendship Mk 600	XP Express Parcel System *Monique*	
PH-HVF	Boeing 737-3K2	Transavia *Johan Cruijff*	
PH-HVG	Boeing 737-3K2	Transavia *Wubbo Ockels*	
PH-HVJ	Boeing 737-3K2	Transavia *Nelli Cooman*	
PH-HVK	Boeing 737-3K2	Transavia *Evert van Benthern*	
PH-HVM	Boeing 737-3K2	Transavia	
PH-HVN	Boeing 737-3K2	Transavia	
PH-HVT	Boeing 737-3K2	Transavia	
PH-HVV	Boeing 737-3K2	Transavia	
PH-KFD	F.27 Friendship Mk 200	N.L.M. *Jan Moll*	
PH-KFE	F.27 Friendship Mk 600	N.L.M. *Jan Dellaert*	
PH-KFG	F.27 Friendship Mk 200	N.L.M. *Koos Abspoel*	
PH-KFI	F.27 Friendship Mk 500	N.L.M. *Bremen*	
PH-KFK	F.27 Friendship Mk 500	N.L.M. *Zestienhoven*	
PH-KFL	F.27 Friendship Mk 500	N.L.M.	
PH-KJA	BAe Jetstream 3102	NetherLines	
PH-KJB	BAe Jetstream 3102	NetherLines	
PH-KJC	BAe Jetstream 3102	NetherLines	
PH-KJD	BAe Jetstream 3102	NetherLines	
PH-KJF	BAe Jetstream 3102	NetherLines	
PH-KJG	BAe Jetstream 3102	NetherLines	
PH-KJH	Saab SF.340A	NetherLines	
PH-	Saab SF.340A	NetherLines	
PH-	Saab SF.340A	NetherLines	
PH-	Saab SF.340A	NetherLines	
PH-KLC	Fokker 100	K.L.M. *Gerard Mercator*	
PH-KLD	Fokker 100	K.L.M. *Jan A. Leeghwater*	
PH-KLE	Fokker 100	K.L.M. *Geradus J. Vossius*	
PH-KLG	Fokker 100	K.L.M. *Johannes Blaeu*	
PH-KLH	Fokker 100	K.L.M. *Christiaan Huygens*	
PH-KLI	Fokker 100	K.L.M. *Antonie van Leeuwenhoek*	
PH-KLK	Fokker 100	K.L.M. *Chris H. D. Buys Ballot*	
PH-KLL	Fokker 100	K.L.M. *Hendrick A. Lorentz*	
PH-KLN	Fokker 100	K.L.M. *Pieter Zeeman*	
PH-KLO	Fokker 100	K.L.M. *Jan H. Oort*	
PH-MBN	Douglas DC-10-30CF	Martinair *Anthony Ruys*	
PH-MBP	Douglas DC-10-30CF	Martinair *Hong Kong*	
PH-MBT	Douglas DC-10-30CF	Martinair	
PH-MBZ	Douglas DC-9-82	Martinair *Prinses Juiliana*	
PH-MCA	Airbus A.310-203	Martinair *Prins Bernhard*	
PH-MCB	Airbus A.310-203CF	Martinair *Prins Maurits*	
PH-MCD	Douglas DC-9-82	Martinair *Lucien Ruys*	
PH-MCE	Boeing 747-21AC (SCD)	Martinair *Prins van Oranje*	
PH-MCF	Boeing 747-21AC (SCD)	Martinair *Prins Claus*	
PH-MCG	Boeing 767-31AER	Martinair	
PH-MCH	Boeing 767-31AER	Martinair	
PH-SAD	F.27 Friendship Mk 200	N.L.M. *Evert van Dijk*	
PH-SFA	F.27 Friendship Mk 400	N.L.M.	
PH-SFB	F.27 Friendship Mk 400	N.L.M.	
PH-SFC	F.27 Friendship Mk 400	XP Express Parcel System *Karin*	
PH-SFE	F.27 Friendship Mk 300	Schreiner Airways	
PH-SFH	F.27 Friendship Mk 600	XP Express Parcel System	
PH-TVC	Boeing 737-2K2C	Transavia *Richard Gordon*	
PH-TVH	Boeing 737-222	Transavia *Neil Armstrong*	
PH-TVR	Boeing 737-2K2	Transavia/K.L.M.	
PH-TVU	Boeing 737-2K2	Transavia	
PH-TVX	Boeing 737-2K2	Transavia/K.L.M.	
PH-XPS	F.27 Friendship Mk 600	XP Express Parcel System	

Note: K.L.M. also operates Boeing 747-306s N1295E, N1298E, N1309E, N4548M and N4551N.

PK (Indonesia)

PK-GIA	Douglas DC-10-30	Garuda Indonesian Airways	
PK-GIB	Douglas DC-10-30	Garuda Indonesian Airways	
PK-GIC	Douglas DC-10-30	Garuda Indonesian Airways	
PK-GID	Douglas DC-10-30	Garuda Indonesian Airways	
PK-GIE	Douglas DC-10-30	Garuda Indonesian Airways	
PK-GIF	Douglas DC-10-30	Garuda Indonesian Airways	

Notes	Reg.	Type	Owner or Operator
	PK-GSA	Boeing 747-2U3B	Garuda Indonesian Airways
	PK-GSB	Boeing 747-2U3B	Garuda Indonesian Airways
	PK-GSC	Boeing 747-2U3B	Garuda Indonesian Airways
	PK-GSD	Boeing 747-2U3B	Garuda Indonesian Airways
	PK-GSE	Boeing 747-2U3B	Garuda Indonesian Airways
	PK-GSF	Boeing 747-2U3B	Garuda Indonesian Airways

PP (Brazil)

PP-VMA	Douglas DC-10-30	VARIG
PP-VMB	Douglas DC-10-30	VARIG
PP-VMD	Douglas DC-10-30	VARIG
PP-VMQ	Douglas DC-10-30	VARIG
PP-VMS	Douglas DC-10-30	VARIG
PP-VMT	Douglas DC-10-30F	VARIG Cargo
PP-VMU	Douglas DC-10-30F	VARIG Cargo
PP-VMV	Douglas DC-10-30	VARIG
PP-VMW	Douglas DC-10-30	VARIG
PP-VMX	Douglas DC-10-30	VARIG
PP-VMY	Douglas DC-10-30	VARIG
PP-VMZ	Douglas DC-10-30	VARIG
PP-VNA	Boeing 747-2L5B (SCD)	VARIG
PP-VNB	Boeing 747-2L5B (SCD)	VARIG
PP-VNC	Boeing 747-2L5B (SCD)	VARIG
PP-VNH	Boeing 747-341 (SCD)	VARIG
PP-VNI	Boeing 747-341 (SCD)	VARIG
PP-VOA	Boeing 747-341	VARIG
PP-VOB	Boeing 747-341	VARIG
PP-VOC	Boeing 747-341	VARIG

RP (Philippines)

Note: Philippine Airlines operates four Boeing 747-2F6Bs which retain their U.S. registrations N741PR, N742PR, N743PR and N744PR and two 747-283Bs EI-BTS and N4502R.

S2 (Bangladesh)

S2-ACE	Boeing 707-351C	Bangladesh Biman *City of Tokyo*
S2-ACO	Douglas DC-10-30	Bangladesh Biman *City of Hazrat-Shar Makhdoom (R.A.)*
S2-ACP	Douglas DC-10-30	Bangladesh Biman *City of Dhaka*
S2-ACQ	Douglas DC-10-30	Bangladesh Biman *City of Hz Shah Jalal (R.A.)*
S2-	Douglas DC-10-30	Bangladesh Biman

S7 (Seychelles)

S7-1HM	Boeing 767-2Q8ER	Air Seychelles
S7-2HM	Boeing 707-324C (Super Q)	Air Seychelles
S7-4HM	Boeing 707-324C (Super Q)	Air Seychelles

SE (Sweden)

SE-CFP	Douglas DC-3	S.A.S. *Fridtjof Viking*
SE-DAK	Douglas DC-9-41	S.A.S. *Ragnvald Viking*
SE-DAL	Douglas DC-9-41	S.A.S. *Algot Viking*
SE-DAM	Douglas DC-9-41	S.A.S. *Starkad Viking*
SE-DAN	Douglas DC-9-41	S.A.S. *Alf Viking*
SE-DAO	Douglas DC-9-41	S.A.S. *Asgaut Viking*

Reg.	Type	Owner or Operator	Notes
SE-DAP	Douglas DC-9-41	S.A.S. *Torgils Viking*	
SE-DAR	Douglas DC-9-41	S.A.S. *Agnar Viking*	
SE-DAS	Douglas DC-9-41	S.A.S. *Garder Viking*	
SE-DAU	Douglas DC-9-41	S.A.S. *Hadding Viking*	
SE-DAW	Douglas DC-9-41	S.A.S. *Gotrik Viking*	
SE-DAX	Douglas DC-9-41	S.A.S. *Helsing Viking*	
SE-DBH	Douglas DC-8-63	Scanair *Dana Viking*	
SE-DBK	Douglas DC-8-63	Scanair *Sigyn Viking*	
SE-DBL	Douglas DC-8-63	Scanair *Bodil Viking*	
SE-DBM	Douglas DC-9-41	S.A.S. *Ossur Viking*	
SE-DBO	Douglas DC-9-21	S.A.S. *Siger Viking*	
SE-DBP	Douglas DC-9-21	S.A.S. *Rane Viking*	
SE-DBR	Douglas DC-9-21	S.A.S. *Skate Viking*	
SE-DBS	Douglas DC-9-21	S.A.S. *Svipdag Viking*	
SE-DBT	Douglas DC-9-41	S.A.S. *Agne Viking*	
SE-DBU	Douglas DC-9-41	S.A.S. *Hjalmar Viking*	
SE-DBW	Douglas DC-9-41	S.A.S. *Adils Viking*	
SE-DBX	Douglas DC-9-41	S.A.S. *Arnljot Viking*	
SE-DDR	Douglas DC-9-41	S.A.S. *Brun Viking*	
SE-DDR	Douglas DC-9-41	S.A.S. *Atle Viking*	
SE-DDS	Douglas DC-9-41	S.A.S. *Alrik Viking*	
SE-DDT	Douglas DC-9-41	S.A.S. *Amund Viking*	
SE-DDU	Douglas DC-8-62	Scanair *Knud Viking*	
SE-DEB	S.E.210 Caravelle 10R	Pelican Express	
SE-DEH	S.E.210 Caravelle 10B	Transwede	
SE-DEI	BAe 146-200QT	Malmo Aviation (TNT)	
SE-DFD	Douglas DC-10-30	S.A.S. *Dag Viking*	
SE-DFE	Douglas DC-10-30	S.A.S. *Sverker Viking*	
SE-DFF	Douglas DC-10-30	S.A.S. *Solve Viking*	
SE-DFH	Douglas DC-10-30	S.A.S. *Rurik Viking*	
SE-DFR	Douglas DC-9-81	S.A.S. *Ingsald Viking*	
SE-DFS	Douglas DC-9-82	S.A.S. *Gaut Viking*	
SE-DFT	Douglas DC-9-82	S.A.S. *Assur Viking*	
SE-DFU	Douglas DC-9-82	S.A.S. *Isulv Viking*	
SE-DFX	Douglas DC-9-82	S.A.S. *Ring Viking*	
SE-DFY	Douglas DC-9-81	S.A.S. *Ottar Viking*	
SE-DGA	F.28 Fellowship 1000	Linjeflyg	
SE-DGB	F.28 Fellowship 1000	Linjeflyg	
SE-DGC	F.28 Fellowship 1000	Linjeflyg	
SE-DGD	F.28 Fellowship 4000	Linjeflyg	
SE-DGE	F.28 Fellowship 4000	Linjeflyg	
SE-DGF	F.28 Fellowship 4000	Linjeflyg	
SE-DGG	F.28 Fellowship 4000	Linjeflyg	
SE-DGH	F.28 Fellowship 4000	Linjeflyg	
SE-DGI	F.28 Fellowship 4000	Linjeflyg	
SE-DGK	F.28 Fellowship 4000	Linjeflyg	
SE-DGL	F.28 Fellowship 4000	Linjeflyg	
SE-DGM	F.28 Fellowship 4000	Linjeflyg	
SE-DGN	F.28 Fellowship 4000	Linjeflyg	
SE-DGO	F.28 Fellowship 4000	Linjeflyg	
SE-DGP	F.28 Fellowship 4000	Linjeflyg	
SE-DGR	F.28 Fellowship 4000	Linjeflyg	
SE-DGS	F.28 Fellowship 4000	Linjeflyg *Svea*	
SE-DGT	F.28 Fellowship 4000	Linjeflyg *Tora*	
SE-DGU	F.28 Fellowship 4000	Linjeflyg *Ulla*	
SE-DGX	F.28 Fellowship 4000	Linjeflyg *Kryss*	
SE-DHA	S.E.210 Caravelle 10B	Transwede	
SE-DHB	Douglas DC-9-83	Transwede	
SE-DHC	Douglas DC-9-83	Transwede	
SE-DHD	Douglas DC-9-83	Transwede	
SE-DHF	Douglas DC-9-83	Transwede	
SE-DHG	Douglas DC-9-87	Transwede	
SE-DHH	Douglas DC-9-83	Transwede	
SE-DHN	Douglas DC-9-83	Transwede	
SE-D	Douglas DC-9-87	Transwede	
SE-DHS	Douglas DC-10-10	Scanair	
SE-DHT	Douglas DC-10-10	Scanair	
SE-DHU	Douglas DC-10-10	Scanair	
SE-DHX	Douglas DC-10-10	Scanair	
SE-DHY	Douglas DC-10-10	Scanair	
SE-DHZ	Douglas DC-10-10	Scanair	
SE-DIA	Douglas DC-9-81	S.A.S. *Ulvrik Viking*	
SE-DIB	Douglas DC-9-87	S.A.S. *Varin Viking*	
SE-DIC	Douglas DC-9-87	S.A.S. *Grane Viking*	

SE/SP

Notes	Reg.	Type	Owner or Operator
	SE-DID	Douglas DC-9-82	S.A.S. *Spjute Viking*
	SE-DIE	Douglas DC-9-82	S.A.S. *Stenkil Viking*
	SE-DIF	Douglas DC-9-87	S.A.S. *Hjorulv Viking*
	SE-DIH	Douglas DC-9-87	S.A.S. *Slagfinn Viking*
	SE-DII	Douglas DC-9-82	S.A.S. *Askold Viking*
	SE-DKO	Boeing 767-383ER	S.A.S.
	SE-DKR	Boeing 767-383ER	S.A.S.
	SE-IRF	F.27 Friendship Mk 600	S.A.S. *Vinge Viking*
	SE-IRG	F.27 Friendship Mk 600	S.A.S. *Vigge Viking*
	SE-ITH	F.27 Friendship Mk 600	S.A.S. *Visbur Viking*
	SE-ITI	F.27 Friendship Mk 600	S.A.S. *Vidar Viking*
	SE-IVR	L-188CF Electra	Falcon Cargo
	SE-IVS	L-188CF Electra	Falcon Cargo
	SE-IVT	L-188CF Electra	Falcon Cargo
	SE-IVY	V.815 Viscount	Baltic Aviation
	SE-IZU	L-188CF Electra	Falcon Cargo
	SE-KBP	FH.227E Friendship	Malmo Aviation
	SE-KBR	FH.227E Friendship	Malmo Aviation
	SE-KGA	FH.227B Friendship	Malmo Aviation
	SE-KGB	FH.227B Friendship	Malmo Aviation
	SE-KGC	F.27 Friendship Mk 600	Malmo Aviation (TNT)
	SE-	BAe 146-200QT	Malmo Aviation/TNT

Note: Malmo Aviation operates Fairchild F.27 registered LN-BSC.

SP (Poland)

	SP-LBA	Ilyushin IL-62M	Polskie Linie Lotnicze (LOT) *Juliusz Sowacki*
	SP-LBB	Ilyushin IL-62M	Polskie Linie Lotnicze (LOT) *Jgnacy Paderewski*
	SP-LBC	Ilyushin IL-62M	Polskie Linie Lotnicze (LOT) *Joseph Conrad-Korzeniowski*
	SP-LBD	Ilyushin IL-62M	Polskie Linie Lotnicze (LOT) *General Wladystaw Sikorski*
	SP-LBE	Ilyushin IL-62M	Polskie Linie Lotnicze (LOT) *Stanislaw Moniuszho*
	SP-LBF	Ilyushin IL-62M	Polskie Linie Lotnicze (LOT) *Fryderyk Chopin*
	SP-LBH	Ilyushin IL-62M	Polskie Linie Lotnicze (LOT)
	SP-LBI	Ilyushin IL-62M	Polskie Linie Lotnicze (LOT)
	SP-LCA	Tupolev Tu-154M	Polskie Linie Lotnicze (LOT)
	SP-LCB	Tupolev Tu-154M	Polskie Linie Lotnicze (LOT)
	SP-LCC	Tupolev Tu-154M	Polskie Linie Lotnicze (LOT)
	SP-LCD	Tupolev Tu-154M	Polskie Linie Lotnicze (LOT)
	SP-LCE	Tupolev Tu-154M	Polskie Linie Lotnicze (LOT)
	SP-LCF	Tupolev Tu-154M	Polskie Linie Lotnicze (LOT)
	SP-LCG	Tupolev Tu-154M	Polskie Linie Lotnicze (LOT)
	SP-LCH	Tupolev Tu-154M	Polskie Linie Lotnicze (LOT)
	SP-LCI	Tupolev Tu-154M	Polskie Linie Lotnicze (LOT)
	SP-LCK	Tupolev Tu-154M	Polskie Linie Lotnicze (LOT)
	SP-LCL	Tupolev Tu-154M	Polskie Linie Lotnicze (LOT)
	SP-LCM	Tupolev Tu-154M	Polskie Linie Lotnicze (LOT)
	SP-LCN	Tupolev Tu-154M	Polskie Linie Lotnicze (LOT)
	SP-LHA	Tupolev Tu-134A	Polskie Linie Lotnicze (LOT)
	SP-LHB	Tupolev Tu-134A	Polskie Linie Lotnicze (LOT)
	SP-LHC	Tupolev Tu-134A	Polskie Linie Lotnicze (LOT)
	SP-LHD	Tupolev Tu-134A	Polskie Linie Lotnicze (LOT)
	SP-LHE	Tupolev Tu-134A	Polskie Linie Lotnicze (LOT)
	SP-LHF	Tupolev Tu-134A	Polskie Linie Lotnicze (LOT)
	SP-LHG	Tupolev Tu-134A	Polskie Linie Lotnicze (LOT)
	SP-LHI	Tupolev Tu-134A	Polskie Linie Lotnicze (LOT)
	SP-	Boeing 767-200ER	Polskie Linie Lotnicze (LOT)
	SP-	Boeing 767-200ER	Polskie Linie Lotnicze (LOT)
	SP-	Boeing 767-300ER	Polskie Linie Lotnicze (LOT)
	SP-LSA	Ilyushin IL-18V (Cargo)	Polskie Linie Lotnicze (LOT)
	SP-LSB	Ilyushin IL-18V	Polskie Linie Lotnicze (LOT)
	SP-LSC	Ilyushin IL-18V (Cargo)	Polskie Linie Lotnicze (LOT)
	SP-LSD	Ilyushin IL-18V	Polskie Linie Lotnicze (LOT)
	SP-LSE	Ilyushin IL-18V	Polskie Linie Lotnicze (LOT)
	SP-LSF	Ilyushin IL-18E	Polskie Linie Lotnicze (LOT)

Reg.	Type	Owner or Operator	Notes
SP-LSG	Ilyushin IL-18E	Polskie Linie Lotnicze (LOT)	
SP-LSH	Ilyushin IL-18V	Polskie Linie Lotnicze (LOT)	
SP-LSI	Ilyushin IL-18D	Polskie Linie Lotnicze (LOT)	
SP-LSK	Ilyushin IL-18V	Polskie Linie Lotnicze (LOT)	

ST (Sudan)

Reg.	Type	Owner or Operator	Notes
ST-AFA	Boeing 707-3J8C	Sudan Airways	
ST-AFB	Boeing 707-3J8C	Sudan Airways	
ST-AIX	Boeing 707-369C	Sudan Airways	
ST-AKW	Boeing 707-330C	Nile Safaris Aviation	
ST-ALK	Boeing 707-349C	Trans Arabian Air Transport	
ST-ALL	Boeing 707-338C	Nile Safaris Aviation	
ST-DRS	Boeing 707-368C	Sudan Airways	
ST-NSR	Boeing 707-330B	Sudan Airways	

SU (Egypt)

Reg.	Type	Owner or Operator	Notes
SU-AOU	Boeing 707-366C	EgyptAir *Khopho*	
SU-APD	Boeing 707-366C	EgyptAir *Khafrah*	
SU-AVX	Boeing 707-366C	EgyptAir *Tutankhamun*	
SU-AVY	Boeing 707-366C	EgyptAir *Akhenaton*	
SU-AVZ	Boeing 707-366C	EgyptAir *Mena*	
SU-AXK	Boeing 707-366C	EgyptAir *Seti I*	
SU-BCB	Airbus A.300B4	EgyptAir *Osiris*	
SU-BCC	Airbus A.300B4	EgyptAir *Nout*	
SU-BDF	Airbus A.300B4	EgyptAir *Hathor*	
SU-BDG	Airbus A.300B4	EgyptAir *Aton*	
SU-BKK	Douglas DC-9-51	North African Aviation	
SU-DAA	Boeing 707-351C	ZAS Airline of Egypt	
SU-DAB	Boeing 707-328C	ZAS Airline of Egypt	
SU-DAC	Boeing 707-336C	ZAS Airline of Egypt	
SU-DAK	Douglas DC-9-82	ZAS Airline of Egypt	
SU-D	Douglas DC-9-83	ZAS Airline of Egypt	
SU-D	Douglas DC-9-83	ZAS Airline of Egypt	
SU-EAA	Boeing 707-351C	Misr Overseas Airways	
SU-FAC	Boeing 707-323C	Misr Overseas Airways	
SU-GAA	Airbus A.300B4	EgyptAir *Isis*	
SU-GAB	Airbus A.300B4	EgyptAir *Amun*	
SU-GAC	Airbus A.300B4	EgyptAir *Bennou*	
SU-GAH	Boeing 767-266ER	Egyptair *Nefertiti*	
SU-GAI	Boeing 767-266ER	Egyptair *Nefertari*	
SU-GAJ	Boeing 767-266ER	Egyptair *Tiye*	
SU-GAL	Boeing 747-366 (SCD)	Egyptair *Hatshepsut*	
SU-GAM	Boeing 747-366 (SCD)	Egyptair *Cleopatra*	
SU-	Boeing 767-366ER	Egyptair	
SU-	Boeing 767-366ER	Egyptair	

SX (Greece)

Reg.	Type	Owner or Operator	Notes
SX-BCA	Boeing 737-284	Olympic Airlines *Apollo*	
SX-BCB	Boeing 737-284	Olympic Airlines *Hermes*	
SX-BCC	Boeing 737-284	Olympic Airlines *Hercules*	
SX-BCD	Boeing 737-284	Olympic Airlines *Hephaestus*	
SX-BCE	Boeing 737-284	Olympic Airlines *Dionysus*	
SX-BCF	Boeing 737-284	Olympic Airlines *Poseidon*	
SX-BCG	Boeing 737-284	Olympic Airlines *Phoebus*	
SX-BCH	Boeing 737-284	Olympic Airlines *Triton*	
SX-BCI	Boeing 737-284	Olympic Airlines *Proteus*	
SX-BCK	Boeing 737-284	Olympic Airlines *Nereus*	
SX-BCL	Boeing 737-284	Olympic Airlines *Isle of Thassos*	
SX-BEB	Airbus A.300B4	Olympic Airways *Odysseus*	
SX-BEC	Airbus A.300B4	Olympic Airways *Achilleus*	

SX/TC

Notes	Reg.	Type	Owner or Operator
	SX-BED	Airbus A.300B4	Olympic Airways *Telemachos*
	SX-BEE	Airbus A.300B4	Olympic Airways *Nestor*
	SX-BEF	Airbus A.300B4	Olympic Airways *Ajax*
	SX-BEG	Airbus A.300B4	Olympic Airways *Diamedes*
	SX-BEH	Airbus A.300B4	Olympic Airways *Peleus*
	SX-BEI	Airbus A.300B4	Olympic Airways *Neoptolemos*
	SX-CBA	Boeing 727-284	Olympic Airways *Mount Olympus*
	SX-CBB	Boeing 727-284	Olympic Airways *Mount Pindos*
	SX-CBC	Boeing 727-284	Olympic Airways *Mount Parnassus*
	SX-CBD	Boeing 727-284	Olympic Airways *Mount Helicon*
	SX-CBE	Boeing 727-284	Olympic Airways *Mount Athos*
	SX-CBF	Boeing 727-284	Olympic Airways *Mount Taygetus*
	SX-DBC	Boeing 707-384C	Olympic Airways *City of Knossos*
	SX-DBD	Boeing 707-384C	Olympic Airways *City of Sparta*
	SX-DBE	Boeing 707-384B	Olympic Airways *City of Pella*
	SX-DBF	Boeing 707-384B	Olympic Airways *City of Mycenae*
	SX-DBP	Boeing 707-351C	Olympic Airways *City of Thebes*
	SX-OAB	Boeing 747-284B	Olympic Airways *Olympic Eagle*
	SX-OAC	Boeing 747-212B	Olympic Airways *Olympic Spirit*
	SX-OAD	Boeing 747-212B	Olympic Airways *Olympic Flame*
	SX-OAE	Boeing 747-212B	Olympic Airways *Olympic Peace*

TC (Turkey)

Notes	Reg.	Type	Owner or Operator
	TC-ABA	S.E.210 Caravelle 10B1R	Istanbul Airlines *Mine*
	TC-ADA	Boeing 737-4Y0	Istanbul Airlines
	TC-	Boeing 737-4Y0	Istanbul Airlines
	TC-	Boeing 737-4Y0	Istanbul Airlines
	TC-ALV	Tupolev Tu-134A	Nesu Air
	TC-ARI	S.E.210 Caravelle 10B1R	Istanbul Airlines
	TC-ASA	S.E.210 Caravelle 10B1R	Istanbul Airlines
	TC-	RomBac One Eleven 561C	Istanbul Airlines
	TC-JAB	Douglas DC-9-32	Turk Hava Yollari (THY) *Bogazici*
	TC-JAD	Douglas DC-9-32	Turk Hava Yollari (THY) *Anadolu*
	TC-JAE	Douglas DC-9-32	Turk Hava Yollari (THY) *Trakya*
	TC-JAF	Douglas DC-9-32	Turk Hava Yollari (THY) *Ege*
	TC-JAG	Douglas DC-9-32	Turk Hava Yollari (THY) *Akdeniz*
	TC-JAK	Douglas DC-9-32	Turk Hava Yollari (THY) *Karadeniz*
	TC-JAL	Douglas DC-9-32	Turk Hava Yollari (THY) *Halic*
	TC-JAU	Douglas DC-10-10	Bogazici Air *Jengelky*
	TC-JAY	Douglas DC-10-10	Bogazici Air *Yenikoy*
	TC-JBF	Boeing 727-2F2	Türk Hava Yollari (THY) *Adana*
	TC-JBG	Boeing 727-2F2	Türk Hava Yollari (THY) *Ankara*
	TC-JBJ	Boeing 727-2F2	Türk Hava Yollari (THY) *Diyarbakir*
	TC-JBK	Douglas DC-9-32	Turk Hava Yollari (THY) *Aydin*
	TC-JBL	Douglas DC-9-32	Türk Hava Yollari (THY) *Gediz*
	TC-JBM	Boeing 727-2F2	Türk Hava Yollari (THY) *Menderes*
	TC-JCA	Boeing 727-2F2	Türk Hava Yollari (THY) *Edirne*
	TC-JCB	Boeing 727-2F2	Türk Hava Yollari (THY) *Kars*
	TC-JCC	Boeing 707-321C	Bogazici Air
	TC-JCD	Boeing 727-2F2	Türk Hava Yollari (THY) *Sinop*
	TC-JCE	Boeing 727-2F2	Türk Hava Yollari (THY) *Hatay*
	TC-JCF	Boeing 707-321C	BHY Cargo
	TC-JCK	Boeing 727-243	Türk Hava Yollari (THY) *Erciyes*
	TC-JCL	Airbus A.310-203	Türk Hava Yollari (THY) *Seyhan*
	TC-JCM	Airbus A.310-203	Türk Hava Yollari (THY) *Ceyhan*
	TC-JCN	Airbus A.310-203	Türk Hava Yollari (THY) *Dicle*
	TC-JCO	Airbus A.310-203	Türk Hava Yollari (THY) *Firat*
	TC-JCR	Airbus A.310-203	Türk Hava Yollari (THY) *Kizilirmak*
	TC-JCS	Airbus A.310-203	Türk Hava Yollari (THY) *Yesilirmak*
	TC-JCU	Airbus A.310-203	Türk Hava Yollari (THY) *Sakarya*
	TC-JCV	Airbus A.310-304	Türk Hava Yollari (THY) *Aras*
	TC-JCY	Airbus A.310-304	Türk Hava Yollari (THY) *Coruh*
	TC-JCZ	Airbus A.310-304	Türk Hava Yollari (THY) *Ergene*
	TC-	Airbus A.310-304	Türk Hava Yollari (THY)
	TC-	Airbus A.310-304	Türk Hava Yollari (THY)
	TC-JFA	Boeing 727-264	Bogazici Air
	TC-JFB	Boeing 727-264	Bogazici Air

TF (Iceland)

Reg.	Type	Owner or Operator	Notes
TF-FLE	Douglas DC-8-63	Icelandair	
TF-FLG	Boeing 727-185C	Icelandair *Heim Fari*	
TF-FLI	Boeing 727-208	Icelandair *Fronfari*	
TF-FLK	Boeing 727-276	Icelandair *Zvia*	
TF-FLM	F.27 Friendship Mk 200	Icelandair	
TF-FLN	F.27 Friendship Mk 200	Icelandair	
TF-FLO	F.27 Friendship Mk 200	Icelandair	
TF-FLP	F.27 Friendship Mk 200	Icelandair	
TF-FLS	F.27 Friendship Mk 200	Icelandair	
TF-FLT	Douglas DC-8-63	Icelandair *Nordurfari*	
TF-FLU	Douglas DC-8-63	Icelandair *Austurfari*	
TF-FLV	Douglas DC-8-63	Icelandair *Vesturfari*	
TF-	Boeing 737-408	Icelandair	
TF-	Boeing 737-408	Icelandair	
TF-1SA	Boeing 737-214	Eagle Air	
TF-VLT	Boeing 737-205C	Eagle Air	

Note: Icelandair also operates DC-8s on lease.

TJ (Cameroon)

TJ-CAB	Boeing 747-2H7B (SCD)	Cameroon Airlines *Mont Cameroun*	

TR (Gabon)

TR-LBV	L-100-30 Hercules	Air Gabon Cargo	
TR-LVK	Douglas DC-8-55F	Air Gabon Cargo/Affretair	

Note: Air Gabon operates Boeing 747-2Q2B F-ODJG on lease which will become TR-LXK.

TS (Tunisia)

TS-IMA	Airbus A.300B4	Tunis-Air *Amilcar*	
TS-	Airbus A.300B4	Tunis-Air	
TS-	Airbus A.300B4	Tunis-Air	
TS-IOC	Boeing 737-2H3	Tunis-Air *Salammbo*	
TS-IOD	Boeing 737-2H3C	Tunis-Air *Bulla Regia*	
TS-IOE	Boeing 737-2H3	Tunis-Air *Zarzis*	
TS-IOF	Boeing 737-2H3	Tunis-Air *Sousse*	
TS-JHN	Boeing 727-2H3	Tunis-Air *Carthago*	
TS-JHQ	Boeing 727-2H3	Tunis-Air *Tozeur-Nefta*	
TS-JHR	Boeing 727-2H3	Tunis-Air *Bizerte*	
TS-JHS	Boeing 727-2H3	Tunis-Air *Kairouan*	
TS-JHT	Boeing 727-2H3	Tunis-Air *Sidi Bousaid*	
TS-JHU	Boeing 727-2H3	Tunis-Air *Hannibal*	
TS-JHV	Boeing 727-2H3	Tunis-Air *Jugurtha*	
TS-JHW	Boeing 727-2H3	Tunis-Air *Ibn Khaldoun*	

TU (Ivory Coast)

TU-TAL	Douglas DC-10-30	Air Afrique *Libreville*	
TU-TAM	Douglas DC-10-30	Air Afrique	
TU-TAN	Douglas DC-10-30	Air Afrique *Niamey*	
TU-TAO	Airbus A.300B4-203	Air Afrique *Nouackchott*	
TU-TAS	Airbus A.300B4-203	Air Afrique *Bangui*	
TU-TAT	Airbus A.300B4-203	Air Afrique	
TU-TCF	Douglas DC-8-63CF	Air Afrique *Ndjamena*	

V8 (Brunei)

Notes	Reg.	Type	Owner or Operator
	V8-RBA	Boeing 757-2M6ER	Royal Brunei Airlines
	V8-RBB	Boeing 757-2M6ER	Royal Brunei Airlines
	V8-RBC	Boeing 757-2M6ER	Royal Brunei Airlines

VH (Australia)

	VH-EBA	Boeing 747-238B	Qantas Airways
	VH-EBB	Boeing 747-238B	Qantas Airways
	VH-EBH	Boeing 747-238B	Qantas Airways *City of Parramatta*
	VH-EBI	Boeing 747-238B	Qantas Airways *City of Dubbo*
	VH-EBJ	Boeing 747-238B	Qantas Airways *City of Newcastle*
	VH-EBK	Boeing 747-238B	Qantas Airways
	VH-EBL	Boeing 747-238B	Qantas Airways *City of Ballart*
	VH-EBM	Boeing 747-238B	Qantas Airways *City of Grosford*
	VH-EBN	Boeing 747-238B	Qantas Airways *City of Albury*
	VH-EBO	Boeing 747-238B	Qantas Airways *City of Elizabeth*
	VH-EBP	Boeing 747-238B	Qantas Airways *City of Adelaide*
	VH-EBQ	Boeing 747-238B	Qantas Airways *City of Bunbury*
	VH-EBR	Boeing 747-238B	Qantas Airways *City of Hobart*
	VH-EBS	Boeing 747-238B	Qantas Airways *City of Longreach*
	VH-EBT	Boeing 747-338	Qantas Airways *City of Canberra*
	VH-EBU	Boeing 747-338	Qantas Airways *City of Sydney*
	VH-EBV	Boeing 747-338	Qantas Airways *City of Melbourne*
	VH-EBW	Boeing 747-338	Qantas Airways *City of Brisbane*
	VH-EBX	Boeing 747-338	Qantas Airways *City of Perth*
	VH-EBY	Boeing 747-338	Qantas Airways *City of Darwin*
	VH-OJA	Boeing 747-438	Qantas Airways
	VH-OJB	Boeing 747-438	Qantas Airways
	VH-OJC	Boeing 747-438	Qantas Airways
	VH-OJD	Boeing 747-438	Qantas Airways
	VH-OJE	Boeing 747-438	Qantas Airways
	VH-OJF	Boeing 747-438	Qantas Airways

VR-H (Hong Kong)

	VR-HIA	Boeing 747-267B	Cathay Pacific Airways
	VR-HIB	Boeing 747-267B	Cathay Pacific Airways
	VR-HIC	Boeing 747-267B	Cathay Pacific Airways
	VR-HID	Boeing 747-267B	Cathay Pacific Airways
	VR-HIE	Boeing 747-267B	Cathay Pacific Airways
	VR-HIF	Boeing 747-267B	Cathay Pacific Airways
	VR-HIH	Boeing 747-267B	Cathay Pacific Airways
	VR-HII	Boeing 747-367	Cathay Pacific Airways
	VR-HIJ	Boeing 747-367	Cathay Pacific Airways
	VR-HIK	Boeing 747-367	Cathay Pacific Airways
	VR-HKG	Boeing 747-267B	Cathay Pacific Airways
	VR-HKK	Boeing 707-336C	Air Hong Kong
	VR-HOL	Boeing 747-367	Cathay Pacific Airways
	VR-HOM	Boeing 747-367	Cathay Pacific Airways
	VR-HON	Boeing 747-367	Cathay Pacific Airways
	VR-HOO	Boeing 747-467	Cathay Pacific Airways
	VR-HOP	Boeing 747-467	Cathay Pacific Airways
	VR-HVY	Boeing 747-236F (SCD)	Cathay Pacific Airways *Hong Kong Jumbo*
	VR-HVZ	Boeing 747-267F (SCD)	Cathay Pacific Airways

VT (India)

Reg.	Type	Owner or Operator	Notes
VT-EBE	Boeing 747-237B	Air-India *Emperor Shahjehan*	
VT-EBN	Boeing 747-237B	Air-India *Emperor Rajendra Chola*	
VT-EBO	Boeing 747-237B	Air-India *Emperor Nikramaditya*	
VT-EDU	Boeing 747-237B	Air-India *Emperor Akbar*	
VT-EFJ	Boeing 747-237B	Air-India *Emperor Chandragupta*	
VT-EFU	Boeing 747-237B	Air-India *Emperor Krishna Deva*	
VT-EGA	Boeing 747-237B	Air-India *Emperor Samudra Gupto*	
VT-EGB	Boeing 747-237B	Air-India *Emperor Mahendra Varman*	
VT-EGC	Boeing 747-237B	Air-India *Emperor Harsha Vardhuma*	
VT-EJG	Airbus A.310-304	Air-India *Vamuna*	
VT-EJH	Airbus A.310-304	Air-India *Tista*	
VT-EJI	Airbus A.310-304	Air-India *Saraswati*	
VT-EJJ	Airbus A.310-304	Air-India *Beas*	
VT-EJK	Airbus A.310-304	Air-India *Gomti*	
VT-EJL	Airbus A.310-304	Air-India *Sabarmati*	
VT-ENQ	Boeing 747-212B	Air-India *Himalaya*	
VT-EPW	Boeing 747-337	Air-India	
VT-EPX	Boeing 747-337	Air-India	

Note: Air-India Cargo operates Douglas DC-8s and Boeing 747s on lease from various airlines.

XA (Mexico)

XA-DUG	Douglas DC-10-30	Aeromexico *Ciudad de Mexico*	
XA-DUH	Douglas DC-10-30	Aeromexico *Castillo de Chapultepec*	

Note: Aeromexico also operates DC-10-30 N3878P on lease.

YI (Iraq)

YI-AGE	Boeing 707-370C	Iraqi Airways	
YI-AGG	Boeing 707-370C	Iraqi Airways	
YI-AGK	Boeing 727-270	Iraqi Airways	
YI-AGL	Boeing 727-270	Iraqi Airways	
YI-AGM	Boeing 727-270	Iraqi Airways	
YI-AGN	Boeing 747-270C (SCD)	Iraqi Airways *Tigris*	
YI-AGO	Boeing 747-270C (SCD)	Iraqi Airways *Euphrates*	
YI-AGP	Boeing 747-270C (SCD)	Iraqi Airways	
YI-AGQ	Boeing 727-270	Iraqi Airways	
YI-AGR	Boeing 727-270	Iraqi Airways	
YI-AGS	Boeing 727-270	Iraqi Airways	
YI-AKO	Ilyushin IL-76M	Iraqi Airways	
YI-AKP	Ilyushin IL-76M	Iraqi Airways	
YI-AKQ	Ilyushin IL-76M	Iraqi Airways	
YI-AKS	Ilyushin IL-76M	Iraqi Airways	
YI-AKT	Ilyushin IL-76M	Iraqi Airways	
YI-AKU	Ilyushin IL-76M	Iraqi Airways	
YI-AKV	Ilyushin IL-76M	Iraqi Airways	
YI-AKW	Ilyushin IL-76M	Iraqi Airways	
YI-AKX	Ilyushin IL-76M	Iraqi Airways	
YI-ALL	Ilyushin IL-76M	Iraqi Airways	
YI-ALM	Boeing 747SP-70	Iraqi Airways *Al Qadissiya*	
YI-ALO	Ilyushin IL-76M	Iraqi Airways	
YI-ALP	Ilyushin IL-76M	Iraqi Airways	
YI-ALQ	Ilyushin IL-76MD	Iraqi Airways	
YI-ALR	Ilyushin IL-76MD	Iraqi Airways	
YI-ALS	Ilyushin IL-76MD	Iraqi Airways	
YI-ALT	Ilyushin IL-76MD	Iraqi Airways	
YI-ALU	Ilyushin IL-76MD	Iraqi Airways	
YI-ALV	Ilyushin IL-76MD	Iraqi Airways	
YI-ALW	Ilyushin IL-76MD	Iraqi Airways	
YI-ALX	Ilyushin IL-76MD	Iraqi Airways	
YI-ANA	Ilyushin IL-76MD	Iraqi Airways	

Notes	Reg.	Type	Owner or Operator
	YI-ANB	Ilyushin IL-76MD	Iraqi Airways
	YI-ANC	Ilyushin IL-76MD	Iraqi Airways
	YI-AND	Ilyushin IL-76MD	Iraqi Airways
	YI-ANF	Ilyushin IL-76MD	Iraqi Airways
	YI-ANG	Ilyushin IL-76MD	Iraqi Airways
	YI-ANH	Ilyushin IL-76MD	Iraqi Airways
	YI-ANI	Ilyushin IL-76MD	Iraqi Airways
	YI-ANJ	Ilyushin IL-76MD	Iraqi Airways
	YI-ANK	Ilyushin IL-76MD	Iraqi Airways

YK (Syria)

	YK-AGA	Boeing 727-29A	Syrian Arab Airlines *October 6*
	YK-AGB	Boeing 727-294	Syrian Arab Airlines *Damascus*
	YK-AGC	Boeing 727-294	Syrian Arab Airlines *Palmyra*
	YK-AHA	Boeing 747SP-94	Syrian Arab Airlines *16 Novembre*
	YK-AHB	Boeing 747SP-94	Syrian Arab Airlines *Arab Solidarity*
	YK-AIA	Tupolev Tu-154M	Syrian Arab Airlines
	YK-AIB	Tupolev Tu-154M	Syrian Arab Airlines
	YK-AIC	Tupolev Tu-154M	Syrian Arab Airlines
	YK-ATA	Ilyushin IL-76M	Syrian Arab Airlines
	YK-ATB	Ilyushin IL-76M	Syrian Arab Airlines
	YK-ATC	Ilyushin IL-76M	Syrian Arab Airlines
	YK-ATD	Ilyushin IL-76M	Syrian Arab Airlines

YR (Romania)

	YR-ABA	Boeing 707-3K1C	Tarom
	YR-ABC	Boeing 707-3K1C	Tarom
	YR-ABM	Boeing 707-321C	Tarom
	YR-ABN	Boeing 707-321C	Tarom
	YR-ADA	Antonov 26	Tarom
	YR-ADB	Antonov 26	Tarom
	YR-ADC	Antonov 26	Tarom
	YR-ADE	Antonov 26	Tarom
	YR-ADG	Antonov 26	Tarom
	YR-ADH	Antonov 26	Tarom
	YR-ADJ	Antonov 26	Tarom
	YR-ADK	Antonov 26	Tarom
	YR-ADL	Antonov 26	Tarom
	YR-BCB	BAC One-Eleven 424EU	Tarom
	YR-BCC	BAC One-Eleven 424EU	Liniile Aeriene Romane (LAR)
	YR-BCD	BAC One-Eleven 424EU	Liniile Aeriene Romane (LAR)
	YR-BCE	BAC One-Eleven 424EU	Tarom *(leased to GAS Air)*
	YR-BCF	BAC One-Eleven 424EU	Liniile Aeriene Romane (LAR)
	YR-BCG	BAC One-Eleven 401AK	Tarom
	YR-BCH	BAC One-Eleven 402AP	Tarom
	YR-BCI	BAC One-Eleven 525FT	Tarom
	YR-BCJ	BAC One-Eleven 525FT	Tarom
	YR-BCK	BAC One-Eleven 525FT	Tarom
	YR-BCQ	BAC One-Eleven 525FT	Tarom *(leased to Istanbul Airlines)*
	YR-BRA	RomBac One-Eleven 561RC	Tarom
	YR-BRC	RomBac One-Eleven 561RC	Tarom
	YR-BRD	RomBac One-Eleven 561RC	Tarom
	YR-BRE	RomBac One-Eleven 561RC	Tarom
	YR-IMA	Ilyushin IL-18D	Tarom
	YR-IMC	Ilyushin IL-18V	Tarom
	YR-IMD	Ilyushin IL-18V	Tarom
	YR-IME	Ilyushin IL-18V	Tarom
	YR-IMF	Ilyushin IL-18V	Tarom
	YR-IMG	Ilyushin IL-18V	Tarom
	YR-IMH	Ilyushin IL-18V	Tarom
	YR-IMJ	Ilyushin IL-18D	Tarom
	YR-IML	Ilyushin IL-18D	Tarom
	YR-IMM	Ilyushin IL-18D	Tarom
	YR-IMZ	Ilyushin IL-18V	Tarom
	YR-IRA	Ilyushin IL-62	Tarom
	YR-IRB	Ilyushin IL-62	Tarom

Reg.	Type	Owner or Operator	Notes
YR-IRC	Ilyushin IL-62	Tarom	
YR-IRD	Ilyushin IL-62M	Tarom	
YR-IRE	Ilyushin IL-62M	Tarom	
YR-TPA	Tupolev Tu-154B	Tarom	
YR-TPB	Tupolev Tu-154B	Tarom	
YR-TPC	Tupolev Tu-154B	Tarom	
YR-TPD	Tupolev Tu-154B	Tarom	
YR-TPE	Tupolev Tu-154B-1	Tarom	
YR-TPF	Tupolev Tu-154B-1	Tarom	
YR-TPG	Tupolev Tu-154B-1	Tarom	
YR-TPI	Tupolev Tu-154B-2	Tarom	
YR-TPJ	Tupolev Tu-154B-2	Tarom	
YR-TPK	Tupolev Tu-154B-2	Tarom	
YR-TPL	Tupolev Tu-154B-2	Tarom	

YU (Yugoslavia)

Reg.	Type	Owner or Operator	Notes
YU-AGE	Boeing 707-340C	Jugoslovenski Aerotransport	
YU-AGG	Boeing 707-340C	Jugoslovenski Aerotransport	
YU-AHJ	Douglas DC-9-32	Adria Airways (leased to ZAS Airline of Egypt)	
YU-AHN	Douglas DC-9-32	Jugoslovenski Aerotransport	
YU-AHU	Douglas DC-9-32	Jugoslovenski Aerotransport	
YU-AHV	Douglas DC-9-32	Jugoslovenski Aerotransport	
YU-AHW	Douglas DC-9-33RC	Adria Airways (leased to ZAS Airline of Egypt)	
YU-AHX	Tupolev Tu-134A-3	Aviogenex Beograd	
YU-AJA	Tupolev Tu-134A-3	Aviogenex Titograd	
YU-AJD	Tupolev Tu-134A-3	Aviogenex Skopje	
YU-AJF	Douglas DC-9-32	Adria Airways (leased as G-BMWD)	
YU-AJH	Douglas DC-9-32	Jugoslovenski Aerotransport	
YU-AJI	Douglas DC-9-32	Jugoslovenski Aerotransport	
YU-AJJ	Douglas DC-9-32	Jugoslovenski Aerotransport	
YU-AJK	Douglas DC-9-32	Jugoslovenski Aerotransport	
YU-AJL	Douglas DC-9-32	Jugoslovenski Aerotransport	
YU-AJM	Douglas DC-9-32	Jugoslovenski Aerotransport	
YU-AJT	Douglas DC-9-51	Adria Airways	
YU-AJU	Douglas DC-9-51	Adria Airways Maribor	
YU-AJZ	Douglas DC-9-81	Adria Airways	
YU-AKB	Boeing 727-2H9	Jugoslovenski Aerotransport	
YU-AKD	Boeing 727-2L8	Aviogenex Zagreb	
YU-AKE	Boeing 727-2H9	Jugoslovenski Aerotransport	
YU-AKF	Boeing 727-2H9	Jugoslovenski Aerotransport	
YU-AKG	Boeing 727-2H9	Jugoslovenski Aerotransport	
YU-AKH	Boeing 727-2L8	Aviogenex Dubrovnik	
YU-AKI	Boeing 727-2H9	Jugoslovenski Aerotransport	
YU-AKJ	Boeing 727-2H9	Jugoslovenski Aerotransport	
YU-AKK	Boeing 727-2H9	Jugoslovenski Aerotransport	
YU-AKL	Boeing 727-2H9	Jugoslovenski Aerotransport	
YU-AKM	Boeing 727-243	Aviogenex Pula	
YU-AMA	Douglas DC-10-30	Jugoslovenski Aerotransport Nikola Tesla	
YU-AMB	Douglas DC-10-30	Jugoslovenski Aerotransport Edvard Rusijan	
YU-AMC	Douglas DC-10-30	Jugoslovenski Aerotransport	
YU-ANB	Douglas DC-9-82	Adria Airways	
YU-ANC	Douglas DC-9-82	Adria Airways	
YU-AND	Boeing 737-3H9	Jugoslovenski Aerotransport	
YU-ANF	Boeing 737-3H9	Jugoslovenski Aerotransport	
YU-ANG	Douglas DC-9-82	Adria Airways	
YU-ANH	Boeing 737-3H9	Jugoslovenski Aerotransport	
YU-ANI	Boeing 737-3H9	Jugoslovenski Aerotransport	
YU-ANJ	Boeing 737-3H9	Jugoslovenski Aerotransport	
YU-ANK	Boeing 737-3H9	Jugoslovenski Aerotransport	
YU-ANL	Boeing 737-3H9	Jugoslovenski Aerotransport	
YU-ANO	Douglas DC-9-82	Adria Airways	
YU-ANP	Boeing 737-2K3	Aviogenex Zadar	
YU-ANU	Boeing 737-2K3	Aviogenex Tivat	
YU-ANV	Boeing 737-3H9	Jugoslovenski Aerotransport	
YU-ANW	Boeing 737-3H9	Jugoslovenski Aerotransport	
YU-	Airbus A.320-230	Adria Airways	

YV (Venezuela)

Notes	Reg.	Type	Owner or Operator
	YV-134C	Douglas DC-10-30	Viasa
	YV-135C	Douglas DC-10-30	Viasa
	YV-136C	Douglas DC-10-30	Viasa
	YV-137C	Douglas DC-10-30	Viasa
	YV-138C	Douglas DC-10-30	Viasa

Z (Zimbabwe)

	Z-WKR	Boeing 707-330B	Air Zimbabwe
	Z-WKS	Boeing 707-330B	Air Zimbabwe
	Z-WKT	Boeing 707-330B	Air Zimbabwe
	Z-WKU	Boeing 707-330B	Air Zimbabwe
	Z-WKV	Boeing 707-330B	Air Zimbabwe
	Z-	Boeing 767-200ER	Air Zimbabwe
	Z-WMJ	Douglas DC-8-54F	Affretair *Captain Jack Malloch*

Note: Affretair also operates DC-8-55F TR-LVK.

ZK (New Zealand)

	ZK-NZE	Boeing 747-419	Air New Zealand
	ZK-NZV	Boeing 747-219B	Air New Zealand *Aotea*
	ZK-NZW	Boeing 747-219B	Air New Zealand *Tainui*
	ZK-NZX	Boeing 747-219B	Air New Zealand *Takitimu*
	ZK-NZY	Boeing 747-219B	Air New Zealand *Te Arawa*
	ZK-NZZ	Boeing 747-219B	Air New Zealand *Tokomaru*

ZP (Paraguay)

	ZP-CCE	Boeing 707-321B	Lineas Aéreas Paraguayas
	ZP-CCF	Boeing 707-321B	Lineas Aéreas Paraguayas
	ZP-CCG	Boeing 707-321B	Lineas Aéreas Paraguayas
	ZP-CCH	Douglas DC-8-63	Lineas Aéreas Paraguayas

ZS (South Africa)

	ZS-SAL	Boeing 747-244B	South African Airways *Tafelberg*
	ZS-SAM	Boeing 747-244B	South African Airways *Drakensberg*
	ZS-SAN	Boeing 747-244B	South African Airways *Lebombo*
	ZS-SAO	Boeing 747-244B	South African Airways *Magaliesberg*
	ZS-SAP	Boeing 747-244B	South African Airways *Swartberg*
	ZS-SAR	Boeing 747-244B (SCD)	South African Airways *Waterberg*
	ZS-SAT	Boeing 747-344	South African Airways *Johannesburg*
	ZS-SAU	Boeing 747-344	South African Airways *Cape Town*
	ZS-SPB	Boeing 747SP-44	South African Airways *Outeniqua* (leased as LX-LGX)
	ZS-SPE	Boeing 747SP-44	South African Airways *Hantam*
	ZS-SPF	Boeing 747SP-44	South African Airways *Soutpansberg*

3B (Mauritius)

	3B-NAG	Boeing 747SP-44	Air Mauritius *Chateau du Reduit*
	3B-NAJ	Boeing 747SP-44	Air Mauritius *Chateau Mon Plaigir*
	3B-NAK	Boeing 767-23BER	Air Mauritius *City of Curepipe*
	3B-NAL	Boeing 767-23BER	Air Mauritius *City of Port Louis*
	3B-NAO	Boeing 747SP-44	Air Mauritius

4R (Sri Lanka)

Reg.	Type	Owner or Operator	Notes
4R-ULA	L.1011-385 TriStar 500	Air Lanka	
4R-ULB	L.1011-385 TriStar 500	Air Lanka	
4R-ULC	L.1011-385 TriStar 100	Air Lanka *City of Jayawardanapura*	
4R-ULE	L.1011-385 TriStar 50	Air Lanka *City of Ratnapura*	

4W (Yemen)

4W-ACF	Boeing 727-2N8	Yemenia	
4W-ACG	Boeing 727-2N8	Yemenia	
4W-ACH	Boeing 727-2N8	Yemenia	
4W-ACI	Boeing 727-2N8	Yemenia	
4W-ACJ	Boeing 727-2N8	Yemenia	

4X (Israel)

4X-ABN	Boeing 737-258	El Al (*leased to LAN Chile*)	
4X-ABO	Boeing 737-258	El Al (*leased to LAN Chile*)	
4X-ATD	Boeing 707-331B	El Al/Arkia	
4X-ATS	Boeing 707-358B	El Al/Arkia	
4X-ATX	Boeing 707-358C	El Al/Arkia	
4X-AXA	Boeing 747-258B	El Al	
4X-AXB	Boeing 747-258B	El Al	
4X-AXC	Boeing 747-258B	El Al	
4X-AXD	Boeing 747-258C	El Al	
4X-AXF	Boeing 747-258C	El Al	
4X-AXG	Boeing 747-258F (SCD)	El Al	
4X-AXH	Boeing 747-258B	El Al	
4X-AXQ	Boeing 747-238B	El Al	
4X-AXZ	Boeing 747-124F (SCD)	El Al	
4X-EAA	Boeing 767-258	El Al	
4X-EAB	Boeing 767-258	El Al	
4X-EAC	Boeing 767-258ER	El Al	
4X-EAD	Boeing 767-258ER	El Al	
4X-EBL	Boeing 757-258	El Al	
4X-EBM	Boeing 757-258	El Al	
4X-EBR	Boeing 757-258	El Al	

5A (Libya)

5A-DAI	Boeing 727-224	Libyan Arab Airlines	
5A-DAK	Boeing 707-3L5C	Libyan Arab Airlines	
5A-DIA	Boeing 727-2L5	Libyan Arab Airlines	
5A-DIB	Boeing 727-2L5	Libyan Arab Airlines	
5A-DIC	Boeing 727-2L5	Libyan Arab Airlines	
5A-DID	Boeing 727-2L5	Libyan Arab Airlines	
5A-DIE	Boeing 727-2L5	Libyan Arab Airlines	
5A-DIF	Boeing 727-2L5	Libyan Arab Airlines	
5A-DIG	Boeing 727-2L5	Libyan Arab Airlines	
5A-DIH	Boeing 727-2L5	Libyan Arab Airlines	
5A-DII	Boeing 727-2L5	Libyan Arab Airlines	
5A-DIX	Boeing 707-348C	Libyan Arab Airlines	
5A-DIY	Boeing 707-348C	Libyan Arab Airlines	
5A-DJM	Boeing 707-321B	Libyan Arab Airlines	
5A-DJU	Boeing 707-351C	Libyan Arab Airlines	

Note: Services to the UK suspended.

5B (Cyprus)

Notes	Reg.	Type	Owner or Operator
	5B-DAG	BAC One Eleven 537GF	Cyprus Airways
	5B-DAH	BAC One Eleven 537GF	Cyprus Airways
	5B-DAJ	BAC One Eleven 537GF	Cyprus Airways
	5B-DAL	Boeing 707-123B	Cyprus Airways
	5B-DAO	Boeing 707-123B	Cyprus Airways
	5B-DAP	Boeing 707-123B	Cyprus Airways
	5B-DAQ	Airbus A.310-203	Cyprus Airways
	5B-DAR	Airbus A.310-203	Cyprus Airways
	5B-DAS	Airbus A.310-203	Cyprus Airways
	5B-DAT	Airbus A.320-230	Cyprus Airways
	5B-DAU	Airbus A.320-230	Cyprus Airways
	5B-DAV	Airbus A.320-230	Cyprus Airways
	5B-DAW	Airbus A.320-230	Cyprus Airways
	5B-DAX	Airbus A.310-203	Cyprus Airways
	5B-	Airbus A.320-230	Cyprus Airways
	5B-	Airbus A.320-230	Cyprus Airways
	5B-	Airbus A.320-230	Cyprus Airways
	5B-	Airbus A.320-230	Cyprus Airways

5N (Nigeria)

	5N-ABJ	Boeing 707-3F9C	Nigeria Airways
	5N-ABK	Boeing 707-3F9C	Nigeria Airways
	5N-ANN	Douglas DC-10-30	Nigeria Airways *Yunkari*
	5N-ANO	Boeing 707-3F9C	Nigeria Airways
	5N-AOK	BAC One-Eleven 320AZ	Okada Air
	5N-AOM	BAC One-Eleven 420EL	Okada Air
	5N-AOP	BAC One-Eleven 320AZ	Okada Air
	5N-AOQ	Boeing 707-355C	Okada Air
	5N-AOS	BAC One-Eleven 420EL	Okada Air
	5N-AOT	BAC One-Eleven 320AZ	Okada Air
	5N-AOW	BAC One-Eleven 402AP	Okada Air
	5N-AOZ	BAC One-Eleven 320AZ	Okada Air
	5N-ASY	Boeing 707-351C	EAS Cargo
	5N-ATY	Douglas DC-8-55F	Flash Airlines
	5N-ATZ	Douglas DC-8-55F	Flash Airlines
	5N-AUE	Airbus A.310-221	Nigeria Airways *River Yobe*
	5N-AUF	Airbus A.310-221	Nigeria Airways
	5N-AUH	Airbus A.310-221	Nigeria Airways *Rima River*
	5N-AUI	Douglas DC-10-30	Nigeria Airways
	5N-AUS	Douglas DC-8-55	Gamair
	5N-AVO	S.E.210 Caravelle III	Inter Continental Airlines
	5N-AVP	S.E.210 Caravelle III	Inter Continental Airlines
	5N-AVQ	S.E.210 Caravelle III	Inter Continental Airlines
	5N-AWE	Douglas DC-8-55F	Kabo Air
	5N-AYJ	Boeing 707-351C	Gas Air
	5N-AYS	BAC One-Eleven 416EK	Okada Air
	5N-AYT	BAC One-Eleven 416EK	Okada Air
	5N-AYU	BAC One-Eleven 401AK	Okada Air
	5N-AYV	BAC One-Eleven 408EF	Okada Air

5R (Madagascar)

	5R-MFT	Boeing 747-2B2B (SCD)	Air Madagascar *Tolom Piavotana*

5X (Uganda)

Reg.	Type	Owner or Operator	Notes
5X-ARQ	Boeing 707-338C	DAS Air Cargo	
5X-DAR	Boeing 707-321C	DAS Air Cargo	
5X-UAC	Boeing 707-351C	Uganda Airlines *The Flying Crane*	
5X-UCF	L-100-30 Hercules	Uganda Airlines *The Silver Lady*	

5Y (Kenya)

5Y-AXC	Boeing 707-351C	African Express Airways	
5Y-BBI	Boeing 707-351B	Kenya Airlines	
5Y-BBJ	Boeing 707-351B	Kenya Airlines	
5Y-BBK	Boeing 707-351B	Kenya Airlines	
5Y-BBX	Boeing 720-047B	Kenya Airlines	
5Y-BEL	Airbus A.310-304	Kenya Airlines *Nyayo Star*	
5Y-BEN	Airbus A.310-304	Kenya Airlines *Harambee Star*	
5Y-BFB	Boeing 707-351C	African Express Airways	
5Y-BFF	Boeing 707-323B	African Express Airways	
5Y-	Airbus A310-304	Kenya Airlines	
5Y-ZEB	Douglas DC-8-63	African Safari Airways	

Note: African Safari also operates DC-8-63 which carries the registration HB-1BF.
Kenya Airways operates DC-8-71 EI-BWG on lease

6O (Somalia)

6O-SBS	Boeing 707-330B	Somali Airlines	
6O-SBT	Boeing 707-330B	Somali Airlines	
6O-	Airbus A.310-304	Somali Airlines	

6Y (Jamaica)

Note: Air Jamaica operates its UK services jointly with British Airways.

7T (Algeria)

7T-VEA	Boeing 727-2D6	Air Algerie *Tassili*	
7T-VEB	Boeing 727-2D6	Air Algerie *Hoggar*	
7T-VED	Boeing 737-2D6C	Air Algerie *Atlas Saharien*	
7T-VEE	Boeing 737-2D6C	Air Algerie *Oasis*	
7T-VEF	Boeing 737-2D6	Air Algerie *Saoura*	
7T-VEG	Boeing 737-2D6	Air Algerie *Monts des Ouleds Neils*	
7T-VEH	Boeing 727-2D6	Air Algerie *Lalla Khadidja*	
7T-VEI	Boeing 727-2D6	Air Algerie *Djebel Amour*	
7T-VEJ	Boeing 737-2D6	Air Algerie *Chrea*	
7T-VEK	Boeing 737-2D6	Air Algerie *Edough*	
7T-VEL	Boeing 737-2D6	Air Algerie *Akfadou*	
7T-VEM	Boeing 727-2D6	Air Algerie *Mont du Ksall*	
7T-VEN	Boeing 737-2D6	Air Algerie *La Soummam*	
7T-VEO	Boeing 737-2D6	Air Algerie *La Titteri*	
7T-VEP	Boeing 727-2D6	Air Algerie *Mont du Tessala*	
7T-VEQ	Boeing 737-2D6	Air Algerie *Le Zaccar*	
7T-VER	Boeing 737-2D6	Air Algerie *Le Souf*	
7T-VES	Boeing 737-2D6C	Air Algerie *Le Tadmait*	
7T-VET	Boeing 727-2D6	Air Algerie *Georges du Rhumel*	
7T-VEU	Boeing 727-2D6	Air Algerie *Djurdjura*	
7T-VEV	Boeing 727-2D6	Air Algerie	

Notes	Reg.	Type	Owner or Operator
	7T-VEW	Boeing 727-2D6	Air Algerie
	7T-VEX	Boeing 727-2D6	Air Algerie *Djemila*
	7T-VEY	Boeing 737-2D6	Air Algerie *Rhoufi*
	7T-VEZ	Boeing 737-2T4	Air Algerie *Monts du Daia*
	7T-VJA	Boeing 737-2T4	Air Algerie *Monts des Babors*
	7T-VJB	Boeing 737-2T4	Air Algerie *Monts des Bibons*
	7T-VJC	Airbus A.310-203	Air Algerie
	7T-VJD	Airbus A.310-203	Air Algerie
	7T-VJE	Airbus A.310-203	Air Algerie
	7T-	Airbus A.310-203	Air Algerie

9G (Ghana)

	9G-ANA	Douglas DC-10-30	Ghana Airways

9H (Malta)

	9H-AAO	Boeing 720-047B	Air Malta
	9H-ABA	Boeing 737-2Y5	Air Malta
	9H-ABB	Boeing 737-2Y5	Air Malta
	9H-ABC	Boeing 737-2Y5	Air Malta
	9H-ABE	Boeing 737-2Y5	Air Malta
	9H-ABF	Boeing 737-2Y5	Air Malta
	9H-ABG	Boeing 737-2Y5	Air Malta
	9H-	Airbus A.320-210	Air Malta

Note: Air Malta also operates two Boeing 727s on lease from Gulf Air (US).

9J (Zambia)

	9J-AEB	Boeing 707-351C	Zambia Airways
	9J-AEL	Boeing 707-338C	Zambia Airways
	9J-AEQ	Boeing 707-321C (Cargo)	Zambia Airways

Note: Zambia Airways also operates DC-10-30 N3016Z which is expected to be allocated a 9J registration.

9K (Kuwait)

	9K-ADA	Boeing 747-269B (SCD)	Kuwait Airways *Al Sabahiya*
	9K-ADB	Boeing 747-269B (SCD)	Kuwait Airways *Al Jaberiya*
	9K-ADC	Boeing 747-269B (SCD)	Kuwait Airways *Al Murbarakiya*
	9K-ADD	Boeing 747-269B (SCD)	Kuwait Airways *Al Salmiya*
	9K-AHA	Airbus A.310-222	Kuwait Airways *Al-Jahra*
	9K-AHB	Airbus A.310-222	Kuwait Airways *Gharnada*
	9K-AHC	Airbus A.310-222	Kuwait Airways *Kadhma*
	9K-AHD	Airbus A.310-222	Kuwait Airways *Failaka*
	9K-AHE	Airbus A.310-222	Kuwait Airways *Burghan*
	9K-AHF	Airbus A.300-620C	Kuwait Airways *Wafra*
	9K-AHG	Airbus A.300-620C	Kuwait Airways *Wara*
	9K-AHI	Airbus A.300-620C	Kuwait Airways *Ali-Rawdhatain*
	9K-AIA	Boeing 767-269ER	Kuwait Airways *Alriggah*
	9K-AIB	Boeing 767-269ER	Kuwait Airways *Algrain*
	9K-AIC	Boeing 767-269ER	Kuwait Airways *Garouh*

9L (Sierra Leone)

Services suspended by Sierra Leone Airlines as a temporary measure.

9M (Malaysia)

Reg.	Type	Owner or Operator	Notes
9M-MHI	Boeing 747-236B	Malaysian Airline System	
9M-MHJ	Boeing 747-236B	Malaysian Airline System	
9M-MHK	Boeing 747-3H6 (SCD)	Malaysian Airline System	
9M-MHL	Boeing 747-4H6 (SCD)	Malaysian Airline System	
9M-MHM	Boeing 747-4H6 (SCD)	Malaysian Airline System	

9Q (Zaïre)

Reg.	Type	Owner or Operator	Notes
9Q-CBS	Boeing 707-329C	Scibe Airlift Zaire	
9Q-CBW	Boeing 707-329C	Scibe Airlift Zaire	
9Q-CLG	Douglas DC-8-63CF	Air Zaire *Domaine de la Nsélé*	
9Q-CLH	Douglas DC-8-63AF	Air Zaire (*stored*)	
9Q-CVG	Boeing 707-329C	Katale Aero Transport	
9Q-CVH	Douglas DC-8-55F	Katale Aero Transport	
9Q-CZF	Boeing 707-344	Air Region	

Note: Air Zaire operates Douglas DC-10-30 F-OGQC.

9V (Singapore)

Reg.	Type	Owner or Operator	Notes
9V-SKA	Boeing 747-312	Singapore Airlines	
9V-SKM	Boeing 747-312 (SCD)	Singapore Airlines	
9V-SKN	Boeing 747-312 (SCD)	Singapore Airlines	
9V-SKP	Boeing 747-312 (SCD)	Singapore Airlines	
9V-SKQ	Boeing 747-212F (SCD)	Singapore Airlines	
9V-SMA	Boeing 747-412	Singapore Airlines	
9V-SMB	Boeing 747-412	Singapore Airlines	
9V-SMC	Boeing 747-412	Singapore Airlines	
9V-SMD	Boeing 747-412	Singapore Airlines	
SV-SME	Boeing 747-412	Singapore Airlines	
SV-SMF	Boeing 747-412	Singapore Airlines	
SV-SMG	Boeing 747-412	Singapore Airlines	
SV-SMH	Boeing 747-412	Singapore Airlines	
9V-SQL	Boeing 747-212B	Singapore Airlines	
9V-SQM	Boeing 747-212B	Singapore Airlines	
9V-SQN	Boeing 747-212B	Singapore Airlines	
9V-SQO	Boeing 747-212B	Singapore Airlines	
9V-SQP	Boeing 747-212B	Singapore Airlines	
9V-SQQ	Boeing 747-212B	Singapore Airlines	
9V-SQR	Boeing 747-212B	Singapore Airlines	
9V-SQS	Boeing 747-212B	Singapore Airlines	

Note: Singapore Airlines also operates Boeing 747-312 N116KB, N117KC, N118KD, N119KE, N120KF, N121KG, N122KH, N123KJ, N124KK and N125KL.

9XR (Rwanda)

Reg.	Type	Owner or Operator	Notes
9XR-JA	Boeing 707-328C	Air Rwanda	

9Y (Trinidad and Tobago)

Reg.	Type	Owner or Operator	Notes
9Y-TGJ	L.1011 TriStar 500	B.W.I.A. *Flamingo*	
9Y-TGN	L.1011 TriStar 500	B.W.I.A.	
9Y-THA	L.1011 TriStar 500 (597)	B.W.I.A.	

Note: B.W.I.A. also operates a TriStar 500 which retains its US registration N3140D.

Overseas Registrations

Aircraft included in this section are those based in the UK but which retain their non-British identities.

Notes	Reg.	Type	Owner or Operator
	A4O-AB	V.1103 VC10 ★	Brooklands Museum (G-ASIX)
	CF-EQS	Boeing-Stearman PT-17 ★	Imperial War Museum/Duxford
	CF-KCG	Grumman TBM-3E Avenger AS.3 ★	Imperial War Museum/Duxford
	CS-ACQ	Fleet 80 Canuck ★	Visionair Ltd (stored)/Coventry
	D-IFSB	D.H.104 Dove 6★	Mosquito Aircraft Museum
	EI-AYO	Douglas DC-3 ★	Science Museum/Wroughton
	F-BDRS	Boeing B-17G (231965) ★	Imperial War Museum/Duxford
	F-BGNR	V.708 Viscount ★	Air Service Training/Perth
	F-BMCY	Potez 840*	Sumburgh Fire Service
	LX-NUR	Falcon 50	Kingson Investments/Heathrow
	N1MF	Cessna 421B	Pelmont Aviation Inc/Cranfield
	N2FU	Learjet 35A	Motor Racing Developments Inc
	N3TV	Douglas DC-3	Hibernian Dakota Flight Ltd
	N14KH	Christen Eagle II	R. Frohmayer
	N15AW	Cessna 500 Citation	A. W. Alloys Ltd
	N15SC	Learjet 35A	Sea Containers Associates/Luton
	N18E	Boeing 247D ★	Science Museum/Wroughton
	N18V	Beech D.17S Traveler (PB1)	R. Lamplough
	N47DD	Republic P-47D Thunderbolt ★	Imperial War Museum/Duxford
	N51JJ	P-51 Mustang (463221) ★	B. J. S. Grey/Duxford
	N59NA	Douglas C-47A	Aces High Ltd (G-AKNB)/North Weald
	N71AF	R. Commander 680W	Metropolitan Aviation
	N158C	S.24 Sandringham (VH-BRC) ★	Southampton Hall of Aviation
	N167F	P-51D Mustang (473877)	RLS 51 Ltd/Duxford
	N179P	Vought F4U-7 Corsair	D. W. Arnold/Biggin Hill
	N203DM	D.H.112 Venom FB.54	Aces High Ltd/North Weald
	N230ET	PA-30 Twin Comanche 160	P. Bayliss (G-ATET)
	N260QB	Pitts S-2S Special	D. Baker
	N415FS	F-100F Super Sabre	Flight Refuelling Ltd/Bournemouth
	N417FS	F-100F Super Sabre	Flight Refuelling Ltd/Bournemouth
	N418FS	F-100F Super Sabre	Flight Refuelling Ltd/Bournemouth
	N419FS	F-100F Super Sabre	Flight Refuelling Ltd/Bournemouth
	N425EE	Cessna 425	J. W. MacDonald
	N444M	Grumman G.44 Widgeon (1411)	M. Dunkerley/Biggin Hill
	N490CC	Cessna 551 Citation II	A. W. Alloys Ltd
	N500LN	Howard 500	D. Baker
	N505MH	P-38L Lightning	D. W. Arnold/Biggin Hill
	N535SM	R. Commander 680	J. E. Tuberty
	N750M	Grumman G.44 Widgeon★	L. E. Usher
	N804CC	G.159 Gulfstream 1	American Trans Air/Gatwick
	N900FR	Dassault Falcon 20DC	Flight Refuelling Ltd/Bournemouth
	N900MD	Learjet 36A	MMFI/Gatwick
	N901FR	Dassault Falcon 20DC	Flight Refuelling Ltd/Bournemouth
	N902FR	Dassault Falcon 20DC	Flight Refuelling Ltd/Bournemouth
	N903FR	Dassault Falcon 20DC	Flight Refuelling Ltd/Bournemouth
	N904FR	Dassault Falcon 20DC	Flight Refuelling Ltd/Bournemouth
	N905FR	Dassault Falcon 20DC	Flight Refuelling Ltd/Bournemouth
	N906FR	Dassault Falcon 20DC	Flight Refuelling Ltd/Bournemouth
	N907FR	Dassault Falcon 20DC	Flight Refuelling Ltd/Bournemouth
	N908FR	Dassault Falcon 20DC	Flight Refuelling Ltd/Bournemouth
	N909FR	Dassault Falcon 20DC	Flight Refuelling Ltd/Bournemouth
	N999PJ	M.S.760 Paris 2	Aces High Ltd/North Weald
	N1042B	B-25J Mitchell (430823)	Aces High Ltd/North Weald
	N1344	Ryan PT-22	H. Mitchell
	N1447Q	Cessna 150L	US Embassy Flying Club
	N2700	Fairchild C-119G	Aces High Ltd (G-BLSW)/North Weald
	N2929W	PA-28-151 Warrior	R. Lobell
	N3600X	Dassault Falcon 10	Xerox Corporation/Heathrow
	N3851Q	Cessna 172K	Bentwaters Aero Club/Woodbridge
	N3983N	Agusta A.109A	NSM Aviation
	N4306Z	PA-28 Cherokee 140	USAF Aero Club/Upper Heyford
	N4712V	Boeing Stearman PT-13D	Wessex Aviation & Transport Ltd
	N4727V	Spad S.VII (S4523)	Imperial War Museum/Duxford
	N4806E	Douglas A-26C Invader ★	R. & R. Cadman/Southend

Reg.	Type	Owner or Operator	Notes
N5063N	Beech D.18S (HB275)	Harvard Formation Team (G-BKGM)	
N5237V	Boeing B-17G (483868) ★	RAF Bomber Command Museum/ Hendon	
N5246	Nieuport 28	A. Graham-Enock	
N6178C	Grumman F7F-3 Tigercat	Planesailing Air Displays/Duxford	
N6268	Travel Air Model 2000	Personal Plane Services Ltd	
N6827C	TBM-3E Avenger (V-110)	R. Hanna/Duxford	
N7614C	B-25J Mitchell	Imperial War Museum/Duxford	
N7777G	L.749A Constellation ★	Science Museum (G-CONI)/Wroughton	
N8155E	Mooney M.20A	D. Skans	
N8297	FG-1D Corsair (88297)	B. J. S. Grey/Duxford	
N9012P	C.A.S.A. 352L (1Z+EK)	Junkers Ju.52/3M Flight	
N9089Z	TB-25J Mitchell (HD368)★	Aces High Ltd (G-BKXW)/North Weald	
N9115Z	TB-25N Mitchell (429366) ★	RAF Bomber Command Museum/ Hendon	
N9455Z	TB-25N Mitchell (30210)	Visionair Ltd	
N9606H	Fairchild M.62A Cornell ★	Rebel Air Museum/Earls Colne	
N13631	NA Harvard IV	E. Webster	
N26178	Cessna 550 Citation II	A. W. Alloys Ltd	
N26634	PA-24 Comanche 250	P. Biggs (G-BFKR)	
N30228	Piper J-3C-65 Cub	C. Morris	
N33600	Cessna L-19A Bird Dog (111989) ★	Museum of Army Flying/ Middle Wallop	
N41836	Cessna 150A	US Embassy Flying Club (G-ARFI)	
N43069	PA-28-161 Warrior II	Lakenheath Aero Club	
N43401	PA-28-161 Warrior II	Cabair/Elstree	
N49272	Ryan PT-23	H. Mitchell	
N52113	Bell P-63C Kingcobra	D. W. Arnold/Biggin Hill	
N54558	Cessna F.152	J. J. Baumhardt	
N54607	Douglas C-47A	J. Keen *Maggie May*/Liverpool	
N54922	Boeing Stearman	Yugo Cars	
N60626	Cessna 150J	Lakenheath Aero Club	
N62822	Bell RP-63C Kingcobra	B. J. S. Grey/Duxford	
N88972	B-25D-30-ND Mitchell (KL161)	Fighter Collection/Duxford	
N91437	PA-38-112 Tomahawk	Lakenheath Aero Club	
N91457	PA-38-112 Tomahawk	Lakenheath Aero Club	
N91590	PA-38-112 Tomahawk	Lakenheath Aero Club	
N94466	Curtiss P-40E Kittyhawk 1 (SU-E)	J. R. Paul/Duxford	
N96240	Beech D.18S	J. Hawke (G-AYAH)	
N99153	T-28C Trojan ★	Norfolk & Suffolk Aviation Museum/ Flixton	
N99225	Dornier Do.24T-3 (HD.5-1) ★	RAF Museum/Hendon	
NC88ZK	Boeing-Stearman PT-17	R. Hanna/Duxford	
NC5171N	Lockheed 10A Electra ★	Science Museum (G-LIOA)/Wroughton	
NC15214	Waco UKC-S	P. H. McConnell/White Waltham	
NL314BG	P-51D Mustang (44-73149)	D. W. Arnold/Biggin Hill	
NL1009N	Curtiss P-40M Kittyhawk (FR870)	B. J. S. Grey/Duxford	
NL1051S	P-51D-25-NA Mustang (511371)	Myrick Aviation/Southend	
NL9494Z	TB-25N Mitchell (151632)	Visionair Ltd	
NX47DD	Republic P-47D Thunderbolt (226671)	B. J. S. Grey/Duxford	
NX700HL	Grumman F8F-2B Bearcat (121714)	B. J. S. Grey/Duxford	
NX1337A	Vought F4U-7 Corsair (133722)	L. M. Walton/Duxford	
VH-BRC	See N158C		
VH-SNB	D.H.84 Dragon ★	Museum of Flight/E. Fortune	
VH-UTH	GAL Monospar ST-12 ★	Newark Air Museum (*stored*)	
VR-BEP	WS.55 Whirlwind 3 ★	East Midlands Aeropark (G-BAMH)	
VR-BET	WS.55 Whirlwind 3 ★	British Rotorcraft Museum (G-ANJV)	
VR-BEU	WS.55 Whirlwind 3 ★	British Rotorcraft Museum (G-ATKV)	
VR-BJI	Lockheed Jetstar	Denis Vanguard International Ltd	
VR-CBE	Boeing 727-46	Resebury Corporation	
VR-CBI	BAC One-Eleven 401	Bryan Aviation Ltd	
5N-ABW	Westland Widgeon 2 ★	British Rotorcraft Museum (G-AOZE)	

Radio Frequencies

The frequencies used by the larger airfields/airports are listed below. Abbreviations used: TWR — Tower, APP — Approach, A/G — Air-ground advisory. It is possible for changes to be made from time to time with the frequencies allocated which are all quoted in Megahertz (MHz).

Airfield	TWR	APP	A/G	Airfield	TWR	APP	A/G
Aberdeen	118.1	120.4		Inverness	122.6	122.6	
Aldergrove	118.3	120.0		Ipswich	118.32		
Alderney	123.6			Jersey	119.45	120.3	
Andrewsfield			130.55	Kidlington	119.8	130.3	
Barton			122.7	Land's End			122.3
Barrow			123.2	Leavesden	122.15	122.15	
Belfast Harbour	130.75	130.85		Leeds	120.3	123.75	
Bembridge			123.25	Leicester			122.25
Biggin Hill	134.8	129.4		Liverpool	118.1	119.85	
Birmingham	118.3	120.5		London City	119.42	128.05	
Blackbushe			122.3	Long Marston			130.1
Blackpool	118.4	135.95		Luton	120.2	128.75	
Bodmin			122.7	Lydd	120.7	120.7	
Booker			126.55	Manchester	118.7	119.4	
Bourn			129.8	Manston	124.9	126.35	
Bournemouth	125.6	118.65		Netherthorpe			123.5
Bristol	120.55	127.75		Newcastle	119.7	126.35	
Cambridge	122.2	123.6		North Denes			120.45
Cardiff	121.2	125.85		Norwich	118.9	119.35	
Carlisle			123.6	Panshanger			120.25
Compton Abbas			122.7	Perth	119.8	122.3	
Conington			123.0	Plymouth	122.6	123.2	
Coventry	119.25	119.25		Popham			129.8
Cranfield	123.2	122.85		Prestwick	118.15	120.55	
Denham			130.72	Redhill			123.22
Doncaster			122.9	Rochester			122.25
Dundee	122.9	122.9		Ronaldsway	118.9	120.85	
Dunkeswell			123.47	Sandown			123.5
Dunsfold	124.32	122.55		Seething			122.6
Duxford			123.5	Sherburn			122.6
East Midlands	124.0	119.65		Shipdham			123.05
Edinburgh	118.7	121.2		Shobdon			123.5
Elstree			122.4	Shoreham	125.4	123.15	
Exeter	119.8	128.15		Sibson			122.3
Fairoaks			123.42	Sleap			122.45
Felthorpe			123.5	Southampton	118.2	128.85	
Fenland			123.05	Southend	119.7	128.95	
Filton	124.95	130.85		Stansted	118.15	125.55	
Gamston			130.47	Stapleford			122.8
Gatwick	124.22	118.57		Staverton	125.65	125.65	
Glasgow	118.8	119.1		Sumburgh	118.25	123.15	
Goodwood	120.65	122.45		Swansea	119.7	119.7	
Guernsey	119.95	128.65		Swanton Morley			123.5
Halfpenny Green			123.0	Sywell			122.7
Hatfield	130.8	123.35		Teesside	119.8	118.85	
Haverfordwest			122.2	Thruxton			130.45
Hawarden	124.95	123.35		Tollerton			122.8
Hayes Heliport			123.65	Wellesbourne			130.45
Headcorn			122.0	Weston	122.5	129.25	
Heathrow	118.7	119.2		West Malling			130.42
	118.5	119.5		White Waltham			122.6
Hethel			122.35	Wick	119.7		
Hucknall			130.8	Wickenby			122.45
Humberside	118.55	123.15		Woodford	126.92	130.05	
Ingoldmells			130.45	Yeovil	125.4	130.8	

282

Airline Flight Codes

Three-letter flight codes are now in general use. Those listed below identify both UK and overseas carriers appearing in the book.

Code	Airline	Reg
AAG	Air Atlantique	G
AAL	American A/L	N
AAN	Oasis	EC
ABB	Air Belgium	OO
ABR	Air Bridge	G
ACA	Air Canada	C
ACF	Air Charter Intl	F
ACY	Air City	HB
ADR	Adria A/W	YU
AEA	Air Europa	EC
AEF	Aero Lloyd	D
AEL	Air Europe	G
AFL	Aeroflot	CCCP
AFR	Air France	F
AFW	Air Furness	G
AGX	Aviogenex	YU
AHD	Air Holland	PH
AIA	Air Atlantis	CS
AIC	Air India	VT
ALK	Air Lanka	4R
AMC	Air Malta	9H
AMM	Air 2000	G
AMR	Air America	N
AMT	American Trans Air	N
ANC	Anglo Cargo	G
ANZ	Air New Zealand	ZK
ATI	ATI	I
ATT	Aer Turas	EI
AUA	Austrian A/L	OE
AUR	Aurigny A/S	G
AVD	Air Vendee	F
AYC	Aviaco	EC
AZA	Alitalia	I
AZI	Air Zimbabwe	Z
AZR	Air Zaire	9Q
BAF	British Air Ferries	G
BAL	Britannia A/L	G
BAW	British Airways	G
BBB	Balair	HB
BBC	Bangladesh Biman	S2
BCS	European A/T	OO
BEE	Busy Bee	LN
BER	Air Berlin	N
BEX	Birmingham Executive	G
BIA	British Island A/W	G
BIH	British Intl Heli	G
BKT	Caledonian	
BMA	British Midland	G
BRA	Braathens	LN
BRY	Brymon A/W	G
BWA	BWIA	9Y
BZH	Brit Air	F
CAI	Novair	G
CAX	Connectair	G
CCA	CAAC	B
CDN	Canadian A/L Intl	C
CFG	Condor	D
CLX	Cargolux	LX
COA	Continental A/L	N
CPG	Capital A/L	G
CPX	Cathay Pacific	VR-H
CRL	Corse Air	F
CRX	Crossair	HB
CSA	Czech A/L	OK
CTA	CTA	HB
CYP	Cyprus A/W	5B
DAH	Air Algerie	7T
DAL	Delta A/L	N
DAN	Dan-Air	G
DAT	Delta Air Transport	OO
DLH	Lufthansa	D
DLT	DLT	D
DMA	Maersk Air	OY
DQI	Cimber Air	OY
EAF	Emery Worldwide	N
ECE	London City A/W	G
ECS	Air Ecosse	G
EGY	Egypt Air	SU
EIA	Evergreen Intl	N
EIN	Aer Lingus	EI
ELY	El Al	4X
ETH	Ethiopian A/L	ET
EUI	Euralair	F
EXS	Channel Express	G
EYT	Europe Aero Service	F
FDE	Federal Express	N
FGT	Fairflight	G
FIN	Finnair	OH
FOB	Ford	G
FOF	Fred Olsen	LN
FTL	Flying Tiger	N
GBL	GB Airways	G
GEC	German Cargo	D
GER	Guernsey A/L	G
GFA	Gulf Air	A40
GFG	Germania	D
GHA	Ghana A/W	9G
GIA	Garuda	PK
GIL	Gill Air	G
GMP	Transwede	SE
HBD	Hubbardair	G
HLA	HeavyLift	G
HLF	Hapag-Lloyd	D
HSL	Hispania	EC
IAW	Iraqi A/W	YI
IBE	Iberia	EC
ICE	Icelandair	TF
IEA	Inter European	G
IFL	Interflug	DDR
IKA	Tradewinds	G
INS	Instone A/L	G
IRA	Iran Air	EP
ISL	Eagle Air	TF
ISS	Alisarda	I
ITF	Air Inter	F
IYE	Yemen A/W	4W
JAL	Japan A/L	JA
JAT	JAT	YU
JEA	Jersey European A/W	G
KAC	Kuwait A/W	9K
KAL	Korean Air	HL
KAR	Kar-Air	OH
KIS	Contactair	D
KLM	KLM	PH
KND	Kondair	G
KQA	Kenya A/W	5Y
LAA	Libyan Arab A/L	5A
LAZ	Bulgarian A/L	LZ
LCN	Lin. Ae. Canarias	EC
LDA	Lauda Air	OE
LGL	Luxair	LX
LIM	Air Limousin	F
LIN	Linjeflyg	SE
LIT	Air Littoral	F
LOG	Loganair	G
LON	Ryanair Europe	G
LOT	Polish A/L (LOT)	SP
LTE	LTE	EC
LTS	LTU Sud	D
LTU	LTU	D
MAH	Malev	HA
MAL	McAlpine	G
MAS	Malaysian A/L	9M
MAU	Air Mauritius	3B
MEA	Middle East A/L	OD
MIN	Minerve	F
MNX	Manx A/L	G
MON	Monarch A/L	G
MOR	Morefly	LN
MPH	Martinair	PH
MSO	Somali A/L	6O
NAA	National A/W	G
NCL	National Commuter	G
NCR	Air Sur	EC
NET	NetherLines	PH
NEX	Northern Executive	G
NFD	NFD	D
NGA	Nigeria A/W	5N
NLM	NLM	PH
NWA	Northwest A/L	N
NXA	Nationair	C
OAL	Olympic A/L	SX
OYC	Conair	OY
PAA	Pan Am	N
PAI	Piedmont	N
PAL	Philippine A/L	RP
PAR	Partnair	LN
PAT	Paramount A/W	G
PIA	Pakistan Intl	AP
PSS	Peregrine A/S	G
QFA	Qantas	VH
RAM	Royal Air Maroc	CN
RBA	Royal Brunei	V8
RFG	RFG	D
RGL	Regionair	G
RIA	Rich Intl	N
RJA	Royal Jordanian	JY
ROT	Tarom	YR
RWD	Air Rwanda	9XR
RYR	Ryanair	EI
SAA	South African A/W	ZS
SAB	Sabena	OO
SAS	SAS	SE OY LN
SAW	Sterling A/W	OY
SAY	Suckling A/W	G
SDI	Saudi	HZ
SEY	Air Seychelles	S7
SIA	Singapore A/L	9V
SJM	Southern A/T	N
SKD	Skyguard	G
SLA	Sierra Leone A/W	9L
SLA	Sobelair	OO
SPP	Spanair	EC
STR	Stellair	F
SUD	Sudan A/W	ST
SWE	Swedair	SE
SWR	Swissair	HB
SYR	Syrian Arab	YK

TAP	Air Portugal	CS	TYR	Tyrolean	OE	VIR	Virgin Atlantic	G
TAR	Tunis Air	TS	UAE	Emirates A/L	A6	VIV	Viva Air	EC
TAT	TAT	F	UGA	Uganda A/L	5X	VKG	Scanair	SE OY LN
TEA	Trans European A/W	OO	UKA	Air UK	G	VRG	Varig	PP
THA	Thai A/W Intl	HS	UKL	Air UK Leisure	G	WDA	Wardair	C
THG	Tal-Air	G	UNA	Universair	EC	WDL	WDL	D
THY	Turkish A/L	TC	UPA	Air Foyle	G	WOA	World A/W	N
TMA	Trans Mediterranean	OD	URO	Euroair	G	WWC	Worldways	C
TOW	Tower Air	N	UTA	UTA	F	ZAC	Zambia A/W	9J
TRH	Transavia	PH	UYC	Cameroon A/L	TJ	ZAS	ZAS A/L of Egypt	SU
TWA	TWA	N	VIA	Viasa	YV			

British Aircraft Preservation Council Register

The British Aircraft Preservation Council was formed in 1967 to co-ordinate the works of all bodies involved in the preservation, restoration and display of historical aircraft. Membership covers the whole spectrum of national, Service, commercial and voluntary groups, and meetings are held regularly at the bases of member organisations. The Council is able to provide a means of communication, helping to resolve any misunderstandings or duplication of effort. Every effort is taken to encourage the raising of standards of both organisation and technical capacity amongst the member groups to the benfit of everyone interested in aviation. To assist historians, the B.A.P.C. register has been set up and provides an identity for those aircraft which do not qualify for a Service serial or inclusion in the UK Civil Register.

Aircraft on the current B.A.P.C. Register are as follows:

Notes	Reg.	Type	Owner or Operator
	1	Roe Triplane Type IV (replica)	Now G-ARSG
	2	Bristol Boxkite (replica)	Now G-ASPP
	3	Blériot XI	Now G-AANG
	4	Deperdussin Monoplane	Now G-AANH
	5	Blackburn Monoplane	Now G-AANI
	6	Roe Triplane Type IV (replica)	Greater Manchester Museum of Science & Technology
	7	Southampton University MPA	Southampton Hall of Aviation
	8	Dixon ornithopter	The Shuttleworth Trust
	9	Humber Monoplane (replica)	Airport Terminal/Birmingham
	10	Hafner R.II Revoplane	Museum of Army Flying/Middle Wallop
	11	English Electric Wren	Now G-EBNV
	12	Mignet HM.14	Museum of Flight/E. Fortune
	13	Mignet HM.14	Brimpex Metal Treatments
	14	Addyman standard training glider	N. H. Ponsford
	15	Addyman standard training glider	The Aeroplane Collection Ltd
	16	Addyman ultra-light aircraft	N. H. Ponsford
	17	Woodhams Sprite	The Aeroplane Collection Ltd
	18	Killick MP Gyroplane	N. H. Ponsford
	19	Bristol F.2b	Aero Vintage Ltd
	20	Lee-Richards annular biplane (replica)	Newark Air Musem
	21	Thruxton Jackaroo	M. J. Brett
	22	Mignet HM.14 (G-AEOF)	Aviodome/Schiphol, Holland
	25	Nyborg TGN-III glider	Midland Air Museum
	27	Mignet HM.14	M. J. Abbey
	28	Wright Flyer (replica)	RAF Museum/Cardington
	29	Mignet HM.14 (replica) (G-ADRY)	Brooklands Museum of Aviation/Weybridge
	32	Crossley Tom Thumb	Midland Air Museum
	33	DFS.108-49 Grunau Baby IIb	Russavia Collection
	34	DFS.108-49 Grunau Baby IIb	D. Elsdon
	35	EoN primary glider	Russavia Collection
	36	Fieseler Fi.103 (V-1) (replica)	Kent Battle of Britain Museum/Hawkinge
	37	Blake Bluetit	The Shuttleworth Trust
	38	Bristol Scout replica (A1742)	Historical Aircraft Museum/RAF St Athan
	40	Bristol Boxkite (replica)	Bristol City Museum
	41	B.E.2C (replica) (6232)	Historical Aircraft Museum/RAF St Athan
	42	Avro 504 (replica) (H1968)	Historical Aircraft Museum/RAF St Athan

Reg.	Type	Owner or Operator	Notes
43	Mignet HM.14	Lincolnshire Aviation Museum	
44	Miles Magister (L6906)	Berkshire Aviation Group (G-AKKY)/ Woodley	
45	Pilcher Hawk (replica)	Stanford Hall Museum	
46	Mignet HM.14	Alan McKechnie Racing Ltd	
47	Watkins Monoplane	Historical Aircraft Museum/RAF St Athan	
48	Pilcher Hawk (replica)	Glasgow Museum of Transport	
49	Pilcher Hawk	Royal Scottish Museum/Edinburgh	
50	Roe Triplane Type 1	Science Museum/S. Kensington	
51	Vickers Vimy IV	Science Museum/S. Kensington	
52	Lilienthal glider	Science Museum Store/Hayes	
53	Wright Flyer (replica)	Science Museum/S. Kensington	
54	JAP-Harding monoplane	Science Museum/S. Kensington	
55	Levavasseur Antoinette VII	Science Museum/S. Kensington	
56	Fokker E.III (210/16)	Science Museum/S. Kensington	
57	Pilcher Hawk (replica)	Science Museum/S. Kensington	
58	Yokosuka MXY-7 Ohka II (15-1585)	FAA Museum/Yeovilton	
59	Sopwith Camel (replica) (D3419)	Historical Aircraft Museum/RAF St Athan	
60	Murray M.1 helicopter	The Aeroplane Collection Ltd	
61	Stewart man-powered ornithopter	Lincolnshire Aviation Museum	
62	Cody Biplane (304)	Science Museum/S. Kensington	
63	Hurricane (replica) (L1592)	Torbay Aircraft Museum	
64	Hurricane (replica)	Kent Battle of Britain Museum/Hawkinge	
65	Spitfire (replica) (QV-K)	Kent Battle of Britain Museum/Hawkinge	
66	Bf 109 (replica) (1480)	Kent Battle of Britain Museum/Hawkinge	
67	Bf 109 (replica) (14)	Midland Air Museum	
68	Hurricane (replica) (H3426)	Midland Air Museum	
69	Spitfire (replica) (QV-K)	Torbay Aircraft Museum	
70	Auster AOP.5 (TJ398)	Aircraft Preservation Soc of Scotland	
71	Spitfire (replica) (P9390)	Norfolk & Suffolk Aviation Museum	
72	Hurricane (replica) (V7767)	N. Weald Aircraft Restoration Flight	
73	Hurricane (replica)	Queens Head/Bishops Stortford	
74	Bf 109 (replica) (6)	Torbay Aircraft Museum	
75	Mignet HM.14 (G-AEFG)	Nigel Ponsford	
76	Mignet HM.14 (G-AFFI)	Bomber County Museum/Cleethorpes	
77	Mignet HM.14 (replica) (G-ADRG)	Cotswold Aircraft Restoration Group	
78	Hawker Hind (K5414)	Now G-AENP	
79	Fiat G.46-4 (MM53211)	British Air Reserve/Lympne	
80	Airspeed Horsa (TL659)	Museum of Army Flying	
81	Hawkridge Dagling	Russavia Collection	
82	Hawker Hind (Afghan)	RAF Museum/Hendon	
83	Kawasaki Ki-100-1b	Aerospace Museum/Cosford	
84	Nakajima Ki-46 (Dinah III)	Historical Aircraft Museum/RAF St Athan	
85	Weir W-2 autogyro	Museum of Flight/E. Fortune	
86	de Havilland Tiger Moth (replica)	Yorkshire Aircraft Preservation Soc	
87	Bristol Babe (replica) (G-EASQ)	Bomber County Museum	
88	Fokker Dr 1 (replica) (102/18)	Fleet Air Arm Museum	
89	Cayley glider (replica)	Greater Manchester Museum of Science & Technology	
90	Colditz Cock (replica)	Torbay Aircraft Museum	
91	Fieseler Fi 103 (V.1)	Lashenden Air Warfare Museum	
92	Fieseler Fi 103 (V.1)	Historical Aircraft Museum/RAF St Athan	
93	Fieseler Fi 103 (V.1)	Imperial War Museum/Duxford	
94	Fieseler Fi 103 (V.1)	Aerospace Museum/Cosford	
95	Gizmer autogyro	F. Fewsdale	
96	Brown helicopter	N.E. Aircraft Museum	
97	Luton L.A.4A Minor	Nene Valley Aviation Soc	
98	Yokosuka MXY-7 Ohka II	Greater Manchester Museum of Science & Technology	
99	Yokosuka MXY-7 Ohka II	Aerospace Museum/Cosford	
100	Clarke glider	RAF Museum/Hendon	
101	Mignet HM.14	Lincolnshire Aviation Museum	
103	Pilcher glider (replica)	Personal Plane Services Ltd	
104	Blériot XI (replica)	Now G-AVXV/Duxford	
105	Blériot XI (replica)	Aviodome/Schiphol, Holland	
106	Blériot XI (164)	RAF Museum/Hendon	
107	Blériot XXVII (433)	RAF Museum/Hendon	
108	Fairey Swordfish IV (HS503)	RAF Museum/Henlow store	
109	Slingsby Kirby Cadet TX.1	RAF Museum/Henlow store	
110	Fokker D.VII replica (static) (5125)	Leisure Sport Ltd/Thorpe Park	
111	Sopwith Triplane replica (static) (N5492)	FAA Museum/Yeovilton	
112	D.H.2 replica (static) (5984)	Museum of Army Flying/Middle Wallop	
113	S.E.5A replica (static) (B4863)	Leisure Sport Ltd/Thorpe Park	

Notes	Reg.	Type	Owner or Operator
	114	Vickers Type 60 Viking (static)	Brooklands Museum of Aviation/Weybridge
	115	Mignet HM.14	Essex Aviation Group/Andrewsfield
	116	Santos-Dumont Demoiselle (replica)	Cornwall Aero Park/Helston
	117	B.E.2C (replica)	N. Weald Aircraft Restoration Flight
	118	Albatros D.V. (replica)	N. Weald Aircraft Restoration Flight
	119	Bensen B.7	N.E. Aircraft Museum
	120	Mignet HM.14 (G-AEJZ)	Bomber County Museum/Cleethorpes
	121	Mignet HM.14 (G-AEKR)	S. Yorks Aviation Soc
	122	Avro 504 (replica)	British Broadcasting Corp
	123	Vickers FB.5 Gunbus (replica)	A. Topen (stored)/Cranfield
	124	Lilienthal Glider Type XI (replica)	Science Museum/S. Kensington
	125	Clay Cherub (G-BDGP)	B. R. Clay
	126	D.31 Turbulent (static)	Midland Air Museum store
	127	Halton Jupiter MPA	Shuttleworth Trust
	128	Watkinson Cyclogyroplane Mk IV	British Rotorcraft Museum
	129	Blackburn 1911 Monoplane (replica)	Cornwall Aero Park/Helston store
	130	Blackburn 1912 Monoplane (replica)	Cornwall Aero Park/Helston store
	131	Pilcher Hawk (replica)	C. Paton
	132	Blériot XI (G-BLXI)	EMK Aeroplane Co Ltd
	133	Fokker Dr 1 (replica) (425/17)	Torbay Aircraft Museum
	134	Pitts S-2A static (G-RKSF)	Torbay Aircraft Museum
	135	Bristol M.1C (replica) (C4912)	Leisure Sport Ltd/Thorpe Park
	136	Deperdussin Seaplane (replica)	Leisure Sport Ltd/Thorpe Park
	137	Sopwith Baby Floatplane (replica) (8151)	Leisure Sport Ltd/Thorpe Park
	138	Hansa Brandenburg W.29 Floatplane (replica) (2292)	Leisure Sport Ltd/Thorpe Park
	139	Fokker Dr 1 (replica) 150/17	Leisure Sport Ltd/Thorpe Park
	140	Curtiss R3C-2 Floatplane (replica)	Leisure Sport Ltd/Thorpe Park
	141	Macchi M.39 Floatplane (replica)	Leisure Sport Ltd/Thorpe Park
	142	SE-5A (replica) (F5459)	Cornwall Aero Park/Helston
	143	Paxton MPA	R. A. Paxton/Staverton
	144	Weybridge Mercury MPA	Cranwell Gliding Club
	145	Oliver MPA	D. Oliver (stored)/Warton
	146	Pedal Aeronauts Toucan MPA	Shuttleworth Trust
	147	Bensen B.7	Norfolk & Suffolk Aviation Museum
	148	Hawker Fury II (replica) (K7271)	Aerospace Museum/Cosford
	149	Short S.27 (replica)	FAA Museum (stored)/Yeovilton
	150	SEPECAT Jaguar GR.1 (replica) (XX718)	RAF Exhibition Flight
	151	SEPECAT Jaguar GR.1 (replica) (XZ363)	RAF Exhibition Flight
	152	BAe Hawk T.1 (replica) (XX163)	RAF Exhibition Flight
	153	Westland WG.33	British Rotorcraft Museum (stored)
	154	D.31 Turbulent	Lincolnshire Aviation Museum
	155	Panavia Tornado GR.1 (replica) (ZA322)	RAF Exhibition Flight
	156	Supermarine S-6B (replica) (S1595)	Leisure Sport Ltd
	157	Waco CG-4A	Pennine Aviation Museum
	158	Fieseler Fi 103 (V.1)	Joint Bomb Disposal School/Chattenden
	159	Yokosuka MXY-7 Ohka II	Joint Bomb Disposal School/Chattenden
	160	Chargus 108 hang glider	Museum of Flight/E. Fortune
	161	Stewart Ornithopter Coppelia	Bomber County Museum
	162	Goodhart Newbury Manflier MPA	Science Museum/Wroughton
	163	AFEE 10/42 Rotabuggy (replica)	Museum of Army Flying/Middle Wallop
	164	Wight Quadruplane Type 1 (replica)	Wessex Aviation Soc/Wimborne
	165	Bristol F.2b (E2466)	RAF Museum/Hendon
	166	Bristol F.2b	Now G-AANM
	167	S.E.5A replica	Torbay Aircraft Museum
	168	D.H.60G Moth static replica (G-AAAH)	Hilton Hotel/Gatwick
	169	SEPECAT Jaguar GR.1 (static replica) (XX110)	No 1 S. of T.T. RAF Halton
	170	Pilcher Hawk (replica)	A. Gourlay/Strathallan
	171	BAe Hawk T.1 (replica) (XX297)	RAF Exhibition Flight/Abingdon
	172	Chargus Midas Super 8 hang glider	Science Museum/Wroughton
	173	Birdman Promotions Grasshopper	Science Museum/Wroughton
	174	Bensen B.7	Science Museum/Wroughton